AMERICAN GOVERNMENT

POLITICS AND CITIZENSHIP

MW01483091

AMERICAN GOVERNMENT

POLITICS AND CITIZENSHIP

Jerold L. Waltman

UNIVERSITY OF SOUTHERN MISSISSIPPI

WEST PUBLISHING COMPANY

Minneapolis/St. Paul   New York   Los Angeles   San Francisco

COPYEDITOR	Beth Bulger
COMPOSITION	Carlisle Communications
COVER DESIGN	K. M. Weber
COVER IMAGE	Lowell Williams, "East Elevation of the Capitol Building", originally reproduced in Kit Hinrichs, *Stars & Stripes* (San Francisco: Chronicle Books, 1987).
TEXT DESIGN	K. M. Weber
ARTWORK	Techarts

Production, printing and binding by West Publishing Company.

WEST'S COMMITMENT TO THE ENVIRONMENT

In 1906, West Publishing Company began recycling materials left over from the production of books. This began a tradition of efficient and responsible use of resources. Today, up to 95 percent of our legal books and 70 percent of our college and school texts are printed on recycled, acid-free stock. West also recycles nearly 22 million pounds of scrap paper annually—the equivalent of 181,717 trees. Since the 1960s, West has devised ways to capture and recycle waste inks, solvents, oils, and vapors created in the printing process. We also recycle plastics of all kinds, wood, glass, corrugated cardboard, and batteries, and have eliminated the use of styrofoam book packaging. We at West are proud of the longevity and the scope of our commitment to the environment.

Photo credits appear following the index.

Library of Congress Cataloging-in-Publication Data

Waltman, Jerold L., 1945–
    American government : politics and citizenship / Jerold L. Waltman.
        p.   cm.
    Includes bibliographical references and index.
    ISBN 0-314-01166-8
    1. United States—Politics and government.   I. Title.
JK274.W243 1993
320.973—dc20   92-40913
                                                      ∞ CIP

To Diane

CONTENTS

CONTENTS

THREE
Federalism

FOUR
Civil Liberties and Civil Rights

FIVE
Congress

SIX

The Presidency

SEVEN

The Bureaucracy

EIGHT
The Federal Courts

NINE
Public Opinion and the Media

TEN
Political Parties and Citizen Participation

ELEVEN

Interest Groups and Citizen Participation

Appendices

PREFACE

THOSE OF US who teach the introductory course in American politics face a dilemma our colleagues who offer courses only on European, Asian, African, or Latin American politics routinely escape: most of the students taking the course are citizens of the nation under study, not only analysts of it. To be sure, evaluative issues have to be faced when teaching foreign political systems, but they are decidedly less immediate. To an extent, we, myself included, have often either adopted the model of comparative politics, teaching American politics "as is," or established some normative schemata and shown how our political system falls short of it. This dose of realism is not wrong, in my view, but incomplete. In trying to be analytically sophisticated, we have moved very far away from one of the reasons the course was developed in the first place, and, lest we forget, why political science developed as a discipline.

These points were brought home to me by a personal experience, an address, and two bits of television. The first occurred one day in my American government class as I was discussing the usual theories about why voting turnout is falling (which followed perhaps not coincidentally a unit on the budget). When I asked the class for their thoughts, one student said, "Perhaps so many instructors like you have done such a good job of showing how futile it all is, how many blockages there are between public preferences and public policy. . . ." I immediately replied that neither I, nor anyone else I knew, tried to spread cynicism, that one has to keep hope alive, etc. But it was inadequate, and both I and they knew it. Were we responsible, at least in part, for the decay of citizenship? Was it wishful thinking to believe we could teach how the system works and assume they would get their political values elsewhere? Were we being taken seriously, but not in the ways we hoped?

Soon thereafter, I read Samuel Huntington's 1988 presidential address to the American Political Science Association, in which he touched on the same theme. His main point was that political science grew from a preference for representative government, and elucidating that preference constitutes part of what we are about. Lastly, I was regularly rewatching tapes of the "Eyes on the Prize" series, in preparation for a class, during the semester in which the remarkable stirrings in Eastern Europe occurred.

Both those profound crusades convinced me anew that what people believe can be changed and that what they believe matters. Since then, the serene courage shown by countless ordinary Russians in foiling a military coup has only deepened that belief.

Convinced that there is both intellectual and pedagogical merit in discussing the nature of free government and what it means to be a citizen of this particular free government, I decided I would take that for the focus of this text. I did not wish, however, to follow the theme so laboriously that it skewed the descriptive material that is at the core of the American politics course. I have used theme texts which were so heavily thematic that the substantive chapters were almost contrived. I opted, instead, to lay out the theme in the initial chapter, to let it resurrect itself only lightly throughout the other chapters, and then to address it directly in a boxed supplement to each chapter.

The two models laid out in the first chapter are admittedly oversimplified caricatures, drawn from several intellectual strands. The individualist model pulls together the ideas of liberal participatory democracy, public choice approaches, and the rights based theories of Ronald Dworkin and Richard Epstein. While these frameworks are, of course, incompatible in some areas, what draws them under one roof here is first their emphasis on the atomized individual and how these individuals, as individuals, relate to

In Frank Capra's classic 1939 motion picture Mr. Smith Goes to Washington, *Jimmy Stewart plays a new, idealistic member of Congress who ulitmately triumphs over corrupt interests. Even though movies such as this one are often derided for their naiveté, they send messages about the values and ideals of American society.*

the political order, and second their detachment from any system of absolute values. For the contrasting model, which I label civic democracy, I combined traditional republicanism and elements of Benjamin Barber's "strong democracy." The first could stand alone as a counter model, of course, but I have often found that students have trouble disentangling the portions of it which evolved into later notions of democracy and the portions which are in tension with liberal democracy. Strong democracy, likewise, would provide a useful alternative (as indeed Barber intended), but much of it is based on the same assumptions as the more individualistic theories it seeks to critique, particularly in that it posits no independent status for the public good. I believe these models will be useful to introductory students and are intellectually defensible; the finer points can be left for those who wish to pursue political philosophy in more depth.

I am aware of the dangers and risks in using citizenship as a focus for an introductory course—the usual naive pulp that is offered when that term is used, that it can often lead to a mindless flag-waving at best and jingoism and xenophobia at worst, that there is a danger of imposing our own values on the impressionable young, and so forth. But free government is a preference, and one that every American political scientist I know shares. Merely because something is capable of perversion does not negate its value. I still think we should avoid setting our detailed policy preferences before students; but I think we can talk about free government and citizenship without preaching about the virtues or defects of particular policies. The models of individualist and civic democracy, in fact, are both compatible with a variety of more partisan approaches, such as mainstream liberalism and conservatism. I think we can hold fast to the ideas and ideals of free government and engage in a dialogue with our past and our present, a conversation that is the hallmark of the American political tradition, without having our courses degenerate into narrow partisan diatribes.

In short, I think that what we teach in the American politics course is vitally important, that the approaches taken there percolate outward far beyond the students in our classes. It is an opportune time, given the appearance of embryonic democracies everywhere, to reintegrate serious discussion of democratic citizenship into our courses. Those who sit in our classes are the educated citizenry in whom Jefferson placed so much faith; they will be affected by what we teach, the only question is how.

Organizing an American politics course is largely a matter of taste and intellectual orientation, especially the decision regarding whether the sections on political participation should precede or follow the coverage of institutions. For this reason, I tried to write this text so that each chapter could stand independently of the others. Thus instructors can structure the course any way they choose without losing continuity.

Chapter 13 was written immediately after the 1992 elections. It provides a useful update to several chapters, both in terms of data and generalizations. I endeavored to point out how the 1992 elections confirmed or cast doubt on the propositions offered in the chapters on Congress, the presidency, political parties, and the media.

Tourists visiting the Jefferson Memorial in Washington, D.C. The nation's capital is filled with similar monuments to the country's heroes, ideas, and values.

Ancillaries

American Government: Politics and Citizenship is accompanied by a set of ancillaries the aim of which is to help both teachers and students more fully benefit from using the text. John Lewis of Indiana University at South Bend has prepared a thoughtful and supportive Instructor's Manual with Test Bank. The manual consists of chapter summaries, discussion topics, and additional interesting commentary. The test bank consists of multiple-choice questions as well as essay-style exam questions. Because many instructors who adopt briefer American government texts for their courses do so to be able to supplement the main text with other materials, Professor Lewis has provided a series of suggested course syllabi consisting of unique approaches toward organizing an American government course. Among the suggestions are a course built around The Federalist Papers, current newspapers and periodicals, political biographies, or novels.

A separate item to accompany *American Government: Politics and Citizenship* is an annotated copy of the United States Constitution entitled *A Citizen's Guide To The United States Constitution*, prepared by Professor Louis Morton of Mesa State College of Colorado. The extensive annotations discuss the historical background, ideas and implications of each section, and the amendments to the Constitution. A series of self-testing examinations is found at the end of the annotations. The *Citizen's Guide To The United States Constitution* is free to all adopters and their students upon request.

West's Political Science Video Library contains an array of videos on American government subject matter and is available to qualified adopters. Because the availability of certain videos in the library may change throughout the course of a year, you should contact your West sales representative to find out more about the video program.

Acknowledgments

It is a pleasure to acknowledge the help of many individuals who contributed in some fashion to this book. First, Robert Jucha of West Publishing had faith in the project from its inception, and provided many hours and pages of useful and insightful counsel thereafter. His abilities to see both the big picture and devote attention to detail are unsurpassed. Diane Colwyn, also of West, was unfailingly helpful at many points. Tad Bornhoft guided the manuscript through the production process with as professional and capable a hand as any author could hope for.

My colleagues at the University of Southern Mississippi have cheerfully shared their thoughts about and many years of collective experience in teaching American government—and generously let me raid their bookshelves. A number of reviewers read all or portions of the manuscript. Their work was remarkably professional and a constant source of ideas; but, of course, they share no blame for any defects in the final product. These people included Peter J. Bergerson, Southeast Missouri State University; David E. Camacho, Northern Arizona University; James E. Campbell, Louisiana State University; James O. Catron, North Florida Junior College; Carl M. Dibble, Wayne State University; Patrick Eagan, John Carroll University; Marshall Goodman, University of Cincinnati; Gerard S. Gryski, Auburn University; Allen Hartter, Parkland College; Marjorie Randon Hershey, Indiana University; Samuel B. Hoff, Delaware State College; Robert W. Hoffert, Colorado State University; Lars Hoffman, Lewis & Clark Community College; Leon Hurwitz, Cleveland State University; Anne M. Khademian, University of Wisconsin–Madison; John Klee, Maysville Community College; Robert J. Lettieri, Mount Ida College; Michael Levine, Merced College; John M. Lewis, Indiana University–South Bend; Nancy S. Lind, Illinois State University; Priscilla Machado, United States Naval Academy; Jarol B. Manheim, George Washington University; William P. McLauchlan, Purdue University; John Molloy, Michigan State University; Charles Noble, California State University–Long Beach; Paulette Otis, University of Southern Colorado; William D. Pederson, Louisiana State University–Shreveport; Rene Peritz, Slippery Rock University; Raymond Pomerleau, San Francisco State University; Edward F. Renwick, Loyola University; Theresia Stewart, Elizabethtown Community College; and Louis T. Vietri, University of Maryland–College Park.

I would also like to mention the influence of the history faculty of Louisiana Tech University. During my years there they provided a model of what quality undergraduate teaching should be.

Finally, my family bore many hours of absence and preoccupation. My wife Diane has been not only a continual source of encouragement throughout but an enlightening conversation partner on many of the book's points as well.

I know of no safe depository of the ultimate power of the society but the people themselves, and if we think them not enlightened enough to exercise their control with a wholesome discretion, the remedy is not to take it from them, but to inform their discretion.

THOMAS JEFFERSON

Men are qualified for civil liberty in exact proportion to their disposition to put moral chains on their own appetites.

EDMUND BURKE

ONE

THE FOUNDATIONS OF DEMOCRACY AND THE CHARACTER OF CITIZENSHIP

INDIVIDUALIST DEMOCRACY	CITIZENSHIP AND CIVIC
CITIZENSHIP AND INDIVIDUALIST	DEMOCRACY
DEMOCRACY	DESCRIPTION VERSUS
CIVIC DEMOCRACY	PRESCRIPTION

Wᴇ ʜᴇᴀʀ from every quarter that citizenship is in crisis. Fewer Americans bother to vote than ever before; cooperation with the 1990 census was most disheartening; and the Internal Revenue Service regularly encounters increasing failure to report income and pay taxes.[1] Ironically, this eclipse of citizenship is occurring at the very moment in which new democracies are emerging in Eastern Europe and elsewhere—democracies which often look to the United States for guidance on how to operate a free government. Do we have nothing to offer but cynicism? Too seldom nowadays do we pause to inquire about exactly what makes a "good citizen," or what should be taught regarding democratic citizenship, and by whom.

What does the term *democracy* mean? In truth, it is both a simple and a complex idea. Both the word and the idea derive from the ancient Greeks, whose political organization was based in independent city-states. Some of these were designated by observers as monarchies (in which one person ruled); others were called oligarchies (in which a few people ruled); and a few won the title of democracies (in which the citizens[2] ruled). Democratic practice died with the end of Greek civilization, but the idea was never entirely erased from political theory, even though it lay dormant for many years. Then, from the seventeenth through the nineteenth centuries, several historical and philosophical trends converged which led to the resurrection of democratic ideals and the birth of modern democracy.

The first intellectual seed to sprout was the belief that all people were inheritors of a common humanity. Politically, this meant that people could no longer be viewed as mere subjects of their rulers; instead, they began to take on the status of citizens. The second seed of democracy involved the search for sovereignty, the source of authority for a political order. Whereas the divine will (as interpreted by the Roman Catholic Church) had been the moral basis for the exercise of political power during the Middle Ages, several writers now argued that sovereignty lay with the people of a society, and that concept slowly took hold. Finally, by the late eighteenth and early nineteenth centuries, the conviction that the people should participate in political decisions reawakened, and modern democracy began to blossom.

Democratic theory has splintered over the years; people frequently disagree about precisely what the term means. Nonetheless, the three factors discussed above continue to form a taproot; no matter how much they disagree on particulars, advocates of all forms of democracy find mutual ground here. These three powerful assumptions form the core of all democratic creeds:

1. All citizens are legally equal.
2. Ultimate authority rests with the people.
3. There must be popular participation in political decisions.

Opposite: *As a gesture of patriotism during World War I, these mill workers in Manchester, New Hampshire in 1917 wove a gigantic American flag.*

The fundamental act of citizenship or only one aspect of it? Citizens casting votes in rural Tennessee.

The American political tradition houses two distinctive models, or theories, of democracy. Although they have much in common, the theories present contrasting views on the character of the political order and the proper role of the citizen. Before we make sweeping judgments about the decline of citizenship, therefore, we should examine the concept carefully from both perspectives; perhaps part of the problem lies in how we define citizenship and the expectations that we thereby create.

INDIVIDUALIST DEMOCRACY

The first model, which I shall label *individualist democracy,* begins with the individual as the building block of the political order. Its philosophical base lies in the idea of the intrinsic worth and dignity of each individual; consequently, the state exists for the sake of the individual, not the other way around. Individuals, it is argued, have created the state in the same way they would create legal obligations: through voluntarily contracting with one another. The purposes of government therefore revolve around the enhancement of each individual's life. Each person is the best judge of what is best for her, and should be allowed to pursue that course unless it harms some other individual.

This unabashed pursuit of self-interest spills over into governmental decision making. Participation is the central and guiding concept of this model. It is vitally important to the individualist democrat that (1) there are no barriers to full adult participation, and (2) the rules which structure participation are fair. Further, there must be mechanisms in place to ensure that no group of people is barred from full and meaningful participation.[3] Voting is the primary form of participation for most people, of course, but other forms are accepted and encouraged: letter writing, marches, demonstrations, joining organizations that lobby, perhaps even sit-ins and civil disobedience.

The individualist democrat encourages each individual to participate to the maximum extent of his interests and abilities. The purpose of this drive to participation is to have each individual advocate, without embarrassment, his own interests. If the procedures of the political arena are fair and open, the public interest will emerge as a result of the ensuing clash of private interests. Building on people's natural tendency to be selfish, a good political order is secured, then, by the development of ingenious institutions to channel such self-interest, yielding the maximum amount of satisfaction to the maximum number of people.[4]

There is a close family relationship between this model and the ideal of the free-market economy. Individual consumers in a market economy pursue their own desires. However, the sum of their actions produces the public good: the maximum satisfaction of the maximum number of people. Procedures—such as the enforcement of contracts—must be fair, as in the political individualism described above. The philosophical root shared by the individualist democrat and the free-market economist is the concept that each person's seeking her own satisfaction will serve the public good.

Leadership roles in individualist democracy go to those who are adept at articulating the interests of a group or a variety of groups, and then brokering these interests with those of other leaders, much as a successful businessperson caters to the needs of his customers. The person who can speak best for the elderly, veterans, the poor, cotton growers, union members, small-town residents, etc., will win elections. In the subsequent political melee, she will secure what she can for those whom she represents. Should new groups emerge or people's ideas change, the leader must stay in tune, or else be replaced through the ballot box.

Individualist democrats also glorify personal liberties and individual rights. This position flows from the concept of the sanctity of the individual—a sanctity that carves a sphere around each individual into which no legislative body may tread, no matter how big the majority. The language of rights—right to privacy, right to absolute freedom of speech, right to free exercise of any religion, right to unbridled use of private property, unregulated right to abortion—is critical in individualist democracy. The reach of the state has definite limits, then; policies which bump up against an individual's personal rights are unacceptable. No person or government has the right to penetrate into a zone which should be under the control of the individual. Much of the conflict in an individualist democracy, in fact, is over how far, and in what areas of life, the majority may go in limiting individual choices.

Citizenship and Individualist Democracy

What does individualist democracy require of the good citizen? Primarily, it demands three things: (1) that he pursue his own interests with vigor; (2) that he be sensitive to keeping the rules fair; and (3) that he assert his rights against government to ward off intrusions into liberty.

The pursuit of self-interest is good for several reasons. First, it encourages people to participate, for nothing motivates people so much as their own needs and wants. Second, no one is a better advocate of a particular position than one who is directly affected. Furthermore, the pursuit of self-interest encourages self-reliance. Finally, it assures that, given the multitude of interests in society, all interests have a chance of being heard.

Acquiring political knowledge is quite important for the citizen, for the more understanding people have about the way government works, the more effectively they can pursue their interests. Those who understand the political process will have a decided advantage over less well prepared adversaries. Individualist democrats urge widespread civic education, then, because it will make the playing field more even. Becoming politically knowledgeable, therefore, is part of the pursuit of self-interest.

Individualist democrats hold that the need to assure fairness is partly ethical (the proof of one's commitment to democracy itself), and partly dictated also by self-interest. That is, by keeping the processes fair for today's "losers," one is hedging against the day she may be in the minority. Furthermore, when the processes are truly fair and open, then everyone can win some of the time, securing at least some of what she wants. This is not only good in itself; it also buttresses allegiance to the system, keeping anyone from rocking the boat too severely.

Vigilance in protecting one's rights is essential to check the tendency of any government to seek too much power. Government always needs to be restrained in order to allow maximum discretion to the individual. Obviously, certain rules are necessary for the maintenance of social peace and order, but the pronounced preference should be for the individual over the the government. Whenever government chooses to regulate individual behavior, therefore, it must bear a heavy burden of proof that its actions are truly necessary.

Not all individualist democrats, it should be stressed, agree on every political issue. They disagree among themselves, for instance, about which procedures are most fair. Along different lines, individualist democrats often have sharply differing preferences concerning which individual rights should be accorded priority. For example, many who favor absolute abortion rights for women are unconcerned about property rights, and vice versa. Nonetheless, most important for our purposes is the common ground they share, the common grammar of politics with which they carry on their discussions. Individualist democracy establishes postulates about how the political system works in practice and how it should work, providing many Americans with a set of guidelines about what they should value and how they should act.

CIVIC DEMOCRACY

In contrast to these beliefs stands a model I will call *civic democracy.* Civic democracy does not seek to deny the importance of individuals; however, it begins with the observation that people cannot live outside a political community. Individualism carried to an extreme means loneliness, isolation and even danger. Meaningful life—anything approaching individual fulfillment—is only possible in community. The political community is not constituted, therefore, merely to achieve certain practical projects which individuals find that they cannot do alone, such as law enforcement. The political community provides for the spiritual, emotional, social, intellectual and cultural well-being of its members—not for their physical needs alone.

The notion that politics gives life to the community in this broad fashion carries a corollary: a *public* interest exists which is separate and distinct from the mere aggregation of everyone's private interests. The aim of government policy, then, is to find this public interest and pursue it.

The usual criticism of the concept of the public interest or public good lies in the inherent difficulty of satisfactorily defining it. Unless we turn the matter over to a small elite group, which would clearly be unacceptable in any type of democracy, there is no way to decide if any one person's definition of the public interest is superior to someone else's. Better, the individualist democrats say, to discard the whole notion and rely on the outcome of a fair political contest in which everyone defines the public good as he wishes. However, this rebuttal misses an important point: there is a vast difference between an argument over the meaning of the public interest and a denial that such a thing exists. Mere disagreement over what the public interest is neither negates its existence, nor makes it an irrelevant focus for political debate. A debate over what the public interest is in some policy area is quite a different matter from a debate in which each side promotes only its own interest.

This desire to search for the public interest leads to a critical tenet: the inherent value of government by discussion and deliberation. The civic democrat believes that people are capable of being persuaded by rational argument; this means that both talking *and* listening are vital. The individualist democrat speaks of talk and the "marketplace of ideas," but says little of the obligation to listen. The civic democrat, by emphasizing the search for the public good, is obligated to listen as well as speak, hopeful that knowledge and understanding will grow and better public policies result. "The Quaker meeting, with its periods of silence for reflection and its groping for consensus," says Benjamin Barber, "carries a message for democrats, but they are often too busy articulating their interests to hear it."[5]

Leadership is also somewhat different in a civic democracy. A leader in this model is one who can speak intelligently about public issues and who can persuade the voters that she is genuinely seeking the public interest. Once in office, while not jettisoning the skills of the bargainer, compromiser, and broker, she performs the primary task of offering justifications—well-reasoned and morally acceptable justifications—for her actions.

Another tenet of civic democracy is the inherent legitimacy accorded to public institutions. To the individualist democrat, public institutions are created only as a result of something called "market failure," which occurs when individual actions are not satisfactory. For instance, national defense or law enforcement must be provided by government, because too many people would not "purchase" their shares if the market were allowed to operate.[6] In other areas, such as highway construction, it is simply more efficient to have government provide some services than to allow competition. In general, though, most individualist democrats want to restrict the role of the state as much as is feasible.

The civic democrat, in contrast, wants to create a genuine public sphere. For the civic democrat, public parks, for example, are not merely conveniences and attractive nature preserves. They are places of community focus, allowing citizens to see one another, to mingle, to discuss. An army, for another example, should not consist of "hired hands" whose services have been purchased on the open market; rather, it should be a truly public institution. Parallel arguments can be adduced for public schools, public transportation, and so forth. The civic democrat does not necessarily wish to enlarge the public sector; rather his concern is that the public institutions that do exist be treated as *public* institutions, as valuable components and symbols of public life, not as necessary evils which merely facilitate individual pursuits.

Of absolutely fundamental importance is the role the civic democrat assigns to personal virtue. A monarchy, it has often been noted, will be only as good as its king or queen; a government resting on the people likewise will be only as good as the people are. "The idea of virtue was central to the political thought of the Founders of the American republic . . . It was understood by the Founders to be the *precondition* for [democratic] government, the base upon which the structure of government would be built."[7] In the same vein, another prominent political scientist summarized the Founders' views this way: "It takes more than a perfect plan of government to pursue ordered liberty. Something else is needed, some moral principle diffused among the people to strengthen the urge to peaceful obedience and hold the community on an even keel . . . [Free] government rests on a definite moral basis: a virtuous people."[8]

Unfortunately, though, virtue is not inherent in the human species; it must be taught and nurtured. In many societies, both ancient and modern, the government has emphasized the need for a virtuous people and set about to teach and enforce its notion of virtue. The civic democrat is

Abraham Lincoln delivering his second inaugural address in March 1865. Lincoln stressed several basic themes on citizenship.

opposed, however, to the government's directly undertaking the promotion of virtue, for that would lead to a deadening uniformity, as well as opening the door to totalitarianism. Numerous historical examples of dogmatic attempts to enforce virtue leap to mind, such as the Spain of the Inquisition or the Soviet Union of the Stalinist purges. To guard against the potential abuses of any government-sponsored effort to impose virtue, the civic democrat prefers to put the task of promoting virtue squarely in the hands of those "mediating institutions"—the family, the church,[9] the neighborhood, the school—that lie between the individual and the state. Richard Vetterli and Gary Bryner note that "the American Founders . . . clearly believed that a republic . . . depended upon the quantity and quality of moral virtue in the people, which owes its origins to sources that are prior to and apart from the political system, and which have traditionally been nurtured at the breast, the hearth, the pulpit, the classroom, and in private associations for public ends."[10]

9

TABLE 1–1

Major Features of Individualist and Civic Democracy

	INDIVIDUALIST DEMOCRACY	CIVIC DEMOCRACY
Philosophical emphasis	Individual	Community
Proper motivation for citizens	Self-interest	Public interest and self-interest
The public interest	A sum of the interests of all individuals	An entity apart from each individual's interest
Political leaders	Those who are most successful at appealing to people's self-interest	Those who offer thoughtful solutions to public problems
Political process	Fair and open procedures so that all can pursue self-interest on level playing field	Reasoned deliberation marked by search for the public interest
Public institutions	No inherent legitimacy Preference for private action	Related to sense of community
Rights	Strong emphasis on individual rights	Some emphasis on individual rights, but also consideration of interests of community
Personal behavior	Maximum freedom	Virtue and self-discipline

For civic democrats, then, the health of a democracy rests on the health of these mediating institutions.[11] Government, especially national government, is too remote to be the only bonding agency that ties the individual to the political community. It is in the family, the neighborhood, the church, the lodge, and the recreational club that the individual finds her identity and lives her life. That private life is not disconnected from the role of citizen; on the contrary, private life is a vital part of citizenship.

CITIZENSHIP AND CIVIC DEMOCRACY

What are the obligations of a citizen in the view of civic democrats? Essentially, there are four expectations: (1) that he act virtuously in private and public life; (2) that he consider the public interest as well as his own narrow interest; (3) that he have tolerance and respect for other citizens; and (4) that he develop an attachment to and nurture the mediating institutions of which he is a part.

Acting virtuously is not only morally good for the individual, but also necessary if a system of ordered liberty is to endure. No society can exist without order, and if this order is not to be imposed from above, the only alternative is for the people to act virtuously without coercion. Civic democracy frowns on the idea of excessive regulation of people's behavior; but it frowns equally on behavior that needs regulating. Quite candidly, this means that citizens must exercise a heavy dose of self-discipline. One

John F. Kennedy's inaugural address in January 1961 was the young president's best speech. Its inspiring phrases stirred the imagination of many young Americans for a generation to come.

writer put it more colloquially: "Citizenship sometimes means having to sit up straight and tie your shoes."[12]

The civic democrat believes that people are capable of seeing beyond their immediate circumstances to the good of the society generally. In fact, it is in their self-interest, broadly defined, to do so; who can gain if the entire society is weakened? Good citizens, therefore, should keep the public interest in mind when thinking about public problems and when deciding for whom to cast their vote. This commandment does not require that a citizen jettison her own interest and adopt a totally unselfish outlook at all times. That is both unrealistic and unhealthy. What it asks is that some thought be given to the public interest while one pursues one's own interest. Candidates for public office, therefore, should be evaluated not only on how their positions match up with the citizens' own interests, but also on what kind of moral vision those candidates paint.

Tolerance and respect for one's fellow citizens are essential in a society prizing equality among the citizenry, which is the only option for democracies. This means that the good citizen not only extends common courtesies but truly treats others with a sense of their dignity. Moreover, respect requires listening carefully to other citizens' ideas and messages, assuming all the while that their motives are as good as one's own. Public dialogue leading to wise public decisions is only possible when people listen and weigh as well as advocate.

The civic democrat expects the good citizen to recognize, furthermore, that citizenship is not detached from private life or from the small com-

11

munities to which one belongs. Families, churches, neighborhood organizations, charitable organizations, youth groups, civic clubs—life in these and many more such institutions and associations is part and parcel of citizenship in a civic democracy. The good citizen will cultivate a life in these bodies, for they not only form critical links between the individual and the larger society, but are the vital transmission belts for educating future citizens.

What about participation? The civic democrat is as strongly in favor of widespread participation as the individualist democrat. But the civic democrat does not view participation as a means to secure one's private needs; rather he expects participation to grow naturally out of an active citizenship. It is only a part of good citizenship, not the definition of it. In fact, the good citizen will not consider it an option *not* to participate.

Civic democracy, it must be emphasized, does not entail uniformity of views or lifestyles. It does not dictate the precise meaning of virtue, except at the most general level; it asserts only that virtue is important. Civic democracy does not define the public interest, but merely asserts that there is one. It does not preordain the course of public deliberation, much less the consensus which might emerge, but simply outlines the manner in which debate should be carried on. It does not declare which mediating institutions should be prominent, how they should be structured, or that the same ones are appropriate for each individual, but insists only that their health is important. Nor does civic democracy provide automatic answers to questions of political structure or public policy. Like individualist democracy, it is a framework that serves as an approach to politics and political life.

DESCRIPTION VERSUS PRESCRIPTION

For some time, the academic study of American politics has been dominated by the individualist model. The Constitution, for instance, has repeatedly been viewed as an elaborate attempt to control and channel people's natural selfish desires.[13] But this is at best only a partial truth. In fact, "A great gulf . . . separates the thought of [the Founding Fathers] from that of believers in such later concepts as . . . utilitarianism and simple majoritarian democracy, who denied that principles of justice and virtue can be identified and made the foundation of government."[14] Furthermore, "The Founders believed that the 'auxiliary precautions' [of the Constitution], *combined* with, rather than replacing, individual virtue, might just make it all possible."[15]

Part of the confusion lies in the difference between *description* and *prescription*. The individualist model unquestionably describes how government often works; however, it clearly does not explain everything that happens in politics. In his review of policy making, for example, Steven Kelman finds any number of instances in which members of Congress have taken public needs into account, and other instances in which presidents have pursued policies they thought were in the public interest even though it cost them electorally.[16] Individual citizens also can often be found acting contrary to what the individualist model would predict, as when people set up interest groups to benefit people other than themselves (such as the homeless or prisoners).

In fact, at the most basic level of explanation and description, the individualist model suffers from a debilitating contradiction. Exhorting people to participate in politics to pursue self-interest is futile; it is obvious to most people that the rational pursuit of individual self-interest dictates that energy be spent elsewhere (making money and making love, as one observer put it [17]). In fact, since people continue to vote and to take voting seriously, some factor other than pure self-interest must be at work. Thus, someone viewing everyday American politics could find ample illustrations of both models at work.

Yet, it is when we turn from description to prescription that the differences between the models is most important. If the individualist model is made an "ought" in addition to an "is," it can become a self-fulfilling prophecy. As Steven Kelman says, "self-interest in politics begets self-interest. The more it is believed that people in government are simply out for themselves, the more it will become true that this is the case."[18] Teaching civic democracy, on the other hand, can alter the "is" because people will change their behavior based on their beliefs.

The point is a crucial one. In a related vein, the eminent anthropologist Clifford Geertz reminds us that law has an educative function as well as a social control function,[19] and that the educative aspect should not be overlooked. So too with theories of democracy. What we grow to expect will largely determine what we get; to hold up something as an ideal is in part to bring it into being. Ralph Ketcham writes, "The crux is not what exists, but what is valued and encouraged."[20]

The ideal of self-government has stirred people's imaginations for centuries, and there remains something uplifting about the notion of a society in which the people have no rulers but themselves. As we enter the 1990s, that noble idea is shaking the foundations of the social and political orders in the former Soviet Union, Eastern Europe, South Africa, Central America, and East Asia. Keeping our own democracy healthy is surely the best way we can serve the interests of democracy elsewhere, and that can only be done by building and nourishing healthy citizenship. E. J. Dionne has written recently, "Talk of citizenship and civic virtue sounds utopian. In fact, it is the essence of practical politics. Only by restoring our sense of common citizenship can we hope to deal with the most profound—and practical—issues before us."[21]

....

ENDNOTES

1. See the articles in the *Washington Post Weekly Edition*, May 14–20, 1990.

2. The status of citizen was sharply restricted in most Greek city-states, and there was no belief in the equality of all people. Slavery, for example, was common in many of the democracies.

3. Paper participation as an illusion of actual participation is discussed in John Hart Ely, *Democracy and Distrust* (Cambridge, Mass.: Harvard University Press, 1980), chap. 4.

4. This formulation is known as the philosophy of utilitarianism, whose chief advocate was the nineteenth-century English philosopher Jeremy Bentham.

5. Benjamin Barber, *Strong Democracy* (Berkeley: University of California Press, 1984), 176.

6. This would result from what is known as the "free rider" problem. That is, it would be irrational for an individual to purchase a share of national defense unless he were assured that all other citizens would purchase their shares. Governmental coercion through taxation is the only way to assure such purchases. Thus, everyone benefits from the coercion.

7. Richard Vetterli and Gary Bryner, *In Search of the Republic: Public Virtue and the Roots of American Government* (Totowa, N.J.: Rowman and Littlefield, 1987), 1.

8. Clinton Rossiter, *Seedtime of the Republic* (New York: Harcourt, Brace, 1953), 447.

9. I am using the term "church" here as a shorthand to cover all religious institutions and not as an exclusionary term.

10. Vetterli and Bryner, *In Search of the Republic,* 247.

11. See Peter Berger and Richard John Neuhaus, *To Empower People: The Role of Mediating Structures in Public Policy* (Washington: American Enterprise Institute, 1977).

12. Mark Lilla, "On Civic Liberalism: A Symposium," *The New Republic,* June 18, 1990, 28.

13. One interpretation holds that a faith in civic virtue infused the ideas leading to the break with Britain, ideas which find their political expression in the Declaration of Independence. Afterwards, free governments allowed so many unhealthy passions to become unleashed that political thinkers turned their attention to constructing institutions to control them. The Constitution represents their handiwork. This scenario is laid out most ably in Gordon Wood, *The Creation of the American Republic* (Chapel Hill: University of North Carolina Press, 1969).

14. Ralph Ketcham, *James Madison: A Biography* (New York: Macmillan, 1971), 43.

15. Vetterli and Bryner, *In Search of the Republic,* 6. Emphasis in original.

16. Steven Kelman, *Making Public Policy: A Hopeful View of American Politics* (New York: Basic Books, 1988).

17. Gerald Pomper, "The Contribution of Political Parties to Democracy," in Pomper, ed., *Party Renewal in America* (New York: Praeger, 1980), 7. In fact, it is easy to demonstrate that from a pure self-interest perspective, voting is irrational.

18. Kelman, *Making Public Policy,* 293.

19. Clifford Geertz, *Local Knowledge: Further Essays in Interpretive Anthropology* (New York: Basic Books, 1983).

20. Ralph Ketcham, *Individualism and Public Life* (New York: Basil Blackwell, 1987), ix.

21. E.J. Dionne, *Why Americans Hate Politics* (New York: Simon and Schuster, 1991), 333.

FURTHER READING

1. Bellah, Robert. *Habits of the Heart: Individualism and Commitment in American Life*. Berkeley: University of California Press, 1985.

2. Dionne, E.J. *Why Americans Hate Politics*. New York: Simon and Schuster, 1991.

3. Fowler, Robert Booth. *The Dance with Community: The Contemporary Debate in American Political Thought*. Lawrence: University Press of Kansas, 1991.

4. Reich, Robert, ed. *The Power of Public Ideas*. Cambridge, Mass.: Harvard University Press, 1990.

5. Shklar, Judith. *American Citizenship: The Quest for Inclusion*. Cambridge, Mass.: Harvard University Press, 1991.

6. Sinopoli, Richard. *The Foundations of American Citizenship: Liberalism, the Constitution, and Civic Virtue*. New York: Oxford University Press, 1992.

7. Sullivan, William. *Reconstructing Public Philosophy*. Berkeley: University of California Press, 1986.

TWO

THE CONSTITUTION

IN THE SUMMER of 1787, fifty-five men gathered in Philadelphia, then the largest city in the United States, supposedly to revise the nearly moribund Articles of Confederation. Instead, they quickly turned to drafting an entirely new constitution. Before they were finished, they had traveled through a vast terrain of political theory, as well as engaged in plenty of old-fashioned bargaining. In the end, they produced what William Gladstone, a nineteenth-century British prime minister, once called "the most wonderful work ever struck off at a given time by the brain and purpose of man."[1]

The Constitution has come to serve a dual purpose in American political life.[2] On the one hand, it is an instrument of government, granting and limiting power. It establishes the institutions of government, sets forth how they shall operate, designates how political leaders shall be chosen, and lays out what political authority those who occupy various positions may and may not exercise. In short, it sets forth the rules of political conduct. However, our Constitution has in addition assumed an important symbolic role. It has come in fact to signify all that the nation stands for, becoming over the years an object of veneration and quasi-religious imagery. Chief Justice (and former president) William Howard Taft captured this spirit when he called it our "Ark of the Covenant."[3] Thus, public discourse about it is conducted in respectful tones, and the gravest epithet that can be given to some proposal is that it is "unconstitutional." As such, it lies outside the realm of the morally acceptable.

Moreover, the symbolic role of the Constitution provides a glimpse into the nature of American society. It goes in fact to the heart of how American citizenship is defined and what it means to be an American. For in our society as in few others we define nationality purely in political terms, both legally and symbolically.

What were the origins of this remarkable document? What is its structure? How has it accommodated the political changes which have occurred between the late eighteenth and late twentieth centuries?

DRAFTING THE CONSTITUTION

The fifty-five men who met in Philadelphia did not begin *de novo*. The colonies had existed as political entities for 169 years before the Declaration of Independence in 1776. Several centuries of English political history lay behind that. Moreover, these men were affected by the intellectual currents of their time. In general, they were a well-read elite, with libraries stocked with works on political ideas. Fortunately, though, they were not merely armchair political philosophers; they were fully conversant with practical politics, all having held important public offices. They understood inti-

---

Opposite: *Over 5000 new citizens taking the constitutional oath in Houston, Texas in April 1988.*

mately how governmental institutions worked—and the difference between what was theoretically desirable and what could be adopted in 1787.

The Colonial Background

Colonial government began largely because officials in London did not want to be bothered with colonial problems.[4] The English colonies, in contrast to the French and Spanish, had been settled by private endeavors. No royal officials preceded or accompanied the original colonists. Once society became somewhat settled, there was a need for basic public services such as law enforcement and roads. Feeling little responsibility, the British government told the colonists to take care of these things themselves, starting a long tradition in America of locally based self-help.

Although there was some variation, all thirteen colonies evolved broadly similar structures of government. First in authority was the governor, appointed in most colonies by the king. The governor was the symbol of royal authority in the colony, and in theory possessed vast powers. He controlled the militia and had to approve all laws passed by the legislature. However, although there were notable exceptions, most of the colonial governors were third-rate hacks who had been given undesirable patronage appointments far removed from London. Even the most energetic governors discovered that the king was far away and the colonial legislatures were nearby. Many, if not most, found it easier to cooperate with the legislatures than to fight them; after all, neither the king nor the politicians in London could offer much help.

The legislatures originated in order to levy taxes, since the British government neglected colonial requests for public works. Legislators were elected only by property-holding white males. Although participation was therefore quite limited by our standards, by eighteenth-century norms it was liberal indeed.[5] As a result of the lack of interest in London, legislators gradually assumed a wide array of powers and became accustomed to a large degree of independence.

Because royal governors, even under the best of circumstances, were unfamiliar with colonial conditions, most early charters provided for a council of about a dozen prominent citizens to advise the chief executive. They counseled him regarding appointments and on whether or not to approve acts of the legislatures. Over time, these councils began meeting apart from the governors and forwarding their recommendations after a vote among themselves. Consequently, they drifted closer to the legislatures, and by the time of the Revolution were functioning more as upper houses of the legislatures than as executive bodies.

Intercolonial political contact was minimal, as each of the colonies was tied more closely to London than to its neighbors. There were a few attempts at intercolonial cooperation and even some temporary leagues and compacts. Typically, however, these were formed to deal with some emergency, such as an Indian war, and when the danger passed they disbanded.

It was only with the continuing crises following 1763 that the colonies drew together. The end of the Seven Years' War in that year had left Britain victorious but deeply in debt. British politicians cast covetous eyes at the now-prosperous colonies, arguing that the colonies reaped significant benefits from the empire—benefits for which they should pay.

Perhaps American separation from Britain would have occurred at some time in any event. But in fact, the above conditions, aggravated by monumental political blunders in London, led to a tax revolt. By 1776 the Revolutionary War was being waged, and American political history set on a new course.

At the national level, the war was fought by the hastily convened Second Continental Congress. Its members were chosen by and answered to state legislatures. Because they had no power to tax, money was their main problem. A question arose immediately: what would be done if the United States won the war? A committee was appointed to study this problem and to draft a constitution.

The Articles of Confederation

By 1781 all thirteen states had approved the committee's work, the Articles of Confederation.[6] The design of this document was rather simple: it established a one-house Congress, with no executive branch and no court system. Each state was entitled to between two and seven representatives in the Congress, but votes were cast by states. State governments paid their representatives' salaries and could replace a member of their delegation at any time. The only stipulation was that no one could serve more than three out of any six years.

The powers given Congress were considerable. It could conduct foreign affairs, declare war, coin money, establish weights and measures, deal with the Indians, operate a post office, borrow money, and settle state boundary disputes. In addition, a national budget was to be composed, with each state assessed its share based on the value of land within it. Lastly, Congress could request that the states provide soldiers for the United States in proportion to their population.

These last two elements were the Achilles' heel of the government under the Articles. Since Congress could only request state financial contributions and military support, not require them, the national government was enfeebled. When the supply of either money or the instruments of coercion is controlled by another government, the exercise of authority is dependent ultimately on the approval of the provider (in this case, the states). The situation, in fact, was not radically different from that of the United Nations today.[7] Grandiose schemes may be proposed and all manner of debates held, but action depends on the cooperation of those with money and arms.

Moreover, a gaping hole was national regulation of commerce. Some provisions did limit the states' ability to control foreign commerce, but internal economic affairs were left almost entirely to the states. As events proved, this further hamstrung the central government's authority.

Finally, the Articles were virtually frozen in time, for the unanimous consent of the states was necessary to ratify any amendment. Not surprisingly, there were no successful amendments.

The Declaration of Independence had detailed the problems of strong government run amuck; the Articles gave people a taste of life under weak government. The immediate cause of much of the discontent was a severe economic depression. Once victorious, the United States had been placed outside the British empire's tariff system, which served to interrupt most trading patterns. Bankruptcies and loan foreclosures brought unrest, riots, and even civil rebellions. State governments often reacted by establishing tariffs to protect their own manufacturers, which merely worsened the situation. Requests by Congress to the states for funds were typically given a low priority or brushed aside. No state ever paid all it was asked (they had economic difficulties of their own); North Carolina, as an extreme case, never paid a cent.

In addition to its financial woes, Congress was not taken seriously by foreign governments. With no military force at its disposal, it was ignored. The British, for instance, would not leave their forts in the Northwest, and Congress could do little but plead.

Yet, we must guard against seeing those years as filled with crises.[8] Several important reforms were undertaken by states, and the Congress did pass one of the most far-reaching laws of our history, the Northwest Ordinance of 1787.[9] State boundaries in the west had never been clear, and several claims overlapped extensively. Congress was able to persuade the states to hand over all disputed areas to the national government for administration. The Northwest Ordinance followed, creating the Northwest Territory and setting up a system of territorial government. Most significantly, it provided that when the population reached a certain level, three to five new states would be established, states with equal status to the original thirteen. This enactment set a vitally important precedent for the whole western movement and dramatically shaped our federalism by making all states legally equal. Consider the possible consequences if Congress had provided instead for two classes of states, original and new.

As a whole, however, the experience under the Articles was daunting. Radical movements won election in some state legislatures, particularly Rhode Island, and proceeded to frighten the upper classes by adopting laws such as one which permitted debtors to delay their loan payments. In other places, mob violence threatened established interests and civil order generally. In western Massachusetts, farmers went on a rampage known as Shays' Rebellion, taking over courthouses and burning tax documents that threatened foreclosures on their land.

The Philadelphia Convention

Moderate and conservative leaders from throughout the country were convinced that some type of action had to be taken. The Philadelphia Convention, called to propose amendments to the Articles, resulted.

The 1787 Constitutional Convention in Philadelphia as depicted in a nineteenth century painting.

Much has been made through the years of the differences these men brought to Philadelphia, especially the North–South and large state–small state cleavages.[10] But it is just as important to stress their areas of agreement. First, there was a universal consensus to discard the Articles and start afresh. Second, most agreed that a national government had to be created, with its power derived from the people and with the power to act independently of the states. That is, the central institutions of government must not be dependent on the states for their authority, their money, or their army.

Third, the Philadelphia delegates shared the intellectual heritage of the late eighteenth century. Government, they all agreed, should be based on the people, an idea known as popular sovereignty.[11] There were no monarchists or advocates of dictatorship here. Popular sovereignty is not synonymous with democracy, however. Although they felt government should rest on the people, few of these men believed in widespread public participation. To use Abraham Lincoln's famous terminology, theirs was to be a government of the people and for the people, but only indirectly by the people.[12]

Furthermore, the delegates shared a belief in the rule of law: the idea that government itself must be subject to the law. Those in power should not be able act in an arbitrary or capricious manner. Additionally, they thought that people had certain natural rights which could not be invaded by government. These rights were not given by government, but inhered in the person. A legitimate government respected these rights, and was thereby limited in the scope of its power.

To be sure, those who gathered in Philadelphia differed strongly on a number of issues. For instance, what was the extent of natural rights? Along different lines, some men, including Alexander Hamilton, wanted a lifetime president and a Senate chosen only from among men of substantial property. Others stood by Luther Martin, a prominent member from Maryland, who wanted to limit severely the central government's powers. But these were disagreements within a framework of consensus, which allowed these controversies to be worked out through compromise.

Whenever large groups meet, if no one has proposed an agenda, a lot of time is usually wasted and little gets done. However, if someone has a proposal ready, debate immediately forms around it. Seldom will the proposal be adopted *in toto,* but a framework will have been established and certain issues omitted. It will be much harder to raise new issues than to suggest amendments to the original proposal. Such was the case in Philadelphia.

Before the convention, the Virginia delegation drew up a set of resolutions laying out a proposed structure of government. It is unlikely that any Virginia delegate expected their plan to be fully adopted, but they had seized the initiative.

The Virginia Plan called for a vastly strengthened national government and the establishment of distinct branches. Congress was to have two houses, each with seats apportioned on the basis of population. The lower house was to be elected "by the people of the several States." For the upper house, state legislatures would submit names to the lower house, which would then select the members. A "National Executive" (not yet called a president) would be chosen by Congress for a single term (the length of which was to be specified in a later draft). A national court system was to be set up, consisting of a "supreme tribunal" and such other courts as Congress saw fit to establish. Lastly, a Council of Revision, composed of the National Executive and several judges, would have the power to veto acts of Congress. These vetoes could be overridden by a supermajority in Congress (the actual percentage was not given).

The proposed powers of Congress were enormous compared to those bestowed by the Articles. The Virginia Plan gave Congress all the powers it had previously exercised, along with the ability to act in "all cases in which the separate States are incompetent." Congress would also be authorized to overturn any state law and employ the army against states.

Sensing that the Virginia Plan would undermine the influence of the smaller states, a New Jersey delegate offered an alternative (see table 2-1). In the New Jersey Plan, Congress' structure would remain as it was under the Articles: equal state representation, with members chosen by the legislatures. The New Jersey Plan added an executive branch headed by a committee (of an as yet undetermined size) chosen by Congress. Like the Virginia Plan, New Jersey's also proposed a national court system.

Expansive powers would be given to Congress under the New Jersey Plan as well, including the power to regulate commerce and to tax individuals if the states did not pay their assessments. A few other details, such as making the Federal Executive Committee commander of the armed

T A B L E 2–1

Major Features of the Virginia and New Jersey Plans

	VIRGINIA PLAN	NEW JERSEY PLAN
Structure of Congress	Two houses, both based on population. Lower house popularly elected; upper house selected by lower from lists supplied by states.	One house with equal state representation. Members chosen by state legislatures.
Executive branch	Single National Executive chosen by Congress. One-term limit.	Committee chosen by Congress.
National courts	Yes	Yes
Other significant points	Veto exercised by Council of Revision. Congressional override possible.	Federal Executive Committee put in charge of armed forces. Supremacy Clause

forces, fleshed out the proposal. Of lasting importance, a Supremacy Clause was inserted, making all national laws stand above state enactments.

Obviously, the critical difference in the two plans revolved around representation in Congress. After intense debate, a compromise was worked out, suggested by Connecticut, which in essence substituted the Congress of the New Jersey Plan for the upper house of the Virginia Plan. Most small state delegates were placated, since the compromise assured equal state representation in the upper house (and made this provision unamendable), allowed the state legislatures to choose upper house members, and gave the Senate more powers than the lower house.

The biggest hurdle was behind the delegates, although much more work remained to be done. An executive branch provision had yet to be crafted, details needed to be worked out on the division of powers between the national and state governments, and decisions were yet to be faced concerning slavery.

Even in 1787, most educated people, even many slaveowners, considered slavery an odious practice.[13] This can be seen, for example, in the fact that the framers avoided even using the word, adopting euphemisms like "person held to service or labor" (Article IV). More than likely, all the delegates, both northerners and southerners, would have liked to evade the issue. However, practicality forced it onto the agenda for two reasons. First, southern representatives wanted to count slaves for purposes of representation in the lower house (surely one of the most cynical suggestions ever made), but not in the apportionment of "direct" taxes. The "compromise" was that slaves would count as three-fifths of a person for both purposes.[14] The second matter raised regarding slaves was the cruel and inhumane slave trade. At southern insistence, it could not be outlawed for twenty years.[15]

A slave auction: Slavery in the states remained one of the great unresolved issues of the Constitutional Convention and it was to have tragic consequences throughout the nation's history.

Ratification: Federalists versus Anti-Federalists

When the final draft of the Constitution was completed, the struggle over ratification began; each state held a special convention to vote on the new document.[16] Within each state, a heated debate erupted between the proponents and opponents of the new Constitution, labeled Federalists and Anti-Federalists respectively. The main arguments of the Federalists centered on the need for a strong defense capability and the building of a unified commercial market; at the same time, they stressed the limited nature of the new national government, pointing out that it was only given certain carefully circumscribed powers.

The Anti-Federalists advanced many arguments, but two are especially significant.[17]

First, the Anti-Federalists insisted that the United States was too large and too diverse a society in which to erect a government resting on the people. They felt that self-government was only possible in smaller, more tightly-knit societies, where people's interests were basically similar. Thus, only political systems the size of the states, or even smaller perhaps, could provide the social homogeneity necessary for a true political community. The discord produced by having so many different types of people of varying political interests under one governmental roof would breed uncontrollable conflict, which would in turn produce demands for despotism. If political authority were concentrated at the center, then an "empire," in which some few would rule over the many, would be the inevitable result.

The Federalists contended in rebuttal that America was indeed a political community. The people had fought the Revolutionary War as a people, and were therefore bound to each other as individuals, not only as members of state political communities. Thus, the prerequisites for an American government based directly on the people existed. Furthermore, the Constitution's supporters argued that the checks and balances contained within the Constitution (discussed later in this chapter) would prevent the development of despotism.

Second, the Anti-Federalists criticized the lack of a Bill of Rights. What was to keep the national government from overstepping its bounds and infringing upon the very rights the Revolution had been fought to secure? The Federalists replied that Congress was not given powers to legislate in the areas traditionally protected by bills of rights. Not satisfied with this answer, wavering members of some conventions secured promises that one of Congress' first tasks would be to draw up amendments regarding basic rights. In response, Congress dutifully submitted a set of amendments to the states in 1789; these were ratified as the Bill of Rights in 1791. Thus, in reality, the first ten amendments can be considered part of the original document, inasmuch as they grew out of the same broad political process as the Constitution itself.

The framers had provided that when nine states assented to the Constitution, the new government would begin. Several smaller states ratified immediately, and the required total of nine was reached on June 21, 1788. However, Virginia and New York had still not ratified. A government without either state would have been difficult; one without both, almost impossible. Fortunately, both Virginia and the New York conventions voted affirmatively by late July.

Of special note was a series of newspaper articles written during the struggle for ratification in New York. Authored by Alexander Hamilton, James Madison, and John Jay, but signed "Publius," these *Federalist Papers* urged the adoption of the document. More important in the long run, they provide an incisive commentary on the Constitution by men close to its adoption.

The Constitution was not drafted, in sum, on a clean slate. It is a product of political evolution, its roots fastened in the deep soil of British and colonial history. But political history sets the boundaries of what is possible; it does not determine specific events. The Constitution must also be seen therefore as a product of the political currents and passions of the day. The greatest perceived need was for order; this is not uncommon after a revolution. What is remarkable about the American achievement is not that a stable national government was established; a dictatorship could and oftentimes does accomplish that. What is remarkable and admirable is that the document which had order as its overriding aim also set the stage for continued political change.

Constitution Drafting in Another British Colony

ORGANIZATIONAL THEORISTS tell us that healthy organizations, like psychologically healthy people, learn from their mistakes. The British government, it seems, learned a great deal from its disastrous dealings with the American colonies.

When unrest broke out in Canada in the 1830s, the colonial authorities dispatched a team of investigators, led by the prominent Lord Durham. Acting on their report, Parliament granted a large measure of self-government to these colonies, while at the same time trying to minimize the tensions between English-speaking and French-speaking inhabitants.

As population grew and economic development proceeded, sentiment grew among the British North American colonies (as they were known) for some type of federation. Following a series of conferences in the 1860s, a draft plan was presented to the British government. The British Parliament then passed the British North America Act of 1867, establishing a national government for Canada and dividing governmental powers between the Dominion of Canada and the provinces. In essence, the BNA Act created a parliamentary system at the national level, with a prime minister and cabinet responsible to (capable of being ousted by) a popularly elected House of Commons. As for the federal equation, after witnessing the American Civil War, the Canadian founding fathers opted for a strong central government. Ironically, though, political forces and several important court opinions would in time give Canadians a quite decentralized political system.

The BNA Act, however, did not make Canada an independent country, for two important powers remained in British hands. First, the British courts retained the power to interpret the Act; second, foreign affairs were to continue to be conducted from London. In 1914, for instance, when Britain entered World War I, Canada was declared to be at war also.

In 1931, Britain relinquished its control over the foreign policies of the dominions (which now included Australia, New Zealand, and South Africa, as well as Canada) by the Statute of Westminster. In 1949, at the request of the Canadian government, the British Parliament amended the BNA Act to disallow appeals from Canadian courts

AN OUTLINE OF THE CONSTITUTION

The Enduring Dilemma

At every turn, the Founding Fathers faced the dilemma that had brought them to Philadelphia. On the one hand, the purpose of the Revolution had been the elimination of tyranny. The Declaration of Independence conto British courts. Thus, the Supreme Court of Canada became the ultimate interpreter of the "constitution."

Beginning in the 1930s, there was discussion in Canada of bringing the constitution home, or "patriating" it. By the 1960s the issue of patriation was being widely debated throughout the country. But the debate was not over whether to do it, a point on which almost everyone agreed; it was rather on what the amending formula should be once the constitution was no longer an act of the British Parliament. Although there were several controversial issues, the principal one was Quebec's unease over the status of language rights. Since Quebec is the only predominantly French-speaking province, many in Quebec feared that any type of majority formula might open the door to the other nine provinces' amending away the language protections contained in the BNA Act. Every attempt at compromise ran afoul of Quebec's veto, and the British government was hesitant to hand over the constitution unless there was a consensus in Canada for it to do so.

In 1981 the Canadian federal government, with the backing of the other nine provinces, proposed a new amending formula virtually exempting language rights from amendment and renewed the push for patriation. At the same time, a new Charter of Rights and Freedoms was added. The Quebec government still demurred, but its position was undermined because the Quebec separatists (advocating separation from Canada) had just lost an important provincial election. On March 29, 1982, 115 years to the day after the adoption of the BNA Act, Queen Elizabeth II signed the Canada Act, making Canada fully independent.

A postscript: Quebec later filed a suit challenging the legality of patriation, but lost. The provincial government has since continued to negotiate the terms of a formal acceptance. In the latest round, a package of proposals dealing with Quebec's status and several other matters was submitted to the voters in October 1992; it failed, however, by a significant margin.

Two intriguing questions could be posed: (1) If the British government had taken this path with the American colonies, would the Revolutionary War ever have occurred? (2) If we had remained tied to Britain in some fashion, how would our history and politics have been different? (One noteworthy fact: the British outlawed slavery throughout the empire in 1833.)

tains a long list of abuses which George III had perpetrated against the colonists. Liberty, they agreed, was the goal of good government. Thus, the last thing they wanted was to substitute an American tyranny for an English one. On the other hand, they had seen that if government is too weak, public order, and even liberty itself, can be threatened. They met in Philadelphia in order to give government more teeth. How then to erect a government that could govern, but not pose a threat to the very values

James Madison, the "Father of the Constitution," was a key delegate to the convention and wrote many of the Federalist Papers. *He later was one of the primary authors of the Bill of Rights. Madison continued his service to the country as Secretary of State under Thomas Jefferson and then as the fourth president.*

it was established to uphold? Or, to quote James Madison, rightly called the Father of the Constitution, "In framing a government which is to be administered by men over men, the great difficulty lies in this: you must first enable the government to control the governed; and in the next place oblige it to control itself."[18]

What is the common denominator which links all people that go into politics? Liberal and conservative, young and old, male and female, rich and poor, black, white, Asian, and Hispanic—almost all politicians share this quality: ambition. It may be ambition born of nothing more noble than a crude search for self-fulfillment through possession of power, or it may flow from a genuine desire to serve humanity—but it is ambition nonetheless. Could we separate "good" ambition from "bad" ambition and live happily, if only we could get the "good" people into power? Madison said no, and insisted, further that even if we could, this would not be desirable. Putting people with pure motives into power, he believed, far too often would corrupt them. Have you ever known anyone who was appointed or elected to some office, perhaps in a school or social organization, and whose personality then changed? (If you haven't, you will.) Imagine the temptations which much greater political power brings.

Madison and the other Founding Fathers had therefore a mixed view of human nature. On the one hand, they believed with civic democrats that the citizenry was capable of governing itself and not overstepping the proper limits. "A dependence on the people is no doubt the primary control on the government," Madison insisted. However, he immediately added that "experience has taught mankind the necessity of auxiliary precautions." If people were angels, he argued, no government would be necessary; or if angels appeared from on high (and we could verify that they were indeed angels, he might have added), we would be wise to turn over governing to them. But people are not angels; they are subject to the temptations of office, and may work all manner of mischief if given the opportunity, as individualist democrats will argue. Nonetheless, this very fact can be used to construct an enduring structure of government. Or, as Madison put it, "Ambition must be made to counteract ambition." But these "auxiliary precautions," specifically the intricate structuring of political institutions, should not obscure the responsibilities of the people themselves. They are always "auxiliary" to the need for a diligent and virtuous citizenry.

In simplest terms, the great riddle was solved by granting wide powers to government (although certain areas are still off limits), but structuring the institutions in such a way as to make the exercise of power inordinately difficult. Power is fragmented and parceled out in such a way that no one person or group has much autonomy. Action requires the cooperation of different parts of the governmental machine, which makes action less likely. This is frustrating to those in power because they are ambitious, ambitious usually to do what they think is in the public interest. But Madison's shadow falls over them, and generally speaking, the system has worked to "control itself" as the Founders intended.

The Constitution utilizes three primary mechanisms to "oblige [government] to control itself": federalism, separation of powers, and checks and balances. Federalism is the vertical breaking of power, giving neither federal nor state government the ultimate authority to act in all areas. Separation of powers is the horizontal fragmentation of power at the national level. Checks and balances are the guarantees that none of the three national branches will be able to dominate the others completely. Since federalism will receive detailed attention in chapter 3, the remainder of this section focuses on separation of powers and checks and balances.

Separation of Powers

Separation of powers grows out of the simple idea, popularly attributed to the French political philosopher Montesquieu, that governments do essentially three things: make rules, implement rules, and interpret rules. In the words of politics, they legislate, they execute, and they adjudicate. Consequently, one separates powers by constructing three different institutions and giving one task to each. Thus, we have Congress to legislate, the president to execute (administer) the laws, and the courts to interpret them.

This high school civics statement is not false; however, it is not entirely true, and can in fact be seriously misleading. Closer to the truth is the observation that we have separate institutions sharing powers.[19] Congress, it is true, is the repository of the bulk of the legislative power of the national government. However, some of this power is allocated to the president, and some has been assumed by the courts. In the same vein, the president is indeed the chief administrator, but Congress and the courts share executive power. To complete the circle, a fraction of the judicial power resides in Congress and the presidency.

Therefore, if one wants to study the legislative power of the United States, the inquiry cannot be confined to Congress. The same is true of executive or judicial power. Equally important, each institution does more than legislate, administer, or judge, respectively. To view the president only as an administrator is to miss a number of vital roles played by the presidency in the political system. The president must both legislate and judge, *and* must share the administrative role with others.

However, the symmetry is not perfect, in either constitutional design or practice. The courts can assume less authority from the other two branches than the presidency and Congress can assume from each other. Furthermore, the judicial power is more confined to the courts than is legislative power to Congress or the executive power to the president. In other words, legislative authority is given primarily to Congress, but a healthy fraction is laid at the president's door, and only a small amount is handed to the courts. The executive power falls mostly to the president, but a significant portion is given to Congress, and a minute amount to the courts. Judicial power, in contrast, is allocated mostly to the courts, with only insignificant dollops exercised by Congress and the president.

Checks and Balances

Checks and balances are often lumped together with separation of powers, but the concepts are different. Checks and balances refers to constructing political institutions in such a way that no one of them will be able to assume a commanding position. Since making laws is the most important activity of any government, a strict separation of powers would mean dominance by the legislative branch. Checks and balances involve the delicate political architecture necessary to avoid just that eventuality. Checks and balances are of course unnecessary without a system of separation of powers, but separation of powers will not ensure checks and balances. Instead, checks and balances require intricate tinkering with methods of choosing people for office, their terms of office, and, most important, the power allocated to those in authority.

METHODS OF CHOOSING OFFICE-HOLDERS   In reality, we have four national political institutions, if we sever Congress into its two houses. Under the original Constitution, the House of Representatives was the only directly elected body of the four. Senators were chosen by state legislatures, and the president by an ill-defined and indirect system of electors (more on that in chapter 6). Judges were given their seats through an agreement between the president and the Senate.

Note that four different methods are employed. In spite of the fact that all rest ultimately on the people, different combinations of "the people" are required to produce majorities in each house of Congress and in the electoral college. In practice, this means that those who sit in these positions will be responsive to different political interests. Even with the democratization of the presidential election system, the House of Representatives, elected as well by all the people, often has a different political complexion from the president. This is not the result of a conspiracy or a fault in the constitutional system; on the contrary, it is exactly how the Constitution was designed to work. The same truth applies to the Senate, and even more to the Supreme Court.

Note further that the role of each institution in the choice of the others is minimized. Only in the case of judges are others involved directly, and even the choice of judges requires the cooperation of two other institutions. Recall the Virginia Plan, which proposed that Congress should choose the president. If such were the case, that fact alone would undercut the independence of the president, who could be elected only by making deals with powerful interests in Congress. The president would enter office with a stack of political IOUs to members of Congress, and to them only. By unchaining congressional and presidential selection mechanisms and giving them three different representational bases, the Constitution takes a large step toward balancing political power.

TERMS OF OFFICE   To further ensure checks and balances, the terms of office are differentiated: two years for the House of Representatives, four years for the president, six years for senators, and life for judges. This makes it much less likely that a political coalition can take power and institute change quickly. Making only one-third of the Senate replaceable every two years adds one more impediment to the concentration of power.

THE ALLOCATION OF POWER   As important as the choice of leaders and their terms of office are, they are secondary to the ways in which power is actually distributed. First, as previously mentioned, all three institutions share power in various ways; this leads to natural frictions. Second, this power-sharing occurs within a structure that gives each institution a core of secure authority and the tools to protect that core. It was the Founders' hope that ambitious people would use these tools to try to carry out their own ambitions; in the process, they would check other ambitious people doing likewise.

An entire treatise could be written on the checks and balances woven into the Constitution.[20] The major ones are outlined here; more detailed discussions will be reserved for later chapters.

Let us examine first the presidential-congressional axis, with particular regard to general legislative power. Congress must pass all laws, but the president is told to "from time to time give to the Congress information of the state of the Union, and recommend to their consideration such measures as he shall judge necessary and expedient." Clearly, the Founders intended the president to be much more than a passive onlooker waiting for Congress to act. Most presidents have eagerly taken up this role, pushing Congress to enact certain laws. In addition, the president is given a veto power when Congress finishes its work. However, Congress may override this veto by a two-thirds vote in both houses. As a result of this give-and-take, the president is intimately involved in the legislative process throughout every congressional session. This drama, in fact, is the center of day-to-day American politics; check today's newspaper for confirmation.

Complicating this never-ending game of check and checkmate are other areas of conflict. Only Congress can declare war and raise and equip an army, for instance. The president, however, is commander-in-chief (which, by the way, solves another central problem of constitutional governance: how to exert civilian control over the military). The president's authority as commander-in-chief is absolute, including a right to lead armies in the field. Congress, though, can always rein in presidential military adventures simply by reducing (or even eliminating) the armed forces at the president's disposal.

Money is a ubiquitous feature of politics, and here Congress reigns supreme. Any program or administrative agency can be ground to a halt by budget manipulation. A president would have no executive branch to operate without congressional approval.

Congress also holds the ultimate weapon: the power to remove the president from office. To do so, an impeachment resolution is adopted in the House by a simple majority. Then, a trial is held in the Senate, with a two-thirds vote needed to remove the president. Some people argue that since the House has passed only one presidential impeachment resolution in 200 years, and that one failed in the Senate, the procedure is ineffective. However, that argument mistakenly identifies the reality of power with its practical use. If two people are arguing and one places a gun on the table, the gun does not have to be fired to have an influence on their deliberations. One clear illustration of this principle occurred in 1974. After his commission of assorted crimes came to light, Richard Nixon resigned because impeachment and removal were imminent. No president ever forgets that a very big cannon lies just out of sight.

All the powers discussed above involve both houses of Congress; the Senate, however, as an heir to the old colonial councils, shares the president's executive powers more completely than does the House. Senate approval must be obtained for all ambassadorial, all judicial, and major executive appointments. While ambassadors are no longer of much importance and the Senate ordinarily approves most executive appointments, the selection of judges is always important and often controversial. In addition, although presidents have the power to negotiate treaties, the

Senate must consent to them by a two-thirds vote. Presidents have frequently found that senators can be quite recalcitrant on both these matters, and that conflict here can easily spill over into other areas.

In sum, the initiative ordinarily lies with the president to pursue a chosen agenda. In this game, the president possesses a number of high trump cards, notably the veto, since veto overrides by Congress are very difficult to obtain. In return, Congress holds plenty of cards, including the highest trump, impeachment. If protracted, intense, and irresolvable conflict ever came, Congress would win.

Relations between the president and the Supreme Court and between Congress and the Court are less regular, but important, nonetheless. The Court's most important power—judicial review, the power to declare laws and presidential acts unconstitutional—is not granted directly by the Constitution, but implied by it. Judicial review is a central facet of the American political system; it will be taken up again in chapter 8.

Because the Court can stop the execution of any law by declaring it unconstitutional, on paper it appears to be more powerful than the other two branches. However, that is a facile reading of the situation. The most dramatic way to check the power of the Court is to amend the Constitution—a method which will be discussed in the following section. However, more subtle forces also serve to check and balance the Court. First, Congress can impeach and remove any Supreme Court justice or other federal judge, by the same method used to remove the president.[21] Furthermore, Congress sets the size of the Court, which could be a critical matter if Congress and the president together opposed the Court on some vital issue. Congress could merely decide that a certain number of seats be added to the Court, and the president could appoint compliant judges. In addition, lower court structure and certain matters of jurisdiction (determination of the types of cases a given court can hear) are controlled by Congress. These can be (and have been) manipulated to curb judicial power.

A president's weapons against the Court are more subtle still. Aside from granting pardons, the president has no arrows to shoot directly at the courts. Nonetheless, it is important to understand that courts are dependent on the executive branch to enforce their decisions (and sometimes on the legislature to vote to allocate the required money). Only a few presidents have defied the courts outright. President Andrew Jackson is supposed to have said contemptuously when the Supreme Court handed down a decision he opposed, "John Marshall [then Chief Justice] has made his decision, now let him enforce it."[22] More often, presidents have stalled enforcement, or enforced a law so unenthusiastically that the decision has lost much of its impact. After the Supreme Court held segregated schools to be unconstitutional in 1954, for example, President Eisenhower moved very slowly and cautiously to employ the enforcement powers at his command. Thus, it took years of subsequent litigation before southern schools were fully integrated.

Although it takes time, presidents ultimately win the day through appointments. Judges die and retire and are replaced by people representing

(text continued on page 36)

BOX 2–1

The Constitutional Framework for Formulating Public Policy

How do individualist and civic democrats evaluate the Constitution in terms of how it sets the "rules of the game" of politics?

The two creeds are in general agreement about one thing: the role of the Bill of Rights and other protections for basic rights and freedoms. Individualist democrats place a high premium on individual liberty, and therefore support measures to secure it. The Bill of Rights guarantees a great deal of personal autonomy to the individual and prohibits government from intruding into several areas of life. As mentioned in chapter 1, individualist democrats differ in the priority they attach to the rights cataloged in the Bill of Rights, but they all agree on the importance of individual rights.

Civic democrats share this attachment to individual rights, although they more often raise questions about community needs. Individual rights are important to civic democrats because they both allow room for individuals to make their own life choices and restrict the scope of government. Civic democrats would argue, though, that in some cases the needs of the community must be considered, as in the prosecution of criminals or the control of hate speech. As a whole, however, civic democrats also support the ideal of the Bill of Rights. Thus, both sets of democrats agree that certain terrain is off limits to legislatures and executives.

The two types of democracy diverge in their attitude toward the way the Constitution dictates that government must make policy. Laws must be passed by Congress and either signed by the president or passed again by a two-thirds majority if the president exercises the veto. Almost everyone agrees that on the face of it, this is a "fair" procedure. The fundamental question then is whether the basic political structure of Congress and the presidency—in particular the way the holders of these offices represent the public—is truly fair.

Individualist democrats would answer that fairness is sorely lacking. In the individualist democratic ideal, individual preferences should be added up and policy should follow the desires and wishes of the greatest number. Each individual's vote or participation should count the same as everyone else's: no more, no less. Political institutions therefore should facilitate the translation of public wishes into public policy. The Constitution clearly contains several impediments to this type of democracy.

While the House of Representatives comes closest to this ideal in that all its members are elected

BOX 2-1

by approximately the same number of people, the Senate and the presidency do not. The Senate is the most blatantly unfair institution in this sense. Giving each state two senators creates gross inequality, since each state does not contain one-fiftieth of the population. The least populous twenty-six states contain 18.02 percent of the population. This means that a little over *nine* percent of the country's citizens (a majority in those states) can elect enough senators to block any policy, no matter how much it is desired by other citizens.

To a lesser degree, the presidential election system produces similar results. Counting votes by states magnifies the power of some voters (according to experts, the voters of very populous and very small states). However, the skew in representation is less pronounced in the choice of presidents than in the choice of senators.

Moreover, the Constitution uses its other institutional arrangements to deflect the head-counting favored by individualist democrats. Federalism, separation of powers, and checks and balances are often buffers between public wishes and public policy. Translating public desires into public policy works imperfectly in such a system, if at all. The very inertia created by those devices militates against action generally, and the fact that opponents may checkmate a proposal by winning only once when laws are being considered can seriously inhibit carrying out what the majority wishes.

Civic democrats are prone to worry less about these problems and emphasize the system's virtues. First, they point out that the fragmented institutional structure insures that there will be widespread and thorough public debate on the issues. There are so many public forums allowing proponents and opponents to square off verbally that hastily and poorly conceived policies are seldom adopted. The very slowness of our policy process is also a way of guaranteeing sustained public debate. Alternatives can be thoroughly clarified and the search for the public interest performed in earnest.

Second, civic democrats contend that there is more to representation than counting numbers. People are not merely interchangeable automatons. Until people are clothed in their political interests, whatever these may be, they cannot really be represented. In a large and diverse society it is important to have a number of access points for these various interests. And as imperfect as it is, the Constitution multiplies the opportunities for representation by building three national representative institutions and fifty-one governments.

Would the Virginia Plan have suited individualist democrats better than the Constitution? Why or why not?

new political outlooks. This happens not only on the Supreme Court level but in lower federal courts as well. The fact that many issues are shaped significantly at the lower levels of the federal judicial system gives the president ample opportunity to exercise influence. President Reagan, for instance, devoted a good deal of effort to finding and appointing lower court judges who shared his orientation.

Furthermore, the practical limits on their power are not lost on the judges. They are usually middle-aged people who have years of government experience. They understand quite well the pragmatic limitations of courts, and this affects the decisions they make. Judges know that to push their claims to power too far would result in their having less authority, not more. Rather than being all-powerful, the Court is surely what Publius called it, "the least dangerous branch."[23]

Taken together, these checks and balances have stood the test of time. Occasionally, those in control of one institution or another have increased their power, but it has never lasted. The balancing mechanisms have swung into place. It is a cumbersome machine, to be sure, but when measured by the Founders' goal of preventing tyranny, it gets high grades. One British commentator said of our system that it set up the Congress to watch the president, the president to watch Congress, and the Supreme Court to watch them both.[24] That analysis comes pretty close to the truth. He might have added that the three institutions expend so much energy watching each other that they accomplish less than they might—ingeniously serving the end of limited government.

Yet, there is a downside to these limits—an important downside. A government that has trouble doing bad things has trouble accomplishing good things. The very institutional arrangements which are bulwarks against tyranny can also impede beneficent public policies. The quality of our public services, for example, is generally admitted to be low by the standards of other advanced industrial countries. Part, but not all, of the reason is our creaking, inefficient system of government. The dispersal of power prevents tyranny, but also leaves many desirable and desired public projects undone or done poorly. What we gain in liberty we lose in public convenience. Apparently, though, Americans are willing to make that trade-off.

CONSTITUTIONAL CHANGE

No constitution can afford to remain static. If it is to retain political significance through time, it must be adaptable to changing social and economic circumstances; otherwise it will calcify and have to be discarded. Some process of amendment is essential, therefore, to induce flexibility. At the same time, amending a constitution cannot be made too easy. If it is amended frequently, it will soon lose its distinctiveness and become merged with ordinary legislation, and in the American case its symbolic role would be undermined. A middle ground must be found, with an amending procedure that is rather difficult but not too difficult. Our Constitution has been amended twenty-seven times (as of 1992), but if we discount the first ten amendments, we are left with seventeen. On the average, then, one amendment has been made about every 12 years.

The Process of Formal Amendment

An amendment must pass through two separate stages: proposal and ratification. The first of two ways to propose an amendment is for both houses of Congress to pass it by a two-thirds vote. The second alternative, which has never been used, is for two-thirds of the states to petition Congress to call a convention to propose amendments. Despite not being utilized in the past, the second method continues to attract attention, and periodically a significant number of states request a convention (most recently, over the so-called balanced budget amendment).[25] Constitutional experts are uncertain as to how such a convention would work. Would members be elected? How? Would the convention be limited to a specific agenda set by Congress in the call? It is truly a wild card in the Constitution, and some of the hesitancy to employ it may stem from memories of what happened the last time an American Congress called a convention to propose amendments to the constitution.

After proposal, the amendment must be ratified. Again, there are two ways that this may be done. The first method is for the legislatures of three-fourths of the states to approve the amendment; the other is for special conventions to be called in each state, and for three-fourths of these to vote yes. All amendments except the twenty-first (which repealed the eighteenth) were ratified through the first procedure.

Usually ratification goes smoothly, but a few questions have arisen through the years. How long can an amendment remain available for ratification? Congress cured this problem beginning in the 1930s by attaching a seven-year limit. But can Congress extend the time by simple majority, as it tried to do in 1978 with the ill-fated Equal Rights Amendment? (The issue became moot in this instance because three-fourths of the states failed to ratify even with the extension.) Can a state legislature vote "no," then "yes"? "Yes," then "no"? (The Supreme Court has hinted that the first kind of change in vote is permissible, but the second is not.)

The two methods for both proposal and ratification can be used in any combination, giving four possible ways to amend the Constitution. Congress chooses the method of ratification, even if the convention were to be used for proposal.

Amendments after the Bill of Rights

If we examine amendments 11 through 27, we find that they fall into fairly identifiable groups by time period (see table 2-2). Amendments 11 and 12 were adopted early (in 1798 and 1804 respectively) to iron out technical defects regarding lawsuits against states and the way presidential electors'

FIGURE 2–1
The Formal Amending Process

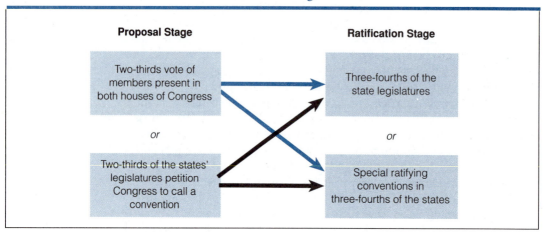

TABLE 2–2
Constitutional Amendments Adopted after the Bill of Rights

AMENDMENT NUMBER	SUBJECT
Eleven (1798)	Forbade lawsuits against states by non-citizens
Twelve (1804)	Required ballots of electors to be cast separately for president and vice-president
Thirteen (1865)	Abolished slavery
Fourteen (1868)	Required that states may not deny any person due process of law or equal protection of the laws
Fifteen (1870)	Established that right to vote cannot be denied because of race
Sixteen (1913)	Empowered the levy of a federal income tax
Seventeen (1913)	Provided for popular election of senators
Eighteen (1919)	Instituted prohibition
Nineteen (1920)	Established that right to vote cannot be denied because of gender
Twenty (1933)	Required presidential and congressional terms to begin in January
Twenty-one (1933)	Repealed number eighteen
Twenty-two (1951)	Established two-term and ten-year limit for president
Twenty-three (1961)	Granted presidential electors for District of Columbia
Twenty-four (1964)	Prohibited poll taxes
Twenty-five (1967)	Provided for presidential succession and disability
Twenty-six (1971)	Lowered voting age to eighteen
Twenty-seven (1992)	Mandated that pay raises for members of Congress cannot take effect until after a new congressional election.

Just as citizens today protest politically, women in the early twentieth century marched demanding the right to vote, often at great personal risk.

votes were to be cast. The Thirteenth, Fourteenth, and Fifteenth Amendments ratified the result of the Civil War. The most important of these has been the Fourteenth, which contains clauses prohibiting states from depriving "any person of life, liberty, or property, without due process of law" or denying "to any person within its jurisdiction the equal protection of the laws." These two formulations have provided grounds for legions of controversial court cases through the years, and the flow shows no signs of abating. (See chapter 4.)

The next four amendments were products of the Progressive Era before World War I, a time of great faith in institutional reform and economic liberalism.[26] The Sixteenth Amendment (1913) allowed Congress to levy an income tax, overturning a decision of the Supreme Court which had found an earlier income tax constitutionally defective. The Seventeenth (1913) and Nineteenth (1920) were attempts to infuse more democracy into the political system, mandating direct election of senators and women's suffrage respectively. The Eighteenth Amendment (1919) was the curious attempt to write prohibition into the Constitution. It was repealed fourteen years later by the Twenty-first Amendment, after generally failing to curb the consumption of alcohol. The Twentieth Amendment, also

Patrons of a New York City bar celebrating enactment of the Twenty-first Amendment, which repealed prohibition.

adopted in 1933, merely moved the date for beginning a new presidency and Congress from March to January.

The Twenty-second Amendment (1951) was a response to Franklin D. Roosevelt's breaking of the two-term tradition set by George Washington. It provided that no one could be elected president more than twice or serve more than a total of ten years.

Amendments 23 through 26 were products of the 1960's; numbers 23, 24, and 26 were designed to increase participation and make government more responsive, while number 25, dealing with presidential succession, was induced by the Kennedy assassination.

The Twenty-third Amendment (1961) gave the District of Columbia the same number of presidential electors as the least populous state. The Twenty-fourth (1964) outlawed the poll tax, a pernicious device used mostly by southern states to discourage voting. The Twenty-sixth Amendment (1971) extended the right to vote to eighteen-year-olds.

The Twenty-fifth Amendment established an orderly method of succession in the event of a presidential or vice-presidential vacancy. In the past, when the vice-presidency became vacant, through either death or the elevation of the incumbent to the presidency, the office remained unfilled. A procedure was now set up to allow appointment of a new vice-president. It also tried to grapple with what could be an enormous problem under modern conditions: a severely disabled or mentally impaired president who refused to step aside. A complex process involving the vice-president, the cabinet, the Speaker of the House, and the president pro tem of the Senate was established to allow the vice-president to become acting president. The first part of the amendment has been used twice since then with no hitch. Fortunately, the second provision, which could prove much more troublesome, remains untested.

The Twenty-seventh Amendment has had a most unusual history. Proposed originally in 1789 along with the Bill of Rights, it provided that a pay raise for members of Congress could not take effect until after a congressional election had been held. Six states' legislatures ratified it immediately, but it dropped from view shortly thereafter. Then, responding to the groundswell of anger directed at Congress in 1992, state legislatures began ratifying it again, with the required 38 reached in May of that year.

In the 1980s there were a spate of suggestions for serious constitutional amendments—including banning abortion, outlawing school busing for racial balance, and requiring a balanced federal budget—but only the balanced budget amendment came close to adoption. Undoubtedly, at some future date a reform movement will secure another set of constitutional amendments, but as the backers of the above amendments have found out, it will take overwhelming political backing.

Informal Change of the Constitution

As important as formal amendments are, they do not tell the whole story. Constitutional change, broadly defined, is a much more continuous and informal process.

At the top of the list of informal methods of change is judicial interpretation. No important political document is self-evident in meaning, if for no other reason than that human language lacks the precision necessary for that feat. Interpretation is essential if a document is to affect human action. Moreover, our Constitution is filled with vague phrases, of which anyone able to read English can grasp the thrust, but about which sensible and learned people will have intense disagreements. Translating these inherently loose phrases into specific rules for governmental conduct is a vital political task, for while it is intriguing to engage in abstract arguments over their meanings, someone's decisions must be authoritative. Long ago, we decided to allocate this task to the Supreme Court (see chapter 8). By applying the language of the Constitution to novel situations, and occasionally by directly overturning previous interpretations, the Supreme Court keeps the document alive.

A cogent example of informal change of constitutional understanding through judicial interpretation grew out of Congress' attempt to regulate child labor. The "commerce clause" of the Constitution (Article I, Section 8) reads, "Congress shall have the power to regulate commerce . . . among the several states." In 1895 the Supreme Court had ruled that the word "commerce" was restricted to buying and selling and therefore did not include manufacturing.[27] Congress was consequently without power to regulate manufacturing, including the working conditions found in factories. Around the turn of the century, Congress adopted several laws banning the shipment or movement of lottery tickets, spoiled food, and prostitutes in interstate commerce (that is, commerce crossing state lines) and the Supreme Court had upheld each of these enactments. At President Woodrow Wilson's urging, Congress decided to adopt this strategy to abolish child labor. The Child Labor Act of 1916 forbade the shipment across state lines of any product that had been manufactured by child labor.

The law was challenged in court, and the Supreme Court voided it in 1918.[28] The Court's opinion stressed that this law was a "prohibition," not a "regulation" and therefore outside Congress' authority. How was this different from the three cases of prohibition mentioned above? The Court argued that these products were all harmful, whereas the products manufactured by child labor were harmless in themselves. In 1924 Congress responded by adopting a constitutional amendment giving it authority to regulate child labor; however, the amendment was never ratified by the necessary three-fourths of the states.

In 1938 Congress was considering a wide-ranging Fair Labor Standards Act setting minimum wages and maximum hours in manufacturing. Its enforcement mechanism was the same as before: banning from interstate commerce the shipment of any product manufactured contrary to the act. Opponents of child labor managed to add a section virtually identical to the 1916 act.

When the law came before the Supreme Court in 1941, the Court saw things differently than it had seen them before.[29] Congressional power to "regulate" commerce, the justices said, was complete: it covered the prohibition of the flow of any product whatsoever.

The result of this case has been momentous. It signaled a complete turnaround in the constitutional domains of state and national governments. Congress now has virtually unlimited ability to control national economic affairs, whereas before 1941, its scope was severely restricted. Yet the words of the Constitution have not been altered; Congress still has the power only to "regulate commerce among the states." But those words are now taken to mean something vastly different from their meaning in the early days of this century, thanks entirely to the Supreme Court.

While this example is rather dramatic in that there was a direct reversal, it is not all that unusual. Ordinarily, however, the Supreme Court changes the meaning of the Constitution's words and phrases more gradually. But the general point still holds, that significant constitutional change occurs through court decisions rather than formal amendment.

Although the Supreme Court is the official interpreter of the Constitution, political convention and custom have an effect as well. Presidents begin a certain practice and Congress accedes, for instance. Over time, legitimacy attaches to the practice, and it becomes an accepted part of normal politics. Or, political parties, which are not mentioned in the Constitution at all, evolve and structure the way elections are held and power organized within Congress. There are dozens of similar habits and conventions which shape how government works.

Two examples may illustrate the influence of political convention on government. Before we entered World War II, President Roosevelt concluded several agreements with the British government using "executive agreements" rather than treaties. As chief executive of the United States, he signed an agreement with another chief executive promising to do certain things (in this case, furnish destroyers to Britain). Although senators have complained (correctly) that this undermines the senatorial role in treaty making, the practice has been used extensively by every president since. Now, only the gravest issues (such as arms control) or the most trivial ones are handled by treaties. In the former case, Congress would insist on involvement in such weighty matters, and in the latter case, the president does not care deeply about the subject at hand.

A second example of convention influencing government is the nature of the office of Speaker of the House. By custom, the majority party meets to agree on a candidate before an election is formally held by the whole House. The majority party's candidate is always easily elected. From that position, the Speaker is expected to become the party's leader in Congress, helping the president's program if her party controls the White House, or leading the charge against the president if control is split between parties. This convention is in sharp contrast to the British House of Commons, where the Speaker (by custom) is expected to be strictly non-partisan.

The Constitution, then, is the foundation stone of American government, but it is not immutable. The formal words can be changed, although they seldom are. Only the most potent and persevering political forces can secure adoption of an amendment. On a more practical level, the Supreme Court and customs and conventions can mediate political change into constitutional change.

The Constitution as Symbol

The American Constitution is much more than merely a set of rules for political conduct, important though that function is. It has become a symbol of national identity itself, and it has taken on the aura of the sacred.[30] (During the Constitution's bicentennial in 1987, it was displayed as a religious icon might be in other societies. The setting was the Second Bank of the United States in Philadelphia, designed, appropriately enough, in imitation of a Greek temple. Inside, solemn crowds filed by to pay homage.) Indeed, this symbolic character of the Constitution is intimately connected to how we define American citizenship.

Half a century ago, Supreme Court Justice Felix Frankfurter, a naturalized citizen born in Austria, said, "American citizenship implies entering upon a fellowship which binds people together by devotion to certain feelings and ideas and ideals summarized as a requirement that they be attached to the principles of the Constitution."[31] When a new citizen is being inducted today into American society, he or she is required to take the following oath, which by implication lists what is expected of all citizens:[32]

1. to support the Constitution of the United States;
2. to renounce and abjure absolutely and entirely all allegiance and fidelity to any foreign prince, potentate, state, or sovereignty of whom or which the petitioner was before a subject or citizen;
3. to support and defend the Constitution and the laws of the United States against all enemies, foreign and domestic;
4. to bear true faith and allegiance to the same; and
5. (a) to bear arms on behalf of the United States when required by the law, or (b) to perform noncombatant service in the Armed Forces of the United States when required by the law, or (c) to perform work of national importance under civilian direction when required by the law.

The central place of the Constitution in this oath is self-evident. Three of the points refer to it directly, including the all-important first one. According to this oath, loyalty to the Constitution's precepts is the fundamental and defining characteristic of American citizenship. A cynic might say that such a loyalty can mean anything because no particular interpretation is demanded. Thus, any person can read anything she chooses into it. However, that contention is simply false. It is true enough that the Constitution is ambiguous and subject to a variety of interpretations; however, it does stand for certain principles.[33] Many types of governments and many political philosophies are ruled out absolutely by the Constitution. One cannot believe in monarchy, dictatorship, the suspension of civil liberties, an established church, a caste system, or a host of other ideas and still take the above oath in good faith. Clearly, then, the Constitution does contain certain positive values; disputes about its meaning are disputes within that framework.

While the requirement of fidelity to the Constitution is a positive act of citizenship, it is also a limited one. It is highly significant that one's identity as an American citizen is confined to the political sphere. To become an Israeli citizen, in contrast, one must prove Jewish lineage. Similarly, although the legal requirements are somewhat looser, it would be difficult to become truly French or German, since those terms carry important cultural connotations. But to be an American requires a political commitment only.[34] American citizenship does not presume any certain religious, cultural, racial, ethnic, or family attachments. The American community one belongs to, whether by birth or naturalization (and significantly, there are no differences, save the ability to become president), is a political community—and solely a political community. Alongside that membership can stand any number of other attachments and commitments, the diversity of which gives America its vibrant social pluralism. In America we have restricted the scope of citizenship to the acceptance of certain political norms—those contained in the Constitution—and have made political community entirely separate from other forms of community.

Summary

The roots of the American Constitution are traceable to our British heritage and colonial political practices. During the Revolutionary War, the Articles of Confederation were drafted to serve as a constitution for the newly independent country. The Articles provided for a single-house Congress with vast powers on paper. But Congress could not levy taxes, raise an army, or regulate commerce. Further, amendments to the Articles were almost impossible, since all thirteen states had to concur. Even so, some important legislation was adopted during these years, especially the Northwest Ordinance.

Economic distress and civil disorder led moderate and conservative leaders to call a convention to amend the Articles. Once in Philadelphia, the delegates decided to create a national government, one that rested on the people and could act directly on them, rather than having to operate through the states.

The Virginia Plan offered a starting point for debate. It proposed a powerful two-house Congress with seats allocated according to population; a chief executive; and a national court system. New Jersey's plan sought to maintain the influence of the small states by keeping representation in Congress equal for each state, but it also gave the new national government increased powers and added the important Supremacy Clause. Compromise was achieved when Connecticut suggested having two houses of Congress: one apportioned on the basis of state population, and the other composed of two representatives from each state. Designs for an independent executive and a national court system fleshed out the plan.

The battle over ratification pitted the Federalists against the Anti-Federalists. Anti-Federalists stressed that the United States was too large to be a genuine political community, and also pointed out the absence of a Bill of Rights. Federalists challenged the first contention but agreed to sponsor a Bill of Rights soon after ratification, a promise which they kept.

The Founding Fathers faced a critical dilemma in framing the actual institutions of the new national government. On the one hand, they feared that those in power might be tempted to assume too much power and become tyrants. On the other, they wanted a government that was strong enough to govern internally and protect the nation from foreign enemies. Their path out of the dilemma was to give government significant powers but to fragment political authority through the mechanisms of federalism, separation of powers, and checks and balances.

Our system of separation of powers is best described as three institutions sharing power. The president and Congress in particular share legislative power, a fact which guarantees conflict. Checks and balances are designed to prohibit any one institution from becoming too powerful. Three vehicles for ensuring checks and balances are the methods of choosing office-holders, their terms of office, and the allocation of power to each institution, the last of which is of especial importance. Each institution places important checks and balances on the others, keeping any one from becoming too powerful. As a whole, these checks and balances have worked well in preventing tyranny. However, they have also contributed to making government slow to act and sometimes unresponsive.

Constitutional change is accomplished both formally and informally. There have been twenty-seven formal amendments, although the first ten can realistically be considered part of the original document. The other seventeen have mostly come in clusters during such periods as the aftermath of the Civil War, the early twentieth century, and the 1960s. Significantly, several of the amendments have increased participation in politics. Informal change comes chiefly through changing interpretations made by the Supreme Court, but also through political conventions and customs.

The importance of the Constitution as an instrument of government is matched by the importance of its role as a political symbol. The American community is defined largely as a political community, and the Constitution is the sacred symbol of that community. Citizens are expected to show a loyalty to it which transcends political divisions. To understand the importance of the Constitution in American political life, one must appreciate its symbolic role as much as the details of political architecture which it contains.

ENDNOTES

1. Quoted in Calvin Jillson, *Constitution Making: Conflict and Consensus in the Federal Convention of 1787* (New York: Agathon Press, 1988), 2.

2. A classic essay on the dual role of the Constitution is Edward S. Corwin, "The Constitution as Instrument and as Symbol," *American Political Science Review* 30 (1936), 1071–85.

3. *Bailey v. Drexel Furniture Co.,* 259 U.S. 20 (1922).

4. An excellent study of one colony which illustrates the evolution of most is David Jordan, *The Foundations of Representative Government in Maryland* (New York: Cambridge University Press, 1988). A more broadly based source is Donald S. Lutz, *The Origins of American Constitutionalism* (Baton Rouge: Louisiana State University Press, 1988).

5. See for example Robert and Katherine Brown, *Virginia, 1705–1788: Democracy or Aristocracy?* (East Lansing, Mich.: Michigan State University Press, 1964).

6. A good essay on the Articles is Donald S. Lutz, "The Articles of Confederation as the Background to the Republic," *Publius* 20 (1990), 55–70.

7. There is also a close parallel between the situation under the Articles and the framework of government established when the Soviet Union disintegrated. Even the name the former Soviet republics chose, The Commonwealth of Independent States, would have fit the government established under the Articles quite well. The fate of the Commonwealth may have signaled what would have happened to the United States had we tried to continue under the Articles.

8. See Richard Morris, *The Forging of the Union, 1781–1789* (New York: Harper and Row, 1987) for an overview of these years.

9. The importance of this law is discussed in Peter Onuf, *Statehood and Union: A History of the Northwest Ordinance* (Bloomington: Indiana University Press, 1987).

10. A thorough study of the convention is Jillson, *Constitution Making.*

11. This important concept is discussed in Edmund S. Morgan, *Inventing the People: The Rise of Popular Sovereignty in England and America* (New York: Norton, 1988).

12. The oft-quoted phrase is from Lincoln's Gettysburg Address. A delightful pictorial essay about the address is Harold Holzer, "A Few Appropriate Remarks," *American History Illustrated* 23 (November 1988), 36–46.

13. Actually, there were more abolitionist societies in the South than in the North in the late eighteenth century. The cotton gin's invention soon made slavery so profitable, however, that the nascent Southern anti-slavery movement was overwhelmed. On slavery, see Eugene Genovese, *Roll, Jordan, Roll: The World the Slaves Made* (New York: Pantheon Books, 1974).

14. The South got a very good deal under this arrangement, for direct taxes were never levied and whites continued to have inflated congressional representation until 1861.

15. Congress in fact abolished the slave trade on the first day it could legally do so (January 1, 1808).

16. The ratification drama is portrayed in Michael Gillespie and Michael Lienesch, *Ratifying the Constitution* (Lawrence: University Press of Kansas, 1989).

17. A good summary of the Anti-Federalist position can be found in Herbert Storing, *What the Anti-Federalists Were For* (Chicago: University of Chicago Press, 1981).

18. This quotation is from *Federalist,* no. 51, as are the subsequent ones in this section. There are many editions of *The Federalist Papers.* An especially useful one is edited and introduced by Garry Wills (New York: Bantam Books, 1982).

19. This approach was first elaborated by Richard Neustadt in his influential book *Presidential Power* (New York: Wiley, 1960).

20. Philip B. Kurland and Ralph Lerner, *The Founders' Constitution: Major Themes* (Chicago: University of Chicago Press, 1987).

21. There is a slight technical difference. When the president is tried in the Senate, the Chief Justice presides.

22. Cited in David O'Brien, *Storm Center: The Supreme Court in American Politics,* 2d ed. (New York: Norton, 1990), 367.

23. *Federalist,* no. 78.

24. Alistair Cooke, *America* (New York: Knopf, 1973), 145.

25. In 1988, thirty-two states, only two short of the required two-thirds, petitioned Congress for a convention, but no additional states have since added their names to the request (as of January 1993). In July of 1990 the balanced budget amendment came to the floor of the House, but failed by seven votes. In June 1992 the House tried again, this time defeating the measure by nine votes. See John Cranford, "Defeat of Budget Amendment Fans Anti-Deficit Flames," *Congressional Quarterly Weekly Report,* June 13, 1992, 1683–88.

26. A good analysis of this period from the perspective of one of the parties is David Sarsohn, *The Party of Reform: Democrats in the Progressive Era* (Jackson: University Press of Mississippi, 1989).

27. *United States v. E. C. Knight Co.,* 156 U.S. 1, 15 S. Ct. 249 (1895).

28. *Hammer v. Dagenhart,* 247 U.S. 251, 38 S. Ct. 529 (1918).

29. *United States v. Darby,* 312 U.S. 100, 61 S. Ct. 451 (1941).

30. A poignant reminder of this can be seen in the actions of those who dissent most fervently in our society. They sometimes show contempt for the basic symbols of the political system, by such actions as burning an American flag. Very seldom, though, do they burn a copy of the Constitution; on the contrary, they cling to its protections.

31. Quoted in Sanford Levinson, *Constitutional Faith* (Princeton, N.J.: Princeton University Press, 1988), 3.

32. 8 United States Code, Section 1448.

33. See Gary Jacobsohn, *Pragmatism, Statesmanship, and the Supreme Court* (Ithaca, N.Y.: Cornell University Press, 1977); Sotrios Barber, *On What the Constitution Means* (Baltimore: Johns Hopkins University Press, 1984); and Harvey C. Mansfield, *America's Constitutional Soul* (Baltimore: Johns Hopkins University Press, 1991).

34. For a discussion of this concept as well as some contrasting ones, see Michael Walzer, "What Does It Mean to be An American?" *Social Research* 57 (1990), 591–614.

FURTHER READING

1. Ackerman, Bruce. *We the People.* Vol. 1, *Foundations.* Cambridge, Mass.: Harvard University Press, 1992.

2. Barber, Sotirios. *On What the Constitution Means.* Baltimore: Johns Hopkins University Press, 1984.

3. Goldwin, Robert and William Schambra, eds. *How Democratic is the Constitution?* Washington: American Enterprise Institute, 1980.

4. Kammen, Michael. *A Machine that Would Go of Itself: The Constitution in American Culture.* New York: Knopf, 1986.

5. Levinson, Sanford. *Constitutional Faith.* Princeton, N.J.: Princeton University Press, 1988.

6. Mansfield, Harvey. *America's Constitutional Soul.* Baltimore: Johns Hopkins University Press, 1991.

7. Marshall, Burke, ed. *A Workable Government? The Constitution after 200 Years.* New York: Norton, 1987.

8. McDonald, Forrest. *Novus Ordo Seclorum: The Intellectual Origins of the Constitution.* Lawrence: University Press of Kansas, 1985.

9. Wills, Garry, ed. *The Federalist Papers.* New York: Bantam Books, 1982.

THREE

FEDERALISM

Federalism, it is often said, is the premier American contribution to the art of governing, for it offers a unique solution to the age-old problem of the territorial organization of political power. All governments, except those of such micro-states as San Marino, Andorra, and Monaco, must establish subunits of some kind. Even such basic governmental functions as law enforcement, not to mention the panoply of services provided by the modern state, can seldom be accomplished by central direction alone. The exact ways in which territorial political relationships are structured and people's loyalties tied to different levels of government, however, varies enormously from country to country.

Countless debates over central-local relations in other countries have seen the American example invoked, usually as a model to be emulated. Federalism is certainly a central feature of our own political system. Without an appreciation of its dynamics, even a rudimentary understanding of American politics is impossible, as almost no aspect of our domestic politics and public policy is untouched by it.

The Foundations of Federalism

Federalism needs first to be defined, a task perhaps best accomplished by examining what it is not. At one extreme of a continuum are *unitary governments*. In countries with such systems, the local governmental institutions are purely creatures of the central government. Central authorities create the governments, define their geographical boundaries, allocate certain powers to them, and determine how local officials are to be chosen. These subnational governments have no legal autonomy, and act only within the guidelines established by the national government. France and Britain are both examples of unitary political systems, with ultimate authority vested in the center. In both these countries, if local political officials act contrary to the wishes of national leaders, they are easily controlled, perhaps even ousted. For example, several years ago a political enemy of former British Prime Minister Margaret Thatcher used his position as head of the Greater London Council to criticize vehemently Mrs. Thatcher's policies. In response, she pushed a bill through Parliament (controlled by her political party) which simply abolished the Council, and with it the position of her nemesis.

Confederal government, in sharp contrast, exists when the national government is the creature of its constituent parts. This occurs most often when a group of sovereign political systems surrender some of their powers to a set of central institutions, but retain ultimate authority for themselves. Recall that the government under the Articles of Confederation was of this type. Another American example is the Confederate States of America (note the name). More recently, a confederation composed of Malaya

Opposite: *Many important decisions affecting citizens are made in the fifty state capitals. Pictured is the Indiana state capitol building in Indianapolis.*

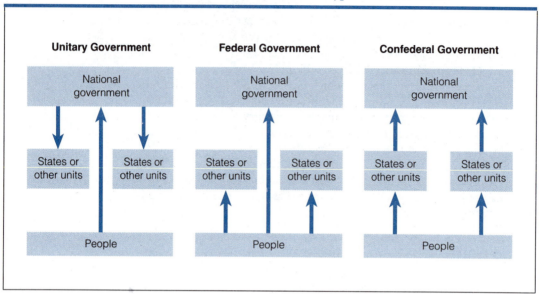

FIGURE 3–1

The Flow of Political Authority in Three Types of Government

(now called Peninsular Malaysia), Singapore, and North Borneo had a brief existence from 1963 to 1965. The temporary nature of each of these governments points to an important generalization about confederations: they are inherently unstable. The reason for their collapse is not hard to see. Inevitably, a political issue arises in which one or more of the subnational governments will not accede to the decisions made at the national level. When this happens, those sitting in central institutions have no way to coerce the recalcitrant local leaders. Once breached, the structure of national power is difficult to reestablish, and in time it dissolves.[1]

For a country to be federal, neither of the above situations can exist. In essence, federalism is characterized by two levels of government, each with its own source of political authority. Thus, neither can destroy the other. Each bases its claim to govern on something apart from the authority of the other level. Neither has given the other its existence; both are independently rooted. Naturally, this structural fact alone gives a distinctive shape to politics in nations which opt for federalism. To reinforce this observation, ponder for a moment how different American politics would be if, say, the president appointed the governors of the fifty states, or, conversely, if the federal treasury were still reliant on state contributions.

A surprisingly large number of countries have adopted federalism over the years. Usually, they have one of three characteristics: they are geographically large (only China among large countries has a unitary government); they have two or more distinct language or ethnic groups (as does Switzerland); or they are made up of previously independent political systems (as is Germany). In some countries, of course, such as Canada and the United States, more than one of these conditions prevail.

Why did the framers of our Constitution create a federal political system? The answer is simple: they had no practical alternative.[2] However, it must be stressed that they had no well-thought-out theory of federalism (in fact, federalism is one of those areas of political life in which the theory developed after the practice); instead, they were merely dealing realistically with the American political universe of 1787.

The states had existed as independent political entities for over a century (in some cases, much longer) and had developed habits of and institutions for governing. The loyalties of the populace were more often than not to their respective states; more importantly, all public officials were state officials. Any proposal to make the states wards of a national government would have upset deeply ingrained political institutions and threatened the position of every officeholder in the country. Such a plan of government, moreover, would have stood no chance whatever of ratification. On the other hand, the framers were meeting in the first place because the Articles had proved too weak to hold the nation together. Hamstrung by the difficulties discussed in chapter 2, the Articles represented a plan of government no one wished to replicate.

In short, the Founding Fathers wanted to create a national government; if they were to accommodate their notions of popular sovereignty, the only way to do so was to rest the national government firmly on the authority of the people. Further, it had to be given ample power to conduct its own affairs and implement its own decisions. At the same time, the states were political givens. The result was a pragmatic but untidy compromise.

THE CONSTITUTIONAL DIVISION OF POWERS

Richard Leach, an expert on American federalism, has said that "while there is no doubt that the framers visualized two levels of government, each exercising power over the nation's affairs at the same time, they failed to make clear what should be the precise relationship between them."[3] Thus, while any analysis of federalism must begin with the Constitution, the document forms only a skeleton, and often one whose contours are uncertain. The issues addressed in the Constitution are the divisions of power between the two levels of government, relations between the states, and the obligations the national government has to the states.

The Spheres of National and State Power

Because ours is a limited government, there are powers that are forbidden to both levels of government. Neither, under the original portions of the Constitution, may pass an *ex post facto* law or a bill of attainder,[4] or grant titles of nobility. The Bill of Rights (as interpreted by the courts after 1925)[5] also contains a number of important prohibitions which limit the powers of both levels of government—prohibitions pertaining especially to speech, religion, and criminal trials.

53

Additionally, there are certain powers forbidden to the states specifically, such as signing a treaty with a foreign country, coining money, and impairing contractual obligations. The first two prohibitions were designed to secure national control over foreign affairs and economic policy; the third, to restrain radical movements then powerful in some states.

On the positive side, Article I, Section 8 contains a long list of powers granted to the federal government, many of which were clearly aimed at remedying the defects in the Articles of Confederation. In addition to the powers granted Congress under the Articles, the new Constitution gave Congress the ability to regulate interstate commerce, to tax, and to raise and equip an army. At the end of this list of "enumerated" powers is the vitally important "elastic clause," stating that Congress has all power "necessary and proper" to carry out the enumerated powers. As will be seen shortly, this clause has been interpreted quite broadly.

Augmenting these sweeping grants of authority, the Supreme Court has held that the federal government has a number of inherent powers, most of which deal with foreign policy. That is, by the very fact of its existence, the federal government assumes the attributes of an international state. Even if these powers are not spelled out in the Constitution, therefore, they can be inferred from the structure of government itself.

Not all grants of power to the national government are exclusive, however. Some of the enumerated powers, chiefly the power to tax, may be exercised by the states as well. These shared powers are labeled "concurrent powers" in constitutional idiom.

Lastly, and most confusingly, there are those who argue that the Constitution contains reserved powers—reserved, that is, to the states. This idea derives from the Tenth Amendment:

> The powers not delegated to the United States by the Constitution, nor prohibited by it to the States, are reserved to the States respectively, or to the people.

What does this mean? If the phrase following the final comma had been omitted, it would mean a great deal indeed, giving great power to the individual states. However, the phrase "or to the people" virtually removes all meaning from the clause. Where else would such powers lie but with "the states" or "the people"? Consider the ways in which "the people" could decide to use the national government to exercise some "powers" as this clause authorizes them to do. We can certainly infer that "the people" are doing just that, if a democratically elected Congress and President adopt some particular law. Many constitutional scholars contend, therefore, that the Tenth Amendment is meaningless, and the Supreme Court has tended to agree. Others, however, argue that the Tenth Amendment must have been put in for some reason, and that it should at least be viewed as a preference for state action, especially in the states' traditional areas of concern (education, law enforcement, and so on).[6]

Relations Between the States

To supplement this structure of vertical federalism, the Constitution contains some provisions regarding horizontal federalism: the relations between states. For instance, states are compelled in Article IV to grant validity to documents from other states (the "full faith and credit" clause); to allow citizens of other states to enjoy the same privileges as their own citizens (the "privileges and immunities" clause); and to turn over criminals who flee across state lines (the "extradition" clause). The general purpose of the first two clauses is obviously to encourage the free flow of goods and people among the states—in essence, to create a nation.

National Obligations to the States

The Constitution also spells out two obligations that the national government owes to the states. The national government must guarantee to each state a "republican form of government"; this clause has seldom been invoked.[7] The national government is also obliged to protect the states from invasion and help them put down domestic unrest. In this clause, it is not clear whether the latter can be done without a request from the state government involved. Usually, state and local officials are pleased to have the help of federal troops, as when rioting and looting broke out in Los Angeles in 1992 in the wake of the not-guilty verdicts given to four police officers charged with beating a black motorist. On occasion, however, presidents have moved troops into a state over the protest of a state government (to quell labor unrest in Illinois in 1894, for example, and to enforce a court order to integrate the University of Mississippi in 1962). However, most often the states have welcomed federal assistance of this sort.

This recitation of constitutional powers leads to two observations. First, only the vaguest outline of how the federal system is designed to work can be gleaned from the Constitution. Second, if government is not to come to a standstill, there is a need for some person or body to interpret the grants of power in specific instances. In other words, the federal system needs an "umpire" to settle disputes about the distribution of power between the two levels. The need for an umpire is endemic to all federal systems, even those in which the division of powers is spelled out much more clearly than ours is. Human language has inherent limitations, for one thing; for another, inevitably political change leads to unforeseen situations.

THE SUPREME COURT AND FEDERALISM

In the United States, we have assigned the role of interpreting grants of power to the Supreme Court; many of its cases, even down to the present, have dealt with the proper allocation of federal and state powers. The vague language of the Constitution must continually be applied to live controversies. The Court must, in the words of Frederick Davenport, make the words of the Constitution "march" through time.[8]

To appreciate the difficulty of the Court's task, consider the "commerce clause" (Article I, Section 8, clause 3):

> The Congress shall have the power to regulate commerce with foreign nations, and among the several states, and with the Indian tribes.

This sounds clear enough. But what is "commerce"? Is it only the buying and selling of goods? Or does it encompass the transportation and manufacture of goods? Does the clause give Congress the power to proscribe certain articles from movement in interstate commerce? And what if Congress chooses not to regulate a given industry? Does that mean the states can regulate it until Congress decides to do so, or does the power belong exclusively to Congress? Further, what if a state adopts a law for another purpose—say, health—that places a burden on commercial activity that crosses state lines? Does that law unconstitutionally infringe on the power of Congress? All these questions arise from actual cases; a moment's reflection will show that all involve much more than abstract political theory. To the steamboat company, the steel manufacturer, the manufacturer using child labor (or the child), the insurance company, or the railroad, the impact of such a decision on economic well-being would be critical.

Although there are many exceptions, the general historical trend has been for the Supreme Court to favor the claims of the national government. At times, to be sure, the states have won important legal victories, but the tendency toward centralization is unmistakable. In fact, an early case (in 1819) established much of the thrust of future court decisions. Had it gone the other way, it is possible that our national political history would be very different.

Reacting to strong pressures from large business interests, Congress chartered a national bank—the Bank of the United States—in 1816. The bank's opponents, who held sway in several states, did not concede defeat. Instead, they set about to utilize the power of state governments to check, if not destroy, the power of the bank.

Legislators in Maryland hit on the idea of levying a special tax on the branches of the Bank of the United States operating in Maryland. The tax was set so high that the inability to pay it would have driven the bank from Maryland—and other states were watching. Officials of the bank refused to pay the tax, whereupon the head cashier was taken to court.

When *McCulloch v. Maryland*[9] reached the Supreme Court, there were two issues. First, Maryland argued that the power to establish a bank was not granted by Article I, Section 8. Indeed, the word "bank" appears nowhere in the Constitution at all. Therefore, Congress had exceeded its authority and the law was unconstitutional. Second, as a fall-back position, Maryland contended that even if the law creating the bank were constitutional, a state tax law was plainly constitutional.

John Marshall, Supreme Court Chief Justice from 1801–1835. Early Court decisions such as McCulloch v. Maryland *did much to establish the powers of the states vis-à-vis the federal government.*

The Court disagreed with the state on both counts. Although the power to create a national bank was not explicitly granted, it could easily be seen as "necessary and proper," in order to carry out such powers as coining money and borrowing on the credit of the United States. Of course, setting up a national bank was not the only way to accomplish these goals, but the Court said that if the end were legitimate, the means Congress chose to reach it was up to Congress alone. The "elastic clause" thus became quite elastic indeed. As for the tax, Chief Justice John Marshall made one of his most famous statements: "The power to tax is the power to destroy." In effect, if Maryland's tax were allowed to stand, a policy of the national government would be a policy everywhere but in Maryland; this would rob it of its designation as a national policy. Therefore, Maryland's tax must fall, since it would destroy the character of our government itself.

It is easy to see what the implications would be had Maryland won this point. Any state that disagreed with any federal policy would simply levy a destructive tax on the activity within its boundaries. In other words, the federal policies could only be enforced in the states that approved them. Given the range of federal policies, at least one state would probably object to each one. If such were intended to be the case, why did the Constitution give the national government any coercive powers? *McCulloch v. Maryland* was the first of a long string of defeats for those who have mobilized state power to challenge federal authority in court.

McCulloch v. Maryland as well as the commerce clause cases alluded to earlier illustrate a vital point about such disputes. Very few people are philosophically committed to either the federal or the state level of government; what they want is to have certain policies adopted or blocked, and they fashion their arguments accordingly. Any time some group is waxing eloquently about the virtues of either national or state government, you would be well advised to look behind the words. Not long ago, for instance, business groups often touted the idea that economic regulations, such as factory safety rules and pollution standards, were best left to the states. It was not coincidental that liberals who pushed stiff regulations were then generally more powerful in the national government. But then, when a few states started enacting tough anti-pollution laws, many business spokespersons became strong friends of the position that only the federal government should regulate such areas. For example, seventeen states have laws which hold oil companies liable for *all* damages resulting from oil spills. In 1990, oil interests tried to convince Congress to enact the Oil Pollution Act of 1990, which would have set damage limits and preempted the state laws.[10] Congress failed to pass this act, however, and the state laws stood. When disputes are settled at one level, the outcomes often differ significantly from what they would be if pushed to the other level. Thus, powerful interests will fight to have their projects dealt with in one arena, with others fighting just as hard to have them addressed in the other.

THE POLITICAL CONSEQUENCES OF FEDERALISM

American federalism is therefore shaped by politics; but our politics is also shaped by federalism. Comprehending both these truths is an essential starting point for any intelligible understanding of the American political system. Yet, the edifice of federalism is not neutral; political outcomes are skewed by it. Not necessarily determined, but skewed. Some of these effects on our political life are clearly beneficial, others clearly harmful, but most mixed.

Advantages of Federalism

First, almost by definition, federalism permits diversity within unity. While the strength of a national government is available to conduct foreign affairs and provide for defense, there is room for diversity in other areas of political life. People in Minnesota might want Norwegian taught in their schools, for example, while French is taught in Louisiana and Spanish in New Mexico. A different limit for game fish might be needed in Colorado from that thought best in Alabama. People in Nevada might want divorce to be more easily obtained than do people in South Carolina. Officials in

Illinois might believe that the needs of higher education are best served by a statewide system of independent two-year colleges and a small number of four-year schools, while Indiana's leaders might prefer four-year branches of the state's universities. All of these variations are made simple by the federal system. The rich diversity of American life, rather than a stale uniformity, can be reflected in state public policies.

A second advantage is that federalism creates governments that are "closer to the people." There are actually two aspects to this feature of federalism. One is that because there is a smaller number of people to be governed in a state, each person has more say. Citizens will consequently be more involved in state government, and feel they can identify more closely with the flow of public life. The other is that the bonds of community are tighter at the state level, in part because there is less diversity. This point harkens back to the Anti-Federalists' belief that citizenship is stronger in a more homogeneous community. For instance, even though a state such as Texas is rather diverse, there is a sense of distinctive identity among its people. In less heterogeneous states, such as Iowa, Vermont, Oregon, or Indiana, the sense of community is stronger still. These bonds of community interact with the smaller, more human scale of state politics, to enhance feelings of belonging and citizenship.

Third, a federal system does serve to unclog the national agenda. Imagine if Congress had to consider not only the issues it now addresses, but also all those dealt with each year in the fifty state legislatures, many of which are intensely controversial but local in their effects. Suppose, for example, that teacher, police, and fire personnel pay scales had to be set by Congress; that marriage and divorce law were national; and that all professional licenses (those of lawyers, real estate agents, barbers, etc.) were granted by the national government. The need to decide these matters would spread congressional and presidential time even thinner, detracting from their ability to deal with pressing national concerns.

Closely related to this is the fourth advantage, that a federal system creates more political access points. In unitary countries, citizens that want some action taken or a new policy adopted can go only to the national government. If they fail there, they have no other options. In our system, though, there are fifty state capitals to which our citizens may have recourse. A few victories there will not only secure part of their goal, but also give them a boost in their efforts to obtain national action. These multiple access points are especially important, according to many, for minorities and groups advocating new programs. Two recent examples are the movement to secure aid for the handicapped and the non-smoking movement. Although both ultimately secured national action, their initial victories were at the state and local levels.

Furthermore, the presence of multiple access points may couple with the capacity states have to be diverse to foster innovation. During the Depression of the 1930s, a candidate for governor of California campaigned on a radical program called "End Poverty in California." When asked, President Franklin D. Roosevelt said of it:

(text continued on page 62)

BOX 3–1

Civic Democracy, Communities, and the Public Interest

TWO ASPECTS of the civic democratic creed relate to federalism: the emphasis on community and the search for the public interest.

The emphasis on community makes civic democracy compatible with federalism, especially in a diverse society such as the United States. By allowing flexibility for local and regional differences through the diffusion of political authority, federalism strengthens the bonds of community. Along with the Anti-Federalists, civic democrats extol the benefits of smaller, more homogeneous communities. Indeed, toleration and encouragement of the diversity that results is often held to be one of the great accomplishments of American life.

Searching for the public interest involves constant debate and discussion. To the civic democrat's mind, everyone should agree beforehand that there is a public interest and that the role of public debate is to move toward it. The debate should be reasoned and enlightened, with all participants having the obligation to listen as well as to speak. Federalism seems to be a good system for this type of debate, in that it allows many discussions to be held in forums smaller and more accessible than the national one.

However, these attractive ideals run into severe difficulties when three conditions prevail: (1) some action must be taken; (2) the issue has moral overtones; and (3) the local community is divided.

Regarding the first, the civic democratic ideal can be threatened at the point where talk must yield to action. In some cases, if no consensus can be reached, a decision can be postponed, and discussion continue. In others, though, the issue itself is whether to do something or to do nothing, and to postpone a decision is in effect to decide. On the second matter, political issues vary on any number of dimensions, and one important factor is how closely an issue touches sensitive moral nerves. Transportation and tax policy are central issues of public policy, for instance, but they are only tangentially related to deep moral concerns. Abortion and school prayer, on the other hand, are two examples of issues in which morality is central. On the third condition, it is always comforting to talk of community and conjure up images of small Midwestern or New England towns, urban ethnic enclaves, or even suburban neighborhoods. However, in truth, many American localities are rife with cleavages. The simple fact that people live near each other does not mean that they share value commitments.

The issue of obscenity provides an apt illustration of this problem. The legal doctrine is that obscenity is not protected by the First Amendment guarantee of freedom of speech. For years, the Supreme Court struggled to develop a definition of obscenity and then apply it. In time, "obscene" material became defined as material which appealed solely to "prurient interests" or was "patently offensive." However, the definition still had to be applied on a case-by-case basis. In 1973 the Court decided to turn the issue over to states and localities, reasoning as follows:

BOX 3–1

Under a national Constitution, fundamental First Amendment limitations on the powers of the States do not vary from community to community, but this does not mean that there are, or should or can be, fixed, uniform national standards of precisely what appeals to the "prurient interest" or is "patently offensive." These are essentially questions of fact, and our nation is simply too big and too diverse for this Court to reasonably expect that such standards could be articulated for all 50 States in a single formulation. . . . To require a State to structure obscenity proceedings around evidence of a *national* "community standard" would be an exercise in futility. . . .

It is neither realistic nor constitutionally sound to read the First Amendment as requiring that the people of Maine or Mississippi accept public depiction of conduct found tolerable in Las Vegas or New York City. . . . People in different States vary in their tastes and attitudes, and this diversity is not to be strangled by . . . imposed uniformity. . . .[We therefore] hold that [obscenity] can be regulated by the States . . . and . . . that obscenity is to be determined by applying "contemporary community standards."[1]

Presumably, after receiving such an opinion from the Court, states and communities would then pursue a debate on where the public interest lay, and adopt policies accordingly, in line with the civic democratic ideal. But can they do this? Enter the three factors noted above.

First, this is a decision that cannot be delayed. Doing nothing is precisely the "action" that some believe to be in the public interest. Thus, putting the decision off is for all practical purposes making a decision.

Second, this issue is very likely to be cast in moral terms, which makes compromise very difficult. Typically, devotees of absolute free speech (not to mention the sellers of pornography) would stand against many religious groups and feminists. Suppose all of these people honestly listened to one another's arguments and carefully weighed them, as civic democrats advocate, yet still remained committed to their positions. What then—more debate and discussion? Again, that would mean victory for those opposed to regulation.

Third, what is a "community" in the context of this Court opinion? A small Utah town has rather clear community standards. One might say also that the inherently cosmopolitan ethos of a city leads to a "live-and-let-live" outlook on matters like obscenity. However, many American states and communities are quite diverse. Think about college towns, such as Bloomington, Indiana and Norman, Oklahoma; ethnically diverse counties, such as those in the Arkansas delta and various parts of Texas; places with many transplanted residents, such as several Florida and California counties; and cities which are large but which possess a more traditional culture, such as Indianapolis and Minneapolis. What exactly is a "contemporary community standard" in any of these places?

In short, when an issue such as this is thrust at the community, the ideal of civic democracy breaks down. Can individualist democracy address it any better? Is this issue so atypical as to be an exception that does not damage civic democracy as an ideal?

---

[1]*Miller v. California*, 413 U.S. 15, 93 S.Ct. 2607 (1973).

Well, they might be elected in California. What difference, I ask you, would that make in Duchess County, New York, or Lincoln County, Maine? The beauty of our state-federal system is that the people can experiment. If it has fatal consequences in one place, it has little effect upon the rest of the country. If a new, apparently fanatical, program works well, it will be copied. If it doesn't you won't hear of it again."[11]

States can become therefore "experimental laboratories" for new ideas. If these ideas work, they can be emulated and perfected by other states, and even the national government. If they prove unworkable, the damage is limited to one state. The gubernatorial candidate Roosevelt referred to lost, by the way; however, a steady stream of policy innovations—old age pensions, income taxes, prison reform, abortion reform, unemployment insurance, to name a few—have been adopted by states before becoming national policies.

A sixth advantage of federalism, many contend, is that it is an aid to limited government and the protection of individual rights. Like the fragmenting of power horizontally through separation of powers, some argue that the fragmenting of governmental power vertically reduces the capacity of any government to tyrannize its citizens. Each level possesses less power than would a central government under a unitary system, and so is restrained from exercising unwarranted control over people's lives. Federalism helps provide a bulwark, then, against arbitrary and capricious government.

Disadvantages of Federalism

Some critics insist that our federal system has serious disadvantages and decidedly unfortunate consequences.

In the first place, diversity is not always desirable. Allowing states to decide a particular question may mean that a large national majority is frustrated merely because it constitutes a minority in one or more states. Historically, this has been especially true with regard to southern states and race relations. First slavery and then segregation continued in the south long after a national consensus had been reached that these were evils which should be expunged from our society. The power that state governments exercised over voting, education, transportation, marriage laws, law enforcement, professional certification, and court systems held back for over a hundred years the effort to bring a modicum of justice to African Americans. The lesson, more generally, is that if a majority in a state or region feels intensely enough about something, it can use the state government as a blunt instrument to make national policy goals inordinately difficult to achieve.

Racism is only one example—and one not confined solely to the south, as California's treatment of Japanese immigrants at the turn of the century shows—of the general proposition. On many important issues, to allow states freedom of action is to turn people's fates over to a minority of the citizens. Often, a consensus that can be hammered out nationally, on such

States work hard to recruit business and industry and often compete among themselves for jobs. This Nissan auto plant landed by Tennessee was a major prize.

an issue as capital punishment, for example, will be undermined by the actions of local minorities in control of state governments.

A corollary is that the very smallness of many state governments makes them easier prey to manipulation by elites. Far from being the "communities" extolled by federalism's supporters, states are often in the hands of powerful elites who use them to shape policies to support their own status. Delta planters in Mississippi, copper mine owners in Montana, oil interests in Oklahoma, and coal mining companies in Kentucky are cogent examples from the recent past. To say that these people spoke for a community is to be completely naive about the character of politics in these states. State governments, it turns out, may be close to only certain people.

Moreover, even if a state government wishes to resist the influence of powerful groups, it often lacks the political and administrative capacity to do so. To be sure, the largest states have populations and budgets that surpass those of many independent countries. On the other hand, the smaller states simply do not have the resources to take on large interests, particularly large corporations. A comparison between General Motors and Wyoming is instructive in this regard: GM has annual revenues of about $123,500 million; Wyoming, of about $2,250 million. Therefore, leaving matters such as industrial regulation, for instance, to the states, is to pit pygmies against giants in some cases.

Closely akin to this problem is the "state competition" argument.[12] Every state wants to hold on to its present industries and to attract others. In bidding for these industrial sites, the states end up offering corporations any number of lucrative incentives. Taxes are often forgiven, for instance,

Some Notes on Canadian Federalism

CANADIAN FEDERALISM differs in three major respects from federalism in the U.S. First, even with the addition of the Charter of Rights and Freedoms in 1982, government in Canada is not legally limited as American government is. Nothing lies outside the scope of government action; the question is merely which level of government may undertake a particular action. A law is only considered unconstitutional in the sense that a particular level of government is forbidden to exercise a particular power. In practice, of course, Canadian government is no more repressive than ours, since Canadians value limited government as much as we do. They simply trust that the widespread belief in those values, particularly by those who sit in government, will provide an adequate check on political power; we definitely do not have this trust. We will return to this contrast again in chapter 4.

Second, Canada has only ten provinces, as compared to our fifty states: this difference has important structural implications, even though the two countries have similar regional population disparities. For example, an amending formula such as ours (with three-quarters of the states ratifying) would be all but unworkable. It would require the assent of eight provinces, which would be difficult to obtain. More importantly, Ontario and Quebec together contain about sixty-two percent of the population; hence, if an amendment could be ratified by the other eight provinces, it might represent the wishes of a relatively small fraction of the population. The same thing can happen in the U.S., of course, but the large number of states and the similarities many of them share make it much less likely. Then, there is the problem of the upper house of the national legislature. To give equal representation to all ten provinces would unacceptably magnify the political power of Prince Edward Island (about 127,000 of Canada's twenty-seven million people). Again, this issue is germane in the U.S. also, but Wyoming's overrepresentation is diluted because it comprises only one-fiftieth of the total representation. PEI's would be one-tenth of total representation. Also, the American disparity between states is not so great: Cal-

and construction costs are frequently financed partially with public funds. The net effect of these recruitment and retention wars is to have states adopt policies that are far too probusiness. In 1991, for example, some ninety states, counties, and cities competed for a $1 billion repair facility to be built by United Airlines. Indianapolis landed the project, offering $291 million in tax credits and public funding of construction.[13] Even the threat of leaving a state can often win a firm (or a sports franchise)[14] generous concessions. These considerations thus condition and taint state politics in an unhealthy fashion, the critics contend.

ifornia has fifty-six times more people than Wyoming, but Ontario has seventy-six times more than PEI. Canada's solution has been to assign Senate seats by a combined consideration of province and region: Ontario and Quebec receive twenty-four each, the Western Provinces twenty-four, and the Atlantic Provinces twenty-four, plus three each for the two territories. In any event, Canada's Senate is appointed, not elected, and much less powerful than ours.

Third, and most dramatically, Canada's federalism is inextricably tied to its major cultural and linguistic divide. Since the French Canadian population is concentrated in Quebec, every aspect of federalism raises language and cultural issues. Quebec argues that the Canadian nation was founded by "two races," and that she is a province "not like the others." Quebec's insistence on using provincial power to protect French Canadian language and culture enormously complicates the operation of the federal system. This is a common pattern in federal systems which have ethnic minorities which are geographically concentrated. Furthermore, another federal complexity which Canada illustrates is the problem of minorities within minorities. About twenty percent of Quebec's population is English speaking, and there are small French-speaking minorities in several other provinces. Under what circumstances should they be able to look to Ottawa (the national capital) or the courts for protection? Recently, for instance, Quebec moved to curtail the right to an English-language education. The courts voided this law, but the problems of dual and triple loyalty remain.

Imagine for a moment that the Reconstruction governments had stayed in power in five Deep South states, say South Carolina, Georgia, Alabama, Mississippi, and Louisiana. Imagine further that through the years substantial numbers of whites had moved out, enough to leave each of the five states with a black majority. Now, do you suppose that the politics of our federalism would be different? How? (Incidentally, Mikhail Gorbachev once suggested that the solution to racial problems in the U.S. would be to set up a few black states.) In what ways do you think our notions of group loyalty and citizenship might have been affected, if any?

One clear disadvantage of federalism is that many modern problems transcend state lines. Pollution is a prime example. Neither acid rain nor industrial pollutants in Lake Michigan respect state boundaries, for instance. As the number of environmental problems steadily mounts, states simply lack the jurisdictional reach to address many of them. In addition, many metropolitan areas have spilled over state lines, leading to all manner of problems in transportation, police and fire protection, taxation, and even such decisions as whether to use daylight savings time.

Of equal importance, federalism helps to perpetuate economic and social inequalities. In any society, there will be regional differences in income and opportunity; however, the effects can be more easily mitigated under a unitary government. For example, a child growing up in rural Mississippi has a much smaller chance of securing a good education than does a rural child of equal ability who is reared in Iowa; that disparity is aggravated by federalism. The greater resources Iowa has available to devote to education, even if the political will is equal in the two states, will make a dramatic difference in the life opportunities of these two children. The Mississippian is much more likely to remain poor because of the sheer accident of birth than perhaps he would be in a unitary system. At the level of higher education, consider what would happen to enrollment patterns if every public university in the country stopped charging fees to out-of-state students. Federalism, therefore, plays a role in keeping the income distribution static and highly inegalitarian; wealthy areas stay wealthy, and poorer ones stay poor.

Finally, without question, federalism is inefficient and cumbersome. Our public policies are a bewildering array of financial and administrative entanglements between national and state governments, requiring a mammoth amount of paperwork and coordination. All the energy, time, and personnel this coordination consumes dissipates the effort which could be devoted to solving the problems which the policies seek to address in the first place. Economic estimates of this "hidden cost" of federalism are difficult to come by, but it must be staggering. Further, the bewildering complexity federalism generates makes it harder for citizens to hold government accountable. Not only ordinary citizens but frequently experts as well cannot determine who is actually responsible for governmental decisions, since authority is so divided and fragmented. Consequently, even though federalism creates governments "closer to the people," it may actually impede and frustrate popular control.

Although all of these problems are serious drawbacks, federalism, on the whole, has probably had a beneficial effect on the United States. It has been peculiarly suited to our localized style of democracy, and to fusing a national political community while retaining the flavor of diversity. Its greatest failing, clearly, has been in its failure to overcome racism. Before we celebrate too many virtues of federalism, let us also recall that it took a bloody civil war to settle its most basic issue, the nature of the constitutional union.

Prominent political scientist William Riker wrote of federalism in 1964:

> The main beneficiary throughout American history has been Southern whites, who have been given the freedom to oppress Negroes, first as slaves and later as a depressed caste. Other minorities have from time to time also managed to obtain some of these benefits, e.g., special business interests. . . . But the significance of federal benefits to economic interests pales beside the significance of benefits to the Southern segregationist whites. The judgment to be passed on federalism in the United States is therefore a judgment on the values of segregation and racial oppression. . . . Thus, if . . . one disapproves of racism, one should disapprove of federalism.[15]

But there is a serious fallacy with that line of reasoning. There is no guarantee that with a unitary system southerners would not have succeeded in making their policies national. It could be that the same federalism that allowed for slavery and segregation also served to aid abolitionism and the civil rights movement. It was state governments in such places as Massachusetts and Wisconsin (whose Supreme Court declared unconstitutional the infamous Fugitive Slave Law)[16] which provided a legal cover for the abolitionists and which, a hundred years later, began the civil rights movement by loosening their own segregation laws. Without federalism, these protections and opportunities for reform would have been unavailable. Even in the area of race, then, the record of federalism is mixed.

FEDERALISM AND FINANCE

To many people governmental finance is a rather boring subject, composed of the endless study of tables, graphs, and arcane equations. Yet, money and political authority are inextricably linked. Knowing who has the power to raise and spend the money will solve many political puzzles. If modern state governments were entirely financially self-sufficient, for example, they would be more politically independent. To the extent, though, that their fiscal pipeline runs to Washington, their scope for decision making is limited. The intergovernmental financial equation is therefore a critical political component of federalism.

The Growth of the Grant System

At the outset, it should be noted that intergovernmental financial linkages are nothing new: they have existed since the earliest days of the Republic. The Northwest Ordinance of 1787 provided grants to the states for school construction and operation. The first Congress also acted to assume the states' Revolutionary War debts. In 1837 the federal government had such an embarrassingly huge surplus that it decided to distribute it to the states. In 1862 the Morrill Act established federal grants for higher education, to form the land-grant colleges.

Nevertheless, by the turn of the century, there were only five federal grant programs in operation. The number and scope expanded somewhat before World War I and rather steadily thereafter, the centerpiece being the adoption of the federal highway program in the 1920s. Still, by 1964 there was a total of only 51 grant programs. Then a literal explosion occurred, with 530 in place by 1971. The number stabilized during the 1970s, and in the 1980s the Reagan administration tried to scale back both the number of programs and the financial commitment to them, with some success.[17] In the 1990s, new battles are shaping up over the grant program (see table 3–1).

TABLE 3–1

Federal Grants to State and Local Governments
1955–1990

YEAR	TOTAL (BILLIONS)[a]	PERCENTAGE OF STATE AND LOCAL REVENUE	PERCENTAGE OF FEDERAL BUDGET
1955	$ 12.7	10.2%	4.7%
1960	24.7	14.5	7.6
1965	35.4	15.1	9.2
1970	61.2	19.0	12.3
1975	87.1	22.6	15.0
1980	105.9	25.8	15.5
1985	94.1	20.9	11.2
1990	100.9	17.9	10.9

Source: Advisory Commission on Intergovernmental Relations, *Significant Features of Fiscal Federalism,* 1991, vol. 2 (Washington: Government Printing Office, 1992), table 24, p. 50.

[a] Amounts are in 1982 dollars.

The impetus for the early development of the grant program is partly traceable to the growth of a national industrial economy. However, it was the adoption of the federal income tax in 1913 that above all else transformed the American fiscal landscape. While the federal coffers filled, state and local governments, continuing to rely heavily on sales and property taxes, watched their collections lag behind. The reason for this disparity is that income taxes are more sensitive to economic growth; that is, as incomes grow, receipts from the income tax will grow rapidly. To be sure, property and sales tax receipts will increase also, as people buy more expensive homes and purchase more goods, but they will grow much more slowly than the intake from income taxes.[18]

With the sustained economic growth of the 1950s and 1960s, the tax balance shifted even more toward Washington. By the 1960s, it appeared possible for government to take on many tasks which had been thought too expensive in the past. President Johnson's activist social policy was the immediate catalyst for most of the new grant programs; soon, however, all types of political interests were seeking grant programs for their pet projects.

Of course, the national government could have established its own administrative system to carry out the various policies. However, many favored funneling the money to state and local governments, charging them with carrying out whatever task was at hand: flood control, remedial education, pollution abatement, road and bridge construction, health care, law enforcement training, urban redevelopment, etc. With this huge transfer of funds (in 1991, $152 billion was paid by the federal government to state and local governments) came political battles over the operation and control of the programs. Before discussing how the political forces matched up in this contest, we need to examine the different types of grants.

Types of Grants

All grant programs have three different features: the matching requirement, the method of distribution, and the limitations on how the money may be spent.

Many federal grant programs require state and local governments to contribute a portion of their own money—usually from 10 percent to 50 percent—to receive a grant. The purpose of this is to be sure the state or locality is committed to the program and serious about undertaking it. The major example of this type is the federal highway program. Some other kinds of grants have no matching requirement, entailing no commitment of state or local funds. This, of course makes these grants more attractive to state and local governments, since they seem to provide "free" money.

On the question of how the money is distributed, there are two approaches. Under the first, the *formula method,* every subnational unit which qualifies receives a certain amount. For example, the program which aids school districts in providing hot lunches for low-income children distributes its monies based on the percentage of such children in the district. If a grant is made through the *project method,* though, state and local governments must file an application, specifying why the grant is needed. Federal authorities then have some discretion as to whether to award the money or not. The so-called "community development" grants (for such things as park renovation) are of this type.

But the most important classification of grants involves how the money may be spent: whether the funds constitute a categorical grant, a block grant, or revenue sharing.

Categorical grants are those in which the federal government gives money to a state or local jurisdiction for a specific purpose, and it may be spent for that purpose only. Examples would be grants for such things as building a hospital, developing a reading program for low-achieving elementary pupils, purchasing a communication system for a police department, and constructing a sewage system. Naturally, a detailed accounting must be provided, and federal auditors have the right to examine the books.

Block grants are monies provided with only a general governmental purpose assigned, such as education, transportation, or law enforcement. It is up to the state or local government to decide how to spend the money within these broad rubrics. Though accounting and audits occur here also, the requirements are much looser.

Lastly, *revenue sharing* permits the most local flexibility, in that monies are given to subnational governments with no stipulations attached. Any projects which local officials deem most needed in their own communities can be addressed with the funds. Officials are responsible only to the voters who elected them. Explicit revenue sharing was begun in the early 1970s at the initiative of the Nixon administration. It was terminated in 1987 as the federal deficit burgeoned, and seems unlikely to be reinstituted. However, it remains at least an available alternative.

Major metropolitan areas often form special governmental units to handle problems which involve a city and its suburbs. An example is the Bay Area Transit Authority, which oversees Bay Area Rapid Transit (BART) in the San Francisco/Oakland area.

There is no agreed-upon "best way" to handle federal grants. Each has advantages and disadvantages which are readily apparent. The categorical grant method insures that the money will be spent as directed, but it involves heavy administrative burdens. Detailed plans must be developed by local authorities and inspections must be carried out by federal officials. Another obvious problem is that not every state or locality needs the same services, but if there is grant money available, applications tend to be filed anyway. The categorical approach therefore not only introduces inflexibility into the programs, but also wastes a great deal of money. Block grants allow flexibility, but may be wasteful as well. There is more temptation for local officials to use the federal funds for expenditures they planned to make anyway. That is, nothing new is accomplished, but federal funds are used instead of locally-generated funds. Moreover, giving such wide discretion to local authorities means that some of them may spend the money for things sharply at variance with national goals. Revenue sharing carries the virtues and defects of the block grant system to an extreme.

Politics and Federal Grants

The main criteria for grant evaluation, as one might expect, are political. At first glance, it would seem that federal authorities would prefer categorical grants, while state and local officials would lean toward block grants and revenue sharing. With categorical grants, the "feds" can be sure the money is being spent the way they desire—a natural orientation, if they have raised the money in the first place. Furthermore, it is much easier to attach "strings," or conditions on taking the money, to categorical grants. For example, according to Title IX of the Education Amendments of 1972, if a college accepts federal funds, it must certify that it does not practice sex discrimination. Another example is the Davis-Bacon Act, which provides that on construction projects using federal funds, wages at prevailing union rates must be paid to workers. If block grants (or more preferably, revenue sharing) are used, on the other hand, local officials not only have much more discretion, but are often freed of these compliance provisions, which they usually view as burdensome.

There is some truth in this model of federal-state conflict. Nevertheless, it obscures as much as it enlightens, for it views the two levels of government as unified entities, which they most certainly are not. The "federal government" includes several entities concerned with grants, including Congress, the president, and the various executive agencies. Seldom do these have coordinated goals and outlooks. Likewise, states are not monoliths. They also have the three traditional branches of government, along with numerous administrative agencies. What this means is that there may be more vertical integration than horizontal integration. For example, federal education officials may be far more similar in outlook and policy preferences to their state counterparts than they are to members of Congress. (In fact, most people who work in the U.S. Department of Education arrive there from posts in state education systems.) The same holds for state education bureaucrats in relation to their legislators. In practice, therefore, we frequently find career officials at both levels arrayed against elected politicians. In one typical scenario, federal education personnel might want a categorical grant program, under which they could transfer funds directly to state education departments and local schools. State educators might prefer this also, since they could now deal with like-minded people, and not have to be dependent on state legislators, who, they fear, would muddy the water. Exactly the same pattern prevails in such areas as law enforcement, welfare, and health.

Furthermore, these "strings" that state and local politicians continually complain about are not put there for the sole purpose of "dictating" to subnational governments. They are put there because some interest group—labor unions, for instance, in one example cited above—wants them there. These conditions can prevent the group's having to fight fifty separate battles when the money comes to be spent. Any interest group that can convince Congress to attach a certain condition to a grant has won its battle (or at least, it has won an important round; executive authorities may still have to be convinced to be diligent in enforcing the condition—perhaps even in court). Remember, too, that if Congress attaches a particular condition, that is some evidence that it represents a national consensus.

In actuality, although many state and local politicians loudly claim to want more discretion, in truth they often want nothing of the sort. With discretion comes responsibility—and political heat. It is frequently easier politically to be enmeshed in categorical grants. Money can be spent without raising local taxes, and the beneficiaries are pleased. If anyone objects to various aspects of a grant program, the local politician can point to the structure of the program and say that her hands are tied.

The vertical alliances postulated above (such as between federal and state education officials) would seem to give rise to a natural counteralliance between elected politicians at both levels, but that is not necessarily the case. State and local politicians are quite content to let Congress raise the necessary taxes and settle the interest group battles over categorical spending. Without too much effort, state and local politicians often get to actually spend the money, with visible local results and visible local jobs (and sometimes, unfortunately, a little local corruption).

Taken together, these elements explain why there is so little support for proposals which surface from time to time (as in the early 1980s) to "return" certain programs to the states. In 1982, President Reagan proposed handing over several important programs to state governments; to sweeten the deal, he offered to simultaneously cut federal excise taxes (taxes on purchases of specific products, such as jewelry and tires) to allow the states a tax base from which to fund these programs. Somewhat surprisingly to many in the administration, there was little support, and no enthusiasm, among state politicians. Their reasons were that services to their citizens might be interrupted by a shift to state responsibility, and— significantly—that they would have had to vote to reimpose the cancelled taxes. Since few politicians relish the notion of levying any kind of tax, this prospect was most unappealing.

In addition, many state officials understand quite clearly that the "tax capacity" of each state is not equal. If income were spread evenly by population among the states, then each would have about the same ability to generate its own revenue. But that is far from the case. If Reagan's proposal had been adopted, poor states would have had only two choices: to cut the level of service, or to raise taxes even beyond the current federal level. It is small wonder that the proposal appealed to neither governors nor legislators in a large number of states.

One important consequence of the federal grant system, as it is presently constituted at least, is that coupled with the federal income tax, it does mitigate some of the disparities we discussed earlier. The income tax takes proportionally more from states populated by high-income people. If grant formulas were based only on population, this practice alone would effect some redistribution from wealthy to poor states. However, many grant formulas also give substantial weight to the percentage of low-income people within a unit of government; this further serves to do a mild Robin Hood trick. Table 3–2 provides graphic verification of this. Either a cut in income taxes or a diminution of the federal grant program would alter this pattern significantly.

It is important to go another step in this analysis. That a "state" benefits from a policy does not mean that each individual in that state also benefits. For example, a wealthy Mississippian might be better off with a reduction

TABLE 3–2

Federal Expenditures versus Federal Tax Collections, 1988–1990,
Or: Each State's Gain Compared to its Pain

STATE	ANNUAL FEDERAL EXPENDITURES, 1988–90 (MILLIONS)	ANNUAL FEDERAL TAX COLLECTIONS, 1988–90 (MILLIONS)	EXPENDITURE PER DOLLAR OF TAX BURDEN
New Mexico	$ 8,500	$ 4,000	$2.10
Mississippi	9,900	5,700	1.73
North Dakota	2,900	1,900	1.52
Virginia	34,700	23,000	1.51
South Dakota	2,800	1,900	1.51
Utah	6,200	4,200	1.46
Montana	3,200	2,200	1.43
Alabama	15,600	11,100	1.41
Idaho	3,700	2,600	1.40
Hawaii	5,300	3,900	1.36
West Virginia	6,200	4,700	1.33
Missouri	23,000	17,600	1.31
South Carolina	12,200	9,300	1.30
Arkansas	7,900	6,100	1.30
Maryland	25,100	20,400	1.23
Kentucky	12,200	9,900	1.23
Maine	4,600	3,700	1.22
Alaska	3,000	2,400	1.21
Arizona	13,600	11,200	1.21
Louisiana	14,100	12,000	1.19
Nebraska	5,900	5,100	1.17
Oklahoma	11,200	9,600	1.16
Colorado	13,800	11,900	1.16
Tennessee	16,800	14,700	1.14
Washington	19,200	17,100	1.13
Wyoming	1,700	1,500	1.13
Iowa	9,800	8,800	1.11
Kansas	9,200	8,700	1.05
Florida	47,000	46,100	1.02
Rhode Island	3,900	3,900	1.01
Oregon	8,900	8,900	1.00
Massachusetts	27,800	28,000	0.99
Pennsylvania	42,500	43,900	0.97
Georgia	20,000	20,700	0.96
North Carolina	18,900	19,900	0.95
Texas	54,200	57,200	0.95
Ohio	35,800	38,200	0.94
California	108,900	116,300	0.94
Nevada	3,800	4,100	0.93
Vermont	1,700	1,800	0.93
Minnesota	14,400	16,000	0.90
Indiana	15,900	18,000	0.88
Wisconsin	14,200	16,400	0.87
New York	65,200	80,100	0.81
Connecticut	14,800	18,500	0.80
Michigan	26,300	35,200	0.75
Delaware	2,100	2,800	0.75
Illinois	34,500	47,800	0.72
New Hampshire	3,400	4,700	0.72
New Jersey	26,100	41,400	0.63

Source: Significant Features of Fiscal Federalism, 1991, vol. 2, table 28, pp. 56–57.

in income taxes accompanied by a cut in grant funds, since he will probably not benefit directly from the grants to his state.[19] Conversely, a poor New Yorker may be hurt by federal grant cuts and helped not at all by an income tax cut.

The financial dimension of federalism has been as important as court decisions, if not more important, in shaping the allocation of powers between the national and the state governments. Moreover, an understanding of intergovernmental finance will provide an important window onto the character of American politics at any given moment.

FEDERALISM AND BIG CITIES: A SPECIAL CASE

Big cities are an anomaly in the federal system. In population and budget, the largest of them dwarf several states, but constitutionally they are purely subdivisions of their respective states. Except for Washington, D.C., they have no direct link to the national government, but arguably, some national policies are more important to their fates than to most states'.

As for population, each of our eight largest cities has more people than does any of the ten smallest states. The thirteenth largest city is larger than six states. The six largest cities also each had budgets in the late 1980s that exceeded those of the eight smallest states.[20]

Legally, cities are creatures of state governments. Within themselves, states are unitary political systems, which means that they entirely control the structure and operation of all local governments. States may redraw local boundaries, rearrange local governmental institutions, and redefine the scope of local public authority any time and for whatever reason they wish to do so.

The legal powers of city governments become subject therefore to statewide politics. States can broaden or curtail the ability of cities to act, depending on the wishes of the legislature. It is not uncommon for a state to have a number of laws that apply "only to municipalities with a population in excess of _____ ," when there exists only one city of that size in that state.

Another consequence of this umbilical cord is the entanglement of state and city finances. Cities' taxing powers are given only by the legislature, and may be altered or withdrawn at will. State tax and expenditure policies also affect cities, for in the states we see the national redistribution system in miniature. No city or county receives benefits exactly proportional to what it pays in. In the past, it was not unusual for large cities to contribute the lion's share to a state revenue system because of the concentration of commercial activity there, only to watch as legislators deemed it wise to spread the fruits throughout the state. Today, with declining income levels in central cities, the cities often put in more claims than they do tax dollars.

State legislative politics are therefore a vital ingredient in determining the shape of urban government and the quality of urban life. Until the 1960s, states did not follow the "one person, one vote" rule in apportioning seats in their legislatures. Overall, cities were substantially underrepresented; this diminished their political clout. When urban issues were raised, a solid phalanx of rural and small-town legislators were either uninterested in or hostile to big-city needs. In 1964, the Supreme Court held that both houses of state legislatures had to reflect population.[21] The rejoicing among urban interests was short-lived, however; ironically, at the very moment of this decision, suburban growth was exploding and central cities were losing population. As a result, the real beneficiaries of the new rules have been suburbanites, who often harbor anti-urban attitudes equal to those of rural Americans. Big cities in the 1980s and early 1990s fared little better in most legislatures than they had a generation earlier.

Yet, big cities, or more accurately the constituencies that make up big cities, are not without political influence. The facts that incumbents in the House of Representatives from some urban areas (who are usually Democrats) tend to serve for many terms and that the Democrats have long controlled the House have translated into key committee assignments for some urban representatives. Further, the statewide character of U.S. Senate races makes large cities important. It is difficult in many states to win a Senate seat without carrying or at least making substantial inroads into the big-city vote. Thus, some representatives and senators are sympathetic when approached by mayors and other city officials. The presidential election system too provides some opportunity for cities. The need to carry large states can give the urban areas within those states an influential role.

Nonetheless, the big-city vote has been of declining importance, particularly in recent presidential elections (neither Reagan nor Bush paid much attention to urban voters), but also in Senate contests. The reasons lie both in the declining population of central cities and in the lower rate of voter turnout among the less affluent, who now disproportionately inhabit our larger cities. Still, urban interests have friends in Congress, and sometimes in the executive branch. Urban problems and politics remain the subject of debate at the national level, even though there is no direct legal link.

The chief ingredient in the national-local linkage is money. Federal programs are especially important to big cities. Their limited fiscal powers, combined with a population more in need of public services than the average, create continual financial pressures. Without the grant programs of the federal government, even in the budget-tight early 1990s, many American cities would probably go bankrupt.

But our largest cities are politically important in many more ways than merely being financial dependents of the national government. They contain, after all, most of our cultural and artistic heritage. Many of them have institutions, buildings, landmarks, and facilities that are national treasures. Furthermore, the arts continue to flourish primarily in big cities. To have our cities decay would be to rob ourselves of something very significant, to say nothing of the fate of those who live there. American cities have therefore a national importance, despite the localized nature of their governments.

The flight of the affluent (of all races) from our central cities has left behind escalating social pathologies. The living conditions in some areas of our inner cities have become frightening indeed, and in truth, there are zones in which such basic public services as law enforcement have all but broken down. In some places, the Postal Service even sometimes has to suspend mail deliveries.[22]

Experts disagree (as they almost always do) over the causes of and cures for this deplorable situation. To some, only a massive, direct national financial commitment will suffice to revitalize these areas. Others argue that government policies are the problem, and the sooner they are terminated, the sooner self-reliance will flourish. In a middle position, proponents of "enterprise zones" (tax breaks and other "carrots" to entice businesses to locate in depressed areas) call for government to create the conditions necessary for private investment to bring about an economic renaissance.

It seems unlikely that the national government will soon abandon "urban policy." Too many political interests and too much national heritage is at stake. What is clear is that in important ways federalism will affect and be affected by how the national government treats big cities.

One last point worth mentioning is that America's cities and the relationships they enjoy with their states are as diverse as our society. We tend to think of the older industrial cities of the Northeast and Midwest as prototypes of American urban areas. However, places such as Albuquerque, Phoenix, San Antonio, Portland, and Oklahoma City are sizeable cities. Social and economic conditions in these cities do not necessarily parallel those in Cleveland or St. Louis, and an urban policy which does not consider these variations will be ill-conceived indeed.

FEDERALISM AND CONTEMPORARY POLITICS: THE REJUVENATION OF STATE AND LOCAL GOVERNMENTS

From the end of World War II to the late 1970s, the federal system was shaped by a pronounced growth in the relative power of the national government. In part, the rapid lacing together of national economic and transportation systems created a need for uniform policies in these areas. From the 1940s on, the Supreme Court aided this trend by interpreting national power broadly in contrast to the narrow scope given it by the pre–1937 Court. We have seen this, for example, in chapter 2, in the decision regarding the scope of the commerce power. The prominent place taken by war and by foreign affairs in our post-war politics gave another impetus to the accretion of national authority. The far-reaching responsibilities of the United States in world politics and the gravity of the issues absorbed political attention, all of which was focused on Washington. The communications revolution, particularly the advent of television, allowed national figures to speak directly to the people, which enhanced their political reach and diminished the role played by intermediaries. As a result, those with serious political ambitions turned increasingly toward careers in national politics, leaving state and local matters to less talented hands. All these trends were aided and abetted by the bountiful revenue

TABLE 3-3

State and Local Expenditures, 1950–1990

YEAR	EXPENDITURES (MILLIONS)[a]	EXPENDITURES PER CAPITA[a]	PERCENTAGE OF GROSS NATIONAL PRODUCT
1950	$130.1	$ 855	14.3%
1955	155.2	934	16.9
1960	198.0	1,095	18.2
1965	262.2	1,351	17.8
1970	341.8	1,666	20.1
1975	404.8	1,874	22.8
1980	421.4	1,850	22.5
1985	449.7	1,879	24.6
1990	541.7	2,154	23.3

Sources: *Significant Features of Fiscal Federalism, 1991,* vol. 2, tables 21–22, pp. 41–43; *Economic Report of the President,* 1991, (Washington: Government Printing Office, 1991) table B-3, pp. 290–92.

[a] All figures in 1982 dollars.

collected by the federal government through the income tax. With the exception of foreign affairs, none of these features was unique to the United States; centralization characterized the politics of other federal systems also. In Canada, for example, the federal government assumed vast new responsibilities and became more than ever the paymaster of the provinces.

An additional factor in the United States was the shameful behavior of and extravagant claims made by southern governors and other public officials as they fought the civil rights movement. "Standing in the schoolhouse door" to resist desegregation and foolish talk of "interposition" (putting a state government between the federal government and a state's citizens) eroded the popular legitimacy of state action. Any responsible public figure who spoke favorably of state power ran the risk of appearing to condone a variety of unsavory actions, finally including violence. Moreover, as case after case involving these futile gestures came to the Supreme Court and state power was overruled, the weight of these precedents and their centralizing doctrines spilled over into other cases involving federalism, eroding the legal legitimacy of state action as well.

A recitation of these historical trends, however, should not make us fall prey to a common logical fallacy. Simply because the relative power of the national government grew during these years, it does not follow that the absolute power of the states shrank. The total power exercised by government at all levels in fact grew after the war, although there was a greater increase in power in the nation's capital. Measured by both expenditures and number of employees, state and local governments were hardly static in this period, much less withering (see tables 3–3 and 3–4).

The states were far from becoming mere administrative appendages of the federal government. Wide-ranging areas of public policy remained

TABLE 3–4

State and Local Employment, 1952–1989

YEAR	TOTAL STATE AND LOCAL EMPLOYEES	EMPLOYEES PER 10,000 OF POPULATION
1952	4,522,000	257
1962	6,849,000	321
1972	10,964,000	442
1982	13,071,000	468
1989	14,765,000	513

Source: Significant Features of Fiscal Federalism, 1991, vol. 2, table 117, p. 218.

firmly under their control, and their actions affected citizens' lives in countless ways. Further, it must be remembered that federalism is written into the very structure of the national government itself: in elections to the Senate by state; in the electoral college; and in the fact that the Supreme Court is linked to state judicial systems. There was no chance that the only people who would soon be interested in state boundaries would be Rand-McNally, as Senator Everett Dirksen once charged.

Nonetheless, the growth in national power and the linkage forged between ordinary citizens and the national government was unmistakably the dominant thrust of the post-war era. In the 1980s, though, several of these trends were weakened, if not reversed. As a result, state and local governments have undergone conspicuous rejuvenation.[23]

To a degree, the turnabout is traceable to the shifting balance between foreign and domestic policy. A changing world has reduced the salience of foreign policy, freeing us to pay more heed to domestic problems. Furthermore, most conservatives and many liberals have expressed doubts about the efficacy of the federal government's role in solving social problems.

Of equal import, federalism is no longer the captive of civil rights issues. The major legal battles here have all been won, removing their clouding effect from all other issues. Southern state governments themselves, in fact, have been transformed in the process, thanks largely to the Voting Rights Act of 1965. Overt racists have either changed positions, in their public stances anyway, or been routed from office. African Americans have entered elective politics in significant numbers. As of 1990, there were more than 4,300 black elected officials in the eleven states that comprised the Confederacy, including a governor and several members of Congress.

The Supreme Court is another harbinger of change. The elevation of William Rehnquist to the position of Chief Justice is especially noteworthy in this regard. Rehnquist has a formidable intellect, and one of the key components of his judicial philosophy is deference to state authority.[24] He is more hesitant than most justices have been in the immediate past to apply the strictures of the First and Fourteenth Amendments (see chapter 4) to circumscribe state power, whether to aid church-related schools or to regulate abortion, for example. If he is able to forge a consensus to push this notion even further, state governments will find themselves with ever more policy flexibility.

At the same time, the federal deficit crisis makes it most improbable that new grant programs will be instituted; on the contrary, further cuts in current ones are more likely. Thus, states will have a smaller federal money tree to shake, and will be forced by circumstance to make serious choices about their priorities (most state constitutions forbid deficit financing). Searching for greater cost-effectiveness, they may well discover more innovative and less expensive ways to deliver services (by "contracting out," for instance, and by using nonprofit organizations).

As a result of all these trends, the states are showing signs of renewed political vitality.[25] A new breed of politician has emerged in state political circles, most visibly at the level of governor. The change was epitomized in the title of a book on this theme: *Goodbye to Goodtime Charlie*.[26] As these more dynamic governors have assumed office, they have brought with them a host of new and generally younger people into state administrative positions. Consequently, many of the most innovative reforms and interesting administrative techniques are now being pioneered at the state level.[27] Politics in many state capitals has become a lively and robust affair.

Accompanying this revitalization has been a spate of state constitutional revision, with an eye toward modernizing political and administrative structures. In a parallel development, state courts have shown an increased interest in state constitutional interpretation, an almost moribund field twenty years ago. As but one example, the Texas Supreme Court recently held that the state's system of school finance violated the state constitution.

The upshot of all this will probably be a burst of even greater vitality in state politics. That is, as more and more important issues are decided in state legislatures, state governors' mansions, and state courts, political interests will turn their attention there. Most likely, citizen involvement in state government will rise, since people will see how their lives are being affected by decisions made at the state and local level. State political battles will also probably become sharper, as the losers learn that they cannot prevail upon either Washington or the federal courts. But the outcomes will not be the same in all the states; the end result perhaps will be more policy diversity than we have been accustomed to.

It is important, nonetheless, to keep this shifting balance in the federal system in perspective. Over 18 percent of state and local expenditures still come from the federal treasury (down from nearly 26 percent in 1980). Furthermore, as the federal financial commitment has lessened, congressional majorities have turned increasingly to regulation, often under the authority of the commerce clause. In 1980, for example, there were thirty-six significant federal regulations which applied to the states; in the 1980s, twenty-five more were added. Those affecting the environment and civil rights are listed in table 3–5.

T A B L E 3–5

Major Environmental and Civil Rights Measures Adopted in the 1980s
Which Regulate State and Local Governments
(New Laws and Amendments)

ENVIRONMENTAL MEASURES

Hazardous and Solid Waste Amendments of 1984
Asbestos Hazard Emergency Response Act of 1986
Safe Drinking Water Act Amendments of 1986
Water Quality Act of 1987
Lead Contamination Control Act of 1988
Ocean Dumping Ban Act (1988)
Clean Air Act Amendments of 1990

CIVIL RIGHTS MEASURES

Voting Rights Act Amendments of 1982
Voting Accessibility for the Elderly and Handicapped Act (1984)
Age Discrimination in Employment Act Amendments of 1986
Education of the Handicapped Act Amendments of 1986
Handicapped Children's Protection Act of 1986
Civil Rights Restoration Act of 1987
Fair Housing Act Amendments of 1988
Americans with Disabilities Act (1990)
Education of the Handicapped Act Amendments of 1990

Source: Timothy Conlan, "And the Beat Goes On: Intergovernmental Mandates and Preemption in an Era of Deregulation," *Publius* 21 (Summer 1991), 52.

SUMMARY

Federalism stands in contrast to unitary governments—in which power is concentrated at the center—and confederations—where ultimate authority rests with the states making up the nation. Our Founding Fathers chose federalism because no practical alternative existed, even though many of them would probably have preferred a more centralized system.

The Constitution provides an ambiguous framework of forbidden, enumerated, inherent, concurrent, and reserved powers. Beginning with *McCulloch v. Maryland* in 1819, the Supreme Court has tended to favor the expansion of national power. Behind these court decisions have stood various political interests which stood to either gain or lose, depending on the level at which decisions were made.

Federalism has several claimed advantages: it allows unity within diversity; it creates governments closer to the people; it unclogs the national agenda; it provides many access points to government; it encourages experimentation and innovation; and it contributes to limited government. Critics, however, point to the negative aspects of federalism: unhealthy diversity; the control of several states by small elites; the political and administrative weakness of some states; the drain on public resources created by economic competition among the states; the public problems that spill over state boundaries; the perpetuation of inequalities; and the inefficiency which characterizes federalism.

The financial consequences of federalism constitute an important dimension of American political life. Federal grants to states and localities began in the nineteenth century, but grew immensely in the 1960s. Lately, the grant system has witnessed cutbacks, but remains substantial. The federal government's financial picture, first colored by the income tax and then by ballooning deficits, accounts for much of the change.

Grants can require matching funds or not, and can be distributed either by a set formula or through project applications. Categorical and block grants are both used, and revenue sharing was employed in the past. Each has advantages and disadvantages, but politics is often the chief element involved when decisions are made.

America's largest cities are tied both to their respective states and to the federal government. As their financial needs have grown, federal policy has come to have a greater impact on cities than on other local governments. With declining populations and economic bases, big cities continue to suffer escalating problems.

Although from the end of World War II to the 1970s, increasing centralization characterized American federalism, now state and local political vitality is flourishing. National economic growth, the communications revolution, the saliency of foreign policy, and the civil rights movement all fostered augmented federal power in the three decades after World War II. However, in the 1990s the growing concern with domestic problems, the end of southern resistance to civil rights, a gradual shift on the Supreme Court, and federal financial woes are reawakening political vigor in the states. But the federal fiscal role is still large, and Congress has increasingly turned to regulation to influence state policy.

ENDNOTES

1. The new political arrangements taking form as the old Soviet Union passes away will make interesting watching in this regard.

2. The framers' view of federalism is explained in Martin Diamond, "What the Framers Meant by Federalism," in Laurence O'Toole, ed., *American Intergovernmental Relations* (Washington: Congressional Quarterly Press, 1985), chap. 2.

3. Richard Leach, *American Federalism* (New York: Norton, 1970), 8.

4. An *ex post facto* law is one that prohibits some activity and applies retroactively to conditions existing before the date the law is passed. A bill of attainder is an act that names a particular person and spells out a punishment. In the first case, a legal activity is made illegal retroactively; in the second case, someone is found guilty without a trial. Both of these measures were used by the British Parliament from time to time.

5. The First Amendment to the Constitution in particular applied only to the national government. In 1925 the Supreme Court held that the

Fourteenth Amendment (1868) made the First Amendment applicable to the states also (*Gitlow v. New York,* 268 U.S. 652, 45 S.Ct. 625). This issue arises again in chapter 4.

6. The Supreme Court discussed the amendment extensively in *FERC v. Mississippi,* 456 U.S. 742, 102 S.Ct. 2126 (1982).

7. The only time of any significance this clause was used occurred in 1842 when a virtual civil war broke out in Rhode Island. *Luther v. Borden,* 48 U.S. (7 Howard) 1 (1849).

8. Frederick Davenport, *The Bacon Lectures on the Constitution of the United States* (Boston: Boston University Press, 1939), 347.

9. 17 U.S. (4 Wheat) 316 (1819).

10. This case and others are discussed in Timothy Conlan, "And the Beat Goes On: Intergovernmental Mandates and Preemption in an Era of De-regulation," *Publius* 21 (1991), 43-57.

11. Quoted in Frances Perkins, *The Roosevelt I Knew* (New York: Viking, 1964), 124.

12. See David Robertson and Dennis Judd, *The Development of American Public Policy: The Structure of Policy Restraint* (Boston: Little, Brown, 1989).

13. *Chicago Tribune,* October 24, 1991, sec. 3, p. 1.

14. When the Chicago White Sox threatened to move to St. Petersburg in 1988, the state of Illinois appropriated $150 million to build the team a new stadium.

15. William Riker, *Federalism: Origin, Operation, Significance* (Boston: Little, Brown, 1964), 152-53.

16. The Fugitive Slave Law was part of the Compromise of 1850 which allowed California to enter the Union as a free state. The law made it much easier for slaveowners to reclaim runaway slaves in federal court and established criminal penalties for anyone aiding their escape (a provision aimed at the Underground Railroad). In 1854 the Wisconsin Supreme Court voided the law and then refused to take notice of the United States Supreme Court's 1859 review of that ruling. In the meantime, several other northern states enacted "Personal Liberty" laws designed to block the national act by establishing heavy administrative roadblocks to the act's enforcement.

17. David Nice, *Federalism: The Politics of Intergovernmental Relations* (New York: St. Martin's Press, 1987), 55-57.

18. Actually, receipts from the income tax will grow at a greater rate than the rise in income because of "bracket creep." The income tax is "progressive"; that is, each successively higher "bracket" of income is taxed at a higher rate than the bracket below it. For example, let us say the tax rate structure is such that the first $10,000 (or, lowest "bracket") is taxed at 5 percent, the second $10,000 at 10 percent, and all income above $20,000 at 15 percent. With a $19,000 income, a person would pay $1,400 ($500 + $900). Now, say she receives a 10 percent raise, putting her income at $20,900. She will now pay $1,635, which is a 17 percent increase. In fact, governments can even cut taxes and still have more revenue. Assume, for instance, that the rates are cut to 5 percent on the first $10,000, 9.5 percent on the second $10,000, and 13 percent on the amount over $20,000. The Treasury will collect $1,567 in taxes, still quite an increase from the original $1,400. In short, if incomes grow, politicians have the best of all possible worlds: they can cut taxes and still have more money to spend.

19. The careful student, especially one who has studied economics, will ask about the "multiplier effect," which often makes affluent citizens in poor states more dependent on federal grants and payments than they think. Consider, for example, an Oldsmobile dealer in Alabama. She is probably in favor of cutting all kinds of federal domestic programs, especially if they are called "welfare," and would likely feel that none of her customers would be hurt. But there is an economic chain reaction at work: a food stamp recipient patronizes the local supermarket, increasing employment and profits in the grocery business; the manager of the supermarket buys shoes at the local shoe store; the owner of the shoe store builds a bigger house; and the construction company owner buys an Oldsmobile with his increased profits. A decrease in the food stamp budget will reverse these effects, and may indeed hurt the dealer's sales.

20. U.S. Bureau of the Census, *Statistical Abstract of the United States, 1991* (Washington: Government Printing Office, 1991), table 477.

21. *Reynolds v. Sims,* 377 U.S. 533, 84 S.Ct. 1362 (1964).

22. See *Los Angeles Times,* September 19, 1989, sec. 2, p. 1.

23. See John Harrigan, *Politics and Policy in States and Communities,* 4th ed. (New York: Harper/Collins, 1991), chap. 1, for a discussion of the turnaround in state politics.

24. A lucid explanation is contained in Sue Davis, *Justice Rehnquist and the Constitution* (Princeton: Princeton University Press, 1989).

25. See Carl Van Horn, "The Quiet Revolution," in Carl Van Horn, ed., *The State of the States* (Washington: Congressional Quarterly Press, 1989), chap. 1.

26. Larry Sabato, *Goodbye to Goodtime Charlie,* 2d ed. (Washington: Congressional Quarterly Books, 1983).

27. A good survey of recent state innovations can be found in David Osborne, *Laboratories of Democracy* (Cambridge, Mass.: Harvard Business School Press, 1988).

FURTHER READING

1. Anton, Thomas. *American Federalism and Public Policy.* New York: Random House, 1989.

2. Elazar, Daniel. *American Federalism: A View from the States.* 3d ed. New York: Harper and Row, 1984.

3. Elazar, Daniel. *Exploring Federalism.* Tuscaloosa: University of Alabama Press, 1987.

4. Leach, Richard. *American Federalism.* New York: Norton, 1970.

5. Nice, David. *Federalism: The Politics of Intergovernmental Relations.* New York: St. Martin's, 1987.

6. Reagan, Michael and John Sanzone. *The New Federalism.* New York: Oxford University Press, 1981.

7. Wright, Deil. *Understanding Intergovernmental Relations.* 3d ed. Pacific Grove, CA: Brooks/Cole, 1988.

FOUR

CIVIL LIBERTIES AND CIVIL RIGHTS

CIVIL LIBERTIES and civil rights are often considered to be identical, but there are differences between the two. Civil liberties rest on the foundation stone of individual autonomy and limited government. They are at the philosophical base of constitutional government itself, and constitute our most basic protections against an overextended and arbitrary state. Civil rights, on the other hand, primarily (although not exclusively) refer to the right to be free from unjust classifications.

Civil liberties, moreover, are based solely on the Constitution, especially the guarantees found in the first ten amendments, collectively known as the Bill of Rights. Civil rights, on the other hand, can either be granted by the Constitution or flow from a statute. The Fourteenth Amendment is the major constitutional source of civil rights, but Congress has also conferred a number of them by law.

One important characteristic that civil liberties and civil rights have in common is that the lifeblood of both flows heavily through the courts. The judiciary is called upon to referee and settle disputes in this domain of government more than in any other. Here law and politics are consequently married more closely than anywhere else.

CIVIL LIBERTIES

In one guise or another, absolutism is the political theory on which most governments have been built. Their sphere of authority over the people is unlimited, and there is no right to question official decisions. In the eighteenth century, some political theorists began to argue that the individual is the proper moral unit of the political order, and that every person has certain inalienable rights that cannot be invaded by any government. This branch of European political thought was transplanted to America, and flowered into the list of liberties contained in the Bill of Rights.

The ideas of liberty and citizenship are in fact closely intertwined. As long as government is absolute, the people are not citizens, but mere subjects, to be acted upon by an overbearing state. To be sure, the actions of such a state need not be malevolent or wicked. Indeed, the state could act quite paternalistically, and truly seek to care for its subjects and meet their needs. But that is the antithesis of both citizenship and liberty. When the individual came to be seen as the building block of the political order, liberty automatically became the paramount goal of government. At the same time, the transition from subject to citizen occurred. The state is now an outgrowth of the citizenry, not vice versa. Thus, both liberty and citizenship are based on the view that the individual is sacrosanct.

Each of the rights or liberties laid out in the Bill of Rights is, significantly, asserted *against* government. None of these fundamental liberties is unimportant, but some relate more to the conditions and governmental

Opposite: *The jury box of the courtroom in the Lawaca County Courthouse, Halletsville, Texas. Civil liberties and civil rights cases often begin in places such as this.*

abuses of the eighteenth century. For example, the Third Amendment prevents the quartering of troops in private homes without the owner's consent. Of the others, three stand out for their continuing relevance to political life: those involving freedom of expression, freedom of religion, and the right to a fair trial.

Originally, each of these three liberties was forged in an age when the major political goal was the chaining of monarchical governments. However, democratization has not made them any less salient. The fact that those in power are now elected is not in itself adequate to assure that government will not tread on the civil liberties of minorities. These civil liberties therefore are checks on the authority of any government, no matter how chosen.

In the following pages we will examine a number of important Supreme Court cases. They are of course only a minute sample; these particular cases were chosen primarily because they illustrate the dilemmas involved in issues of free expression, religious liberty, and the right to a fair trial, rather than because they represent the most recent statement on these matters. The contours of civil liberties are ever changing, as each year brings a fresh crop of difficult cases to court. But the issues raised below should provide a beginning framework for understanding current cases.

Two brief technical notes need to be made before we embark on a survey of these three civil liberties. First, the First Amendment in particular, and most of the others by implication, apply only to the federal government. In 1833 the Supreme Court held explicitly that the Bill of Rights did not apply to the states.[1] The Fourteenth Amendment (1868), however, seemed to imply that the Bill of Rights now did apply to the states, although it was not until 1925 that the Supreme Court broached the subject. Currently, the doctrine of "incorporation" holds that the Bill of Rights is applicable to the states through the Fourteenth Amendment.[2] This is quite significant because many more civil liberty questions have arisen at the state level than have surfaced at the federal level. Second, only the federal and state governments have constitutional standing. Constitutionally, all local governments and their officials are purely creatures of the states. This is important to know because a large number of the cases involving civil liberties grow out of the activities of local officials—police officers, school principals, school boards, city councils, and so forth.

Freedom of Expression

As you read this, someone somewhere is very likely being silenced, imprisoned, or tortured for expressing opposition to a government. The idea that you can criticize government yet still be loyal, not to mention the idea that you have a right to criticize, was a long time coming in human history. In many places this right is still not acknowledged. It is perhaps our most hard-won and most precious right.

It is not, however, without controversy. An individual's right to free speech often collides with other rights, and with the simple need to maintain order. Some questions you might ponder: Is all speech (political and non-political) covered, no matter what its content? Does the right extend to any forum whatever, under any and all circumstances? When, if ever, does the right of the government to protect national security trump the right to free expression? Are symbols "speech"? Does expression ever become action, and if so, where does the protection of free expression end?

The First Amendment provides that "Congress shall make no law . . . abridging the freedom of speech, or of the press." Supreme Court justices have divided into three basic groups regarding the meaning of this sentence. The absolutist position takes the words at face value: "no law" means *no* law. Another group has argued for a "balancing" approach, contending that freedom of expression is given no special status in the Constitution, and the prohibition must be read in light of the whole document. Free expression must always be balanced against other provisions, such as those giving the federal government responsibility for foreign affairs, and the right to a fair trial. Between these two lie the "preferred position" advocates. Free expression, they believe, is so fundamental to our political life that it must always assume a preferred position when being weighed against other needs. Government will always bear a heavy burden of proof when it tries to regulate expression, but the bar is not absolute.

FREEDOM OF SPEECH   The earliest Supreme Court case dealing with freedom of speech arose during World War I (*Schenck v. U.S.*).[3] Congress had established a military draft to raise manpower for the army and had provided that anyone interfering with the operation of the law would be guilty of a federal crime. Charles Schenck published a pamphlet in which he urged young men to refuse induction into the army. He was arrested, tried, and convicted for interfering with the implementation of the draft law, despite the fact that no one had taken his advice. In his appeal to the Supreme Court, he argued that he had only spoken and not acted, and hence his conviction violated the First Amendment. Justice Oliver Wendell Holmes spoke for the Court in upholding the government. Speech, he said, was not an absolute right. One cannot falsely shout "Fire!" in a crowded theater and use freedom of speech as a shield against prosecution for causing harm. If, considering the time, place, and circumstances of the speech in question, there is a "clear and present danger" that the speech will lead to law-breaking, it does not fall under the First Amendment. Holmes was roundly criticized for this test, because it opened a wide door for governments to claim some kind of danger. Throughout the 1920s and 1930s, the test was expanded: speech could be banned when it had a "bad tendency," rather than presenting any truly clear and present danger.

In the aftermath of World War II, another important free speech case came to the Court, *Terminiello v. Chicago* (1949).[4] A private group had rented a lecture hall and scheduled several speakers. A crowd began to gather outside to protest the meeting and the speakers. Tempers grew and the police were called. When Terminiello came to the podium, he verbally

Justice Oliver Wendell Holmes, author of the Court's opinion in Schenck v. United States, *served on the court from 1902–1932.*

lashed out at the crowd and assorted groups he considered enemies. Violence threatened, and the police commander felt that his best move was to shut Terminiello up. When he refused to stop speaking, Terminiello was arrested for breach of the peace, and the two groups quickly dispersed. Terminiello, however, insisted that the city ordinance empowering police to take action to prevent a riot was unconstitutionally applied to him. The Supreme Court agreed, saying that as long as he was only speaking and not urging his listeners to do anything, his right to speak could not be infringed simply because what he said offended someone else. In a democracy we must expect provocative, even insulting, speech, and government must protect those who speak.

Terminiello was an *invited* speaker at an arranged gathering, and the protesters outside had *purposely* placed themselves near the speaker. Suppose the speaker comes to where others are with the intention of insulting them? Skokie, Illinois is a predominately Jewish suburb of Chicago and home to a number of Holocaust survivors. In 1978, the Nazi Party of America requested a permit from the city council to hold a parade and rally in Skokie. The city council refused on two grounds. First, there was almost a certainty of violence which the police might not be able to control. Second, the "speech" involved here could pose real psychological damage to Skokie residents. For those who survived the horrors of Nazi concentration camps to see people in storm trooper uniforms bedecked in swastikas goosestepping past their homes to hold a rally in a nearby park could be severely traumatic. In court, Skokie pressed the point that the village was not trying to ban the Nazi Party, but merely to prevent it from having its march there. The place of the proposed "speech" made it more than speech; it was a deliberate attempt to inflict harm on innocent people. The courts, however, stuck by the *Terminiello* rule.[5] Speech, no matter how despicable, must be protected. (Incidentally, after winning in court, the Nazi Party decided to hold its rally elsewhere.)

The issue of the use of symbols as speech was raised in the Skokie case; this had been addressed explicitly years earlier in *Tinker v. Des Moines Independent Community School Dist.*(1969).[6] On a certain day in 1965, people opposed to the Vietnam war were asked to wear black armbands. John Tinker showed up at his Des Moines high school wearing one, and refused to accede to the principal's request to remove it. The Court held that the armband was speech, and once again, the principal's fear that other students' reactions might disrupt the school day did not warrant the state's interfering with free speech.

As part of a protest connected with the 1988 Republican convention in Dallas, Gregory Johnson and a group of followers burned an American flag and chanted, "America, the red, white, and blue, we spit on you." Although the speech itself was allowed to go unmolested, Johnson was arrested on the basis of a Texas law making it a crime to "desecrate . . . a state or national flag." Johnson had obviously touched a very sensitive nerve, and many felt that the flag was somehow different from other symbols. The Supreme Court, though, said that the very sensitivity of the symbol required that Johnson's "speech" be covered by the First Amendment. He wanted to argue a particular political point, and burning the flag was a graphic way of doing just that.[7]

One passage in the Court's opinion seemed to imply that a critical defect in Texas' law was its almost unlimited breadth. Congress, although rejecting President Bush's suggestion of passing a constitutional amendment, drew up a very restrictive statute outlawing flag burning. The Court, however, struck down this effort also.[8]

All of the above cases involve political speech by an individual. What about "speech" by a business firm, either political or non-political? In general, the Supreme Court has held that speech of this type is also protected by the First Amendment. Massachusetts, for example, had a law that prohibited corporations from sponsoring advertising regarding political issues in which the company had no direct stake. The aim was to protect the integrity of public debate and the electoral process from the unwarranted influence of wealthy corporations. However, the Court held that corporations are covered by the First Amendment in the same way as individuals, and voided the law *(First National Bank v. Bellotti)*.[9]

In the non-political area, or what is called "commercial speech," the major case involving free speech is *Virginia Pharmacy Board v. Virginia Citizens Consumer Council*.[10] Virginia law made it illegal for pharmacists to advertise the prices of drugs. The Court found this to be an unconstitutional infringement on the free speech of a pharmacist who might wish to inform the public of his prices. This holding has led to other cases which have struck down laws regulating the advertising of other services (such as those of abortion clinics), as well as advertising by lawyers and other professionals. The scope of the free speech provisions of the First Amendment is therefore very broad.

FREEDOM OF THE PRESS   Freedom of the press is a sibling to freedom of speech after the fact of publication (as with the *Schenck* case above). There are three unique aspects of journalistic freedom, however: whether prior restraint of publication can be exercised, the status of school-sponsored newspapers, and reporters' protection of their sources.

In general, the Supreme Court has held that there must be no prior restraint, but this does not mean that a publisher is free from civil or criminal action after publication. It is still possible to bring libel suits or for the government to seek criminal penalties (for publishing military secrets, for example). What is ordinarily unacceptable is government's moving to stop the act of publication.

In 1931 the Supreme Court struck down a Minnesota law banning "malicious, scandalous, and defamatory" newspapers from circulating.[11] The most serious case, though, involved a stolen government report, dubbed the Pentagon Papers, obtained by the *New York Times* in 1971.[12] When the government learned that the *Times* planned to publish the material, it began a court action to prohibit it on the basis that sensitive national security information would be divulged. The Court, though badly divided, refused to grant any prior restraint, but cautioned the *Times* editors that they could be subject to criminal prosecution. The report was published in its entirety, and the only result was political embarrassment. However, could there be cases that would warrant prior restraint on national security grounds?

A writer for *The Progressive* magazine, using only public sources available to anyone, wrote an article critical of America's nuclear policies.[13] Pentagon officials obtained a copy of the piece before publication, and several experts said it contained information that could enable someone to build a hydrogen bomb. Reluctantly, the Carter administration asked a federal judge to prohibit publication. During the court proceedings, another periodical published a similar article containing the same information, and the case was dropped. In retrospect, it does seem rather silly to believe that if any foreign government had had the desire and the requisite technical capacity to build a hydrogen bomb, it would not already have dug out the information, which was all public. What if the facts had been different, though, and the information had been classified? Could prior restraint be justified then?

A special variant of the prior restraint problem concerns press coverage of criminal trials. The right to a fair trial is as fundamental to our system of justice as a free press is to our political discourse. In the interest of the pursuit of a fair trial, then, can a judge "gag" the press, especially its coverage of pretrial events? The most significant case in this field was *Nebraska Press Association v. Stuart* (1976).[14] A gruesome murder in a small Nebraska town led a trial judge to fear that pretrial press coverage would make it impossible to find unbiased jurors. Thus, he issued a gag order barring any press reports before the trial began. The Supreme Court, however, struck the order down. In the words of the Court, the case presented "a confrontation between prior restraint imposed to protect one vital constitutional guarantee and the explicit command of another that the freedom to speak and publish shall not be abridged. We reaffirm that the guarantees of freedom of expression are not an absolute prohibition under all circumstances, but the barriers to prior restraint remain high and the presumption against its use continues intact." The preferred-position doctrine is clearly evident in these words.

Newspapers sponsored by high schools present a special problem. They are part of the press, but they have an affiliation with a school and are often part of the curriculum. In *Hazelwood School District v. Kuhlmeier* (1988),[15] such a paper planned to run a story dealing with pregnancy among students and another on how divorce among parents affected students' lives. The principal cancelled the stories primarily because he feared that although fictitious names had been used, the students and their parents could be identified. The student editor then brought a suit. The Supreme Court said that although high school students clearly do not automatically forfeit their constitutional rights when they enter the campus, producing a newspaper as part of a class requirement gives school authorities some control. The principal therefore acted within his scope of authority. The justices emphasized that the right to impose restrictions rested on the paper's relation with the school, not on the substance of the articles. The regular press, they stressed, would have been free to publish the stories without censorship.

Lastly, there is the delicate matter of forcing reporters to divulge information to law enforcement authorities or in court. Journalists argue that they cannot do their jobs if they do not provide anonymity to their sources. Others feel that any citizen is obligated to provide known information about criminal activities. In *Branzburg v. Hayes* (1972),[16] a reporter had written a story about people manufacturing hashish. He was brought before a grand jury and asked for their identities, which he refused to provide. The Supreme Court held that he had no special immunity simply because he was a reporter. Since then, several reporters have gone to jail (normally only briefly) for similar refusals. Several states since have enacted "shield laws" to allow journalists to maintain the confidentiality of their sources.

Civil Liberties in Canada

THE APPROACH TO civil liberties in Canada has a distinctly different slant from that in the United States. The British North America Act (1867) contained no provisions whatsoever relating to rights. In 1960 the Canadian Parliament passed a statute called the Bill of Rights, which laid out the standard civil liberties. However, the government retained the power to suspend them in emergencies. In 1982, as part of the new Canadian constitution, a Charter of Rights and Freedoms was adopted.

Section 2 of this charter contains most of the civil liberties, sections 7 to 14 specify the rights connected with fair trials, and section 15 establishes equality rights. The parallels with our Bill of Rights and the Fourteenth Amendment are obvious. For comparison, let us look at section 2:

> Everyone has the following fundamental freedoms:
> (a) freedom of conscience and religion;
> (b) freedom of thought, belief, opinion and expression, including freedom of the press and other media of communication;
> (c) freedom of peaceful assembly; and
> (d) freedom of association.

This is basically a restatement of our First Amendment. However, there are two important qualifications, section 1 and section 33. Section 1 reads as follows: "The *Canadian Charter of Rights and Freedoms* guarantees the rights and freedoms set out in it subject only to such reasonable limits prescribed by law as can be demonstrably justified in a free and democratic society."

In other words, when a court is considering a civil liberties case, such as one involving freedom of speech, it can judge by no absolutist position, nor really even a strong "preferred position" doctrine. The national or provincial government may be able to persuade the court that some regulation of speech or the press is "reasonable" under the circumstances. (Think of the *Skokie* case.) It is up to the court to weigh these words in each case, of course, but even their presence in the constitution means that the liberties have a lower status than those found in our First Amendment.

Then there is section 33, which contains these words, astounding to one schooled in the American tradition:

Religious Liberty

The phrase "separation of church and state" is often bandied about loosely in public debate, as if it were a constitutional requirement. What the First Amendment actually says is worth quoting: "Congress shall make no law

"Parliament or the legislature of a province may expressly declare in an Act of Parliament or of the legislature, as the case may be, that the Act or a provision thereof shall operate notwithstanding a provision included in section 2 or sections 7 to 15 of this Charter."

This "notwithstanding clause" as it is called, simply means that the national parliament or that of any province can insulate a law from judicial invalidation by declaring that it falls under this section. Someone charged under such a law then will not be able to seek the protection of a court. The law cannot be held unconstitutional, no matter what its provisions.

Liberties in essence are guaranteed unless (1) the court thinks the exception is justified under section 1 or (2) the legislative body which passed the law also inserted a notwithstanding clause under section 33. The legal protections for civil liberties are therefore much more tenuous in Canada than in the United States.

The differences can be seen in the 1985 case of Ernest Zundel, author and publisher of a zany book called *The Hitler We Loved and Why*, which, among other things, denied that Jews were persecuted by the Nazis. He was tried and convicted of violating an Ontario law that made it illegal to publish any *false* information that might "cause injury or mischief to a public interest." The courts held that the law passed the test set out in section 1 of the Charter. No law with that kind of wording could be sustained under the First Amendment.

This whole approach to civil liberties is a clear example of the contrast between the way Canadians view government and the way Americans do. To Americans, the powerful assertion of rights against government flows from a skepticism both about the motives of those in power and about the benevolence of government in general. Canadians, on the other hand, are quite comfortable with a government which possesses a vast reservoir of legal powers. The civil liberties of Canadians rest to a much greater degree than ours on cultural bases, on a trust that those in authority will act in the public interest and not abuse the liberties and rights of the people. Not that we do not have a strong cultural devotion to civil liberties; quite the contrary. We simply prefer it to be reinforced and overlaid with very strict legal prohibitions, whereas Canadians believe that the cultural bases are sufficient.

Which, if either, of the two models of democracy does this Canadian tradition seem to draw on?

respecting an establishment of religion, or prohibiting the free exercise thereof." Note that there are two distinct clauses, and that they forbid two quite different things.

Disputes about the appropriate relationship between religious institutions and government stretch back to the earliest days of colonial settlement. Although the Constitution sets out a tolerably clear position, it does

More Americans attend weekly religious services than the citizens of any other Western nation. The enduring strength of religious institutions may be attributable in part to our commitment to both non-establishment and free exercise.

not settle every question. Moreover, religion almost by definition stirs people's most intense emotions. When courts are pulled into these disputes, there is likely to be an outburst of passion, whatever decision they render.

ESTABLISHMENT OF RELIGION   The establishment clause has stirred much more controversy than the free exercise clause. Free exercise cases, as we shall see, ordinarily involve the practices of small religious groups and do not affect the majority, except perhaps in a symbolic fashion. The law under scrutiny is never declared unconstitutional and overturned, only its application to the specific group falls. In an establishment clause case, however, a minority religious group brings a suit to invalidate entirely a law approved by a majority in the legislature, presumably with popular backing. If they win, the majority loses—a recipe for political controversy.

There have been three major areas of establishment clause jurisprudence: state aid to parochial schools; attempts by majority religious groups to use the public schools to teach their own doctrines; and the placing of religious symbols on public property.

The defining case in the first area is *Everson v. Board of Education* (1947).[17] A New Jersey school district provided transportation at public expense to all children within the district, whatever school they attended. Several taxpayers objected in court on the basis that the practice supported Catholic schools and therefore was an establishment of religion. The

Court held, however, that the benefits were going to all children as a public service, much as police and fire protection are provided to churches and other religious institutions. This became known as the "child benefit theory."

Other cases began to stream to the Court as states sought ways to aid the financially strapped Catholic school system. In 1968, for instance, the Court upheld a New York law providing non-religious textbooks to parochial school students.[18] In 1973, however, the court struck down a New York state income tax deduction for tuition paid to private schools.[19] But in 1983, a Minnesota law was upheld which allowed a deduction for tuition payments to any school, public or private.[20] Since public schools, of course, do not ordinarily charge tuition, the effect was the same as that in New York. Many legal experts are unable to discern any consistent rationale for these decisions, leaving a state of confusion in the law.[21]

Regarding the use of public schools to inculcate religious values or as a forum for religious exercises, there is more consistency but more controversy. In 1962 the Court held that opening prayers led by a teacher were unconstitutional.[22] In the succeeding years states have tried a variety of tacks to get around this decision, but with little success. The issue continues to foment debate and substantial majorities of the American public continue to tell pollsters they favor having prayers in public schools. The latest attempt to reintroduce prayers occurred when Alabama mandated a "moment of silence" in which students would be encouraged but not required to pray. The Supreme Court found, however, that the law had a clear religious purpose, and struck it down.[23] Undoubtedly we have not witnessed the final scene in this play.

An intriguing case came from the Louisiana legislature's attempt to require the teaching of creationism—the belief that the biblical account of the creation is literally true—on an equal basis with evolution in its high school biology courses.[24] The bill's sponsors had been careful to avoid any reference to religion in preparing the measure, and vowed it had only educational purposes. Its goal, they said, was only to broaden students' minds by exposing them to alternative ideas. This rather transparent position was cast aside by the Court, which held that this was a religiously based law no matter what the state maintained. It was an attempt to use the public schools to teach religious doctrine, and therefore unconstitutional.

The third area, the placing of religious symbols on public property, appears to many people to be the proverbial tempest in a teapot. The cost of the symbols is negligible and little harm seems to be done. However, the issue goes to the heart of our political order and of the character of American citizenship. In graphic form, it asks whether the state should be identified with a particular religious tradition, or any religious tradition. The major case is *Lynch v. Donnelly* (1984).[25] Before this case, the Court had normally struck down all religious displays on public property. Here, Pawtucket, Rhode Island used a park to set up a Christmas display which contained a combination of religious and secular symbols of the season. The Court held that since the display as a whole merely celebrated the Christmas season, which is both secular and religious, it did not violate the establishment clause. Critics derisively dubbed the holding the "reindeer rule." Even many religious people objected to the decision, saying that it debases religious symbols to throw them up alongside reindeer and elves.

What is the proper relationship between religion and citizenship? We have established a purely secular political order in the United States through the First Amendment and the admonition in Article VI that "no religious test shall ever be required as a qualification to any office or public trust under the United States." Legally, therefore, American citizenship is absolutely divorced from religious belief or observance. In practice, though, religion is a vital component of American life and politics, and intertwined with citizenship. Many of the personal attributes we associate with good citizenship, for example, are often taught and reinforced in religious institutions. Furthermore, religious institutions and religious leaders are major participants in the public dialogue and hold up an important moral mirror to public policies and politics in general. Without these contributions, both the practice of citizenship and the vibrancy of our political debate would be impoverished.

Naturally, good citizenship does not require a religious commitment. That is precisely the point of keeping the state secular. Personal values, religious or non-religious, are completely outside the scope of government. At the same time, everyone can acknowledge the healthy role religion can play in democratic citizenship, so long as it remains entirely voluntary and non-coercive.

FREE EXERCISE OF RELIGION   The purpose of the free exercise clause is straightforward enough: to allow people to worship as they please. In our day, any direct government regulation of worship services is all but unthinkable. What happens instead is that a law passed for some other purpose comes up against some minority's religious preferences. Usually, these groups are small and without political influence, and occasionally they are unpopular as well.

An early case, *Reynolds v. U.S.* (1878), illustrates the point well. The domestic relations law of Utah territory compelled monogamous marriages. The Church of Jesus Christ of Latter Day Saints taught polygamy, however. When one of its members was charged with breaking the law, he pleaded free exercise. The law could not constitutionally be applied to him, since it interfered with his right to free exercise of religion. The Supreme Court rejected this view with the following argument:

> Laws are made for the government of actions, and while they cannot interfere with mere religious belief and opinions, they may with practices. Suppose that one believed that human sacrifices were a necessary part of religious worship, would it be seriously contended that the civil government under which he lived could not interfere to prevent a sacrifice?[26]

In short, one cannot use free exercise to violate the criminal law. Many critics, though, have noted that the Court did not draw a distinction between criminal laws designed to protect others and those which have other purposes. It is hard to see human sacrifice as equivalent to the organization of Mr. Reynolds' family, as long as the arrangement was entirely voluntary on everyone's part.

In 1972 the Court was called on to apply the rule again in *Wisconsin v. Yoder*.[27] The Old Order Amish believe that modern technology is tainted with evil, and prefer to lead a rustic agricultural life totally detached from society. They feel, in light of their tenets, that education beyond the eighth grade is useless, if not counterproductive; this position violated Wisconsin's compulsory school attendance law. When Amish parents refused to send their children to school, the state brought them to court. If the rule of *Reynolds* were followed, clearly a decision for the state would be expected. Moreover, the state's position appeared even stronger here, since its goal is the welfare of the child. Should she decide to leave the Amish community as an adult, she would need a secondary education. The state would not be attempting to interfere with Mr. and Mrs. Yoder's free exercise rights as they related to themselves. The Supreme Court, nonetheless, decided the case in favor of the Amish. The reasoning is rather patchy; the basic holding is that the rule still stands, but an exception is made for the Amish, since they are such upstanding people and have made noteworthy contributions to American life.

A more recent case takes us back to the *Reynolds* position. Alfred Smith and others worked as drug rehabilitation counselors in Oregon. One of the conditions of their jobs was that they personally remain drug-free. As members of a Native American religious tradition, they ingested small amounts of peyote during certain ceremonies. Although there was no evidence that this act impaired their job performance, the fact that peyote was illegal in Oregon led to their dismissal. When they sought unemployment benefits, their applications were rejected. They charged that this infringed on their right of free exercise. The Supreme Court, though, held that Oregon's law forbidding use of the drug was not a violation of free exercise, and therefore the state could deny them unemployment compensation.[28]

Right to a Fair Trial

Historically, the taproot of all civil liberties lies in criminal procedure. So long as government can use the criminal courts to punish political opponents, there can be no liberty. The great Magna Carta of 1215 dealt primarily with limitations on the king's authority to try dissident barons in England; over the years, those rights were slowly expanded and applied to the populace as a whole. As former Supreme Court justice Felix Frankfurter once said, "The history of liberty has largely been the history of observance of procedural safeguards."[29]

The first constitutional guarantee of note in this field is the right to counsel. The Sixth Amendment says that "in all criminal prosecutions, the accused shall enjoy the right . . . to have the assistance of counsel for his defense." For years this was interpreted to mean only that an accused person had the right to secure his own private counsel. In 1963, however,

The Supreme Court has established detailed rules for arrest and interrogation procedures for persons suspected of committing a crime.

in the landmark case of *Gideon v. Wainwright*,[30] the Supreme Court held that the state had to provide counsel to indigent defendants in criminal trials. That right has since been expanded to cover pretrial proceedings and posttrial hearings (such as revocation of parole).

The second item, much more controversial than the first, is the exclusionary rule. Introduced throughout the country by the decision in *Mapp v. Ohio* (1961),[31] the exclusionary rule prohibits prosecutors from introducing any evidence that was obtained illegally, (without the proper warrants, for example). In recent years, the Court has loosened somewhat the circumstances under which evidence will be excluded from court, giving the police more flexibility.[32] Prosecutors and the police still complain, though, that this rule hampers their enforcement efforts; however, the evidence is not conclusive.[33] This is a uniquely American approach to police malfeasance. In most other countries, including England, all relevant evidence can be introduced at trials, but police officers may be disciplined for exceeding their authority.

Finally, the Court has placed strict limits on police interrogation methods. In *Miranda v. Arizona* (1966),[34] the Court insisted that suspects be given explicit warnings about the use of their statements and that they be informed of their right to have an attorney present—at public expense, if need be. Since *Miranda,* several cases have chipped away at the decision, but the framework remains intact. In the last few years the controversy which erupted when the decision was announced has subsided. For the most part, police seem to have learned to live with the ruling.

BOX 4-1

The Possession of Rights versus The Exercise of Rights

SHOULD THE good citizen exercise all her rights to the fullest extent possible? To the individualist democrat, the answer is an unqualified "yes." Rights create the framework for the pursuit of individual satisfaction, pleasure, and profit. Thus, each person should feel free to do anything the law does not forbid, and it should forbid little. What is the point in having rights if people do not exercise them?

The civic democrat takes a rather different position. He agrees with the individualist democrat that rights should be as expansive as legally possible. But simply because one has a "right" to do something does not mean that it is good for him to do it. Prudence and self-discipline dictate a more circumscribed approach—refraining from exercising rights fully, and urging others to do the same.

Take the problem of pornography. The individualist democrat probably advocates unbridled freedom of expression.[1] There should be no government-sponsored censorship of any type, and people should be free to read and view whatever they like. Thus, the issue of pornography is only an issue of freedom versus censorship. Most civic democrats would join this opposition to government censorship, worrying that the costs of any such policies, morally and practically, would far outweigh any possible benefit. Hence, they would support the *legal* right of people to produce, sell, and read pornography. However, they would also vigorously support voluntary campaigns against pornography. They have no qualms about labeling much of it as filth and a poison to healthy social life.

For example, civic democrats probably would not support radical feminists and some evangelical Christians in their attempts to ban pornography by city ordinance, as was tried in Minneapolis and Indianapolis. However, they would sympathize with the idea behind the move—that pornography is degrading to women—and would eagerly join educational efforts, and even demonstrations and boycotts of advertisers, in an attempt to eradicate it, or at least lessen its prevalence.

It is not censorship or a sign of weak attachment to the First Amendment to believe that people acting in their own interest and in society's should not do what they may have a legal right to do. Thus, the civic democrat steadfastly defends legal rights he or she would never use, and at the same time feels perfectly comfortable trying to convince others to constrain their behavior also.

Should there be limits, though, even to legal and peaceful demonstrations and boycotts of this sort? That is, is there a point at which the social and economic pressures on people not to exercise a legal right constitute, in effect, a cancellation of the right? If so, should the courts establish guidelines to ensure that people can exercise their legal rights without undue molestation? Or, should educational efforts be directed at those who demonstrate and boycott as well, and it be left solely to the judgment of individual citizens to determine when the line separating appropriate from inappropriate behavior is crossed (assuming all along, of course, that what they are doing is legal and peaceful)?

---

[1] I insert the word "probably" because individualist democrats always have to grapple with the problem of majoritarianism. If a majority of individuals pursuing their own self-interest want to have censorship, why shouldn't they? The only answer the individualist democrat has to fall back on is the basic nature of certain rights. But if there are no transcendental political values, then the existence of those rights must be defended on purely utilitarian grounds, which is a tenuous reed to lean on.

CIVIL RIGHTS

The history of civil rights in this country is intimately connected to the history of the black minority. After the Civil War, the Thirteenth, Fourteenth, and Fifteenth Amendments were added to the Constitution, and Congress enacted several far-reaching civil rights laws. The Thirteenth Amendment abolished slavery; the Fourteenth made everyone born in the United States a citizen, and forbade states from depriving "any person of life, liberty, or property, without due process of law," or denying "to any person within its jurisdiction the equal protection of the laws"; the Fifteenth provided that a citizen's right to vote "shall not be denied or abridged by the United States or by any State on account of race, color, or previous condition of servitude." Civil Rights Acts were passed in 1866 and 1875 which provided for, among other things, equal access to housing and public accommodations. Enthusiasm for enforcement of either the

Alabama state police block voting rights marchers at Edmund Pettus Bridge March 9, 1965. The scene sparked a national outrage, and led to the passage of a Voting Rights Act of 1965.

amendments or the statutes soon waned, however. The Fourteenth Amendment even became transformed into a barrier to state business regulation. The due process clause quoted above was read by the courts to disallow any regulations that reduced the value of property (including such intangibles as profits). In time, though, the promise of these documents was reawakened, and a slow march toward equality began. By the 1970s and 1980s, the idea of civil rights had grown to include a number of other groups in addition to African Americans.

Race and Civil Rights

BACKGROUND It is hard in the 1990s to visualize race relations in America only forty years ago. Schools were segregated—legally throughout the south, and by custom elsewhere. Blatant job and housing discrimination permeated every sector and corner of the society. Almost no professional or skilled craft job opportunities existed for African Americans (outside such enclaves as black schools), no matter what one's training or skills. Signs in transportation terminals in many cities indicated different areas for "colored" and "white." All-white police forces openly treated blacks with contempt (or worse) virtually everywhere. Such amenities as water fountains and rest rooms were separate throughout much of the nation. Before 1948, blacks were even segregated and confined to menial tasks in the military. To be black in America was to be relegated to the fringes of society—to be isolated, ignored, and often openly loathed.

In 1896 the Supreme Court had given judicial sanction to the "separate but equal" doctrine.[35] Louisiana law dictated that railroads provide separate coaches for blacks and whites. A man who was seven-eighths white (by law, being one-eighth black made you black) refused to sit in the black coach. The Supreme Court, over only one dissenting vote, said the Fourteenth Amendment phrase "No state . . . shall . . . deny to any person within its jurisdiction the equal protection of the laws" meant that a state could require separate facilities so long as they were "equal." Even if a grain of justice could be found in this formulation, it was evident that there was plenty of political will to enforce the "separate" part, but none to enforce the "equal" portion.

In the 1930s, the National Association for the Advancement of Colored People (NAACP) began a deliberate attack on this doctrine. The NAACP did not then feel prepared to challenge the rule head-on, but rather concentrated its energies on demonstrating how unequal conditions were. For example, in 1938 the NAACP won a suit charging that Missouri's policy of paying out-of-state fees for blacks to attend law school elsewhere while maintaining a publicly supported institution for whites alone was not "equal treatment."[36]

World War II proved to be a great watershed in American racial history, partly no doubt because American racial policies were uncomfortably close in practice to the professed ideas of the Nazis. In the years immediately following the war, African American plaintiffs won a string of suits in the areas of housing, voting rights, and access to higher education.[37]

BROWN V. BOARD OF EDUCATION AND ITS LEGACY In 1951, the NAACP launched what was to become *Brown v. Board of Education* (of Topeka, Kansas it should perhaps be noted), arguably the most famous case in Supreme Court history. A unanimous court held that separate schools were inherently unequal, and therefore unconstitutional.[38]

During the political earthquake that followed *Brown,* an important ambiguity in the case went almost unnoticed. Did the decision require states only to stop legally segregating children by race? Or, did it create in the African American child a right to be free of the stigma imposed by segregated schools? There is a momentous difference, for the first means that compliance is accomplished merely by repealing a law, while the second imposes an obligation on a state government to take positive steps to integrate its schools.

For nearly twenty years the question was moot, since southern states fought the end of segregation with all manner of legal ruses and subterfuges. Finally, in the early 1970s, the legal battles were all won; the issue then shifted to the north, and segregation caused by housing patterns. In *Keyes v. School District No. 1* (1973),[39] the Court held that the Denver

Lawyers George Hayes, Thurgood Marshall, and James Nabrit, Jr. on the steps of the Supreme Court after winning the 1954 Brown v. Board of Education *case. Marshall later became a Supreme Court justice himself.*

school system was in actuality segregated, and ordered system-wide busing. In 1974, the Court faced the problem of adjacent school districts with gross disparities in the numbers of blacks and whites, when it took up a case from the Detroit area.[40] No amount of busing within the city of Detroit could create integrated schools, since the city schools were overwhelmingly African American. Nonetheless, the court backed off from forcing cross-district busing. Some analysts believed that this case was a retreat from the commitment to integrated education; however, dozens of school districts, north and south, have since been found guilty of segregation and forced to implement busing to correct it.

In practice, though, the plans often run up against "white flight" (an action frequently taken by affluent blacks, as well) to private and suburban schools. Ironically, after a few years of busing, school districts often end up more segregated than they were before, with fewer black children attending school with white children than were doing so earlier.[41] In 1990, a federal district judge ordered the Kansas City school district to levy a new set of taxes to engage in a 500- to 700-million-dollar building program in an effort to attract whites back to the city's public schools. The Supreme Court upheld the building order, only altering the district judge's explicit tax provision, saying that the city could decide itself how to raise the money.[42] It is unclear, though, whether this move will rebuild the urban school system.

The fate of our large urban school systems affects several aspects of American life. To the extent that these schools are underfunded and therefore offer inferior educational opportunities, they contribute to more inequality in our society. To the extent that they do not prepare people for useful careers or higher education, they damage our economic competitiveness. But perhaps most important, as they decay, a vital public institution is being destroyed. Public schools are a prime example of the intertwining of public institutions and citizenship, for they do more than mold the lives of the young—they also provide a sense of focus for a community, knitting strong threads of citizenship by tying peoples' fates together. If fewer people care about the public schools, then life becomes more private and less public, and an important bond that ties people to one another is dissolved. Thus, the future of the public schools is important not only for educational reasons, but also because it has implications for how citizens interact with each other.

VOTING RIGHTS The right to vote is fundamental to the meaning of citizenship in a democratic society for two reasons. First, it allows the individual to have a voice in the shape of public policies. Second, it is important for the sense of self-worth and the feeling of dignity that it provides.

For years, African Americans had been systematically denied this basic right in the states of the south. While the Fifteenth Amendment forbade exclusion from the franchise on the basis of race, any number of clever and insidious provisions permeated southern voting statutes. The earliest barred all illiterates from voting, unless someone related to them could vote in 1861 (which happened to be the year the Civil War started!). The Supreme Court struck down this obvious maneuver in 1915.[43] State laws were then enacted to require applicants to read anything given to them, or to interpret any provision of the federal or state constitution to the satisfaction of the local voting registrar. Local officials understood exactly how they were to exercise this power.[44] In addition, all types of other devices were employed, such as the poll tax (outlawed by the Twenty-fourth Amendment).

Congress skirted this issue for years, partly because of southern opposition, but partly also because of a hesitancy to venture into an area traditionally left to the states. In 1957 and 1960, statutes were passed gingerly addressing the issue of denying legitimate voters the right to vote in federal elections. Implementation was cumbersome, however, since it required the filing of a suit by the Department of Justice, which meant registering one voter at a time. In 1965, only 6.7 percent of the voting-age blacks in Mississippi were registered.[45] The ugly and unprovoked attack by Alabama police on peaceful voting-rights marchers at the Edmund Pettus Bridge in 1965 changed all this by igniting public opinion. The congressional log jam was finally broken, and the Voting Rights Act of 1965 became law.

In brief, the act provided that in any county with a history of racial discrimination in voting, federal registrars would be sent to enroll voters. It also compelled those jurisdictions to submit any future changes in voting procedure to the Department of Justice for approval before final adoption. In one day Congress revolutionized southern politics.

Nowhere in the south do African Americans now face any legal impediments to voting. The major issue in the 1990s is redistricting, particularly as political boundaries are redrawn everywhere in light of the 1990 census. Should everything from congressional districts to local city council seats be drawn in such a way as to insure a certain number of black majority districts? Take Mississippi's legislature as an example. Its lower house has 122 members, and roughly 36 percent of the state's population is black. (In 1991 there were twenty-two blacks in the House.) Complicating the picture are the facts that blacks have a higher birth rate than whites, and that many districts have a heavy outmigration of young adult blacks. This means that a district with a bare majority black population will probably not have a black majority voting-age population. Furthermore, as is evident from every study of voting, turnout tends to decline the farther one goes down the socioeconomic ladder. In Mississippi, this factor alone means that black turnout is usually lower than white turnout. African American political leaders argue, therefore, that a black majority district must have at least a 60-percent black population. The Department of Justice has tended to adopt this figure as a rule of thumb. But does this really maximize black political influence? What happens to those blacks not in majority black districts? When new black majority districts are drawn, do the resulting smaller number of blacks in white majority districts have reduced political clout? In 1992, Mississippi created thirty-eight

Federal registrars were sent to enroll new voters in numerous southern counties in the wake of the Voting Rights Act of 1965. This photograph was taken at Canton, Mississippi, January 15, 1966.

black voting-age majority districts for its state house, leaving only small numbers of black voters in the other eighty-four. Today, therefore, the right to vote is largely secure, but issues surrounding the quality of voting remain.

PUBLIC ACCOMMODATIONS AND EMPLOYMENT   Public accommodations and employment were two issues addressed by the far-reaching Civil Rights Act of 1964. Until then, blacks were typically barred from all white restaurants and hotels in the south. The act forbade such discrimination, and has been almost universally successful. Employment issues, in stark contrast, have proved much more difficult.

The act has manifestly done away with open discrimination. Yet, two aspects remain controversial. One is the question of proof of discrimination in court. Is the mere fact that an employer's work force contains few or no African Americans sufficient proof of discrimination, or is it only one piece of evidence to be weighed with others? The Supreme Court held to the former position at one time, but has recently moved to the latter.[46] This decision spawned a heated debate in Congress over whether to amend the law or not (see chapter 8). The other matter is whether white males can claim the protection of the act even though they were not its intended beneficiaries (more on this later in this chapter).

Clearly, the country has made gargantuan strides in forty years. African Americans are commonly found in political office, serving in countless positions from school board members to governors. In 1990 there were 7,335 black elected officials, over 4,300 of whom were in the south.[47] In the professions, in business, in academia, in the civil service, in the military, and in the judiciary, the number of blacks in leadership posts seems startling at first, considering where we stood in 1961. Nonetheless, a discouragingly large number of blacks are still marginalized from the mainstream of American life—still ill-educated, ill-fed, ill-housed, and with few attractive job opportunities. The opening of the doors of opportunity has led to an influx of the talented, the relatively affluent, the educated, and the lucky into virtually every stratum of American society. For a significant percentage of blacks, however, daily life is little better than it was thirty or forty years ago; many believe that it is even worse. The situation of many African American citizens remains our most poignant dilemma. We are still far from the society pictured by Martin Luther King's "I Have a Dream" speech.

Gender Issues and Civil Rights

Women have historically fared better legally in the United States than they have elsewhere in the world. In the nineteenth century, U.S. women obtained the right to hold property and have equal standing in court before most European women did. Wyoming granted women the right to vote in 1869, and most non-southern states followed suit within a few years. In 1920 women acquired the right to vote nationally, with the passage of the Nineteenth Amendment.

Nevertheless, gender equality before the law was nowhere complete. As late as 1948, the Supreme Court upheld a Michigan law which prohibited women from being bartenders.[48] A variety of gender distinctions permeated the legal system, to say nothing of social customs and employment practices.

Overt and direct gender discrimination has more or less been terminated by constitutional interpretation and statutory law. The equal protection clause of the Fourteenth Amendment has been held to apply to gender, although in a slightly more attenuated form than to race.[49] The Civil Rights Act of 1964 covers employment discrimination on the basis of gender as well as race, and a variety of other laws guarantee equal treatment in other areas.

TABLE 4-1

Major Steps on the Long March to
Full Legal Equality for Black Americans

YEAR	LEGAL ENACTMENT OR CASE	RESULT
1865	Thirteenth Amendment	Abolished slavery.
1866	Civil Rights Act of 1866	Granted general civil rights to freed slaves, including right to buy and sell real estate without discrimination.
1868	Fourteenth Amendment	Declared all ex-slaves to be citizens. Provided that states could not deny any person due process or equal protection of the law.
1870	Fifteenth Amendment	Stipulated that right to vote could not be denied on grounds of race.
1875	Civil Rights Act of 1875	Declared public accommodations to be open to all. (Declared unconstitutional by Supreme Court in 1883.)
1896	*Plessy v. Ferguson*	Instituted "separate but equal" doctrine.
1938–1953	Several carefully planned NAACP lawsuits	Improved blacks standing regarding graduate admissions, access to housing, and voting rights.
1954	*Brown v. Board of Education*	Declared segregation in public schools unconstitutional.
1964	Civil Rights Act of 1964	Declared public accommodations to be open to all; outlawed discrimination in employment.
1965	Voting Rights Act of 1965	Required that federal registrars be sent to areas with history of voting discrimination. Required all boundary changes in certain states affecting voting to be cleared with Department of Justice.

The most vexing philosophical and hence legal question is whether or not—and if so, to what extent—the state may take account of actual gender differences in setting public policies. There are basically three positions. The first takes the view that it is perfectly proper for the state to consider gender differences, as long as this does not deprive women of any benefit or subject them to any special burden. If the classification is for a benign or neutral purpose and reasonably related to some valid state objective, then it should be condoned. The second position takes society's basic outline as given, and simply demands no special treatment for anyone. It holds that classifications are inherently discriminatory against women, even when they are ostensibly designed to grant them special status. In this view, these laws are outmoded attempts to impose a paternalistic system on women, which serves to keep them in an inferior rank. A third position argues that men and women are indeed different, but that all social institutions are pervasively masculine, since men have always been in charge. Therefore, the law must remake the current institutions of society along feminist lines, to make equality real.[50]

Two cases can serve to illuminate the dilemmas. Oklahoma had a statute allowing women to purchase beer at eighteen years of age, but required men to be twenty-one.[51] The state's position was that since men between the ages of eighteen and twenty-one as a group cause more alcohol-related automobile accidents, the law was a reasonable way to secure highway safety. The Supreme Court disagreed on Fourteenth Amendment grounds, noting that to sustain such a gender classification would require a very high level of proof, something that was absent here. *Michael M. v. Superior Court of Sonoma County* (1981)[52] is perhaps an even more difficult case. Statutory rape was defined in California as sexual intercourse with a female under the age of eighteen. The defendant (a seventeen-year-old male) admitted having intercourse with a seventeen-year-old female, but contended that the law was unconstitutional, since it did not apply to both genders. Under such a law, a thirty-year-old woman who had sex with a sixteen-year-old male would be guilty of nothing. Although the Supreme Court was badly split over the issue, the majority held that the law was valid. It was, said the Court, a reasonable approach to preventing teenage pregnancy, which was undesirable. In the words of Justice Rehnquist:

> We need not be medical doctors to discern that young men and young women are not similarly situated with respect to the problems and the risks of sexual intercourse. Only women may become pregnant and they suffer disproportionately the profound physical, emotional and psychological consequences of sexual activity. . . .
>
> The question thus boils down to whether a State may attack the problem of sexual intercourse and teenage pregnancy directly by prohibiting a male from having sexual intercourse with a minor female. We hold that such a statute is sufficiently related to the State's objectives to pass constitutional muster.

The dissenting justices argued stridently that California in the statutory-rape case had shown no more proof than had Oklahoma in the drinking-age case that its policy helped reach its stated goals; however they failed to convince the majority.

Any number of related issues—child custody; the availability of alimony only to women; pregnancy leaves; differing rates for life insurance; and draft registration, to name a few—have also come to the courts.[53] In general, the Supreme Court has adopted the first position of the three laid out above: that gender classifications are acceptable as long as they bear reasonable relation to a valid goal and are not discriminatory against women.

Professional women in particular have made significant strides in the workplace, in part because of equal employment legislation.

The Gulf War in 1991 triggered debate on another issue: the role of women in combat. Congress had kept women from combat assignments by law; many believe that this practice limited their promotion possibilities in the military. At the end of the war, Congress dropped the ban on women's service in combat positions. Also, the call-up of both spouses from reserve and National Guard units in some cases raised the question of leaving children without either parent at home.

But the most hotly debated gender issue in recent years has undoubtedly been abortion. Using the Ninth Amendment and parts of various other amendments, in the late 1960s and early 1970s the Supreme Court created a generalized "right to privacy."[54] It was first applied to overturn a Connecticut law forbidding the use of contraceptives, but soon it was expanded to cover a number of areas of personal autonomy.[55] In 1973 in *Roe v. Wade*,[56] the Court held that the right to privacy extended to the first trimester of pregnancy, thereby preventing a state from interfering with a woman's body during this time. Opposition flared from many quarters, including most visibly the Roman Catholic Church. In the ensuing years, states tried various formulas to regulate abortion, but they were uniformly struck down by the courts. In 1989, however, the Supreme Court decided *Webster v. Reproductive Health Services*,[57] in which they did not directly overturn *Roe*, but did allow states more regulating room. Abortion returned to the political arena, with battles waged in state legislatures over new regulatory policies. Louisiana and Pennsylvania quickly enacted laws more restrictive than the one upheld in *Webster.* In 1991, the Court upheld controversial rules issued by the executive branch that forbade clinics receiving federal funds from providing abortion counseling.[58] In June 1992 the justices voted 5–4 to uphold most of the restrictions in the Pennsylvania law, but did not explicitly overrule *Roe.*[59]

It is important to remember that even if *Roe v. Wade* were overturned, this would only *allow* the states to regulate abortion, not compel them to do so. Without question, the types of regulations, if any, would vary enormously among the states. The federal system would once again have produced a diversity of public policies, as discussed in chapter 3.

Other Groups in American Society

Civil rights issues have not been confined to African Americans and women. Both Native Americans and Hispanics have pressed demands on a variety of fronts, and Asian Americans have begun to follow suit. The handicapped and homosexuals have demanded employment rights; the former have also insisted on access rights to public buildings, while the latter have called for access to benefits normally reserved for heterosexual couples (such as retirement and insurance programs covering public employees). Age has also become a civil rights issue—particularly in employment, but elsewhere as well. Laws penalizing illegitimate children have also come under fire, and have generally been repealed or struck down by the courts.

Of all these groups, only illegitimate children have gained explicit constitutional status for their civil rights through the Fourteenth Amendment. The others have all had to press for legislation at the local, state, and federal level. Some, especially the handicapped, have succeeded admirably; all have scored some significant victories. Civil rights is a powerful claim in American politics, and those who can throw its mantle around themselves have a strong political advantage.

Affirmative Action

The Fourteenth Amendment and various congressional statutes now protect African Americans, women, and sometimes other minorities. Any law or practice which discriminated against these groups would be held invalid as a matter of course. But another important question arises. The commands of the Constitution and the statutes on their face speak only of equal treatment; can these commands rule out even policies designed to help the very groups for whom a law is passed?

According to one line of thought, the answer is yes: all racial and gender classifications are insidious and unconscionable. Equal treatment can only mean equal treatment for *everyone*—including white males. The other side contests this view, holding that neither the Fourteenth Amendment nor the civil rights laws were enacted to help white males, and that therefore they should not be able to call upon them for protection. Behind the legal arguments, of course, lie very real benefits such as university admissions, scholarships, and jobs.

Some affirmative action programs—that is, programs which give an explicit preference to minorities or women—have been set up at the behest of the courts themselves. Alabama's state police department, for example, to compensate for years of nefarious discrimination, was ordered to promote one black trooper for each white one (if qualified applicants were available) until each rank in the force was 25 percent black.[60] These types of affirmative action programs do not stir nearly as much controversy as those adopted by institutions which have no (or at least no recent) history of overt discrimination. When these latter types of institutions create affirmative action programs, their justification is that they correct for more generalized discrimination prevalent in the society.

The central case remains *Regents of the University of California v. Bakke* (1978).[61] Sixteen out of one hundred places in the medical school's entering class were reserved for minorities. Alan Bakke was a white male whose grades and test scores fell below those of eighty-four white applicants, but above those of several of the minority admittees; this meant that had he been a member of a racial minority, he would have been admitted. The Supreme Court struck down this plan, and ordered Bakke admitted. However, the Court said that race could be one of the factors weighed in an admission process. In practice, this has allowed universities and other types of institutions to continue their affirmative action programs in admissions and hiring.

The legal escape hatch for affirmative action can be seen clearly in *Johnson v. Transportation Agency* (1987),[62] a case involving the Civil Rights Act of 1964 rather than the Fourteenth Amendment, but raising essentially the same issue. Santa Clara County in California had adopted an affirmative action program whose goal was to have all job categories reflect the composition of the county's work force. When a dispatcher's job came open, the applicants, two of whom were Diane Joyce and Paul Johnson, were given a rating score based on tests, training, and experience. Joyce received a 73; Johnson, a 75. Joyce received the position, and the Court was told that gender was only one of several factors considered by the supervisors. The Court found for the county on this basis.

Affirmative action suffered a blow in 1989, however, in the case of *Richmond v. J. A. Croson Co.*[63] Richmond, Virginia had set aside 30 percent of its purchasing budget for minority businesses. A white contractor who felt he was deprived of business only because he was white took the matter to court. The justices struck the policy down, mostly it seems because of the mathematical exactitude of the formula, which raised shades of *Bakke*.

Affirmative action will no doubt continue to be a hot and divisive political issue. In late 1991, for example, the White House issued a policy paper curtailing affirmative action in the executive branch. It touched off a whirlwind of criticism and was quickly withdrawn.[64] The philosophical equivocations involved (do rights inhere in individuals or in groups?), combined with the economic benefits at stake in professional school admissions and jobs, guarantee affirmative action a place never far off the political or legal agenda. The political divisions it generates are more complex than they may appear at first glance. It not only pits white males against blacks, other minorities, and women. It divides white males, for instance, along class and age lines, for those who bear the costs of the policies are typically the less affluent and the young.[65] Affirmative action can drive a wedge between blacks and women since over three-quarters of American women are white. Further, some minorities, particularly Asian Americans, see affirmative action as aimed against them, not for them. Some black political leaders also question the wisdom of the policy. Does it perpetuate dependency and a sense of inferiority?[66] Could it be harmful in the long run, since it may sap the strength of black institutions such as black colleges by draining off the leadership cadres? Furthermore, does it detract attention from other programs which actually may aid more African Americans, such as revitalizing inner-city neighborhoods and schools?

SUMMARY

Civil liberties and civil rights are important, even defining, aspects of American politics. Civil liberties are the basic guarantees of personal liberty found in the Bill of Rights; civil rights are principally those rights that liberate citizens from unjust classifications, finding their source in both the Fourteenth Amendment and statutes.

Although all the civil liberties contained in the Bill of Rights are important, free expression, religious freedom, and the right to a fair trial are central. In the area of free expression, the preferred-position doctrine seems to hold sway on the Court as opposed to either the absolutist or balancing approaches. In our day, almost all speech, including symbolic speech, no matter how hurtful or offensive to others, and no matter where "spoken," seems to be covered by the First Amendment's protection. As for press freedom, the general rule has been "no prior restraint," even in national security cases and the coverage of criminal trials. Two chinks in the armor of complete press freedom, though, are the censorship allowed for high school newspapers and the forcing of reporters to reveal their sources to criminal investigators.

Religious controversies have long been a staple of American politics, and can stir intense passion. The First Amendment has two religious clauses. One prohibits an establishment of religion; the other allows free exercise of religion. All three aspects of the establishment clause—state aid to parochial schools, religion in the public schools, and religious symbols on public property—have been controversial. The Court has pursued a meandering path regarding how much aid states may give to parochial schools, leaving the law in a confused state. Without exception, however, the Court has forbidden the introduction of religion into public schools, whether through prayer (direct or indirect) or through curricular dictates. The Supreme Court has recently changed course concerning symbols, and now allows them if they are intermingled with secular displays. The Supreme Court has interpreted free exercise to mean that someone cannot claim it as a justification for breaking the criminal law; however, an exception was allowed for the Amish.

The right to a fair trial is historically the source of all other rights. One example of the numerous procedural issues involved in this area is the provision of legal counsel. Counsel are now provided at public expense to all criminal defendants. The exclusionary rule, which bars the introduction of any tainted evidence at trials, has been adopted by the Supreme Court, but it remains controversial and uncertain in its impact. Since 1966, police have had to provide detailed warnings to suspects and refrain from questioning them without a lawyer present.

The history of civil rights is almost synonymous with the history of African Americans. Although the amendments and laws adopted in the immediate aftermath of the Civil War held great promise, the status of blacks soon degenerated into a form of apartheid. After World War II, the Supreme Court moved slowly toward equality, finally sounding the death knell of the "separate but equal" doctrine in 1954. It took nearly twenty years, but legal segregation is now gone forever. At the moment, the Court has been grappling with the problems of school segregation caused by housing segregation, and so far has not found a successful way to deal with resegregation when whites leave inner-city school systems.

For many years African Americans were kept from entering southern voting booths by a variety of legal tactics. The Voting Rights Act of 1965 overwhelmed southern resistance and led to an enormous increase in black voting, and to significant black political power. Now, intricate issues of redistricting occupy those concerned with voting rights. The Civil Rights Act of 1964 demolished segregated public accommodations and began an attack on job discrimination. Though great strides have been made in the last forty years, our society is still very far from one of complete racial justice.

Civil rights concerns have moved from issues of race alone to encompass gender discrimination and the treatment of various other groups. Women have succeeded in having the legal barriers that kept them in an inferior position removed. Lately, the Supreme Court has taken the position that a state may draw a gender distinction if it is reasonably related to a valid policy goal and does not penalize women. Abortion remains as feverishly contested an issue as when the Supreme Court made it a woman's constitutional right in 1973. Recent decisions seem to be inching toward the overturning of *Roe v. Wade,* which would return the issue to the states.

Affirmative action is also a controversial part of the civil rights debate. The *Bakke* case seems still to provide the guiding legal doctrine: that race and gender can be used as one factor in making decisions, but cannot stand alone. With its disparate benefits and costs, affirmative action will likely remain a contentious issue.

ENDNOTES

1. *Barron v. Baltimore,* 32 U.S. (7 Pet.) 243 (1833).
2. This is one of those statements that is basically true but not entirely so. There are several versions of the incorporation doctrine, and the Su-

preme Court has never settled on any one. See any constitutional law casebook for a more detailed discussion.

3. 249 U.S. 47, 39 S.Ct. 247 (1919). This was not the first time the issue arose. During the administration of John Adams, Congress enacted the Alien and Sedition Acts, which contained some highly suspect provisions. They were never contested in court, however, and the Jefferson administration let them expire. See James M. Smith, *Freedom's Fetters: The Alien and Sedition Laws and American Civil Liberties* (Ithaca, N.Y.: Cornell University Press, 1956).

4. 337 U.S. 1, 69 S.Ct. 894 (1949).

5. *Village of Skokie v. National Socialist Party of America,* 69 Ill. 2d 605, 14 Ill. Dec. 890, 373 N.E. 2d 21 (1978).

6. 393 U.S. 503, 89 S.Ct. 733 (1969).

7. *Texas v. Johnson,* 491 U.S. 397, 109 S.Ct. 2533 (1989).

8. *U.S. v. Eichman,* 496 U.S. 310, 110 S.Ct. 2404 (1990).

9. 435 U.S. 765, 98 S.Ct. 1407 (1978).

10. 425 U.S. 748, 96 S.Ct. 1817 (1976).

11. *Near v. Minnesota ex rel. Olson,* 283 U.S. 697, 51 S.Ct. 625 (1931).

12. *New York Times v. U.S.,* 403 U.S. 713, 91 S.Ct. 2140 (1971).

13. *The Progressive* devoted an entire issue to the case when it was finally resolved, in November 1979. The case never got beyond the federal district court. *United States v. Progressive, Inc.,* 467 F. Supp. 990 (W.D. Wis. 1979).

14. 427 U.S. 539, 96 S.Ct. 2791 (1976).

15. 484 U.S. 260, 108 S.Ct. 562 (1988).

16. 408 U.S. 665, 92 S.Ct. 2646 (1972).

17. 330 U.S. 1, 67 S.Ct. 504 (1947).

18. *Board of Education v. Allen,* 392 U.S. 236, 88 S.Ct. 1923 (1968).

19. *Committee for Public Education v. Nyquist,* 413 U.S. 756, 93 S.Ct. 2955 (1973).

20. *Mueller v. Allen,* 463 U.S. 388, 103 S.Ct. 3062 (1983).

21. See Leonard Levy, *The Establishment Clause* (New York: Macmillan, 1986).

22. *Engel v. Vitale,* 370 U.S. 421, 82 S.Ct. 1261 (1962).

23. *Wallace v. Jaffree,* 472 U.S. 38, 105 S.Ct. 2479 (1985).

24. *Edwards v. Aguillard,* 482 U.S. 578, 107 S.Ct. 2573 (1987).

25. 465 U.S. 668, 104 S.Ct. 1355 (1984).

26. 98 U.S. (8 Otto) 145 (1878).

27. 406 U.S. 205, 92 S.Ct. 1526 (1972).

28. *Employment Division v. Smith,* 494 U.S. 872, 110 S.Ct. 1595 (1990).

29. *McNabb v. United States,* 318 U.S. 332, 347, 63 S.Ct. 608, 616 (1943).

30. 372 U.S. 335, 83 S.Ct. 792 (1963).

31. 367 U.S. 643, 81 S.Ct. 1684 (1961).

32. This area of the law is enormously complicated. Some of the exceptions to strict interpretation of the exclusionary rule are discussed in *Michigan v. Long,* 463 U.S. 1032, 103 S.Ct. 3469 (1983) and *U.S. v. Ross,* 456 U.S. 798, 102 S.Ct. 2157 (1982).

33. See Donald Horowitz, *The Courts and Social Policy* (Washington: Brookings, 1977), chap. 6.

34. 384 U.S. 436, 86 S.Ct. 1602 (1966).

35. *Plessy v. Ferguson,* 163 U.S. 537, 16 S.Ct. 1138 (1896).

36. *Missouri ex rel. Gaines v. Canada,* 305 U.S. 337, 59 S.Ct. 232 (1938).

37. *Shelley v. Kraemer,* 334 U.S. 1, 68 S.Ct. 836 (1948); *Smith v. Allwright,* 321 U.S. 649, 64 S.Ct. 757 (1944); *Sweatt v. Painter,* 339 U.S. 629, 70 S.Ct. 848 (1950).

38. 347 U.S. 483, 74 S.Ct. 686 (1954). The story of this case is admirably told in Richard Kluger, *Simple Justice* (New York: Knopf, 1975).

39. 413 U.S. 189, 93 S.Ct. 2686 (1973).

40. *Milliken v. Bradley,* 418 U.S. 717, 94 S.Ct. 3112 (1974).

41. See Alan Ehrenhalt, "Busing and the Urban Schools: The Remedy That Refuses to Die," *Governing,* June 1991, 11–12.

42. *Missouri v. Jenkins,* 495 U.S. 33, 110 S.Ct. 1651 (1990).

43. *Guinn v. United States,* 238 U.S. 347, 35 S.Ct. 926 (1915).

44. An undergraduate professor of mine told the story that a registrar of voters in a rural Louisiana parish kept a Chinese newspaper in his desk drawer as the reading material for any black applicant. After looking at it for a few minutes, one black man reportedly said, "Well, I can't read this fine print down here, but the headline says 'There are not going to be any black voters in this parish for a long time.'"

45. Abigail M. Thernstrom, *Whose Votes Count? Affirmative Action and Minority Voting Rights* (Cambridge: Harvard University Press, 1987), 2.

46. *Wards Cove Packing Co. v. Atonio,* 490 U.S. 642, 109 S.Ct. 2115 (1989).

47. U.S. Bureau of the Census, *Statistical Abstract of the United States, 1991* (Washington: Government Printing Office, 1991), Table 432.

48. *Goesaert v. Cleary,* 335 U.S. 464, 69 S.Ct. 198 (1948).

49. See the discussion in Ralph Rossum and Alan Tarr, *American Constitutional Law,* 3d ed. (New York: St. Martin's, 1991), chap. 16.

50. See Catherine MacKinnon, *Feminism Unmodified* (Cambridge: Harvard University Press, 1987) for a summary of the first two and a defense of the third.

51. *Craig v. Boren,* 429 U.S. 190, 97 S.Ct. 451 (1976). This case was brought to the Court before the federal government used its highway funds to make states raise the legal drinking age to 21.

52. 450 U.S. 464, 101 S.Ct. 1200 (1981).

53. See Rossum and Tarr, *Constitutional Law,* chap. 26, for a summary.

54. *Griswold v. Connecticut,* 381 U.S. 479, 85 S.Ct. 1678 (1965).

55. See Charles Fried, "Privacy," *Yale Law Journal* 77 (1968), 475–93.

56. 410 U.S. 113, 93 S.Ct. 705 (1973).

57. 492 U.S. 490, 109 S.Ct. 3040 (1989).

58. *Rust v. Sullivan,*___U.S.___, 111 S.Ct. 1759 (1991). See also *New York Times,* May 24, 1991.

59. *Planned Parenthood v. Casey,* ___U.S. ___, 112 S.Ct. 2791 (1992).

60. *United States v. Paradise,* 480 U.S. 149, 107 S.Ct. 1053 (1987).

61. 438 U.S. 265, 98 S.Ct. 2733 (1978).

62. 480 U.S. 616, 107 S.Ct. 1442 (1987).

63. 488 U.S. 469, 109 S.Ct. 706 (1989).

64. *Los Angeles Times,* November 22, 1991.

65. See Frederick Lynch, *Invisible Victims: White Males and the Crisis of Affirmative Action* (Westport, Conn.: Greenwood Press, 1989).

66. See Stephen Carter, *Confessions of an Affirmative Action Baby* (New York: Basic Books, 1991).

FURTHER READING

1. Baer, Judith,. *Equality under the Constitution: Reclaiming the Fourteenth Amendment.* Ithaca, N.Y.: Cornell University Press, 1983.

2. Brigham, John. *Civil Liberties and American Democracy.* Washington: Congressional Quarterly Press, 1984.

3. Glendon, Mary Ann. *Rights Talk: The Impoverishment of Political Discourse.* New York: Free Press, 1991.

4. Hemmer, Joseph. *The Supreme Court and the First Amendment.* New York: Praeger, 1986.

5. Kluger, Richard. *Simple Justice.* New York: Knopf, 1975.

6. Levy, Leonard. *The Establishment Clause.* New York: Macmillan, 1986.

7. Lewis, Anthony. *Gideon's Trumpet.* New York: Random House, 1964.

8. Simon, James F. *The Antagonists: Hugo Black, Felix Frankfurter and Civil Liberties in Modern America.* New York: Simon and Schuster, 1989.

9. Sunstein, Cass. *After the Rights Revolution.* Cambridge: Harvard University Press, 1990.

10. Urofsky, Melvin. *The Continuity of Change: The Supreme Court and Individual Liberties, 1953–1986.* Belmont, Calif.: Wadsworth, 1991.

FIVE

CONGRESS

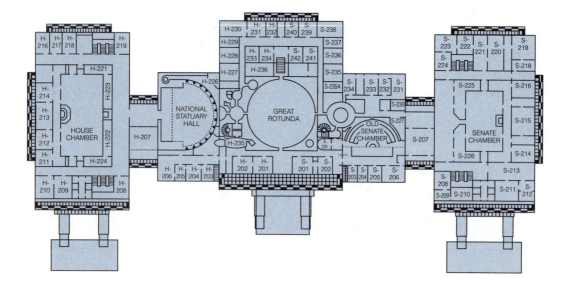

THE CREATION of a legislative body, or congress, was a given at the constitutional convention. Not only were representative assemblies used in each state, but the Stamp Act Congress (called in 1765 to protest British taxes), the Second Continental Congress (which fought the Revolutionary War), and the Congress under the Articles of Confederation were the sole precedents for national government in the new nation. The only questions were how it was to be structured and what its powers were to be. In the end, a two-house body was established with different representational bases, terms of office, and methods of election for each. Together they were handed an array of important powers and given the financial and military wherewithal to carry them out—if the members could forge a consensus among themselves. Here, then, is a microcosm of the American political system: enormous power lies at ready command, but pronounced fragmentation of the structure places formidable barriers before its exercise.

It is also helpful to remember that Congress plays two important political functions, or more prosaically, that there are "two Congresses."[1] On the one hand Congress is a representative assembly of individuals, who come from different parts of the country and who therefore represent different political interests. Although the system of geographical representation is imperfect in providing equal access to all portions of the public, it still makes Congress a potpourri of people pushing different agendas: programs important to such diverse groups as farmers, union members, veterans, Hispanics, loggers, homeowners, food stamp recipients, etc. At the same time, Congress is a law-making body for the nation as a whole. In one sense, these two functions are complementary, for the major reason representation exists is to make certain that laws reflect public preferences. The wider the representation the better the laws, according to general democratic theory. Yet, is it necessarily true that if all the parts are represented the public interest will be served? Will anyone in Congress stand outside the narrow interest and speak for the general one?

These two faces of Congress are closely related to the differences in individualist and civic democracy. Individualist democracy stresses the pursuit of self-interest by voters and officeholders, and believes that the public good will emerge through bargaining and compromise. Congress is an obvious site for this type of interplay. Civic democracy, on the other hand, emphasizes that people should and often do consider more than their narrow self-interest when voting, and that there is a public interest worth debating and pursuing. Thus, both elections for Congress and the behavior of its members need to be examined from this perspective also.

The fact is that evidence can be found to support both models, and members of Congress feel the cross-pressures of the two Congresses each day. Elected as they are from districts and states, they must speak for the dominant groups there; if they do not, they will very likely be replaced. Though the political links forged with these groups remain strong, most

---

Opposite: *Diagram of the second floor of the U.S. Capitol.*

members of Congress also have a sense of public duty, and are not immune to arguments regarding the public interest. They often find themselves determining how much weight they should give to the national interest, and how much to local needs. When should one take priority over the other?

POWERS OF CONGRESS

For convenience, the assortment of powers granted Congress by the Constitution can be divided into two categories: major powers and minor powers. One group of powers which are of the first type deals with national finance and monetary matters, such as the power to levy taxes, the right to borrow money on the national credit, the power to authorize all federal expenditures, and the exclusive right to coin money. Another group of major powers concerns foreign and military policy: the rights to declare war, to raise and equip an army and navy, and to call the state militias (the National Guard, in contemporary terms) to national service. The authority to establish a post office and the power to flesh out the court system below the Supreme Court also lie with Congress, as does the power to set rules for naturalization of new citizens.

One of the most far-reaching of the major powers is the authority to regulate domestic and foreign commerce. Since the 1930s, the term "commerce" has been so broadly interpreted by the courts that few activities seem to lie outside its meaning. For example, when Congress wanted to end racial discrimination in restaurants and motels in 1964, it disguised the law as a commercial regulation, a move which was upheld by the courts.[2]

Supplementing these are a handful of important but relatively minor powers. Congress is to make uniform laws for bankruptcy, to establish weights and measures, and to set rules for copyrights. It is also directed to pass laws controlling piracies and other mischief on the high seas. Lastly, it is given the authority to administer the "seat of government."

All these powers, major and minor, have been expanded by the "elastic clause," which we encountered in chapter 3. It grants Congress the power "to make all laws necessary and proper for carrying into execution the foregoing powers."[3] In general, as in *McCulloch v. Maryland*,[4] the courts have been very generous to Congress when they have had to interpret this clause.

Furthermore, Congress has discovered that the ability to provide grants to state and local governments is the ideal policy lever with which to regulate matters lying outside its direct scope. Terms and conditions can be attached to federal grants (which, after all, the states voluntarily accept) that will accomplish Congress' goal.[5] For instance, when Congress wished to raise the drinking age to twenty-one, it had no direct authority to do so. However, Congress merely made federal highway grants conditional on states' changing their own laws, which, after much carping and some foot-dragging, all of them did. (See chapter 3 for a more extended discussion.)

Through these grants of power, through court rulings, and through its own policy innovations, Congress as a body has at its disposal a vast reservoir of power to direct and oversee virtually every aspect of American life.

A few additional powers are vested in the Senate alone, powers which regularly entangle it with the president. For one, the Senate must approve all treaties by a two-thirds vote. This power is not as important as it once was, because presidents have resorted through the years to executive agreements: essentially, written understandings between two heads of government. That is, the chief executives of two countries each promise to undertake some action; as long as the action lies within the scope of their powers and both follow through, their nations are committed. There are limits, however, to a president's use of this instrument, and really important matters—arms control, major shifts in trade policy, contingent military commitments, and transfer of American property (such as the Panama Canal)—are still accomplished by treaty, and therefore subject to Senate approval.

The Senate must also acquiesce in presidential appointments to ambassadorships, the federal judiciary, and major administrative offices (such as cabinet posts and the headships of various agencies). Ambassadors are seldom important politically in this age of instantaneous communication, and only occasionally does the Senate reject an administrative appointee. Even then, it is usually over some personal transgression rather than a policy disagreement. The only recent example of this happening was the Senate's rejection of John Tower as George Bush's secretary of defense. Tower's alleged alcoholism and sexual indiscretions simply discredited him in too many senators' eyes. However, severe questioning can be used to scold or threaten the administration, a tactic Senate Democrats adopted, for instance, when President Bush nominated Robert Gates to head the Central Intelligence Agency. Gates had been closely identified with the controversial Central American policy of the Reagan administration, and the shadow of various improprieties still lingered, even though none were linked directly to Gates. Judicial appointments, however, now loom larger than ever. As the courts have waded ever more deeply into controversial areas of public policy, the tug of war over who is appointed to judgeships has intensified, as illustrated most recently by the Clarence Thomas hearings (see chapter 8).

Across the capitol, the House has only one special power: the right to introduce all revenue legislation. This power is largely symbolic, in that these bills may be freely amended in the Senate.

Structure of Congress

The Senate consists of two senators from each state. They serve six-year terms, with one-third elected every two years, staggered in such a way that the two representing a given state are not chosen at the same time.[6] Originally, senators were chosen by state legislatures, but the Seventeenth Amendment (1913) changed this practice to direct election.

In contrast, the entire House of Representatives is elected every two years, and has been chosen by popular election since the beginning.[7] States are granted seats on the basis of population, a census being constitutionally required every ten years to redistribute the seats. The total number of House seats is not established in the Constitution, but is instead set by statute. Throughout the nineteenth century, the size was periodically expanded to accommodate the growing number of states and rapidly increasing population. In 1929, the "permanent" number of House seats was set at 435. Since then, after each census this number of seats has been allocated among the states by a set formula, with the proviso that each state must have at least one representative.

After the census numbers are compiled, anyone with a calculator can assign the seats to the states.[8] What anyone with a calculator cannot do is to divide the states with more than one representative into districts.[9] Even in states which have the same number of seats as they had before the census, seldom can the old district lines be used, because there will have been internal shifts in population. According to a 1964 Supreme Court decision, all districts must contain approximately the same number of people—but obviously there are an infinite number of ways this can be done.[10] Furthermore, the Voting Rights Act of 1965 provides special protection for minorities; in essence, their voting strength cannot be "diluted" by the districting.[11]

The actual drawing of the lines is done by the state legislatures, which injects state politics directly into the districting. In many states, political party cleavages constitute the determining factor; in others, it is racial fissures, urban-rural splits, personality conflicts, or one of a welter of other pertinent variables. Naturally, in large states, several of these elements can enter into the equation simultaneously. "Gerrymandering" is a pejorative term that is used to describe the flagrant drawing of district boundaries to help political friends and hurt political enemies, along either party or other lines. In truth, it is impossible to draw neutral lines, and all districts are gerrymandered to some degree, in that they favor some political interests over others. In the cases of purposeful gerrymandering, the age-old tactics are "cracking" and "packing," as illustrated in figure 5-1.

Suppose the state of Fenwick is allocated four representatives and has a population divided into quadrants, with a history of party voting as illustrated in the first map in figure 5-1. Suppose further that the Republicans control the legislature in 1991 and are in a sharply partisan mood. They can draw the lines as shown in the second map and secure three Republican seats, *if* the voting patterns remain stable.

While it is often true that logic plays some role in these decennial exercises, as for example when a moderate-sized city and its hinterland are made one district, or an area of the state with a distinct economic base, such as wheat farming or cattle ranching, is kept within one district. However, the process is inherently political. Redrawing the congressional district lines is in fact one of the most important tasks state legislatures undertake, for it helps shape the face of political power within the House and thus the nation for a decade.

FIGURE 5–1
Congressional Districting in Fenwick

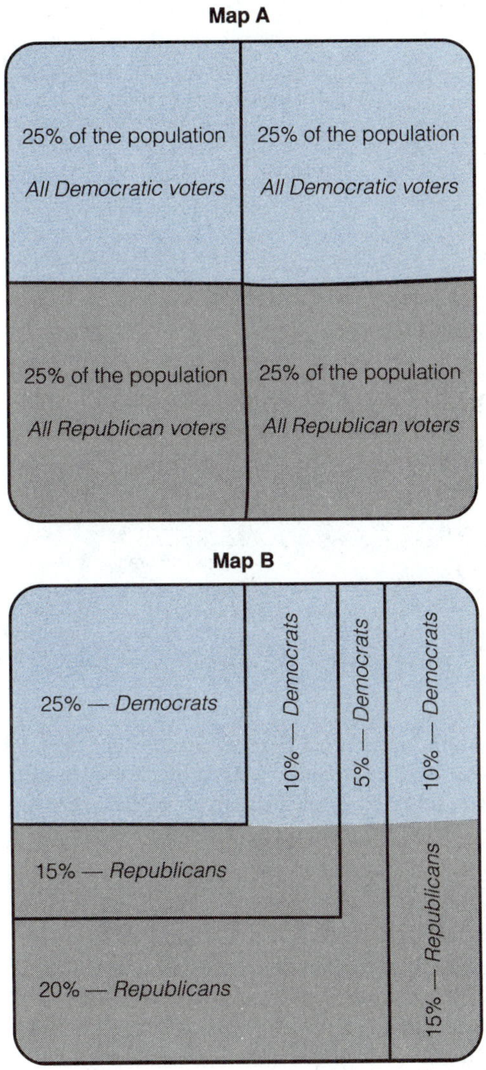

Map A

25% of the population	25% of the population
All Democratic voters	*All Democratic voters*
25% of the population	25% of the population
All Republican voters	*All Republican voters*

Map B

25% — Democrats

10% — Democrats

5% — Democrats

10% — Democrats

15% — Republicans

15% — Republicans

20% — Republicans

After the 1990 census, Fenwick was entitled to four House seats. Twenty-five percent of the state's population lived in each of the state's four quadrants, and had voting histories as shown in map A. The Republicans controlled the legislature, however, and drew the lines as shown in map B. The likely result is that Fenwick will be represented in the House by three Republicans and one Democrat, even though the parties split the vote evenly.

FIGURE 5-2

Newly Drawn Fourth Congressional District in Illinois

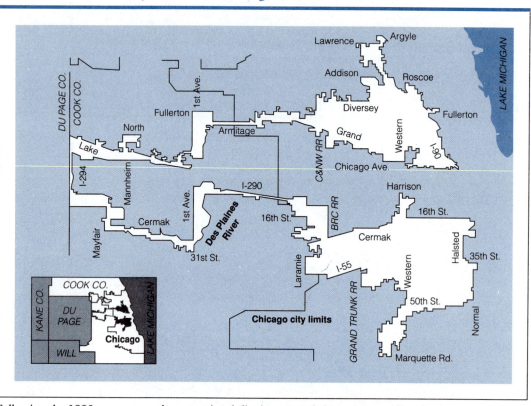

Following the 1990 census several congressional districts around the country were redrawn to enhance the likelihood of minority representation. The irregular outline of the fourth district of Illinois created a concentration of Hispanic voters. In 1992, Louis Gutierrez was elected to Congress from this district, becoming the first Hispanic representative from the Chicago area.

THE POPULAR CONNECTION
Congressional Elections

How and when elections are conducted, who runs, who votes, and the outcomes are all clearly important in a representative democracy. In the Founders' minds, the House would be more in touch with swings in the public mood, given its direct popular connection and its short term. It would, they thought, be subject to rapid turnover and contain more political radicals than the other branches. The Senate, with its disproportionately rural representation, its indirect election, and its longer, staggered terms would be the more conservative body, serving as a check on any radical impulses the House might have.

Curiously, things have not quite worked out that way. Recent figures show that in most years senators are more likely to be defeated in bids for

Members of the House of Representatives are sworn in at the beginning of a new session, January 1991.

reelection than House members, although incumbents are heavily favored in both. Of the House members who sought reelection, 98 percent won in both 1986 and 1988, and 96 percent won in 1990.[12] For the Senate, the reelection rates for incumbents who ran in the same three years were 75 percent, 85 percent, and 97 percent respectively. These results would surely surprise the Founding Fathers. As for which house is more conservative, that depends on how "conservatism" is defined. In the 1980s, the House was more liberal in a policy sense than the Senate on most issues. However, its liberalism was made up primarily of a devotion to the status quo liberal programs enacted during earlier Democratic administrations, while it was a conservative president and his political allies in the Senate who were trying to change them. Thus, it was the House which waged political battle to block the more change-oriented Senate. In that sense, the roles laid out for the two houses were reversed.

Why are senators more electorally vulnerable than House members? Part of it may be that House members spend more time securing their home political bases. That is, knowing they face election every other year, they concentrate more on being spokespersons for their districts and cultivating their constituents' goodwill than on being national lawmakers. Senators, in contrast, are more tempted to focus on Washington politics and devote more of their energies to national policy making. Ironically, then, a shorter term may make for more political security, not less. Another factor is that most senators have a more heterogenous electorate, making it harder to please everyone. Furthermore, Senate races seem to attract more serious challengers, such as former governors, sitting House members, and other public figures, offsetting some of the advantages of incumbency.

Getting and Staying Elected

The legal requirements for running for Congress are minimal: a candidate must be at least twenty-five years of age for the House and thirty for the Senate; must have at least seven and nine years of citizenship respectively; and must be an inhabitant of the state from which he seeks election. The filing of a set of papers in the state capital usually suffices to qualify a person to run in the Democratic or Republican primary, which is the first key to understanding the behavior of members of Congress. Potential candidates may seek the endorsement or help of local, state, or national party figures, but such endorsements are not essential for making a successful race. Anyone can run as a Democrat or a Republican simply by expressing a desire to do so.

If more than one candidate files for the party, a primary is conducted: that is, an election within one party to select the nominee. Generally, organized political parties provide little help to one candidate or the other during these contests, since both claim to want to represent the party at the general election. Supposedly, after the primary the party organization will swing behind the winning candidate at the general election; however, in practice it may not do so, or the party organization may be so weak that its influence is negligible anyway. Candidates rely heavily, therefore, on personal organizations.

Consequently, many new members are not beholden to party leaders when they arrive in Washington. Furthermore, as long as they can successfully run in the primary and the general election in their state or district, they cannot be unseated, a fact which erodes the influence party leaders in Congress or the White House can exercise over ordinary mem-

Senator Arlen Spector of Pennsylvania campaigns for re-election in 1992. The value of incumbency is strong for members of Congress, but 1992 was marked by an anti-incumbency sentiment among the voters.

bers. Of late, however, party support during campaigns has become more important. Both parties have congressional committees which have begun to actively recruit candidates and partially finance many—activities they can now undertake, since they have more money than they had in years past (see chapter 10). Hence, some new members do arrive in Washington in the debt of the party leaders. As we will see shortly, party voting is rather high and has been rising, even though it is ultimately voluntary.

In reality, successfully challenging an incumbent, whether senator or representative, is a formidable task. First, the incumbent has a big lead in name recognition. She will have been on news programs, had her picture in the paper, and been seen at dozens of public events. Second, the sitting member has resources at her command that are partially funded by the taxpayers. Her staff can quickly turn its attention from congressional business to the campaign; in fact, elections are never far from their minds. The "franking" privilege (free use of the mails by members of Congress) is of enormous benefit. Technically, partisan material cannot be mailed out under the frank, but the stream of newsletters, brochures, and copies of speeches leaving Washington is obviously aimed at doing more than merely informing the public. Unsurprisingly, the volume of mail going out under the frank increases dramatically in election years. In 1989, for instance, only 599 million pieces went out from congressional offices, compared to 805 million in the election year of 1988—at a cost of over $82 million to the taxpayers.[13]

Money is another ingredient. The average expenditure per candidate for House campaigns in 1990 was $284,000; for Senate races, $2,600,000. Incumbents, though, averaged $399,000 in the House contests and $3,500,000 in those for the Senate; challengers, on the other hand, struggled with less than half of those budgets: only $103,000 and $1,700,000 respectively. Whence the disparity? The simple answer is that those who contribute the most money to politicians are usually interested in access—and they know the reelection odds (see chapter 9). Therefore, they give heavily to incumbents, further reinforcing their chances. Finally, incumbents always argue, with some justification, that they have seniority and political clout, and that this will help the state or district. Senior Senator Quentin Burdick of North Dakota once based his entire campaign on a simple theme: "Burdick's Clout is North Dakota's."[14] He won.

Effects of Incumbency

Any organization needs the regular infusion of new blood if it is not to calcify, a truism especially germane to the institutions of representative democracy. Ideally, legislators are to be drawn from the citizenry at large and never become detached from them. Otherwise, there is the danger not only that those who make the laws will not be in touch with ordinary people, but also that they will become a permanent political class who regularly exempt themselves from the laws everyone else must obey.[15]

James Madison wrote in *The Federalist* (#57) that the House of Representatives "can make no law which will not have its full operation on themselves and their friends, as well as on the great mass of society. This has always been deemed one of the strongest bonds by which human policy can connect the rulers and the people together. It creates between them that communion of interests and sympathy of sentiments of which few governments have furnished examples, but without which every government degenerates into tyranny." During the Clarence Thomas hearings in 1991, a good bit of public discussion centered on the fact that Congress has exempted itself from its laws on sexual harassment, as well as a variety of other employment-related matters. A few months later, revelations of persistent overdrafts at the House bank caused a public uproar. Is this, many asked, precisely the danger Madison warned against, and a result of excessive incumbency?

Incumbency can also freeze the political balance of power in time. Political changes in the electorate will not be reflected in Congress, leaving the institution in a time warp. The rise in incumbency, for instance, has mostly favored the Democrats, who have controlled the House of Representatives since 1954. However, the last decade has witnessed a decline in the number of people who identify themselves as Democrats, and between 1968 and 1988 only one Democrat won a presidential election. The House, therefore, according to some critics, is the least representative of our branches of government.

As a result, a movement has begun to impose term limits on members of Congress. George Will wrote that "Term limits are needed as an auxiliary precaution against the perennial lust for power."[16] Will and others believe that it would be quite healthy to introduce more turnover—both for the sake of keeping the rulers and the ruled in closer touch with each other, and to force the lawmakers to live with their own rules. But others argue against term limits for two reasons: first, that the key is getting good people into office, and that there is no guarantee that term limits will do that; and second, that setting term limits would deprive people of the right to choose whomever they wish to represent them.[17] The debate became more than academic in 1991, when Washington state put a term limits law on the ballot for a public referendum.[18] Although the polls gave the measure an early 70-percent approval rating, as the campaign wore on that support eroded, and it was ultimately defeated. Interestingly, this measure would have applied to incumbents as well as new office-holders, meaning that every member of the House from Washington state would have had to retire by 1994. The congressional delegation, led by Speaker of the House Tom Foley, launched a determined battle against the proposal, arguing that the state's clout in Congress would be irreparably damaged if the proposal passed.[19] Apparently, this contention swayed a lot of votes. In the end, the proponents of term limits vowed to fight on in spite of this defeat.[20]

Meanwhile, voters were venting their anger at incumbents across the country. Senator Alan Dixon of Illinois and several House members from various parts of the nation were defeated in primary fights, and many other races were closer than expected. The political fallout soon reached Washington, and by late April 1992 there were already more voluntary resignations from the House of Representatives (fifty) than at any time since World War II. (See chapter 13 for a discussion of the 1992 congressional elections.)

It is important, though, not to overstate the degree or effect of incumbency. First, even at its peak, the high rate of incumbent success was not the same thing as having no turnover. In 1992, 61 percent of all House members had been in office twelve years or less; thirty years earlier this figure was 65 percent. On the Senate side, fifty-three Senators had twelve or fewer years of service in 1992, compared to sixty-seven in 1961 (but seventy in 1987). Evidently, then, many members retired after one or a few terms, and the voters had a chance to send a fresh face to Washington.

Second, even though they appear statistically to be very safe, members of Congress seldom feel this way.[21] The best strategy for victory, most seem to think, is to scare away powerful challengers. In the eyes of most senators and representatives, any weakening of their majorities will bring forth serious opposition. During political scientist Richard Fenno's extensive travels with representatives from all over the country, he was struck by how much they talked about their "one close race," and related regularly the woeful tales of a colleague who had been beaten (as a few always are).[22] Most members labor assiduously, therefore, at keeping their political base secure, because they fear what might happen. Thus, incumbency does not necessarily translate into political aloofness and a lessening of political accountability.

Public Evaluations of Congress

From one perspective, the success rate of incumbents is puzzling. Polls continue to show that Americans distrust Congress and have a generally low opinion of the institution.[23] Stand-up comedians always find ample material on Capitol Hill (continuing a tradition stretching back to Mark Twain and Will Rogers) and cartoonists continually picture members of Congress in unflattering ways. If, as Richard Fenno asked in 1974, we disdain Congress as a body, "How Come We Love Our Congressmen So Much?"[24]

After roving about with several House members in their home districts, Fenno decided that the answer to this question lies in the fact that most citizens draw a sharp distinction between Congress and *their* representative. One's own representative is seen more often than not as the embodiment of local values in contrast to "those others." Members of Congress, somewhat ironically, encourage negative views of Congress in that they "run *for* Congress by running *against* Congress."[25] That is, they stress their affinity with the "home folks" and blame other members for Congress' shortcomings. By belittling the influence of powerful "others"— committee chairs, the conservative coalition, the liberals, the farm bloc,

TABLE 5-1

Why People Voted As They Did in 1986 House Races

REASON FOR CHOICE	PERCENTAGE OF VOTERS
Personal qualities of candidate	37
National issues	31
Local/state issues	19
Other or combination	2
No opinion or all	11

Source: CBS News–*New York Times* Poll, April 14, 1986.

city slickers, southerners, the East Coast Establishment, or whatever—the local representative plays on his constituents' disdain for Congress. Even this strategy has its limits, though, as the rising tide of anti-incumbent feeling in 1992 demonstrated.

Moreover, it seems that more people base their vote on personal factors than on any other single criterion. They want someone they can trust and with whom they identify. Once that bond of trust is built with the voters, negative views of Congress as a body do not affect it. One representative confided about his constituents, "They don't know much about my votes. Most of what they know is what I tell them. They know more what kind of a guy I am. It comes through in my letters: 'You care about the little guy.'"[26]

Seemingly, therefore, significant numbers of people consider more than a candidate's policy positions when they enter the voting booth. To be sure, they want someone who will defend the needs of the district and bring home large slices of federal pork. But they also want something more. James Madison again: "The aim of every political Constitution is or ought to be first to obtain for rulers men who possess [the] most wisdom to discern, and [the] most virtue to pursue the common good of society."[27] To some degree, then, when people vote for someone's general character, and not for or against particular policy positions, they are giving life to what Madison said.

A PROFILE OF THE MEMBERS

What types of people are elected to Congress? By any measure, they are not a cross section of the American population. They are more white, more male, more educated, and wealthier than average.

Congress has always been and remains predominantly white, but that is changing, albeit slowly. The number of African Americans has steadily increased from three in 1961 to twenty-six in 1991. But this figure is still only 5 percent of the membership, while about 12 percent of the population is black. Women are even more underrepresented: only thirty of them sat in the 102nd Congress (1991–92), a bare 6 percent for a group

T A B L E 5-2
Blacks and Women in Congress, 1961–1991

YEAR AND GROUP	HOUSE	SENATE	TOTAL
Blacks			
1961	3	0	3
1971	13	1	14
1981	17	0	17
1991	26	0	26
Women			
1961	18	2	20
1971	13	1	14
1981	19	2	21
1991	28	2	30

Source: Adapted from Norman Ornstein, Thomas Mann, and Michael Malbin, *Vital Statistics on Congress, 1991–92* (Washington, D.C.: Congressional Quarterly, Inc., 1992), 38–39.

constituting over half the population. Yet, the House had only twenty female members thirty years before. Worthy of mention also is the fact that these gains for African Americans and women have occurred almost entirely in the House.

In the area of religion, Congress is somewhat more representative. Twenty-seven percent of the members are Catholic, about the same percentage as Catholics in the general population; 8 percent report being Jewish, not dramatically different from the proportion of Jews in the overall population. Protestants and those who profess no religion (a rare claim) make up the remainder; however, there are serious skews within Protestantism. For example, there are fifty-nine Episcopalians (11 percent), although only about 1 percent of Americans are Episcopalian. The obvious reason for this is social class.

Aside from gender, social class in fact is what most acutely separates Congress from the general population. Educationally, almost all members are college graduates and many hold postgraduate degrees. Most came to Congress from high-status occupations and enjoy incomes (and inheritances) far above the national average.

The crucial question, though, is how much all this matters. On some issues, groups of members do tend to vote together: African Americans on civil rights legislation; Jews on Middle East policy; women on matters of equal opportunity. On some other issues, there is a traceable indirect influence, such as Catholic members' votes on abortion bills. However, in none of these cases are these people the only ones who support the positions in question. Many, if not most, white male members support civil rights and equal opportunity legislation, for example. Otherwise, neither type of legislation would ever pass. Aid to Israel and pro-life positions attract diverse coalitions, not ones exclusively composed of Jews and Catholics.

TABLE 5–3

Occupations of Members of Congress:
102nd Congress (1991–1992)

HOUSE	
Occupation	*Number of Members*
Law	183
Business or banking	157
Public service/politics	61
Education	57
Journalism	25
Agriculture	20
Engineering	7
Law enforcement	5
Medicine	5
Professional sports	3
Labor leadership	3
Entertainment	2
Clergy	2
Aeronautics	1
Military	1

SENATE	
Occupation	*Number of Members*
Law	61
Business or banking	32
Education	10
Journalism	10
Agriculture	8
Public service/politics	5
Aeronautics	1
Professional sports	1
Clergy	1
Military	1

Source: Adapted from Ornstein, Mann, and Malbin, *Vital Statistics on Congress, 1991–92,* 22 & 28.

Note: Several members listed more than one occupation.

Social class is the most vexing and the most intangible variable in this regard. Most members of Congress have led fairly comfortable lives, far removed from a factory floor, a coal mine, a lobster boat, or the inside of an eighteen-wheeler. Do their unspoken assumptions on taxes, health care, factory safety, and housing translate into biased legislation? In one sense, they clearly do. In another sense, though, the answer is less clear. Some of the most affluent members, for example, are often the most forthright spokesmen for the disadvantaged, with Senator Edward Kennedy standing as the most conspicuous contemporary example. Furthermore, many members have close electoral ties to unions, social welfare organizations, civil rights groups, and other organizations based in the less-well-off sectors of the population, and this influences the positions they take and the votes they cast.

It is the voters, after all, who send the members, and to whom the members look to retain their seats. One need not be black or female, for instance, to court black and women voters. A good example of this principle is Congressman Mike Espy of Mississippi's black-majority Second District. When Espy, who is black, first ran in 1986, he won by securing almost all the black vote and ceding the white vote to his opponent. Since then, though, he has worked hard to meet the needs of farmers of both races in his heavily agricultural district. In subsequent elections, he has won the backing of many white farmers, and now has a secure political base among them. Thus, even though Espy is neither white nor a farmer, these people believe he attends to their interests. In short, a representative may be effective even if he or she does not share a group's traits.

Thus, Congress need not be a demographic cross section to be representative and adopt policies that accord with public preferences. At the same time, the vast underrepresentation of any group can have serious repercussions for political legitimacy: how much citizens identify with the political system. Inherently, people seem to attach more legitimacy to decisions made by people like themselves (otherwise, well-run empires like the British would not have crumbled). Especially in a society that values equality among citizens, it is important that people feel a personal link with those who sit in the councils of power. Thus, if a sizeable group is left disaffected, this can have potentially far-reaching consequences. To the extent, then, that Congress becomes more of a reflection of the American population, it will probably become more legitimate.

INTERNAL POLITICS
House-Senate Differences

Aside from the special powers given the Senate regarding treaties and appointments, and the requirement that revenue legislation be born in the House, the formal legislative powers of the two houses are equal. However, there are significant differences in the styles of the two chambers, and in the ways that decisions are made in each. Size alone accounts for many of the differences. Obviously, for instance, each senator's vote is more than four times as important as each House member's. This affects both presidential courting of legislators and the importance lobbyists attach to each type. Furthermore, the House's immense size means that the rules of procedure must be tightly structured if chaos and stalemate are not to ensue. If each House member spoke for only fifteen minutes every other week, for example, more than fifty hours per week would be consumed. In contrast, the Senate is more relaxed and informal, allowing much wider latitude to senators' idiosyncrasies—too much, according to some. Senator J. Bennett Johnston (D-La.) quipped that "The Senate is run for the convenience of one senator to the inconvenience of ninety-nine."[28]

The relative smallness of the Senate creates a deference for each senator which is reinforced by notions of "upper houseness," the longer term, and the symbiotic relationship with the presidency in foreign policy and judicial politics. Senators consider themselves to be quite important people, and view any slight upon themselves or their colleagues as a denigration of their office.

Moreover, in the House there is an unwritten rule that if a member wants to acquire influence, she needs to specialize. In the Senate, on the contrary, the tradition encourages senators to become generalists and speak out on a variety of national issues. The Senate, too, is an important breeding ground of presidential candidates, while traditionally the House is not.[29]

Committees

Committees are by far the most important organizational feature of Congress. They are, according to a classic phrase of Woodrow Wilson's, "little legislatures."[30] Two simple realities generate the need for committees. First, both houses are too large to conduct business with any efficiency. The breaking of a house into committees allows more legislation to be considered, and in far greater detail. Second, no member can possibly possess expertise in the multitude of issues that flood into Congress. Committees allow members to select one or two areas and spend time getting a grasp on the issues and policies germane to these areas. Time constraints and the need to specialize affect both houses to some degree, although, as mentioned above, they are much more sharply pronounced in the House than they are in the Senate.

The most important type of congressional committee is the *standing committee*. These are permanent committees composed of members from only one house. The House currently has twenty-two and the Senate sixteen, the size of which varies from twelve to fifty-seven.[31] Most House committees have about forty members, while the Senate's average about twenty members. Even these numbers are not small, especially in the House, and a committee's jurisdiction can often be wide-ranging. Therefore, most committees further divide into subcommittees. The House Agriculture Committee, for example, has the following subcommittees: Conservation, Credit and Rural Development; Cotton, Rice and Sugar; Department Operations, Research and Foreign Agriculture; Domestic Marketing, Consumer Relations and Nutrition; Forests, Family Farms and Energy; Livestock, Dairy and Poultry; Tobacco and Peanuts; and Wheat, Soybeans and Feed Grains. It is in these forums, then, 135 of which existed in the House and 87 in the Senate during the 102nd Congress, that the real work of legislation is most often done.

The chief task of standing committees and subcommittees is to consider bills referred to them and send to the floor those they recommend. Typ-

Confirmation hearings of Robert Gates before the Senate Intelligence Committee, September 1991. Gates was nominated by President Bush to head the Central Intelligence Agency.

ically, committees and subcommittees hold hearings on bills they are working on, inviting proponents and opponents to make statements or answer questions; at the conclusion, they add amendments and frame a report. Dissenters at either level may file their own reports if they so wish.

However, committees are free to, and sometimes do, undertake investigations to determine if legislation is needed concerning a certain problem. (More often, though, this is done by select committees, discussed below.) They also provide an oversight function, in that they frequently call administrators to explain what is and is not working in a particular program. This is an especially favorite tactic of appropriations committees, which oversee the doling out of money.

Committees represent the dilemma of the two Congresses in miniature. Their activities are a delicate balance between searching for beneficent public policy and accommodating the political interests which continually envelop them. The atmosphere of each is always highly charged politically, and interest groups watch them very closely. Members know that quite often campaign contributions come more easily to those who seem attentive to the needs of affected groups. Nonetheless, members do (sometimes, at least) discuss and argue about the merits of legislation. Aggregating the interests of those most closely affected by the committee's acts always tugs against the public interest, and there is no easy way to reconcile the two.

Both houses also use *select committees,* which are temporary bodies charged with some special task, usually an investigation. The most recent noteworthy example was the 1987 Iran-Contra Committee of the Senate; the most famous in history was the Senate Watergate Committee which sat through the summer of 1974. Select committees rather than standing committees are used for this purpose, both because the latter are busy with

135

Upper Houses and Federalism in Australia and Germany

WHY HAVE A BICAMERAL, two-house, legislature? One classic answer is that it provides a second look at legislation, warding off ill-conceived, shortsighted, or unwise proposals. Another oft-cited justification is that different interests can be represented by having different-sized districts for the two houses.

In federal systems one of the houses, usually the upper house, often takes on functions which give life to the federal dimension of the political system within the national institutions. Seats in upper houses are frequently not divided solely or at all on the basis of population, and the governments of the states are sometimes the ones who choose the members rather than the voters directly. The United States is unique in that equal legislative power is granted to both houses. In most federal democracies the lower house, by law or by custom, has assumed far more political importance than the upper house. Australia and Germany are more typical.

Australia always makes for interesting comparisons with the United States, for when its constitution was drafted in 1901 many features of the American system were consciously copied. Thus, even though the legislative branch is called Parliament, the two houses bear the same names as ours. Further, the system of representation is an adapted version of ours. Seats in the House of Representatives are apportioned by population while each state (another borrowed term) has equal representation in the Senate. With only six states, though, the states are given twelve senators apiece (plus there are two each from the capital territory and the Northern Territory). Senators are elected by popular vote for six-year terms; elections are held every three years for half of each state's delegation.

Although the two houses are almost constitutionally equal, the political balance of power has tilted decidedly toward the House of Representatives. The primary reason for this has been that Australia chose to import its executive branch from Britain's system rather than that of

legislation and because the creation of a select committee will itself guarantee attention to the issue.

From time to time, Congress has experimented with joint committees (composed of members from both houses); these have been only marginally successful however. Great fanfare usually accompanies their formation, but the lack of a firm political base normally undermines their effectiveness. The only major one now operating is the Joint Economic Committee, which publishes many useful studies but has very little direct influence on policy.

the United States. The prime minister and the cabinet are selected by the House of Representatives (usually largely from among its own members) and they may be removed by the lower house on a simple majority vote. Therefore, most important political activity long ago gravitated to the House of Representatives. The Senate has not been driven into oblivion by any means; occasionally it forces significant changes in measures clearing the lower house. But its stature is clearly below that of the House of Representatives. In Australia, no truly ambitious politician would give up a seat in the House of Representatives to run for the Senate, the converse of the United States.

Germany presents a somewhat different pattern. There are two legislative chambers, the *Bundestag* and the *Bundesrat*. The former is the popularly elected house and the seat of political power. According to the constitution, the *Bundesrat* has equal legislative power only on laws affecting the federal system. On all other matters a simple majority vote in the *Bundestag* overrides the *Bundesrat*. The number of federal issues is large, however, since most domestic laws are administered by the states.

Each German state is allocated three to five seats in the *Bundesrat*, depending on its population. The government of each state chooses its delegation and may replace them at any time. Interestingly, the votes of each state must be cast as a bloc. Ordinarily, this means that the political party which governs in the state legislature will determine how the votes are to be cast, even though the minority party is usually given a seat or two.

As in Australia, Germany's executive branch (headed by a chancellor) is chosen by and responsible to the lower house alone. Sensing its inferior position, over the years the *Bundesrat* has focused its attention almost exclusively on the technicalities of federal issues. Generally, it has avoided direct confrontations with the *Bundestag*.

Thus, even though the fusion of executive power with the legislative authority of the lower house has diminished the power of the upper house in both countries, the Senate in Australia and the *Bundesrat* in Germany remain significant. They are useful reminders of the federal character of these governments; moreover, their role in public policy making, providing a "second look," is often far more than incidental.

A special type of committee is known as a *conference committee*.[32] A single bill will often pass the two houses in slightly, or even perhaps fundamentally, different form, necessitating the drawing up of a compromise version before it can be sent to the president. A conference committee composed of members from each house (typically of delegations from the committees which examined the bill) irons out the differences; then, both houses must approve the final draft.

The Workings of Standing Committees

Since standing committees are so important, the process of assigning members is critical both to congressional careers and to public policy. Richard Fenno found that members pursue three goals in seeking committee assignments: reelection, influence within Congress, and "good" public policy.[33] Different committees appeal, therefore, to different members, and perhaps to the same member at different stages of his career. Ordinarily, junior members seek committee assignments which will solidify their political base at home—for example, Agriculture for rural members; Merchant Marine and Fisheries for seacoast members; and Public Works and Transportation for almost anyone. On the other hand, Appropriations and Rules (House only) attract those aiming at building influence within Congress. Foreign Relations (Senate) and Ways and Means (House), in turn, allow more opportunity for policy influence.

Committee assignments are more important in the House than in the Senate. In the former, not only is there less opportunity to participate in floor debate, but the rules normally allow only one major committee assignment, while senators serve on two major committees and one minor one. A House member's career can consequently be materially helped or damaged by her committee assignment. Paul Simon of Illinois, who has served in both chambers, noted, "In the House, you are restricted by your

A representative looks over the budget report at a meeting of the House Budget Committee.

committee. But in the Senate, you're not tied down. You have a lot more room to exert influence."[34]

Initially, the membership of each committee is divided between the parties in the same ratio as the seats in the parent house. Selection of the specific Democrats and Republicans then lies with each party's caucus (the organization of all the party members in that house). The four caucuses operate similarly: each sets up a committee of its own to make the assignments, which are then ratified by the entire caucus. Practically, in most circumstances parties manage to give each member his preference. If there are conflicts, the usual procedure is to defer to seniority, but as always, there are exceptions.

Within the committee, leadership is in the hands of the committee chair. The party which is in the majority controls selection of all the committee chairs. In the past, all four caucuses followed a strict seniority rule: the longest continuously-serving majority party member was automatically designated chair. In the mid-seventies, the House Democratic Caucus changed this, mandating that all chairs be chosen by a secret ballot of the caucus. Immediately, three long-serving but especially unpopular chairs were stripped of their offices. Although seniority settled back in as the accepted practice, in 1985 the caucus dumped the most senior member of the Armed Services Committee, and put the seventh-ranking Democrat in his place.

At the same time that it adopted this reform, the House Democratic Caucus loosened the control which chairs had on their committees. Before the change, committee chairs often ruled their domains with a heavy hand: they controlled the agenda, the budget, and the staff, and appointed the chairs of all subcommittees. The most important change involved this last task; now, a particular subcommittee chair is elected by the members of the majority party on that subcommittee. Furthermore, it became harder to "stack" subcommittees, since a new rule said that every Democrat on a committee could choose to be on one subcommittee before anyone else received a second assignment. The net result of all these modifications has been to strengthen subcommittees and diffuse power within Congress. Committee chairs are still powerful, but must now rely more on the power of persuasion than they ever did before.

Lastly, another reform of the mid-seventies called for open committee meetings; in the past, committees had often met in "executive session." While this change has had a generally wholesome effect, it has made the intricate bargaining necessary to craft compromise proposals much more difficult. Congressmen are often loathe to compromise in public what they would freely give up in private, fearing electoral reprisal. This may have had the unintended effect of adding more force to local interests at the expense of national needs. When reforms are proposed to make members of Congress more "accountable," one must always consider *to whom* they will be more accountable. Many observers of Congress argue, though, that informal meetings and telephone conversations have simply replaced the closed session, that just as many "deals" are struck behind closed doors as before, and that nothing has really changed.

Political Parties

Political parties are not only important in assigning members to committees. They are, first of all, the primary groups to which all members belong, and from which they draw their identity (the occasional independent or maverick excepted). Further, both houses are organized around political parties, especially when leaders are selected.

Nominally, the Senate's presiding officer is the vice president, but he rarely attends, and can cast a vote only in case of a tie. Sensing this likelihood, the Constitution's drafters called for the Senate to choose a *president pro tempore* to fill in for the vice president. Normally, this is a symbolic honor given to a senior member of the majority party, who in turn hands the gavel over on most days to various junior members.

Each Senate party christens one of its own as its leader. Together, the majority and minority leaders usually work out a schedule for the Senate's floor time. Each of them also tries to act as spokesperson for her party; however, the streak of independence with which most senators are afflicted impedes this task considerably. Only an adept politician with a strong personality—such as Lyndon Johnson, majority leader from 1955 to 1961—can impose his will on other senators. Both parties also choose *whips,* whose main function is to count the yes and no votes on important legislation ahead of time. In doing their jobs, whips act as important channels of two-way communication between the leaders and the rank and file.

In the House, parties loom a bit more prominently, and the party organizations exercise more influence. The Speaker of the House, selected by the majority party, is expected to be a pivotal party figure. If she is of the same party as the president, she necessarily becomes a key liaison between Congress and the White House. If party control of the House and White House is split, then it customarily falls to her to be the opposition's "point man." Hers will be the major voice which challenges the president publicly on vital issues, and she will have a strong say in decisions about which bills should receive concerted opposition and which should be overlooked. During the Reagan presidency, for example, Tip O'Neill played this role quite effectively. Then, the scandals which dogged his successor, Jim Wright, shortened Wright's tenure and undermined his leadership while in office. The next Speaker, Tom Foley, easily fell in with George Bush's "bipartisan" approach early in the Bush years, but their relationship became strained as the 1992 elections approached.

How effective are parties at organizing votes on the floor? In many European parliaments, parties are often quite cohesive, with members voting together on all but rare occasions. In the United States, however, cohesion is not nearly that common. If "party unity votes" are defined as those votes in which a majority in one party votes against a majority in the other, only about 45 percent of floor votes are party unity votes in most Congresses. Conversely, this means that over half the votes are not along party lines. However, no other variable—region, age, ideology, etc.—will statistically predict as many votes as will party. Thus, while party voting is

T A B L E 5-4

The Power of the Conservative Coalition:
Votes and Victories
1960–1990

	HOUSE		SENATE	
	Votes[a]	Victories[b]	Votes[a]	Victories[b]
1960	20%	35%	22%	67%
1965	25	25	24	39
1970	17	70	26	64
1975	28	52	28	48
1980	16	67	20	75
1985	13	84	16	93
1990	10	74	11	95

Source: Reprinted with permission from Ornstein, Mann, and Malbin, *Vital Statistics on Congress, 1991–92*, 201.

[a] Votes = percentage of votes pitting the conservative coalition (Republicans and southern Democrats) against liberals (northern Democrats)
[b] Victories = percentage of the conservative-vs.-liberal votes which were won by conservative coalition

rather low by comparison with voting in other countries, party cohesiveness is far more important an influence on voting than any other factor. Given the looseness of party organizations and the independent route candidates must follow to get to Congress, it is perhaps surprising that party voting is as common as it is. Moreover, its importance seems to be growing, and that seems to be related to changes which have occurred within each of the parties.

For many years, critics argued that Congress was dominated by a conservative coalition composed of Republicans and southern Democrats. In table 5-4, columns 1 and 3 show the percentage of total congressional votes in each house (examined every five years) in which a majority of southern Democrats and Republicans faced off against a majority of northern Democrats. Columns 2 and 4 in the table show the percentage of those votes that the conservatives won. At their peak, the coalitions split on about a quarter of the votes, with the conservatives victorious far more often than not.

In recent years, however, the coalitions have become more fragmented, and fewer floor votes seem to split Congress in this fashion; instead, the split now comes more often along pure party lines. The major reason the coalitions have been replaced by the parties is the transformation of southern politics. Southern Democrats are much more liberal now than they were in the past, particularly on civil rights issues.[35] Thus, the Democratic Party in Congress is not nearly as ideologically diverse as it once was.

For their part, the Republicans have also become a more ideologically grounded party. Liberal Republicans, most of whom came from the northeast, are a steadily vanishing breed, while a coterie of very conservative

Republicans from the south has entered Congress. Consequently, both parties are more ideologically cohesive than before, and a more significant gulf separates them.

Another result of the increased ideological homogeneity within the congressional parties has been an enlarged role for party leaders, especially but not only among the House Democrats.[36] When the parties were more diverse, members hesitated to give leaders much authority, since it would strengthen one faction or another. Now members can comfortably grant more power to their leaders, because they are more willing to follow where they know the leaders will lead.

Special Groups

In addition to parties, there are a variety of other groups to which members belong. Some are organized as factions by party members within one house; examples from the House of Representatives include the Democratic Study Group (a bloc of more liberal members), the Conservative Democratic Forum, the House Wednesday Group (moderate Republicans), and the Republican Study Committee (Republican conservatives). Others are bipartisan, but still contained within one house: examples include the Conference of Great Lakes Congressmen, the House Beef Caucus, the Senate Coal Caucus, and the Senate Western Coalition. Still others are bipartisan and bicameral, such as the Congressional Black Caucus, the Military Reform Caucus, and the Congressional Soybean Caucus. Some of these are important organizations which hold regular meetings, issue reports, and push legislation. Others are more informal, more akin to an organized network of interested members that can be activated according to need. This latter type is often associated with various trade and product groupings. They can be very powerful in a narrow area of policy, such as soybean price supports, especially if they work closely with the affected interest groups.

THE LABYRINTH OF LEGISLATION

Making laws lies at the heart of most congressional activity. In the 101st Congress (1989–90) 650 bills were enacted, out of over 10,000 introduced.[37] Obviously, the life of every American is affected in some way by which bills get passed and which do not.

Introducing a bill is relatively simple: a representative or senator merely files it with the proper officials in his house. One bill might be the product of a member's ruminations about some public problem, although even here she is likely to have drawn on substantial staff help. At another time, an interest group might suggest a bill and have a friendly legislator introduce it. Sometimes select committees end their work with proposals for bills. The major source of legislation, though, is always the president and his subordinates. Ordinarily, the president presents a package of legislative proposals, his "program," which will inevitably occupy a great deal of the attention of Congress. The dynamics of the president's program and its effect on his relations with Congress are discussed in the next chapter.

The standard route for bills is laid out below. At times, however, these procedures will be circumvented. A pressing emergency can galvanize Congress into speedy action; all that is legally required is passage by floor votes in both houses.

After a bill is introduced, it is assigned to a standing committee. In the House, the Speaker parcels out bills to the various committees; in the Senate, the presiding officer does so. In both cases, the assignment is subject to being overturned by majority vote. Occasionally, the decision as to which committee is given a bill is of critical importance: Education and Labor, for example, may be known to be sympathetic to a new inner-city training program, while Banking, Finance, and Urban Affairs may be openly hostile to it. Its fate may therefore be decided very early.

The chair and his allies on the standing committee largely determine which bills will be taken up; this means that most bills end their lives here. Complex bills—most important bills—are often carved up and given to different subcommittees; however, if the bill is relatively succinct, it may be given to only one subcommittee. Subcommittees then hold hearings at which interest groups and government officials offer testimony and members ask a variety of questions, often with a partisan hue. When hearings are concluded, the subcommittee begins its "markups," drafting a revised bill with amendments. Seldom will a bill emerge from a subcommittee as it came in. Some amendments involve technical matters and do not affect the content of the bill; others may strengthen or weaken critical aspects of the measure. One strategy often used by opponents of a bill—at this stage and elsewhere—is to attach such an odious amendment that the support for the bill will dissolve. It is not unknown for even a bill's sponsor to vote against a bill after it has been "amended to death."

Bills, in whole or in part, are then reported to the parent committee. Sometimes new hearings are held at the committee level, but usually there is only another markup session, with a vote finally taken on whether to recommend that the bill pass or not. If it is reported favorably, it must now compete for a place on the calendar.

In the Senate, a Rules and Administration Committee formally controls the calendar, but the real decisions lie, as noted earlier, with the majority and minority leaders. In the House, things are more complex. Recall that the rules of the House are much more rigid. Various floor rules are available which tightly limit debate and set the approach to amendments: some rules allow for no amendments; other rules permit only certain types; and still others allow general amendments. The House Rules Committee decides which bills will be brought up when and which rule they will follow. Technically, this committee is charged only with overseeing the smooth flow of business. However, where politics can enter, it usually does. The Rules Committee, or more accurately a majority of the committee, can delay floor action or attach an unfavorable rule to a bill members dislike. More often, committee members can let their displeasure be known through the congressional grapevine, and have a standing committee make whatever alterations they desire. At one time, the Rules Committee exercised a virtual veto power over legislation; this power was used primarily to thwart civil rights bills opposed by the southern oligarchy which controlled the committee. Its influence is now more limited, but it is still a major power center in Congress. For this reason it is one committee that does not follow the party-ratio rule for allocating seats: on the Rules Committee, the majority party normally insists on a healthy two-to-one division. Since the mid-1970s, the members from the majority party have been appointed by the Speaker.

Can a standing committee or the Rules Committee kill a bill simply by sitting on it? In the Senate, this is unlikely, if influential senators want it brought to the floor. In the House, there is a procedure called a *discharge petition* that can be used to pry bills out of hostile committees. However, it needs 218 signatures to succeed, a number which is seldom obtainable. Sometimes, though, just the fact that a discharge petition is circulating will spur a committee into action.

Once a bill is on the floor, the House-Senate differences become even more evident. In the House, the bill's floor manager, usually the chair of the committee which considered it, will be given half an hour or so (time he may share with others) to explain the measure. The ranking minority member of the committee, or other opponents, will be allotted an equal amount of time to offer criticism, none of which makes much difference. An abbreviated debate may follow, and depending on the rule used, amendments may be offered. Very few amendments secure House assent, though. A vote is then held, and if the whips have done their homework, the conclusion is usually foregone. Occasionally, House votes are dramatic and surprising, but that is rare. In short, once a bill has been worked over by a House committee, it is seldom voted down on the floor.

In the Senate, the committee report is less sacrosanct and the debate less stage-managed. Floor time is sought by more people, and amendments are more frequent. Furthermore, the Senate has an odd rule which allows the *filibuster:* the practice of unlimited debate to delay passage of a bill, whether or not what is said is germane to the bill. The Senate has been entertained by readings of recipes for Louisiana shrimp and the Sears and Roebuck catalog during these marathons. As it stands now, *cloture* (the ending of debate) can be imposed if sixty senators so vote. After the vote, debate on that bill is restricted to thirty more hours. Filibusters, or threatened filibusters, are most effective at the end of a session, when several important bills are awaiting floor action. By tying up the Senate's calendar at a critical juncture, the opponents may be able to secure substantial concessions, even if the bill is not killed.

If the bill survives House and Senate floor votes, it is ready to be transmitted to the president. Important and controversial legislation seldom passes both houses in exactly the same form, however. The task of working out the differences falls to a conference committee, composed of an equal number of senators and representatives; this committee is more often than not a meeting of bipartisan delegations from the committees

The Typical Path of a Successful Bill

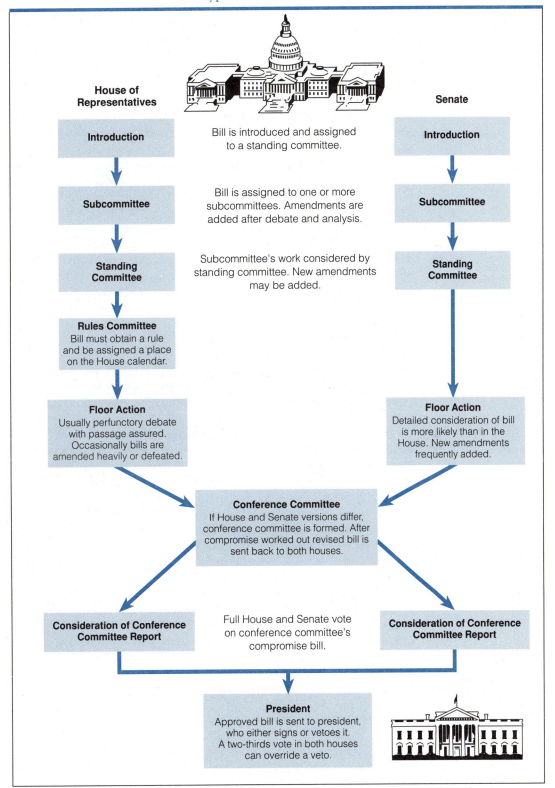

House of Representatives

Introduction

Subcommittee

Standing Committee

Rules Committee
Bill must obtain a rule and be assigned a place on the House calendar.

Floor Action
Usually perfunctory debate with passage assured. Occasionally bills are amended heavily or defeated.

Bill is introduced and assigned to a standing committee.

Bill is assigned to one or more subcommittees. Amendments are added after debate and analysis.

Subcommittee's work considered by standing committee. New amendments may be added.

Senate

Introduction

Subcommittee

Standing Committee

Floor Action
Detailed consideration of bill is more likely than in the House. New amendments frequently added.

Conference Committee
If House and Senate versions differ, conference committee is formed. After compromise worked out revised bill is sent back to both houses.

Consideration of Conference Committee Report

Full House and Senate vote on conference committee's compromise bill.

Consideration of Conference Committee Report

President
Approved bill is sent to president, who either signs or vetoes it. A two-thirds vote in both houses can override a veto.

which handled the bill. When the compromise version is completed, each house must approve the conference committee's handiwork; this approval is almost always given.

The bill now goes to the president, who has several choices. He can sign it into law, or allow it to become law merely by letting it sit on his desk for ten working days. Or, he can veto it and return it to Congress. If both houses then vote by a two-thirds majority to override the president's veto, the bill becomes law anyway.

From even this truncated survey of the lawmaking process, two conclusions are easily drawn. First, ample time is provided for extended public discussion of pending legislation. Almost any person or group that wishes to do so can express an opinion, write an article, call a representative, circulate petitions, or organize demonstrations. Hastily drawn or ill-conceived legislation rarely escapes public scrutiny. Second, the cards are heavily stacked in favor of the opponents of any proposed new law. Getting a bill adopted means getting over every hurdle, while opponents have to manage only a single victory. Moreover, opponents have ample opportunity to water the bill down, perhaps to the point of gutting it.

This latter fate particularly befalls bills which bestow relatively small benefits on a large number of people, but impose the costs on a small group. An illuminating example is automobile fuel efficiency standards. During the oil crunch of the mid-1970s, government-dictated fuel efficiency standards seemed a good way to encourage conservation. Failing to stop the bill's passage, the auto makers turned their efforts to putting off the day when the regulations would take effect. They were successful, and the measure has had little subsequent impact. On several occasions since then, the manufacturers of American cars have sought extensions and typically received them, publicly arguing that they cannot possibly meet the deadlines (in spite of the fact that most foreign-made cars exceed the requirements).[38] The reality is that the auto makers would have to downsize their cars and make smaller profits per unit; this, they believe, would eat into their overall profits. This same pattern occurs in a variety of other settings, especially when some powerful group is being forced to do something it does not want to do.

In sum, the American legislative process is quite slow and cumbersome. It encourages extended discussion, but has a built-in preference for the status quo. Consequently, new programs are inordinately difficult to establish; however, once established, they are equally difficult to abolish.

Staffs and Media Relations
Congressional Staffs

One of the hidden centers of power in Congress is the congressional staff: full-time employees of members, committees, and congressional support agencies.

Each member of the House and Senate is allocated a budget for hiring staff. Representatives receive a uniform amount while senators' stipends vary by the size of their state. Some of the staff perform routine clerical jobs, but others are deeply involved in policy making. Trusted aides often inform members about the policy implications of legislation, or advise them on which measures should be pushed, and which ignored. More directly political advice—what the polls are saying; whether a campaign should be launched for higher office; etc—also often emanates from staff people. Whatever their formal job description, their chief task is to advance their boss's political career. Oftentimes, this means devoting attention to constituents' needs: speeding up a passport application, helping a small town get a sewage grant, sending a flag to an elementary school, and so forth. These personal staffs have expanded markedly in recent years. In addition, representatives and senators seem to be concentrating more of their staff in district offices where they can more visibly perform these chores—a trend which some observers believe has helped contribute to the reelection success of incumbents.

All committees and subcommittees also have staffs (some exceeding one hundred people), which are appointed in varying proportions by the chair and the ranking minority member. These people are often experts in the policy areas covered by the committee's writ, and their influence can be very important. If the chairman has a close working relationship with key staff people, he may delegate much of the research, scheduling of witnesses, and sometimes dealings with other members of Congress to them. Particularly in the Senate, where expertise is more thinly spread, staff influence on committee decision making is prevalent. At times senators have even sent committee staff members to conference committee meetings to hammer out compromises with the representatives.

In addition, Congress has created four specialized nonpartisan agencies to which members may turn for help. The Congressional Research Service will provide background information or detailed research on any topic for any member. The General Accounting Office is both a financial auditor and a policy monitoring agency. That is, it conducts audits to ascertain whether money has been spent legally, and also does studies to measure the effectiveness of agencies in carrying out their missions. The Office of Technology Assessment was established to keep members abreast of the implications of technology; its skill level is high, although its influence has varied. Last, the Congressional Budget Office constitutes a bank of expertise on economic and budgetary matters which is a counterweight to the presidentially controlled Office of Management and Budget.

Table 5-5 shows the growth of the staff serving Congress, now numbering the size of a small city. Do these people, unelected by anyone and outnumbering the members thirty-nine to one, exercise too much power?

Several factors serve as protection against this possibility. First, most of the staff members of congressional offices and committees are relatively young people fresh from college or professional school, full of ideas and ambition. The great majority of them do not stay in their staff jobs for an extended period of time, using them instead as stepping-stones to other

---

BOX 5-1

Civic Democracy in Congress?

THE STUDY OF CONGRESS provides ample material for the individualist democrat. It is easy to catalog any number of instances in which members have worked to advance the narrow, parochial interests of their states or districts. While they sometimes clothe their positions with appeals to the general interest, it is clear that whatever they are pushing will bestow benefits primarily on a few. Electing members of Congress by local districts and by states, in fact, guarantees that they will be advocates for these locally based interests rather than for national ones.

But do members of Congress *always* push the narrow interests of their own constituents, with no thought to the broader interests of the nation? Or, does at least a shadow of civic democracy, with its aim of reasoned deliberation and a search for the public interest, appear in Congress? It seems so. For example, on the great issues of politics, such as war and peace or the confirmation of Supreme Court justices, there is evidence that members are indeed swayed by rational argument. Ethan Bronner found in his study of the nomination of Robert Bork for the Supreme Court that during that episode many senators listened to the arguments and carefully weighed them.[1] In the late 1970s, two journalists who accompanied individual senators for a sustained period of time were surprised by how often serious discussions of the public interest were undertaken.[2] More recently, Congress passed the Tax Reform Act of 1986, in spite of the fact that it was opposed by almost every special interest in the country.[3] There is support, then, for Steven Kelman's conclusion that "public spirit, even in Congress, lives."[4]

Even, in fact, when it comes to that most narrow issue of all—the federal pork barrel—concern for the public interest is not entirely absent. Take the matter of closing military bases. Nothing is closer to the heart of any member of Congress than her military base. These facilities generate hundreds, if not thousands, of jobs, along with substantial collateral spending. Every member of that body will fight strenuously, therefore, to protect a local base and keep it operating.

The end of the Cold War, however, opened the door on an opportunity to scale back American military commitments. This was obviously in the public interest on several counts. Here was a clear clash, then, between national and local interests. Members of Congress could have made their local needs primary

jobs in government, law firms, universities, think tanks, and interest groups. Thus, turnover dilutes any lasting collective influence. Further, while staff members do important work, they are fully responsible to the members. Aside from those in the nonpartisan service agencies, all staff are hired and fired at will by legislators. If a staff member has influence, it is

---

BOX 5–1

and opted to ignore national needs. They easily could have kept overall defense spending high enough to keep all the bases open, or simply have shifted money from other defense needs to finance the bases.

However, Congress chose to close some bases, devising an ingenious, and not altogether irrational, way to accomplish the task. It created an independent body called the Defense Base Closure and Realignment Commission. The Defense Department was ordered to compile a list of bases it no longer needed, given the changed world climate. The commission would examine the list and delete any base it thought worth saving. The list then would go to the president, who had to approve or disapprove it *in toto*. If he approved, the bases would be closed, unless both houses of Congress voted to overturn the entire report. In effect, once the recommendation

left the hands of the commission, it would be a package deal.

The Pentagon handed its list of obsolete bases to the commission in April of 1991. After all the expected appeals and cries of anguish, the commission removed only four bases from the list. On July 10, President Bush approved the list and sent it to Congress. On July 30, the House voted down a motion (60–364) to discard the report. Naturally, all sixty votes were from members with bases scheduled to be closed. A second list is due from the Defense Department in 1993, and a third in 1995; then, the same rules will apply.

From one perspective, the whole exercise seems designed to help everyone avoid responsibility. Congress, after all, is given constitutional authority over providing for the military, and should therefore make the critical decisions itself. From another perspective, though, this can

be seen as an attempt to serve the public interest. Congress could have taken the easy route and kept every base open. Realistically, some political cover had to be provided for members who had bases slated to be phased out. Thus, even in this supersensitive area for local political interests, consideration of the public interest was not completely absent.

---

[1] Ethan Bronner, *Battle for Justice* (New York: Doubleday, 1989).
[2] Bernard Ashball, *The Senate Nobody Knows* (New York: Doubleday, 1978) and Elizabeth Drew, *Senator* (New York: Simon and Schuster, 1979).
[3] See Jeffrey Birnbaum and Alan Murray, *Showdown at Gucci Gulch: Lawmakers, Lobbyists, and the Unlikely Triumph of Tax Reform* (New York: Random House, 1987). The authors call the law a "miracle that defied all the lessons of political science, logic, and history" (p. 285). Perhaps those lessons were all grounded in individualist democratic models, and hence were flawed.
[4] Steven Kelman, *Making Public Policy: A Hopeful View of American Government* (New York: Basic Books, 1988), 66.

because a member of Congress has given it to her. As long as there are competing sources of information and advice and the staff does not develop into a coordinated bureaucracy, there are therefore built-in checks on its power.

TABLE 5–5

The Growth of Congressional Staffs, 1965–1989

EMPLOYEE ASSIGNMENTS	NUMBER OF EMPLOYEES		
	1965	*1977*	*1989*
Members' staffs	5,804[a]	10,496	11,406
Committee and Subcommittee staffs[b]	1,080	2,804	2,999
Service agency staffs	4,509	6,444	6,292
Total	11,393	19,744	20,697

Source: Adapted from Ornstein, Mann, and Malbin, *Vital Statistics on Congress, 1991–92,* 126, 130, 135.

[a] 1967 figure.

[b] Standing committees only.

Congress and the Media

Nothing underscores the difference between Congress as a collection of individuals and Congress as a national law-making body as much as media coverage. A sharp cleavage exists between local news media, which focuses most often on the individual members, and the national media, whose attention is taken up with national politics and national political issues. Legislators, of course, are hungry for any media attention they can get, but they are acutely aware of the differences in the two markets.

Local newspapers are a godsend to senators and representatives. Most of them, for instance, will print press releases from a member's office with minimal editing. Sometimes a legislator "writes" a column (typically drafted by an aide) which many small weeklies and neighborhood papers will eagerly reprint. If local newspapers run an independently generated story concerning the member from the state or district, it is almost always laudatory.

Local television stations are also a valuable outlet for members of Congress. They can always get air time, by granting an interview when back in the district or state, or appearing on local talk shows. Local reporters are seldom versed in the details of legislation or the workings of Congress and the questions are usually "soft balls." In addition, the House and Senate, as well as both parties, have lavish facilities for taping television footage which can be fed to local stations, hoping they will use it in their newscasts, which of course they often do. The government-funded studios are not supposed to be used for political purposes, but as with the postal frank, the line between providing information and campaigning is wafer-thin. The studios operated by the parties, of course, are openly political.

National newspapers, such as the *New York Times,* the *Washington Post,* and the *Wall Street Journal,* maintain highly capable staff reporters to cover Congress on a full-time basis. These reporters usually write stories dealing with national issues, such as taxation, foreign policy, and the deficit; while they frequently quote individual representatives, they have other sources of information if they need it. They occasionally write articles focusing on one member, but usually only scandals will elicit sustained coverage. The national networks and talk shows likewise are geared to issues of national concern, and can secure any number of experts other than legislators. House members in particular find it very difficult to penetrate the national television networks until they have quite a bit of seniority, and then usually only in their areas of expertise.

National media coverage is important, if not vital, for those who desire a national policy profile, or who have eyes on higher office. However, appearing in either the national print or the national broadcast media may have minimal effect back home. Few people in most districts read the *New York Times* or other national papers, so that even a scandal reported there may not be politically crippling. Appearing as an interviewee on a national news program is too brief an affair to have much effect, and the political talk shows are watched more by the national political elite than by local political influentials. A college professor somewhere may think that Congressman Jones botched it when he tried to explain the impact of German unification, but the president of the Smithville Chamber of Commerce is unlikely ever to hear of the interview.

Local and national media, then, serve different audiences, have different criteria for evaluating members of Congress, and are viewed differently by the members themselves. Local outlets serve to enhance a member's electoral links with her state or district; national ones, to provide a forum for political elites—a distinction which reinforces the "two congresses" concept.

The Postwar Evolution of Congress

Both the Depression of the 1930s and World War II consolidated power in the hands of the president. Postwar political trends—especially foreign policy crises, the rush of economic growth, and even the civil rights revolution to a degree—continued to push power toward the presidency. A few legislators, primarily the senior committee chairs, were individually powerful in certain policy areas; however, the political temper of the two decades following World War II favored the executive, and even the courts, over Congress.

Lyndon Johnson and Richard Nixon pushed executive power and executive claims to power to unprecedented heights. In time, the Vietnam War and the scandals associated with Watergate provoked a reaction in Congress. Congressional leaders set about to reorganize themselves and to curtail executive dominance in two key areas: the budget and foreign policy.

The reorganization moves of the 1970s have been discussed above. To recapitulate, their immediate effect was to strengthen subcommittees and make committee chairs more responsive to sentiment within the majority party. By the late 1980s, though, the growing ideological cohesiveness of the parties was giving party leaders more stature and more power. Pronounced decentralization thus gave way to recentralization.[39]

Congress also made changes in its approach to the budget: Congress altered its budgetary calendar, created budget committees in both houses, and established the Congressional Budget Office. Although the CBO has become one of the most creditable sources of information in Washington, the budget committees are weakened by the fact that taxes and appropriations are both considered in other committees. The new timetable has had no noticeable effect whatever.[40]

The budget crises generated by the combination of tax cuts and spending increases enacted during the Reagan administration pushed Congress to seek other solutions. The dichotomy between specific interests and the general interest and the two Congresses discussed in the introduction comes home pointedly in budget politics. All citizens want budget restraint—except in the areas that affect them. Members of Congress dare not give in to cuts in programs beneficial to their constituents, for fear that others will merely take advantage of this act of self-sacrifice. With 535 people guarding any number of different programs, trying to rein in spending is all but impossible. Aware of its own inability to grapple successfully with this dilemma, in 1985 Congress resorted to the Gramm-Rudman-Hollings law. In essence, it provided that if future Congresses did not cut the deficit to a given amount, across-the-board cuts would go into effect (with certain exceptions, chiefly social security). In one view, Congress was acknowledging its own lack of will, like a dieter who removes food from the house; from another angle, though, this was a politically shrewd way to give its role of national policymaker more teeth (and provide political cover when the cuts came).

However, Gramm-Rudman-Hollings has yet to make much dent, for two reasons. The first is that it has so many loopholes that it is not nearly as extreme as it sounds. For example, either a recession or a war will suspend it. The second is that various tricks of creative accounting (or "smoke and mirrors" in budgetary parlance) allow several escape hatches from its ax. The major charade here is moving expenditures "off budget," so that the "budget" is closer to being balanced, but the spending continues. In the early nineties, budgetary deficits remain a central political issue, even during the recession that began in 1991.

Regarding foreign policy, the most significant flexing of congressional muscle was the War Powers Resolution of 1973. Passed over President Nixon's veto, the resolution was designed to curb the habit presidents had of sending troops abroad under their authority as commander-in-chief, without asking for formal congressional approval. The resolution had three provisions:

1. The president must officially notify Congress within forty-eight hours of any deployment of American troops into hostile action.
2. Within sixty days (or ninety days if he declares it an emergency), the president must seek approval from Congress for the keeping of the troops on foreign soil. If he does not, or if Congress withholds approval, the soldiers automatically come home.

3. At any time during the sixty- or ninety-day period, Congress may vote by resolution to withdraw the troops; the president may not veto this resolution.

Presidents from Nixon to Bush have argued that the law is unconstitutional, and many constitutional scholars agree.[41] As one major argument goes, Congress should not be able to bind the president by a resolution which by-passes the ordinary law-making process (by being exempt from the veto). In addition, many critics say the law is politically unwise, in that it gives an adversary advance notice of when troops may be withdrawn. In any event, the core of the act has yet to be tested. Presidents have more or less complied with the notification procedures, even while saying they need not do so. During the Persian Gulf War, the only event to date during which the other provisions would have applied,[42] President Bush asked Congress to vote its approval before hostilities began. Thus, the act remains untested in court.

Has Congress successfully reasserted itself and engineered a greater balance between legislative and executive power? The answer is uncertain. Presidential power certainly appears less grandiose than it did under Johnson and Nixon, but that may have resulted as much from public opinion and political circumstance as from congressional action.

Jimmy Carter's presidency was overwhelmed by continual bickering with members of Congress, caused both by his status as an outsider and by his inept handling of congressional egos.[43] Congress could do little to seize the initiative and the dispersal of power that occurred in the immediate aftermath of the reforms of the mid-1970s wrought havoc with most of Carter's legislative proposals.

President Reagan, particularly in his first term, demonstrated a certain mastery of Congress by his ability to reach beyond Washington to rally public support, and by his wooing of the remaining conservative Democrats. But as the Reagan presidency wore on, the Democrats in Congress, and particularly in the House, became better organized and were frequently able to block the president's initiatives.

George Bush's presidency has been characterized by a strong desire to build bipartisan ties. During his early months, Bush entertained a steady stream of legislators at social occasions, emphasized vague, general themes, and avoided controversy. The Persian Gulf War gave him a brief wave of popular acclaim and a respite from congressional criticism. As the economic recession deepened and the 1992 elections approached, though, relations became more strained.

Thus, these three presidencies offer a mixed picture of congressional power. Clearly, it would be very difficult for Congress to capture the political initiative in any circumstances. That would require extraordinary ideological cohesiveness in the majority party, very skillful leadership, and most likely a weakened presidency. Nonetheless, as we shall see in chapter 12, Congress can leave its imprint on policy, even when the president is relatively popular and opposed to congressional priorities. As long as it retains the power to make laws and control the budget—powers granted by the Constitution—Congress will be a critical part of the political system. It may temporarily cede some of its natural power to the president, as it did after World War II, but in time the checks and balances in the system will give those who sit in Congress the incentive and the means to influence the course of events.

SUMMARY

Congress is both a representative assembly of individuals and a body for the making of national laws. It has enormous powers at its disposal, but political realities—bicameralism, weak political parties, and decentralized decision making—stand in the way of their exercise. Its direct grants of power to set national economic and commercial policy and to exercise substantial leverage over foreign policy have been supplemented by a co-operative Supreme Court and innovations such as the federal grant. The Senate's connection to the executive in the appointment process and in treaties gives an added dimension to congressional power.

Electoral politics is central to Congress. Although incumbents are highly successful, there has been substantial turnover in the last decade, and there is no evidence that public wishes are being ignored on Capitol Hill. Congress is still unreflective of the population demographically, but some change has occurred in the last two decades. Representation of the peoples' interest may not be directly tied to legislators' traits, but legitimacy may be.

Congress' internal politics give weight to committees and political parties—the first is a decentralizing force, the other a centralizing one. The independent electoral campaigns members wage to get to Washington and the power of committees and subcommittees tug mightily in a decentralizing direction. Only when Congress' own leaders can agree among themselves and when they can control votes are the centralizing forces capable of asserting themselves; neither of these happens very often. Even so, party influences are important, and members vote more often with their fellow party members than with any other grouping.

The legislative process is normally slow and cumbersome. Proponents of a bill must clear a number of hurdles and fight unfriendly amendments. While this procedure allows for thorough public debate, it makes government inherently slow-moving.

Members of Congress turn to both their staffs and the media to connect them with the public; their staffs also provide help in performing their legislative chores. A sharp divide separates the local from the national media, and members of Congress rely far more on local news media for electoral purposes. Congressmen's reliance on staff for policy help expands the influence of this unelected corps of people on public policy. However, staff turnover and the fragmentation of staff hierarchies dilutes the control they can have over policy decisions.

Congress was weakened by the Cold War and the domestic economic trends of the postwar years. During these years, power crept to the White House and to the courts. In the 1970s, responding to the debacle in Vietnam and the Watergate scandal, Congress tried to reassert itself through internal reforms, new controls over the budget, and a new dictate on military adventures abroad. These moves have been only partially successful. They appear to have given a piece of the action to more members, but that has not necessarily strengthened the institution itself. Ronald Reagan proved that an astute (or lucky) president with popular backing can still control the political agenda.

Congress' constitutional position guarantees that it will always be a force in American politics. Presidents and judges may nibble away at its powers, often with congressional acquiescence or even encouragement, but those who sit in Congress will never allow it to become merely a showpiece. The political interests of those who look to Congress at any given point will ensure its continued political vitality. Ultimately, the political strengths and weaknesses of the American people will manifest themselves in Congress. It is a political mirror of the citizenry, revealing how we see ourselves. Voters, after all, choose their representatives and much of what these representatives do and how they behave relates to what their constituents expect of them. The legislators the voters send to Washington and voter expectations of them will, it is trite but true, affect the quality of American life.

ENDNOTES

1. This concept is borrowed from Roger H. Davidson and Walter J. Oleszek, *Congress and its Members,* 3d ed. (Washington: Congressional Quarterly Press, 1990).

2. *Heart of Atlanta Motel v. United States,* 379 U.S.241, 85 S.Ct. 348 (1964).

3. U.S. Constitution, Article I, sec. 8.

4. 17 U.S. (4 Wheat) 316 (1819).

5. When the federal grant programs first began, Massachusetts brought a case arguing that the "choice" was an illusion, and the conditions therefore illegal. The Supreme Court disagreed, noting that nothing in the law compelled Massachusetts to accept the grant. *Massachusetts v. Mellon,* 262 U.S. 447, 43 S.Ct. 597 (1923).

6. Sometimes there are simultaneous elections for two state Senate seats, such as when there is a death or resignation. One of the seats is then for an abbreviated term.

7. The actual constitutional provision is that "electors in each state shall have the qualifications requisite for electors of the most numerous branch of the state legislature" (Article I, sec. 2). In 1787, only males possessing a certain amount of property qualified to vote, but it was the broadest electorate of its time.

8. Actually, this is not as simple as it sounds, since there are various mathematical ways to deal with the fractions. See David Butler and Bruce Cain, *Congressional Redistricting: Comparative and Theoretical Perspectives* (New York: Macmillan, 1992) for a complete discussion of redistricting.

9. States are now required by law to have single-member districts, but it has not always been so.

10. *Wesberry v. Sanders,* 376 U.S. 1, 84 S.Ct. 526 (1964).

11. The position of the courts in this complex area is summarized in Rhodes Cook, "Map-Drawers Must Toe the Line in Upcoming Redistricting," *Congressional Quarterly,* September 1, 1990, 2786–2793. For a thorough discussion, see Abigail Thernstrom, *Whose Votes Count? Affirmative Action and Minority Voting Rights* (Cambridge, Mass.: Harvard University Press, 1987).

12. Unless otherwise noted, all statistical data in this chapter is drawn from Norman Ornstein, Thomas Mann, and Michael Malbin, *Vital Statistics on Congress, 1991–92* (Washington: Congressional Quarterly Press, 1992).

13. In 1990, new restrictions were placed on the franking privilege, but few observers expect the additional rules to have much effect.

14. Quoted in Davidson and Oleszek, *Congress,* 86.

15. See David Broder, "An Unchanging House," *Washington Post,* May 8, 1988.

16. George Will, "Perpetual Incumbency Machine," *Washington Post,* November 10, 1991.

17. See Meg Greenfield, "Everyone versus Congress," *Washington Post,* November 5, 1991.

18. The Washington campaign is covered in *Washington Post,* November 7, 1991.

19. An interesting coalition of interest groups also swung into action to defeat the term limits proposal. It included the National Rifle Association, the Sierra Club, the National Organization for Women, the AFL-CIO, the American Association of Trial Lawyers, the National Education Association, and the Philip Morris Company. It comes as no surprise that the only thing these groups have in common is that they all have close links to senior members of Congress. *Washington Post,* November 9, 1991.

20. In 1990, Colorado, Oklahoma, and California adopted term limits for their state legislators—yet another example of how the federal system allows for experimentation.

21. See Thomas Mann, *Unsafe at Any Margin: Interpreting Congressional Elections* (Washington: American Enterprise Institute, 1978).

22. Richard Fenno, *Home Style: House Members in their Districts* (Boston: Little, Brown, 1978).

23. A poll reported by the *Washington Post* in 1989 indicated that 60 percent of the public gave Congress a negative rating. *Post,* May 26, 1989.

24. Richard Fenno, "If As Ralph Nader Says, Congress Is 'the Broken Branch,' How Come We Love Our Congressmen So Much?" in Norman Ornstein, ed., *Congress in Change* (New York: Praeger, 1974), 277–97.

25. Fenno, *Home Style,* 168. Emphasis in original.

26. Fenno, *Home Style,* 153.

27. *Federalist* No. 57.

28. Quoted in Davidson and Oleszek, *Congress,* 326.

29. Neither major party has nominated a House member for president in the twentieth century.

30. Woodrow Wilson, *Congressional Government* (Boston: Houghton Mifflin, 1885), 79.

31. A listing of the committees and subcommittees with their members for the 102nd Congress is available in *Congressional Quarterly,* May 4, 1991.

32. See Lawrence Longley and Walter Oleszek, *Bicameral Politics: Conference Committees in Congress* (New Haven, Conn.: Yale University Press, 1989).

33. Richard Fenno, *Congressmen in Committees* (Boston: Little, Brown, 1973), 1.

34. Quoted in Davidson and Oleszek, *Congress,* 204.

35. The scene of Senator Howell Heflin of Alabama, who looked and sounded like an old-style southern politician who had stepped right out of a novel, criticizing black Supreme Court nominee Clarence Thomas in his 1991 confirmation hearings for not being liberal enough on civil rights captured this transformation perfectly.

36. See Barbara Sinclair, "House Majority Party Leadership in an Era of Legislative Constraints," in Roger Davidson, ed., *The Postreform Congress* (New York: St. Martin's, 1992), chap. 5.

37. This includes both houses. The number of actual bills would be somewhat lower, because many important bills are introduced in both houses at the same time.

38. These matters are surveyed in Allyson Pytte, "Fuel Economy: Japanese Drive a Hard Bargain in Emissions Standards," *Congressional Quarterly,* January 20, 1990, 164–65.

39. See Roger Davidson, "The Emergence of the Postreform Congress," in Davidson, ed., *Postreform Congress,* chap. 1.

40. See Rudolph Penner and Alan Abramson, *Broken Pursestrings: Congressional Budgeting,* 1974–1988 (Washington: Urban Institute Press, 1988).

41. See Stephen L. Carter, "The Constitutionality of the War Powers Resolution," *Virginia Law Review* 70 (1984), 101–34, for a summary and a rebuttal.

42. There was some discussion in 1982 about the act's applicability to President Reagan's deployment of U.S. Marines in Lebanon. However, the marines were withdrawn before the deadlines came, after 242 of them were tragically killed in a terrorist attack on their barracks.

43. See Eric Davis, "Legislative Liaison in the Carter Administration," *Political Science Quarterly* 94 (1979), 287–301.

FURTHER READING

In addition to these books, *Congressional Quarterly Weekly Report* is an excellent way to keep up with what is going on in Congress.

1. Canon, David. *Actors, Athletes, and Astronauts: Political Amateurs in the United States Congress.* Chicago: University of Chicago Press, 1990.

2. Davidson, Roger, ed. *The Postreform Congress.* New York: St. Martin's, 1992.
3. Fenno, Richard. *The Making of a Senator: Dan Quayle.* Washington: Congressional Quarterly Press, 1989.
4. Keefe, William. *Congress and the American People.* 3d ed. Englewood Cliffs, N.J.: Prentice-Hall, 1988.
5. Light, Paul. *Forging Legislation.* New York: Norton, 1992.
6. Maass, Arthur. *Congress and the Common Good.* New York: Basic Books, 1983.

THE PRESIDENCY

FEW ISSUES weighed on the minds of the Founding Fathers more heavily than the structure of the executive branch.[1] Speaking of the presidency, *The Federalist* No. 67 says, "There is hardly any part of the system which could have been attended with greater difficulty in the arrangement of it than this." Experience under the Articles had convinced the Founders that an executive branch was necessary. There was, first of all, no one to provide leadership. Governments, like all organizations, tend to drift if no one sees the broader picture and tries to move others toward the goals he or she envisages. While the Congress under the Articles had elected a presiding officer, actually calling him President of the United States, and divided itself into subject matter committees with chairs, the leadership efforts of all these people were feeble at best. Even had Congress possessed wide-ranging authority, the dilution of leadership which resulted from this diffusion of power would have crippled government. Power dispersed is power hobbled. Second, and of equal importance, there was no way to implement congressional decisions. When Congress passed a law, no one was directly charged with carrying it out. In government, as again in any organization, there are many steps between a decision made and a decision implemented. Without someone who has the specific responsibility to implement laws, those laws may languish, thus muting the effect of government itself.

Yet, while there was a clear consensus among the Founders about the need to create an executive, there were significant disagreements about how to structure it, and what powers to hand the office. In a sense, this was another version of their central dilemma: how to grant power and simultaneously limit it. While these men agreed with Alexander Hamilton that "energy in the executive is a leading character in the definition of good government,"[2] in the background always lay the sordid history of despotism, or power abused. If too much power were concentrated in the executive, it could unhinge the entire political system; but if the executive were impotent, government could become overly weak and perhaps even atrophy.

In the end, the framers pulled together some powers of the British monarch and combined them with some traditional functions of state governors. They tried to be certain that the chief executive would be politically independent of Congress by detaching the method of presidential selection from them; by making chief executive compensation un-

---

Opposite: *President George Bush meeting with senior advisors in the Oval Office.*

touchable during the term of office; and by making it difficult to remove the president. One fact which gave all of them confidence was the understanding that George Washington would be the first occupant of the office. "His presence in New York, the new capital after 1789, legitimized the administration of executive power and, really, the entire experiment in republican government," notes one historian.[3]

Although much has clearly changed since the days of Washington's inauguration, leadership and implementation remain central to the presidential task. In our day, leadership has taken on new dimensions, reaching beyond the institutions of government. A modern president is not only at the center of the machinery of government, but also a leader in the public domain. He now exercises decisive influence in setting the political agenda—in both narrow and broad senses of that term. He obviously proposes laws to Congress, but he also speaks to our more personal and private social concerns. He sets a tone in society that has incalculable consequences. How he conducts himself, what he says, how he defines American society, to which of our instincts he speaks—all these things seep into people's consciences, affecting their views of citizenship and the quality of their everyday lives. The president cannot create virtue where there is none, nor stop all unpleasantness, but he is first citizen of the nation. The picture he paints of and for Americans is as important as it is intangible.

THE CONSTITUTIONAL BASIS OF PRESIDENTIAL POWER

The starting point for any analysis of the presidency must be the Constitution, for from it presidents derive their legal powers to act. Article II, Sections 2 and 3 list the presidential powers, of which the following are the most important:

1. Serving as commander-in-chief of the armed forces;
2. Granting pardons;
3. Negotiating treaties (two-thirds vote of approval in Senate required);
4. Appointing ambassadors, judges, and major federal office-holders (with Senate approval);
5. Giving Congress "information on the State of the Union" and recommending to it "such measures as he shall judge necessary and expedient";
6. Calling special sessions of Congress;
7. Receiving ambassadors from foreign countries; and
8. Taking "care that the laws be faithfully executed."

Additionally, in Article I, Section 7, the president is given the power to veto laws passed by Congress.

Taken as a whole, these provisions create but a skeleton of power, the flesh on which can expand or contract depending on the political situation and the personality of the occupant. During wartime, power naturally gravitates to the president, as military matters transcend all other concerns. In less traumatic times, power can still flow toward the White House if there is a domestic crisis of some sort, such as economic upheaval. During these periods, though, it will take considerable political skill and agility to obtain and exercise political authority, for Congress will be less inclined to defer to the president's judgment alone. In more ordinary times, his political skill will have to be even greater if he seeks to be a powerful president and significantly affect the flow of events.

Roots of the Contemporary Presidency

From 1789 through the first third of the twentieth century, the power of the presidency ebbed and flowed. In the nineteenth century, both Thomas Jefferson and Andrew Jackson rode strong popular victories to power and swept majorities for their party into Congress as well. For a while, this executive-legislative cohesion enabled them to pursue their own programs with minimal opposition. Presidents Abraham Lincoln and Woodrow Wilson presided over massive war efforts, consolidating vast powers in their hands. Theodore Roosevelt capitalized on widespread demands for economic reform, along with a bellicose foreign policy whenever he could find an opportunity for it, to bolster presidential power. However, none of these men were able to pass on their accretions of power to their successors. Within a few years of each of them, or even immediately afterwards, there were weak or ineffectual presidents. The history books give us James Madison, John Tyler, Andrew Johnson, Warren Harding, and William Howard Taft, all of whom helplessly watched, or in some cases encouraged, the seepage of power to other quarters.

Before the Second World War, students of American politics often debated the proper scope of presidential power. Theodore Roosevelt argued that the president is a "steward" of the public interest, and that he should do anything he can—anything that is not specifically forbidden by the Constitution—to pursue that end. Roosevelt wrote that he "declined to adopt the view that what was imperatively necessary for the nation could not be done by the President unless he could find some specific authorization to do it. My belief was that it was not only his right but his duty to do anything that the needs of the nation demanded, unless such action was forbidden by the Constitution or by the laws."[4] In contrast, William Howard Taft argued for what has been labeled the "constructionist" theory of the presidency: "The true view of the executive function is, as I conceive it, that the president can exercise no power which cannot be fairly and reasonably traced to some specific grant of power . . . either in the federal Constitution or in an act of Congress. . . . There is no undefined residuum of power which he can exercise because it seems to him to be in the public interest."[5]

Whatever the theoretical merits of these contending positions, all presidents since 1933 have adhered to Roosevelt's view, arguing that they speak for the American people in a way that no others do, energetically pushing proposals they deem in the public interest, even dreaming of places in history as "great presidents" whose accomplishments long outlive their tenures in office. Some, of course, have been more successful than others, but the point is that all have tried to be powerful and to use that power for certain ends; and by the standards of the nineteenth century, even the least successful have been quite powerful. What has led to this state of affairs, ending the almost rhythmic alternation of strength and weakness in the executive branch?

Sources of Strength

The answer is composed of four principal parts: the changed role of the United States in world politics; the vastly increased role of government in American society; the growth of the mass media; and the democratization of the system of choosing a president.

Both the Civil War and World War I, while they absorbed the energy of the nation for their durations, were followed by rapid demobilizations. The end of World War II, however, was dramatically different. Within a short period, the Cold War punctuated the transition to peace, leading to a massive military buildup, the erection of a system of alliances, and a series of international crises, from Korea to Cuba. The preference of the political system for executive power in wartime, even when the shooting is only intermittent, swung into place. Foreign policy, in one sense, is only a mild version of war, and when it is the dominant item on the political agenda, it is only natural that power will come to rest increasingly at the White House.

At the same time, domestic politics was also pushing power the president's way. Building on the precedents of the New Deal, Franklin D. Roosevelt's wide-ranging program to fight the Depression of the 1930s, Congress enacted a variety of laws establishing governmental responsibility for several new facets of American life, and typically giving the president new powers in the process. Sometimes Congress merely required a report from the president, such as the Economic Report required by the Employment Act of 1946, but other times it handed the chief executive legal authority to act, such as the power to impose wage and price controls. Surveying these developments in 1981, James Sundquist wrote that "the powers of the modern presidency clearly were not wrested by self-seeking chief executives from a struggling but ultimately yielding Congress in a series of constitutional coups-d'état. On the contrary, every transaction embodying a shift in power and influence was one of mutual consent, for the shifts were made pursuant to law, and the Congress wrote and passed the laws."[6] In neither example given above, for instance, did the president seek the new power handed to him.

Another major factor has been the growth of the mass media, particularly television. Until the advent of newspaper pictures (first used extensively in the 1930s) and radio, the president was a distant personage to most Americans: a somber portrait gracing the local post office, or perhaps a fluttering image on a movie newsreel. Now, his face and voice are easily recognized by virtually every adult. This direct bond with the populace at large has not only increased his power by focusing more attention on

President Bush describing the goals of an upcoming trip to Panama and Brazil. Presidents try to link themselves with the grandeur of the office, by speaking with symbols such as Air Force One in the background.

himself (try watching an evening newscast without a story on the president); it has also reduced the influence of intermediaries. Franklin D. Roosevelt discovered a powerful tool in his fireside chats, enabling him to reach beyond the traditional party leaders and local politicos who had been the pre–mass media transmission belts of political communication. Subsequent presidents have made extensive use of their ability to commandeer television and radio time to take their case directly to the people. If the president is successful in building public support, the opposition in Congress to a presidential proposal may well be overwhelmed.

Finally, the process of choosing a president has become more democratized. While the actual election of the president was relatively democratic throughout the twentieth century (if we do not, of course, count the glaring exceptions that generally African Americans could not vote in the south until the 1960s, and that women became eligible to vote only in 1920), the nominating process was oligarchic. Since 1972, though, the nomination process has become much more open to mass participation (details are discussed later in this chapter). As a result, the president can claim more than ever to represent the authentic voice of the people in a way that no other public figure can.

The contemporary presidency, then, is the product of these four forces. Each of them contains the seeds of vast power: a relatively unchecked hand in foreign policy; substantial legal powers to propose new approaches to domestic policy (and sometimes to act), coupled with a huge bureaucracy under his jurisdiction; unparalleled access to the media; and a more direct popular mandate than any other public figure.

Elements of Potential Weakness

Yet, it is important to recognize that each of these four factors may be a constraint on presidential power as well as a source of strength. The freedom to act in foreign policy, for instance, brings responsibility for failure. President Johnson's disastrous course in Vietnam undid the powerful political coalition backing his domestic policies and eventually led to his downfall. Likewise, President Carter's inability to deal effectively with Iran contributed to his image as an embattled man who was in over his head.

Similarly, the grants of domestic power by Congress create political demands that the president in fact act. If inflation is up, employment is down, housing is more expensive, test scores are falling, high school dropout rates are rising, teenage pregnancy is increasing, savings are shrinking, productivity is slipping, gasoline is in short supply, airplanes are unsafe or running late, crime rates are rising, crop prices are falling, riots are engulfing a major city—or even if the ozone layer is shrinking, hurricanes and earthquakes are creating misery, or dry summer fires are burning in the national forests—the president is expected to "do something." Obviously, all of these problems stem from a variety of factors, many of them often far beyond the control of government, much less one person. Furthermore, there is seldom a consensus on what should be done (or can be done), and any presidential proposal is bound to generate political opposition from some quarter.

Media coverage, too, has its downside for the president. While enormous resources are available for the chief executive to dominate and focus the news—timing statements for coverage on the evening newscasts; currying favor with reporters; creating pleasant photo opportunities (with foreign leaders, sports champions, and smiling children, for example)—the constant glare of the cameras can catch the president at awkward times. An incident may be nothing more serious than Lyndon Johnson pulling his dog's ears, Gerald Ford bumping his head, or Jimmy Carter swiping at a rabbit from his canoe (although even these trivialities create images). More serious may be a damaging off-the-cuff remark or a badly timed or insensitive phrase. In addition, the professional journalists who cover the White House can become a nemesis to the president. Most of the reporters assigned to the White House beat are highly talented, and most are favorably disposed toward the presidency in general, and usually even to the current occupant. However, the more energetic among them are always seeking inside stories by developing close contacts with presidential underlings. Inevitably, the game of leak and counterleak begins in every administration as people jockey for position (with the president often as engaged as anyone), and unflattering stories end up in the newspapers and on television. In addition, nothing can catapult a journalist's career upward faster than uncovering corruption or stupidity in high places. Thus, the search is always on.

Democratization is also a double-edged sword. By having to reach farther into the public to receive the nomination, a modern presidential candidate faces a more complex task of coalition building than did his predecessors. The construction of a winning coalition as the contest proceeds through the primary and caucus states can create political commitments which are difficult to shed—both during the general election and, more importantly, once in office. The number and diversity of political IOUs with which a contemporary president enters the Oval Office have therefore increased, and this fact can seriously inhibit his freedom.

SELECTING A PRESIDENT
The Constitutional Commands

Formally, we still select a president the same way we always have, through the cumbersome electoral college. Each state chooses a number of people—a total equal to that state's representation in the House and Senate—to serve as electors. These people may be chosen by whatever method the legislature of the state thinks best, with only the stipulation that no federal officeholders may be electors. The electors then convene in the fifty state capitals and cast ballots for president and vice president, transmitting their choices to Congress.[7] The days of their choosing and voting are designated by Congress in advance. If no candidate receives an absolute majority of the votes, the House of Representatives chooses the president from among the top three vote recipients, with the balloting done by states. (Should no one receive a majority of the vote for vice president, the Senate, with each senator voting as an individual, selects from the top two.)

This was an ingenious way to detach presidential selection from Congress and state governments, but in truth, none of the drafters had the slightest idea how it would work in practice. Apparently, quite a few thought the electors would serve a nominating function, with the actual choice made most often by the House. This notion, and all the other calculations, did not foresee the spread of democratic tenets and the rise of political parties. If they could have peered into the future, of course, many of them would have seen these two developments as a calamity.

In any event, state legislatures soon began turning the electoral choice over to the voters; by the time of the Civil War, only South Carolina's legislature continued choosing electors itself. Within a few years, slates of electors appeared which were pledged to a particular person; this transferred the actual choice among candidates to the voters. Before long, national campaigns were organized by the political parties, who had faithful supporters on an electoral list for each state. Legislatures adopted several practices which made the voters' choices easier, such as grouping the electors by party, or allowing a vote to be cast simply for a certain number of electors pledged to a certain candidate.

FIGURE 6–1
Electoral Votes after the 1990 Census

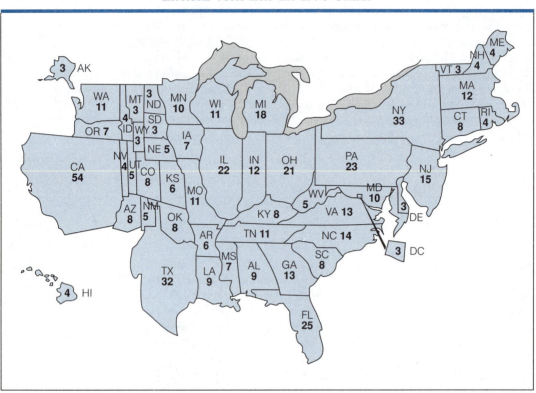

States are drawn in proportion to their number of electoral votes. Each state receives electoral votes equal to the number of its U.S. House representatives plus its two senators.

At the moment, all states choose their electors by popular vote, and all follow a winner-take-all rule. That is, there is only one ballot, and a plurality is sufficient to secure all the electors, or "carry the state."

Problems with the Electoral College

The electoral college is almost universally reviled, and it does have serious drawbacks.[8] As yet, though, there is no consensus on what to replace it with.[9] One oft-cited issue is the "unfaithful elector" problem. Constitutionally, an elector is a free agent, not bound by her pledge.[10] A few electors have in fact voted contrary to their pledges, but this has never affected an election's outcome. In a close election, however, there is always the chance that it could. More likely is the possibility that a candidate could win the popular vote but lose the electoral vote. This could happen if one candidate carried by a slim margin the minimum number of states needed to reach a majority of electoral votes (270), but lost all the other states badly. In fact, in 1988 some Dukakis strategists were conceding the popular vote to Bush, but thought they might be able to carry enough large industrial states by a slight margin and win the electoral vote. Dukakis, however, rejected their advice that he focus his campaign solely in those states in the waning weeks. Had he done so and won, undoubtedly the movement for electoral change would have been given a huge boost.

In the normal course of events, the most serious problem is that the system skews the value of votes. Some groups have their influence magnified, for instance, because they are concentrated in a few large states. The importance of Jewish votes in New York and Hispanic votes in California and Texas are good examples. If either group were spread evenly over the fifty states, its influence would diminish. In contrast, of course, some groups have their voting influence diluted because they are spread among more states. An equally pernicious consequence is the way campaigns are affected by "safe states." Suppose, for example, that candidate A has a lead of 70 percent–30 percent over candidate B in the polls in a given state. Candidate B's backers feel that a concerted push might narrow that lead to 55 percent–45 percent. But why should they make the effort? Even if it is successful, it will count for naught. At the same time, candidate A will probably make only minimal gestures in the state. This situation has two unhealthy consequences. First, regardless of who wins the presidency, the political interests in the above-mentioned state who backed the winner will have less access to the White House than will the winner's allies in other, more marginal states. This is especially true if candidate B is the winner. Second, it is quite discouraging to B's supporters to know that their votes mean nothing. Why, aside from making a symbolic gesture, should they even bother to vote? Surely, some of our cynicism about presidential elections and our dismal turnout figures are rooted here. (In fact, A's backers have less incentive to vote also.)

With this overview of the structure in mind, it is time to step back and examine the process from its inception. The presidential campaign begins literally the day after the previous election, with by far the longest stretch of time devoted to securing the nominations of the two major parties.

The Nominations

According to their rules, both parties nominate their presidential candidates at summer conventions during the election year; then, the campaign between the party nominees traditionally kicks off on Labor Day. Since the reforms of the 1970s, however, the conventions have become the most anti-climactic of affairs, held primarily to rally the faithful, scour the opposition, and showcase the candidate. About the only drama is the choice of a vice-presidential running mate, particularly when the candidate is not the incumbent.

A party convention is made up of delegates representing the membership of that party in each state. Each major party still requires a majority vote of the delegates to secure the nomination; each still goes through a tedious roll call of the states. But since the late 1960s, a change has occurred regarding who the delegates are and how they are chosen. In years past, delegates were usually handpicked by state party bosses of one type or another, although the interaction between the grass-roots party members and the professional politicians varied markedly from state to state. In general, though, party notables came to the conventions with blocs of delegates under their control and struck deals of one sort or another (probably some even in the smoke-filled rooms of legend) before they agreed to throw their support to one or another candidate. Although the concerns of rank-and-file Democrats and Republicans were relevant in that they entered the calculations of the party leaders, the process was largely detached from mass participation.

The Growth of Primaries

During the Progressive era, immediately preceding the First World War, several states adopted the *presidential primary* as a way to democratize the process. Primaries were *party* elections held before the conventions, to allow state voters to express their preferences. Some were merely advisory; others were binding to some degree. Soon after World War I, however, the popularity of the primary declined, as the results had proved disappointing. Turnout was low; the major candidates avoided most of them (fearing a loss would tarnish their image); the primaries were costly; and, of course, the party regulars opposed them.

The populist mood of the 1960s revived the idea of primaries, with the Democratic nomination race of 1968 providing an important catalyst. After President Johnson's withdrawal, Vice President Hubert Humphrey entered the free-for-all, but studiously avoided the remaining primaries. By cultivating the movers and shakers who controlled blocs of delegates—people such as Chicago's Mayor Richard Daley and powerful labor and civil rights leaders—Humphrey secured the nomination. The tumultuous convention which resulted was a Pyrrhic victory for the old order, however.

In the wake of that disaster, made all the more poignant by Humphrey's loss, a party reform commission was appointed which crafted a new set of rules, the details of which we will discuss in chapter 10. The upshot was that by 1972 it was barely conceivable, and by 1976 it was unthinkable, that any viable candidate could come to the convention without a string of impressive primary victories. At the state level, the same impetus to reform created the wave of new primaries that the revised rules seemed to favor. Even those states which retained some form of caucus method for delegate selection (party meetings at local and other levels) passed laws opening the caucuses up to anyone desiring to participate.

The Democratic presidential candidates debating in Goffstown, New Hampshire, early in the 1992 primary season. From left to right are Tom Harkin, Bill Clinton, Bob Kerrey, Paul Tsongas, and Jerry Brown.

Results of the Reforms

The central place now assumed by primaries and open caucuses has had several important effects on presidential aspirants. First, it has dictated an earlier decision for entering the race and backed the whole process up many months. The fact that the early caucuses and primaries are crucial means that presidential hopefuls must get to work early to build an organization and support in those states. Poor early showings are now fatal. Second, the type of campaign mounted and the organization this necessitates have changed significantly. When the focus was on canvassing delegates, political contacts, phone calls, and low-key visits were the modus operandi. Now, a campaign must be waged to woo the voters; this requires especially high-visibility appearances and mass media advertising.

The early primaries and caucuses are of particular importance. Iowa holds its caucuses first and New Hampshire's primary follows soon afterwards—both in February. It is commonly recognized that these early contests are vital. But must this be so? If a candidate were from the west, for example, why should she not make only token efforts in Iowa and New Hampshire, waiting to fight her best fight on more friendly soil? After all, Iowa and New Hampshire are atypical states by any measure; in addition, the two states combined send only a handful of delegates to the conventions.

The reason that all the candidates make serious efforts in these two states is the role public perceptions and the media have come to play.

TABLE 6-1

Methods and Dates of Selecting Convention Delegates

STATE	DELEGATE SELECTION METHOD	1992 DATE
Iowa	Caucus	February 10
New Hampshire	Primary	February 18
Maine	Caucus	February 23
South Dakota	Primary	February 25
Colorado	Primary	March 3
Georgia	Primary	March 3
Idaho	Caucus (D) Primary (R)	March 3
Maryland	Primary	March 3
Minnesota	Caucus	March 3
Utah	Caucus	March 3
Washington	Caucus (D) Primary (R)	March 3
North Dakota	Caucus	March 5–19
Arizona	Caucus	March 7
South Carolina	Primary	March 7
Wyoming	Caucus	March 7
Nevada	Caucus	March 8
Delaware	Caucus	March 10
Florida	Primary	March 10
Hawaii	Caucus	March 10
Louisiana	Primary	March 10
Massachusetts	Primary	March 10
Mississippi	Primary	March 10
Missouri	Caucus	March 10
Oklahoma	Primary	March 10
Rhode Island	Primary	March 10

continued

When most candidates announce for the presidency, they are virtually unknown outside their own states. When it has no incumbent, a political party normally produces in the neighborhood of ten candidates. Since this is too many for the general public to digest, the early primaries serve to narrow the field.

Yet, it is curious and complex how this narrowing occurs. It may not be by "winning" or "losing" that some are given the mantle to carry on and others are forced to give up their aspirations. Gazing into some political crystal ball, the media's campaign-watching gurus speculate beforehand about how well the various candidates should do in the Iowa caucuses and the New Hampshire primary. Our western candidate alluded to above, for example, would probably be slated for a rather low finish. These prognostications establish intangible "benchmarks." A candidate who then does

TABLE 6-1

Methods and Dates of Selecting Convention Delegates—*continued*

STATE	DELEGATE SELECTION METHOD	1992 DATE
Tennessee	Primary	March 10
Texas	Primary and Caucus (D) Primary (R)	March 10
Illinois	Primary	March 17
Michigan	Primary	March 17
Connecticut	Primary	March 24
Vermont	Caucus	March 31
Alaska	Caucus	April 2
Kansas	Primary	April 7
New York	Primary	April 7
Wisconsin	Primary	April 7
Virginia	Caucus	April 11
Pennsylvania	Primary	April 28
District of Columbia	Primary	May 5
Indiana	Primary	May 5
North Carolina	Primary	May 5
Ohio	Primary	May 5
Nebraska	Primary	May 12
West Virginia	Primary	May 12
Oregon	Primary	May 19
Arkansas	Primary	May 26
Kentucky	Primary	May 26
Alabama	Primary	June 2
California	Primary	June 2
Montana	Primary	June 2
New Jersey	Primary	June 2
New Mexico	Primary	June 2

better or worse than the watchers have predicted is either heralded as a "winner" or tagged as a "loser." Momentum is established or lost; contributions go up or down; political writers treat her more or less seriously; television newspeople clamor for interviews or practice avoidance; campaign aides are hailed as geniuses or derided as fools.

Very soon, the field is narrowed to two or three party hopefuls, and the victor is usually decided by mid–primary season. There is then a lull, during which the winner—now the candidate for that party—tries to garner the backing of the defeated and prepare for the convention. Some initial sparring with the opposing party takes place, but the emphasis is on healing the wounds within the party.

The party convention is carefully stage-managed by the candidate's people. Several prominent figures are solicited to give partisan speeches, particularly the one that opens the convention: the *keynote address*. The nomination itself goes like clockwork, while speculation mounts on a vice-presidential choice. Finally, the acceptance speech concludes the affair. Usually, a candidate touches on the themes he will emphasize during the campaign, and commentators watch carefully both the speech's substance and its style. Another stage in measuring this person's ability to be president has been entered.

The General Election

With the two major party candidates facing each other, the goal now is to obtain a majority of electoral votes.[11] This means appealing to enough voters so that the candidate carries enough states to obtain 270 electoral votes. Voters, however, are not only autonomous individuals; they are also members of multiple and overlapping groups and groupings: farmers, dentists, machinists, loggers, suburbanites, veterans, African Americans, Hispanics, southerners, Catholics, the elderly, homeowners, parents, feminists, and so forth ad infinitum. A campaign strategy must be developed that will put together a coalition of enough of these voters located in the proper states to win. At the same time, people are not merely a composite of their various group characteristics. Many seem to have a view of citizenship that makes them strive at least to consider the public interest when voting. Thus, effective campaigns are based on both the individualist and the civic models of democracy.

An appeal based solely on the needs of various groups is therefore likely to fail. However, people cannot be expected to transcend fully the needs of the groups to which they belong and a candidate who does not make some of these appeals will also be likely to lose. On one level, then, the campaign is pitched at specific groups, promising such things as no cuts in social security; new help for cities with harbors; aid for education; more help for small farmers; and so on. Naturally, an attempt is also made to avoid saying anything that would offend any group, since there is always a chance that some members of each group will swing the candidate's way. On another level, most candidates try to push ideas involving the public interest, attempting to attach people to larger purposes than their own narrow interests. The fact that candidates continue to do this is some evidence that the public interest is indeed important to the voters. If people only voted according to their personal interests, politicians would surely have found that out by now, and given up long ago any attempt to argue for the public interest. What the citizenry believes, therefore, is critical in influencing how candidates for public office behave.

While this contest over issues is going on, simultaneously an equally important contest is being waged in the realm of character, personality, and image. Both candidates try to appear—and the press measures their ability to appear—"presidential." What this entails is difficult to state with any precision, but is no less real for being intangible. The kiss of death is a candidate's looking foolish or acting out of control, but even less dramatic failings will draw sustained commentary. Ronald Reagan's 1984

Political ads often create lasting impressions of a presidential campaign. Left: The famous "Girl with a Daisy" ad used by the Johnson campaign in 1964 implied that Senator Barry Goldwater could not be trusted with the future of the country in the nuclear age. Right: This Bush ad from 1992 sought to raise concerns among voters that his opponent, Governor Bill Clinton, would raise their taxes.

campaign suffered a blow in his first debate with Walter Mondale when he appeared forgetful and absent-minded, bringing suggestions that perhaps his age was beginning to show. In 1988, Michael Dukakis brought little but ridicule on himself when he tried to ride in a tank with a helmet on, and appeared at a forest fire in Wyoming in newly bought cowboy boots. Bill Clinton was dogged throughout the 1992 campaign by questions about his sex life, draft history, and marijuana use.

By and large, these images are direct and indirect media creations. The images of a candidate's performance are sent directly into the homes of the voters, where people can form their own judgments. But media commentary also plays a role. If print and broadcast journalists start saying a candidate's image is "unpresidential," that opinion has some weight, and it may become self-reinforcing. Sometimes a candidate can overcome a negative image, as Reagan did in 1984; for other candidates, such as Dukakis, the problem only gets worse as the campaign wears on.

Finally, election day comes: the first Tuesday after the first Monday in November. For one of the candidates, the months and perhaps years of campaigning will have come to naught; she will most likely be only a footnote in the history books. As for the other, he has about two months to prepare to become president. The two critical tasks at this point are putting together a team to lead the executive branch and preparing to deal with Congress.

THE PRESIDENT AND THE EXECUTIVE BRANCH

We often hear references to "the administration" in news reports and political commentary. Altogether, this term refers to the roughly twenty-five hundred people a president can appoint when he assumes office, and who will depart with (or before) him. In everyday conversation, though, this is a shorthand way to describe the top one hundred or so people who occupy administrative and advisory positions near the president. Government organization may sound like a dry and tedious subject in contrast to the drama and excitement of campaigns, but it is necessary to grasp who sits where; who reports to whom; who has what authority; and what people's career interests are, in order to understand how government works.

On paper, almost all federal employees, both civilian and military, report to the president. However, both military personnel and career civil servants have working lives which will span several administrations. Thus, while they are loyal to the president in a general sort of way, and some may even be enthusiastic backers, their deepest loyalties are to their agencies and their careers within them. Every president has had his frustrations with the entrenched military services and the federal bureaucracy as he has sought to bend them to his own purposes. Presidents' experiences in this regard will be discussed in more detail in chapter 7.

Cabinet Secretaries

Turning to the appointees, the most visible members of a presidential administration are the cabinet secretaries. These people head regular government departments which have a legal responsibility for program administration. The various departments, along with their budgets and numbers of personnel, are presented in table 6–2. Moving down the organizational ladder, the president can also appoint several assistant or deputy secretaries in each department.

A cabinet officer has two vital functions to perform. First, she gives the president policy advice in her area of expertise; second, she administers her department. In theory, this structural arrangement should work fairly well. The president should receive expert advice from those actually overseeing the programs, and policy direction should be set by the president's people, since they sit atop the departmental organization. Civil servants should provide information to the secretary for her use in advising the president, and then dutifully carry out whatever their political masters bid them do.

As with all plausible ideas, there is some truth to this model. However, politics, human nature, and organizational reality have their effects too. First of all, cabinet secretaries and their politically appointed assistants are not only the president's people. Powerful interest groups will strive hard to influence the appointment of secretaries, and a president would be courting trouble if he completely ignored the wishes of farm groups regarding the secretary of agriculture, business interests concerning the secretary of commerce, or educators in choosing the secretary of education. He may choose, of course, to risk antagonizing a few groups (particularly if he drew little support from them in the election), but he cannot exercise a free hand in every appointment. Then, too, there will

TABLE 6–2

Cabinet-Level Executive Departments

DEPARTMENT	DATE ESTABLISHED	1991 BUDGET (millions)	1991 PERSONNEL
State	1789	4.4	25,400
Treasury	1789	276.2	160,200
Defense[a]	1789	316.9	969,100[b]
Interior	1849	6.9	72,300
Justice	1870[c]	9.0	84,100
Agriculture	1889[d]	60.1	110,300
Commerce	1903[e]	2.6	39,000
Labor	1913[e]	32.6	17,700
Housing and Urban Development	1965	27.6	13,600
Transportation	1966	31.0	66,000[f]
Energy	1977	16.1	17,800
Health and Human Services	1979[g]	222.9[h]	121,100
Education	1979[g]	27.5	4,600
Veterans Affairs	1988[i]	33.2	217,700

[a]Began as War Department. Present name adopted in 1947.

[b]Civilian employees only. An additional 2,125,700 military personnel also fall under the Department of Defense.

[c]An Attorney General with cabinet rank was appointed in 1789, but a separate department was not created until 1870.

[d]Established in 1862 but not given cabinet status until 1889.

[e]Original title was Commerce and Labor. Labor was broken off as separate department in 1913.

[f]Does not include 37,700 Coast Guard personnel, since they have military status.

[g]A Department of Health, Education, and Welfare was created in 1953. In 1979 it was divided into these two departments.

[h]Does not include social security payments, since they are from a separate trust fund. In 1991, they constituted an additional $269,800 million.

[i]Established as an independent agency in 1930. Given cabinet status in 1988.

have to be a certain amount of ethnic, gender, and regional balancing. As a result, it is not uncommon that a president may not even have met some of his cabinet before he extends them an invitation to office. Thus, the trust that is needed in close working relationships must be built from scratch.[12]

A second obstacle to cabinet officers' effectiveness is that once in office, cabinet secretaries and their underlings naturally must spend far more time running their departments than consulting with White House people. Like anthropologists who often become attached to the cultures they study, these people can end up seeing primarily the "department point of view." Most importantly, that point of view is unlikely to support any policy that trims budgets or people from the department. The Department of Agriculture, for example, would not advise implementation of a program which eliminated half the department. Thus, when a secretary offers advice to the president, that advice is more often than not tainted by the needs of the department she heads. While this does not make the advice useless, it makes it less than objective and not always geared to the president's political needs.

Some presidents have believed they could counter this tendency by having the cabinet meet collectively and using it as a decision-making committee. Seldom does this work out, for several reasons. First, most cabinet members have little or no expertise outside their own areas, and are hesitant to make suggestions to their colleagues. Of more importance, though, is the fact that unlike cabinet members in parliamentary systems, their political fates are only loosely tied together (see comparative politics box in this chapter). Cabinet members relate to the president on a one-on-one basis, rather than as a body. Furthermore, they have not worked as a team in the past, and are unlikely to do so again. Most secretaries have echoed the blunt sentiments of a former official of the Carter administration: "Policy gets made on a one-on-one relationship between each cabinet secretary and the president."[13]

The Executive Office of the President

Franklin D. Roosevelt, sensing all these inadequacies, argued for the establishment of several agencies whose sole function would be to give the president advice. Freed from the burdens of operating programs, presumably they would offer advice that was more objective and more useful to the president politically. Congress finally consented to this proposal in 1939. Through the years, Congress has added several new agencies, bureaus, and councils to the presidential advisory establishment, and has grouped them loosely under the "Executive Office of the President" (EOP). The Executive Office thus has little cohesiveness, and the president really determines how much to rely on each agency.

The most important of the agencies under this roof is the Office of Management and Budget (OMB). Until World War I, Congress wrote the federal budget by itself, with only minimal intervention from the White House. Faced with the complexities of modern budgets, though, in 1921 Congress asked the president to send it a proposed budget each fiscal year. To aid the president in preparing this budget, a Bureau of the Budget was created in the Treasury Department. In 1939, the Bureau was moved to the new Executive Office, allowing it to report directly to the president. In 1970, President Nixon expanded its functions and renamed it. It now stands as a major agency of government, as the federal budget has become an ever more central tool of economic management and political controversy. Its influence extends beyond the budget in a narrow sense, however. All executive agency proposals to Congress for new bills must be cleared with the OMB, to make certain they are in accord with the president's budgetary priorities. Further, President Reagan decreed that all new federal regulations had to be accompanied by an analysis of costs and benefits and submitted to the OMB for review.[14] The OMB is headed by a director, appointed by the president with Senate approval; ordinarily, this person is a major figure in formulating the administration's economic policy.

Worried about how President Truman was making foreign policy decisions, a Republican-dominated Congress created the National Security Council in 1947. By law, it consists of the president, the vice president, the secretary of state, and the secretary of defense. Supposedly, the president

T A B L E 6–3
The Executive Office of the President

AGENCY	DATE ESTABLISHED
Office of Management and Budget[a]	1921
Council of Economic Advisers	1946
National Security Council	1947
Special Representative for Trade Negotiations	1963
Council on Environmental Quality	1969
Office of Policy Development	1970
Office of Science and Technology Policy	1976
Office of Administration	1977
National Critical Materials Council	1984
Office of National Drug Control Policy	1988

[a]Originally housed in the Department of the Treasury and called the Bureau of the Budget. Moved to EOP in 1939 and renamed in 1970.

is to use the council to air security issues and coordinate intelligence. Truman subverted that intent by seldom calling it into session. Eisenhower, however, liked the setup, used it often, and appointed a Special Assistant for National Security Affairs, a sort of executive director of the Council. Later presidents convened the council off and on, but the role of the special assistant grew steadily as presidents increasingly leaned on them for foreign policy advice. In many cases, the NSC special assistant became more important than the secretary of state, and a bureaucratic struggle for the president's ear between these two officers has been common in every administration. Sometimes those working in the NSC have hatched foreign policy schemes of their own, stepping over the line between advice and operations: it was here, for instance, that the infamous Iran-Contra scandals were carried out. The NSC special assistant's powers, though, depend on each president. George Bush, for example, relied more on his secretary of state and less on the special assistant.

In 1946, after long controversy, Congress passed the Employment Act of 1946, committing the federal government to management of the American economy.[15] One provision of the act created the Council of Economic Advisers and located it in the Executive Office of the President. The council consists of three people (one designated as chair) who report to the president. Traditionally, these people have been academic economists on leave from universities. The chair is far more important than the other two members, and presidents have often but not always relied heavily on his views. Naturally, the chairman has to compete for influence with the president's other economic advisers, the secretary of the treasury, the director of the Office of Management and Budget, and various officials such as the head of the Federal Reserve banking system.

In addition to these entities a variety of other offices are housed in the EOP (see table 6–3). But these three are the major players, and illustrate the range of organizational types gathered here.

The White House Staff

Augmenting these officials is the personal staff of the president, located within the White House itself. (Technically, the White House Staff is part of the Executive Office of the President, but in practice it functions as a separate body.) These people have no duties assigned by law, and do not require Senate confirmation. The president is free to organize this staff according to personal preference, and here more than elsewhere, government business and partisan politics blur. Some White House staffers have specific jobs, such as the presidential press secretary and the director of congressional relations. Others maintain contact with important groups in American society, meanwhile tending the president's political interests in these fields. Jimmy Carter, for example, had people responsible for liaison with consumers, women, the elderly, Jews, Hispanics, white ethnic Catholics, Vietnam veterans, gays, blacks, labor unions, and business.[16] Still others have innocuous-sounding titles, but are close to the president personally, and therefore important members of the administration.

Most presidents designate one staff member as chief of staff; this person handles the president's appointments, directs the rest of the staff, and generally speaks for the White House, and usually, therefore, has some influence over almost every decision.[17] If given enough discretion by the president, the chief of staff can become almost an assistant president.

The Vice Presidency

Constitutionally, the vice president has only two functions: to preside over the Senate and to be ready to assume the presidency in case of death or incapacitation of the president. Since presiding over the Senate is a largely ceremonial task (the vice president can vote only in the case of a tie), most vice presidents have been bored with the job.

Presidents customarily assign the vice president a variety of public relations and political chores. They are sent to speak to various groups, usually those already in the administration's corner, and as presidential substitutes to various relatively unimportant events in foreign countries (such as the funeral of the president of some small country). Seldom have vice presidents been brought into the inner circles of an administration, and none has ever functioned as an assistant president.

The reasons for this are rooted in how the "veep" is chosen. The vice presidential candidate in each party is chosen personally by the presidential candidate, ordinarily with a bloc of voters in mind. John Kennedy selected Lyndon Johnson to bring Texas into the Democratic fold and give the ticket a chance in other southern states; Johnson, in turn, chose Hubert Humphrey to solidify his base among liberals; Jimmy Carter picked Walter Mondale for the same reason, and to appease the party regulars he had campaigned against to win the nomination; Ronald Reagan chose George Bush because he was the runner-up in the nomination race and Reagan felt he could placate Republican moderates this way; Bush selected Dan

Quayle because of his youth, his midwestern roots, and his ties to the conservative wing of the party. The political credentials these men brought to the ticket were useful in each case; however, these same political credentials have made presidents wary of them once in office. They have an independent political base and are not dependent on the president to keep their job (for four years at least). Most presidents therefore find it expedient to consign their vice presidents to the shadows.

A clear exception was Jimmy Carter, and a lesser exception was Ronald Reagan. Carter was sensitive about his status as a Washington outsider, and drew on Mondale's intimate familiarity with Congress and the federal government. By all accounts, the two men developed a close working relationship, and Mondale was an influential member of the administration. Reagan held a weekly private lunch with George Bush; apparently, the two men shared thoughts on politics and public issues. However, Bush was not present during most decision-making sessions during the Reagan years. In a return to form, Vice President Quayle remained all but invisible during most of the Bush presidency.[18]

THE PRESIDENT AND CONGRESS

The interaction between the president and Congress is the central drama of American politics. Few things a president wishes to accomplish are possible without legislation—either entirely new laws or modifications to old ones. Thus, the president and Congress are inextricably linked together.

The President's Program

Since the 1930s, all presidents have come into office with some formulation of policy goals, called a "program." At times this has had some grandiose name, such as the New Frontier or the Great Society. At others, it was composed of detailed campaign promises, such as those made by Ronald Reagan in 1980. At still other times, the candidate will only have addressed broad-gauge issues and provided no specifics—the approach taken by George Bush in 1988 when he avowed to be the "education president" and be an advocate for the environment. Even in this case, though, the candidate had a general line of policy which he wished to pursue.

After the election is over and the details of the transition are worked out, the president must prepare a legislative package. It is important, first, to develop a clear sense of priorities. Priorities are essential, for no president can secure action on every bill he favors, and if he spreads his efforts too thinly, none may pass. Hence, getting the major initiatives hammered into specific legislation and lining up political support for them is a vital early undertaking.

Moreover, a president is well advised to move quickly. Immediately after an election, there is always a "honeymoon" period in which the opposition

President Franklin D. Roosevelt signing the Social Security Act of 1935. Bill signings of landmark laws are often well-publicized ceremonial occasions.

is licking its wounds; the victory is fresh; public and party support is usually high; and the new president cannot as yet be blamed for any failures. One key Reagan aide in 1980, for example, advised his boss thus: "Things could go very badly during the first year, resulting in incalculable erosion of GOP momentum, unity, and public confidence. . . . A golden opportunity for permanent conservative policy revision and political re-alignment could be thoroughly dissipated before the Reagan administration is even up to speed."[19]

Steering the Program through Congress

After piecing together his legislative program, the president must now shepherd the bills through the legislative maze. As was evident in the discussion on passing a law in the previous chapter, this is an arduous exercise. Four factors will largely determine his success or failure: party loyalty, ideology, the president's interpersonal skills, and the president's popularity.[20]

American political parties are much more loosely organized than those in many democracies. A president therefore cannot dictate to members of his own party in Congress the way they should vote. Nonetheless, ties of party are important. A president's fellow partisans in Congress are in the same political family, after all, and are his natural allies. Furthermore, the record of the party, of which the president is the symbol, is what many members will be forced to defend in their constituencies. Recall that political party is still the best single predictor of how members of Congress will vote.

Ideology is also an important factor. Although the terms "liberal" and "conservative" are somewhat vague, there is a pronounced tendency for opinions to cluster under these headings. That is, there are identifiable groups of conservatives, moderate conservatives, moderate liberals and liberals in both the House and the Senate. Moreover, these groupings spread across the parties, although there are more conservatives and moderate conservatives among Republicans than among Democrats, and more liberals and moderate liberals among Democrats than among Republicans. This ideological spread allows a president to reach across party lines to garner support for particular policies. For example, Ronald Reagan depended on the support of conservative Democrats to pass his tax and budget policies in 1981. Were it not for this ideological factor, modern Republican presidents would be particularly disadvantaged. If party alone were determinative, they would never have been able to secure the passage of any legislation, since the Democrats have controlled the House since 1954.

Interpersonal skills include both simple human courtesy and the ability to bargain. Like anyone else, members of Congress like to be treated with dignity. A president who remembers to send birthday cards, calls to congratulate them on a child's wedding, or asks them to breakfast occasionally will build a reservoir of goodwill. Conversely, a president who appoints someone who is brusque to head his Office of Congressional Relations, as Jimmy Carter did, will be making unnecessary trouble for himself. It is in the process of bargaining, though, that a president needs to be adept. The bargaining he must do is made more difficult by the fact that he has little to give and, except for the veto, few sanctions he can impose. Most members are safe from threats of electoral retribution, and an attempt by a president to campaign against someone would probably backfire in any event. As Anthony King put it, in the eyes of a member of Congress, "the president . . . cannot help you to secure reelection, and it is most unlikely that he will be able, to any significant degree, to raise or lower your standing on Capitol Hill. He lives in his political house at one end of Pennsylvania Avenue; you live in your political house at the other end. He needs you, but on the face of it you have no great need of him."[21] Presidents can dole out modest bits of patronage (judgeships and other appointments), and there are some things they can do for members (promise to support or not oppose pet projects of theirs). But their primary tools relate to persuasion: by charm, and by appeals to the public interest.

It is important not to overlook the importance of appeals to the public interest. While most members of Congress are certainly sensitive to the dominant political groups of their states and districts, they are not immune to rational argument and persuasion. They are unlikely, of course, to vote consistently against these core interests, but on a variety of issues, many members are at least open to hearing what the president and his people have to say.

The occasion of a State of the Union speech gives the president a major opportunity to persuade Congress to act on his policy initiatives while, at the same time, letting him reach millions of citizens through the media. Here, President Ronald Reagan gives the State of the Union address in 1987.

Yet, perhaps the most potent weapon a president has is the ability to reach beyond Congress to the public.[22] The transportation and communication technology that is now available has made this an increasingly popular option for presidents. If a president can stimulate support for his proposals in the public, this will be heard in Congress. The most dramatic way to accomplish this is with a nationally televised speech. Ronald Reagan, for instance, with his natural feel for the camera, was the master at this. After Reagan's 1981 speech urging support for his tax and budget cuts, for example, former Speaker of the House Tip O'Neill said, "We are experiencing a telephone blitz like this nation has never seen. It's had a devastating effect."[23] Other presidents have been less successful, and sometimes have failed miserably. However, if the speech does result in an upswing in public backing for the president's policy, or better yet, if a Reagan-like flood of letters and telegrams to Congress can be evoked, this can overpower the opposition. Depending on the issue, presidents have other strategies to rally public support. They can make speeches before various groups around the country, or prominent citizens can be brought to the White House to be "briefed" on proposals, with the hope that they will return home and sway others.

TABLE 6–4

Presidential Vetoes and Overrides since 1961

PRESIDENT	VETOES	OVERRIDES
John Kennedy	21	0
Lyndon Johnson	30	0
Richard Nixon	43	7
Gerald Ford	66	12
Jimmy Carter	31	2
Ronald Reagan	78	9
George Bush[a]	36	1

[a]Through October 1992.

The Veto Power

In the Virginia Plan, the original proposal at the constitutional convention, a "negative" over legislation was to be given to a Council of Revision, composed of the president and a segment of the judiciary. The Constitution opted for handing a modified power to negate legislation to the president, providing that it could be overridden by a two-thirds vote in both houses of Congress.[24]

The grounds for the exercise of the presidential veto (which means in Latin, "I disapprove") were left uncertain. Several early authorities argued that it could only be employed when the president had constitutional objections to a bill, while others contended it could be used for policy reasons. In any event, the first few presidents used it sparingly. Andrew Jackson changed this, however, wielding the veto power frequently in his battles with Congress. Since then, presidents have not hesitated to make use of it to block, or attempt to block, legislation they oppose.

Vetoes occur most often, naturally, when party control of the White House and Congress is divided. Yet the veto, like all political weapons, is just as important when it is not used as when it is. It becomes an important element in the political bargaining between the president and Congress.

Presidents do not sit idly by while Congress debates laws, whether they are the president's proposals or bills sponsored by members of Congress. Presidents often threaten vetoes in an attempt to have bills they dislike modified or to stave off hostile amendments to their own bills. If a bill passes by less than a two-thirds margin, the president can usually kill the measure with confidence, since it is unlikely that those who voted against the original bill will now join in an effort to override the veto. However, some of the president's party or ideological supporters may be in favor of the bill; in such a case, the costs of incurring their wrath must be weighed: their votes may well be needed later on. However, it can happen that when a bill passes by a two-thirds margin and the president is determined to veto it, some members who originally voted for the bill will now vote to uphold the veto, out of support for the president. Typically, these are members whose commitment to the bill is lukewarm anyway.

Congress has developed a stratagem for complicating the president's choice: the "rider." Suppose a majority short of two-thirds supports some particular bill to which the president is opposed. Later, when a bill the president supports is up for consideration, the majority may attach the first bill as an amendment, or rider, in effect combining the bills. Technically, bills are supposed to deal with one subject, but the categories are often flexible enough that topics which are only marginally related can be combined in one overall bill. If the combined package passes, the president is faced with the decision whether to accept the whole measure or none of it.

In sum, presidents are involved in the legislative process from beginning to end: from the proposal of bills to the signing of the bills into law. The political initiative lies primarily with the president, whose proposals usually dominate the congressional agenda. Working to secure adoption of as much of the presidential "program" as possible, he becomes the Congress' chief lobbyist. Beginning with a core of party and ideological supporters, she must keep them in her camp and also reach out to others, in order to secure enough votes to pass each bill. Unfortunately, the president cannot use the same coalition for each bill, and must begin each struggle anew. This is perhaps the ultimate example of fragmented policy making; it is no wonder, as we shall see in chapter 12, that it leads to fragmented and often incoherent policy.

The President and the Public

The relationship between the president and the public is of the utmost importance. First, his standing with Congress and the "Washington community" in general will be intimately connected to his standing with the public. Just as importantly, though, his relationship with the public will symbolize the degree of trust and approval Americans give to their public institutions.

Public Approval Ratings

Public opinion polls are the most visible and most closely watched gauges of presidential popularity. Since the 1940s, the Gallup organization has asked a sample of Americans each month: "Do you approve of the way _____ is handling his job as president?" The results of these polls since 1961 are presented in figure 6–2.

Three general trends tend to emerge. First, during periods of international crisis, the percentage of the population which approves of the president rises dramatically. Second, there is a tendency for support to slip over time. And third, bad economic times lead to a drop in support.

When an international crisis occurs, there is the age-old tendency to "rally around the flag." The president's premier role in foreign policy, the general latent support which usually accompanies presidential dealing with foreign nations, and the natural desire to close ranks all lead to this outcome. However, the outburst of support may be only temporary. Especially if the crisis drags on, or worse, if there is failure in its handling, the approval ratings may well plummet. Moreover, it is often more the drama of the moment than support for the president's policies that leads to the upsurge. For instance, during the Vietnam War, presidential approval ratings rose whenever either a troop pullout or an increase in the level of military activity was announced.[25] That is, decisive action, not the substance of that action, is often what draws support.

Regarding the second trend, presidents ordinarily enter office with the best wishes even of those who have voted against them. In time, however, the positions they take and the concrete proposals they develop inevitably create opposition. Presidents also often are guilty of raising false hopes during the campaign: this may lead even some of their supporters to become disenchanted. For example, as a candidate, John F. Kennedy had promised to desegregate public housing "with the stroke of a pen." Once he was in office, though, other priorities took over, and Kennedy was also hesitant to create further opposition among some southern congressmen. Although he eventually signed the executive order, the delay eroded his support among civil rights leaders. Likewise, Ronald Reagan talked up much of the agenda of fundamentalist Christians during the campaign of 1980. In office, though, Reagan did little besides give speeches before these groups; this cost him some of their support.

Economic conditions, in contrast to many aspects of public policy, is a subject about which people are generally informed; inflation and unemployment are not abstractions. When times are good, presidents tend to receive and take the credit; conversely, when the economy is in the doldrums, they tend to be blamed.

Interestingly, surveys continue to turn up the fact that general economic conditions are correlated more closely with people's evaluations of the president than are their personal situations. That is, even if they face no prospect of being unemployed themselves, people will more likely rate a president negatively if the overall unemployment rate is rising than if it is not.[26] Apparently, therefore, there is evidence that civic democracy is involved in the way Americans rate the president. The spectacle of fellow citizens out of work seems to touch a chord of concern for others that would be missing if people were thinking only of their own interests.

In many ways, of course, it is unfair for presidents either to take credit or to be forced to absorb the blame for foreign affairs or economic conditions. Often, the causes of international crises or economic performance are far beyond a president's control. But as Samuel Kernell argues, "So be it. Fairness is less important than motivating them to deal with the country's problems."[27]

Attempts to Influence Public Opinion

Presidents obviously do not merely watch the ups and downs of public approval ratings. Instead, a great deal of effort is expended by presidents and their

FIGURE 6–2
Presidential Approval Ratings

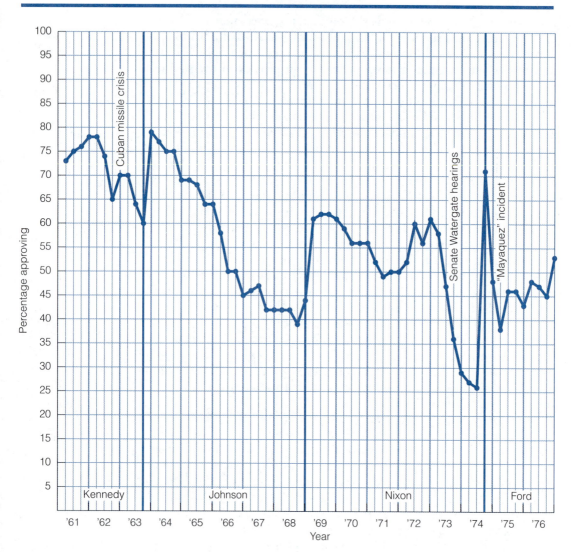

Source: Gallup polls.

aides to generate positive feelings in the public for presidents and their policies. Every effort is made, for example, to be certain the media presents favorable images. Chief executives are continually pictured chatting with children, chopping wood, strolling on the beach, or attending church, to make them appear folksy; or, they are photographed talking seriously with foreign leaders, to make them seem in charge and knowledgeable.

Presidents also take time to speak before a variety of groups—sometimes to accent symbolism, sometimes to keep old political allies in

FIGURE 6–2

Presidential Approval Ratings—*continued*

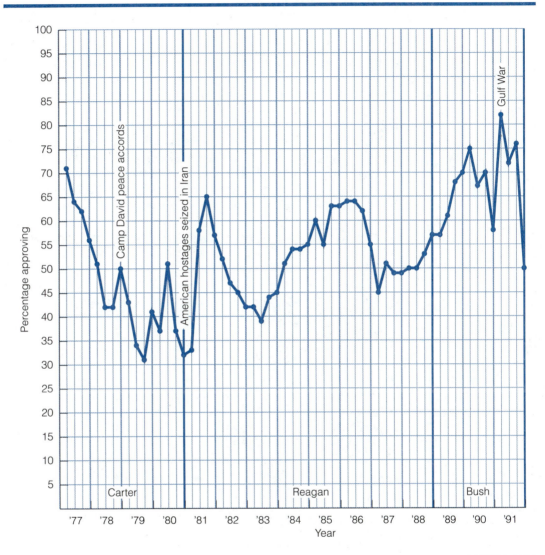

the fold, sometimes to reach out to groups who have not supported them. Few presidents can bypass the opportunity to accent symbolism by speaking to veterans groups on Veterans Day, for example, or at at least one college graduation (appropriately clad, of course, in each instance). Democratic presidents often speak to labor unions and Republicans to business interests of one sort or another, to gratify their respective political allies. A venture such as President Bush's appearance before black groups during Black History Week in 1991 is an instance of a president's efforts to forge links with a hitherto non-supportive group.[28]

Presidents and Prime Ministers

ALTHOUGH THE OFFICE of chief executive in a parliamentary system shares some similarities with the American presidency, there are significant differences. British and Canadian prime ministers, to take two pertinent examples, face different situations with regard to their legislative institutions, their cabinets, and their staffing arrangements.

A prime minister is chosen by Parliament, which means in effect the majority party in Parliament. Each party (let us assume that there are only two parties, for simplicity's sake) chooses a leader prior to the national election, both of whom will be candidates for Parliament. When it is known how many seats in Parliament each party has won, the leader of the winning party becomes prime minister. Therefore, by definition, she will have a working majority in Parliament and will be spared the continual coalition building in which an American president must engage. Occasionally, both British and Canadian prime ministers will introduce bills that stir opposition within their parties, but on most crucial matters the parties are generally cohesive. After all, few members want to see their own party fail and then have to face the voters at the next election.

Another critical difference is the nature of the cabinet. In parliamentary systems, the cabinet members (usually called ministers) are all selected from within Parliament. Therefore, the choices a prime minister has are much more restricted than those of a president. Furthermore, these people usually will have served for a substantial time together in Parliament: they will not be strangers to each other. Of critical importance in both Britain and Canada is the doctrine of collective responsibility. In essence, Parliament (actually the lower house) can remove the entire cabinet, but only the entire cabinet, any time it chooses to do

Some presidents adopt a more or less regular media event, such as President Reagan's Saturday radio addresses. These inevitably made the evening news, and were discussed by commentators over the weekend. Jimmy Carter tried a series of "town meetings" which were well covered.

The White House, in short, is a huge public relations firm. Critics have charged that this continual emphasis on creating favorable publicity detracts from the actual process of governing. There is a danger, they argue, that presidents and their chief associates will become so caught up in this media barrage that they will begin to believe that it represents reality. Most of those who have worked in the White House discount this, noting that the president is usually too smart a politician to allow that to happen. They understand, or at least claim, that people will ultimately form their judgments primarily on performance. Jody Powell, Carter's press secretary, so. Thus, the political fates of all the members in the cabinet are tied together in a way that is completely unknown in the United States.

By convention, and because of practical politics, the cabinet is seen as an important entity in itself. It is the "buckle" that ties the legislative and executive branches together: the members are not merely executive officers who serve the prime minister. In theory, and to a large degree in practice, important policy decisions are made in the cabinet as a body. Significantly, the prime minister is often called "the first among equals." In truth, in the last two decades, both the British and Canadian prime ministers have gathered more power into their own hands, decreasing that of the cabinet. However, both cabinets are still far more important than their American counterpart.

Another important difference flows from the conventions of cabinet government. That is, the prime minister has a much smaller personal staff than does the American president. There is a small prime minister's office (larger in Canada than in Britain), but it is a faint shadow of the Executive Office of the President. Therefore, a prime minister must rely more heavily than a president on cabinet members and civil servants.

Lastly, the fact that a prime minister (and the other ministers) are members of Parliament leads to a procedure called "Question Time." On designated days, each minister must be prepared to answer questions from other members. This gives the opposition an opportunity to embarrass the government of the day and make it explain its policies. No British or Canadian prime minister can avoid the arrows of the opposition, therefore, as easily as an American president can.

There is no definitive answer to the "which system is better?" query. As an exercise, though, one might consider these two questions: (1) What structural changes would have to be made to implement a parliamentary system in the United States? and 2) What effect, if any, would that have on the type of person who became chief executive?

---

argued that as for public relations, "the impact is marginal. The substance of what you do and what happens to you over the long haul is more important, particularly on the big things like the economy."[29] Good public relations efforts cannot hurt, but they cannot create genuine public support if there is none.

The President as First Citizen

Much of what has been said about public relations is tied to the president's relations with others in government, primarily members of Congress. A president wants high public approval ratings because they will help him secure what he wants from Congress. At the same time, there is another dimension to the president's relations with the public.

(text continued on page 194)

BOX 6-1

Presidential Leadership in the Two Models of Democracy

BARBARA KELLERMAN, a student of presidential leadership, has argued that to be an effective leader, a president needs "political intellect," which consists of two items:

(1) an appreciation for and skill in the art of politics and political bargaining, and

(2) a vision of American society that will inspire people to move along the path the president desires.[1]

Both individualist and civic models of democracy concur on the necessity for the first quality. Nothing can be accomplished in any government without the willingness of its leaders to line up followers: this means, everywhere and at all times, "playing politics." It is in the second realm that the two models diverge; and they diverge most significantly on the source of the vision.

According to the individualist model, each individual is to pursue her own goals with as much ardor as suits her. Naturally, like-minded people will find it useful to combine into groups, since they can have more effect on public policy if they do so. Interest groups will advocate various self-serving policies to those in government.

Congress will be especially prone to hear the voices of particular interest groups. The geographical election system will emphasize particular interests, since different groups will be dominant in the various constituencies. Bargaining and compromise will ensue, and something akin to the national interest will be the outcome.

The individualist democrat acknowledges that the president occupies a unique position in the political system. As the only nationally elected official (excepting, of course, the vice president), he is the only person who can claim to speak for the national public interest. He has faced the voters in their entirety; therefore, his political position is something near to an amalgamation and assimilation of all the various interests of the nation. His perspective is different, therefore, from that of anyone in Congress, because only the president can claim to speak for the voters as a whole, to articulate the national interest. But the national interest for which he speaks is not separate from the special interests, but the sum of them.

Civic democracy contests this view. There is indeed, its advocates argue, a public interest that is not merely the sum of all citizens' private interests. While all politicians should pursue the public interest, the president is uniquely positioned to seek and to argue for it. As befits her central role in the system of government, the presi-

BOX 6-1

dent must be the major figure in the ongoing public debate over the attempt to define and push toward the public interest. It is not merely because she is in a position to amalgamate the special interests that her role is critical, but because if leadership is to come, it must come from her. If she does not stake out a moral vision of society that calls citizens to something beyond themselves, then it is unlikely that anyone will, for no one else commands such a stage. If the president does not seek to make that vision a reality, then there will be political drift. It is for this purpose, civic democrats argue, that Hamilton wanted to place "energy" in the executive.

However, just because presidents have a vision of the public interest and pursue it, that does not mean that all will be well. Consider Presidents Johnson and Nixon and the Vietnam War. Both men thought this war was in the public interest, and both

continued fighting it in spite of the obvious damage it was doing to their own short-run political interests. Putting aside the relative merits of their war policy for a moment, we might ask if this is an example of civic democracy.

The answer is no: the manner in which the presidents chose to pursue the war destroyed whatever moral credibility their policy may have had. Lyndon Johnson decided on war in 1965 without being honest with the citizenry. Quite simply, he led the country into war with lies and duplicity. He did not make his case to Congress or the people, lay out his view of the necessity for the war, and ask for their backing; he simply fought it by executive fiat, and never told the truth. Richard Nixon's chief failing, on the other hand, was a refusal to believe that his opponents were as motivated by public spirit as he. Instead, he disdained them, called them "enemies" or worse, and used

the apparatus of government to harass them. Respect for one's fellow citizens and their views is a basic requirement of civic democracy: it cannot be ignored by presidents at will. Therefore, the war in Vietnam was not an example of civic democracy, even though it could have been.[2]

How was President Bush's handling of the Persian Gulf War different from Vietnam? Generally, is war different from all other policies? If so, how?

---

[1] Barbara Kellerman, *The Political Presidency* (New York: Oxford University Press, 1984).
[2] Of course, even if Johnson and Nixon had acted differently, the inherent problems and tragedies of the war might not have been avoided. However, it would seem that if in 1965 Johnson had engaged in the sustained public debate called for in the civic democratic model, the flaws and inconsistencies in the reasoning supporting large-scale American intervention would have become more evident. Two good books to consult on this matter are Doris Kearns, *Lyndon Johnson and the American Dream* (Cambridge: Harvard University Press, 1976) and Larry Berman, *Planning a Tragedy* (New York: Norton, 1982).

People in modern society are as affected as any humans by the pictures their leaders paint. In the United States, for instance, our political tradition is filled with a number of laudable attributes, as well as with several that are rather unsavory. By his actions and through his words, a president can either speak to our better selves, making us better democratic citizens, or open bottles of venom. The president's character, his utterances, how he bears himself, the people he surrounds himself with, the themes he plays upon—all these will affect the image people have of American society and their place in it. Naturally, the president cannot and does not alone create the intangible "public mood." A variety of other objective factors and voices have a role also. But, as first citizen, the president has an important voice; the sense of national purpose he gives and the historical direction he points out do have an impact. The president not only represents and characterizes an age, but has a major role in creating it. The presidency is not only a "bully pulpit" to harangue political opponents, as Theodore Roosevelt called it; it is also a pulpit from which to give homilies on the moral character of political life. Franklin D. Roosevelt once observed that "the presidency is preeminently a place of moral leadership."[30]

THE PRESIDENT AS INTERNATIONAL LEADER

Presidential leadership on the world stage is somewhat different from domestic political leadership.[31] A president has more discretion available when it comes to formulating goals and developing specific policies. His constitutional and legal powers, especially his status as commander-in-chief, are more open-ended, and there are fewer domestic political obstacles to carrying out his policies. Normally, the public is only moderately informed about foreign policy, and there are fewer interest groups active. In fact, some analysts have argued that the roles are so different that we really have "two presidencies" occupied by the same person: one for domestic politics and one for international affairs.[32]

Although presidents have more flexibility in world politics, they face unique challenges, since to accomplish their goals they must influence foreign leaders. The tools at the disposal of presidents are, paradoxically, both more and less forceful than those they can use in the domestic realm. On the forceful end is, of course, raw military power. The use or threatened use of American military might casts a long shadow. However, its utility is usually limited. First, it is limited by the costs it incurs. During the days of the Cold War, for instance, it was always sobering to consider the consequences of an actual military showdown with the Soviet Union. In even a limited nuclear war, tens of millions could have perished. Even with a weaker but substantial military power, such as Iraq, many feared that the cost of military action would be high in both lives and money. In other instances, such as when dealing with allies, its use is inconceivable anyway. No president would dream of threatening Canada or France with military punishment for disobeying American wishes.

American troops prepare to storm Iraqi defenses during the Gulf War. The President's power as commander in chief extends to all matters of strategy and tactics.

The economic levers a president can use are more often brought into play. Congress has given the president fairly broad authority on several economic fronts in dealing with foreign nations. For example, the president can grant or withhold "most favored nation status," which has significant trade consequences. In addition to these discretionary manipulations, Congress will usually approve additional aid requests to a country if a president lobbies hard enough for it. Most often, however, the president's major, if not only, option is persuasion. Foreign political leaders, who have goals and priorities of their own, must somehow be convinced that what the U.S. president wants is in their best interest.

Iraq's invasion of Kuwait posed all these dilemmas. President Bush sought to convince Saddam Hussein to withdraw, but to no avail; finally and decisively, he employed military force to accomplish his goal. Simultaneously, he had to build a consensus among other nations—Britain and the other European countries, the Soviet Union, Japan, the other Arab states, and Israel—that his policies were the best ones to deal with the crisis.[33] Ultimately, he succeeded on every front, at least in the short run.

This episode demonstrated graphically the crucial position, as well as the limitations, of American power and presidential leadership. It is hard to imagine that without American leadership the military and diplomatic force could have been marshalled to defeat Iraq. Nevertheless, without the cooperation and acquiescence of the other nations involved, the operation would have been all but impossible.

Looking back, from the end of World War II until the 1970s, domestic and foreign policy remained largely divorced from each other, and the "two presidencies" were consequently relatively distinct. World politics and American policy were dominated by the confrontation between East and West, the Communist nations and the "Free World." Outside this bipolar system of alliances stood a bloc of nonaligned nations, most of whom were relatively poor. Presidents' tasks in foreign policy revolved therefore around U.S. relations with the Soviet Union, with U.S. allies, and with the so-called Third World. In general, our dealings with the Soviets were adversarial, as we sought to contain their desire to spread communism. Nonetheless, arms control was always on the agenda, and there were intermittent discussions throughout the period. As for our allies, the central task was keeping them committed to our strategies for dealing with the Soviets. Although our major allies, such as Britain, France, West Germany, and Canada, were equally opposed to Soviet expansionism, they often thought alternative methods, such as increasing trade, were more productive. Third World countries were interested primarily in economic development and growth. At the same time, many of them had regional security problems, and long-standing animosities with their neighbors (such as the Indian-Pakistan conflict) which were more important to them than East-West relations. Thus, they frequently wanted economic aid and weapons from anyone who would provide them.

In the early 1990s, these categorizations and the policies surrounding them have faded away. Communism has all but collapsed, and the Soviet Union has broken apart. Western European nations and Japan long ago recovered their economic strength after the devastation of World War II, and are now decidedly less inclined than they once were to follow the American lead. Meanwhile, the complexities of regional politics, particularly but not only in the Middle East, have made the old Third World category completely obsolete.[34]

At the same time, two other trends have eroded the barrier between foreign policy and domestic politics and the type of political situation a president encounters in each, pulling the "two presidencies" closer together. First, foreign policy has become subject to more domestic political debate.[35] From the late 1940s until the Vietnam War, a deep bipartisan consensus existed about both the goals and the tactics of our foreign policy. Since Vietnam, that consensus has broken down, and political opponents do not hesitate to challenge the president's views. In recent years, foreign policy has become nearly as controversial as domestic policy; only when shooting starts, as in the war against Iraq, is there a temporary suspension of most partisan debate. Modern presidents are therefore now faced with a situation in which they must increasingly sell their foreign policies to a domestic audience as well as to foreign leaders.

Second, the globalization of the economy has blurred the distinction between the foreign and domestic spheres. Almost every domestic economic decision now has international ramifications, and almost every foreign policy decision has domestic economic ramifications. Our labor market policies, for instance, affect the prices of American goods in international markets. Our deficit is heavily financed by borrowing from foreigners: this means that our budgetary policy affects the strength of the

Presidents meet regularly with foreign leaders. Here, George Bush is pictured in Munich, Germany at a meeting of the leaders of the seven most industrialized countries.

dollar in international currency markets. The dollar's value in turn affects the costs of imports and exports. Even such a seemingly domestic matter as public education is not immune from this trend. If American workers are less well trained than their foreign counterparts, our productivity lags, and with it our competitiveness. Conversely, any international trade agreement we make, or any tariffs we impose, will affect hundreds, if not thousands, of American jobs, and the prices of any number of consumer products. Another example of the intertwining of foreign and domestic policy is the way our policy in the Middle East can have an effect on the price of oil; this has a chain reaction in energy policy and the economy generally. In short, there is no way to insulate domestic policy from international concerns, and vice versa.[36]

Nonetheless, in spite of the fact that the line between foreign and domestic policy has diminished, it has not been abolished. And the president still has more discretion in foreign policy than in domestic affairs, even if it is not as great as it once was. Managing foreign policy now bears increasing resemblance to constructive leadership in domestic politics, although the two are not identical. The "two presidencies" are now indeed closer together, but not fully merged.

PRESIDENTIAL POWER: A CONCLUDING NOTE

How much power does a contemporary president really have? The question seems a curious one even to ask, since the president controls such vast resources, and sits atop a huge executive branch. Yet, some observers have argued that the presidency is essentially a weak office, and the president more a glorified clerk than a strong leader.[37]

The basis of this claim is that there are so many checks on presidential action that the president is enfeebled. Few members of Congress owe any political debts to the president, who has no sticks to force them into line. Career civil servants are more loyal to their departments and agencies than to the president; in any event, the sheer size of the federal establishment makes direct control from the White House difficult if not impossible. Even the cabinet secretaries and other appointees—supposedly the chief executive's allies in carrying out presidential objectives—often work primarily to further their own political careers or become prisoners of the departments they head, and as often as not end up subverting the president's policies.

Accordingly, so this thesis goes, the president's only real power flows from the ability to *persuade:* to convince members of Congress, career civil servants, and even executive agency heads to carry out *the president's* plans and programs. The power to persuade these people is dependent in turn on two factors: the president's reputation among the Washington establishment (those in or near government and the national press), and presidential prestige among the general public.

There is an undeniable element of truth in this picture. A president of the United States, after all, is not a dictator or a military leader, or even a prime minister backed by a unified political party, but the chief executive of a sprawling, diverse democracy with a system of separation of powers and checks and balances. Nonetheless, many experts believe the picture sketched above to be an exaggeration.[38] First, they point out that if a president selects subordinates carefully, choosing people who share the president's goals and are energetic in pursuing them, the chief executive can indeed effect change in the lower levels of government. Second, a president can personally make things happen on a variety of fronts. Particularly in foreign policy, and most particularly when military action is involved, a president's choices are decisive. Even on the domestic side, though, the president has extensive legal authority to issue a significant number of executive orders, most of which are routinely implemented by the relevant agencies. Third, although the president cannot command Congress, neither is he powerless in dealing with the legislative branch. The president always holds the political initiative, and vetoes are a direct source of power which can often force Congress' hand. And, as Ronald Reagan showed, a president on occasion can successfully appeal to the public and break a congressional logjam.

In short, both images must be kept in mind when appraising presidential power. A president holds enormous power, both that authorized by the Constitution and that which has accumulated through the workings of the modern political conditions surveyed at the outset of this chapter. At the same time, however, the president is hemmed in by various constraints—some constitutional, others products of those same modern conditions. No president is ever reduced purely to persuasion, but on the other hand, none can ever rely on orders alone.

SUMMARY

The presidential office was established to cure one of the major defects of the Articles of Confederation: a leaderless government and a subsequent lack of implementation. The constitutional powers granted the office are vast, but a particular president's power depends on that individual's political skills and the political circumstances surrounding that presidency. Post–World War II conditions have favored strong presidents, but the same elements that make for this strength can create important constraints.

The process of selecting a president is rooted in the electoral college, but both the election and the nomination process have been democratized. Primaries have backed the campaign up several months and increased the role of the press in winnowing the field of candidates.

Presidents sit atop the executive branch, but do not entirely control it. Cabinet secretaries are often caught between a president's objectives and the needs of their departments. The Executive Office of the President can be an important management tool, since it is composed of advice-giving agencies. Most presidents rely heavily on the White House staff, and on the chief of staff in particular.

To be successful in domestic policy, a president must design and champion new legislative initiatives. In trying to push a program through Congress, the president must rely on party loyalty, ideology, interpersonal skills, and public approval. A critical constitutional weapon in presidential dealings with Congress is the veto.

A president's public approval ratings are singularly important: the chief executive must make a concerted effort to secure public backing—both personal and with regard to policy. The percentage of Americans approving of the president's performance tends to slide over time, but can be dramatically affected by events, such as a foreign crisis or an economic plunge.

The position of the United States in world politics has made the president an important international leader. While the modern chief executive is no longer as free to act as were the immediate postwar presidents, today's president still wields enormous power and influence on the world stage.

As a result of its constitutional position and modern political conditions, the office is both strong and weak. There is a great deal of power at the disposal of the president, but the chief executive often must persuade others to go along with his objectives.

ENDNOTES

1. The debate over the executive branch is discussed in R. Gordon Hoxie, "The Presidency in the Constitutional Convention," *Presidential Studies Quarterly* 15 (1985), 2–24.

2. *The Federalist Papers,* No. 70.

3. Michael Kammen, *People of Paradox: An Inquiry Concerning the Origins of American Civilization* (New York: Vintage, 1972), 54.

4. Quoted in Larry Berman, *The New American Presidency* (Boston: Little, Brown, 1987), 55.

5. William Howard Taft, *Our Chief Magistrate and His Powers* (New York: Columbia University Press, 1916), 138.

6. James Sundquist, *The Decline and Resurgence of Congress* (Washington: Brookings, 1981), 4.

7. At least one of their choices must be from a state other than their own. This effectively prevents presidential and vice presidential candidates from coming from the same state.

8. It does have a few defenders, though. See Judith Best, *The Case against Direct Election of the President: A Defense of the Electoral College* (Ithaca: Cornell University Press, 1975).

9. See Lawrence Longley and Alan Braun, *The Politics of Electoral College Reform* (New Haven: Yale University Press, 1975).

10. A few states do have laws requiring electors to vote as they have promised.

11. A good account of the last several elections can be found in Herbert Asher, *Presidential Elections and American Politics: Voters, Candidates, and Campaigns since 1952* (Belmont, Calif.: Brooks/Cole, 1992).

12. See Hugh Heclo, *A Government of Strangers* (Washington: Brookings Institution, 1977).

13. Colin Campbell, *Managing the Presidency: Carter, Reagan, and The Search for Executive Harmony* (Pittsburgh: University of Pittsburgh Press, 1986), 63.

14. The OMB did not however have the legal authority to cancel proposed regulations. The Reagan people hoped to ferret out regulations they deemed to be unnecessary and impede the issuance of regulations in general.

15. The story of this act is told in Stephen K. Bailey, *Congress Makes a Law* (New York: Vintage, 1950).

16. John P. Burke, "The Institutional Presidency," in Michael Nelson, ed., *The Presidency and the Political System,* 3d ed. (Washington: Congressional Quarterly Press, 1990), 392–93.

17. A most enlightening discussion among former presidential chiefs of staff can be found in Samuel Kernell and Samuel Popkin, eds., *Chief of Staff: Twenty-Five Years of Managing the Presidency* (Berkeley: University of California Press, 1986).

18. A useful summary of the role of recent vice presidents can be found in Joseph Pika, "Bush, Quayle, and the New Vice Presidency?" in Nelson, ed., *The Presidency and the Political System,* chap. 20.

19. *Washington Post,* December 14, 1980.

20. These variables are drawn from Jon R. Bond and Richard Fleisher, *The President in the Legislative Arena* (Chicago: University of Chicago Press, 1990).

21. Anthony King, "A Mile and a Half is a Long Way" in Anthony King, ed., *Both Ends of the Avenue* (Washington: American Enterprise Institute, 1983), 236.

22. See Samuel Kernell, *Going Public* (Washington: Congressional Quarterly Press, 1986).

23. *Congressional Quarterly Weekly Report,* August 1, 1981, 1374.

24. An analysis of the veto can be found in Robert Spitzer, *The Presidential Veto: Touchstone of the American Presidency* (Albany: State University of New York Press, 1988).

25. John Mueller, *War, Presidents, and Public Opinion* (New York: Wiley, 1973).

26. Kernell, *Going Public,* 193.

27. Kernell, *Going Public,* 173.

28. Bush's appearance at the ceremonies honoring Martin Luther King's birthday in 1992 could be seen in this light also. However, this appearance can also be seen as one of those actions of presidents that transcend ordinary politics and reach for something higher. Does it say something about the vitality of American citizenship that if he had tried to make a political ploy out of this appearance, it would have led to strong public disapproval?

29. Quoted in George Edwards, *The Public Presidency* (New York: St. Martin's Press, 1983), 88.

30. Quoted in Richard Neustadt, *Presidential Power and the Modern Presidents: The Politics of Leadership from Roosevelt to Reagan* (New York: Free Press, 1990), xv.

31. A good analysis of the president's role in world politics is Barbara Kellerman and Ryan Barilleaux, *The President as World Leader* (New York: St. Martin's Press, 1991).

32. Aaron Wildavsky, "The Two Presidencies," in Aaron Wildavsky, ed., *Perspectives on the Presidency* (Boston: Little, Brown, 1975), 448–61.

33. Furthermore, he had to steer approval of the war through the United Nations.

34. An interesting survey is Cecil Crabb and Kevin Mulcahy, *Presidents and Foreign Policy Making from FDR to Reagan* (Baton Rouge: Louisiana State University Press, 1986).

35. See I. M. Destler, Leslie Gelb, and Anthony Lake, *Our Own Worst Enemy: The Unmaking of American Foreign Policy* (New York: Simon and Schuster, 1984).

36. This is the theme of Richard Rose, *The Postmodern President: George Bush Meets the World,* 2d ed. (Chatham, N.J.: Chatham House, 1991).

37. The person most associated with this view is Richard Neustadt. See his *Presidential Power.*

38. See Thomas Cronin, *The State of the Presidency,* 2d ed. (Boston: Little, Brown, 1980), chap. 4, for example.

FURTHER READING

1. Barber, James D. *The Presidential Character.* Englewood Cliffs, N.J.: Prentice-Hall, 1985.

2. Berman, Larry. *The New American Presidency.* Boston: Little, Brown, 1987.

3. Davis, James W. *The President as Party Leader.* Westport, Conn.: Greenwood Press, 1992.

4. Kellerman, Barbara and Ryan Barilleaux. *The President as World Leader.* New York: St. Martin's Press, 1991.

5. Kernell, Samuel. *Going Public: New Strategies of Presidential Leadership.* Washington: Congressional Quarterly Press, 1986.

6. Lowi, Theodore. *The Personal President: Power Invested, Promise Unfulfilled.* Ithaca, N.Y.: Cornell University Press, 1985.

7. Nelson, Michael, ed. *The Presidency and the Political System.* 3d ed. Washington: Congressional Quarterly Press, 1990.

8. Neustadt, Richard. *Presidential Power and the Modern Presidents: The Politics of Leadership from Roosevelt to Reagan.* New York: Free Press, 1990.

9. Spitzer, Albert. *The Presidential Veto: Touchstone of the American Presidency.* Albany: State University of New York Press, 1988.

SEVEN

THE BUREAUCRACY

THERE ARE PROBABLY FEW, if any, Americans who have not complained about the pathologies of "bureaucracy" at one time or another. Public opinion surveys continually document that this antipathy is widespread, and runs through all social and economic groups. Furthermore, Americans continue to believe that "there are too many bureaucrats," and that they are high-handed and uncaring. In response, few politicians can resist the temptation to blast the bureaucracy and bureaucrats, fixing blame upon them for whatever woes are worrying people at the moment.

However, when people are asked how they perceive specific agencies and the personnel in them, they report remarkably high levels of satisfaction.[1] Furthermore, any proposal to curtail or abolish a particular agency brings legions of shrill defenders in Congress and the public. It must be those "other" bureaucrats, that no one ever seems able to find, who are the problem. More seriously, the truth is that Americans detest bureaucracy in the abstract but want a multitude of government services.

And there's the rub. A handful of government policies are self-implementing: adopting a national anthem is one example (but even it has to be printed). Most public policies, though, require an organization of some type to carry them out. In short, public policy is the source of bureaucracy, and the more tasks the government takes on the larger will be the public service.

Yet, the spirit of bureaucracy, no matter how necessary it is to governance in the modern world, is in tension with the spirit of democracy in two important respects. First, the defining characteristic of bureaucracy is a system of offices linked in a chain of command, with authority flowing from the top down. The model of a bureaucracy is, of course, a military organization. This very notion of hierarchy is anti-democratic, for it rests upon inequality of authority and restricted participation. In contrast, democracy stresses widespread participation and equality of participation. No bureaucracy can adopt the democratic mode for its internal operations, since this would lead to chaos. (Imagine the condition of an army that voted on strategy.)

Second, much of the power of modern bureaucracies rests on expertise. That is, those who staff a bureaucratic agency possess knowledge and skills which the general public does not possess. The regulation of nuclear energy; the negotiation of an arms control treaty; the purification of water; and the teaching of reading are all tasks for which special preparation and training is required. "Leaving such matters to the experts" is not an irrational approach to the many technical issues that beset modern life. Nevertheless, the democratic ethos rests upon the idea that the people are the best judges of the appropriate approach to and direction of public policy. It is a belief in the wisdom of ordinary people, possessing no special skill or aptitude in the myriad of issues facing contemporary governments.

Opposite: *The vast, sprawling complex of government offices known as the Federal Triangle, near the capitol in Washington, D.C.*

Resolving these tensions is a critical dilemma of modern politics, and not only in the United States. On the one hand, bureaucracies are endemic to political life in advanced industrial society; on the other, an overly bureaucratized polity could erode the health of a democracy. For citizens who become bureaucrats, there is a danger that these two roles will come into conflict. Is our polity too bureaucratized, and does too much power rest with these non-elected officials?

DIMENSIONS OF THE AMERICAN BUREAUCRACY

The first noteworthy fact about our bureaucracy is that most Americans who work for government do not work for the federal government. Total federal civilian employment in 1991 was 3.0 million (not counting an additional 2.1 million military personnel), while 4.5 million people worked for the states, and another 11.0 million for local governments.

Is the bureaucracy, in particular the federal bureaucracy, too big? That depends, naturally, on what it is compared to. In 1821 the federal government employed 6,914 people, compared to today's 3.0 million. Even measured as a percentage of the population, the growth is gargantuan: the 1821 personnel constituted only one-twentieth of 1 percent of the population, whereas today federal employment makes up over 1.05 percent of the population.[2] However, remember that in 1821 the army and navy were minuscule, as befitted a small power (and equipped with single-shot muskets and wooden ships); there were no veteran's benefits to speak of; no air traffic controllers were needed; factory safety legislation of any kind was nonexistent; there were no federally funded highways; and there were certainly no social benefits (such as grants and loans to college students). Delivering the mail, in fact, was the only major national domestic function.

Since the end of the Second World War, the federal establishment has grown very little, as is evident in table 7–1. As a percentage of the pop-

TABLE 7–1
Federal Civilian Employment since 1950

	FEDERAL CIVILIAN EMPLOYMENT (thousands)	U.S. POPULATION (thousands)	FEDERAL EMPLOYEES PER 10,000 PEOPLE
1950	2,117	151,684	139.6
1955	2,378	165,275	143.9
1960	2,421	180,671	134.0
1965	2,538	194,303	130.6
1970	2,881	204,879	137.2
1975	2,897	215,973	134.1
1980	2,876	227,757	126.3
1985	3,021	239,279	126.2
1989	3,133	248,762	125.9

Note: Figures are computed from *Statistical Abstract of the United States, 1990* and *1991.*

ulation, federal employment has actually shrunk. Moreover, in comparison with the growth in the budget, personnel growth has lagged far behind.

However, these figures can be deceptive, for three reasons. First, many state and local employees are funded by the federal government, such as those who are paid through the grant system discussed in chapter 3. Second, a number of ostensibly "private" businesses are essentially appendages of the federal government, the prime example being major defense contractors. They have no other customer for many of their products, and are often wholly dependent on tax dollars for their support. Third, a substantial sum of federal expenditures goes each year to researchers and consultants of various sorts. For example, grants to scientists to study cancer or AIDS do not directly increase government employment, but those persons are basically working for the government. There is nothing pernicious or necessarily undesirable in any of these arrangements. The point is only that the number of people employed by the government, broadly conceived, is higher than the number given above.

THE STRUCTURE OF THE EXECUTIVE BRANCH

The Constitution is virtually silent on the question of executive organization. The only directly relevant provision empowers the president to solicit written advice from department heads.[3] To Congress has fallen the tasks of creating and structuring the executive branch.[4] It cannot be stressed too strongly that the organization of government agencies is not merely a matter of management science, of selecting the "best" structural arrangement and neatly arranging who reports to whom. Where an agency is located in government, how it is organized, and to whom it reports will have a significant impact on how it implements the policy with which it is charged.

Executive Departments

At the heart of the federal government are the fourteen *executive departments*. (These are listed in table 6–2 in the previous chapter.) The first Congress created three of them: State, Treasury, and War (now Defense). In addition, an attorney was engaged to represent the United States; this was the forerunner of the Department of Justice. From this core, the departmental structure has grown to include the departments of Agriculture; Commerce; Education; Energy; Health and Human Services; Housing and Urban Development; Interior; Labor; Transportation; and Veterans Affairs. Each of these is headed by a secretary who reports to the president and holds cabinet rank.[5] Most importantly, these agencies are all charged with the operation of programs, and most are organized in the mold of a classical bureaucracy. To illustrate, the organization chart of the Department of the Interior is reproduced as figure 7–1.

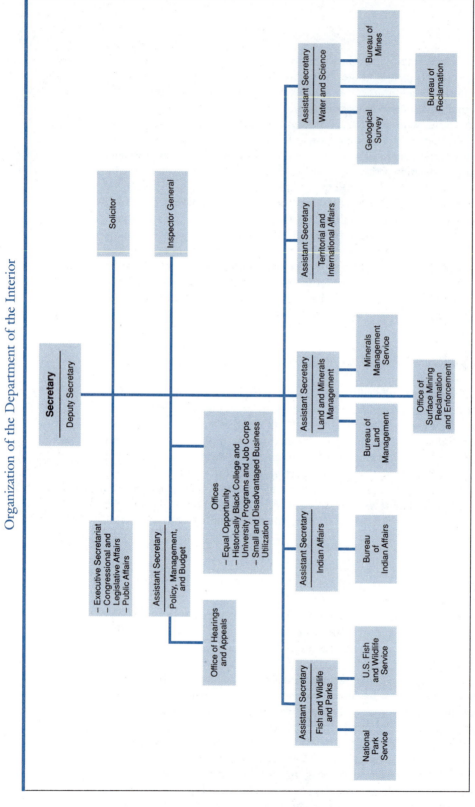

FIGURE 7-1

Organization of the Department of the Interior

Source: United States Government Manual, 1991–92.

208

Note that on this chart, the "bureau" level is where actual operation of programs seems to begin. Above that, we mostly find people with rather general titles and no specific program duties. In fact, across the federal government, the bureau is the key organizational unit. It is used in the actual designation of some units (such as the Federal Bureau of Investigation (FBI) and the Bureau of Land Management); in other units, the concept is present but the name differs ("office" or "service" are common alternatives). Most executive departments, in common with Interior, are collections of these semi-autonomous bureaus. In most cases, the "bureau chief" is a career civil servant who has served in the bureau for many years; those above her are political appointees.

The early departments might be called *core departments,* in that they are concerned with the core functions of government and serve broad general needs of the country as a whole. The Agriculture Department, in contrast, was the first *service* or *clientele* department, established in 1862 and given full cabinet status in 1889. Quite clearly, its purpose was to serve and promote the needs of a particular segment of society. Over the years, other groups—business, labor, educators, and most recently veterans—have succeeded in getting Congress to establish departments for them. Often, these departments, as was the case with Agriculture, have been formed by elevating a previously existing agency or bureau to full department status. Thus, the Department of Labor was detached from the Department of Commerce in 1913; the Department of Education was erected simply by removing the Office of Education from the Department of Health, Education, and Welfare; and the Department of Veterans Affairs involved merely changing the status of the Veterans Administration (which had been an independent agency, as described below).

Another type of department is what might be called a *conglomerate.* For any one of several reasons—usually a desire to give a policy area more visibility—several existing government programs are gathered together in a new department. This process is what led to the creation of the Departments of Housing and Urban Development; Transportation; Energy; and what was once Health, Education, and Welfare (created in 1953 and now rechristened Health and Human Services since the removal of all education programs in 1979). The remaining conglomerate department, Interior, has been a catchall since its establishment (in 1849), and often is the birthplace of bureaus which are later removed to become full-fledged departments or parts of other conglomerates.

Independent Agencies

Alongside the executive departments are a number of *independent agencies* (independent, that is, of any executive department). These agencies are headed by a director or an administrator (or someone with a similar title) who is appointed by the president with Senate approval and serves at the president's pleasure. Some examples of these bodies are the National Aeronautics and Space Administration (NASA), the Central Intelligence

Agency (CIA), and the Environmental Protection Agency (EPA). In most cases, the internal structure found in such an agency is much like that of a regular executive department.

Why did Congress use this form of organization, and why have these agencies not been consolidated into departments? The answer to the first question varies with each agency. In NASA's case, for instance, many members of Congress wanted to keep the space program free from military control, and the independent agency form seemed to offer the best hope of doing that. In the case of the CIA, the sensitive nature of its mission dictated that it should be directly under presidential control. As for the Environmental Protection Agency, environmental advocates wanted the agency to have visibility, but knew that they did not have enough support to make it a full-scale department. (In time, we probably will have a Department of the Environment).[6]

The answer to the second query is more uniform: each independent agency wishes to retain its direct access to the president and its own budget. If any of them were merged into regular departments, they would not only have to go to the president through a department secretary, but also have to fight for resources within their departments. Each of these agencies, therefore, struggles to keep its autonomy from the departments.

Independent Regulatory Commissions

Several important public bodies bear the designation *independent regulatory commission*. As the Industrial Revolution matured and government policy figured ever more prominently in economic affairs, new types of administrative organization were sought. Although sentiment for extended economic regulation grew in the late nineteenth century, there was concern that politicians could manipulate economic regulations for short-term political advantage. Thus, a constitutional hybrid was created when the first major economic regulatory act was passed in 1887, and the Interstate Commerce Commission was born. To this day, it remains the prototype of the independent regulatory commission.[7]

Structurally, the ICC consists of five commissioners appointed by the president with Senate approval, for staggered seven-year terms. By law, no more than three may be from one political party. The president also designates one of the commissioners as chair. A law of Congress gives the ICC broad regulatory power over several forms of surface transportation. Within the guidelines of the act, the commission may issue rules and regulations; enforce those rules; and hold hearings if a business thinks those rules have been unfairly applied. The ICC exemplifies, therefore, the way commissions exercise in miniature fashion all three powers of government—or quasi-legislative, quasi-executive, and quasi-judicial powers.

The rationale for establishing these commissions which now dot the administrative landscape—the Federal Communications Commission; the

The panel on General and Plastic Surgery Devices, a unit of the Food and Drug Administration, voting to restrict the availability of silicon breast implants, February 20, 1992.

Nuclear Regulatory Commission; the Securities and Exchange Commission; the Federal Trade Commission; and a host of others—remains the same: a desire to provide some insulation from partisan politics. The regulation of various types of businesses is, of course, a highly technical and complex matter, but policy issues are always present also. By passing a general law and making the appointments overlap, Congress hoped to put the regulatory commissions at arm's reach from executive or legislative meddling. Commissions are still tethered by the law, which Congress can always amend. Also, over time, presidents can affect the drift of regulatory policy through appointments, particularly if they serve two terms.[8] There is a perpetual tension, however, between independence and political accountability, and the independent regulatory commission is not a perfect answer to that dilemma.

One independent regulatory body that is worthy of special mention is the Federal Reserve Board, which regulates the national money supply.[9] Established in 1913, it consists of seven commissioners (called "governors") who are appointed by the president with Senate confirmation, as usual. The governors serve fourteen-year terms which are staggered so that one expires every two years.

The Federal Reserve Board (popularly called the "Fed") clearly illustrates the strengths and weaknesses of the commission system. Determining the amount of money which should be in circulation is not only a technical matter: it is also a critical factor in the nation's economic health and directly affects people's well-being and livelihoods.[10] If Congress and/or the president retained control over this vital area, undoubtedly the Fed would be manipulated for short-term electoral advantage, (bringing interest rates down immediately before an election, for example). This would be unhealthy for the country in the long run. On the other hand, elected politicians, and elected politicians only, are ultimately accountable in a democracy, and they should make the central choices in such an important area as economic policy. Oftentimes, in fact, presidents have a clear-cut economic strategy and are unable to convince the Fed to cooperate. In a democracy, in other words, it is simply not possible both to have policymakers held accountable and to remove politics.

Foundations, Endowments, and Institutes

To promote scientific research and encourage the arts and humanities, Congress has established a number of *foundations, endowments,* and *institutes.* The National Science Foundation (NSF), for example, provides grants for basic scientific research, while the National Cancer Institute and the National Heart Institute conduct research in these specialty areas. The National Endowment for the Arts (NEA) and the National Endowment for the Humanities (NEH) are parallels of the NSF. Most are governed by a board appointed by the president with Senate approval. Usually, the appointees are distinguished scientists, artists, or writers, and encounter no opposition. At times, though, there is controversy. In February 1992, for example, the head of the NEA resigned under pressure from the president, and some suggested appointees for the NEH created dissension.

Ordinarily, these agencies operate in obscurity, with only those professionals directly concerned even aware of their activities. Occasionally, however, public controversy erupts, as it did in 1989 when Senator Jesse Helms criticized some of the NEA's grants. The arts projects which were funded seemed obscene to Helms, and he moved to restrict the types of projects NEA could fund. This provoked a lively public debate on the whole issue of government funding for the arts. Usually, though, these agencies distribute their largess without serious political oversight.

Government Corporations

Another administrative device used by the federal government is the *government corporation.* Normally, these are set up to operate some semicommercial enterprise: one which provides a service and charges fees. The largest and best known is the United States Postal Service, which was transformed into a government corporation in 1970. Other examples are the Tennessee Valley Authority, which generates electricity, and Amtrak, which operates the nation's passenger train service. Making these entities somewhat independent by putting them on a commercial footing affects how they do business, but it does not remove politics entirely. Congress forces the Postal Service to carry the government's mail free, for example, and members of Congress are often found pressuring Amtrak not to abandon certain lines.[11] Few of these enterprises clear a profit; they are reliant, therefore, on congressional subsidies, a fact which often generates continual debate over their operations and policies.

Government Service Organizations

Lastly, small bureaucracies serve the needs of the three constitutional branches. We have already encountered the Executive Office of the President and the White House staff in chapter 6, as well as the Congressional Budget Office and other congressional agencies in chapter 5. In addition, recall that each congressional committee and subcommittee has a staff, as does each member of Congress. Similarly, the judicial branch has a number of employees who serve as clerks and aides of various types. Taken together, all of these are small in comparison to the rest of the federal government; nevertheless, because they are near the centers of power, they are decidedly influential.

RECRUITMENT

Staffing government has always been a contentious issue. Everyone agrees that we should have capable and honest employees in government, but beyond that, people's preferences and ideals diverge, often sharply. Several questions arise. How politically loyal to the current administration should civil servants be? Should government employees mirror the citizenry in the society which they serve? Is it better to have a career civil service or is a system of in-and-outers preferable? What is the proper balance between specialists and generalists?

The Early Years

George Washington had a firm notion about those whom the federal government should employ. In November of 1789 he wrote, "In every nomination to office I have endeavored as far as my own knowledge extended, or information could be obtained, to make fitness of character my primary objective."[12] While aptitude to perform the task at hand was important, Washington's emphasis on character was designed primarily to secure the legitimacy of the new government. He feared that any shortcoming in the realm of honesty and probity might undermine the precarious base upon which the new government rested. As a whole, those whom he chose were highly educated "gentlemen" who served admirably.

213

BOX 7–1

Voluntary Organizations and the Public Sector

WE STRESSED in the first chapter that a healthy civic democracy generates widespread participation in voluntary institutions. In the United States we have a long tradition of a lively non-profit sector, one that undertakes an amazing variety of services which clearly add to the public good: feeding the hungry; housing the homeless; educating children; teaching literacy skills to adults; providing counseling; maintaining shelters for abused spouses and children; and so forth.

What is the proper and most desirable relation between these institutions and the government? One position holds that all, or at least most, social ser-

vices are best performed by voluntary organizations, and that government should stay its hand, except perhaps to encourage more participation by volunteers.

But this approach falters at two points. First, it assumes that voluntary organizations can meet all needs. Many social problems are so vast that they overwhelm the voluntary

sector. Second, leaving the addressing of a recognized social problem to voluntary organizations turns over a public problem to non-governmental personnel. For instance, perhaps caring for the elderly is defined as a problem worthy of public policy. If only voluntary organizations address it, no one can be sure that they do so in a way that is consistent with public desires. The decisions about which people to help and under what conditions would be made without any public input. There would be no way to guarantee that public ideas on fairness and equity were followed. At best, the result would be uncoordinated and haphazard; at

The Spoils System

Even when the Jeffersonians took over in 1801, they retained most of the Federalist officeholders, and the subsequent Democratic-Republican presidents continued more or less to follow Washington's practice.[13] By the 1820s, though, the democratization bred by the ever-expanding frontier, aptly symbolized by the election of Andrew Jackson, ushered in a new era.[14] Jackson detested the "gentlemen," and the social class from which they came. He immediately began a wholesale housecleaning and filled the vacant posts with his own political backers, generally men of much lower attainments than their predecessors. How else, he argued, could he be assured of their loyalty? If the jobs were too complex to be done by

BOX 7-1

worst, it would be contrary to public intents.

Could some type of government framework be established, perhaps using public funds, that would leave the implementation in the hands of private organizations? We could then have the public ideology prevail, while obtaining the greater efficiency and commitment of the private nonprofit sector.

However, this intuitively attractive approach has problems and drawbacks. The first is that it runs up against our traditional separation of church and state. Many of the voluntary social service organizations are connected with religious organizations; distributing public money to

them or forcing them to follow public "guidelines" would present clear constitutional problems. At the same time, it is at least arguable that such a step might undermine the vitality of the voluntary sector. If, for instance, the voluntary sector became largely dependent on public funds, donors might adopt a mentality which states, "I have already paid my taxes for that." Furthermore, if these organizations became subject to government regulations, even benign ones, they might soon come to resemble the very public bureaucracies they were supposedly replacing.

Nevertheless, the ideal of a public-private partnership is not always doomed.

If care is taken not to intertwine the organizations too much, there is room for innovation and service in the public interest. How do you think arrangements could be best structured?

Clearly, the ideals of a civic democracy oblige citizens sometimes to seek public ends through means other than government. But the line of responsibility is not entirely clear. When does too heavy an emphasis on the voluntary sector, as important as it is, show a lack of confidence in democratic government? In the final analysis, truly public problems call for public solutions—a conclusion no citizen confident in the capacity of self-government should shy away from.

ordinary people, then the tasks should be simplified. This blatant use of patronage, or the "spoils system," to reward loyal followers was clearly linked to the growth of political parties as the engine of popular representation. In time (1841 to be exact), Jackson's followers were themselves turned out of office and replaced with the victors of that day.

Throughout the middle years of the nineteenth century, this spoils system was the chief method of recruiting government employees, from the highest ranks down to the lowest. While it did lead to presidents having enormous discretion to shape and control the bureaucracy, the seamier side of the spoils system soon emerged. Corruption and the expansion of offices purely to find places for appointees were all too common. Moreover, the president's time and energy were drained by the need to deal with patronage, for there were always far more office-seekers than positions.

"In Memoriam—Our Civil Service As It Was." Cartoonist Thomas Nast's view of the spoils system, 1877.

Even during the Civil War, Lincoln was deluged with people seeking offices for themselves or friends and relatives.

Birth and Development of the Merit System

Discussions about creating a "merit system" had been going on for some years when President James Garfield was assassinated by a disappointed office-seeker in 1881. In response, Congress passed the Pendleton Act in 1883, setting up the federal civil service.[15] A Civil Service Commission was created to develop examinations and oversee recruitment. Candidates would be given an examination geared to the job they were seeking; supervisors could then choose among the top three scorers. Once appointed, the civil servant could only be removed for "cause." However, the act originally covered only a fraction of federal employees.

Through the years, the coverage of the civil service was slowly expanded. Typically, a new administration would make all the appointments it could, then extend civil service protection to them. While this approach casts doubt on the commitment of Congress to the merit principle, it did extend the civil service recruitment procedures when the offices were filled the next time around.

The next major reform was the Hatch Act of 1939. Its goal was to ensure a politically neutral civil service by prohibiting political activity of any sort (except voting) by civil servants. Although it seemed to be succeeding in this purpose, in 1973 several civil servants challenged the law in court, arguing that it deprived them of their First Amendment rights to freedom of speech. Here we can see a conflict between the citizen as a participant and the citizen as a career employee subject to popular control through election. If civil servants were as free as ordinary citizens to engage in political activity, the spoils system could and probably would creep back into place. However, to fasten political disabilities on one class of citizens threatens to detach them from the body politic, thereby running the risk that they will develop even greater self-definitions as bureaucrats. The Supreme Court recognized the dilemma, but cited Congress' discretion in structuring the executive branch, and upheld the act.[16]

While most analysts agree that overall the system erected by the Pendleton Act is beneficial, it has developed drawbacks. For one, civil servants recruited for specialist tasks who serve their entire careers in one agency inevitably become both parochial and committed to the status quo. Each major government agency, in consequence, has taken on a certain life of its own, and those who work in it have developed predictable attitudes and outlooks. Efforts, even by the president, to direct the agency are considered to be "interference," and are strongly resisted. Franklin D. Roosevelt lamented:

> The Treasury is so far flung and ingrained in its practices that I find it is almost impossible to get the action and results I want. . . . But the Treasury is not to be compared with the State Department. You should go through the experience of trying to get any changes in the thinking, policy, and action of the career diplomats and then you'd know what a real problem was. But the Treasury and the State Department put together are nothing compared with the Na-a-vy. . . . To change anything in the Na-a-vy is like punching a feather bed. You punch it with your right and you punch it with your left until you are finally exhausted, and then you find the damn bed just as it was before you started punching.[17]

In a similar vein, Jimmy Carter noted, "Before I became President, I realized and was warned that dealing with the federal bureaucracy would be one of the worst problems I would have to face. It has been worse than I had anticipated."[18]

The Carter Reforms

At Carter's urging, after much debate and sparring, Congress passed the Civil Service Reform Act of 1978. Among its major provisions were these:

1. Formation of the Senior Executive Service. These people would be generalist government managers, who would be paid on the basis of performance and could be transferred among various agencies.

The French ENA and the Training of Bureaucrats

WHEN THE FRENCH MONARCHS were consolidating their hold on the country in the seventeenth and eighteenth centuries, they built a centralized bureaucracy in order to undermine the administrative power of local nobles. In time, the nobles became social parasites, and the bureaucracy the major instrument of government. In order that talented individuals be attracted, positions carried high compensation and social prestige. Competition was keen to secure these jobs, and the children of civil servants came to enjoy enormous advantages. The bureaucracy became almost a caste, and took on a life of its own.

After the upheavals of the French Revolution, which stretched from 1789 to 1815, the political philosopher Alexis de Tocqueville noticed a curious phenomenon: the same people were still running the bureaucracy. Who, he asked, really governs France? Although the bureaucracy claimed to be politically neutral and able to serve any government, was not its first priority protecting its own position? Could a democratic government, or indeed any government, ever hope to control it?

After World War II, which had split French loyalties, there were a flurry of "reforms" of the bureaucracy (and much else). One of these was the creation of the *Ecole National d'Administration* (ENA) to train the future bureaucratic elite. It is now the most important school in the country.

Each year, fewer than one hundred candidates are selected from among university graduates, after a rigorous examination. Fewer than one in ten who even dare to take the exam pass it. Successful candidates spend two years in intensive study of the art and science of public administration. When they graduate (at age twenty-five), they are all offered high positions in the civil service, and they will rise quickly. Most will remain in the service their entire careers. The alumni of the ENA comprise an elite within an elite.

2. Establishment of new procedures for removing incompetent and indolent civil servants.

3. Creation of new protections for "whistle-blowers": those who expose waste or abuse in government agencies. In the past, such people often had their careers damaged by those above them in the hierarchy, who were eager to protect the agency from negative publicity.

Although all of these reforms have had some effect, they have not constituted the far-reaching overhaul that Carter desired. The SES has not notably improved the management of government agencies or brought forth the breath of fresh air that was hoped for. The new procedures for dismissal are still inordinately cumbersome and remain ambiguous in their

The training provided at ENA assures France of a highly talented pool of people to run the bureaucracy. No other country's top bureaucrats surpass their level of knowledge and technical expertise. However, these career bureaucrats are all but cut off from life in the society they are supposedly administering. Almost all come from the upper middle class, and a very high number are, as in the past, children of high-ranking civil servants.

Ironically, one of the purposes of ENA was to break the class stranglehold the upper middle class had on the controlling positions in the civil service. Its examinations were to be open to all. In theory, they still are. But to stand a realistic chance, one must have attended an academic high school and studied at the Institute for Political Studies. Very few working class or even middle class children can manage this. Thus, the ENA has merely solidified the hold of the upper middle class.

Occasionally, someone floats the idea that the United States should establish a National Academy of Public Administration (or an institution of similar name), which would be funded by the federal government, to train a group of politically neutral but highly competent bureaucrats. They could be given, for example, expedited paths into the Senior Executive Service. What results do you think the establishment of such an Academy would have?

It is well to consider the words of Elizabeth Sanders: "The American national bureaucracy has always been politicized. Unlike European bureaucracies, which sank their roots in a time of monarchical absolutism, national administration in the United States grew up in the rough and tumble of democratic politics. Pushed and pulled to serve alternating partisan, regional, and institutional goals, it has never been able to achieve broad legitimacy as a system for the marshaling of neutral policy expertise."[1]

---

[1] Elizabeth Sanders, "The Presidency and the Bureaucratic State," in Michael Nelson, ed., *The Presidency and the Political System,* 3d ed. (Washington: Congressional Quarterly Press, 1990), 431.

impact. Perhaps they simply make civil servants more cautious when dealing with their superiors. Lastly, the protections for whistle-blowers have not proved very effective.

Contemporary Issues

Several additional issues are also now being debated, the most controversial of which is affirmative action. If strict reliance on the system of competitive examination results in a government work force that is highly unrepresentative, specifically one that includes few members of minorities,

TABLE 7–2

Women in Federal White-Collar Occupations, 1989

CLASSIFICATION	PERCENTAGE OF FEMALES
Grades 1–6	74.8
Grades 7–10	53.5
Grades 11–12	32.9
Grades 13–15	17.0
Grades 16–18	9.1
Total	48.7

Source: Statistical Abstract of the United States, 1991.

Note: The grades (called General Schedules) cover most employees in the executive departments and the independent agencies. Grade 1 is the lowest classification and grade 18 the highest.

should the system be altered? Clearly, competence and expertise are valued in the public service; but issues of legitimacy are also germane (remember George Washington). Can a public service that is awkwardly unrepresentative of the citizenry secure the political backing necessary to make the political system work smoothly? If a representative (or near-representative) public service is desirable, what other goals should be sacrificed to attain it?

Another issue percolating through the always-shifting waters of public administration is that of "comparable worth." Many feminists argue that occupations traditionally filled by women pay less than others requiring comparable (or less) skill which men have usually taken. Therefore, the government should take the lead in reforming the structure of occupational compensation by grading each occupation according to the level of skill and training needed, and then equalizing pay among equal jobs. Critics argue, first, that whatever inequities existed in the past are being rapidly eroded by market forces and, second, that the whole exercise would be a bureaucratic nightmare.

TABLE 7–3

Minority Employment in the Executive Branch, 1989

CLASSIFICATION	PERCENTAGE OF BLACKS	PERCENTAGE OF HISPANICS
Grades 1–4	28	7
Grades 5–8	22	6
Grades 9–12	11	5
Grades 13–15	6	3
Total	16	5

Source: Statistical Abstract of the United States, 1991.

Note: These figures do not include postal service employees or armed forces personnel.

This last contention is one of the ironies of many "reforms" of the bureaucracy, actual and proposed: almost any reform creates more bureaucrats.[19] If, for instance, you want to monitor more carefully the expenditures or work habits of bureaucrats, you must employ people to do that—and then hire people to monitor the monitors. Or, in order to reorganize, restructure, realign, or otherwise redo pay scales, grades, organizational design, or work routines, people must be hired to do it. More often than not, the result of reorganizations is more offices, as many would-be "reformers" have learned to their chagrin. President Carter, for example, roundly criticized the Civil Service Commission. Before he left office he had succeeded in having the commission abolished, but in its place now stood two new offices—the Office of Personnel Management and the Merit Systems Protection Board—which together performed the old commission's functions. President Reagan, to cite another example, came to office vowing to cut the bureaucracy, but when he left the White House there were more people working for the federal government than there had been when he entered (see table 7–1).

An older but no less significant issue is the veteran's preference. Traditionally, veterans have had five points added to their examination scores (ten if they were disabled). Moreover, there are a variety of rules that give veterans other types of preferences, such as added protection from layoffs. Detractors criticize this practice as a deviation from a strict merit principle, while supporters, particularly veterans groups, contend that it is only just to give veterans employment preference in the government they have served to protect.[20] Ironically, the preference works both with and against affirmative action. Minorities make up a disproportionate share of the contemporary military and therefore stand to benefit more than whites; fewer women than men, on the other hand, have been able to avail themselves of the preference.

POLITICAL CONTROL OF THE BUREAUCRACY

While it is certainly true that vast power is often exercised by bureaucratic officials, it does not follow that "the bureaucracy" as an institution is powerful. Depicting "the federal bureaucracy" as an autonomous power center overlooks the fundamental nature of American political organization, and is simply inaccurate. First, the bureaucracy is not monolithic. It is wrong to give the impression that "the bureaucracy" is a single entity, as was the body of mandarin bureaucrats of ancient China. The American bureaucracy, in contrast, represents dispersed power, and often different agencies work at cross-purposes. Second, the political branches and the courts have final control over every aspect of the bureaucracy. And, third, outside political interests are often watching bureaucratic behavior. These matters are best examined by looking at the relationship between bureaucratic agencies and the three branches of government.

The President and the Bureaucracy

On paper, all the personnel of the executive departments and the independent agencies report to the president. In theory, therefore, commands flow downward and are obediently carried out. But presidents seldom feel that they are truly in charge of the executive branch. A different statement of the same problem lamented by Franklin D. Roosevelt and Jimmy Carter and quoted earlier in this chapter comes from Harry Truman: "I thought I was the president, but when it comes to these bureaucrats, I can't do a damn thing."[21]

But this is an overstatement. In fact, if presidents want something done and devote their attention to it, it will be done. No agency can resist or subvert the direct and persistent commands of a president. Realistically, presidential laments aside, most government employees recognize the president's general line of policy, and even if they are not enthusiastic about it, they will not often sabotage it. The norms of government service and the need to obey political superiors are important in shaping how American bureaucrats act. They are, after all, American citizens, who are committed by and large to democratic norms and who understand and respect the nature of democratic government.

Other than their direct attention, presidents have three tools to influence the behavior of bureaucratic agencies. The first and most significant is the appointment power. There are practical and political limitations, of course, on those whom a president may appoint to the senior posts in the various agencies. Someone with no scientific credentials cannot be handed the top job at NASA, and a person with no legal background cannot be appointed Attorney General. Also, certain interest groups will struggle to influence the appointees to various agencies. Yet even within these confines, the president's choices are wide. The types of people put into a senior position by the president will set a tone and a direction for the entire agency. The influence flow is two-way: the political appointees do often begin to see things from the agency's point of view, but the political appointees also bring the priorities of the administration with them, and they can be important agents of change.[22]

Second, by a longstanding arrangement, any proposed legislation coming from an executive agency must be cleared with the Office of Management and Budget, and hence with the White House. Thus, no agency may submit proposals to Congress that run counter to the president's program. A president and his chief aides can employ this legislative clearance procedure to impose a coherence on the president's program and keep agencies in line.

Third, the president has important budgetary powers. The executive budget compiled by the president and the Office of Management and Budget is, of course, not the final word, but presidential recommendations are important. Congress ordinarily modifies these presidential requests to suit its own purposes, but the initial budget figures often set important benchmarks, and presidents may use their political leverage to secure cuts in programs which are not favored by the White House, or programs in agencies they find uncooperative.

Still, presidents are usually dissatisfied, and want to affect the bureaucracy even more than they do. This is largely because they come into office fresh from an election victory and have a program they want to impose on the government. From their perspective, any foot-dragging or recalcitrance on the part of the bureaucracy is undesirable. Whenever bureaucrats do not carry out the president's priorities, they may be accused of subverting democracy. If the president were the only elected official, that would be true. But the fact of the matter is that Congress has a say in all this, and the priorities of its leaders may not (and probably will not) match the president's. Bureaucrats are often caught in this cross-fire, and what appears to a president to be insubordination is in truth merely a result of our separation of powers.

Congress and the Bureaucracy

Congress' most important attribute is its power to enact laws, including those affecting the bureaucracy. It is elementary but of fundamental importance that no one passes a law or creates a bureaucracy except Congress. Government agencies cannot take any action that is not sanctioned by a specific law of Congress. Any time Congress is dissatisfied with the way an agency is implementing the law, therefore, it can simply change the law.

For several years, Congress wrote a legislative veto provision into many acts which authorized the issuance of administrative rules and regulations. Within a given time, say ninety days, from the announcing of a new rule, Congress (or sometimes either house) could annul the rule by simple majority vote. This practice obviated the need to pass new legislation, which is cumbersome and time-consuming. However, in 1983 the legislative veto was declared unconstitutional.[23] In its place, though, have grown up a number of informal "understandings" that agencies will inform congressional committees of new rules, and that if sufficient opposition emerges, they will be rescinded.[24]

Congress, moreover, is not reluctant to use legal means, or the threat of legal changes, to affect agency behavior. In the mid-1970s, for instance, the Federal Trade Commission (which regulates unfair trading practices) issued new rules on advertising requirements for used car dealers and funeral homes.[25] Strong protests from the affected industries led Congress to go on a rampage of threats, accompanied by a chorus of complaints about "runaway bureaucracy." In short order, the proposed regulations were withdrawn.

A second item in Congress' control is the final say in the budget. Only Congress, it should be recalled, can actually authorize the expenditure of money. This means that the budget of any agency may be cut or increased purely at the discretion of Congress. (The Supreme Court has ruled that

Federal Reserve Board chairman Alan Greenspan testifying before the House Ways and Means Committee, January 1990.

the president may not refuse to spend the money once it has been appropriated.)[26] Additionally, Congress can reshuffle the funds within an agency's budget, forcing cuts in some programs and increases in others. Because most agencies have no other source of funds whatever, the budget is like a fuel line. If it is squeezed, even only slightly, agencies must and will respond.

Still another power Congress can exercise is that of reorganization. All agencies are created by Congress, and their legal and organizational structures are under its control. Thus, for example, one way to punish an agency would be to transfer it from a friendly department to a hostile one. Or, its work could be hampered by the imposition of new procedures, such as a requirement to clear certain actions with another department.

Although we have been speaking of Congress as a whole, most of the dealings between agencies and Congress are channeled through standing committees. In fact, committees in both the House and the Senate are formally charged with "oversight" functions.[27] This leads to frequent hearings in which bureau chiefs or others are asked to explain how their programs are working, and to what effect. At times, citizens, interest groups, or the General Accounting Office (the congressional auditing agency) also testify at these hearings. Frequently, the hearings are followed by reports, which may suggest changes in the law or in an agency's structure.

By all accounts, bureau chiefs and other agency personnel take these hearings very seriously. Herbert Kaufman, for instance, found that bureaucrats put a good deal of emphasis on how well they perform during these sessions.[28] One senator who chaired an oversight committee told a researcher, "I just know that the ones I oversee are on the phone and in the

TABLE 7–4

Changing Amounts of Time Spent on Oversight by
Congressional Committees

	TOTAL COMMITTEE WORK DAYS	OVERSIGHT DAYS	PERCENTAGE OF WORK TIME SPENT ON OVERSIGHT
1963	1,820	159	8.7
1973	2,513	290	11.5
1983	2,331	587	25.2

Source: Joel Aberbach, *Keeping a Watchful Eye: The Politics of Congressional Oversight* (Washington: Brookings, 1990), 35.

office all the time. I think the hearings do it. You just have to demonstrate some serious interest . . . and make suggestions. On the whole they welcome them. . . . They know that they need you to go to bat for them at OMB. So it can become a very mutually supportive and pretty constructive relationship."[29]

Most indicators point to an upsurge in congressional oversight activity over the last fifteen years, as depicted in table 7–4.[30] Joel Aberbach has offered four reasons for this shift.[31] First, the public now puts a higher value on how well existing programs work than on setting up new ones. Members of Congress sense political payoffs, then, in focusing some of their energies there. Second, there is a real or imagined scarcity of resources. Thus, how the money is spent has become more important. Third, there are lingering effects of the congressional response to the Nixon presidency. Congressional sensitivities were ruffled when Nixon tried to bypass Congress and oversee the bureaucracy alone. Fourth, the internal reforms of the 1970s, particularly the growth of subcommittees, has increased congressional capabilities in the area of oversight.

Courts and the Bureaucracy

Courts have always had jurisdiction over bureaucratic activity when interpretations of law were at issue. For example, tax laws often contain complex definitions, and businesses and individuals have long had the right to challenge in court the Internal Revenue Service's reading of the provisions. Or, if any agency denied a benefit, such as a veteran's pension, to a recipient, the disgruntled applicant could seek redress in the courts.

Since World War II, and especially since the late 1960s, however, the role of courts in the life of executive agencies has grown exponentially. One cause of this was passage of the Administrative Procedures Act in 1946,[32] but a more important one has been the changing assumptions with which the judges have approached administrative law.

The Administrative Procedures Act set out a series of steps that administrative agencies must take before they can issue a new rule. The basic requirements are that the rule must be within the scope of legislation; that the rule be clearly stated; that public notice be made; that interested parties be given ample opportunity to comment; and that some advance warning be given regarding the date of implementation. The act also provides that an affected party may challenge a rule in court if these procedures are not adhered to. Only a few cases have actually gone to court, but the impact of the act has been to make agencies sensitive to legal procedures and the precedents courts have set.

Of greater significance has been the judicial and legislative loosening of "standing" requirements, a change that has opened the door to a hoard of suits challenging the substance or content of agency decisions. Traditionally, courts had not allowed private citizens or interest groups to challenge decisions by government officials, arguing that their interest was too remote and that that was the purpose of the political branches. In the 1960s, however, that requirement was modified so that suits by individuals or groups claiming to represent some substantial segment of the public (veterans, blacks, environmentalists, consumers) or even the general public are now common.

For example, the testing methods used by the Food and Drug Administration (FDA) before it approves new drugs or before it requires the manufacturer to remove a previously sanctioned drug from the market are quite controversial.[33] Everyone wants helpful drugs approved quickly and harmful ones barred from the market, but opinions differ sharply over how much risk is acceptable in balancing these factors. In years past, this was a matter for debate between the experts at FDA, Congress, and the current administration, with pressures all around from drug companies and consumer groups.

In 1970 a public interest group filed a suit maintaining that a correct reading of the statute governing the FDA dictated the conclusion that the procedures used to remove dangerous drugs from the market were too slow, a contention with which the courts agreed. After the decision, the FDA shifted some of its resources to meet the new guidelines imposed by the court, and also, quite logically, tightened its testing procedures for new drugs. Naturally, this move slowed down the approval time for new drugs. When the Reagan administration took office, the FDA was prodded to relax these stringent testing procedures and get new drugs into the hands of doctors and hospitals more quickly (a position endorsed by AIDS activists, among others). A consumer group, though, filed a new series of suits challenging the revisions; these suits dragged on in the courts for several years. The point here is not that the Reagan administration's proposals were better than the consumer group's or vice versa; it is rather that the courts became a key player, alongside the experts, members of Congress, and the administration.

The Occupational Health and Safety Administration (OSHA) provides another cogent example. Its main function is to issue rules and regulations regarding workplace safety, and then to see that they are enforced. In a familiar pattern, agency public health experts, Congress, and administrations continually vie for influence, with business and labor groups actively lobbying on every front. Almost without exception, when rules are issued, labor groups claim that they are too lax and business interests aver that they are burdensome, unnecessary, and too costly. Not only do these two groups complain in public, however; both often go to court. Business suits challenging the rules are based on the traditional legal rationale discussed above. What is novel is that unions routinely file suits arguing that the agency is not adhering to its statutory responsibilities as spelled out in the law, a contention with which the courts often agree.

In short, many government agencies are frequently in court justifying their decisions to judges. Naturally, what is decided in court affects the internal procedures of other agencies, casting the "shadow of litigation," as it is called. As a result, lawyers are now indispensable throughout the bureaucracy, and their influence within agencies has risen. Some analysts believe that a major consequence of these suits has been to make bureaucracies even more cautious than they normally are. Fear of being challenged in court makes them hesitate to undertake any but the most timid actions that can be justified under the statute.

Local Governments and the Federal Bureaucracy

There is evidence that local officials have some impact on the federal bureaucracy, even though there is no formal role for them. A few studies have shown that several federal agencies which have field offices throughout the country develop some "play in the joints" (some flexibility, that is), which allows federal officials at the lower levels of the organization to exercise discretion. The wishes and desires of local elected officials then becomes one of the factors they consider as they go about their tasks. For instance, one research team found that the enforcement of several factory safety rules by OSHA was more lax in Republican-dominated (and hence more pro-business) counties and more rigid in counties controlled by the Democrats (and hence more pro-labor).[34] Thus, federal agencies are penetrated not only by national elected officials but by local ones as well.

BUREAUCRACY AND ACCOUNTABILITY

It is still true that a certain amount of power inheres in any bureaucracy, and that this power can lead to abuse. But are American bureaucracies semi-autonomous fiefdoms detached from political responsibility? The foregoing paragraphs tend to paint the opposite picture: a bureaucracy subject to diverse and perhaps debilitating control by all three branches, and even by local politicians. A pervasiveness of controls, not their absence, seems to be the main theme.

What may be overlooked in such a survey is that the American bureaucracy is shaped by the separation of powers and by federalism. In a political system which fuses legislative and executive powers and downplays judicial power (such as that in Britain), bureaucracies are best held accountable by being placed under department heads who are responsible to the legislature.[35] In our fragmented system, with multiple centers of elected officials, control is as much in evidence, but it is dispersed. American bureaucracies become a prey to interinstitutional politics, particularly the continual struggles between Congress and the president.

When Presidents Roosevelt, Carter, and Truman were bemoaning their lack of control over the bureaucracy, they were simply making another comment on their relations with Congress. The agencies were responding to the political realities of congressional pressure. Likewise, when members of Congress complain about "runaway bureaucracy," they are usually only complaining about the fact that the agency is responding to other political forces, either the president or perhaps other factions in Congress. The problem (if it really is a problem) is not a lack of control, but the fact that the controllers speak with many voices. No one can please three masters. So long as our constitutional system disperses power, there will be cross-pressures on the bureaucracy.

A final issue regarding accountability raises once again the potential conflict between the roles of citizen and of public servant for those who staff the bureaucracy. To what extent does the good citizen-bureaucrat owe allegiance to the set of politicians currently holding office, as opposed to her obligations to the Constitution and the mass of the citizenry generally? If the elected officials ask her to carry out policies she genuinely believes are unconstitutional and contrary to the spirit of democratic government, what should she do? Most graphically, this dilemma can be seen in the military. Suppose a president ordered the military to stage a coup. The clear ethos of democracy says that soldiers should obey a civilian commander-in-chief; however, a coup clearly violates the nature of the government established by the Constitution. Should military commanders disregard the Constitution in order to save it? But if military commanders are given the authority to refuse orders which *they believe* to be unconstitutional, the door to bureaucratic irresponsibility swings wide open.

Of course, an order for a coup to be carried out is most improbable in the United States. In the everyday life of bureaucracy, though, career officials must exercise a degree of discretion. When, if ever, should they rely on their own views of what the constitutional system commands (assuming naturally that this is a sincere belief and not a mere cover for selfish action)?[36] Or, should they always simply carry out the desires of elected politicians? There is no comfortable answer to this dilemma. If we expect conscientious citizens as opposed to mindless functionaries to staff the bureaucracy, the dilemma will be ever present.[37]

BUREAUCRACIES AND INTEREST GROUPS

A critically important factor in bureaucratic life is an agency's relationship with interest groups. At least four different patterns can be detected.

First, there are agencies which have a very close relationship with contractors and suppliers, but with few other parties. These may be large agencies charged with high-level political matters, such as the Defense Department, or they may be small and routinized, such as the United States Mint. The Defense Department is closely intertwined with the producers of weapons systems—so much so that the line between public and private is often blurred. The heavy economic stakes pull in members of Congress, since they all want contracts for businesses in their states and districts. The close relationship is most evident at budget time, when any cuts in the armed forces budget will be opposed by the firms which stand to lose contracts, and usually by the members of Congress from affected districts. In the case of the mint, the relationships it enjoys with such firms as copper and silver mining concerns are less visible and have less total impact. Sometimes even here, however, a proposal will trigger intense lobbying. In 1990, for instance, an idea floated around Washington to do away with the penny and the one-dollar bill, since inflation had changed the needs for currency. The copper mining companies and those firms which sell ink for paper money launched a campaign against the proposal, and it died.

Second, there is a relationship, found most often in the clientele agencies, of almost total symbiosis. Departments such as Agriculture, Education, Labor, and Veterans Affairs see themselves as spokespersons for their clients within government. Importantly, with the exception of labor, none of them has an opposition group; there is no anti-farm, anti-education, or anti-veterans lobby. Furthermore, both the agency and the interest groups develop close working relationships with the congressional committees in their area. This cozy relationship is sometimes called an "iron triangle." The consequence for policy is that it is difficult for outsiders—other members of Congress, or even the president—to penetrate the iron triangle. The permanency of the personnel in all three corners of the triangle, especially when compared to the temporary tenure of the people sitting atop the executive branch, gives them an inherent advantage. However, though it may be difficult to penetrate iron triangles, it is not impossible. Presidents and their allies in Congress can fracture, if not crush them if they are determined enough. Nonetheless, the alliances within them are always powerful.

A third pattern emerges in regulatory agencies. Rather than being created to help a clientele, this type of agency is created to regulate it in the public interest. Typically, it is a sector of the economy that is being regulated, such as nuclear power, trucking, railroads, airlines, the stock exchanges, broadcasting, etc. Although it is not universal, a common pattern has been for the agency to show a great deal of vigor in its early years, as energetic administrators establish a new regulatory framework.[38] Over time, as the regulated business exercises influence over appointments and enthusiasm flags, the agency becomes tamed, or even captured, by the industry it is supposed to be regulating. It can turn (and some agencies have turned) into a perversion of the original intent. The regulatory body may be used to keep prices artificially high and to keep potential competitors out of the field. Nonetheless, no matter how much the agency is transformed in practice, the legal framework remains one of regulation,

FIGURE 7–2

The Iron Triangle in Veterans' Benefits Policy

Department of
Veterans Affairs

House and Senate
Veterans Affairs Committees

Veterans Groups ("The Big Three")
American Legion
Veterans of Foreign Wars
Disabled American Veterans

and the adversary relationship may be rekindled by new presidential appointees. Presidents Carter and Reagan, for instance, dramatically jolted the love affair between the Federal Aviation Administration and the major airlines.

Finally, there are conflict-laden agencies, whose tasks fall in the political battleground of two or more hostile groups. A clear example is OSHA, whose difficulties are noted above; another is the Environmental Protection Agency. Congress has empowered the EPA, for instance, to issue regulations setting the acceptable discharge levels for a number of pollutants. Environmental groups and business firms constantly lobby the agency to tighten or loosen the regulations. Every regulation and every revision is certain to be attacked by one or the other (at times by both simultaneously) as being either too lax or too strict. Furthermore, there are several environmental groups, which do not always agree, as well as a multitude of different types of businesses. Every group and business has its supporters and detractors in Congress, and seldom can the president be counted on for unqualified support. Hence, conflict continually swirls around the agency, since it can please no one. (We will revisit this state of affairs in chapter 12.)

SUMMARY

Bureaucracies are inherently undemocratic in their hierarchical structure and their heavy emphasis on expertise, but at the same time are necessary in the governing of any modern, complex society. The American federal bureaucracy is large (but not as large as the state-local sector), and has remained remarkably stable over the last forty years. A number of different organizational forms are used by the federal government: executive departments, independent agencies, regulatory commissions, foundations, and government corporations. Each has distinct characteristics and decided political consequences.

George Washington began a system of recruitment for the public service based on character and ability, but Andrew Jackson initiated a spoils system in the 1820s. Later, a merit-based civil service, which now covers most federal workers, was established. President Carter secured several reforms, but their impact has not been great. Contemporary issues such as affirmative action, comparable worth, and the veteran's preference continue to provoke debate about the virtues of merit versus other considerations.

Although the bureaucratic abuse of power is always possible, American bureaucracies are subject to a number of important political checks. The president has significant appointment and budgetary powers, in addition to a legislative clearance procedure. Congress controls the legal framework and the budgets of all government agencies. In practice, congressional committees exercise the oversight power, and the importance of this activity in the work of the committees seems to be growing. For their part, courts exercise influence over bureaucracies by insisting that they follow judicial readings of the law, not their own.

An important determinant of how a bureaucracy operates can be found in the relations it has with interest groups. These range from cooperative ones with suppliers, through clientele symbiosis and regulation of various bodies, to the pressure of cross-cutting conflict-laden situations.

ENDNOTES

1. See the surveys cited in Charles Goodsell, *The Case for Bureaucracy,* 2d ed. (Chatham, N.J.: Chatham House, 1985), chap. 2.

2. These data are from two compilations, *Historical Statistics of the United States* (Washington: U.S. Department of Commerce, 1977) and the *Statistical Abstract of the United States 1990* (Washington: U.S. Department of Commerce, 1991).

3. Article II, Section 2. The President "may require the opinion in writing, of the principal officer in each of the executive departments, upon any subject relating to the duties of their respective offices."

4. A good basic survey of the structure of the executive branch is Peter Woll, *American Bureaucracy,* 2d ed. (New York: Norton, 1977), although it has become somewhat dated in detail. See also James Fesler and Donald Kettl, *The Politics of the Administrative Process* (Chatham, N.J.: Chatham House, 1991).

5. Recall from chapter 6 that these department heads are appointed by the president with Senate approval. They may be removed at any time, however, by the president.

6. President Bush in fact suggested this, but did not push for it.

7. An older but still valuable study of these bodies is Marver Bernstein, *Regulating Business by Independent Commission* (Princeton, N.J.: Princeton University Press, 1955). The fate of these commissions in the 1980s is discussed in Larry Gerston, et al., *The Deregulated Society* (Pacific Grove, Calif.: Brooks/Cole, 1988).

8. Presidents may not remove members of these commissions, since their terms are fixed. See *Weiner v. United States,* 357 U.S. 349 (1958).

9. The role of the Federal Reserve Board is carefully analyzed in Donald Kettl, *Leadership at the Fed* (New Haven, Conn.: Yale University Press, 1986).

10. The chief consequence of the Fed's action is change in interest rates. If there is more money in circulation, interest rates tend to fall, and vice versa. Thus, the affordability of homes and major purchases, such as automobiles, will be directly affected; this will in turn have an impact on the construction and manufacturing sectors of the economy.

11. See David Baron, "Distributive Politics and the Persistence of Amtrak," *Journal of Politics* 52 (1990), 883–913.

12. Quoted in Leonard D. White, *The Federalists: A Study in Administrative History* (New York: Macmillan, 1948), 258.

13. See Leonard D. White, *The Jeffersonians: An Administrative History* (New York: Macmillan, 1951).

14. Again, one of the best sources is a book by Leonard D. White, *The Jacksonians: A Study in Administrative History* (New York: Macmillan, 1954).

15. The standard history is Ari Hoogenboom, *Outlawing the Spoils: A History of the Civil Service Reform Movement, 1865–1883* (Urbana: University of Illinois Press, 1961). See also Justus Doenecke, *The Presidencies of James A. Garfield and Chester A. Arthur* (Lawrence: University Press of Kansas, 1981), esp. 96–101.

16. *U.S. Civil Service Commission v. National Ass'n of Letter Carriers,* 413 U.S. 548, 93 S.Ct. 2880 (1973).

17. Quoted in Graham Allison, *Essence of Decision* (Boston: Little, Brown, 1971), 86.

18. Larry Berman, *The New American Presidency* (Boston: Little, Brown, 1987), 109.

19. The ultimate example of this tendency exists in Italy. A number of years ago that country's government set up a Ministry for the Reform of the Bureaucracy, which has its own huge bureaucracy and produces innumerable studies and analyses. However, it has had virtually no success in cutting down on the size of the bureaucracy. We usually assign such studies to temporary bodies, such as the Grace Commission of the Reagan administration. Its effect seems to have been minimal also.

20. Of course, one way to solve this problem would be to have universal military conscription. Most continental European democracies, it may be worth noting, have universal male military conscription.

21. Berman, *New American Presidency,* 99.

22. B. Dan Wood and Richard Waterman, "The Dynamics of Political Control of the Bureaucracy," *American Political Science Review,* 85 (1991), 801–828.

23. See Barbara Craig, *Chadha: The Story of an Epic Constitutional Struggle* (New York: Oxford University Press, 1988).

24. See Louis Fisher, *Constitutional Dialogues* (Princeton, N.J.: Princeton University Press, 1988), 224–28.

25. The rules were not particularly draconian. They required funeral homes to tell customers the price of each individual item in the funeral package, and used car dealers to post on the window of the automobile a list of any known defects. See Kenneth Clarkson and Timothy Muris, eds., *The Federal Trade Commission since 1970* (Cambridge: Cambridge University Press, 1981).

26. *Train v. City of New York,* 420 U.S. 35, 95 S.Ct. 839 (1975).

27. See Joel Aberbach, *Keeping a Watchful Eye: The Politics of Congressional Oversight* (Washington: Brookings, 1990).

28. Herbert Kaufman, *The Administrative Behavior of Federal Bureau Chiefs* (Washington: Brookings, 1981).

29. Aberbach, *Watchful Eye,* 196.

30. To give another example, in 1970 the Pentagon was requested to supply 36 reports to Congress. By 1985, that number had grown to 1,172. James Q. Wilson, *Bureaucracy* (New York: Basic Books, 1989), 244.

31. Aberbach, *Watchful Eye,* 191–193.

32. A brief discussion of the APA and its operation can be found in Phillip Cooper, *Public Law and Public Administration* (Englewood Cliffs, N.J.: Prentice-Hall, 1983), chap. 5.

33. The discussions in this example and the next are drawn from Jeremy Rabkin, *Judicial Compulsions: How Public Law Distorts Public Policy* (New York: Basic Books, 1989), chaps. 6 and 7.

34. John T. Scholz, Jim Twombly, and Barbara Headrick, "Street-Level Political Controls over Federal Bureaucracy," *American Political Science Review* 85 (1991), 829–850.

35. Even in Britain, though, courts are playing an ever-increasing role in administrative politics. See Bernard Schwartz, *Lions over the Throne: The Judicial Revolution in English Administrative Law* (New York: New York University Press, 1987).

36. This question is not merely academic. During the Nixon years there were attempts to manipulate the Internal Revenue Service and other agencies to harass those whom Nixon and his aides considered political enemies. In many cases the bureaucracies did not comply, or did not comply fully through foot-dragging and other tactics, because officials believed such demands ran counter to the norms of democratic governance and political fair play.

37. At least one scholar believes the answer to any pathologies of the bureaucracy is to ensure that bureaucrats receive in-depth citizenship education, and then use those norms to carry out their tasks. John Rohr, *To Run a Constitution: The Legitimacy of the Administrative State* (Lawrence: University Press of Kansas, 1986).

38. See Louis Kohlmeier's classic, *The Regulators* (New York: Harper and Row, 1969) as well as Gerston, *Deregulated Society.*

FURTHER READING

1. Bryner, Gary., *Bureaucratic Discretion.* New York: Pergammon Press, 1987.
2. Cooper, Terry. *An Ethic of Citizenship for Public Administration.* Englewood Cliffs, N.J.: Prentice-Hall, 1991.
3. Fesler, James and Donald Kettl. *The Politics of the Administrative Process.* Chatham, N.J.: Chatham House, 1991.
4. Nathan, Richard P. *The Plot That Failed: Nixon and the Administrative Presidency.* New York: Wiley, 1975.
5. Ripley, Randall B. and Grace Franklin. *Congress, the Bureaucracy, and Public Policy.* 4th ed. Homewood, Ill.: Dorsey, 1987.
6. Seidman, Harold and Robert Gilmour. *Politics, Position, and Power.* New York: Oxford University Press, 1986.
7. Wilson, James Q. *Bureaucracy: What Government Agencies Do and Why They Do It.* New York: Basic Books, 1989.
8. Woll, Peter. *American Bureaucracy.* 2d ed. New York: Norton, 1977.

EIGHT

THE FEDERAL COURTS

Many PEOPLE BELIEVE that courts are not, or at least should not be, involved in anything so pedestrian as politics. Rather, the courts should remain unsullied and concern themselves only with the law. Others wish to strip the facade of legalism from the courts and face the fact that they are political institutions as much as the presidency and Congress. It is naive and perhaps dangerous to pretend that politics is not being played out in the courtroom.

Both of these views contain an element of truth, but both are also flawed. The first view seeks to force a sharp and unrealistic dichotomy between law and politics, while the second considers them synonymous. The truth is that law and politics overlap, but they are not identical. Courts are unavoidably political institutions—but they are still courts. The politics that goes on here, then, is not exactly like politics conducted elsewhere.

The exercise of political power by courts nonetheless creates a paradox for democratic government: there is an irreducible tension between democratic theory, whether individualist or civic, and judicial power. Any type of democracy must rest on popular control of government, and since federal judges are elected by no one and cannot be removed short of impeachment, their power is always suspect. Yet, judicial power has always been and remains a central part of our political system, and both individualist and civic democrats find ways to justify and support it.

STRUCTURE OF THE COURT SYSTEM

Article III of the Constitution, which establishes the structure and powers of the federal courts, is much briefer than Articles I and II, which set up Congress and the presidency. Only the barest framework is laid out here; legislation and political practice have filled out the details.

"The judicial power of the United States shall be vested in one Supreme Court, and in such inferior courts as the Congress may from time to time ordain and establish," reads Article III. The first congress tackled this matter through the Judiciary Act of 1789; major modifications were made later by the Circuit Court Act of 1891 and the Judiciary Act of 1925.

Opposite: *The facade of the Supreme Court building, Washington, D.C.*

FIGURE 8-1

The American Judicial System

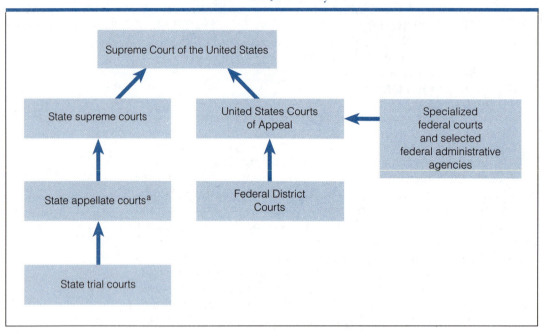

^aNot all states have intermediate courts of appeal; in such states appeals go directly from trial courts to the state supreme court.

Unlike most federal countries, the United States has a dual court system. That is, each of the fifty states and the federal government has its own hierarchy of courts. In other nations, the federal government has only courts of final appeal, and leaves the conduct of trials up to state or provincial courts. At the apex of our system, though, the systems are joined, in that appeals go from state supreme courts to the U.S. Supreme Court (but only if the case raises a federal question). (See figure 8–1.) This is, incidentally, the only formal vertical link in our system between parallel federal and state institutions.

In order to grasp how any court system functions, it is necessary to distinguish between trial and appellate courts. In the former, litigants air their arguments before a judge and possibly a jury. At issue are questions of both fact and law. Appellate courts, in contrast, are designed to hear only questions of law. Normally, appellate courts have more than one judge; in the United States, the usual number is three or nine.

At the base of the federal court system are ninety-four Federal District Courts. There is at least one in each state, and no district crosses state lines. The number of judges assigned to each district varies with the volume of judicial business, from two in Wyoming to twenty-seven in the Southern District of New York. In 1991, these courts heard 241,420 cases.[1]

The country is divided into eleven circuits for the next tier of courts, the Federal Courts of Appeal (see figure 8–2). Decisions of district judges

TABLE 8-1

Major Types of Cases Heard by Federal District Courts (1990)

TYPE OF CASE	NUMBER
Prisoner petitions	42,500
Torts[a]	37,300
Contracts	34,500
Civil rights	19,300
Labor suits	14,700
Real property	9,800
Tax suits	8,200
Social security appeals	7,700
Narcotics violations	7,600
Copyright, patent, and trademark	5,200
Fraud	6,200
Marijuana and other controlled substances	3,800
Weapons and firearms violations	2,900
Illegal immigration	2,000

Source: Administrative Office of the United States Courts, *1991 Federal Court Management Statistics,* 167.

[a]Torts are civil wrongs which require monetary settlements.

involving the interpretation of law may be appealed to these courts. The number of judges assigned to the different Courts of Appeal also varies. Usually, cases are heard by three-judge panels, but occasionally all the justices of a court will be convened to decide an especially important or difficult case. In 1991, the eleven courts heard 42,033 cases.

At the top of the system sits the Supreme Court of the United States. With only a few minor exceptions, its cases come on appeal from either the Courts of Appeal or the state supreme courts.[2] Since 1925, the Supreme Court has had almost complete control over its docket (the list of cases it will hear). Often, therefore, what the Court refuses to hear is as important as what it does hear. If the Supreme Court turns down an appeal, the holding of the next lower court stands; however, this does not signify that the Supreme Court agrees with the way the lower court has decided the case. It merely means that the issue raised is not deemed important enough at this time to warrant Supreme Court resolution. About five thousand appeals are made each year, but the Supreme Court takes only about 6 to 8 percent of these.

Standing outside this neat three-level hierarchy are a number of specialized courts, such as the Court of Military Appeals, the Tax Court, and bankruptcy courts. In addition, a number of executive agencies exercise quasi-judicial powers, such as awarding licenses and setting rates. In both instances, the rulings can be appealed to the federal courts, ordinarily first at the Court of Appeals level. In fact, there is a special Court of Appeals in Washington to hear appeals from the huge number of federal regulatory agencies headquartered there.

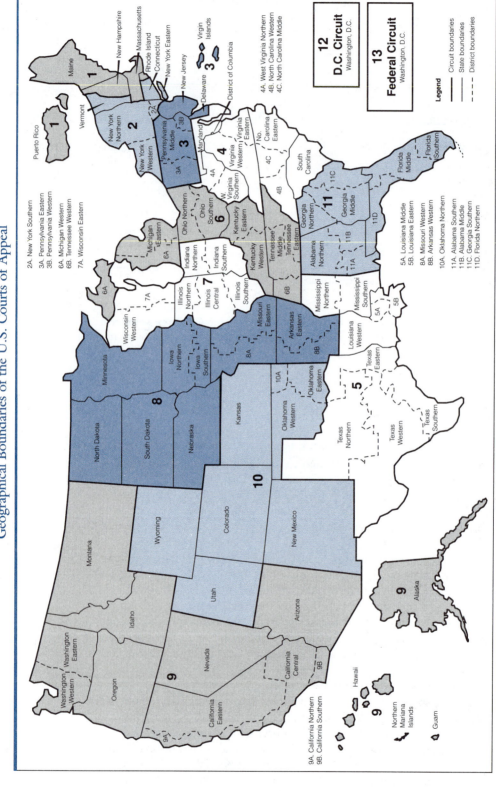

FIGURE 8-2

Geographical Boundaries of the U.S. Courts of Appeal

240

THE COURTS AT WORK

What types of cases do the District Courts hear? Although the issues of federal jurisdiction and procedure are enormously complex (constituting a whole specialty in law schools), there are three major types of cases, two of which are especially important politically. The first type is ordinary criminal and civil suits: counterfeiting, kidnapping, and so forth fall in the former category, while business conflicts between businesses located in different states; trademark infringement; and other similar matters make up the latter. While naturally quite important to the people involved, these cases do not usually raise matters of general public policy.

The second type of case calls for the interpretation of a federal law. Since many of the laws adopted by Congress contain opaque phrases necessitated by political compromise, the interpretations the courts put on statutes can have far-reaching consequences. Some observers believe that Congress in fact sometimes purposely passes the political hot potatoes to the courts by leaving the real decisions to the judges as they fill in the details.[3] Whatever the truth, the broadening reach of the federal government since World War II has significantly increased the importance of statutory interpretation.

The third type of case is of especial importance, calling for interpretation of the Constitution itself. Whenever a person believes governmental authorities have violated the Constitution, either by acting beyond their powers or by failing to undertake what the Constitution commands, he may initiate a suit in the nearest Federal District Court.

At the Court of Appeals and Supreme Court levels, the docket is composed entirely of the second and third types of cases, and only the more important of those.[4] Thus, the decisions in these courts become laden more with overtones of public policy and less with purely technical legal matters. The language is legal, but the reality is highly political.

JUDICIAL REVIEW

Without question, the greatest power of the courts lies in their ability to exercise *judicial review*: the power to declare laws passed by Congress and signed by the president; laws enacted by the states; actions of the president; or actions of local governments or officials to be in conflict with the Constitution, and therefore invalid. This power flows from the fact that the Supreme Court has been assigned the task of interpreting the Constitution. Although who should interpret the Constitution is nowhere specified in the document itself, or even directly implied, judicial review has become so central to our political practice that doing away with it would be little short of revolutionary.

Historians have labored tirelessly trying to decide whether or not the Founding Fathers intended to provide for judicial review. In the final analysis, the evidence is sketchy and inconclusive. Why then did the practice develop? Three answers can be given: the legal/historical answer, the pragmatic answer, and the philosophical answer.

The Legal/Historical Justification

To the lawyer and the historian, we have judicial review because an early case, *Marbury v. Madison* (1803) set the precedent and has been adhered to since. As he left office in 1801, President John Adams, who had lost the election to Thomas Jefferson, appointed a large number of his supporters to various federal offices. Some of the documents certifying several low-level appointees in their offices were inadvertently left in the State Department and not delivered. When the new secretary of state, James Madison, took office, President Jefferson ordered the documents destroyed and made new appointments. William Marbury, a disgruntled Adams appointee for Justice of the Peace for the District of Columbia, went to court to compel Madison to produce his commission to office.

One provision of the lengthy Judiciary Act of 1789 provided that in cases of this sort the plaintiff (the party bringing a suit) should go directly to the Supreme Court. However, Article III of the Constitution had specifically listed the instances in which the Supreme Court has "original," as opposed to "appellate," jurisdiction, and Marbury's case fit none of these. Seizing this inconsistency, the Supreme Court under the leadership of Chief Justice John Marshall[5] declared that the section of the Judiciary Act of 1789 which sought to confer this additional power on the Supreme Court was in conflict with the Constitution and therefore invalid. In short, the Supreme Court alone could interpret the Constitution. Marshall wrote:

> If a law be in opposition to the Constitution; if both the law and the Constitution apply to a particular case, so that the court must either decide that case conformably to the law, disregarding the Constitution; or conformably to the Constitution, disregarding the law; the court must determine which of these conflicting rules governs the case. This is of the very essence of judicial duty.
>
> If, then, the courts are to regard the Constitution, and the Constitution is superior to any ordinary act of the legislature, the Constitution, and not such ordinary act, must govern the case to which they both apply.[6]

Unquestionably, this case set a valuable precedent, but not everyone was convinced. Presidents often claimed in the years that followed, for instance, that they had as much right as the courts to interpret the Constitution. In practical fact, though, it was over half a century later before the Supreme Court struck down another act of Congress. (In this second instance, though, it was not a trivial jurisdictional matter, but a critical part of the compromises by which Congress had sidestepped the issue of slavery in the territories.)[7]

The Pragmatic Argument

The pragmatic argument takes a somewhat different approach, coming to judicial review through a process of elimination. Obviously, the Constitution must be interpreted by someone, and in our system of government there are only four options. The task of interpretation could be assigned to the states, Congress, the president, or the courts.

Should the states take over constitutional interpretation, as was seriously suggested by the Virginia and Kentucky Resolutions in 1798 and by any number of southerners during the lead-up to the Civil War and later during the civil rights years, the results would be disastrous for national unity. Potentially, there would be fifty different interpretations of each clause, leading to certain chaos. This is not, then, a realistic option.

Congress, the institution favored by Thomas Jefferson, is better suited to interpret the Constitution than are the states. However, when would Congress exercise the power of interpretation? Under what circumstances would it pass a law and then declare it unconstitutional? Of course, after an election changed the political composition of Congress, it might declare a law unconstitutional; but a new Congress already has the power to repeal an offending law anyway. Furthermore, imagine how sufficiently Congress could hobble a president if it could interpret her powers under Article II. In effect, to give Congress the power of constitutional review would be to make that power a nullity. If reverence for the Constitution continued, perhaps it would constrain Congress on some fronts, but political pressures would constantly push those who held a majority to find ingenious interpretations that suited their temporary purposes. Constitutional interpretation could not be divorced from simple majoritarian politics.

The third option is that presidents interpret the Constitution—but that idea is equally unsound. Aside from the obvious problem that few presidents have any expertise in this area (of post-war presidents, only Richard Nixon, Gerald Ford, and Bill Clinton have even been lawyers), the veto would become redundant. If the president disliked a congressional enactment, he would simply declare it unconstitutional, and there could be no two-thirds override. Such a power would throw the system of checks and balances into serious disarray.

Thus, by the process of elimination we come to the Supreme Court. The Court has the advantage that its members have at least some claim to expertise. But more importantly, it has the best available distance from the partisan political fray. On a day-to-day basis, the decisions of the Court are less influenced directly by the pull and tug of politics than are those of any of the other branches. Issues can be discussed in the relative tranquillity of the courtroom and the conference chambers, without the distractions of elections. At the same time, the Court is not totally detached from the political system; the judges neither originate from nor reside on Mount Olympus. Judges are chosen by the politicized branches, and continue to be influenced by the intellectual and political currents which swirl around them. Age and death, moreover, assure that the Court's personnel will change, and that the ideas and influences of new political groups will seep into the Court. Thus, the Supreme Court is only semidetached from politics. In an imperfect world, this is not a bad compromise.

Buttressing the pragmatic argument is the issue of federalism which we raised in an earlier chapter. A federal system requires an umpire to arbitrate the competing claims to power made by the two levels of government.

The Supreme Court, 1992. First row, left to right: John Paul Stevens, Byron White, William Rehnquist, Harry Blackmun, Sandra Day O'Connor. Back row, left to right: David Souter, Antonin Scalia, Anthony Kennedy, and Clarence Thomas.

Clearly, the states, Congress, and the president are unfit for this role, since they are the participants in the conflict. The Supreme Court is again an imperfect organ for this task, but it seems to be the best available. If, therefore, the Supreme Court is to interpret the provisions of the Constitution regarding federalism, by implication it should interpret the other parts as well.

Philosophical Analysis

The philosophical argument begins with the proposition that the Constitution is superior to ordinary law. If it is to retain its status as society's basic political charter and simultaneously play its symbolic role (as discussed in chapter 2), it must stand above ordinary law, and ordinary politics. There is a powerful need, therefore, for the Constitution's meaning to be stable and consistent, while still open to gradual change. The Constitution is, in this view, not only an anchor for the social order, but also a compact between one generation and the next.

The Supreme Court has strong credentials as the appropriate institution to be custodian of the Constitution. First, because it is a court, it gives weighty consideration to precedent. Thus, there is a built-in tendency to continue an interpretation handed down from the past, with the burden of proof always lying on the person or group wanting the interpretation changed. Change is possible and indeed almost certain, but it is likely to be evolutionary in nature. Second, the symbolic character of the Constitution is enhanced by the mystique of a robed assembly seated in a "marble temple"[8] to decide the meaning of the Constitution. The Constitution has a quasi-religious property to it, and so does the Court. Finally, because the Court has a continuing membership, it represents and symbolizes the continuity of the political system. Elected politicians may come and go, but the Supreme Court remains. Even during the Civil War, for example, when no southern members of Congress attended and no southern votes were cast in the presidential election of 1864, the Supreme Court, including its southern members, continued to sit. The Supreme Court therefore combines a preference for stability with an openness to change, a strong sense of symbolism with continuity through time.

GUIDELINES FOR THE BEHAVIOR OF JUDGES

A mere consensus that judicial review is proper most definitely does not create a consensus on how judges should approach their task. By what guidelines and criteria should the Supreme Court approach the business of constitutional interpretation?

Judicial Activism versus Judicial Restraint

The first distinction that is usually made is between the schools of judicial restraint and judicial activism.[9] Advocates of judicial restraint believe that judges should give maximum discretion to political majorities at all levels of government. The proper judicial role is to retreat to the sidelines and let democratic political conflict settle most issues of public policy. Only when constitutional violations are clear and unambiguous should the courts overturn decisions taken elsewhere. Judicial activism, in contrast, flows from the belief that the courts are a coequal branch of government, and that judges should act that way. They should not mask their own views of desirable public policy or be reticent to exercise political power when they can. Rather than being an illegitimate foray into democratic politics, judicial activism makes the system of checks and balances work, and any excesses will be easily checked by the other branches. Therefore, judges are justified in advancing their own policy agendas and their own preferences.

There are two major difficulties with this categorization. First, all judges claim to be judicial restrainers, whatever they may be labeled by observers. Restraint is the model of rectitude into which they have been socialized and to which they pay homage, and no doubt in which they sincerely believe. The escape hatch is that they all have *some* areas for which they reserve "special" treatment. Political majorities should of course be given a wide berth, they avow, *except* in a particular domain (freedom of speech; equal protection; the rights of criminal defendants; reapportionment; property rights; etc.). Second, political ideology colors the outlooks of judges and analysts alike. When, that is, the activists are liberal, liberals tend to defend judicial activism, and conservatives to argue piously for

Judicial Review in Germany

Historically, democracy has had a tenuous hold in Germany. In 1871, a number of previously independent German states were united under the Prussian king, to form modern Germany. Although the new German Empire had a two-house parliament (one branch of which was popularly elected) with superficial powers, the real authority lay with the emperor (*Kaiser*) and his chancellor. With Germany's defeat in World War I, the Allies insisted that the emperor be deposed and a democratic government be installed.

Elected representatives met at Weimar to draft a new constitution, to which the city gave its name. On paper, the new document was a model democracy; civil liberties were sweeping, and vast powers were given to the popularly elected parliament. However, economic crises and the growth of anti-democratic groups soon engulfed the fledgling democratic state. In 1933, Adolf Hitler and the Nazis seized power (legitimately, it might be added) and quickly dismantled the shell that was Weimar. The very institutions of democracy had been used to destroy democracy.

After the Second World War, when it became evident that Germany was going to be partitioned, there was a need for a new constitution. Sobered by the experience of Weimar, both German democrats and their American advisers sought new formulas. One idea the Americans insisted on was judicial review.

Judicial review in Germany, though, differs from that exercised by our Supreme Court in two ways. First, it is exercised by a body detached from the regular courts, the Federal Constitutional Court. Second, it is only a court of original jurisdiction.

Cases come to the Federal Constitutional Court in three ways. First, the Federal Government, a state government, or one-third of the mem-

restraint. When conservative activists are in the ascendant, the positions tend to reverse. Liberals find great wisdom in restraint, and conservatives run up an activist banner.

Nonetheless, it is unfair and inaccurate to paint the categories of restraint and activism as merely covers for naked political preferences. Some judges are, in fact, more restrained across a broader range of issues than others. Some justices elevate particular values (such as equality or free market economics) above restraint more often than do some others who share the same political values. Furthermore, justices do change their minds as events unfold. Justice Lewis Powell, for instance, was usually quite restrained. However, in the area of state aid to parochial schools, he voted to strike down even the most circuitous forms of financial help. But bers of the lower house of parliament may seek a ruling on a law before it goes into effect. Second, if a judge encounters a constitutional issue during a trial in the regular courts, he may refer it to the Constitutional Court (and hold the trial in abeyance until a ruling is made). Third, any citizen may file what is called a constitutional complaint, alleging that her constitutional rights have been violated. This third category accounts for about 93 percent of the petitions received. However, the Constitutional Court has a committee of three justices to screen these complaints, and only about 3 percent are actually heard.

Another difference from the United States Supreme Court is that the Constitutional Court is divided into two panels (called *senates*) of eight judges each. The justices serve twelve-year terms, must retire at age sixty-eight, and are ineligible for reappointment. Half the Court's members are chosen by each house of parliament. The upper house designates a special committee of twelve to make its appointments, while the lower house has a direct election. In both cases, a two-thirds vote is necessary; this provision leads to intense bargaining among the political parties, since none has ever had a two-thirds majority in either house. By law, at least three members of each senate must be career judges. Normally, the other five are drawn from the ranks of civil servants, law professors, and politicians. Most high-ranking civil servants and politicians have law degrees, though.

In general, the Federal Constitutional Court has performed well. It has guarded civil liberties, but has not allowed undemocratic groups to use them as a shield to engage in violence or subversive activities. It has challenged parliament from time to time, but has shown a political "sixth sense" about when to defer to the political powers-that-be. Most observers feel that the Court has been a significant component of the post-war German political system, and has made an important contribution to the maintenance of democracy in Germany.

when the legislatures of several states kept returning to court with ever more ingenious formulas, he backed off somewhat. It seems that he realized that rather than taking religious issues out of politics (his stated aim), his decisions were bringing them into politics. Thus, he began voting to allow state political majorities more flexibility.[10]

"Original Intent" versus "Contemporary Values"

Judicial activism and restraint represent broad-based judicial tendencies. What about the more specific approaches to the words and phrases that make up the Constitution? How should they be read?

Organized demonstrations in opposition to Supreme Court decisions are rare. Abortion, though, has been a clear exception. A pro-life rally protesting Roe v. Wade, *April 1990.*

One position is that the words and phrases should be read in light of "original intent."[11] This position holds that to the fullest extent possible, the proper construction to be put on the Constitution is the meaning which those who wrote it intended. There is some logic and some validity in this approach. If some weight is not given to the constraining power of words, they become empty vessels into which any meaning at all may be poured.

However, difficulties abound. What exactly is "intent"? Take the equal protection clause of the Fourteenth Amendment, for example. When it was written in 1868, women had few political rights. Are women therefore to be deprived of the protection of the clause? If we read intent narrowly, presumably so. However, could it not be plausibly argued that the amendment's drafters were trying to create a more egalitarian society, and that while their minds were riveted on the newly freed slaves, they purposely chose a more all-inclusive term?[12] If they had wanted the amendment to remain narrow, they could easily have been more specific.

As a practical matter, moreover, divining original intent is often all but impossible. The Constitution was drafted by fifty-five people and ratified by hundreds of others. The Fourteenth Amendment was drafted by a congressional committee, voted on by two-thirds of both houses of Congress, and ratified by a number of state legislatures. Whose intent should count? And how are we to locate it? Through debates, speeches, writings, and letters? Even when all these are available and are combed thoroughly, the answers are still uncertain in most cases, and in all matters of any importance.

Furthermore, the more extreme form of the "original intent" position can become absurd. Surely, the Founding Fathers knew that political conditions would change: this is one reason they used vague language. To believe that they bequeathed us a political straitjacket would be to convict them of shortsightedness indeed. It calls into question their acknowledged considerable wisdom to argue that they created a system that would purposely stifle political innovation and change.

The competing position, argued most forcefully by former justice William Brennan, emphasizes that judges should consciously weave contemporary values into their constitutional interpretations.[13] This view holds that relying on original intent would wed us to a view of society that sanctioned racism, sexism, and a variety of other tenets which run counter to the values we now hold dear. As our social values have become more sensitive to egalitarianism and the diversity of human needs, the Court should help remake society along these lines. The dead hand of the past should not be allowed to impede progress. There is much that is attractive and admirable in this line of thought as well.

However, this view has problems of its own. If contemporary values are to determine what the Constitution means, does the document have any permanence? Tomorrow's meaning will undo today's interpretation, as today's has negated yesterday's. Have we set out upon a road that undermines the very idea of constitutional stability?

Besides, even if contemporary values are the constellation to which we look, what makes the judges the proper people to steer the political system? Surely the elected branches are, even with all their defects, better gauges of contemporary values than are appointed judges. One has to believe that judges possess some super talent for understanding public values to believe that they surpass legislators in this regard. That type of elitism, of course, runs counter to the reason for democratic government in the first place.

Constitutional Aspiration

Gary Jacobsohn has proposed a middle ground that offers one way out of this dilemma.[14] His approach is to view the Constitution as containing a number of "aspirations." The Constitution, taken as a whole, rests on a certain view of human nature, on an outline of the good society (or at least the political aspect of the good society), and contains a rather clear statement about how government should be structured. When facing the task of interpretation, therefore, judges should look behind the words to the philosophy of the Constitution, and then not move outside that. This approach will not settle specific cases and disputes, since it leaves plenty of room for disagreement. What it does, though, is to provide a general framework—much broader than the "original intent" position, but not nearly so loose as the "contemporary values" one—and a starting point to begin a search for a beneficial and legitimate interpretation. At once, it allows for change, but keeps us in touch with our roots. According to

Jacobsohn, constitutional interpretation should be a philosophical debate, but not one without boundaries.

Because judges exercise real political power, and because constitutional argumentation is the major currency of judicial power, contests over the "correct" approach to constitutional interpretation are endemic to American politics. The approach the justices adopt, therefore, is of far more than intellectual interest, for it will heavily influence how they decide the cases before them, and those decisions will in turn affect the lives of millions of Americans.

SELECTING JUDGES

From the foregoing discussion, it is obvious that determining who becomes a judge, particularly a Supreme Court judge, is a vitally important matter. Law is far from a mechanistic search for correct answers, as many legal philosophers tried to argue in the nineteenth century. Neither is it entirely arbitrary, of course, as some critics have maintained from time to time.[15] But judges do have choices to make, and those choices involve competing values. How they decide and what they decide will be of lasting importance.

Moreover, judges usually serve beyond the terms of the presidents who appoint them. One of the most enduring legacies a president can provide, therefore, is a Supreme Court justice. Only when Justice William Brennan resigned in 1990 did Dwight Eisenhower's direct influence on the court end, thirty years after he left office. John F. Kennedy continues to leave an imprint through Byron White, even though Kennedy has been dead for three decades.

Consequently, judicial appointments at all levels, but especially to the Supreme Court, attract intense political attention. In 1987, the political conflict became more virulent than ever, when President Reagan tried to place Robert Bork on the high court.[16] Civil rights and women's groups found Bork's legal writings and his decisions as an Appeals Court judge alarming, and launched an unprecedented and ultimately successful nationwide effort to defeat him in the Senate. Bork's case was only atypical, though, in the level and intensity of the political activity—not in the fact of it.

District Court and Court of Appeals Appointments

The political activity surrounding the appointment of District and Appeals Court judges is usually of the behind-the-scenes variety, and seldom attracts much public attention. The president is normally not involved directly in the choice of District Court nominees, delegating the collection and sorting of names to subordinates. If one or both senators from the state which has the district court opening are from the same political party as the president, then they will play an important role. In years past, the

Senate had a policy called "senatorial courtesy," whereby if the senator of the president's party opposed a nominee from his state, the entire Senate would reject it. Senatorial courtesy has weakened recently, but presidents still ordinarily seek to accommodate senators from their own parties. If the opposing party controls both Senate seats, the president's people will confer with other leaders of their own party from the state concerned. Many district judges are therefore political allies of senators or other politically influential people, often unknown to the president who "nominates" them.

Presidents Carter and Reagan both tried to influence the appointment of District Court judges more than their predecessors had done. Carter was interested in appointing more women and minorities, and set up a semiformal structure of committees to screen and forward names. Reagan, on the other hand, was determined to find people who were ideologically compatible with his administration, and instructed his subordinates to examine the candidates carefully. Both men were generally successful in their efforts. It is too early to gauge the long-run effect this will have on the nomination process, but if practices such as these continue, the process will be further centralized, and the power of local politicos eroded.

At the Appeals Court level, the president sometimes personally enters the process; the administration generally has a little more flexibility, since each circuit covers several states. However, interest groups, especially those who come to court often, are alert to the persons being nominated. Usually, interest groups and senators try to influence the appointment when it is still under discussion, since inevitably names leak out. Occasionally a public campaign is mounted against a nominee, but it rarely succeeds. For instance, in the summer of 1989, word spread that President Bush was considering Clarence Thomas as a new Appeals Court judge for the Washington, D.C., circuit. Worried that he was perhaps being set up to become Thurgood Marshall's replacement on the Supreme Court (an accurate prognostication, as it turned out), civil rights groups pressured the administration to pass over Thomas because of his strongly conservative views. Then, when that effort failed, they urged the Senate to reject him. He was easily confirmed, however, even though the Senate Judiciary Committee pressed him harder than usual.[17]

Supreme Court Appointments

When it comes to a Supreme Court vacancy, the level of activity and interest in every political quarter reaches a peak. Typically, the attorney general and a few other close confidants of the president are asked to draw up a short list. The president then confers with these aides, and the list is narrowed further. Interviews are often held with the final few candidates. A choice is then made, and the name is forwarded to the Senate. Historically, it seems that four factors have entered into presidents' final decisions: competence and ethics, personal friendship, "representation", and political and judicial philosophy.

COMPETENCE AND ETHICS Legal competence and personal integrity are baseline factors. That is, anyone whose background is suspect, who has limited legal ability, or whose financial or personal history appears unsavory is usually eliminated early on. This is so because, for one thing, most presidents have a high regard for the Supreme Court and do not wish to appoint hacks or con artists. In addition, the press and the Senate will scrutinize the nominee carefully, and it will reflect poorly on a president should his nominee be found wanting. Of course, presidents make mistakes here, as they do elsewhere. G. Harold Carswell, nominated by Richard Nixon in 1971, was characterized by a leading lawyer as having "more slender credentials than any nominee for the Supreme Court put forth in this century."[18] Douglas Ginsburg asked Ronald Reagan to withdraw his nomination after evidence surfaced that he had used marijuana as a student and law professor. In general, however, the nominees have been a remarkably talented lot with high standards of integrity.

PERSONAL FRIENDSHIP Some presidents have nominated close personal friends or associates, although that practice has faded with time. Harry Truman turned to his inner circle for all four of his nominees. Dwight Eisenhower apparently felt he owed Earl Warren a seat on the Court for his support at the 1952 Republican convention. In more recent times, however, the tendency has been to look beyond the president's acquaintances. Reportedly, for instance, Ronald Reagan had never even heard of Sandra Day O'Connor before her name surfaced as aides cast out the net for potential nominees. In her case, she was recommended by other highly respected judges.

REPRESENTATION The Supreme Court, like all political institutions, has been the object of "balancing." At one time in our history, geographical balance was crucial.[19] Currently, that factor has all but disappeared, but it would still be hard to have, say, nine New Yorkers or nine southerners. For years, there were "Catholic" and "Jewish" seats on the Court, and presidents usually replaced one of these retiring justices with another from the same category. These factors too have diminished since World War II, reflecting perhaps the fact that Catholics and Jews are no longer viewed as members of relatively isolated subcultures.[20] Now, African Americans and women are the two groups that seem to have a lock on "seats." When Thurgood Marshall left the Court in 1991, it was all but certain that he would be replaced by a black justice, and should Sandra Day O'Connor retire, it is almost inconceivable that her seat would not be filled with another woman. In essence, this may be one measure of how completely groups have entered the political system and the society generally. When blacks become as fully incorporated into all levels of American society as Catholics are now, the need for a designated black seat will subside. By then, of course, as with Catholics, one or more justices will probably be black, with no one giving it a second thought. Looking into the future, it would seem likely that we may soon have Hispanic and Asian American seats.[21]

POLITICAL AND JUDICIAL PHILOSOPHY Most importantly, however, there is the issue of political and judicial philosophy. There are always many able and qualified people of any gender and background, but a president is looking for something more. In short, liberal presidents strive for liberal justices, and conservative presidents for conservative ones. Indeed, it would be foolish to do otherwise. A president is elected to influence public policy, and choosing a Supreme Court nominee is an important strategy for influencing the course of political history. So long as the criteria of competence and ethics are met, a president does not violate any canons by trying to choose justices whose ideologies are close to the president's own.

Two complications arise, however. Most people prominent and bright enough to make the short list have sophisticated political and legal philosophies which will not perfectly fit with the president's. The president may develop a one-or two-issue "litmus test," but there is no guarantee that that issue will be the dominant one when a particular justice takes her seat. Even if that issue does play a central role, there will be numerous other cases also. To some extent, therefore, every nomination is a presidential gamble. President Eisenhower once muttered that he had made two mistakes as president, ". . . and they are both on the Supreme Court."[22]

The other stumbling block is the need for Senate approval. Most presidents argue that the Senate should restrict itself to examining a nominee's capability—a test most pass easily. However, logically, and certainly realistically, if the president employs political criteria, the Senate is entitled to do so also. Questions about a nominee's judicial philosophy and approach to public affairs are therefore fair game, as are votes based on the answers. In short, this is an important check and balance, which can work only if the Senate is a real player. Presidents' troubles usually arise when the other party controls the Senate and the nomination becomes entangled in legislative-executive politics.[23] Typically, if the president sticks with a moderate, the Senate will confirm him, even if most senators do not share his views. When the president chooses a sharp partisan, however, the nomination can be in trouble, especially if the president is on the political skids. Reagan's nomination of Robert Bork, for example, came during the Iran-Contra affair. His final substitute for Bork, though, the conservative but genial and moderate Anthony Kennedy, sailed through the Democratic Senate. The drama surrounding Clarence Thomas' confirmation was uniquely complex, as questions of ideology and character became entangled with both racial and gender issues, as well as the usual party partisanship.

JUDGES AND CHANGE ON THE COURT Once on the court, however, a justice is free to go where she pleases intellectually, and that may surprise both presidents and senators. "There is a good deal of shallow talk," Justice Felix Frankfurter once wrote, "that the judicial robe does not change the man within. It does."[24] A justice no longer has to curry political favor from anyone for the rest of her life. In addition, the Supreme Court is a unique

253

TABLE 8-2

Justices of the Supreme Court, 1992

	AGE AT APPOINTMENT	STATE OF RESIDENCE	PREVIOUS POSITION
Byron White	44	Colorado	Private practice/Deputy Attorney General
Harry Blackmun	61	Minnesota	U.S. Court of Appeals
William Rehnquist	47	Arizona	Assistant Attorney General
John Paul Stevens	55	Illinois	U.S. Court of Appeals
Sandra Day O'Connor	51	Arizona	State judge
Antonin Scalia	50	Illinois	Law professor/U.S. Court of Appeals
Anthony Kennedy	51	California	U.S. Court of Appeals
David Souter	50	New Hampshire	U.S. Court of Appeals
Clarence Thomas	43	D.C.	U.S. Court of Appeals/Chair of EEOC

Note: William Rehnquist was made chief justice in 1986, at age 62.

body of people; the influence of justices already on the bench, often appointed by presidents with different orientations, has some impact. As time passes—as the justice studies and reads, as she considers new types of cases, as she shares the colleagueship of the court—she may indeed change. Earl Warren, for instance, had been chiefly known as the rather conservative governor of California, but he became one of the most liberal judges ever. Byron White was labeled a liberal when John F. Kennedy appointed him in 1962, but he has moved firmly into the conservative camp. Harry Blackmun was touted as a future member of the conservative bloc when nominated by Nixon, but he has become moderately liberal over the years. Another graphic example of philosophical development was Hugo Black, a senator from Alabama who had once belonged to the Ku Klux Klan. On the Court, though, Black became one of the most ardent defenders of civil rights for African-Americans.[25] The prevailing tendency, nevertheless, has been for justices to remain fairly close to the judicial philosophy they brought to the Court.

Overall, the individuals who have served on the Supreme Court constitute an impressive lot. They have generally been talented lawyers and adaptive thinkers, and have possessed much higher than average ethical standards.

DECISION MAKING WITHIN THE SUPREME COURT

Getting on the Docket

Issues can come to the Supreme Court only in the form of an actual legal controversy, or case. The Court will not issue advisory opinions to either private citizens or government officials. The party which loses in either a Court of Appeal or a state supreme court must formally request that the Supreme Court place that case on its docket. About 5,000 such requests are filed annually, from which about 200 are chosen to receive a full hearing.[26]

As the cases are filed, each justice's law clerks—recent law school graduates serving a year's internship—summarize the major issues raised by the case. Each justice reviews the issue summaries, and the full case, if he so wishes. The justices then meet in conference, usually on Friday, and vote on which cases to place on the docket. According to the rules of the Court, it takes four affirmative votes for a case to be docketed. At this point, there is no indication of how the Court will decide the case, but merely a decision that the issues raised are important enough to warrant the Supreme Court's time.

Briefs

Next, attorneys for both sides are asked to file written briefs: detailed documents setting forth the arguments on their side. Some of the cases, customarily the most significant ones, are also scheduled for oral argument. If so, what ensues is one of the most dramatic events in the American political system. The justices appear fully robed in the ornate court room after a crier announces, "God save the United States and this Honorable Court." Lawyers for each litigant, in formal dress, are given half an hour each to make their presentations. However, justices may interrupt an attorney to ask questions. Many a haggard and time-pressed attorney has watched her precious time evaporate as one justice after another pursued follow-up questions. Some critics say that this is grand theater but accomplishes little. The justices seem to feel, though, that it forces an attorney to compress his best arguments, in contrast to the written briefs, which can cover as many items as the attorney wishes.

Organizations and governments which are not actually parties to the suit, but which stand to be affected by its outcome, often ask the Court to be allowed to file briefs also. For instance, an environmental group or a state school board may see an opportunity or a threat in a pending case. If the Court grants permission, which it habitually does, then a "friend of the court" brief (*amici curiae* brief, in legal lexicon) is submitted. Sometimes these may be significant and raise issues not brought up by the parties to the suit, but they usually only add weight to one side or another.

One special and highly influential friend of the court is the Solicitor General of the United States. This is an anomalous office which straddles the executive and judicial branches of government. The solicitor general is technically located in the Justice Department and is responsible to the attorney general, but also holds status as an officer of the Supreme Court. Two major duties devolve upon the solicitor general. First, he argues any case before the Court in which the United States is a party. If, for example, an individual is charging the federal government with violating the Constitution, the solicitor general defends the government. Second, in cases in which the United States is not a party, the solicitor general is given carte blanche authority to notify the Court of the position of the federal gov-

Justice John Paul Stevens in his chambers with law clerks.

ernment and its justification. A weighing in by the solicitor general on one side of a case or the other, while not decisive, is very important. Justices accord these opinions a great deal of respect at each stage of the case; in fact, the solicitor general wields enough influence to be sometimes called "the tenth justice."[27]

After all the written briefs have been filed and the oral arguments have been heard, the justices retreat to their conference room. The code of secrecy is in effect here, and no one but the nine justices is even allowed in. (If a messenger knocks, by tradition, the junior justice goes to the door.) When the justices enter, they shake hands with one another in a symbolic gesture of the comity of interest and the search for unity. Discussion ensues, and a tentative vote is normally taken at the conclusion.

Opinions

The winning majority must now choose one of its members to draft the majority opinion, or the "opinion of the court." This is the document that sets forth the reasons the Court has decided as it has, and is the only one that has official standing as guidance for lower courts. By the Court's rules, the chief justice, if in the majority, assigns the opinion; if not, then the most senior associate justice in the majority makes the assignment. This is a far from inconsequential power, because it is common, especially in complex cases, for votes to be cast for the same outcome but for different reasons. By emphasizing one argument as opposed to others, an opinion of the court can influence how lower federal and state courts deal with subsequent cases.

If a justice on the winning side is dissatisfied enough with the rationale given in the majority opinion, she may file a concurring opinion setting out her differences. In some cases, several concurring opinions may be written. While these opinions do not affect the official standing of the majority opinion, they do detract from its informal power among lawyers and other court watchers. Further, they can provide important clues to the direction of judicial thinking. A concurring opinion in a 5–4 case, for example, might contain a signal that if the facts were slightly different, the author might have voted the other way. Astute lawyers and watchful interest groups will then be on the lookout for such a case.

Those justices who disagree with the holding and rationale of the Court may write dissenting opinions. While they are technically addressed to the other justices, these exercises in rebuttal really speak to two outside audiences. One is the legal and political community beyond the Court. Dissenting opinions are often aimed at convincing lawyers and others of the soundness of the arguments presented, hoping that they will lead to pressure for change. The other audience is the justices of the future. More than once in the Court's history a dissenting opinion has later become the majority opinion, with the dissenter hailed as a person with great foresight. Some have even become important historical documents in their own right. In the 1896 case of *Plessy v. Ferguson,* which upheld racial segregation in public transportation (and by implication elsewhere), Justice John Marshall Harlan wrote these notable words of dissent: "We boast of the freedom enjoyed by our people above all other peoples. But it is difficult to reconcile that boast with a state of the law which, practically, puts the brand of servitude and degradation upon a large class of our fellow-citizens, our equals before the law. The thin disguise of 'equal' accommodations for passengers in railroad coaches will not mislead anyone, nor atone for the wrong this day done." Segregation laws, he said, "can have no other result than to render permanent peace impossible, and to keep alive a conflict of races, the continuance of which must do harm to all concerned."[28]

All opinions are circulated well before they are published. Hence, those doing the writing have a chance to make additions to refute specific parts of other opinions. It is not unknown for judges to change sides as the opinions are circulated, swayed perhaps by a cogently expressed argument. On Mondays, decisions are announced, and opinions given to the press and public.

Decision making in the Supreme Court, then, is dressed up as a court proceeding, and that fact is not unimportant. It gives a quiet and a dignity to the process that is lacking in the more overtly politicized branches. Yet, the process is infused with political issues at every stage, from the initial screening of the cases to the announcement of the final decision—and as we shall see momentarily, the politics does not stop there. It is important not to let the quietness and the stillness that every visitor feels when entering the Court's majestic building dull this political reality. The still-

Justice Harry Blackmun in his Supreme Court chambers.

ness, Justice Oliver Wendell Holmes wrote, is the stillness of the eye of a storm.[29]

CHECKS ON THE POWER OF THE SUPREME COURT

From one perspective, the Supreme Court is the most powerful institution in the American system. The Constitution is superior to all other laws, and the Supreme Court interprets the Constitution. From its readings of the Constitution, there is no appeal to a higher body.

If state governments, the president, Congress, and lower courts are all constrained by the Constitution, and the Constitution means whatever the Supreme Court decrees, is not the Supreme Court a nine-person dictatorship? Quite clearly, the answer is no. The powerful balances of the Constitution, some readily obvious, some subtle, prevent any possibility of government by the judiciary.

First, there is the option of constitutional amendment. If a strong political consensus exists that the Supreme Court is in error, the actual words of the Constitution may be altered. The Eleventh, Sixteenth, and Twenty-sixth Amendments were all adopted to overturn Supreme Court decisions that defied dominant political values.[30] However, that check is more hypothetical than real in most cases, since securing an amendment to the Constitution is exceedingly difficult. Nonetheless, it is always available as a blunt tool to rein in an overreaching Court.

Second, the justices may be impeached. Distressed by several Court decisions, President Thomas Jefferson had his backers in Congress impeach and remove a federal district judge, and pushed an impeachment resolution through the House against Supreme Court Justice Samuel Chase.[31] In our day, impeachment has fallen into disuse as a revenge tactic for those opposed to specific decisions of the courts, being reserved for instances of moral turpitude.[32] Nonetheless, from time to time members of Congress make noises about impeachment for "judicial tyranny" or some other such aphorism, and in an extreme case might well be moved to carry it through. Given that impeachment requires only a resolution in the House and a two-thirds vote in the Senate, it is a much lower hurdle than a constitutional amendment; however, it is a direct attack on the institution of the court, rather than on one decision. Conceivably, though, impeachment could be used by an enraged Congress to remove one or more justices.

Less dramatically, Congress has control over the size of the Court. The number of justices is not mentioned in the Constitution, and has varied over the years from six to ten. Since 1869, the number has always been nine. Suppose, to give an example of how this power might be used, the Supreme Court were split 6–3 against the Congress and president on some issue of vital importance. Rather than marshalling the political backing necessary to secure an amendment or embarking on the politically bruising route of impeachment, Congress could merely add four seats to the Court. The president would then appoint four justices committed to the presidential and congressional views, and manage to instigate a new case. If all went well, the vote would now be 7–6.

Frustrated by a series of 5–4 decisions which ripped the heart out of his New Deal program for fighting the Depression, Franklin D. Roosevelt decided to try to enlarge the Court. While publicly calling his plan a design to "prevent hardening of the judicial arteries," everyone understood the aim. A torrid political debate followed, with many members of Congress who agreed with Roosevelt's policies hesitant to tamper with the Court. Once the precedent was set, they feared, this tactic would be resorted to frequently. The justices themselves, even those in the minority, campaigned behind the scenes against the bill. Perhaps most important, in the middle of the debate in Congress, a major piece of New Deal legislation was upheld in the Court by a 5–4 vote. The switch by one of the justices was called "the switch in time that saved nine."[33] Fortunately for Roosevelt, within a short time ill health forced two of his staunchest enemies to resign from the Court. Since then there has been no serious movement to increase the Court's size.

Article III of the Constitution provides that Congress shall have a hand in setting the federal courts' jurisdiction. Exactly how far Congress could go in removing jurisdiction is a muddled issue. During Reconstruction, Congress did take away an important area of jurisdiction—and the Court upheld its right to do so. Since then, however, this has not been done, although it is proposed almost every session. If the Court angered enough members of Congress, this pair of scissors would be still available to clip its wings a bit, even if it could not be grounded.

Therefore, Congress alone, and the president and Congress together, have several artillery pieces which could be uncloaked in a political war with the Court. Disgruntled opponents of various decisions of the Court periodically suggest lighting the fuse to one or more, but such moves have gotten nowhere in modern times. In a sense, by not acting, Congress is giving tacit consent to the legitimacy of the Court's deciding these issues, if not an endorsement of the substance of the decisions.

But the subtleties of power are equally decisive. The Supreme Court is a court, after all. It cannot assume the political initiative, inasmuch as it can only take up issues that are raised by the cases filed. To be sure, the judges select the cases, and certainly the wording of their opinions often encourages a person or group to file a case, but the generalization still holds. Congress and the president can move to whatever issues they like, whenever they like; comparatively, the Court is quite restricted.

Furthermore, as Alexander Hamilton observed in *The Federalist* No. 78, courts are "possessed of neither the purse nor the sword" to enforce their decisions. The Supreme Court is only a group of nine people; it has neither money to spend, nor a police force at its command. These resources are under the control of others. Thus, if a court oversteps its bounds, other political actors can simply not enforce its edicts. It is a toothless threat of dictatorship, if ever there was one. In essence, government officials enforce the Court's rulings, and the public obeys (most of the time), because they believe its power is legitimate. That reservoir of beliefs is the Court's final, and only, source of power.

In addition, the recognition of all these factors by the judges themselves further restrains them. Regardless of public opinion on whether they always adhere to it or not, most justices believe that judicial restraint is the only proper stance for a judge. Further, these are practical men and women who have been in public life: they fully understand what Congress and the president could do to them if they so chose. Most important, however, the justices revere the Constitution and the Court, and know that public approval is the cornerstone of political legitimacy, for them and for the governmental system in general. They are loath, therefore, to stir up public antagonism, for they fully appreciate that doing so too often will erode the legitimacy of the Court. The ever-insightful Alexis de Tocqueville said it as well as anyone:

> The power of the Supreme Court Justices is immense, but it is power springing from opinion. They are all-powerful so long as the people consent to obey the law; they can do nothing when they scorn it. Now, of all powers, that of opinion is the hardest to use, for it is impossible to say exactly where its limits come. . . .
>
> The federal judges therefore must not only be good citizens and men of education and integrity, . . . but must also be statesmen; they must know how to understand the spirit of the age, to confront those obstacles that can be overcome, and to steer out of the current when the tide threatens to carry them away, and with them the sovereignty of the Union and obedience to its laws.[34]

THE SUPREME COURT AND PUBLIC OPINION

Observers have long speculated on the exact relationship between the public and the Supreme Court. To what extent should and does the Court listen to the *vox populi*? While the Court is clearly the least democratic branch of government in terms of how its members are chosen, does that mean that it is or should be impervious to public opinion? The nineteenth-century humorist Finley Peter Dunne had his character Mr. Dooley say that "the supreme court follows th' iliction returns."

Few people are so crass as to believe that the Supreme Court justices carefully pore over election returns or read Gallup Polls and try to make their decisions accordingly. However, to believe that public feelings have no impact on the judges is also unrealistic. After all, they live in the culture, and their lives have long been connected to public affairs. The real question is how much does public opinion matter to them, and under which circumstances.

Until recently, most of the writing in this area had been purely speculative and relied heavily on anecdotes collected from here and there. Political scientist Thomas Marshall, however, has now published an extensive study comparing to prevailing public opinion every Supreme Court decision for which a reliable public opinion survey covering the same issue has existed. Naturally, his analysis is confined to the time since the advent of scientific polling, the late 1930s, but he still found 144 instances of matching polls and Supreme Court decisions.

He found that in about two-thirds of the instances the Court decided the same way the public felt. "Overall," he therefore concludes, "the evidence suggests that the modern Court has been an essentially majoritarian institution."[35] Going one step further, he tentatively tried to match poll data with presidential and congressional action. Interestingly, the results were almost the same: about one-third of the time the elected branches are out of step with public opinion as well. Thus, in spite of being further removed from electoral politics, in quantitative terms at least, the Court is as responsive to public opinion as are the more politicized branches.

Marshall also examined the "activist" decisions that overturned legislative enactments, since these are often the most heavily criticized. He found that about half of those decisions were in accord with public preferences. This suggests that judicial activism may not be necessarily undemocratic. "These results challenge the commonly cited view that judicial activism is an essentially countermajoritarian practice."[36]

In a sense, Marshall's framing of the question conforms to the individualist notion of democracy. That is, the sum of individual preferences should be government policy, and the research is designed to find out whether there is a match or not. If, though, the object of politics is government by discussion and a search for the public interest, as advocated by civic democrats, then the query, "How democratic is the Court?" must be measured by other criteria. Perhaps, for instance, even if the Court's activist decisions accord with a momentary majority in public sentiments, it would be better to leave the question to ordinary legislative politics, since that will force discussion and continued debate. Building an enduring and stable consensus behind a policy may be easier if the decisions result from sustained discussion than if they come by judicial fiat, however popular the content of the decision may be.[37]

AN OVERVIEW OF THE SUPREME COURT'S HISTORY SINCE 1890

The history of the Court since 1890[38] falls roughly into five periods: 1890–1937 (the laissez-faire Court); 1937–53 (the Roosevelt Court); 1953–69 (the Warren Court); 1969–86 (the Burger Court); and 1986– the present (the Rehnquist Court).

During the first period, conservative activists dominated the Court, and struck down a wide variety of both state and federal attempts to regulate economic affairs. The consensus among the justices was that constitutionalism and laissez-faire economics (unbridled capitalism, in short) were inextricably intertwined; if one were weakened, the other would also be in peril. Some great dissents were written during this period which contested this view, but it held sway nonetheless.

After President Roosevelt's ill-fated court-packing scheme, fortune smiled on him, and he got the opportunity to make several appointments. In general, these men believed in giving the federal government wide latitude, particularly in economic and military matters. They were somewhat less impressed with the need for state autonomy, however. Whether the states' legal antagonists were individuals or the federal government, the states tended to lose. A few important cases began to take civil rights seriously, with respect to housing, voting rights, and education. By the 1950s, African American groups were receiving an increasingly sympathetic ear from the Court.

In 1953, Earl Warren, a former governor of California and 1948 Republican vice presidential candidate, became chief justice. No one could have predicted that the next thirteen years would witness the most far-reaching liberal activism of the Court's history. Almost immediately the path-breaking *Brown v. Board of Education* case was decided, with Warren skillfully maneuvering to make the decision unanimous.[39] Within a few years, equality had become the basic watchword of the Court. The criminal justice system was virtually overhauled: new restrictions were placed on police behavior (through the exclusionary rule and the *Miranda* warnings), and new protections mandated for court proceedings (counsel was to be provided to the indigent and procedural safeguards were installed in juvenile courts, for instance). Education and employment were the subjects of any number of cases, usually won by minorities. Reapportionment, or making the rule of "one man, one vote" a reality throughout government, from junior college districts to the United States House of Representatives was another area of Court activism. This probably shook more

During Chief Justice Earl Warren's tenure (1956–1969) the Supreme Court greatly expanded civil liberties such as free speech and expression.

political foundations than did any other set of decisions. In the areas of such civil liberties as free speech and expression, the Court almost always sided with the individual.

In his 1968 campaign Richard Nixon stressed that he would appoint judges unsympathetic to these positions.[40] President Johnson botched a plan whereby Earl Warren would resign before the election, so that a liberal could be named in his place.[41] Nixon therefore was handed a plum when he took office. He chose Warren Burger, a stiff man of acknowledged modest ability but staunch conservative leanings. Within three years Nixon had the chance to fill three more seats. In the meantime, analysts kept predicting that the Court would take a sharp conservative direction. In fact, nothing of the sort happened. None of the major Warren Court decisions were overturned, and some in fact were taken further. The Court continued to uphold school desegregation, for instance, and extended equal protection to cover women. In the area of criminal justice, there was some small chipping away at the Warren holdings, but nothing near a wholesale retreat. Freedom of speech and the press continued to enjoy strong protection. Furthermore, some decisions the Burger Court rendered were much more liberally activist than any which had been taken under Warren, particularly the *Roe v. Wade* abortion decision. And, of

BOX 8–1

The Supreme Court and the Two Democratic Traditions

ALTHOUGH BOTH individualist and civic democrats support judicial review, they approach the matter rather differently. The individualistic tradition emphasizes judicial review as a method to insure that political processes are kept fair, and to draw the delicate line between policies adopted by the free play of majoritarian politics and the individual's rights. The civic tradition, on the other hand, stresses the contribution that a court with the power of judicial review can make to lively and intelligent public debate.

According to individualist democrats, it is essential that the processes of governmental decision making be kept fair and open. Of course, exactly what constitutes fair and open decision making is a subject of dispute, and individualist democrats disagree among themselves on the particulars. However, they all agree both on the general goal and on the fact that since the courts are detached from ordinary politics, they can play a useful role in this area. Individualist democrats are equally committed to protecting the legitimate rights of minorities, and here once again, courts are seen as useful instruments in drawing the lines limiting the scope of majority power. But individualist democrats disagree even more vociferously among themselves on this subject than they do regarding fair procedure. They disagree about which rights should be protected (free speech, privacy, property, etc.), and about how much each right should be protected. The courts become a battleground for individualist democrats, as one group pushes for the protection of certain rights (such as complete freedom of speech, including pornography), while simultaneously contending that ordinary majoritarian politics should determine other policies (such as economic regulation). Another faction reverses this, arguing that other rights (such as property rights) should be protected, and majoritarian politics given free reign elsewhere (such as the regulation of pornography). The point is that both groups begin with the same assumption: that the Supreme Court's

course, it was an 8–0 decision[42] which denied Richard Nixon the right to keep his treasured tapes secret, a decision critical to the resolution of the Watergate crisis.

Why did the Burger Court behave in this unexpected fashion? Was it idiosyncratic, or is there some lesson to be drawn here about the life of the Court? One reason for the Burger Court's unpredictably liberal decisions was that some of the justices were not nearly so conservative on most

BOX 8-1

major role is to determine minority rights within the framework of majoritarian politics.

Civic democrats approach the matter differently. To them, politics is about the search for the public interest, and sustained public deliberation and debate is the best method to achieve that end. The Supreme Court, therefore, while not shunning its responsibilities to protect the fairness of governmental decision making and to protect the rights of minorities, should be looked upon primarily for the role it can play in the ongoing public dialogue.

The place of the Court is in fact unique, according to civic democrats. Elected politicians must represent certain constituencies, and of course they have a rather close time horizon: the next election. Thus, while

elected representatives can and do transcend their parochial interests from time to time (see chapters 5 and 6), they cannot (and indeed, should not) be expected to ignore the narrower interests of those who put them into office. The Supreme Court, in contrast, is semidetached from politics, putting the judges in a position to take a broader and less time-bound perspective.

It is reasonable to expect, therefore, that the decisions of the Supreme Court and the justifications given through its opinions strive to keep us in touch with our basic values. The Court is, in short, rather like a moderator or leader in a continuing debate on first principles. It is akin to a collective schoolmaster in a national seminar on the basics of demo-

cratic government and what we stand for as Americans.

The quality of the opinions justices write is consequently of critical importance. If they are sloppy or poorly done, the power of these opinions to persuade and their ability to stir meaningful debate is diminished, and the quality of our democracy suffers. Justices have an obligation, then, to consider decisions carefully, and to write wisely. Citizens, on the other hand, have an obligation to listen to Supreme Court pronouncements with respect—but not awe. They are "class notes" from "experts" on citizenship and democratic government, but they are not the final word. If the class is well conducted, it should inspire further learning and discussion.

issues as many had hoped or feared. Only on matters of criminal justice did they form a solidly conservative phalanx. Another reason was that some of them, particularly Harry Blackmun, became more liberal with time. But in large measure, these unexpected decisions were reached because most of these men were judicial conservatives more fundamentally than they were political conservatives. That is, they respected the Court as an institution, and felt a deep reverence for its precedents. While they might not have voted for a particular liberal precedent had they been on the Court at the time it was established, it was now "the law," and should only be overturned under unusual circumstances. Ironically, by appointing true conservatives, men whose respect for institutional continuity trumped even their own policy preferences, Nixon assured that they would uphold liberal precedents. Of Nixon's four appointments, only William Rehnquist seemed prepared to overturn precedents at a low threshold.

By 1986, however, the tide was turning. Reagan's appointment of Sandra Day O'Connor and Antonin Scalia added two more justices of a decidedly conservative temperament in the policy sense. Meanwhile, Rehnquist's elevation to the position of chief justice gave conservative activism a boost. As for the recent appointees, Anthony Kennedy is something of an ambivalent conservative; David Souter has yet to establish a firm record, but seems solidly middle of the road; and Clarence Thomas' initial opinions hint of strong conservatism. Slowly, then, momentum is gathering for a new judicial orientation.

However, there are crosscurrents and complications. Overturning some decisions, such as abortion, means in effect dumping these issues back into the laps of legislative institutions, which is where restrainers have wanted them all along. Curiously, the attempt to disengage from these controversial issues simply creates more controversy. One of the arguments for restraint is that the courts will become the object of political contentiousness if they wade into these delicate matters. But once the Supreme Court issues a decision, it creates a new status quo; now, the groups which have won in court definitely do not want the issue tossed back into the political arena. This is precisely what has happened in the area of abortion. In some other areas, such as freedom of expression, the Rehnquist Court has stood on firmly libertarian grounds, the prime examples being the two flag-burning cases. In civil rights, however, the Court has begun a retreat from deciding most cases in favor of minorities. It has struck down several affirmative action plans, for example, and cast doubt on policies in several other areas.[43]

Three generalizations can be drawn from this necessarily cursory overview. First, the narrow labels "conservative" and "liberal," as most other labels, are far too simplistic to be of much use when examining justices. The texture of constitutional law and the complexities of judicial philosophy preclude any such facile dichotomy. Second, the Court changes, but rather slowly, and not in the same direction all at once. Third, there is a certain "lag time" between political change and change on the Court, a time which can witness conflict between the political branches and the judiciary. For example, the 1890–1937 Court represented, in general, the dominant political coalition of its day. In the five year transition between Franklin Roosevelt's election and his initial appointments, conflict flared. The New Deal Court, in its turn, by and large deferred to Roosevelt and his successors, minimizing conflict. The Warren Court was in many ways a vibrant extension of New Deal values. Since most of the practices it struck down fell under state jurisdiction, it was opposed most loudly by state governments. At the federal level, a patchwork coalition more or less acquiesced in its decisions. The Burger Court began another shift, but its gradualism and deference to Warren Court precedents was still out of step with the new national coalition that was forming in the late 1970s. Reaganite conservatism was impatient with this approach, and political controversy flared on several fronts. In time, the Court has drifted more to the right, and those who have previously won in Court are fighting a strong rearguard action.

The Court as Part of the Stream of Political Decision Making

The great eighteenth-century general Karl von Clausewitz wrote that "war is a continuation of politics by other means."[44] Viewed from the perspective of the political system as a whole, Supreme Court cases can also be considered politics carried on by other means. Court decisions are not isolated phenomena: they are part of ongoing political jousts. Those who have lost in a state legislature or in Congress come to Court. Once a decision is rendered, the political battle shifts to other fronts: lobbying in Congress; elections; fighting for friendly appointments to administrative agencies; and so forth. No political decision starts or ends with a court decision. To illustrate how this happens, and to once more stress how important statutory interpretation has become, let us look briefly at the recent fate of Title VII of the Civil Rights Act of 1964.

Responding to pressures from civil rights groups, Congress passed this law as part of the package of reforms known as the Great Society. The law provides that "it shall be unlawful employment practice for an employer to fail or refuse to hire or discharge any individual, or otherwise to discriminate against any individual with respect to his compensation, terms, conditions, or privileges of employment, because of such individual's race, color, religion, sex, or national origin."[45]

What does this mean exactly? Clearly, if an employer says to you, "You're black and we don't hire blacks," you win your case. But what if he does not tell you that directly, and yet does not hire you? How can you prove he has violated the law? To simplify a complex answer, there are two basic approaches: the "disparate treatment" test and the "disparate impact" test. In the latter case, all the complainant needs to show is that there is a statistical imbalance between the racial (or religious, ethnic, etc.) composition of the work force from which the employer has drawn applicants for that job and the racial (or religious, ethnic, etc.) composition of the company's employees in that job. Then the burden of proof shifts to the employer, who must demonstrate that there is a "legitimate business purpose" for the disparity. For instance, if 15 percent of the accountants in Metro City are black, and only 1 percent of XYZ Company's accountants are black, a black accountant who has been turned down for a job need only show that fact to the court. XYZ would then be ordered to produce proof of a legitimate reason for this imbalance, a task it would of course find most difficult. Under the "disparate treatment" test, on the other hand, the refused applicant must show that she has been *personally* discriminated against. The statistical imbalance is still relevant, but it is only one item of evidence. (In practice, of course, the greater the imbalance is, the stronger it stands as evidence.) Nonetheless, the burden of proof always rests with the person seeking to prove discrimination.

Until 1989, the courts generally opted for the disparate impact test. This standard of proof was, of course, a boon to civil rights lawyers and those in the protected categories. All that was needed to win a case was a demonstration of statistical imbalance. If employment discrimination cases have to be fought under the disparate treatment standard, they will be hard to win. Establishing an employer's motivations is much more difficult than simply gathering the relevant statistics. Opponents of the disparate impact standard, however, argued that it led businesses to avoid costly lawsuits by resorting to "quotas." Others pointed out that defining the relevant "labor market" was often an arbitrary exercise.

In 1989, the Supreme Court heard the case of *Wards Cove Packing Co. v. Atonio.*[46] Wards Cove had an almost all-white management team and a laboring force composed mostly of native Alaskans and Filipinos. Applying the disparate impact test, lower federal courts found the company guilty of violating the act. On appeal, the Supreme Court overruled and remanded the case to the District Court to be retried under the disparate treatment test. Wards Cove could, of course, still be found guilty of discrimination, but not on the basis of the statistics alone.

Immediately alarmed, civil rights groups began a campaign among their congressional allies to overturn the Supreme Court decision by inserting the disparate impact test into the statute itself. Business groups mobilized their own forces to block any change in the law. President Bush was in a quandary. His natural sympathy was with corporate managers and owners, but he had been courting black political support since his inauguration. Furthermore, many Republicans saw themselves as the protectors of lower-class and lower-middle-class whites who believe, rightly or wrongly, that quotas take jobs away from them. The White House tried to find a formula that would satisfy everyone, and would keep Bush from having to veto something labeled a "civil rights law." Every compromise fell apart, however. Congress then passed its own version of the bill, but Bush vetoed it. An override fell one vote short in the Senate. One senator who voted with the president, however, was defeated in November 1990 (the only senator to fall at this time). In 1991, after intense negotiations, the president came to an agreement with congressional leaders over compromise language, and the bill passed. It is still unclear, though, precisely how the courts will treat the new wording, since it is laden with ambiguity.[47]

In sum, this was a political battle that was waged simultaneously on several fronts. It went from Congress to the Court, back to Congress, to the president's desk, back to Congress, then through a tortuous negotiating process between White House aides and members of Congress, and undoubtedly it will be back in court and will be injected again into political party and election contests in the future. *Wards Cove Packing Co. v. Atonio* therefore was but one stage in an ongoing political contest over the distribution of economic resources and how best to achieve racial justice.

CITIZEN PARTICIPATION IN THE FEDERAL COURTS: A NOTE ON JURIES

Although the courts are often labeled undemocratic in that judges are not elected by the people, service on juries allows the citizenry participation in judicial proceedings—participation often more direct than that which they have in legislative or executive decisions. In a typical year, about 600,000 people are called upon to present themselves for federal jury service, and about 300,000 actually serve as jurors.[48] In addition, an uncounted number serve in state courts.

Federal juries are of two types. *Grand juries* are required by the Constitution (in the Fifth Amendment) before a person can be tried for a serious crime. The function of a grand jury is to hear the evidence the government prosecutors have and decide whether or not an indictment should be issued—in other words, whether there is enough evidence to go to trial.[49] Ordinarily, federal grand juries have between 16 and 23 people, and are empaneled for anywhere from 18 to 24 months. In 1990, 775 grand juries sat for over 10,500 sessions, each of which lasted an average of 5.4 hours. They handled nearly 24,000 cases involving almost 39,000 defendants. Altogether, 207,107 citizens served on these bodies.

While not all cases heard in Federal District Courts have juries, about 11,000 annually do.[50] If a jury trial is called for, a *petit jury* is selected, varying in size from 6 (for most civil suits) to 12 (for criminal cases). Their function is to hear the evidence from both sides and issue a judgment: a monetary settlement in a civil suit, and guilt or non-guilt in a criminal case. In 1990, 110,383 people served on petit juries, for a total of 45,119 trial days.

FIGURE 8-3

Jury Summons: Receiving a summons to jury duty is one of the most direct instances of involvement citizens can have in their local, state, or federal government.

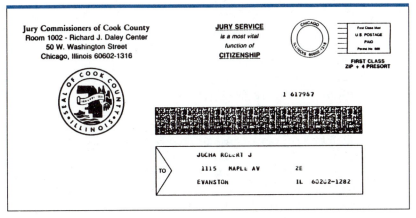

Both grand and petit jurors are chosen at random from voting lists, a fact which introduces an immediate class skew, as we shall see in chapter 10. Furthermore, many people are excused from jury duty because of work or other commitments. Thus, juries are often composed largely of people who have time on their hands, such as those who are retired. Nonetheless, this important feature of judicial proceedings should not be overlooked, either as a central part of the judicial process or as a mechanism whereby ordinary citizens participate in a significant governmental function.

SUMMARY

The federal courts, especially the Supreme Court, are major components of our governmental structure. The United States has a dual court system, with a system of Federal District Courts and Courts of Appeal sitting alongside each state's system.

Although the Constitution does not mention who should interpret its provisions, that power has been assumed by the courts. This leads to judicial review, which gives courts the authority to declare unconstitutional federal and state laws, as well as presidential actions. *Marbury v. Madison* was the first time the Supreme Court claimed this power, which serves as a valuable historical and legal precedent; however, a pragmatic argument and a philosophical argument provide equally convincing rationales for the practice.

Judges can take positions based on either judicial restraint or judicial activism in their approach to the Constitution. At the same time, they seek guidance from original intent, contemporary values, or constitutional aspiration as they read meaning into the actual words and phrases of the Constitution.

Presidential nomination and Senate confirmation of district and appeals court judges normally attracts little public attention. At the Supreme Court level, though, interest is intense. Presidents have historically relied on competence and ethics, personal friendship, representation of various groups, and political philosophy when selecting nominees. The Senate applies its own criteria, with ideology as well as capability playing a role.

The docket of the Supreme Court is controlled by the Court itself. After a case is argued through written and oral briefs, the judges cast votes and write opinions. A majority opinion may be supplemented by concurring opinions or challenged by dissenting ones.

Checks on the power of the Supreme Court include constitutional amendment; impeachment; congressional control of Court size and some matters of jurisdiction; and the lack of enforcement powers. Even though the Court is not directly elected, its decisions seem to match public desires about as often as those of Congress or presidents: about two-thirds of the time.

Since 1890, the Supreme Court has passed through five discernible changes in direction and emphasis. Most recently, a more conservative, and perhaps more activist, movement is taking hold. As has been seen in other periods, the present Court has experienced a lag between a new coalition's victory in national elections and its dominance on the Court.

Supreme Court decisions are not isolated events. Instead, they are a part of the normal stream of politics, as illustrated by the struggle over equal employment opportunities. Losers in one arena shift their energies to others, and consider no loss or victory as final.

Even though the courts are undemocratic in that judges are unelected, nearly 300,000 citizens participate in judicial proceedings each year through service on federal grand and petit juries.

ENDNOTES

1. Administrative Conference of the United States Courts, *Federal Judicial Workload Statistics* (Washington: Government Printing Office, 1991).

2. A good discussion of the flow of cases to the Supreme Court is Lawrence Baum, *The Supreme Court,* 4th ed. (Washington: Congressional Quarterly Press, 1992), chap. 3.

3. Naturally, things are really a bit more complicated than this. R. Shep Melnick has argued that subcommittee members and their staffs know the direction court decisions have been heading, and will insert measures into legislation that sound innocuous but have dramatic consequences. For instance, after lower court decisions in the mid-1970s supporting "appropriate" education for handicapped children, a congressional subcommittee pushed a bill which members said was necessary to bring federal policy into line with the decisions. They then created an elaborate procedural morass for determining what constituted a "free appropriate public education" for handicapped students, a provision which they felt certain the courts would interpret sympathetically. Without debating the merits of educating handicapped children in regular classrooms at public expense, it is important to note that the policy was adopted by an alliance of subcommittee members and the courts. See R. Shep Melnick, "The Courts, Congress, and Programmatic Rights," in Richard A. Harris and Sidney M. Milkis, eds., *Remaking American Politics* (Boulder, Colorado: Westview, 1989), chap. 7.

4. There are times when an ordinary civil or criminal trial will raise a statutory or constitutional issue (say, on the admissibility of evidence) and that question will find its way to the Supreme Court, but the ordinary aspects of the trial will not.

5. There is irony in this fact. Marshall had been the secretary of state under Adams, in whose office the commissions had last been seen. His appointment to the Supreme Court was also an outgoing act of Adams.

6. *Marbury v. Madison,* 5 U.S. (1 Cranch) 137 (1803).

7. *Dred Scott v. Sanford,* 60 U.S. (19 How.) 393 (1856).

8. This is the name by which the Supreme Court building is popularly called.

9. These positions are discussed thoroughly in Stephen Halpern and Charles Lamb, eds., *Supreme Court Activism and Restraint* (Lexington, Mass.: Lexington Books, 1982).

10. Powell's metamorphosis is covered in more detail in Jerold Waltman, "Justice Powell and the Parochial School Cases: A Case for Judicial Statesmanship," *Public Affairs Quarterly* 3 (1989), 61–78.

11. A strong statement of this position is Robert Bork, *The Tempting of America* (New York: Basic Books, 1990). For a critique, see Leonard Levy, *Original Intent and the Framers' Constitution* (New York: Macmillan, 1988).

12. See Judith Baer, *Equality under the Constitution: Reclaiming the Fourteenth Amendment* (Ithaca, N.Y.: Cornell University Press, 1983), chaps. 2–4.

13. He expounds upon this position in "The Constitution of the United States: Contemporary Ratification," *University of Texas Law Review,* Fall 1986, 433–45.

14. Gary Jacobsohn, *The Supreme Court and the Decline of Constitutional Aspiration* (Totowa, N.J.: Rowman and Littlefield, 1986).

15. An excellent introduction to this issue is Edward Levi, *An Introduction to Legal Reasoning* (Chicago: University of Chicago Press, 1949).

16. The saga of this nomination is told in Ethan Bronner, *Battle for Justice: How the Bork Nomination Shook America* (New York: Norton, 1989).

17. See the summary story in the *Washington Post,* March 7, 1990, p. 25. Note the story's placement in the nation's major political newspaper.

18. Quoted in Lawrence Baum, *The Supreme Court,* 3d ed. (Washington: Congressional Quarterly Press, 1989), 33.

19. In the eighteenth and nineteenth centuries, the Supreme Court justices had to ride circuit, that is, actually hold court outside Washington. Each justice was assigned a particular circuit for which he was responsible. Thus, having someone from that circuit was of some importance. Today, each justice technically still oversees a circuit, but this has little practical consequence.

20. Since Abe Fortas retired in 1969, there has been no Jewish justice, but Jewish groups have not been noticeably distressed by this fact. Both Antonin Scalia and Anthony Kennedy are Catholic, but no one seemed to care much, positively or negatively.

21. During the debate over G. Harold Carswell's nomination, Senator Roman Hruska of Nebraska seriously suggested the following: "Even if Carswell were mediocre, there are a lot of mediocre judges and people and lawyers. They are entitled to a little representation, aren't they . . . ?" Most senators apparently did not believe this group deserved a special seat. Quoted in Henry Abraham, *Justices and Presidents,* 2d ed. (New York: Oxford University Press, 1985), 17.

22. Quoted in Elmo Richardson, *The Presidency of Dwight D. Eisenhower* (Lawrence: Regents Press of Kansas, 1979), 108.

23. See Baum, *Supreme Court,* chap. 2.

24. *Public Utilities Commission v. Pollack,* 343 U.S. 466 (1959).

25. One wag quipped that as a young man this justice wore a white robe and went around frightening black people, while as an old man he wore a black robe and went around frightening white people.

26. The careful reader will remember the six to eight percent figure given earlier, which would produce 300 to 400 cases. Two hundred is the number selected for full hearing; the others are disposed of more summarily.

27. Lincoln Caplan, *The Tenth Justice: The Solicitor General and the Rule of Law* (New York: Vintage, 1987).

28. 163 U.S. 537, 16 S.Ct. 1138 (1896).

29. A quote which became the focus of David O'Brien's best-selling study of the Court, *Storm Center: The Supreme Court in American Politics,* 2d ed. (New York: Norton, 1990).

30. In a sense, the Thirteenth, Fourteenth, and Fifteenth Amendments were also adopted to overturn a Supreme Court case, the 1857 decision in *Dred Scott v. Sanford.*

31. Chase, incidentally, had actively campaigned against Jefferson publicly.

32. The only modern attempt that was even semi-serious was an effort in 1969–70 led by Congressman Gerald Ford to have William O. Douglas impeached. Apparently, the move was inspired by the Nixon White House, but it died in a House committee. John Ehrlichman, *Witness to Power: The Nixon Years* (New York: Simon and Schuster, 1982), 122. Ironically, when Douglas retired in 1975, Ford was then president, and had to issue the usual accolades to the departing justice before naming his replacement.

33. Quoted in O'Brien, *Storm Center,* 88.

34. Alexis de Tocqueville, *Democracy in America,* trans. by George Lawrence (New York: Harper and Row, 1966), 137.

35. Thomas Marshall, *Public Opinion and the Supreme Court* (Boston: Unwin Hyman, 1989), 192.

36. Marshall, *Public Opinion,* 192.

37. This point is made forcefully regarding abortion in Mary Ann Glendon, *Abortion and Divorce in Western Law* (Cambridge, Mass.: Harvard University Press, 1987) and more generally in her *Rights Talk: The Impoverishment of Political Discourse* (New York: Free Press, 1991).

38. A readable source on the earlier period is G. Edward White, *The American Judicial Tradition* (New York: Oxford University Press, 1988), chaps. 1–6.

39. 347 U.S. 483, 74 S.Ct. 686 (1954). The fascinating history of this case is best told in Richard Kluger, *Simple Justice* (New York: Knopf, 1975).

40. What he actually promised was to appoint "strict constructionists." He seemed to imply by this phrase what we have labeled "judicial restraint," but a literal "strict construction" would logically lead to activism in some cases. For example, a "strict construction" of the First Amendment would be anything but restrained.

41. Johnson, whose grasp on political reality seemed to be fading at the time, tried to move Associate Justice Abe Fortas to the chief's chair and name Homer Thornberry, a longtime Johnson friend from Texas, to Fortas' seat. Fortas was also a Johnson protégé, and the move seemed to smack of cronyism. However, the Democratic-controlled Senate, even over southern objections, was apparently ready to confirm Fortas when allegations turned up of financial improprieties. Johnson then withdrew the nominations, and Fortas resigned his seat.

42. Justice Rehnquist recused himself since he had served in the Justice Department under President Nixon.

43. For a critical view of the new direction on the Court, see David Savage, *Turning Right: The Making of the Rehnquist Court* (New York: Wiley, 1992).

44. This is the common translation of Clausewitz' words. Bernard Brodie, *War and Politics* (New York: Macmillan, 1973), 2. A more accurate translation is given by Michael Howard, a noted military historian: "War is merely a continuation of political intercourse with the addition of other means." *New York Times,* January 28, 1991, 17.

45. Title VII, Civil Rights Act of 1964, 42 U.S. Code Sec. 2000e–2(a)(1).

46. 490 U.S. 642, 109 S.Ct. 2115 (1989).

47. See Paul Gerwitz, "Fine Print," *The New Republic,* November 18, 1991.

48. Data on juries can be found in Administrative Office of the United States Courts, *Grand and Petit Juror Service in United States District Courts,* annual.

49. Grand juries were seen by the Founding Fathers as another important barrier to an overreaching government. In the leadup to the American Revolution, for example, they had often refused to indict people for damaging British government property and uttering or writing unsavory comments about the authorities.

50. Statutory and constitutional cases do not have juries. In ordinary civil suits (involving money or property), the parties can waive a jury trial and rely on the judge alone. In a criminal case, the defendant (but not the government) has the option of waiving the right to a trial by jury.

FURTHER READING

1. Agresto, John. *The Supreme Court and Constitutional Democracy.* Ithaca, N.Y.: Cornell University Press, 1987.

2. Baum, Lawrence. *The Supreme Court.* 4th ed. Washington: Congressional Quarterly Press, 1992.

3. Bronner, Ethan. *Battle for Justice: How the Bork Nomination Shook America.* New York: Norton, 1989.

4. Goldman, Sheldon and Thomas Jahnige. *The Federal Courts as a Political System.* New York: Harper and Row, 1985.

5. O'Brien, David. *Storm Center: The Supreme Court in American Politics.* 2d ed. New York: Norton, 1990.

6. Tribe, Lawrence. *God Save This Honorable Court.* New York: Random House, 1985.

7. Wolfe, Christopher. *Judicial Activism: Bulwark of Freedom or Precarious Security?* Pacific Grove, Calif.: Brooks/Cole, 1991.

NINE

PUBLIC OPINION AND THE MEDIA

ALL GOVERNMENTS REST ULTIMATELY on public consent. Efforts to contain the passions of the Roman mobs plagued that empire's rulers; when William I conquered England in 1066, one of his first acts was to begin construction on the Tower of London as a stronghold against urban rioters; Italian dictator Benito Mussolini was hanged by his own people during World War II; a coup failed in the former Soviet Union in 1991 because the people would not acknowledge its legitimacy.

Democracy, however, changes public opinion from a practical constraint on government into the foundation stone of political power. The desires and wishes of the citizens, democracy holds, are to play an active role in governmental decision making. Individualist democrats believe that the wishes of the citizenry should be transmitted to the governing authorities as clearly and quickly as possible, and public policy should then reflect those preferences. Civic democrats emphasize the role of deliberation and discussion, trusting that a consensus over the public interest will emerge over time. In the long run, then, they too believe that public policy should coincide with what the people want.

The truth is, though, that the public has only the haziest ideas about the details of most policies. Information about and interest in politics and public affairs are quite scarce throughout most of the public. In fact, it is unrealistic to expect that any large number of people can spend the time and acquire the expertise to be even reasonably conversant with the multitude of policy areas addressed by modern governments. Are both models of democracy, therefore, hopeless ideals, so that governing must (and perhaps should) be conducted with little or no reference to the wishes of the public? Or, are there alternative ways to formulate the link between what the public wants and what government does or should do? To what degree, in fact, has the national government in the United States been responsive to public opinion over the years?

In our technological age, the mass media have assumed enormous importance, as they are the primary way the public receives political information. Thus, the role they play in shaping public thinking is critical. Furthermore, the government itself is affected by the media, if for no other

---

Opposite: *A candidate surrounded by members of the media has become a familiar sight in American public life.*

Hillary and Bill Clinton appearing on the television program "60 Minutes" in January 1992 in an attempt to answer charges about his alleged marital infidelity.

reason than that politicians know they must use the media to communicate with the public. But exactly how do the media link the public and the government?

FINDING OUT WHAT THE PUBLIC THINKS

As democratic ideas became dominant in this country, it was acknowledged that public opinion should be the shaping force in political decision making. Accordingly, throughout the nineteenth and well into the twentieth century, politicians usually used the argument that "the people favored" whatever these politicians were proposing at the time. But their methods for feeling the public pulse—talking to a few prominent citizens, gauging the mood at political rallies, reading newspaper commentary—were haphazard at best. Only the ballot box gave concrete evidence, and that always sent mixed signals, since one issue was seldom decisive in an election.

Only with the advent of public opinion polls in the 1930s was it possible to find out what the public actually thought. Public opinion polls have become a staple of our society, and indeed we know far more than ever before about what people think. Students of public opinion as well as politicians and marketing experts now depend almost entirely on the polls.

This does not mean that all polls are equally valid.[1] There are still many poorly done polls. First, there is the vital question of sample selection.

Call-in polls are especially notorious, since the sample is self-selected. Likewise, the mail-in polls which members of Congress and some newspapers and magazines conduct are seriously flawed. To be valid, a sample *must* be representative of the population about which one is generalizing. These days, sampling is a mathematical puzzle that has largely been solved; samples drawn by the legitimate polling organizations are consequently quite trustworthy. Second, the wording of the questions is of utmost importance. The respondent can be "led," for instance. (*E.g.*: "Do you think agricultural subsidies should be continued so that farmers can make a decent living like everyone else?" or "Do you support the report of a presidential commission that _____?") Biased questions are often used by interest groups and in mailouts from representatives' offices. Objective pollsters, on the other hand, try very hard to keep their question wording from skewing the results. Third, there is the problem of inaccurate answers, which has not been entirely solved. For example, many people hate to admit that they are ill-informed; hence, if a question calls for a simple agree/disagree response, they will just choose one. This off-the-top-of-the-head answering sometimes accounts for the volatility of public opinion polls. The truth is that many people have given the matter no thought at all and really have no opinion.

In spite of the problems of polls, though, they are an indispensable tool for measuring and studying public opinion. As pollsters have perfected their techniques, the good polls have become better and better. When they can be validated by outside criteria, such as voting at elections, they have proved remarkably accurate.

The Structure of American Public Opinion

It is helpful to divide public opinion[2] into three categories or layers: beliefs, attitudes, and opinions. Beliefs are the fundamental values people hold, ideas on the political system in general and the nature of society. Somewhat narrower, political attitudes are the broad general political preferences people have. They constitute what might be called political tendencies, such as liberalism and conservatism. Opinions are the thoughts people have on specific policy questions such as taxes, gun control, government-funded child care, import quotas on Japanese automobiles, the designated hitter rule.

Beliefs

There is almost unanimous agreement among Americans about the fundamentals of the political and economic order. When asked in 1986 how proud they were to be Americans, 89 percent said "very proud," 10 percent "quite proud," and only 1 percent "not very proud."[3] Similar responses are given about the flag, the national anthem, and the pledge of allegiance. Incidentally, this feeling cuts across all social, economic, racial, and religious groups. For instance, among African Americans, often thought to be the most alienated group, 90 percent were "extremely proud" and 10 percent "somewhat proud" to be Americans. Democracy as a form of government also wins wide endorsement, 95 percent in one poll and close to that figure in others.[4]

The economic system too has wide support. In 1975, 90 percent of Americans polled agreed we should make sacrifices if this were necessary to keep our free enterprise system intact. In 1981, 79 percent agreed that "the private business system in the United States works better than any other system yet designed for industrial nations." Only 9 percent disagreed with this statement.[5]

Political tolerance is also quite high, signifying an underlying acceptance of the principles of free expression and minority rights. Fully 85 percent of those polled in one study "believe in free speech for all no matter what their views might be." 93 percent agreed with the statement, "No matter what a person's political beliefs are, he is entitled to the same legal rights and protection as anyone else," and 89 percent with the proposition that "people in the minority should be free to try to win majority support for their opinions."[6]

At least two qualifications must be added to this picture, however. First, when the question of tolerance moves from the abstract to the specific, the supportive numbers erode. A group of political scientists devised an intriguing study to measure the tolerance of specific groups people disliked.[7] They gave people a list of groups (such as atheists, fascists, the Ku Klux

T A B L E 9–1
Tolerance of Least-Liked Groups

SPECIFIC ISSUE RAISED ABOUT LEAST-LIKED GROUP	PERCENTAGE TOLERANT OF LEAST-LIKED GROUP
Members of the _____ should be banned from being President of the U.S.	16
Members of the _____ should be allowed to teach in public schools.	19
The _____ should be outlawed.	29
Members of the _____ should be allowed to make a speech in this city.	50
The _____ should have their phones tapped by our government.	59
The _____ should be allowed to hold public rallies in our city.	34
I would be willing to invite a member of the _____ into my home for dinner.	18
I would be upset if a member of the _____ moved in next door to me.	37
I would be pleased if my daughter or son dated a member of the _____ .	4

Source: John Sullivan, *et al., Political Tolerance and American Democracy* (Chicago: University of Chicago Press, 1982), 67.

Klan, the Black Panthers) and asked which group each person liked least. Then, that respondent was asked several questions about political activity by that group. As reported in table 9–1, many people do not fully support political rights for their least-liked group.

Second, the confidence and trust Americans have in their institutions and leaders has wavered in the recent past. When asked in 1964, "How much of the time do you think you can trust the government in Washington to do what is right—just about always, most of the time, or only some of the time?" only 22 percent said "only some of the time." By 1984, that percentage had risen to 54 percent.[8] In another startling poll from 1986, 66 percent of Americans polled said they believed that "most people with power try to take advantage of people like myself."[9] Table 9–2 shows further evidence of this decline in confidence in the three specific branches of government.

There are conflicting interpretations of this phenomenon. Are Americans registering their distrust and lack of confidence in the institutions, or only in the people now in office? Some analysts believe that a serious crisis lurks only slightly below the surface, and that a dramatic event could immobilize government, since it has so small a reservoir of public trust upon which to draw.[10] On the other hand, two experts who exhaustively reviewed the data contended "that the confidence gap never amounted to a full-scale legitimacy crisis."[11] Jack Citrin put the point more prosaically:

> Political systems, like baseball teams, have slumps and winning streaks. Having recently endured a succession of losing seasons, Americans boo the home team when it takes the field. But fans are more often fickle; victories quickly elicit cheers. And to most fans what matters is whether the home team wins or loses, not how it plays the game. According to this analysis, a modest "winning streak" and perhaps, some new names in the lineup may be sufficient to raise the level of trust in government.[12]

TABLE 9–2

Changing Levels of Confidence in Governmental Institutions

	PERCENTAGE HAVING "A GREAT DEAL OF CONFIDENCE" IN GIVEN INSTITUTION[a]		
	Congress	*Presidency*[b]	*Supreme Court*
1966	42	41	50
1971	19	23	23
1974	17	14	33
1977	16	23	29
1980	18	17	27
1983	20	23	33
1986	21	19	32

Source: Adapted with the permission of The Free Press, a Division of Macmillan, Inc., from *The Confidence Gap* by Seymour Martin Lipset and William Schneider. Copyright © 1983 by Columbia University in the City of New York.

[a]Some questions referred to "the people running _____."
[b]Some questions referred to the entire executive branch.

TABLE 9–3

Percentages Designating Themselves Liberals and Conservatives

	LIBERAL	MODERATE	CONSERVATIVE
1977	20	29	30
1981	18	39	37
1984	17	44	32
1988	21	41	33

Source: CBS News/*New York Times* surveys.

Political Attitudes

Measuring political attitudes is done in two different ways. One method is simply to adopt the shorthand terms of political rhetoric and ask people whether they are liberal, moderate, or conservative. The other is to ask their positions on various policy issues and then assign a label to them based on their responses, again using the categories liberal, moderate, and conservative. Interestingly, the results of the two methods can be somewhat different.

A 1988 CBS News/*New York Times* poll asked people, "How would you describe your views on most political matters? Generally, do you think of yourself as liberal, moderate, or conservative?" The results were 21 percent liberal, 41 percent moderate, and 33 percent conservative (see table 9–3). Two important conclusions stand out: (1) more people are moderate than are in any other category, and (2) more people designate themselves conservative than call themselves liberal. Another 1988 survey asked people their views on ten public issues, and then compiled liberalism/conservatism scores from the responses. They found a breakdown which followed a similar pattern regarding the strength of the center (see table 9–4), but not so much of a conservative tilt.[13] Curiously, as has often been noted, Americans claim to be conservative, but often support liberal policies. That is, they are "ideologically conservative," but "programmatically liberal."

Part of the confusion undoubtedly lies in the terms "liberal" and "conservative." As far back as 1960, researchers found that only a small segment

TABLE 9–4

Distribution of Political Attitudes Based on Policy Responses, 1988

POLITICAL CATEGORY	PERCENTAGE OF ALL RESPONSES
Very liberal	9
Liberal	24
Center (Moderate)	33
Conservative	27
Very conservative	7

Source: National Election Study, 1988.

FIGURE 9–1

FIGURE 9–1

Maddox and Lilie's Four-fold Classification of Political Tendencies

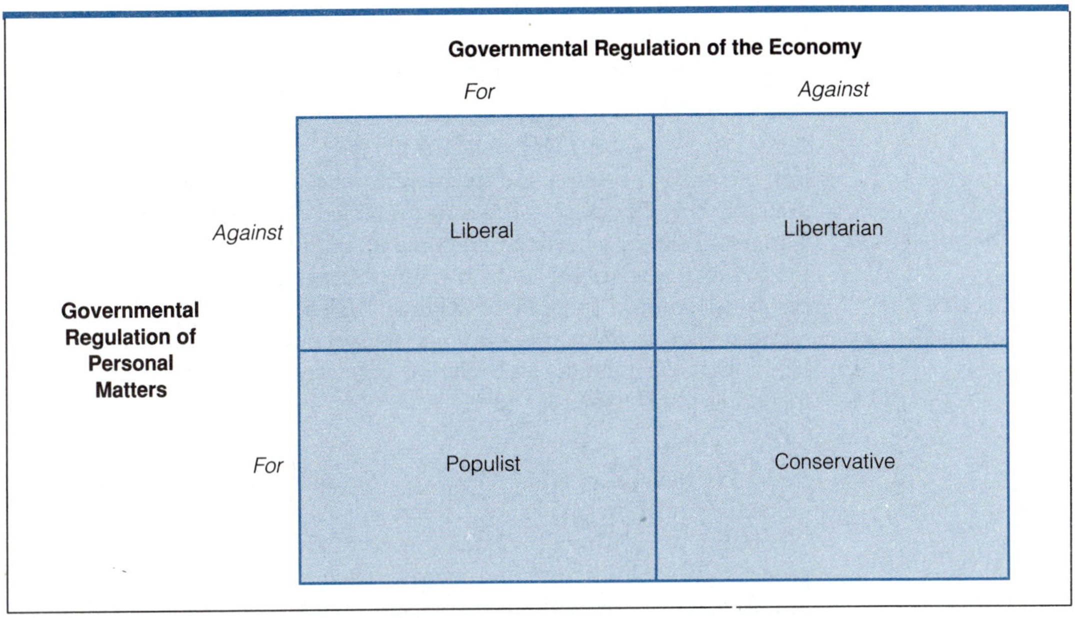

Governmental Regulation of the Economy

	For	Against
Against	Liberal	Libertarian
For	Populist	Conservative

Governmental Regulation of Personal Matters

Source: William Maddox and Stuart Lilie, *Beyond Liberal and Conservative: Reassessing the Political Spectrum* (Washington: Cato Institute, 1984), 5.

of the public understood these terms reasonably well and evaluated politics in terms of a coherent political ideology.[14] Moreover, the meaning of these terms has changed. From the 1930s to the 1950s, being liberal generally meant favoring a greater government role in economic affairs and support for social welfare policies. Now, however, a variety of other issues have emerged—foreign policy, civil rights, abortion, busing, and so forth— which muddy the waters of political classification.

This has led some writers to argue that we need to look beyond the terms "liberal" and "conservative" to understand American political attitudes. William Maddox and Stuart Lilie have proposed a fourfold classification of attitudes (see figure 9–1) that draws on two distinct dimensions.[15] The first revolves around the notion of personal freedoms (such as privacy). The other relates to the degree to which one favors government management of the economy as opposed to free enterprise. Thus, a person could be a pure libertarian (favoring maximum freedom in both personal and economic affairs); a populist (favoring regulation by government of both personal and economic matters); a traditional liberal (favoring a high degree of personal freedom but a large role for government in the economy); or a traditional conservative (favoring government enforcing standards of personal conduct but unfettered economic competition). Reviewing a number of surveys, Maddox and Lilie argue that about a fourth of the public falls into each of these categories.

Opinions

Thanks to the major polling organizations, we have a wealth of information regarding people's opinions on almost every conceivable subject. From all these data, four generalizations stand out.

LOW LEVELS OF PUBLIC INFORMATION   First, the level of information the public possesses and its interest in politics are both quite low. For example, only 29 percent of Americans polled could name their member of Congress; just 23 percent could come up with both countries involved in the SALT negotiations; and only 46 percent knew the first ten amendments constituted the Bill of Rights.[16] Additionally, when asked what matters interest them, respondents always rate politics low. Americans report that jobs, family, and religion regularly absorb more energy than following public affairs.

IMPORTANCE OF "CODE WORDS"   Second, certain words can trigger immediate positive or negative reactions. A good example is "welfare." When this word is used, it leads to overwhelming rejection of whatever program is being discussed. However, when surveys are done about specific welfare policies without mentioning the term, there is solid support for them. People usually want to spend more, not less, on specific welfare state programs—as long as the term is not invoked.[17]

CHANGE   Third, public opinion can change over time. The greatest changes have come in civil rights and foreign policy. Fair employment practices for African Americans, for instance, won the approval of only 42 percent of whites in 1944, but that of 96 percent in 1972. In 1958, 37 percent of whites said they would vote for a black for president, whereas 75 percent said so in 1988. School integration was endorsed by 50 percent of whites in the 1950s but by over 92 percent in 1985.[18] Support for these ideals often breaks down when specific policies are suggested (busing, affirmative action, etc.), but how that breakdown should be interpreted is open to dispute. In foreign policy, the most dramatic shift occurred during World War II. Only a month before Pearl Harbor, a bare 19 percent of respondents thought we should risk war with Japan to protect our interests. By the end of the war, 70 percent favored a continuing international role for the United States, a plateau that stayed steady for twenty years. Support for internationalism dipped somewhat during the Vietnam war, but it has now returned to previous levels.[19]

DIFFERENCES ACROSS SUBGROUPS   Fourth, the aggregate numbers can mask important variations among subgroups. While race is an ever-present dividing line (although a seemingly less and less relevant one),[20] social class, gender, age, religion, and region also affect opinions. Black/white differences in opinion are most pronounced, quite predictably, with regard to such issues as affirmative action and aid to minorities, but they also show up in such areas as economic policy (with blacks being more liberal) and abortion (with blacks opposing it more than whites). These last two differences result, most analysts believe, from the facts that regarding general socioeconomic standing, African Americans tend to be less affluent than whites, and that they are more religious as a whole than whites.

It is not surprising that people in the upper reaches of the social order support fewer government programs for the needy. What may be surprising is that they are also generally more supportive of democratic values. Recall that we noted above that the near-universal consensus on abstract democratic values dissolves when it comes to specific applications. There is a marked differentiation among social classes in this support for democratic norms. The higher one moves up the social ladder, the more support one finds for democratic procedures; this turns upside down the historical pattern of pressure for democracy coming from below. Thomas Dye and Harmon Zeigler have labeled this "the irony of democracy" since it seems to imply that the less democracy you have, the more you will have, and vice versa.[21]

The most significant differences between men and women are found regarding social issues and foreign policy. Pornography brings about the greatest disparity (74 percent of men would allow it, compared to 49 percent of women), but women are also more in favor of gun control and more opposed to capital punishment.[22] In foreign policy, fewer women than men support an aggressive military posture. Incidentally, there is no difference on abortion.[23]

Age, religion, and region also work their effects. It is not merely a matter of the old becoming more conservative (a proposition for which there is mixed evidence), but the issue of formative political events. Those who grew up in the complacent 1950s view the world differently from those reared in the 1970s. Many scholars believe that the political situation one confronts in early adulthood will be personally important throughout one's lifetime. Thus, the Vietnam war or Ronald Reagan's presidency have molded political attitudes for different age groups. Protestants, Catholics, and Jews hold diverse opinions on several subjects (primarily, Jews tend to be somewhat more liberal), but the differences among Protestants are greater than those among the three major groups. Regionally, the south still stands out as the most distinctive section of the country, but that has diminished. Even in the area of civil rights, the south is close to national norms. On some issues other regional cleavages appear; for instance, the west is less supportive of social welfare than are the other regions.

AGENTS OF POLITICAL LEARNING/SOCIALIZATION

What are the sources of people's beliefs, attitudes, and opinions? For most people, fundamental values are planted early in life, but experiences continue to mold and shape their views. Typically, though, those early values serve as a filter through which subsequent learning takes place. As pointed out above, many scholars believe that the years of early adulthood are very important, and that after these years we are unlikely to wander too far from these moorings.

In the study of political learning, or political socialization, it is useful to distinguish between direct and indirect socialization. Direct political socialization refers to matters that are overtly political, whereas the indirect category covers learning which deals with other issues, but which may have political ramifications.

The Family

Time and again, evidence points to the family as the most central agent of socialization.[24] This is not surprising in light of two insights from psychology: the primacy principle and the structuring principle. The first means that whatever is learned first is learned more thoroughly; the second, that what is learned first structures what comes later.

Some family political socialization is direct. Parents tell their children that they should salute the flag, that the Democrats or Republicans are the best party, that the president is wise or inept, and so on. A home environment that stresses politics and political activity will naturally tend to lead a person in that direction. Studies of party activists, for example, have found that most of them came from highly politicized homes.[25]

Much of the family's effect on political socialization is indirect, however. The wider views of the world and other human beings which are presented to children are important. Likewise, the approach parents take towards authority, both in the family itself and externally (whether the police are seen as friend or foe, for example) may shape later attitudes toward political authorities.

Religious Institutions

Churches and synagogues usually reinforce the political values of the family. Some religious teachings, such as those on abortion or peace issues, have a direct political bearing. Others are more diffuse but still important, such as the responsibility one shoulders for the poor. For those given early religious training, these basic values can have very significant political consequences.

Schools

No subject is more fraught with political overtones than the political role of the schools. While the family and religion are viewed as private, the schools are largely public and we enter therefore a different realm. Here government itself has control over what is taught and how.

The commitment of Americans to the political system and its symbols begins early. Public schools, where these children are pledging allegiance to the flag, have traditionally served an important role in teaching citizenship.

Some direct political socialization occurs at all schools. Flags, pictures of George Washington, and copies of the Declaration of Independence and the Constitution bedeck our schools. Saying the pledge of allegiance and singing patriotic songs are rituals familiar to every schoolchild. Voting for offices like class president is a common practice. Then, there is the ubiquitous and usually required high school civics course.

How much effect all this has is uncertain. We should not downplay the impact of the ceremonial features simply because we cannot find a direct effect, however. They carry important messages about social cohesion and the values the polity is committed to, even if they do so at a very abstract level. What passes for a "civics" course is more problematical. Most research documents that such a course seems to have little impact on either the level of political information students have or their interest in politics.[26] (Some critics think this results from their often being taught by members of the athletic department.)

But school has an equally important indirect effect on political socialization. For instance, the first non-family authority figure many children encounter is the teacher. This experience may create feelings that are later transferred to the political authorities. As another example, how the school resolves disputes among students may well color students' views of the fairness of government in general. Further, whether students are treated with respect or demeaned may well establish in them attitudes about what to expect from those who govern in the wider world.

In short, the direct political socialization the school endeavors to provide is important in pointing to socially acceptable ideas and providing certain rudimentary information; but the structure and atmosphere of the school are equally important.

The individualist and civic democratic models clash sharply over the role of the schools. The former stresses teaching the political system "as is," warts and all. Also, the individualist democrat is very hesitant to impose any kind of values on children, professing instead to let each person grow in his or her own direction. Civic democrats believe that teaching how the political system ought to work is as important, if not more so, than painting the political world as it is. Further, civic democrats are more inclined to have the schools share in the shaping of values, especially such values as self-discipline and civic virtue. They argue that to adopt the value-free approach of the individualist democrats itself teaches children that the world ought to be that way, that relativism and the absence of standards are desirable. Individualist democrats reply that when the schools begin teaching civic virtue, this can easily encourage a blind allegiance to the status quo and traditional authority. Conflict over these positions is a persistent feature of the debate over American public education.

The Media

From all indications, the mass media are an important agent of socialization. During the school year the average child between ages two and eleven watches television thirty-one hours a week. According to one study, the typical high school graduate will have spent eleven thousand hours in class but fifteen thousand hours watching television. It seems that during these hours, children pick up not only factual information, but also views about the world beyond their doorstep. "When asked for the sources of information on which they base their attitudes about subjects such as economic or race problems, or war and patriotism, high school students mention the mass media far more often than they mention their families, friends, teachers, or personal experience."[27] Of course, these other agents

Television is a pervasive force in the lives of many Americans.

of socialization have probably provided background values of which the students may not even be aware, but it is interesting nonetheless that they themselves cite the media so often.

College

The effect of college on political socialization has been hotly debated. Generally, students emerge from college more liberal than when they entered, and remain more liberal than those in their age group who have not attended college. But it is not clear that college *causes* them to become liberal.

One study, for instance, found that college-bound high school seniors were already more liberal than their classmates.[28] Furthermore, many of the studies have focused on social rather than economic issues. As we saw when we refined liberalism and conservatism into a fourfold classification, the two kinds of liberalism do not necessarily go together. In fact, surveys of the general population show that those with higher education (and higher incomes) tend to be rather conservative on economic issues, but liberal on social issues.

Peer Groups

From the playground to the office or factory, peer groups exercise an influence over political and other attitudes. With children and adolescents the political overtones are predominantly indirect, but may be potent never-

(text continued on page 292)

Political Beliefs in Canada

OUR BELIEFS about fundamental political values are not shared by all democratic societies. Even in our closest neighbor, not only geographically but also culturally, there is a somewhat different ethos.[1]

The Declaration of Independence speaks of "life, liberty, and the pursuit of happiness." Underlying these ideas is a robust anti-government stance. That is, liberty and the pursuit of happiness are individualistic values. Their realization requires a sharply circumscribed state, one able to exercise few powers.

Canadian founding documents speak, in contrast, of "peace, order, and good government." Not one of these values emphasizes individual freedom from government. Instead, they require the use of government for their achievement.

These differences have continued to mold outlooks down through the years. As the table shows, for example, Canadians clearly prefer a more orderly approach to government, and Americans a more libertarian one. Another interesting study, that not only pointed to differences but might help explain why they persist, found Canadian parents to be much harsher in their disciplinary practices than are Americans.[2]

Support for Liberty versus Order

	PERCENTAGE WHO "BASICALLY AGREE"	
	Canadians	*Americans*
"It is better to live in an orderly society than to allow people so much freedom they can become disruptive."	65	51
"The idea that everyone has a right to their own opinion is being carried too far these days."	37	19
"Free speech is just not worth it if it means we have to put up with the danger to society of radical and extremist views."	36	28
"Free speech ought to be allowed for all political groups even if some of the things that these groups believe in are highly insulting and threatening to particular segments of society."	51	60

Source: Seymour M. Lipset, *Continental Divide* (New York: Routledge, 1990), 111. Original data from Paul Sniderman, *et al.,* "Liberty, Authority, and Community: Civil Liberties and the Canadian Political Culture" (Toronto: Centre of Criminology, 1988).

Both historical and contemporary behavior seem to confirm the differences in values. For example, the settlement of the two western frontiers offers a startling contrast. In the United States, individuals went west on their own initiative. Gunslingers, ranchers, and prospecting miners all led their own lives, often with violence among themselves and against Native Americans. Government came later, with the people themselves having to take the initiative. In Canada, the government established its authority first, largely through the legendary Mounties. Only after government and a set of rules were firmly in place were people allowed to move into an area. The Canadian west had none of the gunfighting and general rancor common in the United States. And although Canada's policy still left much to be desired, the Native Americans were generally treated much better north of the border.

Coming forward a hundred years, in 1987 a Canadian economist wrote, "I have stood on a street corner in Toronto with a single other pedestrian and with not a car in sight, waiting for the light to turn green—behavior unimaginable in most large U.S. cities."

What accounts for these differences in outlook? Most experts believe the answer lies in the fact that the United States has a revolutionary tradition, whereas Canada was founded as a counterrevolutionary society. Our revolution was fought against established authority, and resulted in an anti-government prejudice that has endured. Canada, on the other hand, became home to many of those fleeing the American revolution, including many Anglican priests and government officials. The French-Canadians already there had been sent to New France by the king. Canadians therefore lack the hostility to government that permeates American culture—whether it be in law (in Canada the *government* can appeal in criminal cases); in economic policy (Canadians have much less reverence for free enterprise and a more nearly comprehensive welfare state supported by all parties); or in separation of church and state (unknown in Canada). They also lack the strong strain of individualism and self-reliance that are so important to Americans.

The persistence of these diverse values into the late twentieth century demonstrates how important ideas are in shaping the political order. For as the years have gone by, the objective differences between the two societies have narrowed. The structures of their economies are very similar, and Canada is inundated with American television and movies. Travel is freer across the U.S.–Canadian border than it is anywhere else in the world. Yet the countries remain different in fundamental values, in the nature of their political systems, and in their public policies.

What does the Canadian example tell us about the applicability of our two models of democracy to other societies? Is individualist democracy at all compatible with the Canadian tradition? Does the idea of civic democracy pose a problem also? That is, civic democrats stress civic virtue; but would the civic virtues Canadians believe in be the same as those held up in the United States? If these two models of democracy do not apply to Canada, what model does? Is each country's democracy unique, or are there common threads in democracy and the requirements of democratic citizenship?

---

[1] The information and quotations in this box are all taken from Seymour M. Lipset, *Continental Divide: The Values and Institutions of the United States and Canada* (New York: Routledge, 1990).
[2] Wallace Lambert, *et al.*, *Child Rearing Values: A Cross-National Study* (New York: Praeger, 1979).

theless. In adulthood, the effects continue. The work environment can be one which encourages voting and joining civic groups, or it may be one that places little value on these things. If politics is a usual topic of lunchtime conversation, a person may be pressed to read the newspaper in order to fit in. Similarly, the effects of neighbors and friends can be important.

Political Events

Finally, political events continually affect political learning and political leanings. Some events, such as World War II, are so cataclysmic that the world is never the same again. Other events may jolt people, but not have the dramatic effect which total war does. The war in Vietnam, Watergate, the landing on the moon, the collapse of the Berlin Wall, the 1992 riots in Los Angeles, for instance, were all in this second category. On the whole, though, change is more gradual, and people adjust in marginal ways. Here, we shall see, the role of the media is quite important. The choice of what to cover as news and the angle taken on that news create images that mold people's outlooks. These perceptions, or mental pictures, then affect people's reactions to other events and their evaluations of political leaders, political parties, and the government in general.

PUBLIC OPINION AND PUBLIC POLICY

Many analysts have viewed with skepticism any meaningful role for public opinion in the making of public policy. The documented ignorance and apathy of many if not most citizens, the analysts point out, makes them ill-equipped to participate in public life. Some even go so far as to argue that allowing public opinion to influence public policy is potentially dangerous, since people can be so easily manipulated by unscrupulous politicians with simplistic slogans and grandiose promises. This is the political equivalent of P.T. Barnum's famous quip that no one ever went broke underestimating the intelligence of the American public.

However, two prominent political scientists have recently attempted to rescue the American public's reputation. After careful study of fifty years' polling data, they believe that contrary to what many have argued, public opinion has the following admirable traits: "it is able to make distinctions; it is organized in coherent patterns; it is reasonable, based on the best available information; and it is adaptive to new information or changed circumstances."[29]

Their major thesis is that there is a distinct difference between an *individual's* opinions and *collective* opinion. Individuals, they argue, have long-term preferences and sound general ideas about politics and public affairs. Their short-term responses to issues and events may vary around this central tendency, but if they are polled over the long term, their central values and proclivities become evident. If therefore we examine collective opinion, these preferences should also stand out.[30] It is this collective pattern of opinion to which they attribute the above virtues, not each individual citizen at a given point in time.

Therefore, "even if individual opinions or survey responses are ill-informed, shallow, and fluctuating, collective opinion can be real, highly stable, and . . . based on all the available information. . . . *If* the available information is accurate and helpful (which depends upon the nature of a society's information system), collective opinion can even be wise."[31]

Even if public opinion is more rational and politically sophisticated than its detractors have painted it, though, it is still necessary to ask exactly what its role should be in a democracy. Should it be a direct causal agent? That is, should government sponsor a weekly or even daily poll and immediately act according to its results? Even most individualist democrats, who would be most inclined to give public opinion such a direct role, would hesitate to do this, since the rationality spoken of above is collective, which means it needs to be measured over time. Civic democrats would certainly oppose such a setup not only for this reason, but also because they stress the need for extensive debate and deliberation. Public opinion as a direct and immediate force on the character of public policy would find few defenders, then.[32]

Fortunately, there are three alternative ways of looking at the problem.[33] One of these is the argument that public opinion can set the broad guidelines of policy but leave the details to political elites. Those in power can be pointed in certain directions (such as toward a greater concern for the environment), but with some flexibility to weigh the complexities and tradeoffs (on such specifics as automobile emission standards). Another approach stresses that the public should choose the leaders but grant them flexibility in addressing public problems. Political leaders do what they think best, but if the public disapproves it can change leaders at the next election. Closely related to number two is a third option: after-the-fact reaction to government policies. That is, those in government develop policy, with the public then registering its approval or disapproval.

Taken together, these three alternatives offer practical and feasible ways for public opinion to shape government policy by assigning a role to the public that it can realistically play. These approaches are not based on intimate public familiarity with every question of public affairs. Instead, they rely on the public to set the contours and direction of public policy and to register their approval or disapproval, primarily at election time.

It must be stressed, though, that these alternatives do not call for a dismissive and uninterested citizenry. They place, on the contrary, a great deal of confidence in public judgment and thoughtfulness, even while they push to one side the need for detailed policy expertise. The responsibility of the citizens is not therefore diminished; it is refocused. It becomes the citizens' duty to cultivate judgment, prudence, and a sense of ethics and virtue. If citizens are armed with these attributes, they can play a sustained and healthy role in the formation of public policy. These ideas are all clearly in line with the expectations of civic democracy.

(text continued on page 296)

BOX 9-1

Public Opinion versus Public Judgment

As COFOUNDER and long-time president of a leading firm in the field, Daniel Yankelovich is a major figure in public opinion polling. He has always combined a mastery of the technical skills of his profession with an appreciation of deeper social and political issues. His latest book is a plea for a reorientation in our thinking on how the public can and should affect public policy.[1]

It is easy to demonstrate that the public is largely uninformed about public affairs. Many educated people then take this attitude: "What good are people's views on foreign policy if they do not know where Romania is or on economic policy if they know nothing of how the Federal Reserve System works?" We as a society operate, says Yankelovich, on an assumption that information defines knowledge. Therefore, if a citizen possesses little or no information, his opinion is of little value. This outlook has generated what Yankelovich calls a Culture of Technical Con-

trol, in which those who have the most information make the decisions.

Yankelovich argues that when it comes to matters of public policy, though, the questions are often at heart questions of value choices, and the amassing of more information will not necessarily lead to better decisions. What is desired, in contrast, is judgment. Judgment occurs, Yankelovich believes, when three conditions are met: (1) people accept the consequences of their views, (2) their attitudes are firmly held, and (3) their views are consistent. Ordinary people are quite capable, he thinks, of coming to judgment, with or without a bundle of facts at their command.

However, we must not fall into the opposite trap: letting a respect for public judgment degenerate into a

crude anti-intellectualism. We should not simply elevate every citizen into an armchair (or couch potato) philosopher who is wiser than the experts. The expert has her place too. The point is not that facts are unimportant, but that the expert has no superior claim to shape policy merely because she knows more facts.

What this means is that experts and the public need to be in dialogue with each other. Many experts are, of course, more than willing to share their knowledge with the public and to "educate" them on their areas of expertise. But this is not what Yankelovich has in mind. Dialogue means listening as well as speaking. Experts should indeed share their knowledge and insights with the public, but they should also listen to the concerns of the public, and not dismiss them because the public lacks the requisite information. The public and the experts may not, in fact, even agree on the central question in an area of concern.

BOX 9–1

One example he gives is prison overcrowding. To experts, the issue is whether the conditions constitute cruel and unusual punishment, which is forbidden by the Eighth Amendment. The debate among experts is over striking a balance between the comfort and safety of the prisoners and the efficient administration of the prisons. Several studies have shown that this concern is absolutely irrelevant to most of the public. What they are interested in is *public* safety. Thus, until experts are willing to discuss that topic seriously, they are not in dialogue with the public. This is not to say that the public is correct and the experts wrong, or vice versa, merely that there needs to be a thoughtful discussion between the two.

The theme of Yankelovich's book is closely tied to the contrast between the individualist and civic versions of democracy. Wise public policy does not result, he says explicitly, from either adding up individual's preferences *or* conducting a debate among the political elite, no matter how enlightened or well-intentioned. Instead, it comes from serious and sustained public dialogue. Thus, he believes civic democracy to be both possible and desirable.

Yankelovich proposes a three-step model for how citizens come to public judgment. First, they must be aware of the issue. At this stage, the media are of course a powerful influence. Second, people must "work through" the issue. That is, they must address the fundamental value questions which are raised. Both experts and political leaders have a role to play during this stage, which relies heavily on public debate. Finally, there is the stage of resolution, when the consequences of the public's position have been accepted, the public has come to hold its opinions firmly, and the contradictions have been worked out to make the opinion consistent.

The process of governing in a democracy is never easy, and it is even more difficult in a complex, technological age. However, Yankelovich is right to stress that "self-governance *is* an art more than a science. It concerns itself with ends more than means, with style as well as substance, with wisdom as well as information. All the measurement, number-crunching, poll taking, and computer models in the world cannot substitute for a touch of wisdom—the kind of wisdom that comes with the pursuit of public judgment and is necessary for democratic self-governance."[2]

If we accept Yankelovich's argument, how should we go about modifying citizenship education, in the schools and elsewhere? Should we develop any mechanisms other than elections to bring the public's judgment to bear on the formation of public policy?

[1]Daniel Yankelovich, *Coming to Public Judgment: Making Democracy Work in a Complex World* (Syracuse: Syracuse University Press, 1991).
[2]Yankelovich, *Public Judgment*, 220. Emphasis in original.

HAS PUBLIC OPINION AFFECTED PUBLIC POLICY?

Have the desires of the public actually had much impact on American public policy? Unfortunately, the evidence is sketchy, making it difficult to offer any firm generalizations. However, several studies have tried to tackle the problem.

Alan Monroe, for one, examined a number of issues over a fourteen-year period on which reliable poll and policy data were available.[34] He found that when the public preferred no change in current policy, no change occurred 76 percent of the time; however, when the public wanted a change, that happened only 59 percent of the time. Thus, while the public is more successful at blocking change than at securing it, overall, government still did what the public wished about two-thirds of the time. In another research effort, Benjamin Page and Robert Shapiro looked at the three hundred or so instances between 1935 and 1979 in which they could find a change in the public's views on a particular subject.[35] Their question was how many times government policy had subsequently changed. They found that in those cases in which both public opinion and policy had changed, about two-thirds of the time those changes had matched.

In short, although the congruence is not perfect, neither is public opinion inconsequential. Therefore, it seems that some combination of the three mechanisms sketched out above must be at work. The prescriptive task now is to create within the citizenry those skills which will raise the quality of public judgment and therefore the quality of public policy.

THE RISE OF THE MASS MEDIA

When the Constitution was ratified, a large percentage of the population was illiterate. The "media" consisted of rather expensive newspapers and magazines which catered only to the well-to-do. By the 1830s, rising literacy rates and new technology had given birth to the "penny press," daily urban newspapers which were cheap and geared to mass circulation. Since that time, evolving technology—more rapid printing, photography, radio, television, satellites—has continued to affect the growth and development of the mass media. Since then, too, critics have been debating the political implications of the phenomenon. One group has argued continually that the mass media are a democratizing force, bringing more information to more people and encouraging more widespread participation. Others have feared that the media could be a tool for mass manipulation, either by the media themselves or by governmental authorities. Both the shaping power of technology and the debate continue.

STRUCTURE OF THE AMERICAN MEDIA

Although people often speak of the "mass media" as some kind of unified organization, in fact the various media are rather fragmented and quite competitive. Except for public television and radio, most of the media are controlled by large private business corporations which are guided first and foremost by the profit motive.

Newspapers

Almost every community of any size has a daily newspaper, in which the focus is often heavily on local news, personalities, and events. As for national and international coverage, there is much more uniformity. This is so because few local newspapers maintain reporters in Washington or abroad, making them heavily dependent on the wire services, especially the Associated Press. Sometimes a paragraph is inserted in wire stories to give a local angle (for instance, how a local plant will be affected by new legislation, or how the local member of Congress voted), and each paper composes its own headlines. Otherwise, readers in Tampa, Spokane, and Minneapolis read the identical story.

At one time, ownership of newspapers was mostly local. In the last two decades, however, national newspaper chains—such as Knight-Ridder, Gannett, and Scripps-Howard—have bought many local papers. Gannett, for example, owns eighty-nine daily and thirty-five weekly newspapers (in addition to ten television stations and sixteen radio stations). The twenty-five biggest chains control over half of all daily newspaper circulation in the country, and all group-owned papers account for 77 percent of circulation.[36] Consequently, newspapers are not so firmly rooted in their communities as they once were, and the business side of the paper is of paramount concern to the chain. On the other hand, this shift has also meant that local papers are not so parochial or tied to local political elites, since editors continually move around.

At the top of the newspaper world are a handful of highly influential papers with national elite readerships. The *Wall Street Journal,* the nation's financial organ, is read by business people throughout the country. Its editorial stance is regularly conservative, naturally, and its focus is business news, but its features and analyses carry high prestige. The *New York Times* is almost the official American paper of record, with its motto of "All the news that's fit to print." This aphorism was adopted in 1858 to separate the paper from the New York tabloids, which specialized in the lurid and the sensational. The *Times* offers comprehensive coverage of national and international affairs and maintains its own staff of foreign correspondents worldwide. The *Washington Post* is especially strong in its coverage of the intricacies of national politics. Like the *Times,* the *Post* is read by almost everyone in government every day. Its weekly edition carries a solid array of analytical pieces and caters to a national audience. The *Los Angeles Times* is both a local newspaper for Los Angeles and a national paper, though it is less read outside its home base than are the others. Features published here, though, will receive significant attention. In sum, these papers have an influence that is far greater than their circulation numbers might indicate, because of who reads them.

TABLE 9–5

Circulation of Top Ten Daily Newspapers

NEWSPAPER	CIRCULATION
Wall Street Journal	1,857,000
USA Today	1,348,000
Los Angeles Times	1,196,000
New York Times	1,108,000
New York Daily News	1,098,000
Washington Post	781,000
Chicago Tribune	721,000
Newsday (New York)	714,000
Detroit Free Press	636,000
San Francisco Chronicle	563,000

Source: World Almanac and Book of Facts, 1992 Edition (New York: Pharos Books, 1991), 312.

Magazines

There are three major newsmagazines, *Time, Newsweek,* and *U.S. News and World Report. Time* and *Newsweek* both have fairly sizable circulations (roughly comparable to that of the *National Enquirer*) and through the years they have become more alike. Both present crisp overviews of a variety of stories, sprinkled with some analytical and editorial pieces. *U.S. News* is slanted more to a business clientele and is more purposely conservative in its orientation.

Supplementing these are a number of magazines devoted exclusively to public affairs. They are primarily analytical publications and not designed to convey the news, since their readers will already have digested the factual news from elsewhere. Their readerships are quite small, placing them well below such periodicals as *True Story, Hot Rod,* and *Michigan Living* in circulation. Nonetheless, they are also influential because of who their readers are.[37]

Television

Television has become a pervasive force in American life. Over 97 percent of homes have a set and on a typical evening approximately 100 million people are watching (about 40 percent of the population). As noted above, television viewing supersedes classroom time for adolescents. If further evidence is needed that television watching is ubiquitous, consider that nine months after a power outage in Indianapolis there was a surge in births.

In surveys, more people report getting their news from television than from any other source.[38] Of course, most people watch television for

TABLE 9–6

Circulation of Leading Magazines

MAGAZINE	CIRCULATION
NRTA/AARP Bulletin (formerly Modern Maturity)	22,104,000
Reader's Digest	16,265,000
TV Guide	15,604,000
National Geographic	10,190,000
Better Homes and Gardens	8,007,000
Family Circle	5,432,000
Good Housekeeping	5,153,000
McCall's	5,020,000
Ladies' Home Journal	5,002,000
Woman's Day	4,803,000
Time	4,095,000
Redbook	3,907,000
National Enquirer	3,804,000
Playboy	3,488,000
Star	3,431,000
Sports Illustrated	3,220,000
Newsweek	3,212,000
People	3,209,000
Prevention	3,022,000
American Legion	2,956,000

Source: World Almanac, 1992 Edition, 311.

entertainment, not directly for news or public affairs programming. In fact, about half of those who watch regularly report that they never watch the news. Each network has a thirty-minute evening news program, however, and other public affairs offerings. Some, such as "60 Minutes," achieve substantial ratings successes. Public television sponsors the widely acclaimed "McNeil-Lehrer News Hour," watched by a relatively small but highly educated and informed audience. Finally, there is the Cable News Network (CNN) and C-Span, which offers continual coverage of political material.

Television has been undergoing enormous changes in recent years as cable has made its presence felt. The three major networks—NBC, CBS, and ABC—have claimed a steadily shrinking audience for both entertainment and news programs. As radio did earlier, television channels are turning to "narrowcasting," or finding a specific audience—for sports, religious programs, rock music, movies, comedy, etc.—and catering to it.[39] With this new technology, government policy toward cable television has become controversial. In the Reagan years there was a general relaxation of government oversight of the broadcasting industry, but significant new regulations were imposed by Congress in 1992 (over President Bush's veto).

The newsroom of the Cable News Network (CNN).

SOURCES OF POLITICAL INFORMATION

As noted above, more people say they obtain their information about the political world from television than claim to acquire it from any other source. Supposedly, even though it has been declining, the audience for the network newscasts still exceeds the readership of newspapers. Yet, researchers have found reasons to doubt how much "watching" there really is. It seems that merely having the set on qualifies as "viewing" for many. When people are asked, for instance, to identify stories on the previous evening's newscast, the recall rate is very low.[40]

Those who read newspapers and newsmagazines are, on the whole, substantially better informed.[41] Reading not only requires much more concentration, but the print media can provide far more background material. If an entire script of a thirty-minute television newscast were printed, it would run less than one newspaper page.

But television news coverage is important for two reasons. First, the medium is unmatched for instantaneous coverage. Whenever there are swift-moving events, newspapers are inevitably stale. When the Persian Gulf War broke out, for example, people turned instinctively to television. Second, television provides visual images that affect how people see the world. "The reality that lives is the reality etched in the memories of the millions who watched rather than the few who were actually there."[42] For instance, during the Iranian hostage crisis of 1979–80, the footage of the

The Vietnam War was the first war to be brought home to the public daily via television. This fact contributed to the growing disillusionment and widespread opposition to the war.

unbending Ayatollah and his fanatical followers created a mental picture of Iran that has lasted. During the Gulf War the images that came through were of electronically guided bombs hitting every target and Iraqis surrendering in droves. At best, these are incomplete pictures of both these episodes.

IMPACT OF THE MEDIA ON ATTITUDES

Most early studies concluded that the media had a minimal impact on people's outlooks and attitudes.[43] Three reasons were advanced for this finding, which ran counter to the then-conventional idea that propaganda could mobilize people to mass action. First, most people are anchored in their political beliefs and not overly susceptible to manipulation by an impersonal force. Second, people perceive the news through their own perceptual lens. That is, if they have a favorable image of a candidate or group, new information is seen through that view, merely confirming what is already thought. Third, personal conversations were found to carry far more weight with most people than did the media. The power of the media was therefore declared to be a myth. However, more recent studies have challenged this view, supplying evidence that important cues may be provided by the media, that the political agenda is influenced by media coverage, and that even policy preferences may be affected.

Cues

In the 1976 presidential debates Gerald Ford made an inaccurate statement concerning Poland's government. Most viewers apparently did not understand or thought little of it; a poll following the broadcast revealed that the public declared the debate a draw. The next few days brought forth a barrage of press criticism of the president's gaffe. Follow-up polls then showed that on second thought people believed Carter had won.

Another example can be drawn from the presidential debates of 1984. In the first encounter Reagan appeared somewhat muddled and confused, but that evening's polls showed only a slight leaning toward Mondale's "winning" of the debate. Over the next two days a number of news stories declared that Mondale had clearly won and obliquely raised questions about Reagan's age. Polls then showed the public picking Mondale as the winner by a nearly four-to-one margin. In both cases, it seems the media provided important cues about how events should be interpreted.

Agenda Setting

If government is to be responsive to public opinion, even indirectly, then the subjects people are thinking about are as important as the substance of what they are thinking. Apparently, the media are a major source for people's ideas on which problems need attention.

Three political scientists conducted an interesting experiment by having three groups of people watch the evening news apart from each other for six days.[44] Unknown to the subjects, they saw differently edited versions, one with more stories on pollution, one with more on defense issues, and a third with more on inflation. Before and after the experience they were polled on what they considered the nation's most pressing public problems to be. In all three groups, on the second poll people elevated the importance of the subject on which they had seen the inserted stories.

The Gallup Poll regularly asks people to identify "the most important problem facing the country." Michael MacKuen examined these polls over a fifteen-year period and found that the responses correlated better to media coverage of issues than to actual reality.[45] That is, inflation or crime, for instance, were mentioned more frequently as media coverage of these issues increased, whether or not the inflation or crime rate changed. Seemingly, therefore, the influence of the media in agenda setting is far from negligible.

Policy Preferences

Few people are so gullible that a talking head on television would make them instantly change their views on anything. Could the influence of the media over the long run, though, be more pronounced?

The only thorough study suggests, but does not prove, that the media may have such an influence. A team of political scientists uncovered eighty instances over a roughly fifteen-year period in which public opinion had shifted on a matter of public policy.[46] They then coded the messages contained in the network news programs on these issues, both those enunciated by politicians and interest groups and the observations of commentators and anchors. The most important factor in predicting how opinion changed seemed to be what the media people had said. Although the recorded changes in public opinion were modest, it does appear that over time the messages had had some effect.

Specific instances of commentator effect include their advocacy of campaign contribution limits in 1973; their support for ranking the fight against unemployment ahead of controlling inflation in 1976; and their criticism of President Reagan's tax cuts as primarily of benefit to the wealthy. In each case there was a perceptible movement of public opinion in line with the commentary, even after controlling for the effects of all other factors.

In contrast to the earlier studies, then, later work points to a measured but still important role for the media. The interpretation of events, the political agenda, and opinion on public policy all appear to be influenced to some degree by the media.

IS THERE A BIAS IN THE MEDIA?

If the media possess the power to affect politics in these ways, then the question of possible bias becomes crucial. Even if their ability to control people's thinking falls far short of science fiction fantasies and the Nazi-tainted fears of the 1930s, it is important to examine media use of even limited power.

Two sets of critics contend that there are unmistakable biases in the American media. Conservatives complain that the media have a liberal orientation and bias, and that conservative public figures and ideas are therefore treated unfairly.[47] To shriller critics there is an unseen conspiracy at work, but others simply point out that most journalists are liberals and that those preferences color their reporting: what they select as news and how it is presented.

Ironically, the other fault-finders sit at the opposite end of the political spectrum.[48] They accuse the media of uncritically supporting American institutions, traditional values, and the status quo. Since the media organizations themselves—the networks, television stations, and newspapers—are part of the business world, and usually big business, they uphold the needs of business elites and stifle alternative ideas.

Analyses of working journalists have confirmed that they are substantially more liberal than is the general public. A major study of elite national journalists found tellingly that 54 percent claim to be liberals, compared to 21 percent of the general population.[49] In terms of policy preferences, 80 percent favor affirmative action for blacks and 90 percent a woman's right

University of Oklahoma law professor Anita Hill appearing before the Senate Judiciary committee in 1991 accusing Supreme Court nominee Clarence Thomas of sexual harassment. Many question whether the continued television coverage really informed the public or trivialized the issues at stake.

to have an abortion, for example. In economic policy, though, the preferences turn in a decidedly conservative direction. After carefully inspecting the output of these journalists, the authors offered the guarded conclusion that there is indeed some liberal bias in their reporting.[50]

On the other hand, the media certainly do support the American system. Seldom is any critique offered that would disparage the core institutions and the values which undergird them. Furthermore, on specific economic policies, journalists are quite conservative. A full 70 percent think that private enterprise is fair to workers, for instance, and 63 percent think that less business regulation would be good for the country.

In a way, then, both sets of critics are right. Left-wing critics of journalists are correct in their claim that no fundamental questions are normally raised by the media about the system, especially the economic system. Conversely, right-wing detractors have a point when they criticize the liberal predispositions of journalists regarding social policy.

Nonetheless, there are several offsetting factors. First, journalists have a professional commitment to objectivity. While of course no one is capable of complete objectivity, there are degrees of bias. Though the profession is not formally organized in the way that law and medicine are, there are norms its practitioners take seriously, and objectivity is one of them. Second, competition provides another check on balance and accuracy. Al-

TABLE 9–7
Characteristics of the Journalistic Elite

PERSONAL CHARACTERISTIC	PERCENTAGE OF U.S. JOURNALISTS
White	95
Male	79
From Northeast or north central state	68
From metropolitan area	42
College graduate	93
Politically liberal	54
Politically conservative	17
Seldom or never attends religious services	86

Source: Robert Lichter, *et al., The Media Elite* (Bethesda, Md.: Adler and Adler, 1986), 21–22.

though several media giants indeed own and operate a disproportionate share of newspapers, television, and radio outlets, by no means is their control total. In fact, even though newspaper ownership has become more concentrated over the last few years, television newscasting has become more fragmented. Furthermore, even the major media organizations are quite competitive with each other. Also, there are any number of independent institutions in the media world—small magazines, independent newspapers, and even the foreign press. For example, it was a Lebanese magazine that broke the Iran-contra story. No media source, in short, has a monopoly on information and ideas.

Also, it must not be forgotten that the media do not sit completely apart from American politics and society. Politicians and interest groups expend enormous time and resources trying to use the media for their own ends. The media are the target of manipulation by various interests as much as they are an independent force in themselves. Neither is the public a mere passive bystander. The media endeavor to cover what they think interests the public; thus they do not go about their work with an unrestrained hand when it comes to story selection. Consider the agenda-setting study, for instance, that found media coverage to be directly related to public concerns. The conclusion drawn was that media coverage heightened public concern about an issue. But perhaps the relationship was the other way around; perhaps, that is, the media were merely responding to heightened public interest in inflation or crime, not creating it. After all, newspapers must be sold and television news watched for the media institutions to stay in business.

What does the public think? About 43 percent of Americans believe that the media are biased— 30 percent that they are liberally biased, 13 percent that they are conservatively biased.[51] While it might seem alarming at first glance that nearly half the American people think the media exhibit a bias, it also means that that many people are harder to sway, since they probably discount much of what they see, hear, and read in the media.

In the end, Americans have a great deal of confidence in the media. In a five-nation study, much lower levels of confidence were found in France,

Germany, Britain, and Spain than were noted in the United States.[52] In a 1986 survey, over 80 percent of respondents said all major news organizations could be believed.[53] (The *National Enquirer* got a 14 percent rating.) Also, 85 percent gave both broadcast and print journalists a favorable rating. This compared to favorable ratings of 61 percent for the military and 65 percent for business corporations.

MEDIA COVERAGE OF CAMPAIGNS AND ELECTIONS

Political campaigns and elections are at the heart of any democracy, whether it be based on the individualist or the civic model. They are the primary mechanism by which the citizenry both control and direct government. How citizens are linked to those running for public office, then, is of singular importance.

In our day, this linking role has been assumed almost exclusively by the media, especially in presidential campaigns. Few citizens know anything about the candidates for office or their stands on policy issues except what comes to them via the media. It is ironic, perhaps, that such a vital role is played by an institution that is wholly in private hands and has no responsibility for governing once the election is over.

Media coverage of election campaigns is always subject to a barrage of criticism. The candidates naturally think the press is unfair when it offers anything but enthusiastic backing, but more objective observers are equally critical. Most often, the latter's reproach centers on two facts: the media's tendency to focus on the "horse race" aspect of the campaign (who is ahead by how much, campaign strategy, etc.); and the relentless pursuit of scandal and character failings, especially sensational stories regarding sexual matters.

There is no denying that the media focus heavily on the horse race to the exclusion of serious discussions of the issues. One study of the 1988 election, for example, found that almost two-thirds of newspaper stories dealt with campaign strategy and tactics;[54] another study, of *Time* and *Newsweek's* coverage of the same election, reported that less than 9 percent of the stories on the two candidates dealt with policy.[55] While, of course, the campaign and its attendant drama are important topics, the danger the detractors contend is that this coverage has become so overwhelming that the mass of people act accordingly. "What this emphasis on strategies and performance is . . . likely to do," says Marjorie Hershey, "is to make both voters and reporters into drama critics, judges of how effective the tactic was, not how much sense the candidate made."[56]

The other chastisement administered to the press is its never-ending probe of the personal lives of candidates. Where is the line, it is often asked, between the private and the public when a person is running for president? In 1987, candidate Gary Hart, who had repeatedly been accused of extramarital sexual liaisons, challenged reporters to follow him. Two *Miami Herald* reporters did so and caught him in the act, forcing Hart to withdraw. In 1991 and 1992 the Clinton campaign was rocked by a tabloid story detailing an affair with a former state employee. Major news organizations then reported not directly on the allegation but on the tabloid story. Was either of these stories really useful to voters in making up their minds? Again, surely a candidate's character is a relevant matter for examination in the press; the questions are instead how far into the private the press can go, and to what degree the candidate's personal character should eclipse other issues which are equally germane.

Defenders of the press usually point out that the media merely supply what the public wants; in essence, horse races and sex scandals are what the public seems interested in, since these things sell newspapers and bring up the ratings. Michael Kinsey, writing for *Time,* put it this way: "I may think that a candidate's past or even present sexual activities are completely irrelevant compared with his views on the federal deficit. In fact, that's pretty close to what I do think. But what right do I have, as a journalist in a democracy, to decide that for others?"[57] Referring to the *New York Times* decision to place its story on the tabloid's charges against Bill Clinton at the bottom of the fourteenth page, Edwin Diamond sarcastically said, "The elite 'consensus' will decide what the voting public should be told, when it should be told, and how."[58]

Individualist and civic democrats part company on this issue. Individualist democrats would back Kinsey and Diamond, having media coverage be entirely driven by what people want to see or read. Civic democrats, on the other hand, believe that the press has a civic obligation to foster intelligent public debate. While they would be unlikely to support government regulation to achieve this end, civic democrats would argue that the media should take their responsibilities seriously and not merely cater to the lowest common denominator in the public. Carl Bernstein, one of the two reporters famous for uncovering the Watergate story, recently castigated his fellow journalists for their coverage of campaigns and American life generally. "We do not serve our readers and viewers, we pander to them. And we condescend to them, giving them what we think they want and what we calculate will sell and boost ratings and readership. Many of them, sadly, seem to justify our condescension, and to kindle at the trash. Still, it is the role of journalists to challenge people, not merely to amuse them."[59]

SUMMARY

Democracy places public opinion at the center of politics, but until the 1930s and the advent of modern public opinion polling, no one really knew what the masses of people thought.

Public opinion is commonly divided into three components, beliefs, attitudes, and opinions. American political beliefs are nearly uniform throughout the population, with widespread support for the nation's basic political and economic order. Although confidence has sagged somewhat in the recent past, this has not seemed to pose a serious threat to the legitimacy of the nation's underpinnings. More Americans identify themselves as conservatives than call themselves liberals, but support for liberal policies remains high. Separating economic and social issues provides an insightful fourfold classification which may better describe the structure of American political attitudes. Opinions of the public regarding specific policies are characterized by low levels of information, the importance of code words, change, and variations among subgroups. There are a number of factors which shape political learning, including the family, religious institutions, schools, the media, college, peer groups, and political events.

The extent to which public opinion actually affects public policy is uncertain. Initial research efforts seem to point to an effect in about two out of three cases. Three alternative models which give the public the role of setting the broad outline and direction of public policy (in line with civic democracy) seem better able to describe how this effect works than an idealized version of individualist democracy could.

The media compose a powerful element in American politics. More people get their news from television than from other sources, but newspaper and magazine readers are better informed. Local newspapers carry wire service accounts of national and international news, but most political elites turn to the national papers and public affairs magazines to stay abreast of the political world.

Although the media do not and probably could not directly manipulate public views, they are powerful in giving cues, setting the agenda, and to a degree determining people's policy preferences.

Most national working journalists are decidedly liberal on non-economic issues, far more so than is the public. In some measure, this bias seems to seep into their work. At the same time, journalists strongly support basic American values and institutions. Nonetheless, professional norms of objectivity and the fact of competition reduce the influence of any biases. In general, Americans have a high level of confidence in the media.

Media coverage of campaigns and elections is especially important in a democratic society. The American press has been sharply criticized in this regard for focusing on the "horse race" aspect of the campaign and on character questions while ignoring policy issues.

ENDNOTES

1. An excellent explanation of the issues involved in polling is Albert H. Cantril, *The Opinion Connection: Polling, Politics and the Press* (Washington: Congressional Quarterly Press, 1991), chap. 3. Another solid source on polls is Herbert Asher, *Polling and the Public: What Every Citizen Should Know* (Washington: Congressional Quarterly Press, 1988).

2. A thorough overview of the American public's opinions on a wide variety of issues can be found in Benjamin Page and Robert Shapiro, *The Rational Public: Fifty Years of Trends in Americans' Policy Preferences* (Chicago: University of Chicago Press, 1992), chaps. 3–6.

3. These surveys are summarized in Michael Corbett, *American Public Opinion* (New York: Longman, 1991), 101–102.

4. James Prothro and Charles Grigg, "Fundamental Principles of Democracy: Bases of Agreement and Disagreement," *Journal of Politics* 22 (1960), 276–94. See also Herbert McCloskey, "Consensus and Ideology in American Politics," *American Political Science Review* 58 (1964), 361–82.

5. Seymour M. Lipset and William Schneider, *The Confidence Gap,* rev. ed. (Baltimore: John Hopkins University Press, 1987), 285. For other data on agreement on economic fundamentals, see Lloyd Free and Hadley Cantril, *The Political Beliefs of Americans* (New Brunswick, N.J.: Rutgers University Press, 1967), 129–33.

6. Prothro and Grigg, "Fundamental Principles," and McCloskey, "Consensus and Ideology."

7. John L. Sullivan, James Peirson, and George Marcus, *Political Tolerance and American Democracy* (Chicago: University of Chicago Press, 1982). This approach has been criticized as perhaps overstating the amount of intolerance there is in the public, in that asking people about their least favored group brings out their worst side. See Herbert McCloskey and Alida Brill, *Dimensions of Tolerance* (New York: Russell Sage Foundation, 1983).

8. Corbett, *Public Opinion,* 115.

9. Louis Harris, *Inside America* (New York: Vintage, 1987), 35.

10. Arthur H. Miller, "Political Issues and Trust in Government," *American Political Science Review* 68 (1974), 951–72.

11. Lipset and Schneider, *Confidence Gap,* 438.

12. Jack Citrin, "Comment: The Political Relevance of Trust in Government," *American Political Science Review* 78 (1984), 987.

13. This was a National Election Study poll. It is discussed in Robert Erikson, Norman Luttbeg, and Kent Tedin, *American Public Opinion,* 4th ed. (New York: Macmillan, 1991), 90–91.

14. Philip Converse, "The Nature of Belief Systems in Mass Publics," in David Apter, ed., *Ideology and Discontent* (New York: Free Press, 1964). For a further discussion see Pamela Conover and Stanley Feldman, "The Origins and Meaning of Liberal and Conservative Self-Identification," *American Journal of Political Science* 25 (1981), 617–45.

15. William Maddox and Stuart Lilie, *Beyond Liberal and Conservative: Reassessing the Political Spectrum* (Washington: Cato Institute, 1984).

16. Reported in Page and Shapiro, *The Rational Public,* 10–11.

17. See Tom W. Smith, "That Which We Call Welfare by Any Other Name Would Smell Sweeter: An Analysis of the Impact of Question Wording on Response Patterns," *Public Opinion Quarterly* 51 (1987), 75–83.

18. Erikson, Luttbeg, and Tedin, *Public Opinion,* 63.

19. Erikson, Luttbeg, and Tedin, *Public Opinion,* 66.

20. See the surveys reported and analyzed in *American Enterprise,* January/February 1990, 103. However, see Edward Carmines and James Stimson, *Issue Evolution: Race and the Transformation of American Politics* (Princeton: Princeton University Press, 1989) for evidence on the continuing importance of race as the major cleavage line in American political outlooks.

21. Thomas Dye and Harmon Zeigler, *The Irony of Democracy,* 7th ed. (Belmont, Calif.: Wadsworth, 1987).

22. Corbett, *Public Opinion,* 238.

23. Another interesting fact is that more men than women supported the Equal Rights Amendment. See Rita Simon and Jean Landis, "The Polls: Women's and Men's Attitudes About a Woman's Place and Role," *Public Opinion Quarterly* 53 (1989), 265–76.

24. Fred Greenstein, *Children and Politics* (New Haven: Yale University Press, 1965).

25. Paul Allen Beck and Frank Sorauf, *Party Politics in America,* 7th ed. (Glenview, Ill.: Scott, Foresman, 1992), 129.

26. Kenneth Langdon and M. Kent Jennings, "Political Socialization and the High School Civics Curriculum in the United States," *American Political Science Review* 62 (1968), 852–77.

27. Doris Graber, *Mass Media and American Politics,* 3d ed. (Washington: Congressional Quarterly Press, 1989), 151. The other information in this paragraph is drawn from this book, pp. 150–52.

28. M. Kent Jennings and Richard Niemi, *The Political Character of Adolescence* (Princeton: Princeton University Press, 1974). However, a later study of the same people (called a panel study) seemed to point to some causal effects of the college experience on liberalism. See the same two authors' *Generations and Politics* (Princeton: Princeton University Press, 1981).

29. Page and Shapiro, *The Rational Public,* 14.

30. The reason that collective responses are a substitute for polling the same individuals over a sustained time period results from the statistical procedure known as *aggregation.* For an analysis, see Page and Shapiro, *The Rational Public,* chap. 1.

31. Page and Shapiro, *The Rational Public,* 17. (Emphasis in original.)

32. There are also some other problems, such as intensity (should everyone's opinions be counted equally, no matter how intense their feelings?) and the need for policy stability (should policy change the instant the 50.0001 percentage mark is reached?).

33. These formulations are drawn from Robert Weissberg, *Public Opinion and Popular Government* (Englewood Cliffs, N.J.: Prentice-Hall, 1976).

34. Alan Monroe, "Consistency Between Public Preferences and National Policy Decisions," *American Politics Quarterly* 7 (1979), 3–21.

35. Benjamin Page and Robert Shapiro, "Changes in Americans' Policy Preferences: 1935–1979," *Public Opinion Quarterly* 46 (1982), 24–42.

36. Richard Davis, *The Press and American Politics: The New Mediator* (New York: Longman, 1992), 99.

37. You should sample some of these the next time you are in your college's library. Among them are *America, Commentary, Commonweal, The Nation, National Review, New Leader, The New Republic,* and *The Progressive.*

38. See John Robinson and Mark Levy, *The Main Source: Learning from Television News* (Beverly Hills, Calif.: Sage, 1986).

39. On narrowcasting and its political implications, see Austin Ranney, "Broadcasting, Narrowcasting, and Politics," in Anthony King, ed., *The New American Political System,* 2d version (Washington: American Enterprise Institute, 1990), 175–201.

40. W. Russell Neumann, "Patterns of Recall among Television News Viewers," *Public Opinion Quarterly* 40 (1976), 115–23.

41. Gladys Lang and Kurt Lang, *Politics and Television Re-Viewed,* (Beverly Hills, Calif.: Sage, 1984).

42. Lang and Lang, *Politics and Television Re-Viewed,* 213.

43. See Bernard Berelson, Paul Lazersfeld, and William McPhee, *Voting* (Chicago: University of Chicago Press, 1954).

44. Shanto Iyengar, Mark Peters, and Donald Kinder, "Experimental Demonstrations of the 'Not-So-Minimal' Consequences of Television News Programs," *American Political Science Review* 76 (1982), 848–58.

45. Michael MacKuen, "Social Communication and the Mass Policy Agenda," in Michael MacKuen and Steven Coombs, eds., *More than News: Media Power in Public Affairs* (Beverly Hills, Calif.: Sage, 1981).

46. Benjamin Page, Robert Shapiro, and Glenn Dempsey, "What Moves Public Opinion?" *American Political Science Review* 81 (1987), 23–43.

47. Edith Efron, *The News Twisters* (Los Angeles: Nash, 1971). Senator Jesse Helms of North Carolina was so upset by what he thought was bias at CBS that he once launched an effort to buy the network. It soon fizzled, however.

48. Michael Parenti, *Inventing Reality: The Politics of the Mass Media* (New York: St. Martin's, 1986).

49. Robert Lichter, Stanley Rothman, and Linda Lichter, *The Media Elite* (Bethesda, Md.: Adler and Adler, 1986). See also William Schneider and I.A. Lewis, "Views on the News," *Public Opinion,* August/September 1985, for another survey.

50. The authors did not examine the question of whether the economic conservatism of the journalists also comes through.

51. Schneider and Lewis, "Views on the News."

52. Lawrence Parisot, "Attitudes About the Media: A Five-Country Comparison," *Public Opinion,* January/February, 1988.

53. Michael Robinson, "Pressing Opinions," *Public Opinion,* September/October, 1986.

54. Marjorie Hershey, "The Campaign and the Media," in Gerald Pomper, ed., *The Election of 1988: Reports and Interpretations* (Chatham, N.J.: Chatham House, 1989), 97–98.

55. Thomas Patterson, "The Press and Its Missed Assignment," in Michael Nelson, ed., *The Elections of 1988* (Washington: Congressional Quarterly Press, 1989), 101–102.

56. Hershey, "The Campaign and the Media," 98.

57. Michael Kinsey, "Private Lives: How Relevant?" *Time,* January 27, 1992, 68.

58. Edwin Diamond, "Crash Course: Campaign Journalism 101," *New York,* February 17, 1992, 30.

59. Carl Bernstein, "The Idiot Culture," *The New Republic,* June 8, 1992, 25.

FURTHER READING

1. Berkman, Ronald and Laura Kitch. *Politics in the Media Age.* New York: McGraw-Hill, 1986.

2. Cantril, Albert. *The Opinion Connection: Polling, Politics, and the Press.* Washington: Congressional Quarterly Press, 1991.

3. Davis, Richard. *The Press and American Politics: The New Mediator.* New York: Longman, 1992.

4. Erikson, Robert, Norman Luttbeg, and Kent Tedin. *American Public Opinion.* 4th ed. New York: Macmillan, 1991.

5. Ginsberg, Benjamin. *The Captive Public: How Mass Opinion Promotes State Power.* New York: Basic Books, 1986.

6. Graber, Doris. *Mass Media and American Politics.* 4th ed. Washington: Congressional Quarterly Press, 1992.

7. Key, V.O. *Public Opinion and American Democracy.* New York: Knopf, 1961.

8. Leonard, Thomas. *The Power of the Press: The Birth of American Political Reporting.* New York: Oxford University Press, 1986.

9. Lippman, Walter. *Public Opinion.* New York: Harcourt, Brace, 1922.

10. Page, Benjamin and Robert Shapiro. *The Rational Public: Fifty Years of Trends in Americans' Policy Preferences.* Chicago: University of Chicago Press, 1992.

11. Yankelovich, Daniel. *Coming to Public Judgment: Making Democracy Work in a Complex World.* Syracuse: Syracuse University Press, 1991.

TEN

POLITICAL PARTIES AND CITIZEN PARTICIPATION

DEMOCRATIC INSTITUTIONS have little point if public desires do not affect public policy. In the ideal version of the individualist model, there should be a one-to-one correspondence between the two, governmental institutions being merely the conduit for public preferences. Civic democracy modifies the immediate and direct impact of public opinion through its emphasis on deliberation and discussion, but even here the public's wishes are ultimately determinative.

In a very small society, such as the fabled New England towns, it is possible to establish a direct link between popular participation and government, largely because there is not much distinction between people and government. In a modern nation-state, though, such a direct link is simply impossible. Political parties and periodic elections have developed therefore as the most effective "transmission belts" for channelling public opinion into government's councils. Although they are imperfect mechanisms for performing this function, no one has sketched out any realistic alternative, and no modern democracy has been without political parties. A political party here or abroad may be defined as "a group of officeholders, candidates, activists, and voters who identify with a group label and seek to elect individuals to public office who run under that label."[1]

As befits our status as the pioneer of stable popular government, the United States is the birthplace of the political party. Moreover, our political parties, like our Constitution, have proved remarkably adaptable. During their formative years in the early national period, they were primarily factions within government rather than vehicles for public participation in politics.[2] As the electorate expanded, their office-seeking strategies and their role in organizing government changed. In our own day, they are still evolving, responding to the dictates of television, more centralized government, a more ideological electorate, and a host of new policy issues.

Opposite: *View of the 1992 Republican National Convention held in the Houston Astrodome.*

Some critics have argued that our parties are becoming weaker, and perhaps are even in danger of dying. Since the health of a democracy is closely tied to the health of its parties, these critics argue, there is cause for concern, even alarm. However, others are confident that the parties are merely changing, not perishing, and that what seems like death is really rejuvenation.

THE HISTORY OF AMERICAN POLITICAL PARTIES

Although political parties originated in the early national period,[3] the Founding Fathers would hardly be proud of this legacy. Most of them felt that "factions" detracted from the search for the "public interest" and were therefore unhealthy manifestations of social conflict. James Madison argued strongly in *The Federalist* No. 10 that one of the great objects of the Constitution was to "cure the mischiefs of faction." George Washington, unable to keep factions from developing in either Congress or his own cabinet, somberly warned Americans about the competition of political parties in his farewell address:

"It serves always to distract the public councils and enfeeble the public administration. It agitates the community with ill-founded jealousies and false alarms; kindles the animosity of one part against another; foments occasionally riot and insurrection. It opens the door to foreign influence and corruption."[4]

Washington's sentiments are clearly more akin to civic than to individualist democracy. James Madison, too, believed that government's great purpose was to search for the public interest. However, he was realistic enough to know that people often acted from base self-interest alone. For Madison, therefore, individualist democracy described how politics is often actually conducted—but he did not hold that up as an ideal. Instead, he focused on the ways institutions could be designed to tame and check this tendency. Yet, he never argued that people always acted from pure self-interest; he was a civic democrat in his thinking about how government should and could be operated.[5]

The First Party System

In the formative years, American political parties were only loosely organized groupings in Congress. Soon, though, they took on the trappings of organization, and began the practice of nominating candidates for president and organizing rudimentary campaigns.

A group known as Federalists supported Alexander Hamilton (Washington's secretary of the treasury) and his dual plans for political centralization and the encouragement of economic growth through vigorous government policies (which mostly aided the well-to-do). The Federalists were also skeptical of the growing chorus of demands to expand the franchise beyond the elite of large property-holders. They much preferred a government of "gentlemen," men who had the education, the time, and the "temperament" for public affairs, or put more succinctly, men like themselves.

Their Democratic-Republican challengers were more fearful of centralization and the power it brought. They favored the economic interests of those who were less well off, the small farmers and town artisans. Further, they endorsed the spreading democratic ethos, and with it the lowering of property requirements for the right to vote (a move which would, of course, add to the number of their likely supporters).

In time, the Federalists became an anachronism. Wedded to an idea of government by propertied elites, they could not adapt to new political conditions. Their opposition to the War of 1812 further eroded their credibility. But in the end, they were overwhelmed by the democratic spirit which by the 1820s had won the battle of ideas.[6]

As the Federalists died, the field was left to the Democratic-Republicans, who soon became known simply as Democrats. From 1820 to 1836, no other party nominated a serious presidential candidate. Political conflict in this "Era of Good Feelings" was confined within a single party.

The Second Party System

It was Andrew Jackson's presidency (1829–1837) which reinaugurated two-party politics. Jackson's forceful personality and his strong antipathy to economic elites spawned opposition, an opposition that soon gathered under the umbrella of the Whig party. Both the Democrats and the Whigs were national parties during the ensuing years, with pockets of strength throughout the country. With almost universal white male suffrage, the pool of voters was now larger than ever, and the campaigns more spirited. In general, the cleavage between the parties followed an economic fault line, though not perfectly so. The Whigs represented the more prosperous elements of society, while the Democrats leaned more toward society's lower strata.

Neither party could come to grips with the searing issue of slavery, however, for both had northern and southern wings. As abolitionist sentiment grew, pressure on the parties mounted. In 1854, the Republican party was founded on the platform of no extension of slavery into the territories. Overnight, the Republican party became the vehicle for the anti-slavery forces and drove deep wedges into both of the other parties. In the watershed presidential election of 1860, there were four major candidates: the Republican, a northern and a southern Democrat, and one from the remnant of the Whigs. Abraham Lincoln and the Republicans carried every northern state,[7] precipitating the Civil War.

The Third Party System

After the Civil War and Reconstruction, the United States entered another era of two-party competition; this period, however, was dominated by the

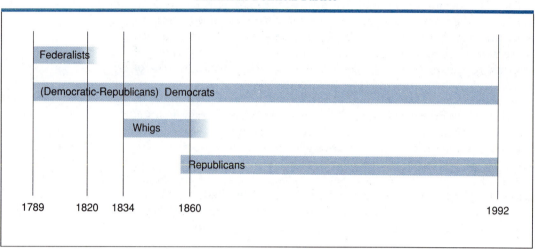

FIGURE 10-1

American Political Parties

Note: Until the 1830's the Democrats were known as the Democratic-Republicans.

Republicans. They won every presidential election between 1860 and 1932 except four. Grover Cleveland won two nonconsecutive terms; a split GOP in 1912 enabled Woodrow Wilson to enter the White House; and looming American participation in World War I kept Wilson there in 1916. To achieve its superior position, the Republican party had forged a diverse coalition. "Its tariff policies attracted new voters on the northeastern seaboard; its land policies solidified the support of farmers in the Midwest; its financial policies, including sound money and government support for railroads, won the votes of merchants and industrialists; and its antislavery policies won it the allegiance of the newly freed black Americans. In short, the Republicans during this era were truly the party of the Union, transcending sectional and class divisions."[8]

The Democrats were relegated to enclaves in the south and in northern urban centers. As whites regained control of southern governments, Democratic loyalties were a precondition for political advancement, the GOP being the party of "occupation" and black voting rights. The "Solid South" was an apt term indeed. In many northern cities, new immigrants began arriving in the 1880s, and Democratic politicians were quick to recognize the political potential they posed. Classic-style political machines, in which social services and jobs were provided to people in return for their votes, grew up in many cities. In national politics, the Democrats continued to speak for the have-nots, or some of the have-nots at least: poor white southerners and poor urban dwellers. By 1892 farmers were feeling the economic pinch associated with rapid industrialization—a discontent which brought many into the Democratic fold, after flirtations with third parties.

The quadrennial national political convention, such as the 1888 Republican gathering in Chicago, once played the dominant role in the presidential nomination process.

The Fourth Party System

The Great Depression of the 1930s and Franklin D. Roosevelt's campaign strategy rearranged the American political landscape. Roosevelt reached beyond the southern and established urban bases of the Democratic party to workers everywhere, and beyond the Eastern European ethnic groups to others, especially African Americans and Jews. Furthermore, Roosevelt was one of the first to see that intellectuals—those who write, speak, or teach about public affairs—have an influence far beyond their numbers, and he cultivated them assiduously. During the dark economic days of the 1930s, the Democrats assembled an overpowering coalition. The Republicans now became the party of enclaves, of smaller midwestern cities and towns, of New England, and of affluent easterners. Between 1932 and 1968, only Dwight Eisenhower, the popular war hero, could pierce the Democratic dominance, but his two terms had no measurable effect on the party alignment.

A Fifth Party System?

Since 1968, however, the wheel has turned again. Republicans won five of the six presidential elections from 1968 to 1988, and almost salvaged a victory in 1976 despite Watergate and a lackluster candidate. The biggest shifts have been among western and white southern voters,[9] both of whom now regularly give Republican candidates large majorities in presidential contests. The Midwest has remained solidly Republican, but New England has dropped out of the GOP column. Urban voters remain heavily Democratic, but the suburbs have become Republican strongholds.

Presidential elections offer an incomplete picture of comparative party strength, however. The Democrats have controlled both houses of Congress since 1954, except for a brief interlude of six years in the Senate. State houses and state legislatures, to say nothing of hundreds of local governments, are dominated by Democrats.

Common Threads among the Party Systems

At least four generalizations may be drawn from this brief historical overview. First, our party system has tended to be a two-party one, and a stable one at that. During each period, there have been only two major parties competing for national office. Only two American parties have ever vanished and only one new entrant has grown to major party status in over two hundred years. Of these, the successful birth and one of the deaths can be attributed to the slavery issue. Had we had no slavery or had we been politically ingenious enough to end the practice without a civil war, we might still be witnessing competition between Democrats and Whigs. We will explore some of the possible causes of the two party-system later in this chapter.

Second, the great dividing line has historically been between society's haves and have-nots. The battle over economic policy, and its attendant distributional consequences, stretches over the history of the parties. James Madison clearly foresaw this when he wrote that "the most common and durable source of factions has been the various and unequal distribution of property. Those who hold and those who are without property have ever formed distinct interests in society."[10]

However, to view party politics as simply a war between those with large bank accounts and everyone else is a vast oversimplification. Other issues have marched across the political stage and had their political repercussions. Neither politics nor political parties are merely concerned with the division of the economic pie.

Third, for over a hundred years we have had the same two remarkably durable parties. Both of them have shown an enviable ability to adapt to new circumstances and conditions. The electorate has expanded exponentially since 1860, from white, mostly Anglo-Saxon, males to virtually all adults; the economy has changed from an agricultural one through an industrial to a postindustrial one; the United States has moved from the periphery to the center of world affairs; communications have been revolutionized several times—through all of this the Democrats and Republicans have survived and prospered.

Finally, voting blocs and political groupings seem to stay with one party for a sustained period but then shift, causing an electoral "realignment."[11]

The dynamics of this process are only hazily understood by political scientists. It seems that a dramatic change in issues is the most likely factor that brings about these shifts in voting patterns.[12] Voting patterns are therefore both stable and changeable at the same time.

THE AMERICAN TWO-PARTY SYSTEM

The dominance of our two major parties over the last 130 years and more has been almost complete. Every president has been either a Democrat or a Republican. Virtually all the members of Congress during this period have carried one of these labels, only a handful coming from third parties or elected as independents. Presently, all fifty governors are Democrats or Republicans, as is nearly every state legislator.[13] Likewise, at the local level Democrats and Republicans sit in almost every jurisdiction which holds partisan elections.

This two-party supremacy is even more striking when viewed from a comparative perspective, most democracies having several major parties. Even those who share a common political heritage with us, such as Britain, Canada, and Australia, exhibit a more modified two-party system. Two major parties are the main players in each nation, but third parties play a significant role, especially at the regional level.[14]

Why does the United States alone among modern democratic nations have such a love affair with the two-party system? At least four explanations can be offered: the institutional structure, the nature and distribution of American political attitudes, the consequences of traditions and laws, and the looseness of the parties themselves.

The Institutional Explanation

The institutional explanation hinges primarily on the presidential election system, but congressional elections play a role also. The presidential election is a one-shot affair, with a majority of electoral votes required for victory. If three major parties habitually contested the presidency, seldom if ever would anyone receive the 270 of 538 electoral votes needed to win (the election would then be thrown into the House of Representatives). This structure has a dual effect. On the one hand, it gives each party a powerful incentive to reach out to as many voters as possible in search of a majority. At the same time, it almost assures that a third-party run at the presidency will be a futile endeavor. Any political leader contemplating such a run will be much better served practically by reaching some type of accommodation with one of the major parties. Further, if a third party does embark on a campaign, voters will be faced with the indisputable argument that their vote will be "wasted," except as a symbolic gesture.

To appreciate more fully the way that the institutional set-up affects party behavior, imagine for a moment that we changed to a popular election with a runoff. A first ballot would be open to anyone. If no one

(text continued on page 324)

Building Political Parties in a New Democracy

IN JUNE OF 1990 Czechoslovakia held its first free elections in forty-four years. It was a moment of triumph and exhilaration for many people, signifying an escape at last from the dark days of totalitarianism. In 1992 the country peacefully and amicably divided itself into separate Czech and Slovak republics. Of all the fledgling democracies in Eastern Europe, many experts give these two countries the best chance of evolving into stable democracies.

Two components of the political life of both republics will be particularly important during the transition: (1) building viable, trustworthy political parties, and (2) finding a role for the discredited Communist party and its followers.

Created as a political entity only in 1918 from the debris of the Austro-Hungarian Empire, Czechoslovakia was not an exceedingly old nation, but it had a long economic and cultural history. During the 1920s and 1930s it was the most prosperous of the countries of Eastern Europe, and the most democratic. Sadly, in 1938–39 it was dismembered by Hitler as a prelude to World War II. After the war, the democratic government returned, and free elections were held in 1946. In 1948 the Communist party staged a coup backed by the Soviet Army. Immediately, all political parties except the Communists were banned. Twenty years later reformers within the Communist party tried to open up the system slightly, although they gave no sign of relinquishing party control. Even these mild reforms were too much for the Soviet leadership, which ordered an invasion and crushed the "Prague spring."

By the 1970s not only was the economy faltering, but intellectuals were increasingly chafing under the heavy-handed restrictions imposed by the state. A group of them formed what became Civic Forum, whose purpose was to build a tiny forum for civic discussion outside state control. Despite repeated harassment by the authorities and the periodic jailing of its leaders, Civic Forum's influence as an anti-Communist force grew steadily. When communism began to collapse all over Eastern Europe, Civic Forum was the logical successor to take the reins of power. In November 1989 its leader, playwright Vaclav Havel, became president.

The free elections followed in June 1990. Twenty-two parties entered the contests for the two houses of the new parliament. On election day, one-half of the eligible voters showed up in the first three hours to vote by paper ballot. Noting that older people were voting first, one pollwatcher told the *New York Times,* "They said they had waited for this for 40 years and didn't want to wait any longer."[1] When the polls closed, fully 96 percent of those eligible had voted.

As expected, Civic Forum outdistanced all rivals, polling 48 percent of the vote. The Communists showed surprising strength, though, with

13 percent; the Christian Democrats, the only other serious party in the campaign, finished a disappointing third with about 10 percent.

The Christian Democrats' fortunes may have been affected by a disturbing sidebar to the election. During the campaign, a Civic Forum official charged that the Christian Democratic leader had collaborated with the Communist secret police. Neither confirming nor denying the indictment, he quickly checked into a hospital and disappeared from public view. Shortly afterward, 166 other candidates quietly withdrew.

This incident points to an ancient problem with transitions from one regime to another: how to handle those who governed in the old days. In Czechoslovakia, for instance, there were about 140,000 secret police informers, and of course everyone who ever worked for the government is tainted in some way. If the new officials embark on a program of wholesale retribution, they will consume valuable political energy, open many old wounds, likely start witch-hunts, and prompt the settling of all kinds of private scores. But if all the collaborators and officials of the old regime merely continue on as before, this can create cynicism of the worst sort. Thus, some cleansing is called for, but not too much. By 1991 Parliament was caught up in a swirling debate on this very question. With the 1992 division of the country, the issue has now merely been transferred to the two new parliaments.

In the Czech republic, Civic Forum still dominates Parliament, and it now faces the practical problem of governing a country. It was forged as an organization to oppose communism; now that that goal has been accomplished and it sits in power, it must fashion policies on the variety of public issues facing any government. Can it develop a consensus behind new policies? Or will disagreements split the party? What will hold it together now? Can it learn to govern as effectively as it once led protests? Can it prepare for the next election, when the opposition will not be the old-line Communists? In short, Civic Forum must now become a regular political party. It is the most legitimate institution in the country, and if it should falter, it could undermine the process of political consolidation.

The unfolding saga of democratization in both parts of the old Czechoslovakia will warrant close watching. If these two countries with brief but important democratic roots can reestablish functioning democracies, perhaps they can offer lessons for others.

Consider how these developments compare with the role of George Washington and the Federalists. Suppose Washington had taken over a government still staffed by British loyalists. Suppose further that the Federalists' competition had been not the Democratic-Republicans but a party linked with the old regime. How might our political history have differed?

---

[1] *New York Times*, June 9, 1990, 5.

received a majority, there would be a runoff between the top two candidates. Under such a system, what incentive would recalcitrant factions and charismatic leaders have to stay within the two major parties? If a candidate failed to get a major party nomination, he could run anyway, and hope to edge into the runoff. The Republican and Democratic nominations would lose much of their value, and most likely parties representing narrow groups and viewpoints would proliferate.

Although they are structured differently, congressional elections also support a two-party system. Throughout the country, there are single-member districts, with only one ballot to elect each member. Thus, factions within states or districts are pulled into coalitions. Picture six hypothetical factions, four with about 20 percent of the voters behind them, and two with about 10 percent each. Two of the big four will have a strong incentive to run a common candidate; this will trigger a response from the others; and so on until the groups coalesce into two parties. With no prize for second place, factions are forced to build coalitions before an election.

Political Values

Two elements of the American system of values come into play in molding the party system. First, there is a broad consensus on basic political values—political *beliefs*, in the idiom of chapter 9. Although the United States is quite diverse ethnically, religiously, and regionally, none of these divisions are so enduring that they create unbridgeable fault lines. There is no pro- or anti-church faction, for example, to rend the nation asunder. No ethnic group feels itself to be so different from other Americans that a political party is necessary to express its goals. There is, in short, a widespread consensus on such fundamentals as the Constitution, basic civil liberties, democratic procedures, and the outline of the economic system.

The other part of the values explanation relates to the distribution of political tendencies, or what we have called political *attitudes*. From figure 10–2 it is evident that small numbers of Americans hover at the extremes of the political spectrum, but the great mass of people lies in the middle. A logical division along party lines is into a moderately "liberal" party and a moderately "conservative" party, with both trying to outbid the other for the center.

Traditions and Laws

Traditions and laws have some role in explaining the maintenance if not the origin of the two-party system. That is, once they are in place, voters and politicians become accustomed to the two parties, and habits of the mind and political practice take on a life of their own. Also, those in power pass laws regarding the structure of elections, campaign finance, and so forth. And as the old saw goes, Republicans and Democrats may not agree

FIGURE 10–2
American Political Tendencies

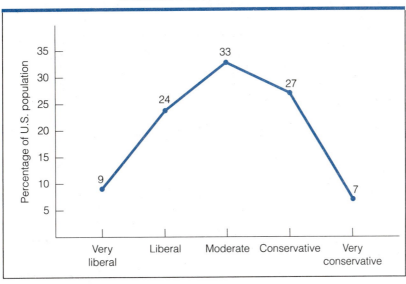

Source: National Election Study, 1988.

on much else, but they agree that they want no further competition. Hence, election laws are tilted against third parties and independents. George Wallace in 1968, John Anderson in 1980, and Ross Perot in 1992, for example, found it difficult and time-consuming even to get on the ballot in several states. In similar fashion, candidates for governor and other state offices have found it difficult to run outside the fold of the two major parties.

Openness of the Parties

Finally, the looseness and permeability of American parties seems to contribute to their dominance. How does one become a Democrat or a Republican? Simply by saying she is, or even just thinking she is. There are no membership dues or cards, no pledges of ideological fidelity to sign, and no induction ceremonies. For a politician to run under the party banner, he need only file the papers to run in a primary and win in that primary. Neither party has any mechanism to purge candidates or officeholders. Thus, those who seek public office have no need to work outside the established party organizations. They can gain all the advantages of a party designation but still retain their independence.

To be sure, the party can often offer candidates or withhold from them inducements such as campaign funds and technical assistance; also, in the case of Congress there are committee assignments to be given or withheld. But in the final analysis, no one can deny a candidate the right to run. As an extreme example, take the case of David Duke, one time Klansman and purveyor of various racial poisons. He entered the Republican primary for a Louisiana legislative seat, and though disowned by an embarrassed national party, he nonetheless won both the primary and the general election. Then he staged (unsuccessful) races for the United States Senate and for the governorship, completely shunned again by the national party. Other unconventional candidates of various political persuasions have also been sources of frustration to party leaders from time to time.

The point of this is that the elasticity of the parties keeps them all-embracing, muting the need for third parties. Almost any political position can find expression within the two major parties, leaving an infertile field for the growth of a new party.

Conclusion

Which of these four bears more weight than the others? Both tradition and the openness of the two parties are arguably as much the consequences of the two-party system as its causes. It seems most likely that the attitudinal factors set the stage for the two-party system, and the institutional structure then begets it. That is, if there were serious and abiding cleavages in the social order, the institutional structures alone would not suffice to overcome their tendencies to divide the nation into hostile groups. Suppose, to take the types of examples that divide some other countries, a third of the society intensely favored a military dictatorship, the establishment of a fundamentalist Muslim state, or the adoption of Croatian or Swahili as the only national language. The presidential and congressional election systems in themselves would not be sufficient to maintain a two-party system. On the other hand, even if the beliefs and attitudes of the society remained as they are, a different institutional structure could push us toward a multiparty setup. The two-party system is thus an outgrowth of the combination of both our social structure and the design of our political institutions.

THIRD PARTIES IN AMERICAN POLITICAL HISTORY

Even though we have had two-party politics in the United States since the 1830s, third parties are a recurring phenomenon in American history.[15] Only one, the Republicans, has ever emerged from the shadows to become a major party, and the circumstances of its early years were surely unique. Since then third parties have been of three types: parties of protest, breakaways, and parties which are mere extensions of interest groups.

Protest Parties

Parties of protest are most often driven by economic distress. Serious economic dislocations, either in the country as a whole or among certain

Theodore Roosevelt campaigning in Elijah, Ohio, as the Progressive party nominee of 1912.

segments (such as farmers or workers) generate demands for action. If the major parties are sluggish in their response, third parties spring up to carry the demand for reform. The best known of these was the People's party or Populist party, founded during the agricultural depression of the early 1890s. In 1892 its presidential candidate received over a million votes and carried five states. In 1896 the Democrats nominated William Jennings Bryan, who, while not a member of the Populist party, held ideas similar to those of Populists.[16] Populist leaders then felt they were left with little choice but to nominate Bryan also, and the party soon eased into oblivion. In the 1920s Robert LaFollette ran on the Progressive party ticket, advocating a renewed set of economic reforms; in 1948 Henry Wallace, a former secretary of agriculture, mounted another campaign under the Progressive label. LaFollette carried Wisconsin and ran reasonably well elsewhere, but Wallace won no states and was buried. Other protest parties, such as the Socialist party, have from time to time won local elections and occasionally elected a member of Congress, but their influence has been short-lived. Excluding Ross Perot's movement, the chief protest party of late has been the Libertarian party, whose candidates for president polled about 0.5 percent of the total vote in 1988 and 1992. Libertarians advocate a complete government withdrawal from economic and social life, as well as an isolationist foreign policy—all in the name of furthering the liberty of the individual.

Breakaway Parties

Breakaway parties are third parties which represent splits within one of the major parties. Dissatisfied with either the nominee or the platform of their party, a faction bolts out of the party and stages its own campaign. By far the most dramatic and successful of these was the Republican bolt in 1912. Former president Teddy Roosevelt lost the nomination fight, as well as an attempt to make the platform more liberal. He then ran as leader of the Progressive party (a popular label with an obviously diverse history), capturing 27 percent of the popular vote and eighty-eight electoral votes— more than the regular Republicans did. The result was, though, that Woodrow Wilson and the Democrats captured the White House. In 1948 and again in 1968, southern segregationists were so dismayed at the civil rights stances of the Democratic party that they launched independent party campaigns. The Dixiecrats of 1948 managed to collect thirty-nine electoral votes with 20 percent of the popular vote. George Wallace's American Independent party ran nationwide in 1968 and garnered 14 percent of the total popular vote, but he had a realistic chance of carrying only southern states. He got forty-six electoral votes for his efforts. Although John Anderson in 1980 steadfastly refused to establish a party to support his independent bid for the presidency, he had sought the Republican nomination earlier in the day, giving his campaign all the earmarks of a bolt.

Interest Groups as Minor Parties

A third type of minor party is really an interest group standing for the moment as a political party. Into this category falls a menagerie ranging from the Prohibition party to the Right-to-Life party. Essentially, these groups run candidates for office to obtain publicity for their chosen causes.

Effects of Third Parties

The effects of third parties are difficult to assess. Interest group parties neither receive nor expect much support. The breakaway factions inevitably disintegrate, but it is not clear whether they are reintegrated into the old party. The progressive faction never really found a home in the Republican Party after 1912, and white southern support drifted noticeably to the Republicans after 1948, becoming an avalanche, in fact, after 1968. The protest parties usually find their issues coopted by one of the major parties. The Populists, for instance, were absorbed into the Democratic party. In this sense, these parties play a useful safety valve function for the political system. They raise issues which the major parties might rather ignore. If the third party strikes a response among the voters, politicians in the major parties, ever mindful of the demands of the electoral system, will reach out to them. New issues and policies are thereby brought onto the agenda, but the two-party system is preserved in the process.

PARTY ORGANIZATION

Technically, each party's quadrennial convention, held in the summer of a presidential election year, is the source of all authority. In addition to selecting the presidential nominee, the convention adopts a platform, passes on the credentials of state delegations, and establishes rules for party operation. Between conventions the parties are both governed by a national committee.

The National Committees

The Democratic National Committee (DNC) consists of around 375 people, including two representatives (one of each gender) from each state party, plus additional people from large states and others with heavily Democratic voting records. Further, there are a variety of representatives from groups of Democrats such as governors, mayors, and members of Congress. The Republican National Committee (RNC), in contrast, is composed of a committeeman and committeewoman from each state (plus the District of Columbia and several territories), along with the chair of each state Republican Party. Currently, it has 165 members.

These differences in composition reflect somewhat different views of the national committee's function. The Democrats have been much more concerned about representation, or more accurately, "representativeness." A substantial amount of effort has been devoted to being certain that the various constituencies making up the party's supporters are given a chance to be heard. The main task the DNC has assumed since the 1970s has been to rule on the acceptability of the state delegations to the national convention in light of this goal. Recently, though, the committee has become more active in fund-raising and aiding candidates for office.

Before the rules regarding representativeness went into effect, each state Democratic party chose its national convention delegates in any way it wished, although there was a credentials committee at each convention to settle the occasional dispute. The procedures varied by state, but the usual pattern was for a few political power brokers, usually a cabal of elected officials such as a governor, a key senator, and perhaps a mayor of a large city, to handpick the delegates. After the bitterly divisive convention of 1968, which pitted the traditional party leaders against the anti–Vietnam war faction, the McGovern-Fraser Commission was appointed to draft new rules for the next convention. Although it has been modified several times since, the basic framework of the McGovern-Fraser report stands: each state delegation should allocate convention seats to various groups, particularly minorities and women. And it has fallen to the DNC, itself reconstituted, to enforce these rules.

The new rules have opened the convention to many more activists who do not hold elective office and are beholden to no one.[17] Seldom now can the politicos come to the convention with a coterie of loyal followers in

TABLE 10-1

Funds Raised by Democratic and Republican National Committees,
1975–1990 (millions)

	DEMOCRATIC NATIONAL COMMITTEE	REPUBLICAN NATIONAL COMMITTEE
1975–76	$13.1	$ 29.1
1977–78	11.3	34.2
1979–80	15.1	76.2
1981–82	16.4	83.5
1983–84	46.6	105.9
1985–86	17.2	83.8
1987–88	52.3	91.0
1989–90	14.5	68.7

Source: Federal Election Commission.

their pocket. Thus, the whole tenor of politics within the Democratic party has changed. Where the old-line state power brokers once met together to draw up various "deals" regarding the platform and the candidate, the newer delegates are much more independent and committed to issues.

The Republicans have been much less concerned with such matters. The party has a few rules encouraging diversity, but they are not binding, and the RNC has no enforcement powers. Both RNC members and state delegations to the national convention are chosen by state party organizations. What the RNC has undertaken with relish is fund-raising. In the mid-1970s, the RNC pioneered the art of direct mail to solicit contributions, a move which paid enormous dividends. Belatedly, the DNC copied these techniques, but has not been nearly as successful.

The Republican riches have been expended in three ways since the 1970s, all of which have enhanced the role of the RNC within the party. First, a general party advertising campaign was established and nourished. Television spots were produced which plugged the party as a whole, with no specific references to candidates or issues. Second, an elaborate system of aid to individual candidates for state and local offices was set up. This aid ranged from direct cash contributions to the providing of professional polls, state-of-the-art television studios, issues experts, and armies of media and campaign strategists. Third, money was provided to strengthen state party organizations.

The common thread in the new activities of both the DNC and the RNC is that both party organizations are more centralized than ever before.[18] The Democrats have gone much further than the Republicans in granting their central organs power over state organizations, but the Republican financial flow chart has had a centralizing tendency also. Candidates aided by the RNC are unlikely to forget the source of their support. While state parties remain power centers, even in the Democratic party, they are relatively weaker now than they were even twenty years ago.

In one sense, what is curious is not the existence of these centralizing tendencies, but their delay in coming. Since the 1930s every other facet of our political life has become more centralized, and clearly voters are more attuned to national issues than to local ones, if turnout is any indication. In addition, all of our other institutions—the media, entertainment, business, labor, etc.— all became national long ago. Only the parties have lagged so far behind. The power now slowly accruing to the national committees could be seen simply as a rather belated response to the transformation of American life.

The National Chairperson

Even though each of the two national committees has the authority to govern its party between conventions, each one meets as a body only intermittently, and when it does this proves rather unwieldy. On a day-to-day basis the work of each party is done by the national chairperson, who usually is devoted full-time to this task.

By custom, the presidential nominee names the chair of his party's national committee; this tradition is a relic of the days when the party was the chief campaign vehicle. If the party is victorious, the chair usually stays on—unless she is offered a job in the administration, in which case the president names a new chair. The losing party's chair normally resigns after the election, with the national committee electing a replacement.

Somewhat paradoxically, when a party controls the White House, the chair's position is weakened. The president is then the symbolic and actual leader of the party, overshadowing the national committee. Naturally, he will want to concentrate political control in the White House, and neither he nor his aides will want an alternative power center developing outside the official presidential circle. A chair's role during these years can still be useful to the party if she concentrates purely on helping state and local candidates; but she cannot be a truly influential figure in the national party.

In contrast, the chair's position is strongest when the party loses. The person who emerges as elected head of the national committee assumes a prominence denied to his winning counterpart. He is a fresh face, appealing to a party which will normally be eager to put the loss behind it. The new chair can thus play an influential role in shaping the party and laying the groundwork for the next campaign. Frequently, he also becomes a visible spokesperson for the party, as Democrat Ron Brown did during the Bush years. By custom also, the party chair is expected to remain strictly neutral as jousting for the nomination begins. When the convention selects the nominee, the chair must offer his resignation. In short, between the election loss and the next convention, the national chairperson can be an important figure within the party, but this takes great skill and adroitness.

Congressional Campaign Committees

Supplementing the national committees are party organizations in Congress. Each house has a party caucus, as discussed in chapter 5, to attend

TABLE 10–2

Funds Raised by the Four Congressional Campaign Committees
1975–1990 (millions)

	SENATE REPUBLICAN CAMPAIGN COMMITTEE	HOUSE REPUBLICAN CAMPAIGN COMMITTEE	SENATE DEMOCRATIC CAMPAIGN COMMITTEE	HOUSE DEMOCRATIC CAMPAIGN COMMITTEE
1975–76	$12.2	$ 1.8	$ 1.0	$ 0.9
1977–78	10.9	14.1	0.3	2.8
1979–80	23.3	28.6	1.7	2.1
1981–82	48.9	58.0	5.6	6.5
1983–84	81.7	58.3	8.9	10.4
1985–86	86.1	39.8	13.4	12.3
1987–88	65.9	34.5	16.3	12.5
1989–90	65.1	33.8	17.5	9.1

Source: Federal Election Commission.

to organizational details and committee assignments. More important for the party itself are the four campaign committees maintained by the caucuses. These bodies have long been dedicated both to protecting incumbents and offering aid to challengers. In recent years these committees have become much more active, a direct result of their being able to raise significant funds through direct mail.

Each committee spends a surprising amount to recruit and train challengers, as opposed to simply aiding incumbents.[19] Although the congressional campaign committees ordinarily work closely with their respective national committees, sometimes conflict surfaces. There may be disagreements, for instance, about who the best challenger might be for a vacant House or Senate seat, and since the campaign committees are organizationally and financially independent, they are not subject to the national committee.

Affiliated Groups

Each party has a set of affiliated organizations loosely connected to the national committee. Often these are set up for certain groups. Two such organizations are the Young Democrats of America and the Young Republican National Federation. Party leaders like to use these two associations to build loyalty among young voters and to recruit party activists. Both youth groups have sometimes refused to play the role of docile appendage, however. The Young Democrats have often passed resolutions condemning party policy (usually for not being far enough to the left), and the Young Republicans have urged the party to adopt a more militant brand of conservatism.

In addition, there are quasi-official organizations of officeholders set up outside the regular party channels. Some pull together those who hold similar offices, such as the Republican Governors Conference. Others have a more explicitly ideological orientation, the most prominent of which is the Democratic Leadership Council. It claims about one hundred members, led by several prominent members of Congress. Its stated purpose, which sometimes strains relations with the DNC, is to lead the Democratic party in a more moderate direction. It was in the DLC that Bill Clinton first gained national visibility.

Finally, there are strictly private groups which are nonetheless all but formally attached to one party or the other. The Committee on Political Education of the AFL-CIO is the best example, since it is virtually an unofficial arm of the Democratic party. Several business groups, such as the Business Roundtable, enjoy a similar relationship with the Republican party.

State and Local Party Organizations

On paper, both parties are fully organized at every level, from that of precinct (usually the smallest voting unit) to that of state central committee. However, there is enormous variation across the country in actual organization. "In some places," notes Samuel Patterson, "parties are strong and vigorous; in other places they are sluggish; in yet others, moribund."[20]

Most precincts have at least a skeleton organization which includes a "precinct captain." In many locales, though, the first major group is at the county level. Here there is invariably a county executive committee and a county chairperson. These officers are ordinarily elected at a county convention, but the practice varies from place to place. County conventions and lower-level meetings as well are usually open to any resident. In some states there are intermediate-level bodies, such as those for congressional districts, between the county committees and the state central committee. As at the national level, a central figure is the chair of the state central committee. In about three-fourths of the states, the chair is elected by the committee; in the remaining states, the state party holds a convention and the selection is made there. In some states, tradition dictates that the governor chooses the chair of her party.

What kinds of people devote their time and energies to attending these meetings and doing party work?[21] Some are elected officials or people who aspire to elective office, but these are a minority. In the past, many party organizations had significant patronage at their disposal, drawing many people who desired to obtain or keep a government job. The amount of patronage has shrunk dramatically, however, thanks largely to civil service laws and a number of court decisions outlawing the practice of wholesale firings and replacements. Recently, the Supreme Court went further by overturning a patronage system for promotion in Illinois, a bastion of patronage politics.[22]

With the erosion of patronage as a motivator for party participation, a new type of activist has emerged. These new activists are largely people of

Volunteers for independent presidential candidate Ross Perot manning a phone bank in the spring of 1992.

middle-class status with higher-than-average educational levels. Some are propelled by a sense of general civic duty, but many more are drawn to party work by ideological concerns. They are intensely dedicated either to some particular issue or to a general political ideology, and view party work as a way to influence government. Several studies have shown, for instance, that Democratic activists are considerably more liberal and Republican activists considerably more conservative than the population as a whole, and that both are fervently committed to their ideologies.[23]

This shift has had important consequences for the parties. When patronage seekers formed the backbone of the parties, the major aim was winning elections, for to the loser went no spoils. Party "bosses" had substantial flexibility to engineer compromises on issues and build coalitions with whoever was willing to deal. The new-style party activists, in comparison, do not have their livelihoods at stake in the electoral success of the party. What they desire is that candidates and the party take the "proper" stance on the issues, a development that has led to much more ideological debate—and more rancor—within the parties.

The rise of this new breed of activists has posed problems for candidates. To secure the nominations of their parties, they must largely conform to the ideological dictates of the activists. In a general election, though, these ideological commitments may turn into liabilities, for the general electorate is neither so conservative nor so liberal as the activists in the Republican and Democratic parties respectively. If candidates moderate their stands on the issues, though, they run the risk of seeing their support within the party evaporate. This dilemma has seeped into presidential nomination politics through the mechanism of the primary. Hailed as a way to give the public more say, the primary has had the unintended effect of magnifying the influence of the activists. The reason is that those who vote in primaries tend to be more partisan, and hence more ideological, than even the party's mass supporters, much less the electorate.

This state of affairs has led some commentators to argue that we need to bring the old bosses back into the picture.[24] For whatever their defects, and they were legion, the bosses wanted first and foremost to win elections. Therefore they sought out more moderate candidates and produced more bland platforms. This was more healthy, these critics charge, because once in government these people were more willing to compromise and less ideological.

Defenders of the new system, though, contend that not only is it preferable to have party activists who are motivated by a commitment to the public interest (however variously defined) rather than by the lure of a job, but also that the present setup moves us a little more closely to a system of "responsible" parties.

THE RESPONSIBLE PARTY MODEL

Many people have argued through the years that democratic government would be enhanced if we had a system built on responsible parties.[25] The word "responsible" is not used here in the sense of moral trustworthiness and sound judgment; rather, it is imported from descriptions of other countries' party systems, chiefly Britain's.

In the ideal form of this model, the two parties develop clear and coherent programs and proposals which are sharply different from each other's. All those who run under one party label subscribe to its program and vow to support it if elected. The voters now have a clear choice and register their desires by voting one or the other party into power. The victorious party proceeds to enact its proposals into law. At the next election, then, the voters know which party to hold responsible for government policy. Consequently, they can choose either to keep the sitting party in power or to substitute the other party.

Although the British system does not in practice work precisely like this, it comes closer to this model than does ours. To develop even an approximation of the responsible party model requires three conditions. First, the parties must draft platforms that are ideologically coherent and different from each other; second, each party must assure that all those running under its label are loyal to the program and agree to help implement it; and third, the victorious party must be able to control enough power in government to be able to pass its program into law.

As we have seen, the first condition is now being met in the United States. Regarding the second, a few tentative steps have been taken in each party, but they have run up against the individualism and localism endemic to the American political tradition.

In 1986, for example, the DNC asked state party leaders who wanted its party-building help to sign a statement that they would not "run a campaign against, and instead run with the national Democratic Party."[26] State leaders rebelled and the policy was withdrawn, but not before Republicans had a field day attacking it as dictatorial. On the Republican side, a 1970s-era RNC policy of "endorsing" a candidate in Republican primaries boomeranged, as unendorsed candidates turned the matter to their advantage: "Who do these people from Washington think they are, telling the good people of _____ how to vote?" Under fire, in 1980 the GOP adopted a rule that the RNC would not endorse a candidate unless state party officials agreed.

As for the third requirement, our system of separation of powers militates against party control of government. With three nationally elected bodies (president, House, and Senate) chosen through a system of staggered elections, the odds do not favor one party's being able to count on controlling all three. Since the end of World War II one party has held all three bodies for a total of only eighteen years (until 1993). This does not even consider the Supreme Court or state governments. In short, radical constitutional surgery would be required to give a political party guaranteed access to enough offices to allow it to enact its program in full. Such a dramatic overhaul in our political institutions would undermine the philosophy on which the Constitution rests: that public policy should be the outcome of slow deliberation and the consensus of multiple and overlapping majorities.

Despite these impediments to instituting a truly responsible party system in the United States, there is something to be said for parties offering coherent programs to the voters and then being held accountable for what happens. Our system allows instead continual rounds of finger-pointing. However, recall that it is the voters who have chosen divided government, of late often handing the Republicans the White House but keeping a firm Democratic majority in Congress. Because our politics has become more ideological, unified party control of the White House and Congress would probably produce more coherent policy. Apparently, though, the voters wanted some of both approaches—until 1992.

PARTY IDENTIFICATION

Table 10–3 depicts the ways Americans have identified themselves politically since 1952. Three trends are worthy of elaboration from these data: the long-term lead that has been enjoyed by the Democrats; the recent gains made by the Republicans; and the decline in the number of people claiming loyalty to either major party.

Democrats have retained a significant margin in party identifiers throughout most of the postwar period. Why then do they not win every election? One reason is that a number of white southerners have continued to select the Democratic party when asked about their affiliation by a pollster, and often still vote Democratic in state and local elections, but pull the Republican lever in national elections. Another reason uncovered by researchers is that as a whole Republicans are more deeply attached to their party than are Democrats.[27] Thus, they wander away less frequently,

T A B L E 10–3

Party Identification Since 1952 (Percentage of Americans)

	PARTY OF IDENTITY		
	Democratic	*Republican*	*Independent*
1952	47	27	23
1956	46	29	23
1960	45	29	23
1964	52	24	23
1968	45	24	29
1972	41	23	34
1976	40	23	36
1980	41	22	34
1984	37	27	34
1988	35	28	36
1990	36	32	32

Source: Center for Political Studies, University of Michigan, for the years 1952–88. *New York Times*/CBS News Poll for 1990 (*New York Times,* January 21, 1990, 24).

Note: For 1990, all those who did not identify with a party were counted as Independents.

less affected by issues and candidate personalities. If the GOP runs an attractive candidate who enunciates popular policies, he may well woo substantial numbers of Democrats; however, the converse is not true. Third, there is a marked difference in turnout figures: Republicans are much more likely to vote than are Democrats. Hence, the voting population has not exhibited as lopsided a Democratic lead as has the general population.

Without question, the Republican party has made meaningful inroads into Democratic strength in the last few years, now standing virtually even with it in identifiers. Partly, this change results from the movement of many white southerners into the Republican party. It is also partly attributable to Ronald Reagan's popularity in the 1980s, a popularity he tried diligently to transfer to his party (unlike Dwight Eisenhower, who made almost no effort to build the party). But the most important trend has been among young people. Traditionally, Democrats have enjoyed the loyalty of young identifiers and first-time voters. Several studies have shown, though, that among people born since 1958, the Republican party leads as the party of choice.[28] It is not clear exactly why this should be happening, but again, Reagan's presidency probably contains much of the explanation. (But see chapter 13.)

The most evident, and to some the most alarming, trend is the erosion of support for both parties and the simultaneous growth in the ranks of independents.[29] In the early years of this trend, many pundits applauded it. Party partisans were seen as unthinking automatons who merely marched to the polls and voted for the party label, whoever the candidate and whatever her program. Independents, by contrast, were thought to weigh the issues and merits of the candidates and choose accordingly. The growth of independents was attributed largely to increasing educational levels.

BOX 10–1

Political Parties and the Two Models of Democracy

How do POLITICAL parties stand in the separate worlds of individualist and civic democrats?

The individualist case was set out years ago in an important book by Anthony Downs, *An Economic Theory of Democracy*.[1] Downs drew an analogy between the business firm and the political party. Business firms try to maximize profits by producing what consumers want, packaging it attractively, and advertising their wares. Political parties do the same, except that they deal in votes rather than dollars. They find out what the voters want and then offer that at election time. Whichever party most pleases the consumers will be victorious.

The major analytical building block of this model is individual preference. It is sovereign, as consumer spending is sovereign in traditional economic theory. People will make a "preference schedule" to "spend" their votes in the same way that they make preference schedules to spend their incomes. The public's preferences are thus aggregated through an election, as in the marketplace, and their desires become public policy.

Civic democrats object to this model, first, because it ignores the substance of the preferences held by individuals. It makes no qualitative distinctions among preferences. One preference is as acceptable as another. Whatever people want is good by definition. Civic democrats take it as a given, in opposition to this position, that some values are better than others.

But civic democrats also object on the grounds that this consumer approach to democracy ignores the role of those who seek public office and political parties in creating people's preferences. Political parties are hardly passive bystanders in the formation of how people feel about public issues— nor should they be. An election is a time of civic education as well as a time for choosing between would-be leaders and parties.

Self-government demands more of its leaders and its parties than the search for and adoption of public whims. Political parties must recognize and take responsibility for their educative role; they must acknowledge that their relationship with the voters is a reciprocal one, not merely a one-way street. In a healthy democracy the parties will stir the political imagination, inspire the public, and appeal to people's better instincts.

This most assuredly does not mean that the parties will necessarily agree on the specifics of policy. Within a civic democracy there is still a wide scope for lively political debate. What is important is the way in which party leaders see their role, and the way in which they seek to carry it out. Civic democrats are persuaded that if political leaders take their educative role seriously and discard the shoe-store-proprietor model of individualist democracy, this will have a significant effect on how the citizenry regard the political system and their place in it.

---

[1] Anthony Downs, *An Economic Theory of Democracy* (New York: Harper and Row, 1957).

However, the underlying reality proved to be more complex. Many independents, it turned out, did not fit the description of the virtuous and careful voter; instead, they were apolitical, with no connection to the political system whatever. As a group, in fact, independents are even less likely to vote than are partisans. Thus, this steadily growing category seemed to indicate alienation more than the emergence of a new breed of informed, discriminating voters. This conclusion has led some critics to argue that the party system itself was weakening if not collapsing, an issue we will take up later in this chapter.

An Anatomy of Party Identifiers

Neither the Democrats nor the Republicans constitute a cross section of society. Place of residence, for example, affects party identification. The most recent comprehensive study[30] showed urban dwellers giving the Democrats a 53-percent to 31-percent majority, while suburban loyalties were almost exactly the reverse: 50 percent to 35 percent in favor of the Republicans. Small towns and rural areas, in contrast, split almost evenly.

A significant gap exists between men and women. Men tend to be Republican by a 45- to 39-percent margin, while women are decidedly Democratic in their sympathies (50 percent, to the Republicans' 40 percent). This "gender gap" is usually explained by the Democrats' more liberal stance on women's rights issues (such as support for the Equal Rights Amendment); the Democrats' reputed reluctance to use force in the international arena; and the Democratic party's commitment to social welfare. The gap is about the same, incidentally, in all age brackets.

The greatest statistical disparity, though, occurs between racial groups, as African Americans claim allegiance to the Democratic party by an overwhelming 86-percent to 4-percent margin. Until the 1930s blacks were solidly Republican, supporting the party of the Emancipation Proclamation. Franklin D. Roosevelt's courting of black voters paid dividends, but as late as 1960 African Americans were roughly evenly split. Then came Lyndon Johnson's civil rights packages and Richard Nixon's "southern strategy," an attempt to win white southern votes; together they transformed the party orientation of the black electorate. As for whites, they are slightly Republican — 46 percent to 41 percent — while Hispanics favor the Democrats 69 percent to 14 percent.

Socioeconomic status, as measured by occupation, education, and income, is the most telling divide apart from race. People who work at executive and professional occupations are staunchly Republican (54 percent to 32 percent), while blue-collar workers are Democratic by a 48-percent to 35-percent margin. Family income breakdowns offer a similar picture. Those receiving under $12,000 a year are 62 percent Democratic, to the Republicans' 25 percent; at the over–$42,000 level, the Republican margin soars to 48 percent, as compared to the Democrats' 37 percent. Education presents an analogous pattern. Those who have not completed high school claim a 59- to 23-percent preference for the Democrats, while college graduates favor the GOP by a 47- to 39-percent margin.

Religious divisions are also evident in party identification. In general, Protestants tend to be Republican (46 percent to 41 percent); Catholics and Jews tend to be Democratic (49 percent to 39 percent and 52 percent to 28 percent, respectively). The Protestant category must be handled with caution, though, since it covers so much diversity. Most African Americans tend to be Protestant, for example. Thus, among white Protestants, the margin favoring the Republicans is even greater than is evident here. But once again, some white Protestants with low incomes (although not self-described evangelicals) tend to be Democratic, while members of upscale Protestant denominations such as Presbyterians and Episcopalians are overwhelmingly Republican.

Catholics' preference for the Democrats is rooted in the ethnic politics of Franklin D. Roosevelt, as Irish, Italian, Polish, and other largely Catholic ethnic groups flocked to the Democrats. Both their ethnicity and their poverty led to Democratic loyalties. Now, however, these ethnic ties have loosened and Catholic income has risen.[31] Hence, socioeconomic factors now tug against traditional Democratic loyalties, and the margin of Catholic support for the Democrats is not nearly so great as it once was. Also, while the Catholic church's liberal teachings on economic policy and its criticisms of military force dovetail nicely with the Democratic party's positions on these issues, the church's stance on social issues (primarily, but not only, abortion) drives a wedge between the faithful and the Democrats. Jewish attachment to the Democrats is normally explained by the generally liberal outlooks held by Jews and the Democrats' long record of support for Israel.[32]

Self-described ideology has a major influence on party identification. Those who style themselves "very liberal" line up 76 percent to 14 percent in favor of the Democrats, while people designating themselves "very conservative" show a 59-percent to 31-percent Republican preference. Those choosing the "somewhat" categories are slightly less partisan: "somewhat liberals" identify themselves 63-percent to 27-percent Democratic, and "somewhat conservatives" 58 percent to 29 percent Republican.

It is important to keep three vital facts in mind. First, these factors overlap to a considerable degree. A white, suburban, Protestant lawyer has several reasons to be a Republican. Conversely, a poor African American who lives in a central city feels very strong pulls toward the Democrats. Second, there are always people who identify against their categorization. Fully one-fourth of people with family income under $12,000 are Republicans, as are 14 percent of those who are very liberal in ideology. Third, there is an important difference between these percentages and the percentages these groups provide in the parties' total bases of support. For example, although blacks are almost unanimously Democratic, they make up only about 12 percent of the population. Thus, even though whites as a group are less loyal than blacks, whites who are Democrats represent more total voters.

VOTING

Citizen participation in politics is of fundamental importance in a democracy, especially in the act of voting. For here all citizens stand on an equal footing, an equality that is as important for symbolic reasons as it is in terms of actual impact. Voting is a concrete embodiment of the belief in citizen equality. But citizen voting has two dimensions. On the one hand, it is a method of influencing both the choice of persons who will occupy the seats of power and the direction of public policy—a tenet clearly in line with individualist democracy. Ordinary citizens have an opportunity to express their preferences, and most research shows that elections do tend to have an impact on public policy. At the same time, viewed more in terms of civic democracy, voting is a collective act, a reaffirmation of one's connection to the broader society and to other citizens. Elections provide legitimacy for the political system not only in the instrumental sense that they designate someone as a winner, but also in the sense that they constitute a ritual symbolizing the richness and worth of collective life.

If large numbers of citizens do not vote, therefore, this raises two types of concerns. First, many people are not represented when government makes decisions. This is not healthy for either these individuals or the society as a whole. Second, the bond that connects citizens to each other and to the social order is undermined. Even assuming that the nonvoters would divide their votes in precisely the same way as the actual voters have, leaving the outcome undisturbed, the national sense of belonging and all-inclusiveness is eroded by their failure to vote.

Turnout in Contemporary America

Voting turnout can be measured in one of two ways: as a percentage of the registered voters, or as a percentage of those eligible to vote.[33] Most observers prefer the latter form of measurement, since registration procedures themselves may affect voting turnout. In 1988, barely 50 percent and in 1992, 55 percent of those eligible turned out to vote for president. This compares to the turnouts of 77 percent for Britain's most recent election and 83 percent for Sweden's.

One factor which surely accounts for some of these cross-national differences is the American registration system. In most European democracies, people are automatically registered to vote, whereas in the United States, a citizen has to initiate the registration procedure. Were we to adopt a European-style universal registration system, most analysts predict that our turnout would rise by about 10 percent.[34] Further, Europeans are called on to vote much less frequently (and usually on the weekend). Nowhere in Europe do voters elect as many officials as in the United States, nor are public referenda on bond issues and the like common. In one five-year comparison of voting opportunities between citizens of

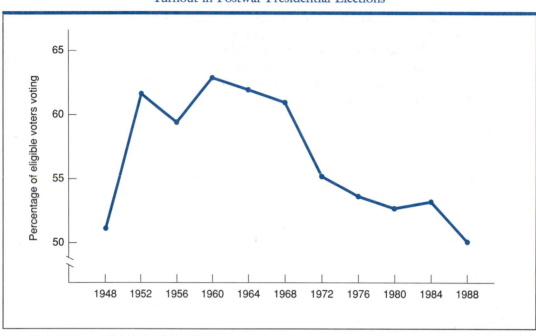

FIGURE 10-3

Turnout in Postwar Presidential Elections

Source: Statistical Abstract of the United States, 1991.

Cambridge, England and those of Tallahassee, Florida, voters in Cambridge went to the polls for four elections (each for a single office), while in Tallahassee, the dutiful citizen was asked to make 165 choices.[35]

Nevertheless, neither the complexities of registration nor the frequency of elections can account for the *decline* in American participation. In 1960, for instance, 62.8 percent of eligible voters turned out for the presidential election, compared to 55 percent in 1992 and a scant 50 percent in 1988.

Ironically, in fact, turnout has fallen during the very years when we might have expected it to rise. For instance, until the 1960s, African Americans were habitually barred from voting in much of the south; this is no longer true. Women long had a lower turnout rate than did men; this was usually explained by their being more removed from the workplace and political discussion. With more women working, this explanation no longer holds. As will be seen below, education is the best predictor of voting, and educational levels have risen markedly in the last forty years. Lastly, registration and residency requirements have been eased substantially. Therefore, even if we accept the "nonvoters are happy" thesis laid out below, there seems to be valid cause for concern—not alarm, but concern. Interestingly, it is the voting rate among white men that has fallen most sharply.

Two explanations have been given for the relatively low turnout. One contention is that those who do not vote are mostly satisfied with the way things are going. Otherwise, they would take the rather minimal trouble to register and vote. They are therefore an inert mass of people who basically support the political system by giving their tacit consent. They rise for the national anthem at a baseball game and watched the Persian Gulf War unfold with as much interest and concern as other Americans had. The alternative thesis is that these people are bitterly alienated from politics and the political system. They see no connection between voting and their lives. Nonvoters, in this view, constitute a serious problem: they make up a large group of people who grant little legitimacy to the political system, and could threaten its stability.

The evidence for either of these two explanations is mixed and inconclusive, as social scientists have yet to uncover enough clues to answer the puzzle of nonvoting.[36] It will be helpful, though, to examine who votes and who does not.

Who Votes?

Two sets of factors separate voters from nonvoters: personal characteristics and psychological attitudes.[37] The list of personal characteristics that are correlated with voting is potentially endless, and political scientists have devoted intense effort to analyzing them. Before surveying the major ones, it is vital to stress that these characteristics do not *cause* people to act as they do. They are simply statistical categories uncovered by researchers; the causes of the behavior may lie elsewhere.

EDUCATION   Socioeconomic status generally is related to turnout, as those with higher incomes and more prestigious occupations vote more frequently than others. However, when all other variables (including those noted below) are held constant, education has the greatest correlation with the likelihood to vote. Across all categories and levels of society, the more education a person has, the more likely he is to vote.

RACE   Blacks vote in fewer numbers than do whites, and African American turnout has been falling. However, since 1964, black turnout has not fallen as much as white turnout has. In 1964, 59 percent of eligible blacks voted in the presidential election, compared to 71 percent of eligible whites. By 1988, the comparable figures were 52 percent and 59 percent. Much of the remaining difference is undoubtedly explained by the disparity in educational levels between blacks and whites.

GENDER   At one time, as noted, men voted in larger numbers than women did. Now, however, women turn out in slightly higher numbers than do men; this means they form a majority of the electorate. This has not occurred because of a surge in female participation, but rather because women's rate of decline in turnout has been lower than that of men.

AGE   In the early years of sophisticated voting studies, a model encompassing a political life cycle was proposed. Voting rates were seen to be low in the early adult years, became greater in middle age, then declined once again with advanced age. Recently, however, this pattern seems to have changed. Those over sixty-five years old have the highest turnout of any age group. Young people, though, are abstaining more than ever. In 1988, for instance, only 36 percent of the eighteen- to twenty-four-year group voted.

This change has two possible, and somewhat contradictory, implications. One is that as more Americans grow older, the political power of the aged will increase dramatically if they maintain their high levels of turnout. Politicians once kissed babies; now they must visit retirement homes. The other implication is that if young voters are voting less often than their parents did at their age, we may be witnessing a generational difference. If so, we may face the long-run prospect of even further reductions in turnout.

Individualist and civic democrats might see this puzzle differently. As the former would predict, are older people voting in large numbers because they have high stakes in government policies (primarily social security), and wish to protect their interests? Or, as civic democrats might claim, was there a difference in the socialization experiences of those who are now elderly, wherein the obligation to vote was stressed more strongly in school and elsewhere?

PSYCHOLOGICAL FACTORS   The first psychological factor which affects voting behavior is partisanship. Those who identify with a political party are more likely to vote than are independents. Also, unsurprisingly, the degree of interest a person shows in politics in general and this election in particular is closely related to voting. Perceptions of civic duty and whether or not a person sees her vote as mattering also play a role.

It is in this area that what people are taught matters so deeply. Why do some citizens have partisan affiliations and develop an interest in politics? What makes for a sense of civic duty and molds a belief that one's vote matters? Although we understand little about precisely how people acquire attitudes and beliefs, we do know that what one is taught in the home, in the school, in the church or synagogue, and by peer groups is extremely significant. While this is an important *descriptive* point on which both individualist and civic democrats agree, the latter also put a great deal of emphasis on the *prescriptive* element of social learning, as noted in chapter 9. If people see voting as more than merely a way to express a preference about leaders and policies, then they will clearly be more likely to vote—and to derive a sense of satisfaction from it.[38]

POTENTIAL ELECTORAL SIGNIFICANCE   Turning to the practical side, what would happen if large numbers of the nonvoters suddenly turned out? The conventional wisdom was that the Democrats would reap the rewards of such an influx, since so many of the nonvoters represent the dispossessed. However, studies of recent elections have challenged that belief. Younger citizens are a substantial component of the nonvoters, and they are often overwhelmingly Republican in their leanings. Any Democratic gains among the poor, therefore, would be cancelled out by the young. For instance, one study of nonvoters in 1988 found that they split 55 percent to 45 percent for George Bush, almost exactly as the electorate did.[39] All of this is speculation, though, and it is not completely clear how these people would vote if motivated to do so.

OTHER AVENUES FOR PARTICIPATION   One factor that must be kept in mind when speaking of voting and declining turnout is that voting is not the only way citizens participate in politics. People write letters to members of Congress and other officials, contribute money to candidates or groups, join and become active in organizations, sign petitions, march and demonstrate—all manifestations of a healthy democracy. Thus, it may not be true that because voter turnout rates have fallen there is less total participation than there was before; it could be that participation has merely changed forms. In fact, as we will discover in the next chapter, citizen interest groups are much more active now than they were two or three decades ago. However, these forms of participation ordinarily show an even more pronounced class skew than voting does. Hence, there may be more participation, but it may be by fewer citizens—a most disturbing trend.

WEAKENED PARTIES? IMPERILED DEMOCRACY?

According to some, our parties have become weak if not enfeebled, a development that poses a serious threat to the viability of our democracy. Almost everyone agrees that democracy cannot function without vibrant political parties. If, therefore, our parties are indeed in a state of decay, there is cause for concern.

Signs of Decline

A brief of three indictments usually constitutes the case for party decline. First, there is the matter of decreasing numbers of party identifiers which we have noted above. If this trend continues, the critics charge, the parties will be without a mass base, making them but shadows of their former selves.

There are two responses to this contention.[40] One is that the data could be read another way. We could interpret the figures as reflecting relatively high party loyalty. In a sense, it is remarkable that 70 percent of the American people still identify with one of the parties, in spite of all the pressures working to erode such attachments. Rising educational levels make for more independence among voters; television's power as a political medium undercuts one of the traditional functions of parties—to serve as a communication link between candidates and the public; suburbanization has made people more difficult to organize. Second, to take the argument apart, a party may not be necessarily any less healthy if those only marginally attached to it turn in their badges, leaving a smaller but more committed set of backers. Taking the logic another step, democracy may be equally well served if the parties have to compete for the votes of more people through offering attractive candidates and issue positions, rather than relying on the automatic backing of most voters.

A second pillar of the case for party decline is the fact that the party "bosses" no longer exercise much control over either nominations or platforms. The chief culprit here is the primary. At the presidential level, primaries are now the only realistic route to the White House. Since the primaries attract a more ideological electorate than do general elections, candidates must appeal to those who will vote in them. Old-line party regulars, or even officeholders, may thus be frozen out of the party's most important single decision.

According to the critics, presidential primaries have another pernicious effect, which is our third piece of evidence of party decline. The primaries have meant that candidates must launch personal campaigns, since several candidates from the same party are squaring off in the initial rounds. Then, when the nomination is secured, the candidate keeps the personal campaign organization intact and all but ignores the party as a whole.

Personal campaigns are also abetted by the shift to partial public funding of presidential campaigns.[41] Significant campaign funds are now provided at public expense and paid directly to the candidates, removing an important resource from the party's hands.

Signs of Vitality

While the primaries and public funding have unquestionably led to an uncoupling of presidential campaigns from the party apparatus, to draw from that a conclusion of party decline is to equate party health with its role in presidential politics alone. The presidency is, of course, the main prize of American politics, but parties contest a plethora of other offices. In this light, the vigor of the party congressional campaign committees compared to those of twenty or thirty years ago would seem to point to increased party health. Moreover, since the DNC has copied the RNC as far as its resources will permit, the level of campaign activities of the national committees is at an all-time high. Anyone witnessing the flurry of partisan activity in Washington and on-site in the race for an open Senate seat or a governor's chair would not speak of party decline.

It must be remembered that the role of the party in government is as important as the party's role in elections. As discussed in chapter 5, the number of "party votes" in Congress seems to be growing, if anything. If the party label is more important in Congress than it has been at any time since World War II, can parties really be said to be declining?

Finally, the strong ideological bifurcation that has taken place between the parties since the 1960s seems to indicate party vitality. At one time, both parties contained substantial representation from liberals and conservatives. To be sure, the political center of gravity was more liberal among Democrats and more conservative among Republicans; but arch-conservative Democrats (often from the south) and liberal Republicans were not unusual. In the last twenty-five years, however, a slow but discernible polarization has occurred. Only a remnant of the conservative bloc remains in the Democratic party, and liberals are increasingly uncomfortable in the Republican fold, at the activist level at least. One need only read the platforms of the two parties in any recent election to see the strident differences in ideology. The point is that a good many people obviously care deeply about where "their" party stands on public issues; this is hardly a sign of organizational weakness. The time people stop caring what an organization stands for is the time organizational decay is likely to set in.

In sum, the evidence for the party decline thesis is incomplete, and the assertion that our democracy is thereby imperiled is surely overdrawn. Our parties have shown an amazing ability to adapt to new issues, new campaign technologies, and new electorates. Remember that the Democrats date to Thomas Jefferson's day and the Republicans to the 1850s. To be sure, the fortunes of both have ebbed and flowed. However, for the parties, as for Mark Twain, reports of their death are most certainly exaggerated.

SUMMARY

Political parties seem to be an essential component of democracy, as they are in evidence everywhere democracy reigns. The American party system has gone through at least four stages, perhaps five. Federalist and Democratic-Republican competition gave way to Democratic dominance, but soon two-party politics reemerged with the birth of the Whigs. The Republican party replaced the Whigs during the Civil War, and became the prevailing party from then until the 1930s. The Democrats then built a coalition that dominated national politics until 1968, when a new period of Republican presidential ascendancy began. However, in this last period the Republicans have not been able to win control of Congress.

Explanations for our two-party system differ. The most convincing is that our consensus on basic values, coupled with the bell-shaped distribution of political tendencies, sets the stage for a two-party system and that the institutional structure, particularly our mode of choosing a president, completes the play. Third parties have risen from time to time, though. Their most lasting effect has occurred when protest parties have raised new issues and have then been absorbed into one of the two major parties.

Parties are organized around their national committees. In recent years, the national committees have assumed a larger role in both parties—Democrats through seeking representativeness, and Republicans through finance. Congressional committees and affiliated groups of various sorts flesh out the party organizations at the national level. In the states, the degree of party organization varies enormously. Throughout the parties' structures, the last two decades have witnessed an influx of new activists: people committed to issues rather than to patronage.

The new ideological orientation of the parties has put the first brick in place for a system of responsible parties. However, the parties' inability to control candidates and, more important, the continuance of divided party control of government has foreclosed the building of a responsible party system in the United States.

Party identification has changed in the last forty years. Fewer people now claim to be Democrats, but this party still holds an edge. Increasing numbers of people are opting out of any party identification. Democrats are concentrated among women, blacks, those with lower incomes, Catholics, Jews, and liberals. The Republicans appeal to men, whites, people in upper income brackets, Protestants, and conservatives.

Voting turnout has been falling in the United States, but no one is certain why this is so or what it means. Turnout varies by race, age, education, and psychological orientation. Gender, a once potent factor, is no longer of any consequence in turnout. The potential political result of nonvoters' coming to the polls is unknown.

The decline in party identification along with the fading power of the party bosses and the personal campaigns now run by candidates has led some analysts to conclude that our parties are losing their place in the political system. But the national organizations have gotten stronger in recent years; party means more in government now than it once did; and the majority of people still identify with a political party, despite several social pressures working against identification. It seems that the parties remain healthy organizations with a central role in governing.

ENDNOTES

1. Larry Sabato, *The Party's Just Begun: Shaping Political Parties for America's Future* (Glenview, Ill.: Scott, Foresman, 1988), 26.

2. See John Hoadley, "The Emergence of Political Parties in Congress, 1789–1803," *American Political Science Review* 74 (1980), 757–79.

3. A good history of the various stages of American party development can be found in William Chambers and Walter Dean Burnham, eds., *The American Party Systems* (New York: Oxford University Press, 1967).

4. Washington's "Farewell Address" in *Writings* (Washington: Government Printing Office, 1940), 35:223.

5. For a good discussion of Madison and his contribution to these two models (although they are not labeled by the same terms), see James Q. Wilson, "Interests and Deliberation in the American Republic, or Why James Madison Would Never Have Received the James Madison Award," address at the 1990 meeting of the American Political Science Association (on Wilson's receiving of the Madison Award).

6. It should be pointed out that there was nothing preordained about the death of the Federalists. The Conservative or Tory Party of Britain,

which had an even more antidemocratic heritage, managed to survive into the age of mass democracy by adapting.

7. New Jersey divided its electoral votes by congressional district and Lincoln did not carry all of these, even though he carried the state as a whole.

8. Robert Huckshorn, *Political Parties in America,* 2d ed. (Belmont, Calif.: Brooks/Cole, 1984), 35.

9. For the change in southern politics, see Alexander Lamis, *The Two-Party South* (New York: Oxford University Press, 1984).

10. *The Federalist,* No. 10 (punctuation modernized).

11. For an analysis and application of this concept, see Jerome Clubb, William Flanagan, and Nancy Zingale, *Partisan Realignment: Voters, Parties, and Government in American History* (Beverly Hills, Calif.: Sage, 1980).

12. See the discussion in James W. Caesar, "Political Parties: Declining, Stabilizing, or Resurging?" in Anthony King, ed., *The New American Political System,* 2d version (Washington: American Enterprise Institute, 1990), chap. 4.

13. Only Nebraska has nonpartisan elections for its legislature, which incidentally is composed of only one house.

14. See Leon Epstein, *Political Parties in Western Democracies* (New Brunswick, N.J.: Transaction, 1980).

15. A good survey of third parties is Steven Rosenstone, *et al., Third Parties in America* (Princeton, N.J.: Princeton University Press, 1984).

16. See Louis W. Koenig, *Bryan: A Political Biography of William Jennings Bryan* (New York: Putnam, 1971).

17. See Warren Miller and M. Kent Jennings, *Parties in Transition: A Longitudinal Study of Party Elites and Party Supporters* (New York: Russell Sage Foundation, 1986).

18. Leon Epstein has characterized this as a move from a confederal to a federal structure which parallels the transition from the Articles of Confederation to the Constitution. See his "Party Confederations and Political Nationalization," *Publius* 12 (1982), 70–121.

19. Paul Allen Beck and Frank Sorauf, *Party Politics in America,* 7th ed. (Glenview, Ill.: Scott, Foresman, 1992), 101.

20. Samuel C. Patterson, "The Persistence of State Parties," in Carl Van Horn, ed., *The State of the States* (Washington: Congressional Quarterly Press, 1989), 169.

21. See William Crotty, ed., *Political Parties in Local Areas* (Knoxville: University of Tennessee Press, 1986) and John McGlennon, *The Life of the Parties* (Lexington: University of Kentucky Press, 1986).

22. *Rutan v. Republican Party of Illinois,* 497 U.S. 62, 110 S.Ct. 2729 (1990).

23. Miller and Jennings, *Parties in Transition.*

24. See David Broder, *The Party's Over* (New York: Harper and Row, 1972) for an early statement of party decline. A more recent work is Martin Wattenberg, *The Decline of American Political Parties, 1952–1988* (Cambridge, Mass.: Harvard University Press, 1990).

25. This concept is elaborated in Austin Ranney, *The Doctrine of Responsible Party Government* (Urbana: University of Illinois Press, 1962).

26. This example and the following one are discussed in Beck and Sorauf, *Party Politics in America,* 108.

27. Beck and Sorauf, *Party Politics,* 185. In 1988, however, a large number of Democrats returned to the fold. 93 percent of strong Democrats and 70 percent of weak Democrats voted Democratic, compared to 87 percent and 67 percent respectively in 1984. (Remember, though, that the percentage of the whole electorate avowing Democratic sympathies has been shrinking. Thus, the 1988 figure is a larger percentage of a smaller base.) Comparable Republican figures were 98 percent and 83 percent in 1988, and 96 percent and 93 percent in 1984.

28. See Helmut Norpoth, "Under Way and Here to Stay: Party Realignment in the 1980s?" *Public Opinion Quarterly* 51 (1987), 376–91.

29. On independents, see Wattenberg, *Decline of American Parties,* chap. 3.

30. All the data in the following paragraphs are taken from Sabato, *The Party's Just Begun,* chap. 4.

31. Actually, Catholic per capita income is now slightly higher than that of Protestants.

32. Examination of these religious data points to the precariousness of any deterministic socioeconomic explanation for party identification. Most Jewish citizens and most evangelical white Protestants identify overwhelmingly against their socioeconomic interests.

33. A good discussion of turnout can be found in L. Sandy Maisel, *Parties and Elections in America* (New York: Random House, 1987), 48–62. See also M. Margaret Conway, *Political Participation in the United States,* 2d ed. (Washington: Congressional Quarterly Press, 1991).

34. Russell Dalton, *Citizen Politics in Western Democracies: Public Opinion and Political Parties in the United States, Great Britain, West Germany, and France* (Chatham, N.J.: Chatham House, 1988), 39.

35. These included 13 city offices, 49 county offices, 40 state offices, 13 federal offices, and 50 referenda. Dalton, *Citizen Politics,* 39, 58.

36. Turnout is discussed in Ruy Teixeira, *Why Americans Don't Vote: Turnout Decline in the United States, 1960–84* (Westport, Conn.: Greenwood Press, 1987). For 1988, see Paul Abramson, *et al., Change and Continuity in the 1988 Election* (Washington: Congressional Quarterly Press, 1990), 103–107.

37. An in-depth discussion of these factors can be found in Michael Gant and Norman Luttbeg, *American Electoral Behavior* (Itasca, Ill.: Peacock, 1991), chap. 3. See also Conway, *Political Participation in the United States.*

38. See Carole Pateman, *Participation and Democratic Theory* (New York: Cambridge University Press, 1976).

39. Sorauf and Beck, *Party Politics,* 225. See also James DeNardo, "Turnout and the Vote: The Joke's on the Democrats," *American Political Science Review* 74 (1980), 406–20.

40. There is also a technical consideration which has bedeviled political scientists. Typically, surveys ask something like this: "Do you consider yourself a Democrat, a Republican, or an Independent?" For those selecting a party, a follow-up question asks whether they are "strong" or "not so strong" supporters of the party; independents are asked toward which party they lean. How should analysts count the leaners?

41. On personal campaigns in general see Martin Wattenberg, *The Rise of Candidate-Centered Campaigns* (Cambridge, Mass.: Harvard University Press, 1991).

FURTHER READING

1. Bartels, Larry. *Presidential Primaries and the Dynamics of Public Choice.* Princeton: Princeton University Press, 1988.

2. Beck, Paul Allen and Frank Sorauf. *Party Politics in America.* 7th ed. Glenview, Ill.: Scott, Foresman, 1992.

3. Conway, M. Margaret. *Political Participation in the United States.* 2d ed. Washington: Congressional Quarterly Press, 1991.

4. Epstein, Leon. *Political Parties in the American Mold.* Madison: University of Wisconsin Press, 1986.

5. Gant, Michael and Norman Luttbeg. *American Electoral Behavior.* Itasca, Ill.: Peacock, 1991.

6. Maisel, L. Sandy. *Parties and Elections in America.* New York: Random House, 1987.

7. Nelson, Michael. *The Elections of 1988.* Washington: Congressional Quarterly Press, 1989.

8. Sabato, Larry. *The Party's Just Begun.* Glenview, Ill.: Scott, Foresman, 1988.

ELEVEN

INTEREST GROUPS AND CITIZEN PARTICIPATION

ROUPS AND ASSOCIATIONS of every type and size are a persistent feature of American society. As has long been observed, we are a nation of joiners. Inevitably, many of these groups turn their attention to government, often because government is doing or contemplating doing something that affects their interest.

The interest group, defined as "an organized body of individuals who share some goals and who try to influence public policy,"[1] is therefore a natural part of democratic politics; in fact, the existence of interest groups is guaranteed by the Constitution, as the First Amendment provides that there shall be no barriers to "the right of the people peaceably to assemble, and to petition the government for a redress of grievances."

At the same time, Americans have always worried about the undue influence of groups. Attacks on the "special interests" are as old as the republic. Social reformers of the early twentieth century, known as muckrakers, produced classic cartoons of bloated and corrupt "trusts" (combinations of business firms) running government and exploiting the people. In our day, some critics argue that interest groups are contributing so much money to political campaigns that they are all but buying seats in Congress. Others see the rise of single-interest groups as injecting so much intensity into politics that government is becoming paralyzed. According to both sets of modern critics, far from being a healthy part of democratic politics, group activity is subverting it.

What types of groups are significant in American politics? What strategies do they employ to achieve their goals? What changes have occurred over the last two to three decades? How much influence do groups really have?

A NATION OF JOINERS

In the 1830s the young French nobleman Alexis de Tocqueville visited the United States and recorded his impressions in *Democracy in America,* a book that has since become a classic. At one point, Tocqueville says, "In no country in the world has the principle of association been more suc-

---

Opposite: *Anti-nuclear protestors being arrested for blocking the entrance to Seabrook nuclear power plant, New Hampshire, March 1990.*

cessfully applied to a greater multitude of objects than in America. . . . In the United States associations are established to promote the public safety, commerce, industry, morality, and religion."[2]

Comparatively speaking, Americans still join groups more often than do the citizens of most other democracies. We outdistance the British, Germans, and Italians, for example, lagging behind only the Scandinavians in the percentage of people who participate in group life.[3] Every American community is suffused with a rich variety of groups and associations.

But the tendency to join is not universal, nor is it spread evenly throughout the social structure. According to the most thorough study, 52 percent of American adults belong to at least one group.[4] However, if labor unions are not included, the number falls to 40 percent.

The class skew is quite pronounced. Of those who have completed no more than grade school, only 10 percent are members of any group other than a union. College graduates, in contrast, report a 56-percent joining rate, with the number jumping to 73 percent among those who have attended graduate or professional school. People in professional and technical occupations join at a rate of 63 percent, and laborers at a rate of only 13 percent (when unions are included, though, this rate rises to 56 percent). Considering income, 55 percent of those in the top brackets join, but only 24 percent of people in the lowest do so. As was true with voting, education has the greatest correlation with the likelihood of joining.

THE PANORAMA OF GROUPS

No one knows for sure how many interest groups there are. A 1946 law requires any group lobbying the federal government to register and file certain reports. However, the law is full of loopholes, and carries no serious penalties for failure to register (and is never enforced in any event). The closest thing to a reliable count is a private publication, *Washington Representatives,* which lists nearly seven thousand groups as active in the capital. The ways these groups break down into categories is presented in table 11–1.

It is immediately evident that business groups predominate. Taking together corporations and trade associations, fully 63.6 percent of the active groups represent business interests. However, we must not make the easy assumption that numbers alone translate into political power. We will take up the critical question of power later in the chapter. For the moment, let us look more closely at some of the major categories of groups, beginning with the economic and occupational groups.

Economic and Occupational Groups

BUSINESS GROUPS   Business is represented by three different types of organizations. First, many large companies, ninety-seven of the top one hundred listed by *Fortune* magazine, for instance, maintain their own Washington lobbying offices.[5]

TABLE 11-1

Interest Groups with Representation in Washington

	PERCENTAGE OF ALL GROUPS
Corporations	45.7
Trade and other business associations	17.9
Professional associations	6.9
Foreign corporations and commercial organizations	6.5
Governmental units (U.S.)	4.2
Citizens' groups	4.1
Civil rights groups (minority, women, handicapped, and elderly)	2.4
Foreign groups other than business	2.0
Educational organizations	1.9
Unions	1.7
Advocacy groups for social welfare and the poor	.6
Other	6.3
Total	100.2

Source: Adapted from *Organized Interests and American Democracy* by Kay Lehman Schlozman and John T. Tierney. Copyright © 1986 by Kay Lehman Schlozman and John T. Tierney. Reprinted with permission of Harper Collins Publishers.

Note: Total does not equal 100% because of rounding.

Next, there are a multitude of trade associations, organizations of businesses in particular sectors of the economy. Some of these were formed in the post–Civil War years as the United States industrialized, and with the years economic diversification has led to massive proliferation. Originally, they were designed to carve up market shares and discourage new entrants into their fields. When federal antitrust laws checked that tendency (at least to a degree), these groups moved to lobbying over tariff and tax legislation. As government activity expanded into regulatory, environmental, and consumer protection areas, trade associations have taken an even greater interest in public policy.

Some of them make the news from time to time, such as the American Petroleum Institute, the Tobacco Institute, and the Association of American Railroads. Others are more specialized, such as the Fertilizer Institute, the Potato Chip/Snack Foods Association, and the National Association of Truck Stop Operators. Hardly any line of business, large or small, is not represented by a trade association, and most American businesses rely heavily on their trade associations to represent their interests.

There are also a number of general business organizations, such as the National Association of Manufacturers, the Chamber of Commerce, and the Business Roundtable. The NAM is the oldest of these, founded in 1895. It represents primarily medium-sized manufacturers, and long had an image of unbending opposition to unions and to progressive legislation in general. Recently, it has tried to shed this legacy and become more open. The United States Chamber of Commerce, founded in 1912 at the invitation of President Taft, tries to represent all business. Its base is in its local chapters, found in almost every town and city in the country. Its national headquarters is in Washington, giving it a natural base from which to lobby. The Chamber's real strength is in retail, wholesale, and service businesses. The Business Roundtable is a relative newcomer, founded in the 1970s as the leaders of the country's largest businesses felt that the other organizations were not adequately representing them. It is made up of the chief executive officers of these large corporations, who contact members of Congress directly rather than relying on paid staff to do it. In general, it has proved quite effective. The member of Congress who cannot find time to meet with a lobbyist from a business organization will usually find time to meet with the head of General Electric.

LABOR UNIONS   Labor unions trace their heritage to the Knights of Labor, formed in 1869. It was only in the 1930s, though, when Franklin D. Roosevelt secured passage of the Wagner Act, that unions really began to prosper.[6] This law provided for government monitoring of elections on whether there should be a union at a plant and outlawed several union-busting tactics which businesses had long used.

In several major economic sectors, such as the steel, automobile, and construction industries, unions established major strongholds. However, rivalries between unions, personality clashes, organizing difficulties among workers in smaller businesses, and sometimes corruption have plagued the union movement. The American Federation of Labor (representing chiefly skilled-worker unions) and the Congress of Industrial Organizations (representing predominately semiskilled and unskilled workers) merged in 1955, but two major unions, the United Mineworkers and the Teamsters, remained outside. The United Auto Workers soon left also (but have since returned). The AFL-CIO is a good example of what is called a "peak organization," that is, an organization of organizations.

Even at their height, unions counted only about 25 percent of all workers as members. The economic decline of the older smokestack industries has hit the unions hard, and membership is now down to around 20 percent of the work force. Furthermore, unions have been slow to adapt to the electronic media age, and the image of union leaders has suffered.[7] However, the AFL-CIO and the older industrial unions are still a significant force in national politics, even if a declining one.

One noticeable change in the last several years has been the growth of white-collar unions, many affiliated with the AFL-CIO. The American Federation of Teachers (AFT) and the American Federation of State, County, and Municipal Employees are symptomatic of this shift in union makeup. In time, their concerns may come to dominate the AFL-CIO's lobbying stance, especially since members of both of these groups are government employees.

FARM GROUPS   Farmers constitute only a minuscule percentage of the work force, but farm groups are among the most politically active interest groups, and arguably among the most successful. There are several general organizations of farmers, but they share power with the associations representing the various crops and herds.

The largest general association is the American Farm Bureau Federation, founded in 1919 as an adjunct to the county agent system. Its orientation has been essentially conservative. The rival National Farmers Union (1955) has been generally more liberal. More militant than either is the American Agriculture Movement, which has fought foreclosures and engaged in other forms of protest.[8]

More real political power now rests with the special farm groups, analogues of the trade associations, since these groups are able to work closely with the powerful subcommittees of the two agriculture committees in Congress. Examples include the Cotton Council of America, the National Corn Growers Association, and the National Cattlemen's Association.

PROFESSIONAL ASSOCIATIONS   The line between a business or occupation and a profession is hazy. Most of the older professions are well organized. The American Medical Association is a very powerful group, as is the American Dental Association. Teachers are represented by the National Education Association (as well as by the AFT).

Almost all the newer professions and a variety of occupations claiming professional status have organizations which are active in Washington. Some examples include the American Institute of Certified Public Accountants, the American Society of Mechanical Engineers, the American Institute of Architects, the National Association of Social Workers, and even the National Association of County Parks and Recreation Officials.

Civil Rights Groups

Organizations of African Americans have long been the leading force in the civil rights field. The National Association for the Advancement of Colored People (NAACP) is the broadest and most visible civil rights organization in the country. Founded in 1909, it began and led the fight for desegregated schools and still remains highly active in a number of areas. The National Urban League sits beside the NAACP in longevity and prestige. Its activities are more centered on research and public education, but it is also an important lobby in Congress. There are a number of other organizations of black Americans, but none has the prestige of these two groups.

Women's groups have a significant but often ignored place in American political history. Some, such as the Daughters of the American Revolution, are longstanding and essentially conservative. In the late nineteenth century the National American Women Suffrage Association and the Women's Christian Temperance Union both aimed at major social reforms; interestingly, each obtained a constitutional amendment within a year of the other.

The League of Women Voters emerged from the Suffrage Association, but it was long a timid, if respected, organization. In 1966 the National Organization for Women (NOW) formed in conscious imitation of the NAACP.[9] In spite of being plagued by internal disputes and suffering several schisms, it remains the premier feminist organization. Although NOW failed to achieve its major goal, ratification of the Equal Rights Amendment, it has succeeded on several fronts.

Other women's organizations worthy of note include the National Women's Political Caucus and the Women's Equity Action League. The former is dedicated to increasing the number of women in public office. WEAL, a NOW breakaway, is more forthright in its claims to equality on a variety of fronts. Legal issues involving women are pursued by several other organizations, but particularly by the Women's Rights Project.

Recently, groups lobbying for civil rights and other benefits for homosexuals and the victims of AIDS have become active. Various ethnic minorities, such as Hispanics, Native Americans, and Asian Americans, have also copied the NAACP format and approaches. Groups representing the handicapped have likewise followed suit.

Civil rights groups have a peak association, the Leadership Conference on Civil Rights. Founded in the 1950s, it now consists of about 150 organizations representing the gamut of organizations sketched out above, along with several religious groups.

Public Interest Groups

One of the most remarkable developments of the last twenty years has been the surge of public interest or citizens' groups. Jeffrey Berry defined a public interest group as "one that seeks a collective good, the achievement of which will not selectively and materially benefit the membership or activities of the organization."[10]

These groups can claim an old and hallowed tradition in American politics, going back at least to the Anti-Slavery Society. Similar groups were founded in the Progressive period before the First World War. The American Civil Liberties Union (ACLU) was formed in 1920 and remains active. Other old-line groups include Americans for Democratic Action (a liberal group), Americans for Constitutional Action (a parallel conservative group), and Americans United for Separation of Church and State.

Most of the newer groups derive their inspiration if not their direct organizational history from the social activism of the sixties—and the response to it. The role of Ralph Nader cannot be overemphasized in this regard. In the mid–1960s, Nader demonstrated that a handful of dedicated reformers could capture the public imagination, take on a corporate giant, and win. The groups that he founded continue to play a conspicuous role in public interest lobbying.

His success inspired a host of new groups pushing consumer, environmental, health, and general "good government" issues. In the last-mentioned category is the prominent Common Cause.[11] Begun by ex-

Consumer advocate Ralph Nader testifying before the Senate Government Operations Subcommittee, March 1966.

cabinet member John Gardner in 1970, Common Cause soon had 100,000 members, and by 1988 it boasted over 300,000. Although it deals with many issues, its main focus is campaign reform. It favors the public financing of congressional campaigns, but believes that failing that, all candidates should disclose the sources of their contributions. Gardner has stressed that "our system is being corrupted and compromised by the power of money to dictate political outcomes."[12]

Another esteemed public interest lobby is Citizens for Tax Justice, which spearheads the movement to shift the tax system in a more progressive direction (that is, with the wealthy paying a greater share than they do now). On the environmental front, there are several citizens' groups, such as the National Resources Defense Council and the Friends of the Earth.

Public interest groups have a reputation for supporting liberal causes, but that is not necessarily the case. In the late 1970s, conservatives learned how to organize and finance citizens' groups of their own. The Pacific Legal Foundation, for instance, stands for free enterprise and the building of nuclear power plants. The Cato Institute is devoted to disseminating conservative ideas on economic policy and other issues, and has been quite successful in securing a hearing. In a sense, too, antiabortion groups, such as the National Right-to-Life Committee, are public interest groups, since they fit Berry's definition.

Other Types of Groups

An almost infinite number of groups are left out of the above classifications, groups representing virtually every sector and facet of American life.

BOX 11-1

Citizens' Groups in the Two Models of Democracy

WHAT DO INDIVIDUALIST and civic democrats make of citizens' groups? Individualists usually see people as pursuing their own interests. Thus, when people who are fairly affluent or people who have never been in jail become advocates for the poor or for prisoners, how does that fit the individualist model? It could be said that they receive personal satisfaction, the "good feeling" that comes from doing good, and that therefore their action is selfish after all. But this surely stretches the definition of "selfish" to the point of making it meaningless, as well as demeaning the motives of a good many activists.

Civic democrats take a more benign view of these matters, believing that the good society requires a commitment of people to

see beyond themselves, and that a proper upbringing and schooling will inculcate those values. Of course, groups of this type can sometimes go overboard in their advocacy, failing to see that the needs of their constituency may have to be balanced against those of others. Nonetheless, trying to give some representation to the traditionally powerless is a noble cause.

What about ideological and value-laden groups, though? People for the American Way and the

American Family Association are examples from opposite ends of the spectrum. PFAW was founded by television producer Norman Lear ("All in the Family," "The Jeffersons") as a counterweight to the religious right. It stands for a maximum of individual liberty and fights censorship and conservative religious influences in general. The American Family Association was founded by a Methodist minister concerned about the amount of violence and sex on television. Its members monitor programs for this type of content. The organization then publicizes the findings and sometimes advocates boycotts of sponsors.

The individualist democrat strongly supports free speech, and would welcome the activities of both

Veterans' groups, such as the American Legion, the Veterans of Foreign Wars, and others, are prominent political actors. Religious groups are notable lobbyists.[13] Some denominations, particularly the Roman Catholic Church, are important political players in their own right. The National Council of Churches, on the other hand, speaks for most mainline Protestants, while evangelicals have their own groups. Reverend Jerry Falwell's Moral Majority (now called Liberty Foundation) was prominent for a brief period, but it faded in importance when Falwell turned his attention elsewhere. Jewish groups constitute another segment of the religious community, and the Conference of Presidents of Major Jewish Organizations coordinates much of their lobbying. The aged are represented by the

BOX 11-1

of these groups, so long as they abided by the law and allowed others to speak. The emphasis is primarily on the right of anyone to organize and advocate at will, creating a "marketplace of ideas."

The crux of the matter for the civic democrat is that these two groups force a lively debate on one aspect of values and public policy, something we perpetually need. Both these groups are rooted in legitimate American traditions. Individual liberty and a secular state are cornerstones of our political ideology; but a respect for decency and a willingness to confront immorality is also part and parcel of our heritage. What is required is a genuine debate, not merely groups of people talking past each other. In other words, we need listeners as well as talkers. The AFA needs to respect the canons of personal liberty and understand that not everyone wishes to follow the lifestyle it favors, and that at some point private censorship becomes as dangerous as government censorship. On the other hand, PFAW needs to treat with respect the values and approaches of people like AFA and be willing to engage them in serious discussion. What television portrays as normal and acceptable is important in forming the nation; that issue, which PFAW has ignored, needs to be addressed.

According to the civic democrat, the search for the public interest requires debate and discussion, not merely a marketplace of ideas where people pick and choose whatever suits them. Respecting other citizens' ideas as legitimate, it should be stressed, does not devalue your own. You can hold fast to your own values and still be willing to talk to other citizens about theirs.

Suppose you were in charge of structuring a meaningful debate between representatives of PFAW and the AFA. What format would you select: Questions from a panel? Questions from the audience? Allotted time for statements and rejoinders? If a panel were chosen and you were to be on it, what questions would you ask of each group? What common ground, if any, do these two groups share?

American Association of Retired Persons, and by several other active groups. In short, almost every classification of Americans is directly represented—except, that is, the poor.

Even the poor, though, have some substitute representation. For example, the Children's Defense Fund, founded by ex–NAACP staff member Marian Wright Edelman, is a respected organization which lobbies for improved conditions for poor children. Similarly, the Food Research and Action Center focuses on food stamp and other food-related problems of the poor, while the National Coalition for the Homeless advocates decent housing for all. Nevertheless, these are not direct organizations *of* poor people, but organizations *for* them.

STRATEGIES USED BY GROUPS

Interest groups pursue a variety of strategies in their quests to shape public policy. Some groups, for reasons related to the types of policy they are interested in, their resource limits, or their own expertise, emphasize one or two exclusively; others operate on a variety of fronts simultaneously.

Lobbying Congress

The mainstay of most interest groups is trying to convince members of Congress to vote in accordance with the groups' positions. This is so basic that our image of lobbying (as well as its name)[14] is connected to Congress. The reason that Congress is the center of so much attention is simple: this is where the laws are written. If a group can win Congress over, no other strategies may be needed.

Since most congressional work is done in committees and subcommittees, lobbyists spend most of their time and effort there. Meeting the members and their key aides face to face is the goal of every lobbyist. "For an organized interest bent on influencing the course of congressional policymaking," two experts write, "there is no substitute for direct contact with individual congressmen and legislative aides."[15] Once given access to key committee members, lobbyists go to great lengths to cultivate their confidence and support.

How are access and support gained? One way is through political action committee contributions to campaigns, a matter we will discuss below. Rarely is an outright bribe given, but this is not unknown, as the infamous Abscam case of 1980 showed. (FBI agents posing as lobbyists passed bribes to several members of Congress in front of hidden video cameras.) More often, the lobbyists arrange things that are completely legal, but surely questionable. In 1981, for example, a lobbyist for Hughes Helicopter arranged a three-day elk-hunting trip for two key committee members right before a vote on a matter vital to Hughes.[16] A much more common practice is inviting the member to speak before a group for a fee. The speech is usually a canned rehash of many others or a series of anecdotes. Congress has placed some restrictions on this practice, but it is still open to abuse. Nevertheless, too much weight must not be given to these dubious practices. Lobbyists and members alike stress that credible information is the lobbyists' stock in trade with most members of Congress. "The most important thing is your trust and integrity,"[17] reported one labor lobbyist. Echoing the same refrain, a lobbyist for a chemical company commented, "You'd better bring good ideas and some facts, and they'd better be accurate."[18]

If the issue moves from the committee to a floor vote and the outcome is uncertain, lobbyists must shift tactics. Ordinarily, they will seek help from friendly members to gain access to people they do not usually work with. Further, they will concentrate on the fence sitters, bypassing those already

Lobbyists waiting outside the meeting room of the House Ways and Means Committee in the Capitol.

committed one way or the other. At times, they will seek coalitions with groups which do have an entree with other members. In other instances, they can try to have their backers in the various members' districts make the contact. Trade associations in particular will often try to find someone, such as an Arkansas plant manager, to ask for a few minutes of the representative's time. Congresswoman X from Arkansas may refuse to see someone from the Paper Clip Institute, but she is unlikely to turn down the plant manager from her district, who will bring the lobbyist along.

The most dramatic ploy is to ask group members or sympathizers to flood their senators and representatives with phone calls, telegrams, and letters. Careful observers have often debated how much difference this really makes. If Congressman Z gets a thousand identically worded post-cards, he knows that they have been orchestrated. However, they have come from his district, sent by people who cared enough about the issue to write. Many congressional staffers report that such mail-ins are taken seriously, and that unless the member has strong commitments, they often sway the vote.[19]

One particularly successful use of this ploy occurred when the American Bankers Association was unable through its usual lobbying methods to keep Congress from adding a provision to the tax law which would have mandated withholding on interest payments.[20] The bankers put together a nationwide blitz, utilizing signs in every bank and flyers in customers' monthly bank statements. Congress was literally flooded with telegrams, phone calls, and letters; in response, the withholding provision was removed, even though both President Reagan and Senate Majority Leader Robert Dole favored keeping it.[21]

Lobbying the Executive Branch

Presidents normally set up an elaborate liaison system to maintain contact with various interest groups.[22] However, much of the contact with these groups flows from the White House to the groups, as the president tries to build support for his policies.[23] Groups, of course, try to obtain some influence over presidential decisions (influencing, for example, the particular aspects of his program which the president is really going to push), but most of the influence runs the other way.

A critical part of lobbying the executive branch involves influencing appointments. Which individuals hold certain positions is terribly important to many interest groups. Here, the group's size, prestige, and relationship to the president's political party are crucial. Labor unions, for instance, virtually control the appointment of a secretary of labor in Democratic administrations, while they are almost ignored by Republicans. Both environmental groups and mining concerns are interested in who becomes secretary of the interior, since that department controls most federal land. In appointments to many of the regulatory commissions, the affected industries become very active, many times with success.

Interest groups may thus find allies or enemies in the politically appointed leaders of administrative agencies. In the Reagan-Bush years, conservative groups often found a welcome mat out to them, which they used to press their own agendas. Liberal groups, in contrast, found themselves largely frozen out.

Below the level of political appointees, interest groups may have access to agencies in what is usually a more formalized process. Many agencies are given substantial discretion to make rules and regulations, but they must adhere to rather arduous procedures. Ordinarily, these procedures call for hearings or opportunities for "public comment." Interest groups use these occasions to make their case for or against a proposed regulation. Since the civil servants are typically well versed in the field, interest groups rely heavily on technical arguments.

The relationship between an interest group and an administrative agency can even approach symbiosis. Agencies need political allies, particularly at budget time, as much as interest groups need favorable decisions. Obviously, this close bonding does not always occur, since ideological hostility often precludes it. Further, even when it does develop, it is not necessarily the result of conniving; people who work regularly in a particular field often view problems in the same way without any *quid pro quo* involved.

The most disturbing aspect of interest group–executive branch relations is what is known as the "revolving door": the practice of people leaving an agency and going to work for groups or firms they have just been dealing with. Who better to hire as your chief lobbyist than a former head of the executive agency? No one—except possibly a former White House aide or a former member of Congress. All these people have something even more important than knowledge: indispensable contacts. Doors will open to them that are shut to all others. Questions arise about more than simply the propriety of this privileged access. Also troubling are the possible influences at work on government officials while they are still in government. These officials are only human; are the prospects of future employment ever on their minds as they make decisions?

The Ethics in Government Act has attempted to cure the most glaring abuses surrounding this practice. It provides that a person may not lobby the agency for which he once worked for a year after leaving government service. While helpful, many feel that the law needs tightening. For example, the term "agency" has been construed very narrowly, diminishing the law's scope. Michael Deaver, a Reagan aide who resigned to set up a lobbying firm, shamelessly sold his ability to contact important people. Reportedly, he received $250,000 for making one telephone call.[24] He was able to avoid the law's strictures because he did not contact the particular unit of the White House in which he had worked. Clearly, some adjustments are needed if the law is to be more than minimally effective.

Litigation

Many groups see the courts as a major arena for pursuing their objectives.[25] The NAACP pioneered the technique of the carefully plotted legal strategy to secure social change.[26] In the ensuing years, other civil rights groups and women's groups have adopted the practice as well. Environmental groups, particularly the National Resources Defense Council and the Environmental Defense Fund, have become adept at employing lawsuits to delay projects such as dams and nuclear power plants. The American Civil Liberties Union is heavily court-oriented, since its area of interest is mostly addressed by the courts.

However, courts are not used only by liberal groups. Business firms have long fought regulatory laws and adverse administrative rulings in court. This is an effective strategy, since sustained delay can often negate a policy in the end. That is, even if the firm loses, conditions may have changed so much by the time the case is settled that the policy is meaningless. In addition, conservative interest groups have learned to use the courts.[27] So far, though, it seems that they have not been as successful as they had hoped.[28] With the slowly changing character of the judiciary, however, that may change.

As mentioned in chapter 8, the Supreme Court allows groups which are not direct parties to a case to file "friend of the court" briefs. This opens another channel for interest groups to influence judicial proceedings; the growth of this practice, though, has paradoxically, muted its influence. The Court now receives so many such briefs and their arguments are so predictable that they have less import than they had a generation ago.

Another factor is judicial appointments. Robert Bork's and Clarence Thomas' nominations to the Supreme Court triggered immense interest group struggles. Most potential justices for either the Supreme Court or the lower federal bench do not generate so much interest group activity, but all nominations for Supreme Court justice bring about some. Interestingly, this involves lobbying both the executive and the legislative branch, with the goal of affecting the third branch. The importance of the judiciary in making critical decisions in our society guarantees that interest groups will make an effort to seat friendly men and women on the bench.

Influencing Public Opinion

Most interest groups strive to create a favorable climate of public opinion for their positions. In these endeavors, astute use of the media is of fundamental importance.

At times, groups purchase advertisements to paint a favorable image of the group and/or solicit support for specific policies. Mobil Oil has spent millions of dollars running in many newspapers and magazines full-page ads which outline the virtues of free enterprise. The National Rifle Association has run a series of ads titled "I am the NRA," depicting a well-known or particularly wholesome-looking person who belongs to the NRA. Planned Parenthood has run similar ads on the need for birth control. Sometimes such ads relate to specific policies; an example is the one the Association of American Railroads ran against a proposed Interstate Commerce Commission regulation which would have permitted longer trucks on the highways.

There are two drawbacks to this strategy. One is that it is enormously expensive. A full-page ad in a major magazine or newspaper can run to nearly fifty thousand dollars. The other is that most people perceive them for what they are: ads.

Sponsoring research and disseminating the results is another often-used strategy. A particularly noteworthy case was the Citizens For Tax Justice report in 1985 that exposed 250 major corporations which had paid no federal income taxes. Newspapers across the country ran stories on the report, and many believe it laid the groundwork for the Tax Reform Act of 1986.[29] The Urban League annually issues a Report on the State of Black America, which is routinely covered by the press. Environmental and consumer groups regularly conduct studies to support their positions. One key advantage of this approach is that it is much less costly, since it is covered by the media as news. Another is that, as news, it seems more objective and believable, even though the quality of research varies considerably. The most enviable position for a group to have, which only a few achieve, is one in which the media seek it out for information. This allows a group to present the facts in its own way and be somewhat selective in the information it provides. However, credibility is most important here. Journalists usually try to be objective, and if a group distorts the facts or puts too much of a spin on the data, it will not be called again.

Demonstrations and Civil Disobedience

The civil rights and anti-Vietnam war movements taught that demonstrations and civil disobedience can be powerful tools. These groups were not the first to use such tactics—the suffragists and the unemployed had applied them much earlier[30]—but the modern groups perfected the tactics and learned how important media coverage is. Today, media coverage, particularly televised footage, is essential to the success of a demonstration.

Traditionally, demonstrations were the chosen tactic of groups with few resources other than a number of supporters. Now, however, all sorts of groups mount demonstrations. In fact, the very proliferation of them has detracted from their effect, since the media tend to ignore all but the very largest.

The most significant national demonstrations of late were the marches conducted by pro-choice and pro-life forces in response to the Supreme Court's 1989 *Webster* decision. Earth Day, though technically more a festival than a demonstration, is another example of successful mobilization that generates substantial publicity. All kinds of other groups continue to make use of demonstrations and marches in hopes of swaying public opinion and policymakers: gays and lesbians, labor unions, pro-life groups, teachers, even Michigan doctors protesting increased liability insurance costs, along with the seasoned veterans of the civil rights and peace movements.

Civil disobedience and creative theatrics can also attract media attention. Martin Luther King, Jr. became the most eloquent modern defender of civil disobedience, and it served the civil rights movement well.[31] Others were quick to learn. The Clamshell Alliance staged sit-ins at a nuclear power facility, had themselves arrested, then refused bail. Greenpeace has refined the tactics of interfering with whaling vessels and other commercial ships. Operation Rescue's members have repeatedly blocked the doors to abortion clinics and been arrested. ACT-UP, an AIDS advocacy group, created a disturbance at Holy Cross Cathedral in Boston.

All these instances resulted in heavy media coverage. However, demonstrations and civil disobedience are very sharp two-edged swords. People may be turned off by what they see, rather than becoming sympathetic. If so, the groups' lobbyists will have more difficulty convincing government officials to take up their case.

All these strategies have proved effective at one time or another. What tends to be most effective, of course, is building public support and carrying on a steady, reliable lobbying campaign at the same time. Groups want and need to be seen as serious and regular participants in policy areas that concern them, not merely perpetual outsiders.

INTEREST GROUPS IN THE STATES

Oftentimes we become absorbed in the role of interest groups in national politics and overlook the fact that they are active in the states as well.[32] If the trends elaborated in chapter 3 continue, and the role of the states and the number of policy areas they touch grows, then interest group politics at the state level will likely become more significant still.

In the past, many states were dominated by one powerful group or a handful of them—usually economic interests of one sort or another, such

367

as tobacco, oil, timber, and mining interests. States with more diversified economies displayed a more pluralistic pattern, but economic groups (including unions in states such as Michigan and Ohio) were always powerful. Today, as more states have increasingly diversified economies and as educational levels rise across the country, interest group patterns are becoming more complex in most places.

Business groups and trade associations (particularly those in fields, such as public utilities and banking, that are heavily regulated by states) are still very active. Professional groups and groups of public employees, especially teachers, have joined the lobbying system in every state, and are often major players. Furthermore, studies of state politics have found that local government units—cities, counties, school districts, and so forth—are significant interest groups in their own right. The reason is that state legislatures control the legal authority of these local units as well as their taxing and spending abilities, and naturally they act to protect themselves.

The degree of influence which interest groups exercise varies widely across the states. In general, where political parties are strong, interest groups tend to be weaker. Parties provide an automatic organizational form for legislators, and party leaders develop a high degree of influence over public policy. Elections and the stances of the parties thus become important determinants of the actions of the legislatures. Likewise, in states with historically and constitutionally strong governors, interest group influence is lessened. If the governor has the power to push her program through the legislature, interest groups have fewer opportunities to penetrate policy-making for their special purposes. Finally, the political culture of a state is important. In some states there is a long and accepted place for interest groups; in others, groups are viewed with suspicion, and therefore often held at arm's length by public officials.

Recently, a team of researchers set out to categorize the states according to the importance of interest groups in their politics compared to other factors such as parties, elections, etc. Each state was classified according to whether the interest groups were a *dominant* political factor; played a *complementary* role to other political institutions and actors; or occupied an entirely *subordinate* position. In nine states, interest groups were deemed to have a dominant role; in eighteen they fell into the complementary category; and in none were they completely subordinate. All the remaining states showed a mixed pattern. Thus, interest groups are nowhere irrelevant, but their influence varies considerably from one state to the next. If state power continues to grow, though, interest groups of all types can be expected to step up their activity in state capitals.

POLITICAL ACTION COMMITTEES

Groups have long supported candidates at election time through making endorsements, providing campaign workers, and giving financial contributions. Today, the most frequently used vehicle for this purpose is the political action committee, or PAC. PACs are organizations designed to

The National Education Association, headquartered in Washington, D.C., has one of the ten largest political action committees.

solic contributions from people and then make campaign gifts to candidates for office.[33]

The Problem of Campaign Finance

The financing of political campaigns has always proved a vexing issue, and has become more so as costs have skyrocketed, thanks largely to television. Presumably, people in a democracy should be free to spend their money to support causes and candidates they prefer. But money easily corrupts the democratic process, for those who give do not always do so for civic reasons alone. They want something in return. Many people and interest groups therefore operate precisely as individualist democrats would predict when it comes to campaign contributions. They have some type of interest, and seek to maximize it through the mechanism of campaign giving. Further, one must always remember that at any given moment those who possess the power to reform campaign laws have benefited from the status quo.

Through the years, some ineffectual statutes were enacted which set limits on the amounts individuals could give and the amounts candidates could spend, while also barring corporations and unions from making contributions. In 1971, however, two far-reaching reforms were enacted. One required candidates to list the source of all contributions over one

369

hundred dollars; the other provided for partial public funding of presidential campaigns by establishing a one-dollar checkoff on federal income tax returns. The Watergate scandal created more pressure for reform, the result of which was the Federal Election Campaign Act of 1974. This act increased the public funding of presidential campaigns (including primaries), but also inadvertently gave birth to the PAC explosion.

The Growth of PACs

PACs were an innovation of labor unions to get around the law forbidding direct union gifts to candidates. The best-known labor PAC has been the AFL-CIO's Committee on Political Education (COPE), which solicited money from individual members and distributed it to friendly candidates. Until 1974, businesses had not been able to set up PACs, largely because of a law which prohibited any government contractor from doing so. Because almost every business of any size sells something to the government, this was a wide blanket. In the early 1970s, courts were considering litigation that could have spelled trouble for the labor PACs. Hence, labor lobbyists requested their congressional supporters to add a provision to the 1974 law which protected their PACs; but there was no way to accomplish this without opening the door to business PACs. Labor leaders believed that few businesses would set up PACs, and that the risk was therefore worth taking. Seldom has an interest group more clearly won a legislative battle and simultaneously shot itself in the foot more completely.

Business and trade association PACs literally took off, in number and in riches. They were given further life by a ruling of the Federal Election Commission that corporate funds could be used to administer the PAC, freeing up for contribution to candidates a larger percentage of the donations from management and stockholders. At the same time, the computer revolution was making a science out of direct-mail solicitations. Ideological and public interest groups found this to be a highly effective means of raising funds, and entered the PAC game in a big way.

Table 11–2 shows how the number of PACs has grown, while table 11–3 classifies them by type. The amounts of money involved are colossal. In the 1990 election cycle, PACs raised $372.4 million and spent $358.1 million. Table 11–4 lists the top ten PACs in terms of expenditure.

Since presidential campaigns now draw heavily on public funds, PACs concentrate most of their energies on congressional races. Who gets PAC money? At first blush, one would think that candidates who are sympathetic to the sponsoring group would receive a PAC's blessing. But that is only partially correct. Ideological PACs do tend to follow this rule. Business and trade association PACs are more flexible, however. In most cases, they give overwhelmingly to incumbents, even if the challenger is more in tune with their goals. The reason? The incumbent is so likely to win, with or without PAC money, that to give aid to his opponent would only alienate him after the election. Usually, then, it is only when a challenger stands a reasonable chance, which is not often, that business and trade

TABLE 11-2

The Growth of Political Action Committees (PACs)

	TOTAL NUMBER OF PACS
1974	608
1976	1,146
1978	1,653
1980	2,551
1982	3,371
1984	4,009
1986	4,157
1988	4,268
1990	4,172

Source: Federal Election Commission.

association PAC money comes her way (if, of course, she is more pro-business than her opponent). Some pragmatic PACs (53 percent in one study)[34] hedge their bets by giving to both candidates. Also, the few victorious challengers at each election often find that PACs are suddenly ready to help them retire their campaign debts.

The Influence of PACs

Many commentators believe that PACs have flagrantly corrupted the political process.[35] The huge amounts of money involved mean that members of Congress are more beholden than ever to special interests. Money has become the basic element of political influence, and those who can give through PACs secure the benefits of public policy. As Senator Robert Dole

TABLE 11-3

Types of Political Action Committees (PACs)

	NUMBER
Corporate	1,965
Labor	372
Non-Connected	1,337
Trade/Membership/Health	796
Cooperative	60
Corporation without stock	151
Total	4,681

Source: Federal Election Commission.

Note: The total in this table does not match that in Table 11–2 because that figure is given as of December 31, whereas this represents an average over the 1989–90 period.

TABLE 11-4

Top Ten Political Action Committees in Spending
for 1989–1990 Election Cycle

NAME OF POLITICAL ACTION COMMITTEE	EXPENDITURE
Democratic-Republican Independent Voter Education Committee	$10,600,000
Realtors Political Action Committee	5,400,000
Voter Guide	5,100,000
American Medical Association Political Action Committee	4,700,000
National Education Association Political Action Committee	4,100,000
Association of Trial Lawyers of America Political Action Committee	3,900,000
American Federation of State, County, and Municipal Employees Political Action Committee	3,700,000
National Congressional Club	3,600,000
National Rifle Association Political Victory Fund	3,500,000
United Auto Workers Voluntary Community Action Program	3,300,000

Source: Federal Election Commission.

(R-Kansas) said, "There isn't [*sic*] any Poor PACs or Food Stamp PACs or Nutrition PACs or Medicare PACs."[36]

PAC executives are quick to point out that they do not expect the recipients of their gifts automatically to support the affiliated group's position. That, they claim, would be unethical. What they want is "access," the chance to argue their case when the time comes. One PAC manager said, "You can't use money to change opinion, but you can use money to get in the door."[37]

Objective studies of the influence PAC money has on congressional voting records are inconclusive.[38] It is difficult to sort out the effect of PAC money from what members would do anyway. However, Representative Les Aspin (D-Wisconsin) points out that "There are various degrees of being for a bill. . . . PAC money can determine a member's intensity as well as position."[39] Recent studies of congressional committees, where after all most of the important legislative work is done, have tended to bear this out.[40] Representative Barney Frank (D-Mass.) adds, "We are the only human beings in the world who are expected to take thousands of dollars from perfect strangers on important matters and not be affected by it."[41]

However, it must also be said that members of Congress work the PACs as much as the PACs work them. Most are quite bold in soliciting PAC funds. "Candidates talk about the corruptive nature of PACs," said the director of one, "and then they turn around the next day and invite PACs to their fund-raisers."[42] Behind these requests often lies the subtle hint that without contributions, access will be closed off. Sometimes the hint is not so subtle. When Representative Tony Coelho chaired the Democratic Congressional Campaign Committee, he told an interviewer, "Access. Access. That's the name of the game. . . . We don't sell legislation; we sell the opportunity to be heard."[43]

The system of financing elections through PACs does have some virtues and some defenders. Two major points usually stand out. First, the disclosure laws regarding PACs are pretty strict, ensuring that the public knows who got what from whom. Formerly, many large contributors were unseen, since they were individuals, and it was unclear to the public what interests they represented. Second, ideological PACs in particular allow citizens to contribute to candidates who share their philosophy but are unknown to them. Thus, they broaden political participation among the ordinary citizenry.

Still, PAC money and pressure has to be worrisome. Although the platitudes about "access" are no doubt mostly sincere, it is well to recall that access is a form of power. The ability to make your case is an enormous advantage if it is denied to the opposing interests. Those denied this opportunity are, of course, primarily the poor and unorganized. While, as we have noted, these groups are not completely without representation, they do not have the luxury of handing out campaign contributions to guarantee access. There is a major difference between having a designated seat at the table and being invited in occasionally. And $358.1 million buys a lot of chairs.

Reforming the Financing of Political Campaigns

The real culprit here is politicians' unending need for money to run effective campaigns. The costs of campaigning have climbed into the stratosphere because of the use and expense of television time. If some way could be found, without violating the First Amendment's free speech guarantee, to limit the amount any candidate could spend, the need for PAC money would diminish. For the time being, given the Supreme Court's stance on the matter, that seems a forlorn hope.[44] The only available alternatives seem to be public financing or requiring the television networks to provide free air time to all candidates. Regarding the first option, it is difficult to believe that the current incumbents, now regularly returned at a rate greater than 95 percent, would hand 535 challengers the means to mount an effective race. As for the second option, the television industry would fight it forcefully, since campaign ads are such a rich source of revenue. Furthermore, the differing circumstances of the two political parties clouds the issue. The Republicans, for their part, raise vastly greater private sums for their campaign committees (see chapter 10), but the overwhelming majority of congressional incumbents are Democrats, so that they have a decided edge in PAC contributions. Until someone solves these dilemmas or public attitudes change in favor of steps like those suggested above, reform will be difficult.[45]

All these matters surfaced in the latest round of attempted congressional reform. In the wake of widespread public anger over the House banking and post office scandals, in April of 1992 Congress passed the most far-reaching campaign finance reform measure since 1974. It would have given House candidates who agreed to limit their private spending to $600,000 another $200,000 in public matching funds. Similar limits were to be set at $1.6 million to $8.9 million for Senate candidates, depending on the size of the state. In the senators' case, though, the public grant would have been in the form of vouchers good for television advertising only. Additionally, limits were to be placed on PAC contributions and political party spending.

President Bush, however, quickly vetoed the bill, criticizing the fact that it did not eliminate PAC funding entirely, and calling it a "taxpayer-financed incumbent protection plan" which would "lead to a raid on the U.S. Treasury to pay for the Democrats' elaborate scheme of public subsidies."[46] An attempted override divided closely along party lines and failed, but Senator David Boren (D-Oklahoma), a leading proponent of public financing, vowed, "We'll be back again and again until we get it passed into law."[47]

THE IMPACT OF INTEREST GROUPS ON PUBLIC POLICY

The real question involving interest groups is not how many and what types there are, what strategies they use, or how much they spend. It is whether or not they have an influence on the contours of public policy. This question is not simple, because influence is not something either present or absent. There are many grades and shades of influence.

Two broad generalizations seem to emerge from the wealth of studies on interest groups and policy. The first is that groups are much more successful at blocking new policy initiatives than they are at getting new laws adopted. This ability to foil new policies flows from the fragmented character of the legislative process and the political system in general. Our structure of government provides so many veto points that groups need only penetrate one successfully to stave off unwanted action. The second generalization is that groups usually have more power over the details of policy than they have over the broad outlines. This is not, however, inconsequential. Details are important in giving life to public policies, and they may be, in fact, all that matters to a narrowly focused group. These two features sometimes combine, as for instance when the American Medical Association fought the adoption of Medicare. When the organization saw that in spite of several successful bouts, the policy stood a good chance of being enacted, it shifted to the content of the program. The AMA managed to help structure Medicare in such a way that it has been a bonanza for doctors.

Interest group influence also varies with the structure of policymaking in various policy areas. We habitually think of interest group politics as arraying one set of groups against another, with one side winning and the other losing. Indeed, this scenario is often played out. Changes in environmental laws, for instance, usually find environmentalists lined up against industry, as when the redwood forests/spotted owl controversy erupted in the late 1980s. Similarly, the fight over the civil rights bill in 1991 (see chapter 8) pitted business against civil rights groups. However, while these are the controversies that make the headlines, largely because they are controversies, they are not the sum and total of politics.

In some policy areas, a second type of situation exists, in which one or more groups has no opponents at all. For instance, there are no anti-veterans groups to fight against veterans' benefits. Similarly, no group opposes the charitable deduction in the federal income tax or seriously objects to the deduction for homeowners' interest payments. Thus, groups such as charities and the National Association of Realtors and the National Association of Home Builders face no real struggles. In these areas of uncontested policy, the organized interests typically get what they desire with only minimal effort.

A third type of policy-making is more complex. Here we find a highly organized group with an intense interest in the policy, but facing loosely organized or apathetic opponents. There are actually three subsets of this type of policy-making.

In the first of these, the benefits are directed to a few people, but the costs are spread thinly among many, and are small to each individual. Agricultural price supports are of this nature. They benefit farmers in a direct and obvious fashion, and government policy is a significant factor in farm incomes. The costs are borne by consumers, who pay perhaps an extra two cents for a loaf of bread. A National Association of Bread Eaters could be a counterweight, but who would bother to join?[48] In the second case, the converse is true: the benefits are widespread, but the costs are loaded onto a few. A good example is automobile safety. The car manufacturers believe, with some justification, that they will bear the costs. Thirdly, there are cases in which lifestyle issues are at stake and intense minorities feel that their values are threatened. The best example is the issue of gun control, in which a dedicated and intense minority mobilizes to fight any regulation of firearms. Those who support gun control are generally less committed and more diffuse. In each of these areas, the odds are usually with the well-organized interest group.

However, it is important to point out that public feelings play a significant role. At one time, the tobacco lobby appeared to be impregnable. But antismoking groups slowly changed public values and perceptions; this change then altered the way the debate was carried on. Civil rights is another poignant example. As important as court victories have been, the greatest change has been in public values. Likewise, current debates over clean air and water are quite different from debates on the same topics twenty years ago. Interest groups which address public values can therefore have an enormous impact over time. All these examples confirm the faith of the civic democrat that what people believe matters.

Thus, in spite of PAC money and interest group pressure, politicians are indeed influenced by public judgments and what might be called "the temper of the times." Incidentally, incumbents need not be replaced in

375

Economic Policy-Making in Austria

DO INTEREST GROUPS have more power in the United States than in other modern democracies? The answer is both yes and no.

In Austria the groups representing business, labor, farmers, and the various professions are established by law. There are a Chamber of Commerce, a Chamber of Labor, a Chamber of Agriculture, and various professional bodies. Further, they are all-encompassing. No person in the work force is permitted to *not* be a member of one or more such groups.

By tradition and law, these groups function as an adjunct to government, if not an actual part of the state. They are regularly consulted on all matters affecting economic policy, either separately or together in various councils and commissions. Throughout the government, advisory groups are filled by delegates from the chambers. Plus, some institutions on which their members sit have legal authority. The Parity Commission, for example, sets prices for about one-third of all products and services.

Once agreement is reached among the chambers, each one is expected to help implement the policy among its members. Thus, when wage settlements are made after bargaining between the peak associations of business and labor, the unions and their local affiliates are expected to acquiesce and not demand higher wages or go on strike. Similarly, if certain percentages are established by the Parity Commission as the maximum for price increases, business firms are required not to raise them above that level.

This system has certain advantages for interest groups. They are guaranteed the access that American groups so ardently and constantly search for. Austrian groups sponsor no PACs. Further, each such group has a legal status which is more than that of a purely private association. But the drawback is that they become virtually part of the state appa-

order for changed value perspectives to work their effects. Elected officials are adept at altering their stances in order to be in accord with their constituents' values. In this sense, the effort devoted to public education campaigns is not wasted, and citizen discussions in coffee shops, bars, schools, churches, and homes are a significant part of the political process.

INTEREST GROUPS AND THE IDEAL OF CITIZEN PARTICIPATION

In both the individualist and the civic democratic models, each citizen should have an equal voice in the shaping of public policy. Whatever their ratus, making independent criticism difficult. When you have helped set the policy, you are in no position to criticize.

It is also evident that the success of the system depends on (1) there being only one general or peak association in each sector, and (2) the associations being all-inclusive. In the United States, for example, there are several general business associations, two major farm groups, and so on. Furthermore, when there are single peak or general associations, such as the AFL-CIO or the AMA, not all unions, workers, or doctors belong. Given this situation and the voluntary nature of American interest groups, American groups would have great difficulty coercing members to go along with any bargain they might strike.

There is sometimes a faint shadow of the Austrian system in the United States. Some governmental bodies have representatives from business, labor, and the general public. Advisory councils, consisting of interest group representatives in fact if not in name, are sprinkled throughout government. During the Nixon administration's ill-fated attempt to impose wage and price controls, the councils which were established to set the figures and implement them were composed of interest group representatives. Later, President Ford held a series of economic summits to try to get various interest groups to come up with an economic strategy. Reaching further back into history, during the 1930s the Roosevelt administration tried to use trade associations to monitor business regulation, but the Supreme Court voided this plan.

In general, we maintain a rather firm line between the public and the private realm. We are hesitant to give a private association anything approaching legal status within government. Yet, this practice is common in many European democracies, not only Austria. The reasons are historical. Remember that their democracies were imposed on states that had accumulated vast powers during the age of absolutism. The separation of state from church, from economic planning, from social morality, etc., has never quite taken hold in Europe.

other differences, both models hold up equality of individual participation as the appropriate ideal.

Yet, the interest group system in contemporary American politics is blatantly inegalitarian. We have seen earlier in the chapter that those with higher educational levels are members of interest groups in grossly disproportionate numbers. Further, PAC money obviously has some effect, even if it is not clear precisely how much and when. The less-well-educated and the less-well-off, who of course are often the same people, are decidedly underrepresented by any measure we might wish to use.

Since this situation is clearly undesirable, what can be done about it? E. E. Schattschneider, a famous political scientist of the postwar era, argued many years ago that maintaining strong political parties was one way to offset the power of interest groups and the inequalities they bring to the political arena.[49] Political parties must compete for votes, and while money and organizational skill obviously count in elections, at least citizens are all on an equal footing in the ballot box. Interest group influence can thus be muted, if not overcome. However, the links political parties have with the electorate have been declining, as we have specified in the last chapter. Moreover, political parties never have been very democratic in their internal workings, and forcing citizens to choose between two candidates and packages of policy proposals does not necessarily increase equality of participation. At best, this is only a partial solution, and one which seems more elusive now than ever before.

Cass Sunstein, a legal theorist, has advocated that the courts play an expanded role, through developing what he calls "rationality review."[50] Courts would review legislative enactments and administrative rulings to determine if they had been adopted to serve a legitimate public purpose. Congress, the state legislatures, and administrative agencies therefore would have to convince judges that they considered the public interest, not merely the special interests of a few, and further, that the measures they chose were rationally related to the ends they sought. (In part, Sunstein argues, this idea would help bring about the type of deliberative discussion favored by civic democrats.) However, putting this type of power into the hands of the courts is an ironic way to make participation more equal, for the courts are the farthest removed from public discussion of all governmental institutions. With their highly formalized procedures and the expense involved in litigation, the courts are much more suited to educated and moneyed elites than are legislatures.[51] It seems highly unlikely that in the long run, relying on courts could increase genuine public participation among all segments of the populace.

Philippe Schmitter, a student of European government, has proposed what may be the most innovative solution.[52] The government would give each citizen a yearly voucher, which he could then divide up among the interest groups of his choice. The groups would then receive funds from the government when they turned in their vouchers. Government would also promise that each group would be consulted in areas affecting its members. Further, each interest group that took the public funds would be required to adopt a charter spelling out that its internal affairs would be run democratically. Thus, each citizen would be assured of having interest groups that spoke for her interests, and would be entitled by law to participate in the internal decisions of the group. Equality among individuals and equality among groups would be enhanced. It is unclear, though, how government could guarantee meaningful as opposed to merely symbolic participation in each group. Also, those in power can be required to listen, but how can they be forced to weigh arguments? Further, it would be almost impossible in a free society to prevent other, truly private groups from forming outside the voucher system and going about their business as they do now.

Perhaps, in the final analysis, the surest way to increase equality of participation is to spread the belief that this is a central political value. If political decisions arrived at through inegalitarian means were viewed as illegitimate by the public, that fact alone would affect decision-making. Perfect equality of participation is probably unattainable, but if it were a more widely held ideal, the actual degree of inequality would be substantially lower than it is now.

SUMMARY

Interest groups are both a healthy manifestation of democracy and a problem for it. The diversity of interest groups mirrors the diversity of American society, but there is a marked imbalance in the population which joins groups. The poor are decidedly underrepresented in all facets of interest group politics. Occupational groups, such as organizations of businesses, workers, farmers, and professional organizations, are active participants in American political life, as are civil rights groups, public interest groups, and a variety of other groups.

Groups pursue their objectives chiefly through lobbying Congress, where access is all-important. In the executive branch, groups often focus on technical details, but also make attempts to influence the appointment process. Litigation is undertaken by many groups, a fact which leads these groups to take an interest in judicial appointments. Building support among the public through such tactics as demonstrations is also a common approach.

Interest groups operate at all levels of government. Although we tend to focus on the work of groups in Washington, groups are active in the states as well. As the states become more important, it is likely that the attention of interest groups to state politics will grow also.

Political action committees have become an important feature of American politics. With significant public funding of presidential campaigns, their funds go primarily into congressional races. As a rule, incumbents reap the bulk of PAC donations. It is unclear, though, exactly how much influence PACs have. At the moment, campaign finance reform is an elusive goal.

Interest groups' effect on public policy is complex. When a group has no opponents or when the opponents are unorganized, group influence is likely to be substantial. When groups have contests with each other, it is always uncertain which group will emerge victorious. Nonetheless, public sentiment is also a weighty factor in the shaping of public policy. The interest group system is highly inegalitarian, even though both models of democracy advocate equality of participation.

ENDNOTES

1. Jeffrey Berry, *The Interest Group Society,* 2d ed. (Glenview, Ill.: Scott, Foresman, 1989), 4. There are any number of other definitions, none of which is entirely satisfactory. The main difficulty with this one is that a political party would fit into it. Interest groups typically do not run can-

didates for political office, whereas that is the main function of political parties. For a discussion of the various definitions, see Mark Petracca, "The Rediscovery of Interest Group Politics," in Mark Petracca, ed., *The Politics of Interests: Interest Groups Transformed* (Boulder, Colo.: Westview, 1992), chap. 1.

2. Alexis de Tocqueville, *Democracy in America* (New York: Colonial Press, 1899), 1:191, 198.

3. Graham Wilson, *Interest Groups in the United States* (New York: Oxford University Press, 1981), 132–44.

4. The figures in this paragraph and the next are drawn from Kay Lehman Schlozman and John Tierney, *Organized Interests and American Society* (New York: Harper and Row, 1986), 59–63.

5. Schlozman and Tierney, *Organized Interests,* 58. This abundance of corporate lobbyists is nothing new. For an historical overview, see Edward Epstein, *The Corporation in American Politics* (Englewood Cliffs, N.J.: Prentice-Hall, 1969). For a more modern analysis, see David Vogel, *Fluctuating Fortunes: The Political Power of Business in America* (New York: Basic Books, 1989).

6. A good history of American unions is Philip Taft, *Organized Labor in American History* (New York: Harper and Row, 1964). A briefer survey can be found in Daniel Benjamin, "Combinations of Workmen: Trade Unions in the American Economy," in S. M. Lipset, ed., *Unions in Transition* (San Francisco: Institute for Contemporary Studies, 1986), chap. 8.

7. Some analysts believe that a renewed business offensive against unions is at least partly responsible for the decline. See Michael Goldfield, *The Decline of Organized Labor in the United States* (Chicago: University of Chicago Press, 1987).

8. In 1978–79, for example, the AAM sponsored a tractorcade to Washington, which incidentally did $3.6 million worth of damage to Washington's streets and parks. Graham Wootton, *Interest Groups: Policy and Politics in America* (Englewood Cliffs, N.J.: Prentice-Hall, 1985), 137.

9. Sara Evans, *Personal Politics* (New York: Knopf, 1979).

10. Jeffrey Berry, *Lobbying for the People* (Princeton: Princeton University Press, 1977), 7.

11. See Andrew McFarland, *Common Cause: Lobbying in the Public Interest* (Chatham, N.J.: Chatham House, 1984).

12. John Gardner, *In Common Cause* (New York: Norton, 1972), 56.

13. See Allen Hertzke, *Representing God in Washington* (Knoxville: University of Tennessee Press, 1988).

14. The term "lobbyist" comes from the old days when legislators frequently gathered in the lobby of the building when business was slow. There they were met by the representatives of various interests who had been hanging around the lobby.

15. Schlozman and Tierney, *Organized Interests,* 290.

16. Schlozman and Tierney, *Organized Interests,* 295.

17. Berry, *Interest Group Society,* 143.

18. Berry, *Interest Group Society,* 144.

19. Berry, *Interest Group Society,* 114.

20. Income tax has long been withheld from wages and salaries as they are earned. Interest and dividends, though, are not subject to withholding, but are taxed once, at the end of the year. People who receive substantial income from these latter sources thus have use of the money throughout the year; this allows them to earn more interest. Plus, the banks are spared the administrative costs of withholding the tax and remitting it to the government. At the same time, though, the government has to wait longer for its tax dollars, and therefore has to borrow more to meet current obligations.

21. Paul Taylor, "The Death of Withholding, or How the Bankers Won a Big One," *Washington Post,* July 31, 1983 and Bill Keller, "Lowest Common Denominator: Why the Bankers Fought Withholding," *Washington Monthly,* May 1983, 32–38.

22. See John Orman, "The President and Interest Group Access," *Presidential Studies Quarterly* 18 (1988), 787–97.

23. A good discussion of presidential mobilization of interest groups is Mark Peterson, "Interest Mobilization and the Presidency," in Petracca, *Politics of Interests,* chap. 10.

24. Berry, *Interest Group Society,* 225. The call, incidentally, did not produce what the client (TWA) wanted.

25. See Stephen Wasby, "Interest Groups and Litigation," *Policy Studies Journal* 11 (1983), 657–70.

26. See Mark Tushnet, *The NAACP's Legal Strategy against Segregated Education, 1925–1950* (Chapel Hill: University of North Carolina Press, 1987).

27. See Lee Epstein, *Conservatives in Court* (Knoxville: University of Tennessee Press, 1985).

28. Karen O'Connor and Bryant Scott McFall, "Conservative Interest Group Litigation in the Reagan Era and Beyond," in Petracca, *Politics of Interests,* chap. 12.

29. Berry, *Interest Group Society,* 106.

30. See Frances Fox Piven and Richard Cloward, *Poor People's Movements* (New York: Vintage Books, 1979).

31. See Martin Luther King, Jr., *The Trumpet of Conscience* (New York: Harper and Row, 1989).

32. The most thorough and comprehensive study of interest groups in state politics is Clive Thomas and Richard Hrebenar, "Interest Groups in the States," in Virginia Gray, *et al.,* eds., *Politics in the American States,* 5th ed. (Glenview, Ill.: Scott, Foresman, 1990), chap. 4. All the information in this section is drawn from this source.

33. See Larry Sabato, *PAC Power* (New York: Norton, 1984) for an overview.

34. Schlozman and Tierney, *Organized Interests,* 253.

35. See especially Elizabeth Drew, *Politics and Money: The New Road to Corruption* (New York: Macmillan, 1983).

36. *Boston Globe,* December 12, 1982.

37. Schlozman and Tierney, *Organized Interests,* 241.

38. Diana Evans, "PAC Contributions and Roll Call Voting: Conditional Power," in Allan Cigler and Burdett Loomis, eds., *Interest Group Politics,*

2d ed. (Washington: Congressional Quarterly Press, 1986), 114–33 and John Wright, "PACs, Contributions and Roll Calls," *American Political Science Review* 79 (1985), 400–414.

39. Quoted in H. R. Mahood, *Interest Group Politics in America: A New Intensity* (Englewood Cliffs, N.J.: Prentice-Hall, 1990), 96.

40. Richard Hall and Frank Wayman, "Buying Time: Moneyed Interests and the Mobilization of Bias in Congressional Committees," *American Political Science Review* 84 (1990), 797–820.

41. Quoted in Berry, *Interest Group Society,* 134.

42. Berry, *Interest Group Society,* 138.

43. Schlozman and Tierney, *Organized Interests,* 253.

44. The Supreme Court has held not only that the First Amendment protects a person's right to spend his money to advocate whatever he pleases, but also that business advertising during a political campaign is also covered by the amendment's strictures.

45. A good discussion of the issues surrounding campaign finance reform can be found in Frank Sorauf, *Inside Campaign Finance: Myths and Realities* (New Haven, Conn.: Yale University Press, 1992).

46. *Washington Post,* May 10, 1992, A7.

47. Beth Donovan, "Senate Sustains Veto of Overhaul Bill," *Congressional Quarterly,* May 16, 1992, 1324.

48. The problems of organizing people under conditions such as these are discussed in Mancur Olsen, *The Logic of Collective Action* (Cambridge, Mass.: Harvard University Press, 1965). But see Jack Walker, *Mobilizing Interest Groups in America* (Ann Arbor: University of Michigan Press, 1991), chap. 5.

49. E. E. Schattschneider, *The Semisovereign People* (New York: Holt, Rinehart, Winston, 1960).

50. Cass Sunstein, "Interest Groups and American Public Law," *Stanford Law Review* 38 (1985), 29–87.

51. It is often argued that courts are used by less-advantaged groups to offset their lack of power elsewhere. However, recent research demonstrates convincingly that that conclusion relies too heavily on the example of the NAACP. See Susan Olsen, "Interest Group Litigation in Federal District Court: Beyond the Political Disadvantage Theory," *Journal of Politics* 52 (1990), 854–82.

52. Schmitter's ideas are contained in an unpublished paper entitled "Corporative Democracy." They are discussed in Jane Mansbridge, "A Deliberative Theory of Interest Representation," in Petracca, *Politics of Interests,* 41–42.

FURTHER READING

1. Berry, Jeffrey. *The Interest Group Society.* 2d edition. Glenview, Ill.: Scott, Foresman, 1989.

2. Browne, William. *Private Interests, Public Policy, and American Agriculture.* Lawrence: University of Kansas Press, 1988.

3. Hertzke, Allen. *Representing God in Washington*. Knoxville: University of Tennessee Press, 1988.

4. Mahood, H. R. *Interest Group Politics in America: A New Intensity*. Englewood Cliffs, N.J.: Prentice-Hall, 1990.

5. Mundo, Philip. *Interest Groups: Cases and Characteristics*. Chicago: Nelson-Hall, 1992.

6. Olson, Mancur. *The Rise and Decline of Nations*. New Haven, Conn.: Yale University Press, 1982.

7. Schlozman, Kay Lehman and John Tierney. *Organized Interests and American Democracy*. New York: Harper and Row, 1986.

8. Smith, Hedrick. *The Power Game: How Washington Works*. New York: Random House, 1988.

9. Stern, Philip. *The Best Congress Money Can Buy*. New York: Pantheon, 1988.

10. Useem, Michael. *The Inner Circle*. New York: Oxford University Press, 1984.

PUBLIC POLICY

PUBLIC POLICY—"what the government says and does about perceived problems"[1]—is central to all politics. Politics is indeed characterized by games of intrigue, the clash of personalities, and the search for personal power. But most of the activity of those in office, those seeking office, and those trying to influence both is directed toward having government do something or not do something. The actual actions of government—laws passed, taxes collected, regulations issued, wars fought, pensions paid, bridges built, medicines approved, student grants awarded, and so on—are at the heart of what it means to govern.

In studying public policy, an important conceptual distinction needs to be drawn between the making of policy and the substance of policy. Policy-making refers to a series of decisions by those with the authority to act. The substance of policy, on the other hand, is the actual content of laws, administrative regulations, and court decisions. Both the way governments make policy and the policies they actually make are of enormous importance for students of politics.

In this chapter we shall take a brief tour of the process of domestic policy-making in the federal government, categorize the different types of domestic policies the government pursues, and examine the tools most often used by government. The discussion will be limited to domestic policy solely in the interest of brevity and clarity. There are important differences in foreign policy-making (in particular, the increased power of the president), which deserve a full discussion, precluded by our lack of space.[2] After we have established a framework for the study of domestic policy, we shall then turn to environmental policy as an example of the way these elements fit together.

THE POLICY-MAKING PROCESS

Dividing any ongoing process into stages is always a bit artificial, akin to dividing the life cycle into the periods of youth, adulthood, and old age, for example. Nevertheless, there are discernible phases to processes such as policy-making (and life), and it is useful to break them down for analysis, even though the stages blend into each other.

Agenda-Setting

The initial stage in all policy-making is agenda-setting.[3] Before any action can be considered, something must be perceived as a problem, and there must be demands for government to act on the matter. Take poverty. Poverty has always existed, but in ancient Rome, medieval England, and

---

Opposite: *Thomas Moran,* The Grand Canyon of the Yellowstone, *1872. Moran's grandiose painting of this Wyoming landform influenced Congress in 1872 to create Yellowstone National Park, the start of the national park system.*

eighteenth-century America, poverty was not considered a problem government ought to alleviate. The results of poverty—crime, riots, and vagrancy—were indeed often viewed as public problems, but poverty itself was not. Only in the mid–twentieth century did a general consensus develop that poverty was a social problem which government could and should address.

When we discuss agenda-setting, we must distinguish between the societal agenda and the governmental agenda. The former consists of all those matters eliciting public concern, and the latter only of the list of issues actually on legislative calendars, court dockets, and the like.

Typically, an issue appears on the societal agenda before it is placed on the governmental agenda. However, there are times when a small but powerful interest group can have an item put on the government's agenda, or when those in government pursue some policy initiatives on their own. Usually, though, a new issue has to attract the attention of a substantial segment of the public, gestate there a while, and then crack the governmental agenda. Some problems, however, never move from the societal to the governmental agenda. The ability to keep something off the governmental agenda is often the most fundamental exercise of political power.[4] Costs of and access to health care, for instance, have long been widely perceived as a social problem; however, the American Medical Association, the health insurance industry, and various other interests have managed to keep this problem off the governmental agenda. Thus, social problems do not automatically become public problems. Keep in mind, though, that doing nothing is in effect a policy. In the case of health care, as in other cases, it is an endorsement of the status quo.

How do issues move from the societal to the governmental agenda? Interest groups play a crucial role in this linking process, but they are not alone. Interest groups pressure members of Congress to introduce bills; lobby presidential candidates to adopt their proposals; and publicize their issue among the voters. Political parties play a function in filtering and consolidating interest group demands. Sometimes, a so-called "policy entrepreneur" will act as a catalyst, heightening interest among the public and galvanizing lawmakers into action. Ralph Nader's work on automobile safety is the major example of this phenomenon, but there are many others.

The exact factors which cause public values to change and thereby breed the conditions for policy change are little understood. Yet, we can observe clearly that public values and attitudes do change. The proper relationships between blacks and whites and the role of women in society are two examples of areas that have undergone substantial change over the years. It seems that the roles of interest groups (such as the NAACP and NOW) and the media are vital, but we must not forget the educative role of government itself. When a shift in public attitudes begins, government endorses the attitude change by taking tentative policy steps, and that probably speeds further change. Moreover, the new laws may create incentives for people to behave in a certain way (say to end job discrimination, for example) and the new patterns of behavior may help change

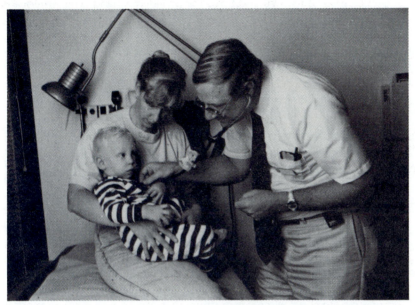

Access to health care is currently a subject of intense controversy. In most western countries, care is free at point of service. In the U.S., a fragmented system of government programs supplement a basically private system.

attitudes further. As stressed in chapter 1, therefore, the moral values which government supports by its words and deeds are important in shaping social values, which in turn affect future policies (and private actions as well).

In light of the importance of changed public values, it would be easy to say that changed public attitudes "cause" shifts in public policy, but that is far too simplistic. There is no automatic one-to-one correspondence between value changes and public policy. First, not all changes in public attitudes result in new policies. Of all the changes that are continually going on in society, only some make it to the governmental agenda, while others remain at the fringes of political activity. Second, value changes do not dictate the specifics of particular policy responses. Those in government will translate public demands into public policies, and there are always a variety of ways to attack a given problem.

Within the federal government, the president is without doubt the major agenda-setter. He can elevate an issue from obscurity to make it the most debated topic in Washington. The particular proposals he sends to Congress, and the ones among those which he really pushes, will be important in determining what Congress considers. Sometimes, of course, events determine the agenda, even for the president. Such conditions as foreign policy crises, major economic difficulties, or unsettling domestic events such as the riots which erupted in Los Angeles in 1992 after policemen were acquitted of beating a black motorist will demand to be addressed. Inside Congress, occasionally a coalition of members may develop an agenda item of its own and force the president's hand. The Americans with Disabilities Act of 1990, for example, was initiated and passed with no presidential leadership. In addition, courts sometimes set the agenda, particularly when the Supreme Court announces a far-reaching and controversial decision, such as the ones on flag-burning and abortion. Nonetheless, the president retains the central role in setting the national agenda.

Policy Formulation

Once an issue is on the government's agenda, it enters the stage of policy formulation. On the surface, this stage is rather straightforward. Both houses of Congress pass a law, which is either signed or vetoed by the president. If it is vetoed, either the veto is overridden by Congress or the law dies. If the law is challenged, the courts either legitimate the new law by upholding its constitutionality or void it.

As with the constitutional descriptions we have encountered before, this is but the skeleton of how policy formulation works. In fact, most of what has been covered so far in this book is in a sense a description of policy formulation. In short, almost everything that occurs within government is directly or indirectly related to policy formulation. If one generalization can be made about American policy-making, it is that its overriding characteristic is fragmentation. The dispersal of power within our political system through separation of powers and federalism makes central coordination and planning all but impossible, except under the most unusual of circumstances (such as war on the scale of World War II). "Policy" consequently is more often than not a series of patchwork decisions rather than a coherent approach to solving a problem.

Some analysts have argued that it is helpful to break the government down into what they call subgovernments.[5] That is, they contend that each policy area—education, transportation, energy, housing, and so on—has a different configuration of power and a different process for making policy. In one subgovernment, the president may be a dominating force; in another, a congressional subcommittee may be the locus of decision making; in a third, a bureaucratic agency may hold center stage.

While the concept of a subgovernment is quite useful, it is important to keep two points in mind. First, the subgovernments are not completely isolated from each other. Some are more autonomous than others, because of either the power possessed by the major actors or the nature of the policy, but none are completely detached from the larger political system. The education subgovernment, for instance, is linked to the employment and welfare subgovernments, as well as others. Further, few subgovernments are immune from general economic and budgetary policy. Second, subgovernments are not static. The process of policy formulation within them is constantly open to change as people and conditions change. A classic case is management of the national forests. For years, the Forest Service balanced recreational needs with the demands of the timber and mining industries. When the environmental movement turned its attention to forest management, though, stressing such issues as species preservation, a whole new constellation of forces and political pressures appeared.[6]

Implementation

After a policy is formally adopted, it must be implemented.[7] Again the constitutional commands are relatively straightforward. The executive branch is charged with carrying out the law, and any uncertainties in the statute are settled by the courts.

Often, Congress hands wide discretion to administrative agencies by empowering them to make rules to carry out the statute. These may be regulations forbidding certain behaviors, such as the dumping of specific pollutants in streams, or guidelines on who is eligible for certain benefits, such as research grants. The drafting of these regulations is far from a rote and mechanical exercise. Frequently, the conflicts generated by the law's passage are simply transferred to the bureaucracy.

Furthermore, laws can be enforced with zeal or laxity. Without violation of the law itself, enforcement can be strict or light, depending primarily on the philosophical position of the person heading an agency. In any presidential administration, the president will push certain objectives more strongly than others. To do this, the president may appoint as heads of administrative agencies people who will seek to bend the agencies' enforcement programs in the desired direction. A president may even appoint to the headship of an agency an individual who strongly opposes the whole program the agency is administering. For example, President Nixon placed an opponent of the antipoverty program in charge of the Office of Economic Opportunity, the agency charged with overseeing federal antipoverty efforts.

Still another element in the implementation stage involves the budget. Few agencies, especially those regulating behavior, have enough money and people to ferret out every violation. Even under the best of circumstances, therefore, choices have to be made. However, one sure way to hamper an agency is to cut its budget. Whatever the wording of a law, if its enforcement is in the hands of an emasculated agency, it will have little impact.

Court decisions are another factor which enters the picture. These may deal with procedural matters, as when a federal court ruled that the Food and Drug Administration's expedited program to remove suspect drugs from the market violated the Administrative Procedures Act, and that a full internal hearing had to be held. Or, a court may interpret the statute itself, to uphold or curtail administrative actions.

Evaluation

As policies are implemented, they are naturally evaluated. Some of these evaluations are technical. Is this particular technique (such as grants to

FIGURE 12–1

The Policy-Making Process

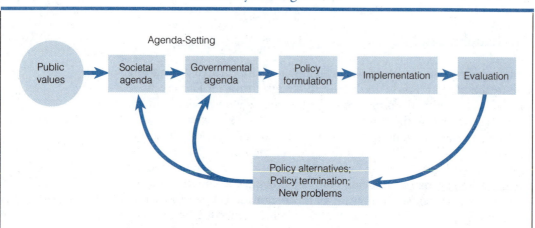

schools to buy computers) accomplishing its goal (teaching students to read faster)? What side effects are occurring, as in the case of airline safety after deregulation?

But many of the evaluations are inevitably political. Even if a policy is "working," many people may be opposed to its goals, or ideologically opposed to a particular technique of implementation. Others may believe that the costs or tradeoffs are too high, even if there are positive results from the policy. Making life unpleasant for welfare recipients, for example, probably does reduce welfare rolls, but many are philosophically opposed to such draconian measures, and many further believe that such steps would lead to higher crime rates and other social pathologies. Raising the tariffs on imported clothing probably does save American jobs (in that foreign clothing will be relatively more expensive), but many are ideologically committed to free trade, and many others believe that there are cheaper and more effective ways to ensure employment opportunities for American workers.

Policy evaluation is therefore a sticky business in which the distorting effects of political ideology and economic self-interest are everywhere. Nonetheless, we should not overlook the fact that many people in both the executive and the legislative branches are fair-minded, and sincerely in search of answers to specific problems. Frequently, however, even the best and most objective research on policy assessment is inconclusive. As but one example, no one seems to have convincing evidence about how best to fight the drug war. As another example, the best way to provide decent housing for low-income people is as elusive now as ever.

Yet, policies do get evaluated, even if haphazardly, and this information is fed back to decision makers. Policies therefore are subject to continual alteration, and sometimes even termination. Interest groups, of course, are always seeking changes in the laws which affect their constituencies. Also, general social changes, such as an increase in the number of older people, can generate calls for changes in public policies. In short, the stage of evaluation brings us full circle, back to agenda-setting.

TYPES OF POLICIES

One way to classify policies is to use the traditional categories of government departments and bureaus, such as agriculture, education, energy, and the like. However, another useful way to look at policies is to examine the kinds of actions that governments undertake. This approach leads to a four-fold classification: distributive policy, regulatory policy, redistributive policy, and symbolic policy.[8]

Distributive Policy

One key government activity is the distribution of benefits, usually money, to groups and individuals. Agricultural subsidies to farmers, grants to local governments for flood control or airport construction, and grants to college students are prime examples of distributive policies.

The hallmark of distributive policy is that the benefits are disaggregated, or broken into small pieces, so that everyone who qualifies can get a bite

Filing for unemployment benefits is one major area in which citizens come into direct contact with public policy.

of the cookie. Resource constraints are seldom limited to a set dollar amount; this means that a benefit can be given to A without threatening B. Hence, no one who benefits will mind that others benefit as well.

Politically, these programs are always popular. The targeted groups are naturally pleased, and the total amount given to any one program is seldom enough to raise taxpayers' ire. Hence, the style of politics found in this arena is one of low conflict and a something-for-everyone approach.

Because distributive policies are so popular and generate such little conflict, they are a favorite of Congress. Often, proponents of a new policy will make it distributive so that wide support can be attracted. For example, in the 1960s, the Model Cities program was initially designed to operate a few small pilot programs in selected cities in order to test whether the idea worked—a plausible approach, one would think. However, there was sustained opposition in Congress to the whole idea; the opposition melted away, though, when the program was broadened to include virtually every major city in the United States.

Another political lesson is that distributive policies are extremely difficult to control. When Presidents Carter and Reagan in turn tried to cut the wasteful federal water projects program, they ran into a stone wall in Congress. No member wanted to see any project cut, for fear hers would be next. The severe problem of closing military bases is another illustration. As pointed out in chapter 5, Congress could accomplish this contentious task in the end only by setting up an independent commission (whose decisions stood unless overturned by an affirmative vote). If Congress itself had had to make the decisions, few members could have summoned the courage to vote to close colleagues' bases, much less their own.

Regulatory Policy

Regulatory policy involves government's regulation of some activity in the public interest. The law normally requires some group of people or organization (most often a business) to do or not do something, and imposes a penalty for any violation.

Government regulations requiring financial disclosure by firms trading on the stock exchanges; specifying maximum allowable automobile emissions or minimum gasoline mileage; demanding the disclosure of interest rates charged by financial institutions; mandating the payment of minimum wages; prohibiting smoking on passenger airlines; and stipulating the types of drugs which require a prescription—all these are examples of regulatory policy.

The politics of regulatory policy are laden with interest group pressures. Most groups being regulated prefer the regulations to be as permissive as possible. Wherever the regulations are written, whether in a congressional subcommittee or in a bureaucratic agency, therefore, interest groups representing the regulated will be present in force. Frequently, of course,

Caring for the elderly has become a major public policy issue as more people live longer.

interest groups speaking for consumers or the general public will also work on an issue. Furthermore, these battles often spill over into the courts as well.

For most regulatory policy, Congress passes a law spelling out the goal to be sought, and turns over the detailed regulation drafting to a federal agency. Sometimes, however, Congress pursues regulatory policy by attaching conditions to federal contracts or grants. One example of this is the requirement that contractors dealing with the federal government must pay union wage rates. Another is that the states must set their drinking ages at twenty-one in order to qualify for federal highway funds. Thus, regulatory policy may merge with distributive policy.

Redistributive Policy

Into the redistributive category fall government programs which explicitly take from one group and give to another. A system of taxation that falls more heavily on the rich than on the poor (called "progressive taxation") is redistributive. Likewise, a law requiring quotas of minorities or women in certain jobs traditionally held by males is redistributive.

Redistributive politics tend to bring out sharply ideological debates. Moreover, they divide the public along class, racial, gender, or other lines, since the winners and losers are clearly identifiable. Ensuing conflicts are often bitter and emotion-laden.

Since redistributive policies raise such contentious debate, public officials usually try to avoid them. One common way is to hide the redistributive effect. The whole federal taxing and spending system redistributes the nation's wealth, but the exact way it operates is so misty that few even see it as redistributive. It is difficult to explain to someone in Connecticut precisely how his taxes are being poured into Mississippi via the federal grant program. Plus, experts differ on exactly how much redistribution there actually is, and exactly whom it affects.

Furthermore, we ordinarily think of redistributive policies as those which take from the affluent and give to the masses. (This is, after all, one of the fears the wealthy had in the eighteenth century about creating a democracy.) However, many government programs transfer wealth from one geographical region to another, or from one sector of the economy to another. For example, federal energy policy has both of these attributes. If it favors oil production, it will shift wealth from non-oil-producing states to those which are awash in oil wells, and from coal mining and other firms to oil companies. Of course, wealth will also be shifted from and to the many people who work for and supply these various industries.[9]

Symbolic Policy

A final area of government policy is the manipulation of symbols. This might involve such a move as the declaration of a public holiday to honor Martin Luther King, Jr. Another example of symbolic policy was the alteration of the official seal of the United States after World War II, to make the head of the eagle face the talon holding the olive branch rather than the talon holding the arrows. Yet another example was the addition in 1954 of the words "under God" to the Pledge of Allegiance.

Another type of symbolic policy is found in the statements of broad objectives which often accompany legislation, indicating overall policy of the federal government, such as the goals that every American have a decent house, that a good job be available for everyone who wants to work, and that each child is entitled to an excellent education. Few realistically expect the specific policy to accomplish these goals, but the goal itself elaborates a value. It does symbolize what the nation would do, if it had sufficient knowledge, skill, and resources. Thus, while these statements are platitudes, they are important in defining the character of a political order.

Sometimes, though, symbolism takes on a more sinister face. The steeply progressive federal income tax schedules of the 1950s and 1960s were long cited as a major example.[10] On paper, the rate tables made it appear that the wealthy were paying enormous sums, which supposedly made ordinary folk feel better about forking over their shares. In practice, though, a variety of loopholes guaranteed that no one actually paid the rates at the top of the table. Political contentment among the masses was thus bought with a mere symbolic gesture. The Tax Reform Act of 1986 improved this deceptive approach to the tax rates by compressing the rate structure into only a few bands and lowering the general rates, although many dodges remain in the law.[11]

TOOLS OF PUBLIC POLICY

Policymakers seek to affect the behavior of individuals and to alter social conditions. In their quest to accomplish this, they have several tools, or strategies, available. Each has certain advantages and certain disadvantages, and each works better or worse depending on the circumstances. The major ones are direct regulation through binding rules, structuring, subsidies and payments, taxation, and moral suasion.

Binding Rules

An obvious way for government to affect society is to pass a law commanding that people behave in a certain fashion. In order to be effective, naturally, the law must carry penalties for those who disobey.

The federal government relies heavily on this strategy in virtually every area of public life. Ordinary criminal laws are an obvious example, but this strategy is also at work in laws such as those forbidding the dumping of toxic wastes, requiring the approval of the Food and Drug Administration for new drugs, preventing any interference with the right to vote, and prohibiting deceptive advertising practices.

When this approach is adopted, those designing the policy must take some precautions. First, they must be careful to specify precisely what is being regulated. Statutes must be drawn very carefully, so that those targeted, and the courts, will understand what is expected. Imprecise laws are an invitation to confusion and avoidance.

Second, policymakers must be astute when setting the sanction. Is a violation to be punishable by a prison sentence or by imposition of a fine? If the penalty is to be incarceration, some thought needs to be given to the odds of the violator's being caught. If the odds are low, the prison term may need to be stiff to have any deterrent effect at all. If a fine is to be levied, as is often the case in economic regulation, another question must be asked: Will the fine be large enough to affect behavior? That is, what if paying the fine is cheaper than stopping the illegal behavior?

A major problem with binding rules is that they must be enforced; this normally means a sizable bureaucracy and a host of inspectors. Not only is this costly, but also the opportunity for abuse is present in the inspectorate. In addition, the very enactment of such edicts and erection of an enforcing bureaucracy creates an automatic adversary relationship between government and those being regulated. While not always undesirable, the atmosphere of conflict can lead to needlessly uncooperative behavior.

Public education is becoming an increasingly crucial public policy issue in the 1990s. Here, a security officer uses a hand-held metal detector to search for guns on students entering a New York City high school.

Structuring

Structuring refers to government actions that structure the relations between private parties. In many cases, structuring is done through such devices as licenses. For example, the broadcast industry is structured through the licensing powers of the Federal Communications Commission. For a variety of private parties (such as advertisers), subsequent transactions are therefore structured by government.

In other cases, a law will set the conditions under which two parties may conduct their transactions, often giving one party the right to bring a lawsuit if the other violates the law. For example, a federal law forbids discrimination by home mortgage lenders on the basis of race. If a lender breaks this law, the rejected applicant need not wait for the government to pursue the matter. She is empowered to bring a suit on her own. In this way, structuring can be linked to binding rules and used merely as a tactic to enforce the law.

Subsidies and Payments

The expenditure side of the budget sheet is a popular policy tool. If you want people to do something, pay them—a strategy employed throughout history. In 1862 the Homestead Act enticed people to settle the west by giving them the land on which they settled. In the same era, huge land subsidies helped build the transcontinental railroad.

Today, crop subsidies to farmers, payments to professors to conduct research, grants to school districts for a variety of programs, and subsidies to employers for job training are a staple of federal policy. One reason that these programs are popular among politicians is that the benefits are focused and the costs are dispersed. But the programs are also effective in that people usually feel more kindly toward government when it pays them to do something than when it compels them. Thus, compliance tends to be higher when payment is involved.

However, a subsidy program has one major drawback: the cost. Since this type of policy is usually distributive, there will be inevitable pressures to widen the scope of a program and keep benefits high. A constellation of beneficiaries, interest groups, and bureaucrats with jobs to protect is almost certain to grow up around the program. When budgets become tight, therefore, these programs are very difficult to cut or reform.

Many payments, such as those listed above, are direct and obvious, whereas others are more indirect. As an example of the latter, in the early days of commercial aviation the government provided contracts for air mail service at highly inflated rates. The goal was obviously to speed the development of commercially viable airlines. The Pell Grant program is another example of indirect payment. By providing aid to students in proportion to their financial need, the program enables many students to attend more expensive private colleges, indirectly channeling funds to these institutions. The goal here is to help maintain the diversity of American higher education.

In some cases, the subsidy is through the mechanism of a tax reduction. Those working parents who pay for child care receive a tax credit for a portion of the costs they incur. At the higher end of the income spectrum, the credit (a direct reduction in taxes) is 20 percent of the amount paid. Thus, if such a family pays $1,000 for child care during the year, the government in effect pays $200 of it, since the parents can subtract that amount from their taxes. Similarly, homeowners receive a deduction for the interest paid on home mortgages.[12] Thus, if someone pays $1,000 in interest in a year and is in a 28-percent tax bracket, the government in effect pays $280 of his housing cost. A large number of subsidies go to both individuals and businesses through similar manipulations of the tax code.[13]

Lastly, government sometimes compels people to participate in a "cross subsidy" program. That is, money is taken from one group and transferred to another. The major example is social security, in which, contrary to popular opinion, those now working support the presently retired.[14] Cross subsidies can bring forth intense opposition if the groups are static.[15] Social security, on the other hand, retains its popularity precisely because everyone hopes to join the beneficiary group.

Taxation

The major purpose of taxation is, of course, to raise money for the government's coffers. However, taxes have long been used to encourage or discourage certain activities.

The federal excise (or sales) tax on cigarettes was doubled in 1986 in an obvious attempt to discourage smoking. A rise in gasoline taxes has been proposed on several occasions as a way to cut our dependence on foreign oil by reducing consumption. Tariffs, that is, taxes on imports, are often manipulated to help American businesses.

Moral Suasion

To some degree, all policies involve moral suasion. If large numbers of people disobey a law, it cannot be enforced—a lesson clearly taught by the experience under prohibition. Any regulatory or tax law, for example, must depend on most people's voluntary compliance. Governments therefore both explicitly and tacitly urge citizens to obey and support the law.

In many other cases, though, government uses moral suasion not to encourage obedience to the law, but more on its own. This can be done either in conjunction with other programs or alone. The "Just Say No" campaign against drugs is a classic example of such an endeavor. Similar efforts to encourage the use of condoms and to urge people to stop smoking have been undertaken.

While these policies are relatively cheap, in the short run they are ordinarily only marginally effective. It is harder to say what their long-run effect is, though. If public attitudes are shifting, as they are towards smoking, government may be a significant voice in the chorus. Further, these campaigns, if long-lasting, may well shape the outlook of future generations. Thus, they should not be dismissed too hastily as merely "ineffectual propaganda."

In sum, those who formulate public policy have a variety of mechanisms at their disposal. All have certain costs and certain probabilities of success. The tool which will or should be chosen to accomplish a given task will depend not only on the nature of the task but on whose cooperation is needed to successfully carry out the policy. An ill-chosen instrument may well cause the entire policy to fail.

ENVIRONMENTAL POLICY AS AN ILLUSTRATION
Agenda-Setting

Although there has long been a conservation movement in the United States, modern environmental politics began in the mid-1960s.[16] The publication of three seminal books—Rachel Carson's *The Silent Spring,* Paul Ehrlich's *The Population Bomb,* and Barry Commoner's *The Closing Circle*—sparked widespread interest in environmental issues. Ecological ideas merged easily with the counterculture of that period, but they also spread remarkably quickly among the general population as well, helped no doubt by such dramatic events as the 1969 Santa Barbara oil spill. Earth Day, April 22, 1970, was a milestone in the growing environmental awareness of the public.

The exact dynamics of how the environmental movement spread from the college-educated elite to the general public are uncertain. However, the role of the media has surely been critical. Coverage of Earth Day 1970 was significant, and by the late 1980s the media barrage on all environmental issues was overwhelming. As noted in chapter 9, though, there is a reciprocal effect at work, as newspapers and news programs seek to cover stories which are of interest to their readers and viewers.

Even though there have been fluctuations, support for environmental issues has grown steadily through the years. In 1973, for example, 45 percent of Americans polled felt that we were spending too little on improving and protecting the environment; a decade later, that number was 54 percent, and by 1988 the number had grown to 62 percent.[17] In 1991, 78 percent of the public identified themselves as environmentalists, and 37 percent of those as strong environmentalists. As for policy, 57 percent reported in 1991 that they favored "immediate, drastic action" to tackle environmental problems, and another 31 percent wanted "some additional action"; only 8 percent expressed a desire to continue as we are.[18] Clearly, environmentalism has become a major feature of the societal agenda over the last twenty years.

Policy Response

Congress has responded to the rising chorus of environmental concern by moving the issue to the governmental agenda and by passing a number of new laws. The first, the National Environmental Protection Act of 1969 (NEPA), declared that it was continuing federal policy "to create and maintain conditions under which man and nature can exist in productive harmony," wording which is an obvious example of the type of symbolic goal-setting discussed earlier in this chapter. The actual provisions of the law (1) established the Council on Environmental Quality in the Executive Office of the President to collect data and advise the president on environmental matters, and (2) required that all federal agencies prepare an "environmental impact statement" (EIS) when contemplating new projects. The NEPA was soon followed by the Clean Air Act of 1970, which regulated the discharge of several known harmful pollutants. Two measures attacked water pollution: the Clean Water Act of 1972 dealt with toxic discharges into streams and rivers, and the Safe Drinking Water Act of 1974 began an effort to clean up groundwater contamination. In 1976, Congress passed the Resource Conservation and Recovery Act, which tried to come to grips with the problem of toxic waste disposal. All of these laws are clearly regulatory and rely heavily on the binding rules strategy; however, distributive policy and use of payments are not unknown. Some environmental laws provide grants to state and local governments, for example, and the pressure is always on to spread them widely, as one might expect.

Further, during this period, substantial acreage was added to the areas designated as national parks, wild and scenic rivers, and wilderness areas.

How much people use private automobiles versus public transportation is heavily influenced by several government policies: monies devoted to highway construction, taxes on gasoline, and fares and safety on public transit, for example.

This policy action does not fit neatly into the categories drawn up above. It is distributive in some ways, in that many states vie for the building of new parks, but it is also often redistributive between economic sectors. The tourism industry and businesses which equip outdoors activities will be helped, for instance, while the timber and mining industries may be harmed. It is also somewhat redistributive in that affluent urbanites gain recreational values at the expense of businesses (such as those involved with timber, again) and workers (such as loggers).[19]

Policy Formulation

As in all American policy-making, the best descriptive term for environmental policy-making is fragmentation. Part of the fragmentation results from the breadth of matters touched by environmental policy: clean air and water, toxic and nuclear waste disposal, and the protection of wildlife and wilderness areas, to name but the major ones. But equally deep-seated factors are the separation of powers, federalism, and overlapping policy domains within the legislative and executive branches.[20]

In Congress several different committees handle major environmental issues, and several more a variety of related concerns (such as transportation, public health, and nuclear weapons). In the Senate, the Environment and Public Works Committee has general oversight responsibilities for the environment and jurisdiction over air and water pollution, toxic substances, hazardous wastes, and ocean dumping. The Energy and Natural Resources Committee, meanwhile, handles national parks, public lands, and wilderness, in addition to energy policy. The Agriculture Committee devotes time to pesticides and soil conservation, among other items. On the House side, the Agriculture Committee has parallel jurisdiction with its Senate counterpart, while the Interior and Insular Affairs Committee handles public lands and forests, irrigation, and petroleum conservation. Concurrently, the Energy and Commerce Committee supervises solid and hazardous waste disposal, the transportation of hazardous materials, and nuclear facilities. Fisheries and aquatic wildlife fall under the Merchant Marine and Fisheries Committee.

A wide variety of interest groups are active in environmental policy. In most policy disputes, a coalition of environmental groups squares off against business interests. However, there are numerous complications and caveats to this simple picture.

Business interests often disagree among themselves about pollution control and other issues. For example, those who have complied with a law sometimes do not wish to see it weakened to give their laggard competitors an advantage. Further, some businesses, such as the manufacturers of pollution control equipment or less damaging pesticides, may favor stronger regulations.

On the other side, the environmental movement is hardly monolithic. Although the major organizations, collectively known as the Group of Ten,[21] often work together, they sometimes take opposing positions, and some environmental groups are not even affiliated with this umbrella organization.[22] Most environmental activists are drawn from the upper middle classes, well-to-do people who have the leisure and income to enjoy the country's beauty and who fear its despoliation. Nonetheless, they sometimes disagree among themselves about how wilderness areas should be preserved or the effectiveness of various environmental measures. Furthermore, some powerful environmental organizations, particularly the National Wildlife Federation, are composed mainly of sportsmen, whose interest in keeping large areas open to hunting and fishing comes into conflict with those wanting to preserve pure wilderness areas.

Presidential leadership is a major factor in environmental policymaking. President Nixon seized the initiative when he created the Environmental Protection Agency by executive order,[23] signed the National Environmental Protection Act, and proclaimed the 1970s the environmental decade. Presidents Ford and Carter continued to support environmental policy development, but energy crises and economic stagnation often conflicted with their environmental goals. When Ronald Reagan entered the White House in 1981, he had an altogether different environmental agenda. Convinced that environmentalists were a fringe group in American society and that environmental regulations were a heavy contributing factor to the country's economic difficulties, he aggressively sought to free business from this "burden."[24] To carry out this objective, he appointed outspoken foes of environmentalism to head the major agen-

The Environmental Protection Agency is charged with overseeing toxic waste dumps.

cies, particularly the EPA and the Interior Department. In addition, budgets for environmental agencies were slashed dramatically whenever possible. The Council on Environmental Quality, for instance, had its budget cut 85 percent.[25] Lastly, Reagan insisted that all environmental regulations be subjected to cost-benefit analysis. Those which could not be justified by showing a margin of benefits over costs were to be cancelled. The problem is that there is an inherent difficulty in determining the long-term benefits which a measure may bring about (such as improved health for future generations), while the costs are immediately evident.

Although the Reagan administration clearly affected environmental policy, it was stymied in its attempt to reverse course completely, because of the separation of powers and divided party control of government. The Democratic-controlled House forcefully fought the changes in the laws that the administration wanted, and softened its budget-slicing as well. Congress even managed to favorably amend several environmental laws, in spite of the administration's staunch opposition. The Resource Conservation and Recovery Act was strengthened in 1984, for instance, as were the Safe Drinking Water Act in 1986 and the Clean Water Act in 1987. Nor did the administration win the battle for public opinion. Membership in virtually all environmental organizations increased significantly during Reagan's tenure, and polls continued to show the public at odds with the president in this area. In May of 1983, 50 percent of those polled said they disapproved of Reagan's handling of the environment, while only 33 percent approved.[26] In December 1984, right after Reagan had buried Walter Mondale in the previous month's election, a 61-percent to 28-

percent majority of Americans said that if forced to choose between economic growth and environmental protection, they would opt for the latter.[27] Similar large majorities continued to support specific environmental laws and most wanted to spend more on environmental enforcement, not less.

When Reagan exited from office, he left a double legacy. He had undeniably wounded some aspects of environmental policy; however, his belligerence may actually have strengthened the environmental movement. The Bush administration compiled a more mixed record. During the 1988 campaign, Bush painted himself as an environmentalist, and some of his early appointees won praise in environmental quarters. Other administration figures were less warmly received by environmentalists, though, and no major legislative initiatives were proposed. By 1992, Bush was at odds with environmentalists, as he took an ambivalent stance on the Clean Air Act and seemed to side with timber and mining companies on western land use matters. The most disappointing position to environmental groups, however, was the administration's lukewarm stance toward the United Nations–sponsored Earth Summit in Rio de Janeiro. The president refused to sign the important Biodiversity Treaty supported by most nations, citing fears that it would hurt the American economy. A hastily-pieced-together program to save tropical rain forests was dismissed by environmentalists as inadequate and a mere ploy to divert attention from the Earth Summit controversy. Thus, while the noisy animosity of the Reagan years subsided, the environmental movement began to have serious doubts about the Bush administration's commitment to environmental issues.

Implementation

Like policy formulation, implementation of environmental policy is characterized by fragmentation. The major executive entity charged with implementing environmental laws is the Environmental Protection Agency. However, the EPA shares implementation with the Interior Department (public lands and national parks, endangered species, wildlife, and wilderness areas); the Department of Transportation (pipeline safety, transport of hazardous materials); the Department of Commerce (weather research, marine resources); the Department of Agriculture (soil conservation and national forests); and the Nuclear Regulatory Commission (licensing and safety regulation of nuclear power plants). In addition, the Council on Environmental Quality, located in the Executive Office of the President, assesses the quality of the nation's environment.

Many of the laws administered by the EPA as well as the other agencies are quite vague and subject to varying interpretations. This circumstance has been the result not only of the usual compromises engineered in Congress, but also of the fact that when these acts were passed, the scientific knowledge was seldom available to allow more specificity. For example, the Toxic Substances Control Act of 1976 (TSCA) ordered the

BOX 12-1

The Citizen and the Environment: The Necessity and the Limits of Public Authority

If POLLUTION is a problem, to what extent is it necessarily a public problem, calling for political action? If public values change and clean air, for instance, assumes a higher priority in people's preferences, will not that fact force automobile makers to produce cars with cleaner emissions, without the need for government action?

This puzzle is often referred to as the "problem of the commons." Imagine a village which has an adjacent pasture on which everyone has the right to graze livestock. It is in everyone's interest that the grazing be limited, so that the resource will both be available to all and remain a viable pasture. Overgrazing could deplete the pasture, making everyone worse off. However, from the "rational" perspective of any one individual, there is no economic incentive for him to limit his own stock's grazing. Similarly, when the "commons"

is the air above a large city, why should any one driver trouble herself to buy a pollution-free automobile, if there is no guarantee that everyone else will?

To forestall abuse of the pasture, there must be some way to limit grazing. In a small village, informal social sanctions may suffice to accomplish this, although occasionally even there penalties may have to be enforced. In a large, impersonal city, informal social pressures are simply impractical for the most part. To accomplish the collective good of clean air, some type of public regulation will be necessary. Problems of the commons

are therefore by their very nature political issues, and clearly many environmental problems fit this category. From the perspective of individualist democrats, therefore, beginning with the assumption that people act in their own self-interest, political action is necessary if environmental problems are to be seriously attacked.

Yet, for the civic democrat, the problem of the commons extends beyond this purely economic logic. The commons—the pasture or the country we inhabit—unavoidably takes on a moral character. It becomes intimately connected with our definition of the community and the nature of its social order. The physical attributes of this land are more than mere economic commodities. Thus, public action is necessary, since the environment, the commons, is an aspect of the community itself.

As a practical matter,

EPA to consider the following factors when deciding whether to limit exposure to such substances, but it gave no guidance on how much weight should be given to each:

The type of effect (chronic or acute, reversible or irreversible); degree of risk; characteristics and number of humans, plants, and animals, or ecosystems, at

BOX 12-1

however, there are limits to public action, here as elsewhere. Consider the problem of throwing trash on the highway or the sidewalk. Individuals find it more convenient to throw candy wrappers or beer cans down than to search for a trash bin. Thus, the commons is damaged. Presumably, public authority could be harnessed to control this behavior. An enormous body of trash police could be employed to patrol every highway, sidewalk, subway, and park in the land. Or, extreme penalties (say, ten years in prison) could be imposed for littering and rigidly enforced on those caught, a move which would probably have a decided deterrent effect. Who would want to live in such a society, though?

In reality, only a sense of personal responsibility and private virtue, as stressed by civic democrats, will keep public areas free of litter. Only when citizens regulate themselves is community life in a free society truly possible. Otherwise, either chaos reigns—trash is thrown about freely—or an oppressive government must be created—a heavy-handed trash police.

Or, circle back to the initial question about the consumer forcing the production of pollution-free automobiles. Changing public values are not unimportant; they do cause business firms to respond. Businesses now focus heavily on their environmental awareness. Of course, much of the recent wave of "green" advertising is phony. Nonetheless, some practices are changing, as pressure from environmentally conscious consumers is felt. For example, commercial fisherman have changed the types of nets they use for tuna-catching to ones less likely to ensnare dolphins.

The use of recycled paper and containers is much more common than it was a few years ago.

In short, securing a clean environment requires a combination of the public and the private. Environmentally concerned citizenship, therefore, particularly for civic democrats, mandates action on two fronts simultaneously. One is the building of respect and support for public authority, not only because public policy is the only feasible way to solve the problem of the commons (a concept which enjoys the support of individualist democrats as well), but also because there is an ethical dimension to the commons; the other is the encouragement, teaching, and practice of private virtue—not only, again, because this produces collectively rational results, but also because it is a key component of civic life in a democracy.

risk; amount of knowledge about the effects; available or alternative substances and their expected effects; magnitude of the social and economic costs and benefits of possible control actions; and appropriateness and effectiveness of TSCA as a legal instrument for controlling the risk.[28]

However desirable from a practical view, the vagueness of environmental laws has often left the EPA adrift, plagued by a deep confusion and

T A B L E   12–1

Major Statutes Administered by the Environmental Protection Agency

Asbestos Hazard Emergency Response Act
Clean Air Act
Clean Water Act
Comprehensive Environmental Response, Compensation, and Liability Act
Emergency Planning and Community Right-to-Know Act
Federal Insecticide, Fungicide, and Rodenticide Act
Marine Protection Research and Sanctuaries Act
Resource Conservation and Recovery Act
Safe Drinking Water Act
Toxic Substances Control Act

uncertainty, and thus open to political crossfire. It simply lacks the resources and knowledge to accomplish the idealistic goals often laid out in statutes, making many environmental laws more statements of principle than guides to actual policy implementation. Further, interest groups continually pressure the EPA to adopt strong or lax regulations; then, the regulations which are eventually issued often end up in court.

Over the years, the courts have also become key players in the implementation process.[29] Several statutes have explicitly allowed citizens to file suits challenging the implementing agency; usually, these are interest group suits. In other cases, the courts have seized on a particular provision of a law and allowed groups to bring suits regarding this provision. For instance, as noted above, the NEPA required all government agencies to prepare environmental impact statements before undertaking any actions. Although the drafters of the law apparently thought this rather inconsequential, interest groups quickly learned that the courts would entertain suits challenging the adequacy of the statements, and thus significant projects such as dams or power plants could be held up while new and more detailed EISs were prepared. In short, the influence of the courts in the implementation of environmental policies has been far from negligible.

Evaluation

Three types of evaluation have occurred in environmental policy. First, there has been a significant accumulation of scientific knowledge. We know far more than we knew twenty years ago about which substances cause environmental degradation or pose threats to human health; how to measure them; and how to control them.

Second, we are still evaluating matters of institutional and policy design.[30] For example, many now feel that the regulation of certain pollutants by medium (water, air, ground) is less effective than a "multimedia" approach that would focus on the type of chemical being discharged. This would still be regulatory policy, and binding rules would remain the tool of enforcement, but the substance of the rules would change. As another example, a sustained discussion has gone on for some time concerning the use of market incentives rather than binding rules to control some types of industrial air and water pollution. Long opposed by environmentalists, market incentives are now being considered as perhaps more workable and effective, if they are carefully structured. In this case, regulatory policy would remain in place, but with a different enforcement tactic. Advocates of market incentives usually propose either imposing a tax on pollutants or having government sell a "license" to discharge certain pollutants (which could be bought and sold by businesses). Businesses would then have an incentive to reduce, but perhaps not eliminate, pollution. Thus, taxes or structuring would be enlisted to enforce regulatory policy. Naturally, all these questions are not only technical but also political.

Finally, we are discovering that the more we think in ecological terms, the more we discover that we did not even know. The number of toxic substances is far greater than it was thought to be a generation ago, and we have discovered that many substances that are relatively harmless when standing alone can be deadly when combined with other chemicals. Many experts refer to these new problems as "second-generation" environmental problems, and believe that they will be much more difficult to solve than those of the first generation. In fact, the frontiers of ecological research now lie at "third-generation" problems, such as the deterioration of the ozone layer and the greenhouse effect—matters which are truly staggering in their implications.

With these second- and third-generation problems emerging, though, we have come full circle. The next critical step, already well advanced in the case of the second-generation problems, is for them to get on the political agenda. The process will then begin all over again.

Policy Linkage

Environmental policy illustrates two final points about public policy. The first is that no policy problem exists in isolation from others.

Energy policy is clearly linked with environmental policy, for example. Many issues related to energy policy—such as the kinds of fuels (oil, coal, etc.) which are to be extracted from the earth, the methods of extraction (strip mining or not), and the location of mines or wells (in national parks?)—are inextricably linked to issues of environmental policy. The retrieval of oil from the Alaska wilderness will lower gasoline prices, but may also do irrevocable harm to wildlife habitats. The construction of hydroelectric dams poses a host of dangers to the ecosphere. The burning of coal to generate electricity leads to air pollution; nuclear plants generate waste. So-called "clean" energy alternatives (such as solar energy) are expensive and problematical.

General economic policy is also closely linked to environmental policy. However, the connections between environmental laws and the operation of the economy are complex and only dimly understood. Environmental

(text continued on page 410)

Environmental Policy-Making in Britain

POLLUTION AND OTHER environmental problems are common to all industrialized countries. Having become industrialized first, Britain has a longer experience with these problems than does any other country.[1] Although environmental legislation in Britain can be traced back to 1273, when Edward I banned the burning of certain types of coal as a public health measure, the first major parliamentary act came in 1873, when the Alkali Inspectorate was created. Several subsequent laws (1881, 1892, and 1906) broadened the number of plants to be inspected and added additional chemicals to the forbidden list.

In the 1950s, there was another round of environmental legislation in Britain. London had long been plagued by its famous fogs, which were in reality smoke from the coal used to heat most homes and businesses. Beginning on December 5, 1952, a weather inversion caused a terrible four-day fog. Up to four thousand deaths were attributed to it. A Commission of Inquiry proposed a wide-ranging bill, which passed Parliament as the Clean Air Act of 1956. Its major provision banned coal furnaces, but at the same time it provided grants to individuals and businesses for the purchase of new heating equipment. In the wake of this act, several other landmark environmental laws were also enacted.

In the 1960s and 1970s, Britain experienced a resurgence of its environmental movement. In response, a cabinet-level Department of the Environment was created in 1970 (which, like the EPA, merely gathered several existing agencies under one roof), and Parliament passed a number of pollution control acts. However, the content of these laws and the manner in which they are implemented are both quite different from those of comparable laws in the United States.

The statutes tend to be very vague, even when compared to ours. They do not specify the pollutants to be banned, nor do they set elaborate timetables. Rather, they declare that the public health is endangered by various conditions, and turn over broad authority to regulatory agencies.

The regulatory agencies then set up what are called "consultative bodies." These are panels of civil servants and people from the businesses to be affected by the regulations; sometimes environmental groups are also represented, but not always. The goal of the consultative bodies is to work out an anti-pollution plan for each individual plant. The regulators are willing to allow some pollution, if the firm will make a good-faith effort to reduce emissions. The head of the Department of the Environment explained its approach this way:

> Except in clearly defined cases, we believe it is better to maintain gradual progress in improving the environment in light of local circumstances and

needs than to operate through the formation of rigid national emission standards which may be in particular circumstances either unnecessarily harsh or insufficiently restrictive.[2]

After the agreements are drawn up, the regulatory agencies rely almost entirely on the voluntary compliance of business. Fines are levied very rarely (the maximum amounts are usually trivial anyway), and court cases are unknown. Thus, throughout the implementation stage, there is an absence of the adversarial tone that so clearly characterizes American efforts. In short, Parliament sets the broad guidelines, public agencies and businesses negotiate the details, and firms then carry out what they have promised.

According to most studies, this approach has been about as effective as ours. British industries tend to follow through on their promises, and the state of the environment has definitely improved. The air in London is cleaner than that in most of the world's urban areas; Britain's rivers, which were once open sewers, are remarkably pollution-free; and the dumping of toxic waste is pretty much under control. Everyone admits that there is still a long way to go, but conditions are certainly no worse in Britain than they are elsewhere.

What accounts for this difference in approach? There are at least four reasons. First, British civil servants, like those in France, command immense respect. Neither British businesspeople nor the public castigate or demean civil servants the way Americans do regularly. Second, there is in Britain little history of fear or suspicion of industry.[3] A deep strain in the American psyche is the conviction that business will get away with whatever it can, making severe regulation necessary. Third, British business has long had a cooperative but deferential relation to public authority. Business interests do not consider government "the enemy" to be fought at every turn. In Britain, the practice of consultation and cooperation, but with public officials always having the last word, has a long tradition. Lastly, the use of private organizations to carry out public policy is not uncommon in Britain, and hardly novel. Remember, for example, that the earliest American colonies were settled as private ventures. Thus, the line between public and private is more blurred than it is in the United States. Incidentally, the government also provides funding for several of the major environmental organizations—up to half, in some cases.

Even though we have none of these elements in our political culture, is there anything to be learned from the British approach that might be useful to us?

---

[1] The material in this box draws on David Vogel, *National Styles of Regulation: Environmental Policy in Great Britain and the United States* (Ithaca, N.Y.: Cornell University Press, 1986).

[2] Vogel, *National Styles,* 76.

[3] The political left in Britain, it is true, has long harbored a strong hostility toward wealthy business owners, but it has been more directed at individuals than at the business corporations themselves. Where we have a history of "trust-busting," for example, British reformers have sought simply to put another set of people in charge of running huge corporations.

controls on certain industries may well cause the prices of their products to rise; this, of course, could lead to decreased production and the loss of jobs. However, the new businesses and jobs created by environmental regulations may more than offset that loss. Seldom, though, will the same people both suffer the loss and enjoy the gain. Environmental controls can also make American products less competitive internationally, at least in the short run, if other countries are less demanding towards their industries. A drop in competitiveness may lead to job loss for American employees, as firms shift their plants to those other (typically less developed) countries.

A variety of other policies are also linked to environmental affairs. Health is one obvious example; transportation is another. Housing prices are affected by the amount of timber that is cut from national forests, and land use planners feel the effect of decisions on waste site locations. In fact, few public policies are untouched in some fashion by environmental policy.

The International Dimension

Finally, environmental policy nicely illustrates the continuing internationalization of political life.[31] We tend to think that political systems, both our own and others, exist in isolation, but that has never been true, and is now farther from the truth than ever.

Some environmental problems directly spill over national boundaries, just as acid rain composed of toxins emitted from industries in our midwest drifts into Canada. In other cases, materials dumped into international waters are carried to foreign shores.

President Bush speaking at the 1992 World Environmental Conference in Rio de Janeiro.

But the most graphic examples of international environmental problems are the greenhouse effect and the depletion of the ozone layer. These calamities know no national boundaries and are clearly beyond the control of any one nation. Only concerted international action can even begin to address them, and so far the record is only mildly encouraging. The Earth Summit of 1992, sponsored by the United Nations in Rio de Janeiro, Brazil, was both a promising step and a graphic example of the multitude of difficulties inherent in international environmentalism.

SUMMARY

Public policy is the ultimate goal of political activity. People want government to perform or refrain from certain tasks. For analytical purposes, it is useful to divide the study of policy into process and substance, or the way policy is made and the content of specific policies.

Agenda-setting, bringing a problem to the attention of those in government, is the first step in the policy-making process. Policy formulation is the next part of the chain, and it ends when a policy is adopted. As bureaucracies and courts then grapple with implementation, evaluations are made and fed back to those in policy-making positions: high executive officials and legislators. Inevitably, policies are modified or perhaps terminated, and new problems are placed on the political agenda.

Policies can be classified in several ways, but breaking them down by the kinds of action government takes provides four useful categories. Distributive policies are especially popular with the public and Congress, since benefits, particularly money, are given to people or organizations. When governments forbid some activity, they are engaging in regulatory policy. Interest groups are especially active when regulatory policies are pursued. Redistributive policy is very controversial and often triggers ideological debate. Symbolic policy has several uses, and its importance should not be ignored.

Policymakers have several tools to employ when seeking their goals. Binding rules; structuring of transactions; subsidies and payments; taxation; and moral suasion can be used either singly or in some combination.

Environmental policy is an apt illustration of the general features of American domestic policy. It got on the political agenda in the late 1960s, through elite agitation and the spread of environmental ideas to the general public. Congress and the president responded with several significant laws and executive actions. As it became a regular part of governmental activity, environmental policy formulation took on the fragmented character of other domestic policies. Several congressional committees have responsibility for environmental affairs. They are all continually monitored and lobbied by business and environmental interest groups, but even within each coalition, goals and strategies sometimes diverge. The president and leading executive appointees, especially the secretary of the interior and the head of the Environmental Protection Agency, also play important roles.

Implementation is as fragmented as policy formulation, with responsibilities scattered throughout government. Further, the courts have assumed a vital role in implementing several environmental policies. Evaluations have continued on both the scientific and the policy design fronts. We have much more scientific knowledge than we had formerly, and policies are often modified accordingly. A growing debate is occurring over how best to attack environmental problems; one issue is whether more reliance should be placed on market incentives. The growing ecological consciousness has led us to uncover truly monumental problems, a "third" generation of environmental issues. All of these evaluations are penetrating the political agenda, although in no rational or coherent form.

Environmental policy illustrates the complexity of public policy. No policy area stands alone; environmental policy is linked to energy, economic, health, transportation, and housing policies, to name only a few. Furthermore, there is a clear international dimension to environmental policy, in part because some pollutants simply cross national boundaries, but in greater part because the looming catastrophes which could be caused by the greenhouse effect or ozone depletion truly threaten the entire planet.

ENDNOTES

1. Randall B. Ripley and Grace A. Franklin, *Congress, The Bureaucracy, and Public Policy,* 4th ed. (Chicago: Dorsey Press, 1987), 1. A brief overview of the field of policy studies is Charles O. Jones, *An Introduction to the Study of Public Policy,* 3d ed. (Monterey, Calif.: Brooks/Cole, 1984).

2. For an analysis of how foreign policy is made, see the essays in Thomas Mann, ed., *A Question of Balance: The President, The Congress, and Foreign Policy* (Washington: Brookings, 1990). A highly readable overview of recent American foreign policy history which weaves in the way decisions are made is John Spanier, *American Foreign Policy Since World War II,* 12th ed. (Washington: Congressional Quarterly Press, 1991).

3. On agenda-setting see Roger Cobb and Charles Elder, *Participation and American Politics: The Dynamics of Agenda-Setting,* 2d ed. (Baltimore: Johns Hopkins University Press, 1983); John Kingdon, *Agendas, Alternatives, and Public Policies* (Boston: Little, Brown, 1984); and Nelson Polsby, *Political Innovation in America: The Politics of Policy Initiation* (New Haven, Conn.: Yale University Press, 1984).

4. For an excellent discussion of how this can work, see Peter Bachrach and Morton Baratz, *Poverty and Power* (New York: Oxford University Press, 1970).

5. See Ripley and Franklin, *Congress, the Bureaucracy, and Public Policy,* 6–10 and throughout.

6. See Paul Culhane, *Public Lands Politics: Interest Group Influence on the Forest Service and the Bureau of Land Management* (Baltimore: Johns Hopkins University Press, 1981).

7. An entertaining and enlightening analysis of implementation is Jeffrey Pressman and Aaron Wildavsky, *Implementation* (Berkeley: University of California Press, 1973).

8. This scheme is a modified version of one made famous by Theodore Lowi. See his *The End of Liberalism,* 2d ed. (New York: Norton, 1979).

9. In fact, sometimes government programs may shift wealth from the less well-off to the more affluent. In some ways the federal tax system does this, particularly through the changes adopted during the 1980s. See Robert S. McIntyre, "The Reagan Legacy," *The New Republic,* September 30, 1991, 11–13.

10. See Murray Edelman, *The Symbolic Uses of Politics* (Urbana: University of Illinois Press, 1964).

11. The Tax Reform Act of 1986 is lucidly discussed in Jeffrey Birnbaum and Alan Murray, *Showdown at Gucci Gulch* (New York: Random House, 1987).

12. A deduction is a reduction in one's taxable income before the tax is figured. A tax credit, as pointed out, is a reduction in the actual tax bill.

13. We would be remiss if mention was not also made of the indirect subsidies given to charitable institutions through the same method. The federal income tax allows (subject to certain limitations) a deduction to be taken for charitable donations. Thus, if a person who is in a 28-percent marginal tax bracket makes a $100 contribution to a church, the United Way, or a college, it will cost him only $72. Because everyone else's taxes must be raised to make up the loss, the institution is in effect receiving a subsidy from the government. You might think about how the class structure is affected by this provision, considering that giving patterns and amounts given vary according to income bracket.

14. See Paul Light, *Artful Work: The Politics of Social Security Reform* (New York: Random House, 1985).

15. In 1989, Congress, with the support of the American Association of Retired Persons, amended the Medicare program to provide for a cross subsidy by rather well-off elderly people of those who were less well-off. The ensuing outcry throughout the country (the chair of the Ways and Means Committee was even jostled by a cane-waving mob) led Congress to repeal the law. See *Los Angeles Times,* November 22, 1989, 1.

16. For an overview, see Samuel P. Hays, *Beauty, Health, and Permanence: Environmental Politics in the United States, 1955–1985* (New York: Cambridge University Press, 1987).

17. Cited in Robert Cameron Mitchell, "Public Opinion and the Green Lobby: Poised for the 1990s?" in Norman Vig and Michael Kraft, eds., *Environmental Policy in the 1990s* (Washington: Congressional Quarterly Press, 1990), 87.

18. *The Gallup Poll Monthly,* April 1991, 10.

19. See the discussion of federal land use policies in Phillip Davis, "Cry for Preservation, Recreation Changing Public Land Policy," *Congressional Quarterly Weekly Report,* August 13, 1991, 2145–52.

20. We are confining the discussion here to federal environmental policy. The states, of course, have their own set of policies, further complicating and fragmenting the picture.

21. The Group of Ten includes The Environmental Defense Fund, Friends of the Earth, the Izaak Walton League, the National Audubon Society, the National Parks and Conservation Society, the National Wildlife Federation, the Natural Resources Defense Council, the Sierra Club, the Wilderness Society, and the Environmental Policy Institute.

22. Notable among these are the "ecowarriors" associated with Earth-First! See Dave Foreman, *Confessions of an Eco-Warrior* (New York: Harmony Books, 1991) for a criticism of the Group of Ten.

23. For those who recall the statement in chapter 7 that only Congress can create a new executive department: Congress has from time to time given the president statutory authority to reorganize existing agencies. Nixon gathered together several programs already in place and simply regrouped them to form the EPA. For a history and critique see Marc Landy, *et al., The Environmental Protection Agency: Asking the Wrong Questions* (New York: Oxford University Press, 1990).

24. For a summary of the Reagan years, see Norman Vig, "Presidential Leadership: From Reagan to the Bush Administration," in Vig and Kraft, *Environmental Policy.*

25. Norman Vig and Michael Kraft, "Conclusion: Toward a New Environmental Agenda" in Vig and Kraft, *Environmental Policy,* 379.

26. Gallup Poll, May 12, 1983.

27. Dennis Gilbert, "Environment," *Compendium of American Public Opinion* (New York: Facts on File Publications, 1988), 126.

28. Quoted in Walter Rosenbaum, *Environmental Politics and Policy,* 2d ed. (Washington: Congressional Quarterly Press, 1991), 15.

29. An excellent case study is R. Shep Melnick, *Regulation and the Courts: The Case of the Clean Air Act* (Washington: Brookings Institution, 1983). For more general coverage, see Lettie Wenner, *The Environmental Decade in Court* (Bloomington: Indiana University Press, 1982).

30. Many of the issues are ably discussed in the essays comprising Sheldon Kamieniecki, *et al., Controversies in Environmental Policy* (Albany: State University of New York Press, 1986).

31. See Lynton K. Caldwell, "International Environmental Politics: America's Response to Global Imperatives," in Vig and Kraft, *Environmental Policy.*

···

FURTHER READING

1. Elder, Charles. *The Political Uses of Symbols.* New York: Longmans, 1983.

2. Hood, Christopher. *The Tools of Government.* Chatham, N.J.: Chatham House, 1986.

3. Jones, Charles O. *An Introduction to the Study of Public Policy.* 3d ed. Monterey, Calif.: Brooks/Cole, 1984.

4. Lowi, Theodore. *The End of Liberalism.* 2d ed. New York: Norton, 1979.

5. Milbrath, Lester. *Envisioning a Sustainable Society.* Albany: State University of New York Press, 1989.

6. Reagan, Michael. *Regulation: The Politics of Policy.* Boston: Little, Brown, 1987.

7. Ripley, Randall and Grace Franklin. *Congress, the Bureaucracy, and Public Policy.* 4th ed. Chicago: Dorsey, 1987.

8. Rosenbaum, Walter. *Environmental Politics and Policy.* 2d ed. Washington: Congressional Quarterly Press, 1991.

9. Tatalovich, Raymond and Byron Daynes, eds. *Social Regulatory Policy: Moral Controversies in American Politics.* Boulder, Colo.: Westview, 1988.

10. Vig, Norman and Michael Kraft, eds. *Environmental Policy in the 1990s.* Washington: Congressional Quarterly Press, 1990.

THIRTEEN

THE ELECTION OF 1992

ALL PRESIDENTIAL ELECTIONS are unique to some degree; however, the election of 1992 has no parallel, chiefly because of Ross Perot's curious and unusual venture into the race. At least two important questions are raised by Perot's candidacy. Will other independents with the financial means step forward in the future to run campaigns completely detached from the political parties, or was this merely an aberration? Will Perot himself, or the movement he galvanized, be a continuing factor in American politics?

But Perot was only a part of the story of this election. While the Democrats broke the Republicans' twelve-year hold on the White House, it remains to be seen whether this will usher in a sixth party system (see chapter 10), or merely be an interesting deviation from regular Republican victories. In addition, turnout rose for the first time in thirty years. Does this signify renewed citizen interest in politics, or will voting rates soon sink once again? Also, during the campaign, the candidates turned to a previously little-used media format, the talk show. Will this become a permanent part of campaign strategy?

Finally, a veritable tidal wave of anti-incumbent anger and frustration was tapped by pollsters before the election. Congressional incumbents, however, were not thrown out wholesale. Nonetheless, there certainly will be a large number of new—and different kinds of—faces in the 103rd Congress. Moreover, everywhere term limits for elected officials was on the ballot, it passed handily.

Bill Clinton's trek to the presidency formally began with an announcement of his candidacy for the Democratic nomination on October 3, 1991. Before he became president-elect a year and a month later, he had to navigate the Democratic primaries, rally his party at its convention, face an incumbent president in a grueling campaign, and win enough votes in enough states to give him a majority in the electoral college.

THE PATH TO THE NOMINATIONS: THE PRIMARIES

In the summer of 1991 the conventional wisdom among both Democrats and Republicans was that President George Bush was assured of a second term. He had skillfully led a popular and not very costly war against an acknowledged tyrant; his approval ratings stood at around 80 percent; the economy seemed reasonably healthy. This aura of invincibility led many of the Democratic party's "heavy hitters"—people such as New York governor Mario Cuomo, Senator Albert Gore of Tennessee, Representative Richard Gephardt of Missouri, and others—to bide their time and wait for

Opposite: *Hillary and Bill Clinton along with Al and Tipper Gore on the night of their election victory. The frequent joint campaign appearances by the candidates and the prominent roles played by their wives were innovations of the 1992 campaign.*

1996, when there would be no incumbent. Republican strategists, meanwhile, were concentrating their efforts on increasing the number of Republican members of Congress.

The first Democrat to announce his candidacy for the presidency was former Massachusetts senator Paul Tsongas, on April 30, 1991. A recovered cancer patient who billed himself as an economic conservative and a social liberal, he had almost no organization, little money, and hardly any name recognition outside his home state. At the time, few people took Tsongas seriously, writing him off as one of the many marginal candidates that usually announce early. By the fall, he had been joined by former California governor Jerry Brown (who had run for the nomination in 1988 as well); Virginia governor Douglas Wilder; Iowa senator Tom Harkin; Nebraska senator Bob Kerrey; and Arkansas governor Bill Clinton. None of the candidates, with the possible exception of Brown, was known nationally, nor was any the clear favorite.

Before long, Wilder dropped out. Iowa's caucuses, the usual site of the candidates' first test, were ceded by all the other hopefuls to Harkin. Thus, New Hampshire's primary shaped up as the first real test. In a once-prosperous state that was plagued by recession, Clinton's simple and focused message—"the forgotten middle class"—played well and gained him the early lead in the polls, despite his southern roots. Then, the Arkansas governor was the subject of a story in a supermarket tabloid which claimed he had had a twelve-year extra-marital affair with a former state employee; shortly afterward, he was buffeted by allegations that he had evaded the draft during the Vietnam war. Although Clinton stood up under the barrage, responding to the infidelity charge in a joint appearance with his wife on "60 Minutes" immediately after the Super Bowl game, his lead evaporated.

When New Hampshire's votes were counted, Tsongas had polled 33.2 percent, Clinton 24.7 percent, Kerrey 11.1 percent, Harkin 10.2 percent, and Brown 8.1 percent. With Clinton severely damaged and Bush's approval ratings beginning to slide, other prominent Democrats toyed with the idea of entering the race. The fact that the filing dates for many of the primaries had already passed kept them on the sidelines however. Meanwhile, Clinton labeled himself "the comeback kid," since he had climbed back up in the polls after the charges had been leveled and his popularity had fallen. Some observers in the press agreed, saying that 20 percent was an important threshold for him to break after all the allegations against him. Furthermore, the pundits attributed Tsongas' win in part to the fact that he was from New England.

Super Tuesday, March 10, was looming as the major test for all the candidates, but before that there were the Maine caucuses, the South Dakota primary, and seven states with primaries or caucuses on March 3. Kerrey won handily in his neighboring South Dakota, but Brown did surprisingly well in the Maine caucuses—wins which gave each of them temporary momentum. After the March 3 contests, the picture was even more scrambled: Clinton won the primary in Georgia (as the pundits said he had to do), Tsongas the one in Maryland, and Brown the one in

Colorado. Harkin led in the Minnesota and Idaho caucuses, while Tsongas emerged victorious in the caucuses held in Utah and Washington. Two days later Kerrey dropped out; four days after that, Harkin followed suit.

The heavily southern character of Super Tuesday worked to Bill Clinton's advantage, although it put him in a "must win" situation, since the media gurus expected him to do well. In any event, Clinton swept all eight southern primaries held that day, running well ahead of Tsongas in the delegate-rich states of Texas and Florida. The Massachusetts and Rhode Island primaries held on the same day were conceded to Tsongas.

One week later, the critical states of Illinois and Michigan were scheduled to conduct their primaries. Here, neither front-runner would be a regional favorite, nor would the still-standing Brown. Clinton polled over half the votes in both states, with Tsongas finishing second in Illinois with 26 percent, but Brown the runner-up in Michigan with the same number. On March 19 Tsongas withdrew; Brown, however, vowed to fight on with his populist message of "taking the country back." The press announced the race over and anointed Clinton the nominee.

On March 24, though, Brown surprised everyone by narrowly winning the Connecticut primary, with 37.2 percent of the vote to Clinton's 35.6 percent. The mainstream press line was now that "the perception is that Clinton has reached a make or break point in his campaign."[1] Had Clinton received another 1.7 percent of the Connecticut vote, however, it is unlikely that would have been the perception. Nonetheless, the battle now moved to New York, Wisconsin, and Kansas, all of which had primaries on April 7. Clinton regained momentum by scoring significant victories in all three; then on April 28 he buried Brown in Pennsylvania.

The following day Clinton went to Washington to meet congressional leaders. While the gatherings were polite enough, each side kept the other at arm's length. Sensing the rising tide of anti-incumbent feeling in the country, Clinton did not want to appear to be too close to the established Washington politicians. Senator Patrick Leahy of Vermont noted that "a presidential candidate wants a big congressional endorsement today about as much as one would from the Mafia."[2]

From then on, Brown was more of a nuisance to Clinton than a serious opponent. Only in vitally important California (with a June 2 primary) did Brown pose even a symbolic threat. There, Clinton won, if not resoundingly: 48 percent to Brown's 40 percent. Officially, Clinton now had enough delegates pledged to him to clinch the nomination. On June 3, he capped his victory by appearing on the Arsenio Hall Show, where he also demonstrated his ability as a saxophone player. Preparations for the New York City convention in one month's time were now under way.

Several noteworthy points emerge from this narrative. First, the primary system had forced candidates to make an early decision on whether to run. Had Bush's approval ratings in October of 1991 been what they were in March of 1992, undoubtedly several more Democrats would have tossed their hats into the ring. By March, though, so many of the filing deadlines were past that it was all but impossible to enter the race at that point.

Inner city and race issues were thrust into the 1992 campaign by three days of rioting in Los Angeles in late April. The riots were triggered by the jury acquittal of police officers accused of brutality against Rodney King.

Second, the early primaries served to narrow the field, as usual. Iowa was no contest this time, with a native in the race. New Hampshire now did the winnowing; when Kerrey, Harkin, and Brown failed to do well in the granite state, their campaigns were in deep trouble. Kerrey won a brief reprieve by winning South Dakota, but both he and Harkin were soon out of the race, as money and support dried up while press coverage painted them as losers. Brown saved himself by doing well in the Maine caucuses, then again by winning Colorado. But his campaign took on an increasingly quixotic nature. He took no large contributions, traveled modestly, and carefully picked the places in which he would fight. It was effectively a Clinton-Tsongas race between the day of the New Hampshire primary and the day Illinois and Michigan voted.

Third, Super Tuesday "worked" in 1992. It has been instituted by southern Democratic leaders in the hope that it would help a more moderate candidate, and perhaps one with a base in the south as well. However, had Clinton not emerged with at least a respectable showing in New Hampshire and survived the March 3 primaries, he might never have had the chance to prove his mettle in the south.

Fourth, the media played its accustomed role in analyzing the field and setting the intangible targets of who should finish where. As the sexual and draft-dodging stories swirled around Clinton's campaign, the media kept an almost daily scorecard of how he should do. After Clinton's appearance on "60 Minutes" brought mostly favorable press commentary, one observer was moved to write: "Consider that he went, in media world, from unknown to front-runner to de-Flowered goods to 'tested' survivor all in a matter of weeks . . . and before a single ballot was cast."[3]

But the appearance on "60 Minutes" foreshadowed an important development in the 1992 campaign. Candidates were discovering that they could use media formats which allowed them to speak directly to the people, without the intervening effect of media commentators. It was an important step, and one that would loom larger as the campaign wore on.

As a sitting president, George Bush was almost assured renomination by his party. However, there were factions in the Republican party that had never warmed to Bush, particularly the ardent conservatives, who felt he had let Ronald Reagan's policy initiatives dissipate. They were especially put off by his 1990 agreement to raise taxes, despite his pledge at the 1988 Republican convention not to do so—the famous "Read my lips; no new taxes" statement.[4]

Newspaper columnist and former Nixon and Reagan aide Patrick Buchanan announced that he was going to challenge Bush in the primaries. Few of his strongly conservative backers believed that Buchanan could actually win. However, they were frustrated with Bush, and saw Buchanan as a vehicle to express that frustration. At the very least, they felt, they could force the president to secure his base among the conservative wing of the party by adopting stances of which they approved.

Buchanan was a lively and caustic speaker who campaigned relentlessly in New Hampshire. On election day he got 37 percent of the vote, not enough to mortally wound the president but enough to be an embarrassment. Though he was nominally on the ballot in most primary states, Buchanan concentrated his fire next in Georgia. Before the Georgia vote, nearly one-third of the Republicans voted for an uncommitted slate in South Dakota (where Buchanan was not on the ballot), a clear blow to Bush. Bush won Georgia and all the subsequent primary states, but did so unimpressively, losing 25 to 35 percent in each outing. Polls seemed to show that many of the votes cast against Bush were not driven by ideology so much as they were being used as a mechanism for registering protests about the state of the economy and a disquiet over "leadership" in general.

Buchanan slogged on through California, finishing there with 27 percent, in spite of pressure from Republican regulars to cease his fire. His campaign, they argued, was merely weakening the president for the fall. After the California primary, Buchanan returned to New Hampshire to inform his supporters: "We go to Houston not to swear fealty to King George. We go to Houston to tell them that the little rebellion that started here has turned into a revolution."[5] He was lobbying the Bush people for a chance to speak to the convention during prime time, a request which they finally granted.

THE CONVENTIONS

Modern political conventions, as noted in chapter 10, are in most cases carefully staged to reach beyond the immediate audience to the larger

New York Governor Mario Cuomo nominating Governor Bill Clinton for president at the Democratic National Convention in July, 1992.

public. They are designed to showcase the candidate, to present an image of unity and competence, and to scour the opposition.

The Democratic convention, under the control of Clinton aides, largely accomplished these objectives. It included, for example, a quarter-hour film portraying Clinton's life, with an especially symbolic moment depicting a 1963 visit to the White House as part of a high school group, during which Clinton shook hands with John F. Kennedy. Governor Mario Cuomo of New York, the party's best orator and champion of the liberal wing, was drafted to give the nominating speech, a task at which he excelled. Further evoking the legendary Kennedy image, Clinton walked from his hotel to the convention floor the night he was nominated, as had Kennedy in 1960. The acceptance speech the following night was crafted in part to lay out Clinton's biography again—his early childhood difficulties, his affection for his mother, lessons learned from a grandfather, and so forth—in order to introduce or reintroduce him to the general public.

Clinton's backers used the platform to tout the themes they deemed important. They were determined to make it sound moderate in substance and in tone, and to distance the party from the ghosts of the recent Democratic past. Some of the traditional themes Democrats usually touch on, such as protecting the weak and vulnerable, were retained; but the platform also included a strong emphasis on economic growth, passages critical of bureaucracy, and a stress on individual responsibility—none of which had been incorporated in earlier years.

Dissidence was also kept to a minimum. Jerry Brown's supporters sported distracting signs on one night, but Clinton's people soon flooded the floor with signs of their own. Although Paul Tsongas, Jesse Jackson, and Jerry Brown were all allowed to speak, they were placed under tight restrictions. Brown, for example, was scheduled before prime time television coverage began. Both Tsongas and Jackson gave only lukewarm endorsements of Clinton during their presentations. However, many observers felt this may have actually helped the nominee since it distanced him from traditional Democratic factions.

The Republicans were, of course, blamed for most of the ills affecting the country. The keynote speeches were overshadowed by other efforts this time around, though. In a highly unorthodox move, several pro-choice Republican women were brought to the podium to criticize President Bush. Two AIDS victims addressed the convention, denouncing the administration's policies. Both candidates' acceptance speeches also heavily criticized Republican policies on a variety of fronts.

In one area, Clinton broke all tradition: the selection of his running mate. First, he made the announcement before the convention began, eliminating the one element of suspense at most modern conventions. But his most important departure from tradition was in the person he chose: Senator Albert Gore of Tennessee. Rather than reaching to another wing of the party or reaching to someone representing another bloc of voters (regional, ideological, demographic), Clinton chose someone from a neighboring state, someone who is a moderate like himself, and someone of the same age, race, and gender. There were some contrasts, to be sure: Gore had Washington experience, whereas Clinton had only held state office; Gore had served in the military during Vietnam; and Gore was more of a hawk in foreign policy than Clinton. In general, though, it was a sharp break with past practice, and something of a gamble.

Although there were some minor glitches, overall the convention went as planned and received good reviews. The party had succeeded this time in avoiding "the exciting, unruly street theater that had helped the Democrats lose five of the last six elections."[6] Instead, Clinton's supporters had redefined the party, "emphasizing youth, traditional family values and mainstream policy visions."[7] The "bounce" in the polls which candidates usually get following a convention was much greater than any others had been in the recent past.[8]

The Republican convention met in Houston under less happy circumstances. Even as the delegates gathered, party officials were expressing concern. Bush had taken another slide in the polls. Buchanan's challenge had pushed the president in a decidedly more conservative direction, but such actions had not really satisfied the more strident elements of the Republican right. At the same time, Bush's wooing of the right had undermined his position among party moderates. Others worried that the image of being weak and vacillating was hurting Bush more than the specific positions he took.

There was little need, of course, to showcase either candidate. Even so, a couple of gestures were made to create positive images of the candidates. Ronald Reagan was brought in to rally the faithful and praise Bush. A nostalgic film on Vice President Quayle mirrored the Democratic convention piece on Clinton.

Cameras panned the usual enthusiastic flag- and sign-waving crowds, but beneath the surface cracks were showing. The platform had provided the first scuffle even before the convention opened, as abortion rights advocates tried to water down its staunch pro-life position. In the drafting committee these advocates mustered only about 20 percent of the votes, but they threatened to take the issue to the floor. No floor fight emerged, though, and their protest was muffled; however, the news-starved media played up the division. Televangelist Pat Robertson (a candidate for president in 1988) and Pat Buchanan were allowed to address the convention; the first by his presence and the second by his words seemed to damage the party more than help it. Buchanan, speaking during prime time, endorsed Bush, but spent most of his time lashing out at those with whom he disagreed. The media gave such heavy coverage to the speech that it was often taken as a metaphor for the convention as a whole. Rightly or wrongly, the convention was painted as intolerant and mean-spirited.

In many ways, the Republican convention was similar to several the Democrats had held in the recent past. Every political convention faces an important dilemma. If the party has a candidate who is not enthusiastically backed by the loyal core of his own party, he is all but doomed. That is, if the base of the party is not energized, an appeal to the voters will seem flat. However, if the candidate preaches the message the party faithful want to hear with the fervor with which they want to hear it, she may alienate the larger electorate. Clinton's convention managers succeeded in keeping Brown and his supporters out of the limelight at their gathering, and made the party appear to be mainstream and moderate. But Buchanan was not Jerry Brown, and Bush's political position was not the same as Clinton's. With his approval ratings continuing to slide, Bush felt he needed the party's core behind him before he launched into the fall campaign. For its part, the "Buchanan brigade" wanted to keep the president on a short ideological leash.

What the Republicans spent plenty of time and effort doing was bashing Democrats. Speaker after speaker sought to link Clinton and Gore to big-spending liberals, the nuclear freeze movement, assorted Democratic constituency groups, and Jimmy Carter. But special invective was reserved for congressional Democrats, who were held to blame for virtually every problem in the republic. A constant floor chant of "clean the House" echoed after each shower of criticism.

Finally, the Republican convention played the one inevitable role of all such affairs when an incumbent president is seeking a second term. It served as the opening round of the chase for the 1996 nomination. Vice President Quayle, Jack Kemp, Senator Phil Gramm, Pat Buchanan, and several others were being watched and evaluated by delegates and the press with that thought in mind—all of which detracted from the effort of the current campaign.

In the end, Bush got a modest boost in the polls after the convention, but not what he and his campaign staff had hoped. The images of an intolerant party overlaid with simmering divisions and a president adrift were not overcome.

THE CAMPAIGNS

The presidential campaign of 1992 was truly unique in American history. Never before had someone from completely outside the political parties, indeed someone who had never held an elective or appointive office of any kind, launched a serious bid for the presidency. Texas billionaire H. Ross Perot announced February 20, 1992 on the "Larry King Live" talk show, aired on CNN, that if volunteers in all fifty states would put his name on the ballot, he would run for president.

Within days, his movement was off the ground, and polls showed him to have surprising strength among the public. By early June, Perot was virtually even with Bush and Clinton. Then, in July, with the fifty-state hurdle nearly complete, he abruptly dropped out of the race. The reason he gave at the time was that the Democratic party had "revitalized itself. They've done a brilliant job, in my opinion, of coming back."[9] On October 1, after hinting as much on several talk shows, he reentered the race. "I thought," he said, "that both political parties would address the problems that faced the nation. We gave them a chance. They didn't do it."[10]

Almost immediately, Perot was invited to participate in the three presidential debates, scheduled to begin ten days later. He dug into his own very deep pockets and spent about $60 million on his campaign. He made few public appearances, relying instead on half-hour television "infomercials," during which he sketched out his economic recovery plan. His major theme was deficit reduction, and the centerpiece of that a 50-cent-a-gallon gasoline tax. Then on October 25, Perot made another surprise move, this time on "60 Minutes." He claimed that he had withdrawn from the race in July because the Bush campaign was planning to disrupt his daughter's wedding, although he admitted he had no proof. Even with this bizarre twist, Perot's support remained at roughly one-fifth of the electorate.

While Perot's erratic behavior distracted the campaigns of the two major candidates, they concentrated primarily on their contest with each other. Clinton was determined from the first to avoid what he and his staff believed were Michael Dukakis' critical errors in 1988. First, Clinton felt that Dukakis had allowed the momentum from the convention to fade away by taking a break before beginning the campaign against the Republicans. Clinton and Gore, in contrast, left the convention immediately to begin an eight-state bus trip through the heartland.

Second, Clinton was convinced that Dukakis had let Bush define him, putting the Democrats on the defensive. Clinton adopted the economy, "change," and leadership as his central themes, and he reiterated them again and again. This kept Bush's record in front of the voters. However,

Clinton rounded out his campaign with other proposals, even if he was not overly specific about details. He spoke often of health care reform, education and training, "investment," and help for the middle class.

Moreover, Clinton could not be attacked in some of the areas that had wounded Dukakis in 1988. His support for capital punishment effectively neutralized the crime issue, for example. For good measure, he quoted from Scripture and the pledge of allegiance during his acceptance speech, establishing a link with voters to whom these texts have high symbolic importance.

The Republican campaign seemed limp from the start. Bush came across as hesitant and unsure of himself, and there was confusion at the top. James Baker, a widely heralded campaign wizard, had been brought over from the State Department, but he could not infuse the effort with the life it had shown in 1988. The president had proposed few domestic policy initiatives, and this was what seemed to be on the voters' minds. Whenever he did bring out some program idea, Bush was faced with the question of why it had not been sent to Congress before now.

Stymied on the domestic policy front, the Bush campaign experts turned elsewhere. First, they stressed the president's accomplishments in foreign policy—especially his presiding over the end of the Cold War—and they pointed to Clinton's lack of experience in this field. Second, the Republicans tried to link Clinton and Gore with several different supposed bogeymen: the Democratic-controlled Congress, the "tax and spend" heritage of the Democratic party, the "malaise" of the Carter years, and environmental extremists (calling Gore "ozone man").

But much of the campaign was devoted to attacking Clinton's character. Bush hammered away at Clinton's inconsistencies in the accounts he had given about his draft status, and argued that Clinton's organizing of anti-war demonstrations in a foreign country while a war was going on was wrong. However, most of this barrage seemed to fall on deaf ears. Polls continued to show that many voters were not influenced by the attacks. Perhaps the fact that similar allegations had been made during the primaries immunized Clinton against the charges. Or perhaps the voters really were ready for a discussion of substantive policies. Whatever the case, Bush's own behavior soon came into question: reports continued to surface that he had not been completely forthcoming about his role in the Iran-Contra affair, nor concerning his pre–Persian Gulf War dealings with Iraq. Naturally, this detracted from the sting of attacks against Clinton.

Finally, the Bush campaign resorted to serving up a litany of supposedly deplorable conditions in Arkansas and implying that Clinton was responsible for them. He was, they argued, the "failed governor of a small state."

Without question, the highlight of the fall campaign was the series of three presidential debates. Congress had established a bipartisan commission after the 1988 election to set up the debates for 1992. The commission chose a somewhat different format from that of 1988: one moderator would ask general questions with the answering candidate determined beforehand, and time allowed for responses from the other candidates. In 1988, there had been a panel of questioners. Bush, however, rejected the

Since the first Kennedy-Nixon debates of the 1960 campaign, presidential debates have become one of the highlights of the fall campaign. There were three presidential debates held in 1992 involving independent Ross Perot, Democrat Bill Clinton, and Republican President George Bush.

altered arrangements, and cancelled the first two debates. After intense negotiations between the campaigns and several compromises on the format, three debates were set up. The first, on October 11, drew a surprisingly large audience (81 million). Perot drove home the deficit problem, and proved to be witty and entertaining in the process. Most polls and observers concurred that while Perot was the most impressive, Clinton bettered Bush. The second and third debates drew increasingly large audiences, 90 million and 99 million respectively. Perot became repetitive, and while Bush seemed to improve each time, so did Clinton. In the second debate in particular, in which an audience of ordinary citizens asked the questions, Clinton performed well.

A significant development occurred during this campaign to which we have already alluded.[11] All the candidates resorted to media formats which allowed them to speak directly to the voters, bypassing the media commentators. The proliferation of radio and television talk shows, spawned by the narrowcasting discussed in chapter 9, provided ample opportunities for the candidates. Clinton was the first to employ the tactic, going on "60 Minutes" after the Super Bowl to answer the tabloid stories alleging extramarital affairs. Similarly, Perot made his campaign debut on "Larry King Live." Soon, he and Clinton were everywhere. Bush was slower to adapt to the newer approach, at first rejecting most invitations, including a chance to appear on MTV. As the campaign closed, though, he made the rounds, even going on MTV. The most thorough use of direct contact with the people was made by Perot. He purchased half-hour and one-hour slots on the major networks to air his views on the economic difficulties facing the nation. Most evaluations of this trend were similar to that of the

(text continued on page 430)

The British General Election of 1992

BRITISH NATIONAL ELECTIONS bear certain similarities to our own: the voters select the chief executive (the prime minister); the choice is more or less confined to the candidates of the two major parties; and the campaign focuses primarily on national issues. However, there are also several significant differences: the structure of the election system, the timing of elections, and the length of the campaign all vary markedly from American practices.

The only election to national office is the one for the 651-member House of Commons. (Although this is the lower of the two houses of Parliament, it dominates policy-making.) The country is divided into 651 constituencies, each of which elects one member. There are no runoffs: whoever gets the most votes on election day wins.

Technically, the House of Commons chooses the prime minister. (More technically, he or she is selected by the queen and the House gives its approval.) However, before the election, each political party selects a leader, who must be a member of the House of Commons. Each party, incidentally, chooses its leader internally; there are no primaries. Then, when the election results are known, the queen "sends for" the leader of the party with the most seats, and invites him or her to become prime minister. The only route to the prime ministership, therefore, is through Parliament. This makes a Perot-type independent candidacy impossible.

British elections do not occur at regular intervals, as ours do. By law, an election must be called within five years of the previous election, but it can fall at any time during that period. The choice of a date is entirely up to the prime minister. Once the decision is made, the election occurs in about four weeks. Campaigns are therefore much shorter than ours. The last election had been held in June of 1987; on March 11, 1992, Prime Minister John Major announced that an election would be held on April 9.

Once a date has been set, each party then selects its candidates for the 651 constituencies (there is no requirement that they live in the constituency), and publishes its "manifesto," the British equivalent of the party platform.

Individual candidates are strictly limited in the amount they may spend on the campaign, currently about fifteen thousand dollars. Television advertising is forbidden at the local level, but each candidate is entitled to one free mailout to every household in the constituency. The bulk of local campaigning is done by standing in public places greeting voters and by going door to door. At the national level, each party is given five free ten-minute television broadcasts. Further, there are no limits at the national level regarding what the parties may spend on general party advertising. In these ads, though, no one's name may be mentioned, not even those of the candidates for prime minister. In 1992, the Conservative party spent about $35 million on such advertising, while Labour spent about $12 million. The third party, the Liberal Democrats, spent about $6 million. Bush and Clinton, in contrast, each received about $55.2 million from the U.S. Treasury. In addition, significant amounts were contributed to both candidates by private individuals and groups.

The British style of campaigning at the national level is not radically different from the American. The leaders criss-cross the country, holding rallies, giving speeches, and granting interviews with the press. Debates among the parties' leaders are not ordinarily part of a campaign, although Labour proposed one this time. (At the constituency level, the candidates usually participate in several debates, however.)

Labour's central campaign theme in 1992 was that the Conservatives (who have been in power since 1979) had neglected public services, particularly the health service. The Conservatives mounted an attack on Labour's tax policies, and argued that Neil Kinnock, Labour's leader, would be an ineffective prime minister. Most polls showed Labour going into the final days of the campaign with a slight lead.

Election day brought a turnout of 77 percent, up from 75 percent in 1987, and the highest rate since 1974. The Conservatives won 42 percent of the popular vote, Labour 34 percent, the Liberal Democrats 18 percent, and other parties 6 percent. The distribution of the vote, though, gave the Conservatives 336 seats, Labour 271, the Liberal Democrats 20, and miscellaneous others 24. Because votes are counted by constituency, the winner of the popular vote usually obtains a larger percentage of seats in the House of Commons than they do of actual votes; this is similar to the effect of our electoral college. In Britain, 42 percent of the popular vote in the 1992 election yielded 52 percent of the seats; here, Clinton got 43 percent of the popular vote, but 69 percent of the electoral vote.

As in the U.S., loss of the election in Britain usually brings a period of soul-searching and finger-pointing for the losing party. Kinnock resigned as Labour leader immediately after the election, and the party replaced him with a veteran of the House of Commons, John Smith. Smith will now lead the opposition in Parliament and try to get the party ready for the next election, which may come at any time before April 9, 1997.

New York Times: Perot's "use of talk shows and the consistently high ratings his 30-minute and hourlong commercials received indicated a voter preference for direct communication from the candidate, and for substance over slash and burn attacks or mawkish advertisements."[12]

Finally, Perot's campaign did have one interesting parallel with most protest parties of the past. In chapter 10, we noted that these parties often raise issues the two major parties would rather ignore. In the 1992 campaign, Perot's continual harping on the budget deficit fit this pattern. Neither Bush nor Clinton really wanted to say much about it, except in the most general way, but Perot's attacks kept the matter squarely before the public. Clinton even thanked him during one of the debates for his efforts on this score. Whether either party will now embrace deficit reduction, though, remains an open question.

AN ANALYSIS OF THE VOTE

Some of the voting trends evident in 1992 were in line with the generalizations offered in this text; some, however, ran counter to what might be expected. (A summary of the 1992 vote is shown in figure 13–1.) Everything about the 1992 election was complicated, of course, by the presence of Ross Perot.

First, turnout was up for the first time in thirty years. Since 1960 the percentage of eligible voters casting ballots had been creeping down with every election, reaching 50 percent in 1988 (see figure 10-3). In 1992, though, 55 percent came to the polls, the highest percentage since 1972. The reasons are unclear, but most analysts believe that Perot's candidacy brought out many who would otherwise have stayed at home. One poll of Perot supporters found that 14 percent said they would not have voted in a Bush-Clinton race.[13] However, the Perot factor does not seem to account completely for the increased turnout. Various barometers indicated long before election day that interest in politics was higher than usual this year; the first presidential debate significantly outdrew the baseball playoff game, for example. Whatever the reason for the higher voter turnout, it is encouraging news.

Second, the electoral college arithmetic proved controlling again (see chapter 6). Figure 13–2 details the vote by state since 1976. Clinton won primarily by carrying the industrial heartland (Ohio, Michigan, and Illinois); the populous eastern states (New York, Pennsylvania, and New Jersey); and the Pacific coast. These nine states alone gave him 204 of the 270 electoral votes he needed to win. To this Clinton added a band of states immediately west of the Mississippi River; all of New England; the border states of West Virginia, Kentucky, and Tennessee; and a scattering of others. No Democrat since Lyndon Johnson has had such a balanced appeal. Bush, on the other hand, was anchored in Texas and Florida, picking up only a handful of other southern, farm belt, and Rocky Mountain states.

FIGURE 13-1

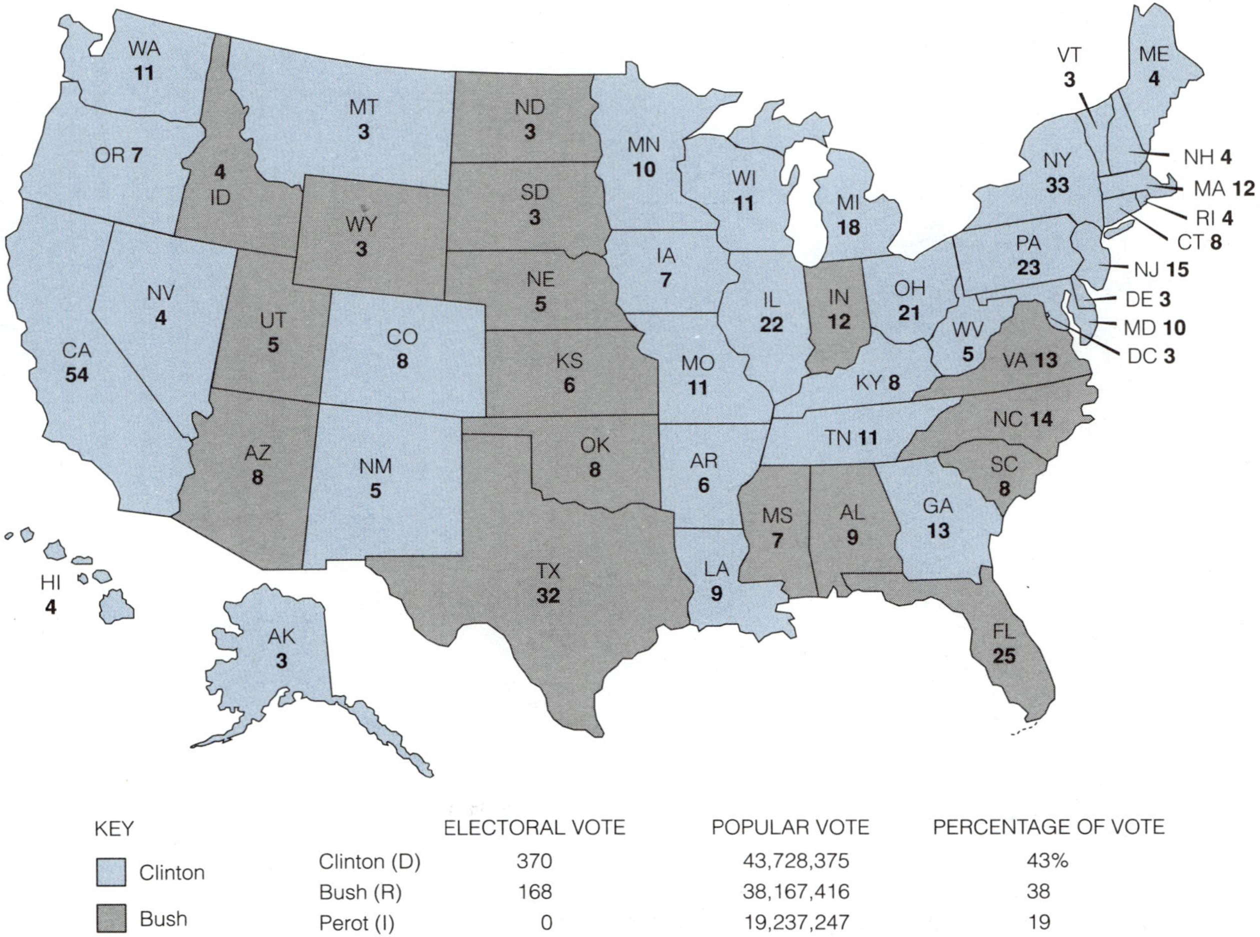

KEY

Clinton

Bush

	ELECTORAL VOTE	POPULAR VOTE	PERCENTAGE OF VOTE
Clinton (D)	370	43,728,375	43%
Bush (R)	168	38,167,416	38
Perot (I)	0	19,237,247	19

ME 4
NH 4
MA 12
RI 4
CT 8
NJ 15
DE 3
MD 10
DC 3
VT 3
NY 33
PA 23
WV 5
VA 13
NC 14
SC 8
FL 25
GA 13
OH 21
KY 8
TN 11
AL 9
MI 18
IN 12
IL 22
MS 7
WI 11
MO 11
AR 6
LA 9
IA 7
MN 10
ND 3
SD 3
NE 5
KS 6
OK 8
TX 32
MT 3
WY 3
CO 8
NM 5
UT 5
ID 4
AZ 8
NV 4
WA 11
OR 7
CA 54
AK 3
HI 4

FIGURE 13-2

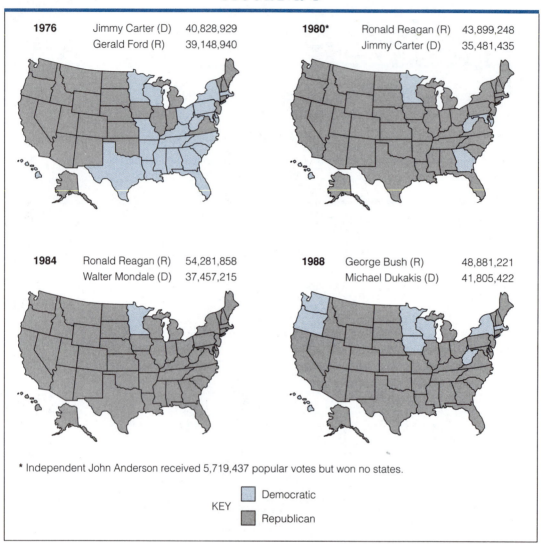

| 1976 | Jimmy Carter (D) | 40,828,929 |
| | Gerald Ford (R) | 39,148,940 |

| 1980* | Ronald Reagan (R) | 43,899,248 |
| | Jimmy Carter (D) | 35,481,435 |

| 1984 | Ronald Reagan (R) | 54,281,858 |
| | Walter Mondale (D) | 37,457,215 |

| 1988 | George Bush (R) | 48,881,221 |
| | Michael Dukakis (D) | 41,805,422 |

* Independent John Anderson received 5,719,437 popular votes but won no states.

KEY ☐ Democratic
☐ Republican

The comparison to 1988 is instructive. Clinton carried every state Dukakis had secured, plus all but one (South Dakota) of the twelve in which Dukakis came within 10 percent. In addition, Clinton carried ten states which had gone to Bush by over 10 percent four years earlier: Arkansas, Georgia, Kentucky, Louisiana, Maine, Nevada, New Hampshire, New Jersey, Ohio, and Tennessee. However, Democrats should not become complacent. In eleven states with a total of 91 electoral votes Clinton's margin of victory was under 5 percent; had he lost all of these he would have still won the election, but with only 279 electoral votes.

One compelling question is how Perot's vote affected the outcome. The major poll found that without Perot in the race, his supporters who would

TABLE 13-1

The 1992 Vote by Gender

	MEN (PERCENTAGE OF ALL MALE VOTERS)	WOMEN (PERCENTAGE OF ALL FEMALE VOTERS)
Bush	38	37
Clinton	41	46
Perot	21	17
Total	100	100

Source: Voter Research and Surveys. Reported in *New York Times,* November 5, 1992, B9.

have voted would have split their ballots exactly evenly between Clinton and Bush. Seemingly, therefore, the outcome would not have been disturbed had Perot not run. However, that conclusion assumes that Perot's supporters in each state would have divided evenly between the two other candidates. Suppose, for example, that the half that would have voted for Bush all live in California, Illinois, Ohio, and Michigan. Moving these voters to Bush's column in those states would have deprived Clinton of 115 electoral votes and have kept Bush in the White House. Unless we are able to find out more detail about the Perot vote though, such a speculation remains just that.

Turning to the popular vote, several salient points are evident. The first is the significant gender difference in both turnout and voting preferences. If both men and women had visited the polls in equal proportions, the electorate would have been roughly balanced; in fact, though, the 1992 voting public was 54 percent female. Clinton clearly outpolled Bush among women (46 to 37 percent) and did better among women than among men (46 to 41 percent). Bush received about the same level of support from both men and women; Perot, in contrast, ran better among men than among women.

As for race and ethnicity, Clinton almost split the white vote with Bush, and beat him badly among most minorities. Remember, though, that these groups make up vastly different percentages of the total electorate. Whites accounted for 87 percent of the total number of votes cast. However, also recall that minority voters, who are not scattered evenly among the states, were critical in a few of the close states (such as Ohio). Perot received his greatest support from whites, with some support from Hispanics and Asians.

The age breakdown is most intriguing. Democrats reversed one major pattern of the last decade: a tendency for young voters to give their preferences to the Republicans. This time Clinton harvested the lion's share from voters between ages eighteen and twenty-nine, with 44 percent. Nevertheless, 22 percent of the under-thirty vote went to Perot, to form his strongest base. Should this 22 percent lean more heavily to the Republicans in the future, Clinton's accomplishment may not mean much in the long run. At the other end of the age bracket Clinton was the clear favorite, as half of those over sixty gave him their vote. It is interesting that

TABLE 13–2

The 1992 Vote by Race and Ethnicity

| | PERCENTAGE OF GROUP VOTING FOR EACH CANDIDATE | | | |
	Whites	*African Americans*	*Hispanics*	*Asian Americans*
Bush	41	11	25	55
Clinton	39	82	62	29
Perot	20	7	14	16
Total	100	100	100	100

Source: Voter Research and Surveys. Reported in *New York Times,* November 5, 1992, B9.

Note: Some totals may not add up to 100% because of rounding.

so many members of this cohort voted solidly against someone from their own generation.

Voting proclivities also varied according to level of education. College graduates split their votes about evenly between Bush and Clinton; however, Clinton bested Bush in every other category. Clinton's two strongest bases, though, were in those voters at both ends of the educational spectrum. Perot's popularity was exactly the opposite; he found his lowest levels among the least and the most educated.

Income shows a fairly predictable pattern. The Republican candidate did better the higher one moved up the income scale; yet note that he still received nearly a quarter of the votes cast by those with very low incomes. Conversely, the Democrats did consistently better the further down the income ladder one went. Interestingly, Perot seemed to do the worst among people most like himself, the affluent, although the $75,000-plus category is too broad to indicate much in this regard. Perot may have done better among those with incomes of $1 million and up.

It is important to stress here in particular, but similarly in all the other groupings, that these categories do *not* represent equal proportions of the electorate. The top and bottom income bands contain 14 percent and 13 percent of the voters respectively. The totals for the other three are 24

TABLE 13–3

The 1992 Vote by Age Category

| | PERCENTAGE OF AGE GROUP VOTING FOR EACH CANDIDATE | | | |
	18-29 years	*30-44 years*	*45-59 years*	*Over 60 years*
Bush	34	38	40	38
Clinton	44	42	41	50
Perot	22	20	19	12
Total	100	100	100	100

Source: Voter Research and Surveys. Reported in *New York Times,* November 5, 1992, B9.

TABLE 13-4

The 1992 Vote by Level of Education

	PERCENTAGE OF EDUCATION GROUP VOTING FOR EACH CANDIDATE				
	Less than high school	*High school graduate*	*Some college*	*College graduate*	*Postgraduate degree*
Bush	28	36	37	41	36
Clinton	55	43	42	40	49
Perot	17	20	21	19	15
Total	100	100	100	100	100

Source: Voter Research and Surveys. Reported in *New York Times,* November 5, 1992, B9.

Note: Some totals may not add up to 100% because of rounding.

percent, 30 percent, and 20 percent. Therefore, 54 percent of the electorate lies in the span of yearly family income between $15,000 and $49,999. When Bill Clinton launched his campaign, he talked incessantly about the "forgotten middle class," and it was here that he won the election. In 1988, for example, Bush received 56 percent of the middle bracket vote.

Religious affiliation broke the vote down very much the way one would predict from the differences in party identification analyzed in chapter 10. Jews were overwhelmingly Democratic in 1992 (78 percent), but Catholics voted for Clinton by a significant margin also (44 percent, to 36 percent for Bush). White Protestants went largely for Bush, and white self-described "born again" Christians voted for him by an even larger margin (61 percent to Clinton's 23 percent). However, in 1988 Bush received 81 percent of the vote of this last group, who make up 17 percent of the voting population. Jews were less enthusiastic about Perot than were either Catholics or white Protestants, but "born again" Christians were not in his corner either.

Both party's partisans stayed with their loyalties in roughly equal percentages. Approximately three-quarters of each group voted for their own

TABLE 13-5

The 1992 Vote by Level of Family Income

	PERCENTAGE OF INCOME GROUP VOTING FOR EACH CANDIDATE				
	Under $15,000	*$15,000– $29,999*	*$30,000– $49,999*	*$50,000– $74,999*	*Over $75,000*
Bush	23	35	38	42	48
Clinton	59	45	41	40	36
Perot	18	20	21	18	16
Total	100	100	100	100	100

Source: Voter Research and Surveys. Reported in *New York Times,* November 5, 1992, B9.

TABLE 13–6

The 1992 Vote by Religious Preference

| | PERCENTAGE OF RELIGIOUS GROUP VOTING FOR EACH CANDIDATE | | | |
	White Protestant	*Catholic*	*Jewish*	*White "Born-Again" Christian*
Bush	46	36	12	61
Clinton	33	44	78	23
Perot	21	20	10	15
Total	100	100	100	100

Source: Voter Research and Surveys. Reported in *New York Times,* November 5, 1992, B9.

Note: Some totals may not add up to 100% because of rounding.

party, while one in ten crossed over. The Democratic victory, though, resulted from three factors. First, independents cast more votes for Clinton (38 percent) than for Bush (32 percent), even though 30 percent of them went for Perot. Second, Democrats still hold a slight edge in party identification, with 38 percent of those voting on November 3 saying they were Democrats, compared to 35 percent who chose the Republican label; this means the Democratic "three-quarters" represents more total votes. Third, slightly more Republicans than Democrats deserted their party for Perot.

Ideology provides a final clue. *Self-described* conservatives and liberals (see chapter 9) split about exactly the same for Bush and Clinton respectively. Sixty-eight percent of the liberals voted for Clinton, while 65 percent of the conservatives sided with Bush; 14 percent of the liberals voted for Bush and 18 percent of the conservatives chose Clinton. Since more voters describe themselves as conservatives than as liberals, such a breakdown would have meant a Bush victory had no moderates voted. But moderates did vote; they gave Clinton 48 percent of their vote, compared to only 31 percent for Bush. In 1988, by way of contrast, Bush received 50 percent of the moderate vote. (There was, of course, no third candidate

TABLE 13–7

The 1992 Vote by Party Identification

| | PERCENTAGE OF PARTY LOYALISTS VOTING FOR EACH CANDIDATE | | |
	Democrats	*Republicans*	*Independents*
Bush	10	73	32
Clinton	77	10	38
Perot	13	17	30
Total	100	100	100

Source: Voter Research and Surveys. Reported in *New York Times,* November 5, 1992, B9.

TABLE 13-8

The 1992 Vote by Ideological Orientation

PERCENTAGE OF IDEOLOGICAL GROUP VOTING FOR EACH CANDIDATE			
	Liberals	Moderates	Conservatives
Bush	14	31	65
Clinton	68	48	18
Perot	18	21	17
Total	100	100	100

Source: Voter Research and Surveys. Reported in New York Times, November 5, 1992, B9.

to siphon these people off.) Clearly, no Democrat can hope to win without doing better than the Republican candidate among the moderates, *if* the conservative and liberal patterns remain the same as those in recent years. Seemingly, at least this time, the Democrats' strategy paid off.

THE CONGRESSIONAL ELECTIONS

The congressional elections of 1992 were fought against a backdrop of three factors: (1) the redistricting required for the House of Representatives; (2) a restive, anti-incumbent mood that seemed to grip the voters; and (3) more women than ever before seeking a place in the halls of power.

Seats for the House of Representatives must be reallocated among the states every ten years, in accordance with population shifts. Several states always gain and several always lose in this process. Moreover, within states, as mentioned in chapter 5, the Supreme Court has ordered that congressional districts contain roughly equal numbers of people, a rule which mandates the changing of boundaries in most states. Complicating the picture this year was a provision of the Voting Rights Act which had been interpreted as requiring that more districts with African American and Hispanic majorities be created. Throughout the country, all these factors produced bitter and complex battles over redistricting, with a number of curious cartographic configurations the result. (See figure 5–3 for one example.) Ironically, Republicans were quite pleased with the effort to chisel out more black-majority districts. Packing African Americans, with their traditional Democratic voting loyalties, into these districts diluted the Democratic vote in other districts, thereby strengthening Republican's chances in a number of states. When the lines were completed, both African American political leaders and the GOP hoped to see their numbers increase. Here as elsewhere, politics makes strange bedfellows.

The anti-incumbent mood of the voters had been simmering for some time. It dominated political discussion in 1990, but seemed to have little concrete impact. By 1992, however, it had been reignited by the House bank and post office scandals and by renewed anger at the direction in which the country was headed. By the fall, fifty-three House incumbents had retired, as had seven senators—a postwar record. One senator and nineteen representatives were defeated in primaries.

Early in the year, 1992 was hailed as the "year of the woman." Several high-visibility candidates for the Senate were symptomatic of this trend. Lynn Yeakel had defeated several Democrats in Pennsylvania for the right to challenge Senator Arlen Specter, who had been instrumental in cross-examining Anita Hill before the Senate Judiciary Committee; in Illinois, a little-known woman, Carol Moseley Braun, defeated Senator Alan Dixon in the primary; and in California two strong women candidates—Barbara Boxer and Dianne Feinstein—were vying for both of that state's Senate seats.[14] In addition, record numbers of women were running for other Senate and House seats.

There were thirty-five Senate races conducted in 1992. Going into the election, Democrats held twenty of these, and Republicans fifteen. The results kept the party ratio as it was, a 58–42 advantage for the Democrats.

Of the thirty-five seats, twenty-seven were contested by incumbents, with only four of them losing. (One of the losing incumbents, though, John Seymour of California, had only served about a year; he had been appointed to fill an unexpected vacancy.) An additional loss, of course, was Dixon's fall earlier in the year. But of the incumbents seeking reelection, a

Democrats Dianne Feinstein, left, and Barbara Boxer together after their simultaneous Senate primary victories in California.

Carol Moseley Braun on election night making history as the first African American woman ever elected to the United States Senate. To her right is her 15-year-old son Matthew.

full 85 percent won. However, several prominent senators—Hollings of South Carolina, Specter of Pennsylvania, Packwood of Oregon, Glenn of Ohio, and Leahy of Vermont—had unusually close races.

Altogether, eleven new senators will take office in 1993. Three of them are former House members, diminishing somewhat the anti-incumbency tide. Significantly, four of the newcomers are women, raising their total number to six. One of them, Ms. Braun, is the first African American senator since Everett Brooke of Massachusetts retired in 1978, and the first African American woman ever to serve in the Senate. Additionally, Ben Nighthorse Campbell of Colorado is the first Native American senator in sixty years.

Redistricting had its desired effect on the House side: more Republicans and more African Americans. The Republicans gained nine seats—far short of what they had hoped, but a significant number considering their loss of the presidency. In the new House, there will be thirty-eight blacks, compared to twenty-five in the previous Congress. Other minorities are also better represented. Hispanics increased their representation in the House, from ten to seventeen.

The voters' supposed distaste for congressional incumbents showed mixed results. Redistricting pitted four incumbents against one another in primaries, while another five were paired in the general election. The avalanche of retirements also removed many vulnerable incumbents.

(text continued on page 442)

439

BOX 13–1

Echoes of Civic Democracy in the 1992 Election

POLITICAL CAMPAIGNS are usually heavily laced with appeals to people's special interests. Candidates and their strategists view voters as blocs of one sort or another, and then tailor their messages to attract a majority of them. There was certainly plenty of that in 1992. At the same time, American campaigns usually contain at least a hint of an appeal to the public interest and other themes related to civic democracy. In 1992, though, the features of civic democracy seemed to come through a little more loudly than they had in the past. This can be seen especially in four areas: Bill Clinton's convention acceptance speech; the central themes of the fall campaign; the Perot candidacy; and the voter turnout.

Clinton's acceptance speech at the Democratic convention clearly drew on the communitarian thread of civic democracy when he labeled his program the "New Covenant," which he defined as "a solemn agreement between the people and their government, based not simply on what each of us can take, but what all of us must give to our nation."[1] He underscored this theme when he reiterated, "We will build an American community again."

In the same speech Clinton also spoke of the all-inclusive nature of the American political community: "We need each other. All of us—we need each other. We don't have a person to waste. . . . There is no them; there's only us. One nation, under God, indivisible, with liberty and justice for all." Further, he linked his New Covenant to our history: "In the end, my fellow Americans, this New Covenant asks us all to be Americans again. Old-fashioned Americans for a new time. Opportunity. Responsibility. Community."

In addition, Clinton's acceptance speech touched on two other elements of civic democracy: the need for citizen action through voluntary organizations and the importance of faith in government. Regarding the first, he said simply and forthrightly, "There is not a program in government for every problem." But he stressed equally, "This election is about putting power back in your hands and putting government back on your side."

George Bush's acceptance speech was woven from a much thinner piece of civic democratic cloth, but it was present nonetheless. In the days before the Republican convention, there had been rumors that the U.S. might get tough on Iraq, and perhaps even instigate military action. Some observers noted that such a move would probably help the president's chances in the election. Bush said in his speech: "Let me make just one aside comment here because of what you've been reading in the paper. This is a political year, but there's a lot of danger in the world. And you can be sure, I will never let politics interfere with a foreign-policy decision. Forget the election; I will do right—what is right for the national security of the United States of America. And that is a pledge from my heart."[2] Only the worst of cynics did not believe that Bush was telling the truth. Most of his speech, however, was devoted to a recitation of his accomplishments and an attack on the Democrats.

BOX 13-1

Clearly, civic democratic themes were crucial to the campaign. Polls showed that the economy and change—two issues Bill Clinton stuck with—were the subjects voters wanted discussed. In one sense, of course, the economy is a purely individualistic issue: people are concerned about their own fortunes. However, it seems that in this campaign, when voters spoke of the economy, their concern transcended their own pocketbooks. In fact, the economy, by any objective measure, was really not in such bad shape, as Bush kept repeating. Growth was steady; inflation was very low; interest rates were down; etc. To be sure, there was unemployment and there were hard-hit areas, but the recession was still milder than most. It seemed to be a sense of unease and foreboding, rather than bread-and-butter economic issues, that was driving many people's views. Michael Lewis-Beck and Tom Rice have written recently that "the overwhelming evidence is that American voters hardly respond to their pocketbooks; instead they seem to care mostly about the nation's economic well-being."[3] So it seemed in the fall of 1992.

This interpretation, that the voters held the concern of civic democrats for the whole nation uppermost, is strengthened by the elusive but real call for "change." Large numbers of citizens indicated to pollsters that they thought the country was headed in the "wrong direction." This position may have been, for many people, a purely selfish response: "I am not doing well and want to do better. I want more government services." However, it also seemed to indicate that many people cared about the fate of the society in the long run.

Ross Perot's candidacy offers another sign that civic democracy was alive in this election. His early attractiveness was based in part at least on the call for citizens to care, get motivated, and get involved for the sake of a purpose larger than themselves. Few volunteers had anything to gain personally by Perot's candidacy. Furthermore, when he reentered the race in October, not a single one of his proposals was designed to appeal to a special group of voters. On the contrary, Perot called for sacrifice, hard work, and higher taxes. That this message appealed to one in five voters, despite Perot's enigmatic personal behavior, surely says something about the vitality of civic democracy in this country.

Finally, there was the increased voter turnout. Many voters apparently felt that this election was important, that going to the polls meant something for the future of the country. There were, to be sure, sharp partisans of Bush, Clinton, and Perot who went to the polls simply because they favored or opposed some particular policy or mix of policies one of the candidates advocated. But media reports from across the nation seemed also to tap a feeling that participation in our great civic ritual was also important, that our faith in democracy had somehow been renewed, that citizenship matters after all.

[1] A transcript of Clinton's speech can be found in the *New York Times,* July 19, 1992.
[2] *New York Times,* August 21, 1992.
[3] Quoted in *Congressional Quarterly Weekly Report,* July 25, 1992, 2153.

Nonetheless, of the 349 incumbents who sought reelection, 325 will be back in the Capitol, a success rate of 93 percent. Nevertheless, there will be 110 new members of the House in the 103rd Congress—over a quarter of the total, and the largest number since 1948.

The anti-incumbent feeling definitely surfaced in another sphere, as fourteen states approved term limits for members of Congress. The constitutionality of these initiatives will undoubtedly be tested in court, and they may not stand up. However, they do seem to signify that many voters are restive for political change, even if they do not always direct this sentiment at their current member of the House or Senate.

Women did relatively well in House races also. Forty-seven women, an increase of nineteen, will be in the new House. This brings their total representation now to about 11 percent.

Congress seems to be inching toward the type of representation we discussed in chapter 5. It is still far from a demographic cross section of the American population, but there is much more diversity than there was in years past. If the hypothesis about such representation increasing legitimacy is correct, then perhaps Congress has taken an important step in reestablishing its connection with the citizenry.

Summary

The Democratic presidential primaries attracted six candidates, none of whom was a nationally established politician. New Hampshire propelled Paul Tsongas and Bill Clinton into a two-way race for the nomination, with Clinton wounded by allegations of extra-marital affairs and draft dodging. Clinton came back in the south, and then delivered a knockout blow to Tsongas in Illinois and Michigan. He suffered a temporary setback in Connecticut, but soon clinched the nomination.

George Bush won all the Republican primaries, but he was harassed by arch-conservative Pat Buchanan, who polled about one-third of the vote in each contest.

The Democratic convention was a departure from those of previous years, in that it avoided serious ruptures and presented a decidedly moderate tone. The GOP convention, in contrast, portrayed an image of harshness and exclusiveness.

Bush's campaign lacked a defining purpose. None of the tactics the Republicans tried seemed to resonate with the voters. Clinton stuck to his central themes of the economy, change, and the need for leadership. Ross Perot hammered away with specific policy ideas to close the federal deficit.

In the end, Clinton received 43 percent of the popular vote, swept thirty-two states and the District of Columbia, and received 370 electoral votes. Clinton did best among women; minorities; the elderly; those with the least and the most education; those with low incomes; Jews and Catholics; Democrats; and liberals.

In Congress, redistricting helped simultaneously to elect more African Americans and more Republicans. Retirements probably softened the expected anti-incumbent surge, but term limits passed in fourteen states. Women did very well in a number of high-profile Senate races and in a number of House races.

ENDNOTES

1. *Congressional Quarterly Weekly Report,* April 4, 1992, 895.

2. *Congressional Quarterly Weekly Report,* May 2, 1992, 1082.

3. Edwin Diamond, "Crash Course: Campaign Journalism 101," *New York,* February 17, 1992, 29.

4. A fascinating account of how those words were placed in Bush's mouth is given in Bob Woodward, "The Anatomy of a Decision: Six Words that Shaped—and May Sink—the Bush Presidency," *Washington Post National Weekly Edition,* October 12–18, 1992, 6–7.

5. *Congressional Quarterly Weekly Report,* June 6, 1992, 1647.

6. *New York Times,* July 19, 1992.

7. *New York Times,* July 18, 1992.

8. Clinton's bounce in the polls was 24 points. Carter had gained 17 points in 1980, Mondale 16 in 1984, and Dukakis 9 in 1988.

9. *New York Times,* July 17, 1992.

10. *New York Times,* October 2, 1992.

11. See the article by Howard Kurtz, "The Year the Candidates Took to the Airwaves," *Washington Post National Weekly Edition,* November 2–8, 14.

12. *New York Times,* November 5, 1992.

13. *New York Times,* November 5, 1992.

14. California had two seats to be filled at the 1992 election: one for a regular six-year term and one for the remaining two years of the term of Pete Wilson, who had resigned in 1990. John Seymour had been appointed to fill Wilson's seat when Wilson was elected governor.

APPENDIX A

THE DECLARATION OF INDEPENDENCE*

IN CONGRESS, July 4, 1776.

A *Declaration by the Representatives of the United States of America, in General Congress assembled.*

When in the Course of human Events, it becomes necessary for one People to dissolve the Political Bonds which have connected them with another, and to assume among the Powers of the Earth, the separate and equal Station to which the Laws of Nature and of Nature's God entitle them, a decent Respect to the Opinions of Mankind requires that they should declare the causes which impel them to the Separation.

We hold these Truths to be self-evident, that all Men are created equal, that they are endowed by their Creator with certain unalienable Rights, that among these are Life, Liberty, and the Pursuit of Happiness—That to secure these Rights, Governments are instituted among Men, deriving their just Powers from the Consent of the Governed, that whenever any Form of Government becomes destructive of these Ends, it is the Right of the People to alter or to abolish it, and to institute new Government, laying its Foundation on such Principles, and organizing its Powers in such Forms, as to them shall seem most likely to effect their Safety and Happiness. Prudence, indeed, will dictate that Governments long established should not be changed for light and transient Causes; and accordingly all Experience hath shewn, that Mankind are more disposed to suffer, while Evils are sufferable, than to right themselves by abolishing the Forms to which they are accustomed. But when a long Train of Abuses and Usurpations, pursuing invariably the same Object, evinces a Design to reduce them under absolute Despotism, it is their Right, it is their Duty, to throw off such Government, and to provide new Guards for their future Security. Such has been the patient Sufferance of these Colonies; and such is now the Necessity which constrains them to alter their former Systems of Government. The History of the present King of Great Britain is a History of repeated Injuries and Usurpations, all having in direct Object the Establishment of an absolute Tyranny over these States. To prove this, let facts be submitted to a candid World.

He has refused his Assent to Laws, the most wholesome and necessary for the public Good.

He has forbidden his Governors to pass Laws of immediate and pressing Importance, unless suspended in their Operation till his Assent should be obtained; and when so suspended, he has utterly neglected to attend to them.

He has refused to pass other Laws for the Accommodation of large Districts of People, unless those People would relinquish the Right of Representation in the Legislature, a Right inestimable to them, and formidable to Tyrants only.

He has called together Legislative Bodies at Places unusual, uncomfortable, and distant from the Depository of their Public Records, for the sole Purpose of fatiguing them into Compliance with his Measures.

He has dissolved Representative Houses repeatedly, for opposing with manly Firmness his Invasions on the Rights of the People.

*The spelling, capitalization, and punctuation of the original have been retained here.

He has refused for a long Time, after such Dissolutions, to cause others to be elected; whereby the Legislative Powers, incapable of Annihilation, have returned to the People at large for their exercise; the State remaining in the mean time exposed to all the Dangers of Invasion from without, and Convulsions within.

He has endeavoured to prevent the Population of these States; for that Purpose obstructing the Laws for Naturalization of Foreigners; refusing to pass others to encourage their Migration hither, and raising the Conditions of new Appropriations of Lands.

He has obstructed the Administration of Justice, by refusing his Assent to Laws for establishing Judiciary Powers.

He has made Judges dependent on his Will alone, for the Tenure of their offices, and the Amount and payments of their Salaries.

He has erected a Multitude of new Offices, and sent hither Swarms of Officers to harass our People, and eat out their Substance.

He has kept among us, in times of Peace, Standing Armies, without the consent of our Legislatures.

He has affected to render the Military independent of, and superior to the Civil Power.

He has combined with others to subject us to a Jurisdiction foreign to our Constitution, and unacknowledged by our Laws; giving his Assent to their Acts of pretended Legislation:

For quartering large Bodies of Armed Troops among us:

For protecting them, by a mock Trial, from Punishment for any Murders which they should commit on the Inhabitants of these States:

For cutting off our Trade with all Parts of the World:

For imposing Taxes on us without our Consent:

For depriving us, in many cases, of the Benefits of Trial by Jury:

For transporting us beyond Seas to be tried for pretended Offences:

For abolishing the free System of English Laws in a neighbouring Province, establishing therein an arbitrary Government, and enlarging its Boundaries, so as to render it at once an Example and fit Instrument for introducing the same absolute Rule into these Colonies:

For taking away our Charters, abolishing our most valuable Laws, and altering fundamentally the Forms of our Governments:

For suspending our own Legislatures, and declaring themselves invested with Power to legislate for us in all Cases whatsoever.

He has abdicated Government here, by declaring us out of his Protection and waging War against us.

He has plundered our Seas, ravaged our Coasts, burnt our towns, and destroyed the Lives of our People.

He is, at this Time, transporting large Armies of foreign Mercenaries to compleat the works of Death, Desolation, and Tyranny, already begun with circumstances of Cruelty and Perfidy, scarcely parallelled in the most barbarous Ages, and totally unworthy the Head of a civilized Nation.

He has constrained our fellow Citizens taken Captive on the high Seas to bear Arms against their Country, to become the Executioners of their Friends and Brethren, or to fall themselves by their Hands.

He has excited domestic Insurrections amongst us, and has endeavoured to bring on the Inhabitants of our Frontiers, the merciless Indian Savages, whose known Rule of Warfare, is an undistinguished Destruction, of all Ages, Sexes and Conditions.

In every state of these Oppressions we have Petitioned for Redress in the most humble Terms: Our repeated Petitions have been answered only by repeated Injury. A Prince, whose Character is thus marked by every act which may define a Tyrant, is unfit to be the Ruler of a free People.

Nor have we been wanting in Attentions to our British Brethren. We have warned them from Time to Time of Attempts by their Legislature to extend an unwarrantable Jurisdiction over us. We have reminded them of the Circumstances of our Emigration and Settlement here. We have appealed to their native Justice and Magnanimity, and we have conjured them by the Ties of our common Kindred to disavow these Usurpations, which, would inevitably interrupt our Connections and Correspondence. They too have been deaf to the Voice of Justice and of Consanguinity. We must, therefore, acquiesce in the Necessity, which denounces our Separation, and hold them, as we hold the rest of Mankind, Enemies in War, in Peace, Friends.

We, therefore, the Representatives of the UNITED STATES OF AMERICA, in General Congress Assembled, appealing to the Supreme Judge of the World for the Rectitude of our Intentions, do, in the Name, and by Authority of the good People of these Colonies, solemnly Publish and Declare, That these United Colonies are, and of Right ought to be, Free and Independent States; that they are absolved from all Allegiance to the British Crown, and that all political Connection between them and the State of Great Brit-

ain, is and ought to be totally dissolved; and that as Free and Independent States, they have full Power to levy War, conclude Peace, contract Alliances, establish Commerce, and to do all other Acts and Things which Independent States may of right do. And for the support of this declaration, with a firm Reliance on the Protection of divine Providence, we mutually pledge to each other our Lives, our Fortunes, and our sacred Honor.

The foregoing Declaration was, by order of Congress, engrossed, and signed by the following members:

John Hancock

NEW HAMPSHIRE
Josiah Bartlett
William Whipple
Matthew Thornton

MASSACHUSETTS BAY
Samuel Adams
John Adams
Robert Treat Paine
Elbridge Gerry

RHODE ISLAND
Stephen Hopkins
William Ellery

CONNECTICUT
Roger Sherman
Samuel Huntington
William Williams
Oliver Wolcott

NEW YORK
William Floyd
Philip Livingston
Francis Lewis
Lewis Morris

NEW JERSEY
Richard Stockton
John Witherspoon
Francis Hopkinson
John Hart
Abraham Clark

PENNSYLVANIA
Robert Morris
Benjamin Rush
Benjamin Franklin
John Morton
George Clymer
James Smith
George Taylor
James Wilson
George Ross

DELAWARE
Caesar Rodney
George Read
Thomas M'Kean

MARYLAND
Samuel Chase
William Paca
Thomas Stone
Charles Carroll,
 of Carrollton

VIRGINIA
George Wythe
Richard Henry Lee
Thomas Jefferson
Benjamin Harrison
Thomas Nelson, Jr.
Francis Lightfoot Lee
Carter Braxton

NORTH CAROLINA
William Hooper
Joseph Hewes
John Penn

SOUTH CAROLINA
Edward Rutledge
Thomas Heyward, Jr.
Thomas Lynch, Jr.
Arthur Middleton

GEORGIA
Button Gwinnett
Lyman Hall
George Walton

Resolved, That copies of the Declaration be sent to the several assemblies, conventions, and committees, or councils of safety, and to the several commanding officers of the continental troops; that it be proclaimed in each of the United States, at the head of the army.

CONSTITUTION OF THE UNITED STATES OF AMERICA*

Ratified 1788

WE THE PEOPLE *of the United States, in Order to form a more perfect Union, establish Justice, insure domestic Tranquility, provide for the common defence, promote the general Welfare, and secure the Blessings of Liberty to ourselves and our posterity, do ordain and establish this Constitution for the United States of America.*

ARTICLE I.

Section 1.

All legislative Powers herein granted shall be vested in a Congress of the United States, which shall consist of a Senate and House of Representatives.

Section 2.

The House of Representatives shall be composed of Members chosen every second Year by the People of the several States, and the Electors in each State shall have the Qualifications requisite for Electors of the most numerous Branch of the State Legislature.

No person shall be a Representative who shall not have attained to the Age of twenty-five Years, and been seven Years a Citizen of the United States, and who shall not, when elected, be an Inhabitant of that State in which he shall be chosen.

Representatives and direct [Taxes][1] shall be apportioned among the several States which may be included within this Union, according to their respective Numbers [which shall be determined by adding to the whole Number of free Persons, including those bound to Service for a Term of Years, and excluding Indians not taxed, three fifths of all other Persons].[2] The actual Enumeration shall be made within three Years after the first Meeting of the Congress of the United States, and within every subsequent Term of ten Years, in such Manner as they shall by Law direct. The Number of Representatives shall not exceed one for every thirty Thousand, but each State shall have at Least one Representative; and until such enumeration shall be made, the State of New Hampshire shall be entitled to chuse three, Massachusetts eight, Rhode Island and Providence Plantations one, Connecticut five, New-York six, New Jersy four, Pennsylvania eight, Delaware one, Maryland six, Virginia ten, North Carolina five, South Carolina five, and Georgia three.

When vacancies happen in the Representation from any State, the Executive Authority thereof shall issue Writs of Election to fill such Vacancies.

The House of Representatives shall chuse their Speaker and other Officers; and shall have the sole Power of Impeachment.

Section 3.

The Senate of the United States shall be composed of two Senators from each State [chosen by the Legislature thereof],[3] for six Years; and each Senator shall have one Vote.

---

*The spelling, capitalization, and punctuation of the original have been retained here. Brackets indicate passages that have been altered by amendments to the Constitution.

[1] Modified by the Sixteenth Amendment.
[2] Modified by the Fourteenth Amendment.
[3] Repealed by the Seventeenth Amendment.

Immediately after they shall be assembled in Consequence of the first Election, they shall be divided as equally as may be into three Classes. The Seats of the Senators of the first Class shall be vacated at the Expiration of the second year, of the second Class at the Expiration of the fourth Year, and of the third Class at the Expiration of the sixth Year, so that one third may be chosen every second Year [and if Vacancies happen by Resignation, or otherwise, during the Recess of the Legislature of any State, the Executive thereof may make temporary Appointments until the next Meeting of the Legislature, which shall then fill such Vacancies.][4]

No Person shall be a Senator who shall not have attained to the Age of thirty Years, and been nine Years a Citizen of the United States, and who shall not, when elected, be an Inhabitant of that State for which he shall be chosen.

The Vice President of the United States shall be President of the Senate, but shall have no Vote, unless they be equally divided.

The Senate shall chuse their other Officers, and also a President pro tempore, in the Absence of the Vice President, or when he shall exercise the Office of President of the United States.

The Senate shall have the sole Power to try all Impeachments. When sitting for that Purpose, they shall be on Oath or Affirmation. When the President of the United States is tried, the Chief Justice shall preside: And no Person shall be convicted without the Concurrence of two thirds of the Members present.

Judgment in Cases of Impeachment shall not extend further than to removal from Office, and disqualification to hold and enjoy any Office of honor, Trust or Profit under the United States; but the Party convicted shall nevertheless be liable and subject to Indictment, Trial, Judgment and Punishment, according to Law.

Section 4.

The Times, Places and Manner of holding Elections for Senators and Representatives, shall be prescribed in each State by the Legislature thereof; but the Congress may at any time by Law make or alter such Regulations, except as to the Places of chusing Senators.

[The Congress shall assemble at least once in every Year, and such Meeting shall be on the first Monday in December, unless they shall by Law appoint a different Day.][5]

Section 5.

Each House shall be the Judge of the Elections, Returns and Qualifications of its own Members, and a Majority of each shall constitute a Quorum to do Business; but a smaller Number may adjourn from day to day, and may be authorized to compel the Attendance of absent Members, in such Manner, and under such Penalties as each House may provide.

Each House may determine the Rules of its Proceedings, punish its Members for disorderly Behaviour, and, with the Concurrence of two thirds, expel a Member.

Each House shall keep a Journal of its Proceedings, and from time to time publish the same, excepting such Parts as may in their Judgment require Secrecy; and the Yeas and Nays of the Members of either House on any question shall, at the Desire of one fifth of those present, be entered on the Journal.

Neither House, during the Session of Congress, shall, without the Consent of the other, adjourn for more than three days, nor to any other Place than that in which the two Houses shall be sitting.

Section 6.

The Senators and Representatives shall receive a Compensation for their Services, to be ascertained by Law, and paid out of the Treasury of the United States. They shall in all Cases, except Treason, Felony and Breach of the Peace, be privileged from Arrest during their Attendance at the Session of their respective Houses, and in going to and returning from the same; and for any Speech or Debate in either House, they shall not be questioned in any other Place.

No Senator or Representative shall, during the Time for which he was elected, be appointed to any civil Office under the Authority of the United States, which shall have been created, or the Emoluments whereof shall have been increased

[4]Modified by the Seventeenth Amendment.

[5]Changed by the Twentieth Amendment.

during such time; and no Person holding any Office under the United States, shall be a Member of either House during his Continuance in Office.

Section 7.

All Bills for raising Revenue shall originate in the House of Representatives; but the Senate may propose or concur with Amendments as on other Bills.

Every Bill which shall have passed the House of Representatives and the Senate, shall, before it become a Law, be presented to the President of the United States; If he approves he shall sign it, but if not he shall return it, with his objections to that House in which it shall have originated, who shall enter the Objections at large on their Journal, and proceed to reconsider it. If after such Reconsideration two thirds of that House shall agree to pass the Bill, it shall be sent, together with the Objections, to the other House, by which it shall likewise be reconsidered, and if approved by two thirds of that House, it shall become a Law. But in all such Cases the Votes of both Houses shall be determined by yeas and Nays, and the Names of the Persons voting for and against the Bill shall be entered on the Journal of each House respectively. If any Bill shall not be returned by the President within ten Days (Sundays excepted) after it shall have been presented to him, the Same shall be a Law, in like Manner as if he had signed it, unless the Congress by their Adjournment prevent its Return, in which Case it shall not be a Law.

Every Order, Resolution, or Vote to which the Concurrence of the Senate and House of Representatives may be necessary (except on a question of Adjournment) shall be presented to the President of the United States; and before the Same shall take Effect, shall be approved by him, or being disapproved by him, shall be repassed by two thirds of the Senate and House of Representatives, according to the Rules and Limitations prescribed in the Case of a Bill.

Section 8.

The Congress shall have Power To lay and collect Taxes, Duties, Imposts and Excises, to pay the Debts and provide for the common Defence and general Welfare of the United States; but all Duties, Imposts and Excises shall be uniform throughout the United States;

To borrow Money on the credit of the United States;

To regulate Commerce with foreign Nations, and among the several States, and with the Indian Tribes;

To establish a uniform Rule of Naturalization, and uniform Laws on the subject of Bankruptcies throughout the United States;

To coin Money, regulate the Value thereof, and of foreign Coin, and fix the Standard of Weights and Measures;

To provide for the Punishment of counterfeiting the Securities and current Coin of the United States.

To establish Post Offices and post Roads;

To promote the Progress of Science and useful Arts, by securing for limited Times to Authors and Inventors the exclusive Right to their respective Writings and Discoveries;

To constitute Tribunals inferior to the supreme Court;

To define and punish Piracies and Felonies committed on the high Seas, and Offences against the Law of Nations;

To declare War, grant Letters of Marque and Reprisal, and make Rules concerning Captures on Land and Water;

To raise and support Armies, but no Appropriation of Money to that Use shall be for a longer Term than two Years;

To provide and maintain a Navy;

To make Rules for the Government and Regulation of the land and naval Forces;

To provide for calling forth the Militia to execute the Laws of the Union, suppress Insurrections and repel Invasions;

To provide for organizing, arming, and disciplining the Militia, and for governing such Part of them as may be employed in the Service of the United States, reserving to the States respectively, the Appointment of the Officers, and the Authority of training the Militia according to the discipline prescribed by Congress;

To exercise exclusive Legislation in all Cases whatsoever, over such District (not exceeding ten Miles square) as may, by Cession of particular States, and the Acceptance of Congress, become the Seat of the Government of the United States, and to exercise like Authority over all Places purchased by the Consent of the Legislature of the State in which the Same shall be, for the Erection of forts, Magazines, Arsenals, dock-Yards, and other needful Buildings;—And

To make all Laws which shall be necessary and proper for carrying into Execution the foregoing Powers, and all other Powers vested by this Constitution in the Government of the United States, or in any Department or Officer thereof.

Section 9.

The Migration or Importation of such Persons as any of the States now existing shall think proper to admit, shall not be prohibited by the Congress prior to the Year one thousand eight hundred and eight, but a Tax or duty may be imposed on such Importation, not exceeding ten dollars for each Person.

The Privilege of the Writ of Habeas Corpus shall not be suspended, unless when in Cases of Rebellion or Invasion the public Safety may require it.

No Bill of Attainder or ex post facto Law shall be passed.

[No Capitation, or other direct, Tax shall be laid, unless in Proportion to the Census or Enumeration herein before directed to be taken.][6]

No Tax or Duty shall be laid on Articles exported from any State.

No Preference shall be given by any Regulation of Commerce or Revenue to the Ports of one State over those of another; nor shall Vessels bound to, or from, one State, be obliged to enter, clear, or pay Duties in another.

No Money shall be drawn from the Treasury, but in Consequence of Appropriations made by Law; and a regular Statement and Account of the Receipts and Expenditures of all public Money shall be published from time to time.

No Title of Nobility shall be granted by the United States; and no Person holding any Office or Profit or Trust under them, shall, without the Consent of the Congress, accept of any present, Emolument, Office, or Title, of any kind whatever, from any King, Prince, or foreign State.

[6]Modified by the Sixteenth Amendment.

Section 10.

No State shall enter into any Treaty, Alliance, or Confederation; grant Letters of Marque and Reprisal; coin Money; emit Bills of Credit; make any Thing but gold and silver Coin a Tender in Payment of Debts; pass any Bill of Attainder, ex post facto Law, or Law impairing the Obligation of Contracts, or grant any Title of Nobility.

No State shall, without the Consent of the Congress, lay any Imposts or Duties on Imports or Exports, except what may be absolutely necessary for executing its inspection Laws; and the net Produce of all Duties and Imposts, laid by any State on Imports or Exports, shall be for the Use of the Treasury of the United States; and all such Laws shall be subject to the Revision and Controul of the Congress.

No State shall, without the Consent of Congress, lay any duty of Tonnage, keep Troops, or Ships of War in time of Peace, enter into any Agreement or Compact with another State, or with a foreign Power or engage in War, unless actually invaded, or in such imminent Danger as will not admit of delay.

ARTICLE II.

Section 1.

The executive Power shall be vested in a President of the United States of America. He shall hold his Office during the Term of four Years, and, together with the Vice President, chosen for the Same Term, be elected, as follows.

Each State shall appoint, in such Manner as the Legislature thereof may direct, a Number of Electors, equal to the whole Number of Senators and Representatives to which the State may be entitled in the Congress; but no Senator or Representative, or Person holding an Office of Trust or Profit under the United States, shall be appointed an Elector.

[The Electors shall meet in their respective States, and vote by Ballot for two Persons of whom one at least shall not be an Inhabitant of the same State with themselves. And they shall make a List of all the Persons voted for, and of the Number of Votes for each; which List they shall sign and certify, and transmit sealed to the Seat of

451

the Government of the United States, directed to the President of the Senate. The President of the Senate shall, in the Presence of the Senate and House of Representatives, open all the Certificates, and the Votes shall then be counted. The Person having the greatest Number of Votes shall be the President, if such Number be a Majority of the whole Number of Electors appointed; and if there be more than one who have such Majority, and have an equal Number of Votes, then the House of Representatives shall immediately chuse by Ballot one of them for President; and if no Person have a Majority, then from the five highest on the List the said House shall in like Manner chuse the President. But in chusing the President, the Votes shall be taken by States, the Representation from each State having one Vote; A quorum for this Purpose shall consist of a Member or Members from two thirds of the States, and a Majority of all the states shall be necessary to a Choice. In every Case, after the Choice of the President, the Person having the greatest Number of Votes of the Electors shall be the Vice President. But if there should remain two or more who have equal Votes, the Senate shall chuse from them by Ballot the Vice President.][7]

The Congress may determine the Time of chusing the Electors, and the Day on which they shall give their Votes; which Day shall be the same throughout the United States.

No person except a natural born Citizen, or a Citizen of the United States, at the time of the Adoption of this Constitution, shall be eligible to the Office of President; neither shall any Person be eligible to that Office who shall not have attained to the Age of thirty five Years, and been fourteen Years a Resident within the United States.

[In Case of the Removal of the President from Office, or of his Death, Resignation, or Inability to discharge the Powers and Duties of the said Office, the same shall devolve on the Vice President, and the Congress may by Law provide for the Case of Removal, Death, Resignation or Inability, both of the President and Vice President, declaring what Officer shall then act as President, and such Officer shall act accordingly, until the Disability be removed, or a President shall be elected.][8]

The President shall, at stated Times, receive for his Services, a Compensation, which shall neither be encreased nor diminished during the Period for which he shall have been elected, and he shall not receive within that Period any other Emolument from the United States, or any of them.

Before he enter on the Execution of his Office, he shall take the following Oath or Affirmation: — "I do solemnly swear (or affirm) that I will faithfully execute the Office of President of the United States, and will to the best of my Ability, preserve, protect and defend the constitution of the United States."

Section 2.

The President shall be Commander in Chief of the Army and Navy of the United States, and of the Militia of the several States, when called into the actual Service of the United States; he may require the Opinion, in writing, of the principal Officer in each of the executive Departments, upon any Subject relating to the Duties of their respective Offices, and he shall have Power to grant Reprieves and Pardons for Offences against the United States, except in Cases of Impeachment.

He shall have Power, by and with the Advice and Consent of the Senate, to make Treaties, provided two thirds of the Senators present concur; and he shall nominate, and by and with the Advice and Consent of the Senate, shall appoint Ambassadors, other public Ministers and Consuls, Judges of the supreme Court, and all other Officers of the United States, whose Appointments are not herein otherwise provided for, and which shall be established by Law; but the Congress may by Law vest the Appointment of such inferior Officers, as they think proper, in the President alone, in the Courts of Law, or in the Heads of Departments.

The President shall have Power to fill up all Vacancies that may happen during the Recess of the Senate, by granting Commissions which shall expire at the end of their next Session.

[7]Changed by the Twelfth Amendment.

[8]Modified by the Twenty-fifth Amendment.

Section 3.

He shall from time to time give to the Congress Information of the State of the Union, and recommend to their Consideration such Measures as he shall judge necessary and expedient; he may, on extraordinary Occasions, convene both Houses, or either of them, and in Case of Disagreement between them, with Respect to the Time of Adjournment, he may adjourn them to such Time as he shall think proper; he shall receive Ambassadors and other public Ministers; he shall take Care that the Laws be faithfully executed, and shall Commission all the Officers of the United States.

Section 4.

The President, Vice President and all civil Officers of the United States, shall be removed from Office on Impeachment for, and Conviction of, Treason, Bribery, or other high Crimes and Misdemeanors.

ARTICLE III.
Section 1.

The judicial Power of the United States, shall be vested in one supreme Court, and in such inferior Courts as the Congress may from time to time ordain and establish. The Judges, both of the supreme and inferior Courts, shall hold their Offices during good Behaviour, and shall, at stated Times, receive for their Services, a Compensation, which shall not be diminished during their Continuance in Office.

Section 2.

The judicial Power shall extend to all Cases, in Law and Equity, arising under this Constitution, the Laws of the United States, and Treaties made, or which shall be made, under their Authority;—to all Cases affecting Ambassadors, other public Ministers and Consuls;—to all Cases of admiralty and maritime Jurisdiction;—to Controversies to which the United States shall be a Party;—to Controversies between two or more States;[—between a State and Citizens of another State;][9]—between Citizens of different States,—

between Citizens of the same State claiming Lands under Grants of different States, [and between a state, or the Citizens thereof, and foreign States, Citizens or Subjects.][10]

In all cases affecting Ambassadors, other public Ministers and Consuls, and those in which a State shall be Party, the supreme Court shall have original Jurisdiction. In all the other Cases before mentioned, the supreme Court shall have appellate Jurisdiction, both as to Law and Fact, with such Exceptions, and under such Regulations as the Congress shall make.

The Trial of all Crimes, except in Cases of Impeachment, shall be by Jury; and such Trial shall be held in the State where the said Crimes shall have been committed; but when not committed within any State, the Trial shall be at such Place or Places as the Congress may by Law have directed.

Section 3.

Treason against the United States, shall consist only in levying War against them, or in adhering to their Enemies, giving them Aid and Comfort. No Person shall be convicted of Treason unless on the Testimony of two Witnesses to the same overt Act, or on Confession in open Court.

The Congress shall have Power to declare the Punishment of Treason, but no Attainder of Treason shall work Corruption of Blood, or Forfeiture except during the Life of the Person attainted.

ARTICLE IV.
Section 1.

Full Faith and Credit shall be given in each State to the public Acts, Records, and judicial Proceedings of every other State. And the Congress may by general Laws prescribe the Manner in which such Acts, Records and Proceedings shall be proved, and the Effect thereof.

Section 2.

The Citizens of each State shall be entitled to all Privileges and Immunities of Citizens in the several States.

[9]Modified by the Eleventh Amendment.

[10]Modified by the Eleventh Amendment.

A Person charged in any State with Treason, Felony, or other Crime, who shall flee from Justice, and be found in another State, shall on Demand of the executive Authority of the State from which he fled, be delivered up, to be removed to the State having Jurisdiction of the Crime.

[No Person held to Service or Labour in one State under the Laws thereof, escaping into another, shall, in Consequence of any Law or Regulation therein, be discharged from such Service or Labour, but shall be delivered up on Claim of the Party to whom such Service or Labour may be due.][11]

Section 3.

New States may be admitted by the Congress into this Union; but no new State shall be formed or erected within the Jurisdiction of any other State; nor any State be formed by the Junction of two or more States, or Parts of States, without the Consent of the Legislatures of the States concerned as well as of the Congress.

The Congress shall have Power to dispose of and make all needful Rules and Regulations respecting the Territory or other Property belonging to the United States; and nothing in this Constitution shall be so construed as to Prejudice any Claimes of the United States, or of any particular State.

Section 4.

The United States shall guarantee to every State in this Union a Republican Form of Government, and shall protect each of them against Invasion, and on Application of the Legislature, or of the Executive (when the Legislature cannot be convened) against domestic Violence.

ARTICLE V.

The Congress, whenever two thirds of both Houses shall deem it necessary, shall propose Amendments to this Constitution, or on the Application of the Legislatures of two thirds of the several States, shall call a Convention for proposing Amendments, which, in either Case, shall be valid to all Intents and Purposes, as Part of this Constitution, when ratified by the Legislatures of three fourths of the several States, or by Conventions in three fourths thereof, as the one or the other Mode of Ratification may be proposed by the Congress; Provided that no Amendment which may be made prior to the Year One thousand eight hundred and eight shall in any Manner affect the first and fourth Clauses in the Ninth Section of the first Article; and that no State, without its Consent, shall be deprived of its equal Suffrage in the Senate.

ARTICLE VI.

All Debts contracted and Engagements entered into, before the Adoption of this Constitution, shall be as valid against the United States under this Constitution, as under the Confederation.

This Constitution, and the laws of the United States which shall be made in Pursuance thereof; and all Treaties made, or which shall be made, under the Authority of the United States, shall be the supreme Law of the Land; and the Judges in every State shall be bound thereby, any Thing in the Constitution or Laws of any State to the Contrary notwithstanding.

The Senators and Representatives before mentioned, and the Members of the several State Legislatures, and all executive and judicial Officers, both of the United States and of the several States, shall be bound by Oath or Affirmation, to support this Constitution; but no religious Text shall ever be required as a Qualification to any Office or public Trust under the United States.

ARTICLE VII.

The Ratification of the Conventions of nine States, shall be sufficient for the Establishment of this constitution between the States so ratifying the Same.

Done in Convention by the Unanimous Consent of the States present the Seventeenth Day of September in the Year of our Lord one thousand seven hundred and Eighty seven and of the Independence of the United States of America the Twelfth. IN WITNESS whereof we have hereunto subscribed our Names.

[11]Repealed by the Thirteenth Amendment.

Go. WASHINGTON
Presid't. and deputy from Virginia

Attest
William Jackson
Secretary

DELAWARE
Geo. Read
Gunning Bedford jun
John Dickinson
Richard Basset
Jaco. Broon

MASSACHUSETTS
Nathaniel Gorham
Rufus King

CONNECTICUT
Wm. Saml. Johnson
Roger Sherman

NEW YORK
Alexander Hamilton

NEW JERSEY
Wh. Livingston
David Brearley.
Wm. Paterson.
Jona. Dayton

PENNSYLVANIA
B. Franklin
Thomas Mifflin
Robt. Morris
Geo. Clymer
Thos. FitzSimons
Jared Ingersoll
James Wilson
Gouv. Morris

VIRGINIA
John Blair
James Madison Jr.

NORTH CAROLINA
Wm. Blount
Richd. Dobbs Spaight.
Hu. Williamson

SOUTH CAROLINA
J. Rutledge
Charles Cotesworth Pinckney
Charles Pinckney
Pierce Butler.

GEORGIA
William Few
Abr. Baldwin

NEW HAMPSHIRE
John Langdon
Nicholas Gilman

MARYLAND
James McHenry
Dan of St. Thos. Jenifer
Danl. Carroll.

AMENDMENT I[12]

Congress shall make no law respecting an establishment of religion, or prohibiting the free exercise thereof; or abridging the freedom of speech, or of the press; or the right of the people peaceably to assemble, and to petition the Government for a redress of grievances.

AMENDMENT II

A well regulated militia, being necessary to the security of a free State, the right of the people to keep and bear arms, shall not be infringed.

[12]The first ten amendments were passed by Congress on September 25, 1789, and were ratified on December 15, 1791.

AMENDMENT III

No Soldier shall, in time of peace be quartered in any house, without the consent of the owner, nor in time of war, but in a manner to be prescribed by law.

AMENDMENT IV

The right of the people to be secure in their persons, houses, papers, and effects, against unreasonable searches and seizures, shall not be violated, and no warrants shall issue, but upon probable cause, supported by oath or affirmation, and particularly describing the place to be searched, and the persons or things to be seized.

455

AMENDMENT V

No person shall be held to answer for a capital, or otherwise infamous crime, unless on a presentment or indictment of a Grand Jury, except in cases arising in the land or naval forces, or in the militia, when in actual service in time of war or public danger; nor shall any person be subject for the same offence to be twice put in jeopardy of life or limb; nor shall be compelled in any criminal case to be a witness against himself, nor be deprived of life, liberty, or property, without due process of law; nor shall private property be taken for public use, without just compensation.

AMENDMENT VI

In all criminal prosecutions, the accused shall enjoy the right to a speedy and public trial, by an impartial jury of the State and district wherein the crime shall have been committed, which district shall have been previously ascertained by law, and to be informed of the nature and cause of the accusation; to be confronted with the witnesses against him; to have compulsory process for obtaining witnesses in his favor, and to have the assistance of counsel for his defence.

AMENDMENT VII

In Suits at common law, where the value in controversy shall exceed twenty dollars, the right of trial by jury shall be preserved, and no fact tried by a jury, shall be otherwise reexamined in any Court of the United States, than according to the rules of the common law.

AMENDMENT VIII

Excessive bail shall not be required, nor excessive fines imposed, nor cruel and unusual punishments inflicted.

AMENDMENT IX

The enumeration in the Constitution, of certain rights, shall not be construed to deny or disparage others retained by the people.

AMENDMENT X

The powers not delegated to the United States by the Constitution, nor prohibited by it to the States, are reserved to the States respectively, or to the people.

AMENDMENT XI (1795)

The Judicial power of the United States shall not be construed to extend to any suit in law or equity, commenced or prosecuted against one of the United States by Citizens of another State, or by Citizens or Subjects of any Foreign State.

AMENDMENT XII (1804)

The Electors shall meet in their respective states, and vote by ballot for President and Vice-President, one of whom, at least, shall not be an inhabitant of the same state with themselves; they shall name in their ballots the person voted for as President, and in distinct ballots the person voted for as Vice President, and they shall make distinct lists of all persons voted for as President, and of all persons voted for as Vice-President, and of the number of votes for each, which lists they shall sign and certify, and transmit sealed to the seat of the government of the United States, directed to the President of the Senate;—The President of the Senate shall, in the presence of the Senate and House of Representatives, open all the certificates and the votes shall then be counted;—The person having the greatest number of votes for President, shall be the President, if such number be a majority of the whole number of Electors appointed; and if no person have such majority, then from the persons having the highest numbers not exceeding three on the list of those voted for as President, the House of Representatives shall choose immediately, by ballot, the President. But in choosing the President, the votes shall be taken by states, the representation from each state having one vote; a quorum for this purpose shall consist of a member or members from two-thirds of the states, and a majority of all the states shall be necessary to a choice. [And if the House of Representatives shall not choose a President whenever the right of choice shall devolve upon them, before the fourth day of March next following, then the Vice-President shall act as President, as in the case of the death or other constitutional disability of the President.][13]—The person having the greatest number of votes as Vice-President, shall be the Vice-President, if such number be a majority of the whole number of Electors appointed, and if no person have a majority, then from the two highest numbers on the list, the Senate shall choose the Vice-President; a quorum for the purpose shall consist of two-thirds of the whole number of Senators, and a majority of the whole number shall be necessary to a choice. But no person constitutionally ineligible to the office of President shall be eligible to that of Vice-President of the United States.

AMENDMENT XIII (1865)

Section 1.

Neither slavery nor involuntary servitude, except as a punishment for crime whereof the party shall have been duly convicted, shall exist within the United States, or any place subject to their jurisdiction.

Section 2.

Congress shall have power to enforce this article by appropriate legislation.

AMENDMENT XIV (1868)

Section 1.

All persons born or naturalized in the United States, and subject to the jurisdiction thereof, are citizens of the United States and of the State wherein they reside. No State shall make or enforce any law which shall abridge the privileges or immunities of citizens of the United States; nor shall any State deprive any person of life, liberty, or property, without due process of law; nor deny to any person within its jurisdiction the equal protection of the laws.

Section 2.

Representatives shall be apportioned among the several States according to their respective numbers, counting the whole number of persons in each State, excluding Indians not taxed. But when the right to vote at any election for the choice of electors for President and Vice President of the United States, Representatives in Congress, the Executive and Judicial officers of a State, or the members of the Legislature thereof, is denied to any of the male inhabitants of such State, being [twenty-one][14] years of age, and citizens of the United States, or in any way abridged, except for participation in rebellion, or other crime, the basis of representation therein shall be reduced in the proportion which the number of such male citizens shall bear to the whole number of male citizens twenty-one years of age in such State.

Section 3.

No person shall be a Senator or Representative in Congress, or elector of President and Vice President, or hold any office, civil or military, under the United States, or under any State, who having previously taken an oath, as a member of Congress, or as an officer of the United States, or as a member of any State legislature, or as an executive or judicial officer of any State, to support the Constitution of the United States, shall have engaged in insurrection or rebellion against the same, or given aid or comfort to the enemies thereof. But Congress may by a vote of two-thirds of each House, remove such disability.

Section 4.

The validity of the public debt of the United States, authorized by law, including debts incurred for payment of pensions and bounties for services in suppressing insurrection or rebellion, shall not be questioned. But neither the United States nor any State shall assume or pay any debt or obligation incurred in aid of insurrection or rebellion against the United States, or any claim for the loss or emancipation of any slave, but all

---

[13]Changed by the Twentieth Amendment.

[14]Changed by the Twenty-sixth Amendment.

such debts, obligations and claims shall be held illegal and void.

Section 5.

The Congress shall have power to enforce, by appropriate legislation, the provisions of this article.

AMENDMENT XV (1870)
Section 1.

The right of citizens of the United States to vote shall not be denied or abridged by the United States or by any State on account of race, color, or previous condition of servitude.

Section 2.

The Congress shall have power to enforce this article by appropriate legislation.

AMENDMENT XVI (1913)

The Congress shall have power to lay and collect taxes on incomes, from whatever source derived, without apportionment among the several States, and without regard to any census or enumeration.

AMENDMENT XVII (1913)

The Senate of the United States shall be composed of two Senators from each State, elected by the people thereof, for six years; and each Senator shall have one vote. The electors in each State shall have the qualifications requisite for electors of the most numerous branch of the State legislatures.

When vacancies happen in the representation of any State in the Senate, the executive authority of such State shall issue writs of election to fill such vacancies: *Provided,* That the legislature of any State may empower the executive thereof to make temporary appointments until the people fill the vacancies by election as the legislature may direct.

This amendment shall not be so construed as to affect the election or term of any Senator chosen

before it becomes valid as part of the Constitution.

[AMENDMENT XVIII (1919)
[Section 1.

[After one year from the ratification of this article the manufacture, sale, or transportation of intoxicating liquors within, the importation thereof into, or the exportation thereof from the United States and all territory subject to the jurisdiction thereof for beverage purposes is hereby prohibited.

[Section 2.

[The Congress and the several States shall have concurrent power to enforce this article by appropriate legislation.

[Section 3.

[This article shall be inoperative unless it shall have been ratified as an amendment to the Constitution by the legislatures of the several States, as provided in the Constitution, within seven years from the date of the submission hereof to the States by the Congress.][15]

AMENDMENT XIX (1920)

The right of citizens of the United States to vote shall not be denied or abridged by the United States or by any State on account of sex.

Congress shall have power to enforce this article by appropriate legislation.

AMENDMENT XX (1933)
Section 1.

The terms of the President and Vice President shall end at noon on the 20th day of January, and the terms of Senators and Representatives at noon on the 3rd day of January, of the years in which such terms would have ended if this article had not been ratified, and the terms of their successors shall then begin.

---

[15]The Eighteenth Amendment was repealed by the Twenty-first Amendment.

Section 2.

The Congress shall assemble at least once in every year, and such meeting shall begin at noon on the 3rd day of January, unless they shall by law appoint a different day.

Section 3.

If, at the time fixed for the beginning of the term of the President, the President elect shall have died, the Vice President elect shall become President. If a President shall not have been chosen before the time fixed for the beginning of his term, or if the President elect shall have failed to qualify, then the Vice President elect shall act as President until a President shall have qualified; and the Congress may by law provide for the case wherein neither a President elect nor a Vice President elect shall have qualified, declaring who shall then act as President, or the manner in which one who is to act shall be selected, and such person shall act accordingly until a President or Vice President shall have qualified.

Section 4.

The Congress may by law provide for the case of the death of any of the persons from whom the House of Representatives may choose a President whenever the rights of choice shall have devolved upon them, and for the case of the death of any of the persons from whom the Senate may choose a Vice President whenever the right of choice shall have devolved upon them.

Section 5.

Sections 1 and 2 shall take effect on the 15th day of October following the ratification of this article.

Section 6.

This article shall be inoperative unless it shall have been ratified as an amendment to the Constitution by the legislatures of three-fourths of the several States within seven years from the date of its submission.

AMENDMENT XXI (1933)

Section 1.

The eighteenth article of amendment to the Constitution of the United States is hereby repealed.

Section 2.

The transportation or importation into any State, Territory, or possession of the United States for delivery or use therein of intoxicating liquors, in violation of the laws thereof, is hereby prohibited.

Section 3.

This article shall be inoperative unless it shall have been ratified as an amendment to the Constitution by conventions in the several States, as provided in the Constitution, within seven years from the date of the submission hereof to the States by the Congress.

AMENDMENT XXII (1951)

No person shall be elected to the office of the President more than twice, and no person who has held the office of President, or acted as President, for more than two years of a term to which some other person was elected President shall be elected to the office of the President more than once. But this Article shall not apply to any person holding the office of President when this Article was proposed by the Congress, and shall not prevent any person who may be holding the office of President, or acting as President, during the term within which this Article becomes operative from holding the office of President or acting as President during the remainder of such term.

AMENDMENT XXIII (1961)

Section 1.

The District constituting the seat of Government of the United States shall appoint in such manner as the Congress may direct:

A number of electors of President and Vice President equal to the whole number of Senators and Representatives in Congress to which the

District would be entitled if it were a State, but in no event more than the least populous State; they shall be in addition to those appointed by the States, but they shall be considered, for the purposes of the election of President and Vice President, to be electors appointed by a State; and they shall meet in the District and perform such duties as provided by the twelfth article of amendment.

Section 2.

The Congress shall have power to enforce this article by appropriate legislation.

AMENDMENT XXIV (1964)
Section 1.

The right of citizens of the United States to vote in any primary or other election for President or Vice President, for electors for President or Vice President, or for Senator or Representative in Congress, shall not be denied or abridged by the United States or any State by reason of failure to pay any poll tax or other tax.

Section 2.

The Congress shall have power to enforce this article by appropriate legislation.

AMENDMENT XXV (1967)
Section 1.

In case of the removal of the President from office or of his death or resignation, the Vice President shall become President.

Section 2.

Whenever there is a vacancy in the office of the Vice President, the President shall nominate a Vice President who shall take office upon confirmation by a majority vote of both Houses of Congress.

Section 3.

Whenever the President transmits to the President pro tempore of the Senate and the Speaker of the House of Representatives his written declaration that he is unable to discharge the powers and duties of his office, and until he transmits to them a written declaration to the contrary, such powers and duties shall be discharged by the Vice President as Acting President.

Section 4.

Whenever the Vice President and a majority of either the principal officers of the executive departments or of such other body as Congress may by law provide, transmit to the President pro tempore of the Senate and the Speaker of the House of Representatives their written declaration that the President is unable to discharge the powers and duties of his office, the Vice President shall immediately assume the powers and duties of the offices as Acting President.

Thereafter, when the President transmits to the President pro tempore of the Senate and the Speaker of the House of Representatives his written declaration that no inability exists, he shall resume the powers and duties of his office unless the Vice President and a majority of either the principal officers of the executive department or of such other body as Congress may by law provide, transmit within four days to the President pro tempore of the Senate and the Speaker of the House of Representatives their written declaration that the President is unable to discharge the powers and duties of his office. Thereupon Congress shall decide the issue, assembling within forty-eight hours for that purpose if not in session. If the Congress, within twenty-one days after receipt of the latter written declaration, or, if Congress is not in session, within twenty-one days after Congress is required to assemble, determines by two-thirds vote of both Houses that the President is unable to discharge the powers and duties of his office, the Vice President shall continue to discharge the same as Acting President; otherwise; the President shall resume the powers and duties of his office.

AMENDMENT XXVI (1971)
Section 1.

The right of citizens of the United States, who are eighteen years of age or older, to vote shall not be denied or abridged by the United States or by any State on account of age.

AMENDMENT XXVII (1992)

Section 1.

No law varying the compensation for the services of the Senators and Representatives shall take effect, until an election of Representatives shall have intervened.

Section 2.

The Congress shall have the power to enforce this article by appropriate legislation.

Federalist Paper #10

November 22, 1787

AMONG THE NUMEROUS ADVANTAGES promised by a well-constructed Union, none deserves to be more accurately developed than its tendency to break and control the violence of faction. The friend of popular governments never finds himself so much alarmed for their character and fate as when he contemplates their propensity to this dangerous vice. He will not fail, therefore, to set a due value on any plan which, without violating the principles to which he is attached, provides a proper cure for it. The instability, injustice, and confusion introduced into the public councils have, in truth, been the mortal diseases under which popular governments have everywhere perished, as they continue to be the favorite and fruitful topics from which the adversaries to liberty derive their most specious declamations. The valuable improvements made by the American constitutions on the popular models, both ancient and modern, cannot certainly be too much admired; but it would be an unwarrantable partiality to contend that they have as effectually obviated the danger on this side, as was wished and expected. Complaints are everywhere heard from our most considerate and virtuous citizens, equally the friends of public and private faith and of public and personal liberty, that our governments are too unstable, that the public good is disregarded in the conflicts of rival parties, and that measures are too often decided, not according to the rules of justice and the rights of the minor party, but by the superior force of an interested and overbearing majority. However anxiously we may wish that these complaints had no foundation, the evidence of known facts will not permit us to deny that they are in some degree true. It will be found, indeed, on a candid review of our situation, that some of the distresses under which we labor have been erroneously charged on the operation of our governments; but it will be found, at the same time, that other causes will not alone account for many of our heaviest misfortunes; and, particularly, for that prevailing and increasing distrust of public engagements and alarm for private rights which are echoed from one end of the continent to the other. These must be chiefly, if not wholly, effects of the unsteadiness and injustice with which a factious spirit has tainted our public administration.

By a faction I understand a number of citizens, whether amounting to a majority or minority of the whole, who are united and actuated by some common impulse of passion, or of interest, adverse to the rights of other citizens, or the permanent and aggregate interests of the community.

There are two methods of curing the mischiefs of faction: the one, by removing its causes; the other, by controlling its effects.

There are again two methods of removing the causes of faction: the one, by destroying the liberty which is essential to its existence; the other, by giving to every citizen the same opinions, the same passions, and the same interests.

It could never be more truly said than of the first remedy that it was worse than the disease. Liberty is to faction what air is to fire, an aliment without which it instantly expires. But it could not be a less folly to abolish liberty, which is essential to political life, because it nourishes faction than it would be to wish the annihilation of air, which is essential to animal life, because it imparts to fire its destructive agency.

The second expedient is as impracticable as the first would be unwise. As long as the reason of man continues fallible, and he is at liberty to exercise it, different opinions will be formed. As long as the connection subsists between his reason and his self-love, his opinions and his passions will have a reciprocal influence on each other; and the former will be objects to which the latter will attach themselves. The diversity in the faculties of men, from which the rights of property originate, is not less an insuperable obstacle to a uniformity of interests. The protection of these faculties is the first object of government. From the protection of different and unequal faculties of acquiring property, the possession of different degrees and kinds of property immediately results; and from the influence of these on the sentiments and views of the respective proprietors ensues a division of the society into different interests and parties.

The latent causes of faction are thus sown in the nature of man; and we see them everywhere brought into different degrees of activity, according to the different circumstances of civil society. A zeal for different opinions concerning religion, concerning government, and many other points, as well of speculation as of practice; an attachment to different leaders ambitiously contending for pre-eminence and power; or to persons of other descriptions whose fortunes have been interesting to the human passions, have, in turn, divided mankind into parties, inflamed them with mutual animosity, and rendered them much more disposed to vex and oppress each other than to cooperate for their common good. So strong is this propensity of mankind to fall into mutual animosities that where no substantial occasion presents itself the most frivolous and fanciful distinctions have been sufficient to kindle their unfriendly passions and excite their most violent conflicts. But the most common and durable source of factions has been the various and unequal distribution of property. Those who hold and those who are without property have ever formed distinct interests in society. Those who are creditors, and those who are debtors, fall under a like discrimination. A landed interest, a manufacturing interest, a mercantile interest, a moneyed interest, with many lesser interests, grow up of necessity in civilized nations, and divide them into different classes, actuated by different sentiments and views. The regulation of these various and interfering interests forms the principal task of modern legislation and involves the spirit of party and faction in the necessary and ordinary operations of government.

No man is allowed to be a judge in his own cause, because his interest would certainly bias his judgment, and, not improbably, corrupt his integrity. With equal, nay with greater reason, a body of men are unfit to be both judges and parties at the same time; yet what are many of the most important acts of legislation but so many judicial determinations, not indeed concerning the rights of single persons, but concerning the rights of large bodies of citizens? And what are the different classes of legislators but advocates and parties to the causes which they determine? Is a law proposed concerning private debts? It is a question to which the creditors are parties on one side and the debtors on the other. Justice ought to hold the balance between them. Yet the parties are, and must be, themselves the judges; and the most numerous party, or in other words, the most powerful faction must be expected to prevail. Shall domestic manufacturers be encouraged, and in what degree, by restrictions on foreign manufacturers? are questions which would be differently decided by the landed and the manufacturing classes, and probably by neither with a sole regard to justice and the public good. The apportionment of taxes on the various descriptions of property is an act which seems to require the most exact impartiality; yet there is, perhaps, no legislative act in which greater opportunity and temptation are given to a predominant party to trample on the rules of justice. Every shilling with which they overburden the inferior number is a shilling saved to their own pockets.

It is in vain to say that enlightened statesmen will be able to adjust these clashing interests and render them all subservient to the public good. Enlightened statesmen will not always be at the helm. Nor, in many cases, can such an adjustment be made at all without taking into view indirect and remote considerations, which will rarely prevail over the immediate interest which one party may find in disregarding the rights of another or the good of the whole.

The inference to which we are brought is that the *causes* of faction cannot be removed and that relief is only to be sought in the means of controlling its *effects*.

If a faction consists of less than a majority, relief is supplied by the republican principle, which enables the majority to defeat its sinister views by regular vote. It may clog the administration, it may convulse the society; but it will be unable to execute and mask its violence under the forms of the Constitution. When a majority is included in a faction, the form of popular government, on the other hand, enables it to sacrifice to its ruling passion or interest both the public good and the rights of other citizens. To secure the public good and private rights against the danger of such a faction, and at the same time to preserve the spirit and the form of popular government, is then the great object to which our inquiries are directed. Let me add that it is the great desideratum by which alone this form of government can be rescued from the opprobrium under which it has so long labored and be recommended to the esteem and adoption of mankind.

By what means is this object attainable? Evidently by one of two only. Either the existence of the same passion or interest in a majority at the same time must be prevented, or the majority, having such coexistent passion or interest, must be rendered, by their number and local situation, unable to concert and carry into effect schemes of oppression. If the impulse and the opportunity be suffered to coincide, we well know that neither moral nor religious motives can be relied on as an adequate control. They are not found to be such on the injustice and violence of individuals, and lose their efficacy in proportion to the number combined together, that is, in proportion as their efficacy becomes needful.

From this view of the subject it may be concluded that a pure democracy, by which I mean a society consisting of a small number of citizens, who assemble and administer the government in person, can admit of no cure for the mischiefs of faction. A common passion or interest will, in almost every case, be felt by a majority of the whole; a communication and concert results from the form of government itself; and there is nothing to check the inducements to sacrifice the weaker party or an obnoxious individual. Hence it is that such democracies have ever been spectacles of turbulence and contention; have ever been found incompatible with personal security or the rights of property; and have in general been as short in their lives as they have been violent in their deaths. Theoretic politicians, who have patronized this species of government, have erroneously supposed that by reducing mankind to a perfect equality in their political rights, they would at the same time be perfectly equalized and assimilated in their possessions, their opinions, and their passions.

A republic, by which I mean a government in which the scheme of representation takes place, opens a different prospect and promises the cure for which we are seeking. Let us examine the points in which it varies from pure democracy, and we shall comprehend both the nature of the cure and the efficacy which it must derive from the Union.

The two great points of difference between a democracy and a republic are: first, the delegation of the government, in the latter, to a small number of citizens elected by the rest; secondly, the greater number of citizens and greater sphere of country over which the latter may be extended.

The effect of the first difference is, on the one hand, to refine and enlarge the public views by passing them through the medium of a chosen body of citizens, whose wisdom may best discern the true interest of their country and whose patriotism and love of justice will be least likely to sacrifice it to temporary or partial considerations. Under such a regulation it may well happen that the public voice, pronounced by the representatives of the people, will be more consonant to the public good than if pronounced by the people themselves, convened for the purpose. On the other hand, the effect may be inverted. Men of factious tempers, of local prejudices, or of sinister designs, may, by intrigue, by corruption, or by other means, first obtain the suffrages, and then betray the interests of the people. The question resulting is, whether small or extensive republics are most favorable to the election of proper guardians of the public weal; and it is clearly decided in favor of the latter by two obvious considerations.

In the first place it is to be remarked that however small the republic may be the representatives must be raised to a certain number in order to guard against the cabals of a few; and that however large it may be they must be limited to a certain number in order to guard against the confusion of a multitude. Hence, the number of representatives in the two cases not being in proportion to that of the constituents, and being proportionally greatest in the small republic, it follows that if the proportion of fit characters be not less in the large than in the small republic, the former will present a greater option, and consequently a greater probability of a fit choice.

In the next place, as each representative will be chosen by a greater number of citizens in the large than in the small republic, it will be more difficult for unworthy candidates to practice with success the vicious arts by which elections are too often carried; and the suffrages of the people being more free, will be more likely to center on men who possess the most attractive merit and the most diffusive and established characters.

It must be confessed that in this, as in most other cases, there is a mean, on both sides of which inconveniencies will be found to lie. By enlarging too much the number of electors, you render the representative too little acquainted with all their local circumstances and lesser interests; as by reducing it too much, you render him unduly attached to these, and too little fit to comprehend and pursue great and national objects. The federal Constitution forms a happy combination in this respect; the great and aggregate interests being referred to the national, the local and particular to the State legislatures.

The other point of difference is the greater number of citizens and extent of territory which may be brought within the compass of republican than of democratic government; and it is this circumstance principally which renders factious combinations less to be dreaded in the former than in the latter. The smaller the society, the fewer probably will be the distinct parties and interests composing it; the fewer the distinct parties and interests, the more frequently will a majority be found of the same party; and the smaller the number of individuals composing a majority, and the smaller the compass within which they

are placed, the more easily will they concert and execute their plans of oppression. Extend the sphere and you take in a greater variety of parties and interests; you make it less probable that a majority of the whole will have a common motive to invade the rights of other citizens; or if such a common motive exists, it will be more difficult for all who feel it to discover their own strength and to act in unison with each other. Besides other impediments, it may be remarked that, where there is a consciousness of unjust or dishonorable purposes, communication is always checked by distrust in proportion to the number whose concurrence is necessary.

Hence, it clearly appears that the same advantage which a republic has over a democracy in controlling the effects of faction is enjoyed by a large over a small republic—is enjoyed by the Union over the States composing it. Does this advantage consist in the substitution of representatives whose enlightened views and virtuous sentiments render them superior to local prejudices and to schemes of injustice? It will not be denied that the representation of the Union will be most likely to possess these requisite endowments. Does it consist in the greater security afforded by a greater variety of parties, against the event of any one party being able to outnumber and oppress the rest? In an equal degree does the increased variety of parties comprised within the Union increase this security. Does it, in fine, consist in the greater obstacles opposed to the concert and accomplishment of the secret wishes of an unjust and interested majority? Here again the extent of the Union gives it the most palpable advantage.

The influence of factious leaders may kindle a flame within their particular States but will be unable to spread a general conflagration through the other States. A religious sect may degenerate into a political faction in a part of the Confederacy; but the variety of sects dispersed over the entire face of it must secure the national councils against any danger from that source. A rage for paper money, for an abolition of debts, for an equal division of property, or for any other improper or wicked project, will be less apt to pervade the whole body of the Union than a particular member of it, in the same proportion as such a malady is more likely to taint a particular county or district than an entire State.

In the extent and proper structure of the Union, therefore, we behold a republican remedy for the diseases most incident to republican government. And according to the degree of pleasure and pride we feel in being republicans ought to be our zeal in cherishing the spirit and supporting the character of federalists.

A P P E N D I X D

FEDERALIST PAPER #51

February 6, 1788

To WHAT EXPEDIENT, then, shall we finally resort, for maintaining in practice the necessary partition of power among the several departments as laid down in the Constitution? The only answer that can be given is that as all these exterior provisions are found to be inadequate the defect must be supplied, by so contriving the interior structure of the government as that its several constituent parts may, by their mutual relations, be the means of keeping each other in their proper places. Without presuming to undertake a full development of this important idea I will hazard a few general observations which may perhaps place it in a clearer light, and enable us to form a more correct judgment of the principles and structure of the government planned by the convention.

In order to lay a due foundation for that separate and distinct exercise of the different powers of government, which to a certain extent is admitted on all hands to be essential to the preservation of liberty, it is evident that each department should have a will of its own; and consequently should be so constituted that the members of each should have as little agency as possible in the appointment of the members of the others. Were this principle rigorously adhered to, it would require that all the appointments for the supreme executive, legislative, and judiciary magistracies should be drawn from the same fountain of authority, the people, through channels having no communication whatever with one another. Perhaps such a plan of constructing the several departments would be less difficult in practice than it may in contemplation appear.

Some difficulties, however, and some additional expense would attend the execution of it. Some deviations, therefore, from the principle must be admitted. In the constitution of the judiciary department in particular, it might be inexpedient to insist rigorously on the principle: first, because peculiar qualifications being essential in the members, the primary consideration ought to be to select that mode of choice which best secures these qualifications; second, because the permanent tenure by which the appointments are held in that department must soon destroy all sense of dependence on the authority conferring them.

It is equally evident that the members of each department should be as little dependent as possible on those of the others for the emoluments annexed to their offices. Were the executive magistrate, or the judges, not independent of the legislature in this particular, their independence in every other would be merely nominal.

But the great security against a gradual concentration of the several powers in the same department consists in giving to those who administer each department the necessary constitutional means and personal motives to resist encroachments of the others. The provision for defense must in this, as in all other cases, be made commensurate to the danger of attack. Ambition must be made to counteract ambition. The interest of the man must be connected with the constitutional rights of the place. It may be a reflection on human nature that such devices should be necessary to control the abuses of government. But what is government itself but the greatest of all reflections on human nature? If men were angels, no government would be necessary. If angels were to govern men, neither external nor internal controls on government would be necessary. In framing a government which is to be administered by men over men, the great difficulty lies in this: you must first enable the government to control the governed; and in the next place oblige it to control itself. A dependence on the people is, no doubt, the primary control on the government; but experience has taught mankind the necessity of auxiliary precautions.

This policy of supplying, by opposite and rival interests, the defect of better motives, might be traced through the whole system of human affairs, private as well as public. We see it particularly displayed in all the subordinate distributions of power, where the constant aim is to divide and arrange the several offices in such a manner as that each may be a check on the other—that the private interest of every individual may be a sentinel over the public rights. These inventions of prudence cannot be less requisite in the distribution of the supreme powers of the State.

But it is not possible to give to each department an equal power of self-defense. In republican government, the legislative authority necessarily predominates. The remedy for this inconveniency is to divide the legislature into different branches; and to render them, by different modes of election and different principles of action, as little connected with each other as the nature of their common functions and their common dependence on the society will admit. It may even be necessary to guard against dangerous encroachments by still further precautions. As the weight of the legislative authority requires that it should be thus divided, the weakness of the executive may require, on the other hand, that it should be fortified. An absolute negative on the legislature appears, at first view, to be the natural defense with which the executive magistrate should be armed. But perhaps it would be neither altogether safe nor alone sufficient. On ordinary occasions it might not be exerted with the requisite firmness, and on extraordinary occasions it might be perfidiously abused. May not this defect of an absolute negative be supplied by some qualified connection between this weaker department and the weaker branch of the stronger department, by which the latter may be led to support

the constitutional rights of the former, without being too much detached from the rights of its own department?

If the principles on which these observations are found be just, as I persuade myself they are, and they be applied as a criterion to the several State constitutions, and the federal Constitution, it will be found that if the latter does not perfectly correspond with them, the former are infinitely less able to bear such a test.

There are, moreover, two considerations particularly applicable to the federal system of America, which place that system in a very interesting point of view.

First. In a single republic, all the power surrendered by the people is submitted to the administration of a single government; and the usurpations are guarded against by a division of the government into distinct and separate departments. In the compound republic of America, the power surrendered by the people is first divided between two distinct governments, and then the portion allotted to each subdivided among distinct and separate departments. Hence a double security arises to the rights of the people. The different governments will control each other, at the same time that each will be controlled by itself.

Second. It is of great importance in a republic not only to guard the society against the oppression of its rulers, but to guard one part of the society against the injustice of the other part. Different interests necessarily exist in different classes of citizens. If a majority be united by a common interest, the rights of the minority will be insecure. There are but two methods of providing against this evil: the one by creating a will in the community independent of the majority—that is, of the society itself; the other, by comprehending in the society so many separate descriptions of citizens as will render an unjust combination of a majority of the whole very improbable, if not impracticable. The first method prevails in all governments possessing an hereditary or self-appointed authority. This, at best, is but a precarious security; because a power independent of the society may as well espouse the unjust views of the major as the rightful interests of the minor party, and may possibly be turned against both parties. The second method will be exemplified in the federal republic of the United States. Whilst all authority in it will be derived from and dependent on the society, the society itself will be broken into so many parts, interests and classes of citizens, that the rights of individuals, or of the minority, will be in little danger from interested combinations of the majority. In a free government the security for civil rights must be the same as that for religious rights. It consists in the one case in the multiplicity of interests, and in the other in the multiplicity of sects. The degree of security in both cases will depend on the number of interests and sects; and this may be presumed to depend on the extent of country and number of people comprehended under the same government. This view of the subject must particularly recommend a proper federal system to all the sincere and considerate friends of republican government, since it shows that in exact proportion as the territory of the Union may be formed into more circumscribed Confederacies, or States, oppressive combinations of a majority will be facilitated; the best security, under the republican forms, for the rights of every class of citizen, will be diminished; and consequently the stability and independence of some member of the government, the only other security, must be proportionally increased. Justice is the end of government. It is the end of civil society. It ever has been and ever will be pursued until it be obtained, or until liberty be lost in the pursuit. In a society under the forms of which the stronger faction can readily unite and oppress the weaker, anarchy may as truly be said to reign as in a state of nature, where the weaker individual is not secured against the violence of the stronger; and as, in the latter state, even the stronger individuals are prompted, by the uncertainty of their condition, to submit to a government which may protect the weak as well as themselves; so, in the former state, will the more powerful factions or parties be gradually induced, by a like motive, to wish for a government which will protect all parties, the weaker as well as the more powerful. It can be little doubted that if the State of Rhode Island was separated from the Confederacy and left to itself, the insecurity of rights under the popular form of government within such narrow limits would be displayed by such reiterate oppressions of factious majorities that some power altogether independent of the people would soon be called for by the voice of the very factions whose misrule had proved the necessity of it. In the extended republic of the United States, and among the great variety of interests, parties, and sects which it embraces, a coalition of a majority of the whole society could seldom take place on any other principles than those of justice and the general good; whilst there being thus less danger to a minor from the will of a major party, there must be less pretext, also, to provide for the security of the former, by introducing into the government a will not dependent on the latter, or, in other words, a will independent of the society itself. It is no less certain than it is important, notwithstanding the contrary opinions which have been entertained, that the larger the society, provided it lie within a practicable sphere, the more duly capable it will be of self-government. And happily for the *republican cause,* the practicable sphere may be carried to a very great extent by a judicious modification and mixture of the *federal principle.*

APPENDIX E

GETTYSBURG ADDRESS

ABRAHAM LINCOLN

November 19, 1863

FOUR SCORE and seven years ago our fathers brought forth on this continent, a new nation, conceived in Liberty, and dedicated to the proposition that all men are created equal.

Now we are engaged in a great civil war, testing whether that nation or any nation so conceived and so dedicated, can long endure. We are met on a great battle-field of that war. We have come to dedicate a portion of that field, as a final resting place for those who here gave their lives that that nation might live. It is altogether fitting and proper that we should do this.

But, in a larger sense, we can not dedicate—we can not consecrate—we can not hallow—this ground. The brave men, living and dead, who struggled here, have consecrated it, far above our poor power to add or detract. The world will little note, nor long remember what we say here, but it can never forget what they did here. It is for us the living, rather, to be dedicated here to the unfinished work which they who fought here have thus far so nobly advanced. It is rather for us to be here dedicated to the great task remaining before us—that from these honored dead we take increased devotion to that cause for which they gave the last full measure of devotion—that we here highly resolve that these dead shall not have died in vain—that this nation, under God, shall have a new birth of freedom—and that government of the people, by the people, for the people, shall not perish from the earth.

SECOND INAUGURAL ADDRESS

ABRAHAM LINCOLN

March 4, 1865

FELLOW-COUNTRYMEN: At this second appearing to take the oath of the presidential office there is less occasion for an extended address than there was at the first. Then a statement somewhat in detail of a course to be pursued seemed fitting and proper. Now, at the expiration of four years, during which public declarations have been constantly called forth on every point and phase of the great contest which still absorbs the attention and engrosses the energies of the nation, little that is new could be presented. The progress of our arms, upon which all else chiefly depends, is as well known to the public as to myself, and it is, I trust, reasonably satisfactory and encouraging to all. With high hope for the future, no prediction in regard to it is ventured.

On the occasion corresponding to this four years ago all thoughts were anxiously directed to an impending civil war. All dreaded it, all sought to avert it. While the inaugural address was being delivered from this place, devoted altogether to *saving* the Union without war, insurgent agents were in the city seeking to *destroy* it without war—seeking to dissolve the Union and divide effects by negotiation. Both parties deprecated war, but one of them would *make* war rather than let the nation survive, and the other would *accept* war rather than let it perish, and the war came.

One eighth of the whole population was colored slaves, not distributed generally over the Union, but localized in the southern part of it. These slaves constituted a peculiar and powerful interest. All knew that this interest was somehow the cause of the war. To strengthen, perpetuate, and extend this interest was the object for which the insurgents would rend the Union even by war, while the Government claimed no right to do more than to restrict the territorial enlargement of it. Neither party expected for the war the magnitude or the duration which it has already attained. Neither anticipated that the *cause* of the conflict might cease with or even before the conflict itself should cease. Each looked for an easier triumph, and a result less fundamental and astounding. Both read the same Bible and pray to the same God, and each invokes His aid against the other. It may seem strange that any men should dare to ask a just God's assistance in wringing their bread from the sweat of other men's faces, but let us judge not, that we be not judged. The prayers of both could not be answered. That of neither has been answered fully. The Almighty has His own purposes. "Woe unto the world because of offenses; for it must needs be that offenses come, but woe to that man by whom the offense cometh." If we shall suppose that American slavery is one of those offenses which, in the providence of God, must needs come, but which, having continued through His appointed time, He now wills to remove, and that He gives to both North and South this terrible war as the woe due to those by whom the offense came, shall we discern therein any departure from those divine attributes which the believers in a living God always ascribe to Him? Fondly do we hope, fervently do we pray, that this mighty scourge of war may speedily pass away. Yet, if God wills that it continue until all the wealth piled by the bondsman's two hundred and fifty years of unrequited toil shall be sunk, and until every drop of blood drawn with the lash shall be paid by another drawn with the sword, as was said three thousand years ago, so still it must be said, "The judgments of the Lord are true and righteous altogether."

With malice toward none, with charity for all, with firmness in the right as God gives us to see the right, let us strive on to finish the work we are in, to bind up the nation's wounds, to care for him who shall have borne the battle and for his widow and his orphan, to do all which may achieve and cherish a just and lasting peace among ourselves and with all nations.

APPENDIX G

INAUGURAL ADDRESS

JOHN F. KENNEDY

January 20, 1961

WE OBSERVE TODAY not a victory of party but a celebration of freedom—symbolizing an end as well as a beginning—signifying renewal as well as change. For I have sworn before you and Almighty God the same solemn oath our forebears prescribed nearly a century and three quarters ago.

The world is very different now. For man holds in his mortal hands the power to abolish all forms of human poverty and all forms of human life. And yet the same revolutionary beliefs for which our forebears fought are still at issue around the globe—the belief that the rights of man come not from the generosity of the state but from the hand of God.

We dare not forget today that we are the heirs of that first revolution. Let the word go forth from this time and place, to friend and foe alike, that the torch has been passed to a new generation of Americans—born in this century, tempered by war, disciplined by a hard and bitter peace, proud of our ancient heritage—and unwilling to witness or permit the slow undoing of those human rights to which this nation has always been committed, and to which we are committed today at home and around the world.

Let every nation know, whether it wishes us well or ill, that we shall pay any price, bear any burden, meet any hardship, support any friend, oppose any foe to assure the survival and the success of liberty.

This much we pledge—and more.

To those old allies whose cultural and spiritual origins we share, we pledge the loyalty of faithful friends. United, there is little we cannot do in a host of cooperative ventures. Divided, there is little we can do—for we dare not meet a powerful challenge at odds and split asunder.

To those new states whom we welcome to the ranks of the free, we pledge our word that one form of colonial control shall not have passed away merely to be replaced by a far more iron tyranny. We shall not always expect to find them supporting our view. But we shall always hope to find them strongly supporting their own freedom—and to remember that, in the past, those who foolishly sought power by riding the back of the tiger ended up inside.

To those peoples in the huts and villages of half the globe struggling to break the bonds of mass misery, we pledge our best efforts to help them help themselves, for whatever period is required—not because the Communists may be doing it, not because we seek their votes, but because it is right. If a free society cannot help the many who are poor, it cannot save the few who are rich.

To our sister republics south of our border, we offer a special pledge—to convert our good words into good deeds—in a new alliance for progress—to assist free men and free governments in casting off the chains of poverty. But this peaceful revolution of hope cannot become the prey of hostile powers. Let all our neighbors know that we shall join with them to oppose aggression or subversion anywhere in the Americas. And let every other power know that this hemisphere intends to remain the master of its own house.

To that world assembly of sovereign states, the United Nations, our last best hope in an age where the instruments of war have far outpaced the instruments of peace, we renew our pledge of support—to prevent it from becoming merely a forum for invective—to strengthen its shield of the new and the weak—and to enlarge the area in which its writ may run.

Finally, to those nations who would make themselves our adversary, we offer not a pledge but a request: that both sides begin anew the quest for peace, before the dark powers of destruction unleashed by science engulf all humanity in planned or accidental self-destruction.

We dare not tempt them with weakness. For only when our arms are sufficient beyond doubt can we be certain beyond doubt that they will never be employed.

But neither can two great and powerful groups of nations take comfort from our present course—both sides overburdened by the cost of modern weapons, both rightly alarmed by the steady spread of the deadly atom, yet both racing to alter that uncertain balance of terror that stays the hand of mankind's final war.

So let us begin anew—remembering on both sides that civility is not a sign of weakness, and sincerity is always subject to proof. Let us never negotiate out of fear. But let us never fear to negotiate.

Let both sides explore what problems unite us instead of belaboring those problems which divide us.

Let both sides, for the first time, formulate serious and precise proposals for the inspection and control of arms—and bring the absolute power to destroy other nations under the absolute control of all nations.

Let both sides seek to invoke the wonders of science instead of its terrors. Together let us explore the stars, conquer the deserts, eradicate disease, tap the ocean depths and encourage the arts and commerce.

Let both sides unite to heed in all corners of the earth the command of Isaiah—to "undo the heavy burdens . . . [and] let the oppressed go free."

And if a beachhead of cooperation may push back the jungles of suspicion, let both sides join in creating a new endeavor—not a new balance of power, but a new world of law, where the strong are just and the weak secure and the peace preserved.

All this will not be finished in the first hundred days. Nor will it be finished in the first thousand days, nor in the life of this Administration, nor even perhaps in our lifetime on this planet. But let us begin.

In your hands, my fellow citizens, more than mine, will rest the final success or failure of our course. Since this country was founded, each generation of Americans has been summoned to give testimony to its national loyalty. The graves of young Americans who answered the call to service surround the globe.

Now the trumpet summons us again—not as a call to bear arms, though arms we need—not as a call to battle, though embattled we are—but a call to bear the burden of a long twilight struggle, year in and year out, "rejoicing in hope, patient in tribulation"—a struggle against the common enemies of man: tyranny, poverty, disease and war itself.

Can we forge against these enemies a grand and global alliance, north and south, east and west, that can assure a more fruitful life for all mankind? Will you join in that historic effort?

In the long history of the world, only a few generations have been granted the role of defending freedom in its hour of maximum danger. I do not shrink from this responsibility—I welcome it. I do not believe that any of us would exchange places with any other people or any other generation. The energy, the faith, the devotion which we bring to this endeavor will light our country and all who serve it—and the flow from that fire can truly light the world.

And so, my fellow Americans: ask not what your country can do for you—ask what you can do for your country.

My fellow citizens of the world: ask not what America will do for you, but what together we can do for the freedom of man.

Finally, whether you are citizens of America or citizens of the world, ask of us here the same high standards of strength and sacrifice which we ask of you. With a good conscience our only sure reward, with history the final judge of our deeds, let us go forth to lead the land we love, asking His blessing and His help, but knowing that here on earth God's work must truly be our own.

APPENDIX H

FREEDOM MARCH ADDRESS

MARTIN LUTHER KING, JR.

August 28, 1963

FIVE SCORE YEARS AGO, a great American, in whose symbolic shadow we stand, signed the Emancipation Proclamation. This momentous decree came as a great beacon light of hope to millions of Negro slaves who had been seared in the flames of withering injustice. It came as a joyous daybreak to end the long night of captivity.

But one hundred years later, we must face the tragic fact that the Negro is still not free. One hundred years later, the life of the Negro is still sadly crippled by the manacles of segregation and the chains of discrimination. One hundred years later, the Negro lives on a lonely island of poverty in the midst of a vast ocean of material prosperity. One hundred years later, the Negro is still languished in the corners of American society and finds himself an exile in his own land. So we have come here today to dramatize an appalling condition.

In a sense we have come to our nation's Capital to cash a check. When the architects of our republic wrote the magnificent words of the Constitution and the Declaration of Independence, they were signing a promissory note to which every American was to fall heir. This note was a promise that all men would be guaranteed the unalienable rights of life, liberty, and the pursuit of happiness.

It is obvious today that America has defaulted on this promissory note insofar as her citizens of color are concerned. Instead of honoring this sacred obligation, America has given the Negro people a bad check; a check which has come back marked "insufficient funds." But we refuse to believe that the bank of justice is bankrupt. We refuse to believe that there are insufficient funds in the great vaults of opportunity of this nation. So we have come to cash this check—a check that will give us upon demand the riches of freedom and the security of justice. We have also come to this hallowed spot to remind America of the fierce urgency of *now*. This is no time to engage in the luxury of cooling off or to take the tranquilizing drug of gradualism. *Now* is the time to make real the promises of Democracy. *Now* is the time to rise from the dark and desolate valley of segregation to the sunlit path of racial justice. *Now* is the time to open the doors of opportunity to all of God's children. *Now* is the time to lift our nation from the quicksands of racial injustice to the solid rock of brotherhood.

It would be fatal for the nation to overlook the urgency of the moment and to underestimate the determination of the Negro. This sweltering summer of the Negro's legitimate discontent will not pass until there is an invigorating autumn of freedom and equality. 1963 is not an end, but a beginning. Those who hope that the Negro needed to blow off steam and will now be content will have a rude awakening if the nation returns to business as usual. There will be neither rest nor tranquillity in America until the Negro is granted his citizenship rights. The whirlwinds of revolt will continue to shake the foundations of our nation until the bright day of justice emerges.

But there is something that I must say to my people who stand on the warm threshold which leads into the palace of justice. In the process of gaining our rightful place we must not be guilty of wrongful deeds. Let us not seek to satisfy our thirst for freedom by drinking from the cup of bitterness and hatred. We must forever conduct our struggle on the high plane of dignity and discipline. We must not allow our creative protest to degenerate into physical violence. Again and again we must rise to the majestic heights of meeting physical force with soul force. The marvelous new militancy which has engulfed the Negro community must not lead us to a distrust of all white people, for many of our white brothers, as evidenced by their presence here today, have come to realize that their destiny is tied up with our destiny and their freedom is inextricably bound to our freedom. We cannot walk alone.

And as we walk, we must make the pledge that we shall march ahead. We cannot turn back. There are those who are asking the devotees of civil rights, "When will you be satisfied?" We can never be satisfied as long as the Negro is the victim of the unspeakable horrors of police brutality. We can never be satisfied as long as our bodies, heavy with the fatigue of travel, cannot gain lodging in the motels of the highways and the hotels of the cities. We cannot be satisfied as long as the Negro's basic mobility is from a smaller ghetto to a larger one. We can never be satisfied as long as a Negro in Mississippi cannot vote and a Negro in New York believes he has nothing for which to vote. No, no, we are not satisfied, and we will not be satisfied until justice rolls down like waters and righteousness like a mighty stream.

I am not unmindful that some of you have come here out of great trials and tribulations. Some of you have come fresh from narrow jail cells. Some of you have come from areas where your quest for freedom left you battered by the storms of persecution and staggered by the winds of police brutality. You have been the veterans of creative suffering. Continue to work with the faith that unearned suffering is redemptive.

Go back to Mississippi, go back to Alabama, go back to South Carolina, go back to Georgia, go back to Louisiana, go back to the slums and ghettos of our northern cities, knowing that somehow this situation can and will be changed. Let us not wallow in the valley of despair.

I say to you today, my friends, that in spite of the difficulties and frustrations of the moment I still have a dream. It is a dream deeply rooted in the American dream.

I have a dream that one day this nation will rise up and live out the true meaning of its creed: "We hold these truths to be self-evident; that all men are created equal."

I have a dream that one day on the red hills of Georgia the sons of former slaves and the sons of former slaveowners will be able to sit down together at the table of brotherhood.

I have a dream that one day even the state of Mississippi, a desert state sweltering with the heat of injustice and oppression, will be transformed into an oasis of freedom and justice.

I have a dream that my four little children will one day live in a nation where they will not be judged by the color of their skin but by the content of their character.

I have a dream today.

I have a dream that one day the state of Alabama, whose governor's lips are presently dripping with the words of interposition and nullification, will be transformed into a situation where little black boys and black girls will be able to join hands with little white boys and white girls and walk together as sisters and brothers.

I have a dream today.

I have a dream that one day every valley shall be exalted, every hill and mountain shall be made low, the rough places will be made plains, and the crooked places will be made straight, and the glory of the Lord shall be revealed, and all flesh shall see it together.

This is our hope. This is the faith with which I return to the South. With this faith we will be able to hew out of the mountain of despair a stone of hope. With this faith we will be able to transform the jangling discords of our nation into a beautiful symphony of brotherhood. With this faith we will be able to work together, to pray together, to struggle together, to go to jail together, to stand up for freedom together, knowing that we will be free one day.

This will be the day when all of God's children will be able to sing with new meaning

My country, 'tis of thee,
Sweet land of liberty,
    Of thee I sing:
Land where my fathers died,

Land of the pilgrims' pride,
From every mountain-side
Let freedom ring.

And if America is to be a great nation this must become true. So let freedom ring from the prodigious hilltops of New Hampshire. Let freedom ring from the mighty mountains of New York. Let freedom ring from the heightening Alleghenies of Pennsylvania!

Let freedom ring from the snowcapped Rockies of Colorado!

Let freedom ring from the curvacious peaks of California!

But not only that; let freedom ring from Stone Mountain of Georgia!

Let freedom ring from Lookout Mountain of Tennessee!

Let freedom ring from every hill and molehill of Mississippi. From every mountainside, let freedom ring.

When we let freedom ring, when we let it ring from every village and every hamlet, from every state and every city, we will be able to speed up that day when all of God's children, black men and white men, Jews and Gentiles, Protestants and Catholics, will be able to join hands and sing in the words of the old Negro spiritual, "Free at last! free at last! thank God almighty, we are free at last!"

APPENDIX I

COMMENCEMENT ADDRESS

RONALD REAGAN

University of Notre Dame, May 17, 1981

FATHER HESBURGH, I thank you very much and for so many things. The distinguished honor that you've conferred upon me here today, I must say, however, compounds a sense of guilt that I have nursed for almost fifty years. I thought the first degree I was given was honorary. But it's wonderful to be here today with Governor Orr, Governor Bowen, Senators Lugar and Quayle, and Representative Hiler, these distinguished honorees, the trustees, administration, faculty, students, and friends of Notre Dame and most important, the graduating class of 1981.

* * *

This Nation was born when a band of men, the Founding Fathers, a group so unique we've never seen their like since, rose to such selfless heights. Lawyers, tradesmen, merchants, farmers—fifty-six men achieved security and standing in life but valued freedom more. They pledged their lives, their fortunes, and their sacred honor. Sixteen of them gave their lives. Most gave their fortunes. All preserved their sacred honor.

They gave us more than a nation. They brought to all mankind for the first time the concept that man was born free, that each of us has inalienable rights, ours by the grace of God, and that government was created by us for our convenience, having only the powers that we choose to give it. This is the heritage that you're about to claim as you come out to join the society made up of those who have preceded you by a few years, or some of us by a great many.

This experiment in man's relation to man is a few years into its third century. Saying that may

make it sound quite old. But let's look at it from another viewpoint or perspective. A few years ago, someone figured out that if you could condense the entire history of life on Earth into a motion picture that would run for 24 hours a day, 365 days—maybe on leap years we could have an intermission—this idea that is the United States wouldn't appear on the screen until 3½ seconds before midnight on December 31st. And in those 3½ seconds not only would a new concept of society come into being, a golden hope for all mankind, but more than half the activity, economic activity in world history, would take place on this continent. Free to express their genius, individual Americans, men and women, in 3½ seconds, would perform such miracles of invention, construction, and production as the world had ever seen.

As you join us out there beyond the campus, you know there are great unsolved problems. Federalism, with its built in checks and balances, has been distorted. Central government has usurped powers that properly belong to local and state governments. And in so doing, in many ways that central government has begun to fail to do the things that are truly the responsibility of a central government.

All of this has led to the misuse of power and preemption of the prerogatives of people and their social institutions. You are graduating from a great private, or, if you will, independent university. Not too many years ago, such schools were relatively free from government interference. In recent years, Government has spawned regulations covering virtually every facet of our lives. The independent and church-supported colleges and universities have found themselves enmeshed in that network of regulations and the costly blizzard of paperwork that government is demanding. Thirty-four congressional committees and almost eighty subcommittees have jurisdiction over 439 separate laws affecting education at the college level alone. Almost every aspect of campus life is now regulated—hiring, firing, promotions, physical plant, construction, record-keeping, fundraising and, to some extent, curriculum and educational programs.

I hope when you leave this campus that you will do so with a feeling of obligation to your alma mater. She will need your help and support in the years to come. If ever the great independent colleges and universities like Notre Dame give way to and are replaced by tax-supported institutions, the struggle to preserve academic freedom will have been lost.

We're troubled today by economic stagnation, brought on by inflated currency and prohibitive taxes and burdensome regulations. The cost of stagnation in human terms, mostly among those least equipped to survive it, is cruel and inhuman.

Now, after those remarks, don't decide that you'd better turn your diploma back in so you can stay another year on the campus. I've just given you the bad news. The good news is that something is being done about all this because the people of America have said, "Enough already." You know, we who had preceded you had just gotten so busy that we let things get out of hand. We forgot that we were the keepers of the power, forgot to challenge the notion that the state is the principal vehicle of social change, forgot that millions of social interactions among free individuals and institutions can do more to foster economic and social progress than all the careful schemes of government planners.

Well, at last we're remembering, remembering that government has certain legitimate functions which it can perform very well, that it can be responsive to the people, that it can be humane and compassionate, but that when it undertakes tasks that are not its proper province, it can do none of them as well or as economically as the private sector.

For too long, government has been fixing things that aren't broken and inventing miracle cures for unknown diseases.

We need you. We need your youth. We need your strength. We need your idealism to help us make right that which is wrong. Now, I know that in this period of your life, you have been and are critically looking at the mores and customs of the past and questioning their value. Every generation does that. May I suggest, don't discard the time-tested values upon which civilization was built simply because they're old? More important, don't let today's doom criers and cynics persuade you that the best is past, that from here on it's all downhill. Each generation sees farther than the generation that preceded it because it stands on the shoulders of that generation. You're going to have opportunities beyond anything that we've ever known.

The people have made it plain already. They want an end to excessive government intervention in their lives and in the economy, an end to the burdensome and unnecessary regulations and a punitive tax policy that does take "from the mouth of labor the bread it has earned." They want a government that cannot only continue to send men across the vast reaches of space and bring them safely home, but that can guarantee that you and I can walk in the park of our neighborhood after dark and get safely home. And finally, they want to know that this Nation has the ability to defend itself against those who would seek to pull it down.

And all of this, we the people can do. Indeed, a start has already been made. There's a task force under the leadership of the Vice President, George Bush, that is to look at those regulations I've spoken of. They have already identified hundreds of them that can be wiped out with no harm to the quality of life. And the cancellation of just those regulations will leave billions and billions of dollars in the hands of the people for productive enterprise and research and development and the creation of jobs.

The years ahead are great ones for this country, for the cause of freedom, and the spread of civilizations. The West won't contain communism, it will transcend communism. It won't bother to dismiss or denounce it, it will dismiss it as some bizarre chapter in human history whose last pages are even now being written.

William Faulkner, at a Nobel Prize ceremony some time back, said man "would not only

479

[merely] endure: he will prevail" against the modern world because he will return to "the old verities and truths of the heart." And then Faulkner said of man, "He is immortal because he alone among creatures . . . has a soul, a spirit capable of compassion and sacrifice and endurance."

One can't say those words, "compassion, sacrifice, and endurance," without thinking of the irony that one who so exemplifies them, Pope John Paul II, a man of peace and goodness, an inspiration to the world, would be struck down by a bullet from a man towards whom he could only feel compassion and love. It was Pope John Paul II who warned in last year's encyclical on mercy and justice against certain economic theories that use the rhetoric of class struggle to justify injustice. He said, "In the name of an alleged justice the neighbor is sometimes destroyed, killed, deprived of liberty or stripped of fundamental human rights."

For the West, for America, the time has come to dare to show to the world that our civilized ideas, our traditions, our values, are not—like the ideology and war machine of totalitarian societies—just a facade of strength. It is time for the world to know our intellectual and spiritual values are rooted in the source of all strength, a belief in a Supreme Being, and a law higher than our own.

When it's written, history of our time won't dwell long on the hardships of the recent past. But history will ask—and our answer determine the fate of freedom for a thousand years—Did a nation born of hope lose hope? Did a people forged by courage find courage wanting? Did a generation steeled by hard war and a harsh peace forsake honor at the moment of great climactic struggle for the human spirit?

If history asks such questions, it also answers them. And the answers are to be found in the heritage left by generations of Americans before us. They stand in silent witness to what the world will soon know and history someday record: that in the third century, the American Nation came of age, affirmed its leadership of free men and women serving selflessly a vision of man with God, government for people, and humanity at peace.

A few years ago, an Australian Prime Minister, John Gorton, said, "I wonder if anybody ever thought what the situation for the comparatively small nations in the world would be if there were not in existence the United States, if there were not this giant country prepared to make so many sacrifices." This is the noble and rich heritage rooted in great civil ideas of the West, and it is yours.

My hope today is that in the years to come—and come it shall—when it's your time to explain to another generation the meaning of the past and thereby hold out to them their promise of the future, that you'll recall the truths and traditions of which we've spoken. It is these truths and traditions that define our civilization and make up our national heritage. And now, they're yours to protect and pass on.

I have one more hope for you: when you do speak to the next generation about these things, that you will always be able to speak of an America that is strong and free, to find in your hearts an unbounded pride in this much-loved country, this once and future land, this bright and hopeful nation whose generous spirit and great ideals the world still honors.

GLOSSARY

affirmative action A public policy mechanism imposed by law or administrative regulation that is designed to redress past discrimination against minorities and women by granting explicit preference in recruitment and employment to members of these groups. (Ch. 4)

agenda A list of specific items of business to be considered at a legislative session, conference, or meeting. (Ch. 12)

agenda-setting Agenda-setting, the first step in the policy-making process, involves, first, identifying issues or problems that the public determines are appropriate for governmental action, and, second, bringing those issues to the attention of the government. (Ch. 12)

appellate courts In the federal judicial system, the circuit courts of appeal are intermediate appellate tribunals with power to review appeals and resolve questions of law in cases arising in the federal district courts within their respective circuits. Many state judicial systems have similar intermediate tribunals. (Ch. 8) *See also* trial courts.

Articles of Confederation This "first constitution," initially agreed to in 1777 and finally approved in 1781, established a confederal national government. Though the Articles gave Congress considerable powers, they failed to provide the national government sufficient authority to raise revenue, quell disorders, or regulate commerce. In 1789 the U.S. Constitution replaced the Articles. (Ch. 2)

bill of attainder A law which declares guilt and prescribes punishment without an appropriate judicial hearing or trial. Article I, Section 10, of the Constitution prohibits the enactment of such bills by either national or state governments. (Ch. 3)

Bill of Rights The first ten amendments to the Constitution, adopted in 1791 shortly after the establishment of the national government, setting forth our most basic personal guarantees against unwarranted government interference with individual civil liberties. These guarantees include the freedoms of religion, speech, press, and assembly; the prohibition against unreasonable searches and seizures; and the right to a fair trial for persons accused of a crime. (Chs. 2, 4)

binding rules An instrument of public policy used to control the behavior of individuals and alter social conditions through the prescription of compulsory rules and sanctions for disobedience of those rules. (Ch. 12)

brief In practice before appellate courts, a brief is a formal, detailed, written document setting forth arguments supporting the legal position of a party in a case before the court. In addition to briefs of the parties, the court may permit briefs from "friends of the court," known as *amicus curiae* briefs, providing legal arguments designed to assist the court in its final resolution of the case. (Ch. 8)

bureaucracy An administrative system of offices staffed by a body of officials whose principal task is to implement governmental policy in a particular area through standardized procedures. Bureaucracies are characterized by a chain of command, with authority flowing from the top down, and by a specialization of duties and expertise. (Ch. 7)

cabinet In the executive branch of the national government, a group of senior leaders personally selected by the president and confirmed by the Senate who generally advise the president concerning matters relating to specified areas of responsibility. Each cabinet secretary directs the activities of a major governmental department, such as the Department of the Treasury, and discharges the statutory responsibility for program administration pertaining to that department. (Ch. 6)

caucus Meeting of party leaders to select party candidates for public office. (Ch. 6)

checks and balances Constitutional concept referring to the construction of national political institutions so that no one of them will be able to become too powerful and dominate the others. Conceptually, checks and balances are unnecessary without a system of separation of powers, but separation of powers alone will not ensure checks and balances. To achieve this balance, the Constitution therefore carefully prescribes methods of choosing leaders, limits and staggers their terms of office, and allocates power in an intricate power-sharing arrangement among the three branches of government. (Ch. 2) *See also* separation of powers.

civic democracy A distinctive theory of American democracy whose principles often contrast sharply with those of the competing theory of individualist democracy. Civic democrats believe that a broad political community, embued with a strong sense of the public interest, is essential to the political order and to individual well-being. According to civic democrats, the proper aim of government is to seek out and pursue this public interest. Contrary to individualist democrats who want to restrict the role of the state, civic democrats view public institutions not as necessary evils but as valuable components of public communal life. Other mediating institutions such as family and church, rather than government, define and nurture moral virtues and bond the individual to the political community. In a civic democracy, a "good citizen" is expected to act virtuously in private and public life; consider the public interest as well as narrow individual concerns; be tolerant of and respect other citizens; and support mediating institutions. (Ch. 1)

civil liberties Fundamental personal freedoms, especially those guaranteed by the first ten amendments of the Constitution (the Bill of Rights), which constitute our most basic protections against arbitrary use of government power. (Ch. 4) *See also* Bill of Rights.

civil rights Those rights, granted by the Constitution or flowing from a statute, that citizens are entitled to assert against government, for example, to free themselves from constitutionally impermissible classifications, or to obtain equal treatment under the laws. (Ch. 4)

cloture Action taken by the Senate to end debate on a bill. At least sixty senators must vote to impose cloture, thereby limiting further debate on the bill to thirty hours. (Ch. 5)

committee amendment Amendment made in committee during the "markup" or revision of proposed legislation. Some committee amendments involve technical matters and do not affect the content of the bill; others may strengthen or weaken critical aspects of the measure. (Ch. 5)

concurrent powers Constitutional powers that are shared by both the national and state governments. Not all grants of power to the national government are exclusive. Some expressly delegated powers, such as the power to levy taxes, can also be exercised by state governments, and are thus said to be concurrent. (Ch. 3) *See also* delegated, exclusive, implied, inherent, and reserved powers.

concurring opinion Formal written opinion by one or more appellate judges that agrees with the ultimate resolution of a judicial issue by the majority of the court but sets forth different reasons for reaching that same conclusion. (Ch. 8)

confederal government Confederal systems of government, such as those created by the Articles of Confederation and the Constitution of the Confederate States of America, exist when the national government is the creature of its constituent parts. A confederal system is formed when a group of sovereign political systems surrender some of their powers to a set of central institutions, but retain ultimate authority for themselves. (Ch. 3)

conference committee Special congressional committee composed of members of both houses of congress whose task is to resolve differences in separate versions of the same legislation passed by the Senate and the House. (Ch. 5)

conglomerate departments Executive departments of the federal bureaucracy, including Health and Human Services, characterized by the consolidation of several existing government programs into one cabinet-level department. (Ch. 7)

congressional district Basic unit of representation for the House of Representatives. States are granted seats in the House on the basis of population. In those states entitled to more than one representative, the state legislature actually establishes the boundaries of the separate districts through a process known as redistricting that is fraught with legal and political cross-currents and sometimes results in "gerrymandering." (Ch. 5) *See also* gerrymandering.

core departments Executive departments of the federal bureaucracy, including State, Treasury, and Defense, that oversee and conduct the most essential functions of government. (Ch. 7)

delegated powers Constitutional powers expressly granted to the national government by Article I, Section 8, including the powers to regulate commerce, provide for the common defense, and coin money. (Ch. 3) *See also* concurrent, exclusive, implied, inherent and reserved powers.

discharge petition Procedural device used with only rare success in the House of Representatives to relieve a committee of its jurisdiction over certain proposed legislation by majority vote of the members and send the bill to the floor of the House. Generally, members attempt to use this device to "pry" a bill from a hostile committee seeking to kill the measure by "sitting" on it. (Ch. 5)

dissenting opinion Formal written explanation by one or more appellate judges of the basis for disagreement with the decision of the majority. (Ch. 8)

distributive policy A type of governmental policy characterized by the distribution of benefits, usually money, to groups and individuals. Examples are agricultural subsidies to farmers, grants to local governments for flood control or airport construction, and grants to college students. (Ch. 12)

docket List or calendar of cases awaiting action before a trial or appellate court. (Ch. 8)

Due Process Clause Constitutional safeguard set forth in the Fifth and Fourteenth Amendments barring arbitrary governmental deprivation of life, liberty, or property. (Ch. 4)

electoral college Gathering of persons selected by the voters of a state as "electors" to formally cast their ballots, as prescribed by the Constitution, for the official election of the president and the vice-president. Each state has a number of electors equal to the total number of representatives from that state in both houses of Congress. In order to be officially elected president or vice-president by action of the electoral college, a candidate must receive at least 270 electoral votes. (Ch. 6)

enumerated powers (Ch. 3) *See* delegated powers.

Environmental Protection Agency Federal administrative agency charged with implementing national environmental laws. President Nixon created the EPA in 1971 by executive order, utilizing his presidential statutory authority to reorganize existing agencies to do so. Though the scope of its authority is broad, the EPA shares its regulatory responsibilities with several other federal entities, such as the Interior Department. (Ch. 12)

Equal Protection Clause Constitutional safeguard set forth in the Fourteenth Amendment forbidding any state from denying equal protection of the laws to any person within its jurisdiction. In the landmark Supreme Court decision of *Brown v. Board of Education of Topeka* (1954), the court ruled that segregated school education is a denial of equal protection of the laws guaranteed to all persons by the Fourteenth Amendment. This constitutional provision offers major protections to persons against governmental discrimination on the basis of race, sex, or national origin. (Ch. 4)

Ethics in Government Act of 1978 Federal law codifying and broadening conflict of interest provisions applicable to senior members of the executive branch by requiring the filing of annual financial disclosure statements and prohibiting certain employment after termination of federal service. (Ch. 11)

exclusive powers Constitutional powers granted to and exercised only by either the national or state governments. Certain constitutional powers are forbidden to the states specifically, such as signing a treaty with a foreign country, coining money, and impairing contractual obligations. Other constitutional grants, such as the authority to levy taxes, are shared by the national and state governments and are thus described as concurrent powers. (Ch. 3) *See also* concurrent, delegated, implied, inherent, and reserved powers.

ex post facto law A law enacted "after the fact" that either makes criminal an act that was legal at the time it was committed or has other adverse retroactive effects on a person accused of a crime. Article I, Sections 9 and 10, of the Constitution, prohibit the enactment of such criminal laws by either the national or state governments. The prohibition does not extend to civil laws. (Ch. 3)

Extradition Clause Article IV of the Constitution requires the return of any person charged with treason, a felony, or other crimes, who has fled from justice and is found in another state, to be returned to the state having jurisdiction over the alleged crime. (Ch. 3)

faction A loosely organized group or clique within a larger political group (such as a party) or within a government whose members share common interests and work in concert to advance those interests in competition with other groups. (Ch. 10)

federalism A system of government, found, for example, in the United States, Canada, and Switzerland, that is characterized by the constitutional division of power between the central government and constituent regional or state governments. (Ch. 3)

Federalists During the ratification process in 1787–88, supporters of the new Constitution, known as Federalists, emphasized the need for a strong defense capability and a unified commercial market, and stressed the limited nature of the new national government. By contrast, the Anti-Federalists, opponents of the Constitution, contended that the United States was too large and diverse to be a genuine political community with a single national government resting on the peo-

ple; they further criticized the Constitution's lack of a bill of rights. This latter criticism eventually brought about the adoption of the first ten amendments to the Constitution in 1791. In the United States' formative years, the Federalists were a loosely organized group wedded to an idea of government by propertied elites which supported Alexander Hamilton's proposals for political centralization and the encouragement of economic growth through vigorous government policies. (Ch. 2)

Federalist Papers A series of newspaper articles authored by James Madison, John Jay, and Alexander Hamilton during the struggle for ratification of the new Constitution in New York in 1788. These Federalist Papers urged the adoption of the Constitution, but, more importantly, provide an incisive commentary on the document by men directly involved in its creation. (Ch. 2)

filibuster A Senate practice, permitted under Senate rules, of unlimited debate to delay passage of a bill, whether or not the content of the "debate" is germane to the bill. (Ch. 5)

floor amendment Amendment made on the floor of either the Senate or the House after the proposed legislation is reported out of committee. In the House, more so than the Senate, floor rules tightly control the members' right to make amendments: some rules proscribe any amendments; others permit only certain types; and still others allow general amendments. (Ch. 5)

formal amendment At its most basic level, formal amendment is the process of constitutional change by one of the methods expressly set forth in the Constitution. The process consists first of the formal proposal of an amendment either by a two-thirds vote of both houses of Congress, or by a constitutional convention called by Congress at the request of two-thirds of the states (a procedure never used). After proposal, the amendment must be ratified by the approval of either three-fourths of the state legislatures, or three-fourths of the special conventions called in each state to consider the amendment. Of the twenty-seven formal amendments to the Constitution (as of 1992), all were proposed by the Congress. All except the twenty-first (which repealed the eighteenth) were ratified by state legislatures. (Ch. 2)

foundations, endowments, and institutes Federal agencies established to promote scientific research and encourage the arts and humanities. Examples are the National Science Foundation and the National Endowment for the Humanities. (Ch. 7)

Full Faith and Credit Clause Article IV, Section 1, of the Constitution requires each state to accord respect to the laws and judicial decisions of another state equal to that given its own. (Ch. 3)

gerrymandering Flagrant drawing of legislative district boundaries in a manner designed to secure some partisan political advantage. (Ch. 5)

Gideon v. Wainwright **(1963)** Landmark Supreme Court decision requiring states to provide counsel free of charge to indigent defendants in a criminal trial. (Ch. 4)

government corporations Federal corporate entities, such as the U.S. Postal Service and the Tennessee Valley Authority, that function as semi-commercial enterprises by providing a service and charging fees for that service. (Ch. 7)

government service organizations Small federal bureaucratic organizations, such as the Executive Office of the President, which serve the administrative support needs of the three branches of the national government. (Ch. 7)

grant system Through the grant system, Congress provides funds to state and local governments for various programs specified by the federal government, such as highway construction, education, and community development. The most important classification of grants specifies how the grant money may be spent. For example, *categorical grants* are those in which the federal government gives money to a state or local jurisdiction for a specified purpose, and it may be spent for that purpose only. *Block grants* are monies provided with only a general governmental purpose assigned, such as education or transportation. Within these broad rubrics, the state or local government decides how to spend the grant money. Lastly, *revenue sharing* permits the most flexibility, providing monies with no strings attached. (Ch. 3)

implied powers Inherent authority possessed inferentially by the national government from those powers expressly delegated to it by the Constitution. For example, the vitally important "elastic clause" contained in Article I, Section 8, empowers Congress to take actions "necessary and proper" to carry out its delegated powers. (Ch. 3) *See also* concurrent, delegated, exclusive, inherent, and reserved powers; Necessary and Proper Clause.

incumbent Person currently holding a particular public office. (Ch. 5)

independent agencies Federal agencies without cabinet-level rank, such as the Environmental Protection Agency and the Central Intelligence Agency, which function directly under presidential control but independently of any cabinet-level executive department. Each such agency enjoys direct access to the president and has its own budget. (Ch. 7)

independent regulatory commissions Autonomous federal bodies, such as the Interstate Commerce Commission, consisting of commissioners appointed by the president with Senate approval, statutorily empowered to issue rules and regulations concerning a specific broad area of national interest, enforce those rules, and hold hearings to resolve disputes concerning their application. The independence and broad authority accorded these commissions reflects the desire to insulate them from partisan politics. (Ch. 7)

individualist democracy A theory of American democracy based on the primacy of the individual as the basic building block of the political order. According to individualist democrats, the state exists for the individual, whose personal liberties and individual rights must be free from unwarranted state intrusion. An individualist democracy expects its "good citizens" to pursue their individual interests vigorously, work hard to assure fairness in governmental processes, and vigilantly protect their individual rights and liberties from government encroachment. Much of the conflict in an individualist democracy centers around the extent to which government, representing the majority of the people, may regulate individual behavior by limiting individual choices. (Ch. 1)

informal amendment In contrast to formal constitutional change, informal amendment occurs through methods not expressly set forth in

485

the Constitution. Informal change can occur, for example, through the process of judicial interpretation of the Constitution (as in the case of the power of judicial review), and by political convention and custom (such as the presidential practice of concluding "executive agreements"). (Ch. 2) *See also* formal amendment.

inherent powers Constitutional powers not spelled out in the Constitution that are inferred from the structure of government itself. For example, by the very fact of its existence, the federal government assumes the attributes of an international state and thus has certain inherent powers to conduct foreign policy. (Ch. 3) *See also* concurrent, delegated, exclusive, implied, and reserved powers.

interest groups Organizations of individuals with shared interests that pursue those interests by influencing governmental actions or policies for specific purposes at all levels of government. (Ch. 11)

judicial activism Approach to judicial decision-making that promotes a broad interpretation of the Constitution and reflects a tendency by judges to consciously weave "contemporary values" into constitutional interpretations. (Ch. 8)

judicial restraint Approach to judicial decision-making, opposed to that of judicial activists, that advocates a stricter interpretation of the Constitution preserving the "original intent" of the Framers as nearly as possible, restraint toward invalidating laws on constitutional grounds, and a belief that the courts should give maximum discretion to political authorities at all levels of government to resolve policy issues. (Ch. 8)

judicial review Power of courts to review legislative and executive actions and to invalidate those actions if they are found to be unconstitutional. (Ch. 8)

jurisdiction Judicial power to administer justice by hearing a case and deciding a controversy. (Ch. 8)

legislative discretion Authority granted by Congress to administrative agencies empowering them to make rules according to their own judgment in carrying out the mandates of a statute. Often, Congress bestows wide discretion on administrative agencies to issue rules and regula-

tions consistent with congressional intent that will govern specific circumstances not addressed in the legislation or foreseen by Congress. (Ch. 12)

legislative veto Congressional invalidation, by simple majority vote, of an executive action taken pursuant to a statute containing a legislative veto provision. In 1983 the Supreme Court declared the legislative veto unconstitutional. (Ch. 7)

lobbyists Persons acting as agents for organized interest groups, associations, or corporations who seek to influence proposed legislation, policy decisions, and administrative actions at all levels of government on behalf of their groups. (Ch. 11)

majority leader Elected leader and chief spokesperson of the majority party in the House of Representatives or the Senate. In the House, the majority leader is subordinate to the speaker of the House, who actually leads the majority party in the lower chamber. (Ch. 5)

***Marbury v. Madison* (1803)** Landmark Supreme Court decision establishing the power of the Court to review acts of Congress as well as state laws and to declare them invalid when found to be in conflict with the Constitution. (Ch. 8)

markup Legislative term for the process of amending or modifying proposed legislation in committee. (Ch. 5)

***McCulloch v. Maryland* (1819)** Supreme Court decision favoring national over state control of the economy. Writing for the Court, Chief Justice John Marshall announced the "implied powers" doctrine, empowering Congress in this case to use the "necessary and proper" clause of Article I, Section 8, to carry out its expressly delegated powers by establishing a national bank. Declaring further that "The power to tax is the power to destroy," the Court struck down Maryland's tax on the national bank, confirming the precedence of national over state law. (Ch. 3)

merit system System providing for the selection and promotion of public employees on the basis of demonstrated merit rather than political patronage. In 1883 Congress passed the Pendleton Act, establishing the federal civil service and thereby replacing the spoils system then governing federal employment practice. (Ch. 7) *See also* spoils system.

minority leader Elected leader and chief spokesperson of the minority party in the House of Representatives or the Senate. (Ch. 5)

***Miranda v. Arizona* (1966)** Landmark Supreme Court decision requiring police to warn persons accused of crimes, prior to interrogation, of their right to remain silent, and to inform them of their right to have an attorney present during interrogation. (Ch. 4)

moral suasion An instrument of public policy used to persuade citizens to obey and support the law or to take some action consistent with policy objectives. The "Just Say No" campaign to discourage drug abuse is an example of the use of moral suasion. (Ch. 12)

Necessary and Proper Clause Article I, Section 8, of the Constitution enumerates the express powers of Congress and further empowers Congress to make all laws "necessary and proper" to carry them out. Also referred to as the "elastic clause." (Ch. 3)

New Jersey Plan A set of resolutions presented as an alternative to the Virginia Plan by the New Jersey delegation to the Philadelphia Convention in 1787. New Jersey's plan sought to maintain the influence of the small states by keeping representation in Congress equal for each state, with members chosen by the legislatures (as under the Articles of Confederation). It also included an executive branch headed by a committee chosen by Congress, and a national court system. The plan expanded the powers of Congress, as did the Virginia Plan, and further included a Supremacy Clause, making all national laws superior to state enactments. In its final form, the Constitution reflected a compromise between the two rival plans by providing for two houses of Congress, one apportioned on the basis of state population, and the other composed of two representatives from each state. (Ch. 2)

oversight committee Congressional committee charged with observing and broadly supervising program implementation by the executive branch. (Ch. 7)

party activists Persons extensively involved in political activities on behalf of a particular political party. (Ch. 10)

party identification An individual's feelings of attachment to a political party and desire to extend personal loyalty to that party. (Ch. 10)

Philadelphia Convention During the summer of 1787, fifty-five representatives convened in Philadelphia at Congress' call to revise the Articles of Confederation. Once in Philadelphia, the delegates decided instead to create a national government that rested on the people and could act directly on them rather than through the states. Their efforts produced an entirely new constitution. By the end of 1788, all thirteen states had completed ratification of the Constitution. (Ch. 2)

policy formulation A key stage of the policy-making process involving the development of courses of action regarding problems on the government agenda and the expression of those courses of action in a precise form, such as legislative acts or administrative regulations. (Ch. 12)

policy implementation Once a governmental policy is properly formulated and adopted, it then must be placed into effect. Inevitably, during this implementation phase, a policy may be modified or even terminated based on feedback or experience. (Ch. 12)

policy linkage Term indicating that no policy problem exists in isolation, but rather is dependent in part on a favorable resolution of other problem areas for its own success. For example, environmental policy is linked to energy, economic, health, transportation, and housing policies, to name only a few. (Ch. 12)

political action committee Organizations formed by business corporations, labor unions, and other special interest groups for the purpose of raising and dispensing funds, including making campaign contributions to candidates for public office, in order to achieve specific political objectives. (Ch. 11)

political access When used to refer to a lobbyist, political access describes the lobbyist's ability to approach and speak directly with governmental policy-makers as part of the lobbyist's effort to influence certain legislation, decisions, or other courses of action. (Ch. 11)

political socialization Process of political learning in which an individual's political values, particularly those of young people, are shaped by interaction with family, religious institutions, schools, the media, peer groups, and political events. (Ch. 9)

popular sovereignty Fundamental democratic concept providing that ultimate political authority resides with the people. (Ch. 2)

president pro tempore Temporary presiding officer of the Senate in the absence of the vice-president. Chosen by senators from their own ranks. Usually the senior member of the majority party in the chamber. (Ch. 5)

presidential party convention Gathering of party delegates from each state during a presidential election year for the purpose of nominating candidates for president and vice-president. (Ch. 6)

primacy principle Whatever is learned first is learned more thoroughly. For example, when describing the process of political socialization, evidence points to the family as the key agent of socialization. (Ch. 9) *See also* political socialization.

primary election Election in which voters determine party candidates for the general election. Primary elections may be open or closed, and may be used also to select convention delegates and party leaders. (Ch. 5)

Privileges and Immunities Clause Article IV of the Constitution provides that the citizens of any one state are guaranteed the "privileges and immunities" of every other state, as though they were citizens of that state. (Ch. 3)

public comment Through a formalized process known as "public comment," citizens, interest groups, and other interested parties are given an opportunity by federal administrative agencies to provide input concerning a proposed regulation. Lobbyists frequently make good use of this chance to influence the interpretation and implementation of legislation. (Ch. 11)

public opinion Grouping of beliefs, attitudes, and opinions people have about specific policy questions. (Ch. 9)

public policy Concept of a government's substantive goals or intentions and its subsequent implementation of those objectives in the form of

laws, regulations, decisions, and other courses of action. (Ch. 9)

redistributive policy Policy characterized by the explicit shifting of wealth or benefits from one group to another through government action. Examples are those government programs that transfer national wealth from one geographical region to another, or from one sector of the economy to another. (Ch. 12)

regulation Rule or order issued by an administrative agency that has the force of law and controls or governs certain activities of an agency, business, and other similar organizations and individuals. (Ch. 12)

regulatory policy Policy characterized by government regulation of an activity in the public interest, requiring groups or organizations (most often a business) to do or not do something, and specifying sanctions for any violations. (Ch. 12)

reserved powers Under the Tenth Amendment to the Constitution, powers not delegated to the national government nor prohibited to the states are reserved to the states. (Ch. 3) *See also* concurrent, delegated, exclusive, implied, and inherent powers.

"revolving door" Practice of federal bureaucrats terminating their employment with an agency to accept a more lucrative position working as a lobbyist, consultant, or executive for groups or firms they dealt with as a federal employee. Congressional concern about this practice was a prime consideration in the passage of the Ethics in Government Act. (Ch. 11)

select committees Temporary congressional committees charged with some special task, usually an investigation. A recent example is the Iran-Contra Committee (1987). (Ch. 5)

separation of powers Constitutional concept referring to the horizontal fragmentation of political power at the national level. As one of three primary constitutional mechanisms designed, in James Madison's words, to "oblige [government] to control itself," separation of powers actually works through a shared power arrangement among the three branches of the national government. (Ch. 2)

service departments Executive departments of the federal bureaucracy, including Agriculture,

Labor, and Education, whose purpose is to serve and promote the needs of a particular segment of society. Also known as clientele departments. (Ch. 7)

solicitor general Federal official who presents the case for the United States to the Supreme Court when the United States is a party. Additionally, the solicitor general has the authority to notify the Court of the legal position of the federal government in any case in which the United States is interested but is not a party. (Ch. 8)

speaker Presiding officer of the House of Representatives, selected by the majority party, who serves as a key liaison between the House and the president. Leader of the majority party in the House. (Ch. 5)

spoils system Blatant use of patronage by victorious politicians or parties to reward loyal partisans with government jobs. At the national level the use of the spoils system was most prevalent during the early to mid-nineteenth century, particularly the Jackson era, and persisted until the establishment of the federal civil service based on the merit system in 1883. (Ch. 7) *See also* merit system.

standing committees Permanent congressional committees composed of members from only one chamber, whose chief task is to consider proposed legislation referred to them and send to the floor the measures they recommend. Currently, the House has twenty-two and the Senate sixteen such committees, with membership ranging from twelve to fifty-seven. Examples are the House and Senate Armed Services Committees. (Ch. 5)

state presidential primary Party election held before the national presidential party convention to allow state voters to express their preference for the party's nominee. Since the early 1970's, the proliferation of presidential primaries and open caucuses has democratized the nomination process and has changed the character of presidential campaigns. (Ch. 6)

structuring Use of government action for policy purposes to organize or arrange the relations between private parties, for example, through the licensing powers of the Federal Communications Commission. (Ch. 12)

structuring principle That which is learned first structures what comes later. For example, the

political values and perceptions gained during one's youth generally will determine the approach one takes toward authority throughout life, and, serving as a conceptual prism, will continue to mold and shape views in later life. (Ch. 9)

subsidies and payments An instrument of public policy by which government entices or persuades individuals to take actions consistent with policy objectives by paying them, for example, in the case of professors, to conduct research. (Ch. 12)

Supremacy Clause Fundamental constitutional concept, set forth in Article VI of the Constitution, which states that the laws enacted by the national government in pursuance of its constitutional powers, and all treaties, are the supreme law of the land. (Ch. 2)

symbolic policy Governmental policy that manipulates symbols in an effort to express national goals or values. An example is the declaration of a public holiday to honor Martin Luther King, Jr. (Ch. 12)

taxation An instrument of public policy long used to encourage or discourage certain activities. (Ch. 12)

term limit Constitutional or statutory restriction governing the number of terms or the amount of time a person can serve in a public office. For example, the president is barred by the Constitution from serving more than two four-year terms. In the early 1990's efforts began in several states to limit the number of terms congressional representatives and senators can serve because of perceived disadvantages to the public of extended incumbency. (Ch. 5)

trial courts Unlike most federal countries, the United States has a dual court system, exemplified by a separate hierarchy of courts in the federal and all state judicial systems. These hierarchies are joined in the United States Supreme Court, which sits atop both federal and state systems. At the base of each of these systems are trial courts which exercise original jurisdiction over civil and criminal cases within their respective jurisdictional authority. Trial proceedings are conducted before a judge and possibly a jury. In criminal cases the duty of the trial court is to determine whether the person on trial committed the offense charged. In civil cases the court generally must resolve questions of fact and law in civil disputes involving multiple litigants. (Ch. 8) *See also* appellate courts.

unitary government Unitary systems of government, found in such countries as France and Great Britain, are characterized by the vesting of ultimate political authority in a central government. In such a system, local governmental institutions are purely creatures of the central government, have no legal autonomy, and act only within the guidelines established by the national government. (Ch. 3)

veto (presidential) Constitutional power of the president to reject acts of Congress. In turn, Congress can override a presidential veto by two-thirds vote of both chambers. (Ch. 6)

Virginia Plan A set of resolutions presented by the Virginia delegation to the Philadelphia Convention in 1787 that proposed a powerful two-house Congress, with seats allocated on the basis of population; a "national executive" chosen by Congress for a single term; a national court system; and a Council of Revision, composed of the national executive and several judges, with power to veto acts of Congress. The plan further empowered Congress to overturn any state law and employ the army against states. The new Constitution reflected a compromise between the Virginia Plan and the rival New Jersey Plan supported by small state delegations at the convention. (Ch. 2) *See also* New Jersey Plan; Philadelphia Convention.

whip Assistant to the majority or minority leader of each house of Congress whose chief tasks are to serve as two-way channels of communication between the leaders and the rank and file, count votes on specific legislation prior to voting, and urge members to support the leadership on certain legislation. (Ch. 5)

INDEX

Page numbers in italics refer to figures; those followed by "n" refer to endnotes.

PHOTO CREDITS